LECTURES ON
EUROPEAN HISTORY, 1789–1914

LECTURES ON EUROPEAN HISTORY 1789–1914

MEN, MACHINES AND FREEDOM

by

JOHN McMANNERS

Emeritus Fellow of St Edmund Hall, Oxford
Professor of History in the University of Sydney

OXFORD
BASIL BLACKWELL
1966

940.28

M 16l

FIRST PRINTED 1966

PRINTED IN GREAT BRITAIN BY
WESTERN PRINTING SERVICES LTD., BRISTOL

PREFACE

I am grateful to Blackwells for their flattering suggestion that I should prepare some of my lectures for publication as a sequel to the Reverend J. M. Thompson's *Lectures on Foreign History, 1494–1789*, a book which enlivened the Preliminary Course for me when I read Modern History at Oxford before the war.

Thompson's two rules for lectures of this sort cannot be bettered—though how one contrives to comply with them successfully, as he did, is quite another question. Firstly, the lecturer must be interesting: at Oxford, because the members of his audience will otherwise fold up their tents and depart; in the Australian universities, because they are pressed men, and humanity and selfish prudence alike dictate that they be reasonably entertained while serving their sentence. Secondly, the lecturer must provoke the emotions of zeal, doubt, anger, curiosity (or whatever else it is) that send his hearers off determined to look at the evidence for themselves. To assist any readers who may be so moved, references are given to a limited number of the more accessible books and articles. The footnotes combine this role, uneasily, with that of recognizing my more obvious obligations, though—as is the way with lecture courses—I cannot hope to recollect chapter and verse to list all my creditors, and I must apologize in advance to writers from whom I may inadvertently have filched an argument or an epigram.

To my colleagues in the History Department of the University of Sydney I must offer especial thanks; Dr. Christina Campbell discussed Emigration with me, Professor John M. Ward looked over the pages on Imperialism, and Mr. R. B. Rose reviewed those on Socialism and the French Revolution; Miss Ruth Teale, my research assistant, helped me over many matters, and unearthed many of the references; while Dr. Fred Stambrook, in what I can only believe was a moment of generous folly, offered to read the whole typescript, and fulfilled his promise gallantly, to my great profit. I have not always taken their advice, and I now fear that they will have all too many opportunities to say 'I told you so'.

J. McM.

v

CONTENTS

CHAPTER I

MEN, MACHINES AND FREEDOM

I

'You won't learn anything by my lectures; so if you have any studies of your own, you had better pursue them.'[1] This is the advice Southey received from his tutor when he went up to Balliol in 1793, at the beginning of our period. The academic world has changed since then, and you can no longer expect to hear such frank admissions; however, I shall subscribe to the second half of the saying and urge you to pursue your own interests, within the limitations that the examination system imposes. Indeed, these lectures are meant to provide a framework of indispensable examinable knowledge about the nineteenth century—the nation states, their leaders, régimes and revolutions, movements of political and social thought, developments in social hierarchies and economic structure—a framework within which you can 'place' the more interesting things that attract your fancy: what Baudelaire thought about sin, or what the ordinary man had for breakfast. The monuments of the age which will constitute its history when everything else about it is forgotten—its novels, symphonies, paintings and scientific discoveries—will be referred to only incidentally, for we shall be dealing, not with the most important things, in an absolute sense, but with the basic historical patterns within which the achievements of culture can be understood and compared. In any case, the cultural legacy of the nineteenth century is so overwhelming that it defies attempts to cram it into a general synthesis. Even in the new, brilliant and dangerous age into which we have now moved, a knowledge of this legacy and a first-hand acquaintance with some of its masterpieces is the groundwork of a civilized mind and the subject matter for the leisures of a lifetime.

II

The most difficult moment for a lecturer in history comes at the very beginning, for the multifarious life of the world moves in a continuous surge and everything, for its explanation, has to be referred to

[1] C. E. Mallet, *A History of the University of Oxford* (1927), III, pp. 178–9.

things that happened before. So how can one start? How, so to speak, can one nose one's vehicle into the uninterrupted stream of traffic?

One device is to choose a convenient base and from it set out upon a tour: in this case, a tour around Europe in the 1780s. You will forgive me if I do not start from distant Sydney Cove where, as the Estates General met in France, the convicts in their 'miserable huts' were rehearsing for the first theatrical performance in Australia, Farquhar's *Recruiting Officer*.[2] Oxford, surely, would be a more convenient and congenial starting point, especially, you might think, because its University, a place of powdered wigs, of dogs and horses, of 'drunkenness and prerogative, or in their language Church and King', was not so exigent in scholarly matters as universities have since become. Lord Eldon got his degree in 1770 by knowing the Hebrew for 'the place of a skull' and by ascribing the foundation of University College to King Alfred; others qualified by translating the pedigrees of racehorses into Latin, devising a syllogism or two, and drinking with their examiners.[3] At Cambridge, things were more strictly organized of course, and in 1788 candidates were asked, 'what was never before heard of', for square roots right up to three places of decimals.[4]

So let us imagine ourselves acquiring a painless degree at Oxford before setting out for the Continent. Then we go to London, and from London to Dover by stage coach, 76 miles in a day; after this a wait, depending on wind and tide, of from three hours to three days, for a boat to Calais; from thence, not being able to afford a hired post chaise, we take the daily 'diligence' to Paris and suffer forty-five hours of jolting, springless travel before reaching our destination.[5] Safely lodged in the cultural metropolis of Europe, it would be pleasant to plan new expeditions further afield; in France itself, with its good roads, bad inns, and brilliant society; to Switzerland, with its newly fashionable mountain scenery, where the innkeepers 'hear all you have to say with the greatest composure but hardly ever abate their charges';[6] to Italy, to 'pick up a few superficial notions of the fine arts from the poor thralls of bigotry and superstition'[7]

[2] A. Birch and D. S. Macmillan, *The Sydney Scene, 1788–1960* (1962), p. 19. (Cf. *Hist. Records N.S.W.*, II, p. 746).
[3] Mallet, op. cit., pp. 159, 165, 164.
[4] D. F. Winstanley, *Unreformed Cambridge* (1935), p. 53.
[5] Constantia Maxwell, *The English Traveller in France, 1698–1815* (1932), pp. 19–20, 27, 106.
[6] G. R. Beer, *English Travellers in Switzerland* (1949), pp. 45–49.
[7] Sir William Jones, cit. M. Kraus, *The Atlantic Civilization: 18th Century Origins* (1961), p. 39.

or, unashamedly, merely to enjoy the carnival at Venice under the lucid skies of Canaletto. One might be more daring and leave the accustomed tourist circuit, going, perhaps, to Lisbon, with its negro slaves, religious processions and assassins who wipe their knives on their cloaks and depart unhindered on their legitimate business;[8] or to 'wild and romantic' Prague; Vienna where Hungarians, Greeks, Turks and Poles in national dress jostle on the sidewalks; [8] and on to Buda where hooded flagellants walk the streets on days of penitence; or northwards to the overgrown village of Berlin around its monumental centre of palaces and barracks, destitute alike of 'industry, commerce or freedom[9]; to Stockholm with its red-painted wooden houses and white stuccoed brick around the deep, crystal-clear harbour;[10] or eastwards into a world of unmade roads and bed-bugs to see the 'palaces and sheds' of Warsaw and the barbaric, tumble-down spaciousness of Moscow, dominated by the onion domes of churches in copper, tin, green and gilt.[11]

Yet, having dreamed a while about the romantic details of our tour as English travellers reported them, I must now draw back and confess that we have no time to complete it. The structure of society in the various states of eighteenth-century Europe is too complex to be studied in detail by those whom an evil fate has constrained to concentrate their studies upon the succeeding century. Austerely, we must forgo the picturesque ramifications of the crystalline, abusive social order of the *ancien régime* to concentrate upon the tensions that were working within to destroy it, and the beginnings of the movements and pressures that were to shape the future. Remember, however, as we do this, that we are making an extreme use of the historian's power of hindsight, for in the 1780s no one in Europe expected startling political, social or industrial change. In 1776, Adam Smith published the *Wealth of Nations*, a masterly treatise built upon the supposition that the economies of the European states were virtually stationary; in the following year, Voltaire, nearing death, reflected that 'the world improves a little, the thinking world, but *le monde brut* will long be a composite of bears and monkeys, and

[8] Rev. C. C. Southey (ed.), *Life and Corresp. of the Late Robert Southey* (1849) I, pp. 68–70; *Journal of William Beckford in Portugal and Spain, 1787–8* (ed. B. Alexander, 1954), *passim*.

[9] N. W. Wraxall, *Memoirs of the Courts of Berlin, Dresden, Warsaw and Vienna in the Years 1777, 1778 and 1779* (2nd ed. 1800) I, pp. 296 (Prague), 351, 376, 100.

[10] W. Coxe, *Travels into Poland, Russia etc.* (1784) in F. F. D. Tennant, *The Scandinavian Book* (1951), p. 22.

[11] Wraxall, op. cit., II, p. 4; P. Putnam, *Seven Britons in Imperial Russia. 1698–1813* (1952), p. 258.

the *canaille* will always be a hundred to one.'[12] The most acute intelligences of the eighteenth century believed in progress as a slow, long haul by the steady pull of commerce, invention and reason; they had no hope of achieving a millenium out of cataclysm, or of suddenly mastering nature by a scientific or technological breakthrough.

III

What then were the new destructive-creative tendencies that were gathering force in Europe in the last years of the *ancien régime*? Essentially, they were three: a population explosion, a political and, to some extent a social revolution, and a 'sudden qualitative and fundamental transformation'[13] of economic life for which sociologists in the 1820s were to coin the name 'Industrial Revolution', on the analogy of the political upheavals of the previous generation. Men and machines were to multiply, and within the new mass industrial civilization which emerged, there was to be a bitter and confused struggle to achieve freedom, variously defined in terms of individual liberties, political franchises, economic equality and national independence. The political revolution was French, the industrial revolution was English, the demographic revolution (with variations from place to place) was Europe-wide. Freely, men chose to fight for freedom; the path of industrialization they followed by a sort of choice, though once the process had begun anywhere, it was ultimately inescapable; their numbers, however, increased by a fatality which they did not understand and which still evades a completey logical explanation.

While pundits were solemnly discussing the numerical decline of mankind since the heroic days of Roman antiquity,[14] the population of Europe was rising at an accelerating pace, from about 120 millions in 1700 to something over 180 millions at the end of the century. By 1798, the fecundity of the contemporary, as against the ancient world, was established, and Malthus issued his famous warning that mankind would inevitably outgrow the means of its subsistence. The increase cannot be ascribed to improvements in medicine or hygiene; the only innovation that looks significant,

---

[12] Cit. Lester G. Crocker, *An Age of Crisis: Man and World in 18th Century French Thought* (1959), p. 211. The point about Adam Smith is made by M. S. Anderson, *Europe in the 18th Century, 1713–88* (1961), p. 337.

[13] E. J. Hobsbawn, *The Age of Revolution, 1789–1848* (1962), p. 29.

[14] D. V. Glass, 'The Population Controversy in 18th Century England', *Population Studies* VI (1952).

innoculation against smallpox, dates from the 'nineties.[15] One is on safer ground in pointing to improvements in nutrition in western Europe, where for two generations there had been no great famines. In Ireland, indeed, the increase seems to have a clearly definable cause; the introduction of the potato. On a milk and potato diet a family could live by cultivating two acres, and as rents were 'elastic', thrift was pointless and young people married as soon as they had money for a licence, committing everything 'to Providence and their potato garden'.[16] But if the Irish explanation applies to some other areas, for example, to south-west Germany, it can hardly be relevant to Russia before 1800, except in some parts of the Ukraine, and only marginally relevant to England. The great rise in the Russian birth rate remains rather mysterious. It was probably connected with the availability of vast empty lands on the eastern and southern borders, into which seigneurs moved with their serfs, or the government sent state peasants, or the serfs themselves migrated as fugitives.[17] In England[18] where, as in Ireland and Russia, it seems to have been a question of a rising birth rate rather than a falling death rate, the explanation must be complex—improvements in nutrition and public order, the operation of a rhythm of acceleration following a period of high mortality in which the unfit had been killed off and marriages delayed, the decline of the guilds with their marriage regulations, and the improvements in agriculture. The relationship between the Industrial Revolution and the demographic rise was probably one of pull followed by push; invention was spurred by a shortage of labour, then an onrush of labour came just as the expanding factories could take it, so that finally, as Adam Smith and Malthus thought, the demand for labour may have helped to produce it. Much of this remains surmise. There were many reasons why population might well have expanded, but it is hard to give each its due weight or to describe their cumulative and interlocking action.

IV

In the long run, the population explosion was to enhance the possibilities of large-scale industrial organization, both by increasing

---

[15] W. L. Langer, 'Europe's Initial Population Explosion; *American Hist. Rev.* LXIX (1963), pp. 1–19.

[16] The Rev. Horatio Townshend (1815), cit. R. N. Salaman, *The History and Social Influence of the Potato* (1949), p. 276.

[17] Jerome Blum, *Lord and Peasant in Russia* (1961), pp. 278–9.

[18] See especially, J. H. Habakkuk, 'English Population in the 18th Century', *Econ. Hist. Rev.* 2nd Ser. VI (2) (1953), pp. 117–33; and *American and British Technology in the 19th Century* (1962), pp. 134–6.

the numbers of consumers and by expanding the labour force. This was hardly evident, however, in the 1780s, for as yet factories of the modern kind were virtually unknown. The biggest employers of labour were the cloth manufacturers, and most of their workers plied their trade at home: a large textile factory in Bohemia, for example, had 297 people working within its walls and 1,400 spinners and 100 weavers under contract in the domestic system.[19] Wherever one went in Europe, in every nook and corner there would be someone spinning or weaving, 'young children, orphans, idiots, vagabonds and even soldiers in Prussian barracks'.[20] Other industries, with the exception sometimes, of mining and metallurgical enterprises and state arsenals and manufactories, would be carried on by comparatively small groups under the paternalistic discipline of the workshop, rather than the impersonal regimentation of the factory, and the industrial working class in towns consisted, generally, of masters and their journeymen, and independent artisans and craftsmen. In all France, there were only two industrial organizations that were sizable by modern standards: the Anzin coal mines, employing 4,000, and the Van Robais textile mill at Abbeville which had 3,000 workpeople engaged within its walls and many more in their own homes. Even in England, the land of the inventions of Kay, Hargreaves and Arkwright, and of the Boulton-Watt steam engine, an intelligent contemporary would have been puzzled to hear that an 'industrial revolution' was in progress. The small scale of the innovations concealed their ultimate potentialities. As late as 1800, all the steam engines in the country were not developing the amount of horsepower that we find necessary today to propel three hundred business men in their separate conveyances from suburb to office.

Industrialization in England was to have two stages: in the first, the inventions in textile manufacture, the steam engine, an infinitely extensible market for cotton goods and an expanding labour force were to make the factory system possible; after this, the locomotive and railways would revolutionize transport and create a vast market for the metallurgical industries. Once these two stages were completed, another era was to begin—which the eighteenth century equally could not foresee, but for which it was making the longer-range preparations—when science was to be brought deliberately into mesh with technology.

Europe had passed the decisive stage in its 'Scientific Revolution'

[19] M. S. Anderson, op. cit., p. 65.
[20] D. Ogg, *Europe of the Ancien Régime* (1965), p. 113. For a clear analysis of the different types of working-class people see G. Rudé, *Revolutionary Europe, 1783–1815* (1964), pp. 27 ff.

in the seventeenth century, and the eighteenth century saw the consolidation and refinement of the achievement: the improvement of
instruments and the sophistication of some branches of mathematics,
the foundation of geology and the systematizing of botany, the crucial
experiments on the nature of heat and the basic discoveries about
electrical phenomena. By the beginning of the nineteenth century,
scientific methodology had reached a fully recognizable modern
form and the way was open for the comprehensive investigation of
Nature which, it seems, will be the decisive factor in all foreseeable
permutations of human civilization.[21] Yet in 1789, though a few
industrialists were showing an interest in science,[22] and lightning
conductors and aids to navigation were evidence to justify new hopes,
not many discoveries of scientists had found a dramatic practical
application. It was not as a lever to change the world or as a force
of destiny that science enjoyed an enormous prestige, but as a supreme
achievement of the disinterested intellect. Polite society gathered to
see Pilâtre de Rozier rising in his hot-air balloon 3,000 feet above the
dome of the Invalides; Arthur Young was mightily impressed by
Mme Lavoisier discoursing on the 'phlogistic theory of inflamma-
bility' while she poured out tea;[23] and Prince Ernest wrote to George
III about his studies at Göttingen to say that 'of all the course of
natural philosophy, electricity is the most interesting'.[24] A century
before the laboratory went into close alliance with the factory, and
a century and a half before the atom bomb, science had, at least,
made a conquest of the drawing rooms.

V

To contemporaries, the expansion of commerce and agriculture may
have seemed a more revolutionary phenomenon than the new
techniques in industry. All three movements were connected, of
course, and in so far as agricultural development needed capital and
industrial development needed both capital and attractive markets,
the commercial boom provided the impulsion for both. 'The century of the Enlightenment', writes M. Morazé, 'was essentially and
primarily the century of commerce.'[25] Between 1717 and 1750 the

[21] A. R. Hall, *The Scientific Revolution, 1500–1800* (1954), p. 364.
[22] A. E. Masson and E. Robinson, 'Science and Industry in the late 18th
Century', *Econ. Hist. Rev.* XIII (2), 1960, pp. 222–44.
[23] Arthur Young, *Travel in France during the years 1787, 1788 and 1789* (ed.
Constantia Maxwell, 1950), p. 82.
[24] *The Later Corresp. of George III*, ed. A. Aspinall, I (1962), p. 442 (9 Sept.
1789).
[25] C. Morazé, *Les Bourgeois conquérants* (1957), p. 8.

external trade of the states of western Europe increased by 400 per cent (in the corresponding period of the next century, the increase was only 130 per cent).[26] From the Americas came Canadian furs, Newfoundland salt fish, Virginian tobacco, South-American gold, silver and dye-stuffs, while vast quantities of manufacturers were sent back in return—and African slaves. From the East came cotton, tea, porcelain, raw silk and spices; light luxury loads, paid for in specie, not goods, so that the Asian trade employed few ships as compared with the Atlantic run. The importance of commerce in European life can be traced in the pattern of its cities. Only twenty had populations of over 100,000, and the largest were capitals of great states, like Paris with half a million and Vienna with 250,000. The next biggest were seaports, especially those of the west—Lisbon, Amsterdam (200,000), Hamburg (130,000), Bordeaux, Cadiz—and, on the Mediterranean, Marseille, Venice and Naples. London, a capital and also the greatest seaport of all, was easily the most populous city in Europe, with something like a million inhabitants. Urbanization was still a phenomenon of courts and of commerce, not of the factory system and the population explosion.

Significantly, the commercial expansion of the eighteenth century was matched by a parallel revolution in agricultural techniques. An increasing population and a leap forward into machine production would be complementary developments multiplying each other's forces by mutual interaction if—and only if—the agricultural system could maintain an increasing food supply. The innovations in farming—scientific crop raising and animal breeding, enclosures and heavy capital investment in consolidated estates—were most obvious in England, though there were signs of progress in the Austrian Netherlands (Belgium), Holland, and in areas of intensive cultivation in the Rhineland and Lombardy. France had its agricultural societies devoted to the new ideas and attended chiefly by reforming townsmen, but the land hunger of the peasants made them unwilling to co-operate with plans of the government to encourage enclosure. The land needed the investment of capital: the money that was sucked up by the unfair and archaic taxation system or, through the channel of rents and feudal dues, went to support aristocratic display or the purchase of offices from the Crown. In Spain,[27] the nobles had little interest in agricultural investment, and the profits of the land went to provide portions for younger sons, who in England would have been sent into commerce or the profes-

---

[26] R. Schnerb, *Le XIX$_e$ siècle* (*Hist. gén. des civilisations*, 1957), p. 44.

[27] A. R. M. Carr, 'Spain' in *The European Nobility in the 18th Century*, ed. A. Goodwin (1953), pp. 48–55.

sions. Most peasant holdings in France were too small to support the cost of improvements; in Spain, the rural population was poorer still and, except in the Basque provinces, Navarre and Catalonia, leases were too short and precarious for improvements to be worthwhile.

East of the Elbe, south of the Apennines and in the Danube basin, the new agriculture could only penetrate on the rare occasions when some great nobleman was willing to experiment on his private demesne, for the actual cultivators of the soil were serfs, (or in a miserable condition very near to serfdom), and most of them remained so until the mid-nineteenth century. 'Attached to the glebe and sold with it', said an English traveller to Poland, 'they are equally strangers to the name and to the possession of freedom.'[28] Those were the days when an Englishman could look out across his moat and take comfort in the working of a law of increasing misery across the map of Europe; Popery and wooden shoes on the other side of the Channel and, as one got further away from home, slavery and no shoes at all.

VI

What was this 'freedom', unknown to Polish serfs and possessed in the highest degree by Englishmen? An English observer of the time might have said that there were three things that the Polish serf lacked. One was membership in a stable, independent national community, for in 1772 Russia, Prussia and Austria shamelessly partitioned half the country and in due course were to divide up what remained. Another was the possession of property and economic opportunity, and the third was the right to participate in political life. We can see these sorts of criteria being applied by an English visitor to Sweden, who compared the lot of the rural population with that of the serfs of other countries, and said that the Swedish peasant, in spite of his poverty and the burdens of tithes, quit rents and post services, 'enjoys the profits of his own labour, and has a voice in the legislature of his country, as a member of the Fourth Estate'.[29] To be free from foreign domination, to enjoy the profits of one's own labour, and to have a voice in the legislature are ideals which can be taken to extreme conclusions; this indeed was to happen in the nineteenth century, whose complicated history has sometimes been simplified into a story of masses of men moving forward through

[28] Wraxall, op. cit., II, pp. 31–3.
[29] Ratcliffe, *A Journey Through Sweden* (1790) in F. F. D. Tennant (ed.), *The Scandinavian Book* (1951), p. 43.

factory smoke towards the beacon lights of nationalism, socialism and democracy. In a later lecture, I must attempt to trace the eighteenth-century roots of these three ideologies, but it would be anachronistic to define freedom at the end of the *ancien régime* in their terms. In 1789, a peculiar pattern of social tensions and social theorizing focused men's minds, especially in France, upon the burning grievances of 'despotism' and 'privilege', and from the battle over these issues sprang the revolution that was to formulate the ideologies that stirred among the masses in the century to come.

There was general agreement in the eighteenth century that monarchy was a necessity in great states, and the anarchy in Poland caused by a weak, elective kingship and the habit of the republican Dutch of turning to the House of Orange in emergencies seemed to prove the proposition. Voltaire, anxious to break the grip of clergy and aristocracy in France, naturally appealed to kings as the agents of regeneration, and some other thinkers of the Enlightenment even spoke of the necessity for 'enlightened despotism'. In fact, however, the *philosophes* never regarded despotism as anything better than a desperate expedient, a necessary evil. [30] If they had thought otherwise, the conduct of the rulers themselves would have soon brought disillusionment. Some of them hobnobbed with literary men in the interests of their public image and used the Enlightenment's ideals of utility, toleration and uniformity of administration as aids to their power; meanwhile, they pursued the paths of *raison d'état*, mercantilism and militarism. Joseph II, an exponent of Machiavellianism in foreign policy, who nevertheless risked his throne in trying to free the serfs in the lands of the Habsburgs, was almost unique in his idealism. Enlightened despotism, indeed, had little substance as a political theory and less still as a political reality. The alliance of princes and *philosophes* was sincere only when directed against the Catholic Church or the privileges of the aristocracy.

Otherwise, what the *philosophes* wanted—what most educated men in France and western Europe wanted—was, not reform at the expense of freedom, but 'liberty under the law'. The king must be under the laws, said an Archbishop, preaching before Louis XVI on the eve of his coronation, with an emphasis some thought scandalous. [31] England, where the courts of justice protected the individual against the executive and America, which had retained the rights of

---

[30] For enlightened despotism see Fritz Hartung's essay (1957, Hist. Association); for the attitude of the *philosophes*, Peter Gay, *Voltaire's Politics: the Poet as Realist* (1959).

[31] J. McManners, 'The Revolution and its Antecedents', in *France: Government and Society*, ed. McManners and J. M. Wallace-Hadrill (1957), p. 171.

Englishmen by disguising them as the inalienable Rights of Man, were incomplete reflections of the ideal set out by Voltaire's Brahmin, of a government in which a man 'obeys the laws alone'.

> 'That is an old reply.
> That does not make it any worse.
> Where is that country?
> We must look for it.'[32]

However great their theoretical powers and however numerous their arbitrary practices none of the monarchs of Europe could wield untrammelled absolute authority. They ruled by buying the collusion of a privileged minority of their subjects. Even in Russia, the throne of the Tsarina was fortified by systematic concessions (at the expense of the serfs) to the aristocracy. In a brilliant and controversial analysis of the west European and American scene, Professor R. R. Palmer[33] has recently argued that everywhere in the 1780s the aristocracies (and these included British and Irish Parliaments, Dutch and Belgian Estates, the Diets of Sweden, Poland, Hungary and Bohemia, the councils of city states in Switzerland and other oligarchical 'constituted bodies') were enlarging their claims and their functions. They could do this under the device of liberty, for since Montesquieu, it was a common opinion, as Gibbon said, that 'the distinction of ranks and persons is the firmest basis of a mixed and limited government'. It is possible that Palmer is attempting to include too many diverse phenomena within a single formula, but his study, by its parallel illustrations, has thrown into relief the working of the pattern in France, where the clash between 'despotism' and 'aristocracy' had reached its most civilized and dangerous complexity.

'We hold our Crown from God alone,' said Louis XV in 1770, 'and the independent power of making laws is solely ours.' In practice, however, the King at Versailles was trapped in a web of protocol and precedence, customary rights and provincial, class and personal privileges which, Frenchmen sometimes argued, differentiated their traditional monarchy from a despotism à la Turque. The nobles had their exemptions from taxation, their monopoly of higher posts in Church and army; the Gallican Church taxed itself and voted its own subventions to the Crown; the Estates of the pays d'états and some of the towns bought off royal taxes and imposed their own; the magistrates of the Parlements were there by inheritance and purchase; the very intendants, chief agents of royal authority in

---

[32] Dictionnaire philosophique, in Gay, op. cit., p. 17.
[33] R. R. Palmer, The Age of the Democratic Revolution, 1760–1800, I (1959).

the provinces, were chosen from a narrow circle at the summit of the magisterial hierarchy of nobles of the robe. The Crown worked against these privileges from above, for the sake of self-aggrandizement and efficiency; the privileged classes replied by challenging the royal 'despotism'. Meanwhile, from below, wherever privilege drew its odious line of demarcation, the resentments of the ambitious and educated were accumulating with revolutionary intensity—to destroy privilege in the social order and also to outface the aristocracy in its bid to annex political leadership when the monarchy became constitutional.

VII

This upsurge against aristocracy and despotism has been called a rising of the 'bourgeoisie'. The validity of this term, with its Marxist overtones, will be discussed later: at least it gives an indication of the social standing of most of the people concerned. Professor Palmer, referring to objectives rather than origins, calls the movement 'democratic', and he has shown that the word 'democracy' and its derivatives, though not often used, were gaining a new meaning that went far beyond the evocation of a polity once practised in the city states of antiquity. Van der Capellan tot de Pol, leader of the left in the Dutch revolution of 1784–7, was spoken of as a 'democrat'; he believed that officials ought to be elected, as in America, and he argued that the Dutch people owned the United Netherlands just as the shareholders owned the East India Company.[34] This did not mean that he was a levelling radical, for the evolving theory of 'democracy' or of 'popular sovereignty' did not necessarily lead to extreme conclusions until the fatal question arose—how ought that sovereignty to be exercised? Even so, by 1789 it was clear that there was a body of opinion in western Europe that was not satisfied to see sovereignty in the hands of a despot, however enlightened, or to suffer the abusive privileges of an aristocracy, however traditional.

Whence came the inspiration of this 'bourgeois' resistance, of this 'democratic' idealism? It is, essentially, the eighteenth-century form of the drive towards equality which Tocqueville regarded as the mainspring of European history, and derived from sources as diverse as Christianity, the invention of gunpowder and the domination of money.[35] The contrast between the spread of commerce and of education on the one hand, and the survival of

[34] Palmer, op. cit., pp. 325–31.
[35] Alexis de Tocqueville, *Democracy in America* (1835; Eng. trans. ed. R. D. Heffner 1956), pp. 26 ff.

unjustified privilege on the other, served as an incitement to action and as a whetstone to revolutionary theory. Intertwined with the demand for equality was the demand for liberty, which the aristocracy was using against despotism, and which the middle classes wished to use against despotism and aristocracy alike. The American revolutionaries contributed to the climate of opinion by exercising the pragmatic right of Englishmen to get rid of a displeasing ruler, but by doing so on principle. The principle was that governments exist to preserve the rights of individuals and derive their authority solely from the consent of the governed. Though the philosophers of the Enlightenment did not speak with a common voice on questions of political theory, their almost universal, common theme was the rejection of the Christian doctrine of original sin.[36] The ideals of liberty and equality, implicit in Christianity, had been obscured by the tendency of rulers to emphasize the incorrigible sinfulness of the ruled; it became common, in the eighteenth century, however, for men to believe that human nature would be ameliorated by education and the rational organization of society. Existing governments, therefore, could not be justified by prescription, but would be judged by the tests of 'nature' and 'utility', and even before Bentham made the formula famous, there was wide agreement to define utility as consisting in 'the greatest happiness of the greatest number'.[37]

But if theories of nature and utility were eminently suited to the criticism of abuses, they were not necessarily incompatible with illiberal government and social injustice—with despotism, for example, if really enlightened, or as events were to show, with an industrialism that ground down men's souls within an ostensibly liberal régime. In the end, the justification for democracy was to be, not that it is either natural or utilitarian, for (except in a devious fashion), it is neither, but in the sentimental hatred of injustice and in the passionate moral conviction that men ought to be treated as equals. It is significant that the democratic ideal arose in western Europe within the generation that saw a unique efflorescence of the humanitarian spirit. The deputies who came up to the Estates General in 1789 knew of Beccaria and Voltaire's campaigns for the reform of the criminal code and of Howard's for the reform of prisons, of recent measures in various states for the abolition of torture or for giving toleration to Protestants, of the anti-slavery

[36] E. Cassirer, *The Philosophy of the Enlightenment* (1951), p. 141; Crocker, op. cit., p. 455.
[37] See R. Hubert, *Les sciences sociales dans l'Encyclopédie* (1923), p. 359; and, generally R. Mauzi, *L'Idée du bonheur dans la littérature et la pensée françaises au XVIIIe siècle* (1960).

agitation in France and England, of the founding of orphanages, charity schools and deaf-and-dumb institutions; they were accustomed to reading literature of a highly sentimental and moralizing kind and to using a special vocabulary of philanthropic *clichés* which seems ludicrous today; they were full of new ideas on education, deeply sympathetic to children, which stemmed from Rousseau and reached their final point of absurdity in Bourdon de la Crosnière's system of alarm bells on the beds in children's dormitories.[38]

The men of '89 were familiar too with the passionately egalitarian writings of Rousseau which, as the old order crumbled, achieved overwhelming popularity and wove themselves into the phraseology and life of the Revolution. Rousseau can easily be misunderstood. He was not one of the *grands seigneurs* of revolutionary speculation who inherited the world of culture like Marx, of money like Engels, or of rank like Saint-Simon and Bakunin, and who dare to follow the logic of their argument into the subversion of existing institutions on the way to utopia. A tortured soul of genuinely humble origins, Rousseau felt his inferiority, masked it by pride—and deliberate simplicity—and in practical affairs always recommended caution and conformity. Even so, he was the most revolutionary of writers. On the other hand, to accuse him of 'totalitarian' tendencies, of a willingness to change the world by revolutionary terror, is nonsense. He specifically denied that *le salut public* (that ominous term) could justify interference with the life of a single individual,[39] and the unanimity of his General Will was a unanimity of love and friendship, a Quaker 'sense of the meeting'.

He was a revolutionary, but in divergent, almost contradictory ways. For himself, he rejected civilization. As a protégé of Mme de Warens, that strange ash-blonde adventuress, he had entered the dream-world of aristocratic leisure, and had established his right to stay there by his writings. Yet, self-consciously and awkwardly he left it, embracing poverty and the life according to nature. The Enlightenment denied original sin: Rousseau affirmed it, but not in man; it was inherent in society. Jean-Jacques, the lover of children and the most sympathetic of educationalists, had five children of his own and abandoned them under the constraints of a viciously unequal social order. Rousseau's hatred of inequality was intensely and

[38] Shelby T. McCloy, *The Humanitarian Spirit in 18th Century France* (1957), p. 230. For literature and vocabulary, see A. Monglond, *Le Préromantisme français* (2 vols., 1930) and P. Trahard, *Les Maîtres de la sensibilité française au XVIIIe siècle* (4 vols., 1931–3), *La Sensibilité révolutionnaire 1789–94* (1936).

[39] R. Derathé, *Jean-Jacques Rousseau et la science politique de son temps* (1950), p. 357.

passionately personal, and he calls us to abandon the corrupt society which battens on the weak and poor. We refuse, of course, so he offers us the alternative of Spartan self-sacrifice to achieve that harmony with our neighbours which is otherwise beyond us. We achieve this under the sovereignty of the General Will: in a sense, we obey only ourselves. The General Will is an impossible and charming fiction which corresponds to deep realities, haunts the imagination and is potentially subversive of all existing institutions. The people are never trapped by their past, they can never surrender their freedom; they have but to meet in due form and the government—be it king, parliament or what you will—is automatically suspended. Rousseau provided theoretical justification for men always and everywhere to do what the Americans did once under the stress of necessity—to blot out the past and start again. This, and not the preaching of ephemeral violence and vengeance is the true revolutionary mentality, however mild the mask behind which it disguises itself, and the coming century was to bring to its aid methods of transforming society and of conditioning men which could not have been foreseen in the generation of Rousseau.

VIII

In the 1780s, Europe was on the verge of a century of revolutionary transformation—industrial, political and social, a century that was to be infinitely rich in literature, painting, music and the works of the human spirit, that was to develop the modern art-sciences of history, geography and sociology, and was to make experimental science the decisive factor for the future of all humanity, that was to create the ideologies around which our lives are still lived and whose clash may yet destroy us. The other continents were helpless before the vast energies and growing technological dominance of the west Europeans, whose foreign offices and counting houses would settle the destinies of the world as they pleased. In 1789, all eyes were fixed on Paris and Versailles as the Estates General met and the triangular battle of Crown, aristocracy and 'democracy' reached its climax. Only a few eccentric thinkers ever speculated on what would happen when Russia awoke from the sleep of barbarism and America was fully populated, enjoying 'the favourable effects of time and of European arts and sciences'.[40] To us, who have seen the meeting of Russian and American armies on the Elbe, all this seems far away and very long ago.

[40] A Venetian opinion on America in 1783 (R. R. Palmer, op. cit., p. 239). For other opinions, M. Kraus, op. cit., pp. 265, 268.

Chapter II

THE FRENCH REVOLUTION: THE DEFEAT OF ARISTOCRACY AND 'DESPOTISM'

I

What was the French Revolution? To the great historian Alphonse Aulard, who wrote avowedly as a supporter of the Third Republic, hostile to both Christianity and Socialism, it was 'the Declaration of the Rights of Man of 1789 and the attempts to realize it'.[1] What then of the Terror? One can imagine how Aulard would have protested if a Catholic writer had defined Christianity simply as the attempts that have been made to realize the Sermon on the Mount; this would have seemed to him a fraudulent procedure designed to evade responsibility for the Inquisition, mercenary popes and religious wars. At the time he was writing it was a device of republican tactics to insist that the great Revolution had been a monolithic unity, which the conservative opposition had to accept or reject as a whole. Hence the importance of a single definition, and an elevated one, such as Aulard provided.

In contrast to his approach, suited to republican historiography in the late nineteenth and early twentieth centuries, we may take another, invented fairly recently by a philosopher of history, Henri Marrou. To Professor Marrou, the phrase 'French Revolution' is meant to evoke 'the tumultuous totality of what we know of all that happened in France and under French influence, between 8 May 1789 and 18 Brumaire Year VIII'—admitting, of course, that the precise dates are disputable.[2] There is a salutary warning in this definition, a warning against the deterministic logic which cannot glimpse the many possible revolutions which our narratives might have contained in place of the Revolution as we know it, a warning against the synthesizing tendencies of general surveys which forget the many folk to whom the Revolution was a series of external circumstances in which their participation was mostly involuntary.

Even so, the 'tumultuous totality' of all that happened in a certain area and between certain dates is not a sufficient description of the historian's term, 'the French Revolution'. If it were, this would

[1] A. Aulard, *The French Revolution: a Political History* (Engl. trans. 1910) IV, p. 282.
[2] H.-I. Marrou, *De la connaissance historique* (1962), p. 166.

imply that here we have a nominalist concept—rather like 'the Middle Ages'—to facilitate discussion, whereas 'the French Revolution' is at once a conventional term like this, and something more. From the middle of the eighteenth century a coming revolution was spoken of in France, and the events of 1789, from the very start, were spoken of as a 'revolution' by contemporaries; the titles of pamphlets and newspapers contain phrases like '*la Révolution actuelle*', '*les Révolutions de Paris*', and so on. At Lyon, a good abbé published a book detecting the 'historical resemblances between the beginnings of the French Revolution and those of the English Revolution which destroyed Charles I'.[3] If we believe the anecdote, there was one specific moment when it dawned on the court that the startling events in Paris were 'revolutionary'; Louis XVI asked if the attack on the Bastille constituted a riot, and the Duc de Liancourt said, 'No Sire, it is a revolution'. However this may have been, it is clear enough that the historian who talks of 'the French Revolution' is not imposing a convenient phrase on the past: he is accepting a phrase, convenient and inconvenient, which the past imposes on him. The 'Revolution' is not contrived as history is being written; it was in men's minds as history was being made.

II

Yet a form of words is not necessarily clearer because men have guillotined each other for it. The content of the Revolution changed, divided, contradicted itself. Though men had talked of the new era to come, they had done so in undramatic terms. The classical education of the *collèges* had familiarized them with the recurring revolutions of the Roman Republic, usually beneficent, while England (1688 rather than 1640) and America provided examples of revolutions which were respectable. What was expected was something like the colourless definition of the *Encyclopédie* (1765), 'a considerable change coming about in the government of a State. This word comes from the Latin *revolvere*, to turn. There are no States which have not been subject to revolutions, many or few.'[4] In 1789, men expected change, regeneration even, but they had no concept of a great destruction, of a fatal, compulsive web of disasters, of an abyss between the old society and the new. Perhaps it was a tragedy that few schools taught Greek, so that educated Frenchmen, who were familiar with the revolutions of ancient Rome, did not know Thucy-

[3] A. Monglond, *La France révolutionnaire et impériale* (1930) I, cols. 270–1.
[4] *Encyclopédie*, XIV (1765), p. 237.

dides' terrible description of the Corcyrean Revolution, so bitterly fratricidal, so distorted by war, as theirs was to be.

The events of 1789 rapidly outran all expectations. Before the end of the year, the *ancien régime* was commonly spoken of, a daring recognition of the breach with the past which quickly supplanted the cautious official *régime précédent*; before another year was out, the forces of the old order had been subsumed under the new term 'counter-revolution'.[5] Thus the Revolution went on, coining its own vocabulary, accumulating its own symbols and religious overtones, monopolizing patriotism, until war came to intensify the process to a morbid degree. The law of 10 October 1793, which declared the government of France 'revolutionary' until the peace, is a landmark in a blurred landscape of changing meanings. Politically, it marks the suspension of ideals in the interest of their preservation. 'The Revolution,' said Robespierre, 'is the war of liberty against its enemies; the Constitution is the rule of liberty victorious and at peace.' To the student of historiography, this is the topographical point where travellers diverge and lose sight of each other, some historians inclining to the principles of '89, spontaneous and liberal, and others to those of '93, the despotic, heroic culmination of the high Revolution. To the student of semantics, here is a reversal of meaning brought about by the imperious pressure of events. Revolution, a political change, strictly speaking cyclical in nature, has become a ruthless, purposeful forward movement, united with the new idea of indefinite progress and the old ideas of *raison d'état*, survival and conquest. Ordinary necessary things became ideological now, because they had to be done expeditiously. There were 'revolutionary' methods of making saltpetre and tanning hides; there was a 'revolutionary logic' which Mercier regarded as 'the eclipse of the human mind'.[6]

When the tumult subsided, who could interpret its tense vocabulary, its frenzies and its innumerable factions? Quinet recalls how, as a boy, he was unable to understand the references to 'Girondins', 'Jacobins', and 'Montagnards' which he met in his reading. They had all been swallowed up in one mysterious word, the 'Terror'; 'to such an extent and so soon had the language of the Revolution ceased to be a living language.'[7] This devitalizing of the terminology which had once enshrined the secrets of the Revolution was also noted—and as early as 1810—by Grégoire; 'Jacobin', he said, which had been the name for a member of a society which began by

[5] F. Brunot, *Histoire de la langue française*, IX (1927), pp. 618–9.
[6] Ibid.
[7] E. Quinet, *Histoire de mes Idées* (n.d., 12th ed.), pp. 75–6,

being patriotic then lapsed into cruelty, was now a term simply meaning those who believed in executing political opponents. So it was with all these words for which they had killed each other— 'as each one attaches to them a nuance according to his own principles or prejudices, their true meaning will, perhaps, one day become a torment to historians'.[8]

In this fashion, the historian has inherited the terms of the revolutionary era, including the term 'the French Revolution' itself, with its dark penumbra of subconscious meaning and its implication of organic unity in which infinite complexities are obscured. To understand it, these complexities have to be unravelled, and six generations of historians so far have variously essayed the task. In two lectures one cannot do more than refer to some of the main lines of interpretation which have emerged, sketch in the main patterns of events, and examine some of the chances by which these patterns became interlocked in unpredictable and tragic ways. Then, in a third lecture rather later, I will look again at the Revolution from the point of view of what came after, seeking in its chaos for the inspirations of some of the great movements that shaped the nineteenth century.

III

Though the French Revolution can never be comprehended in a single definition, I think that we can get near to the essence of the matter in a phrase chosen by Professor Goodwin as a concluding summary for his short history: 'a merciless war between aristocracy and democracy'.[9] We have seen how this theme of a clash between aristocratic and democratic tendencies has been developed by R. R. Palmer into an interpretation of the trend of political events in Europe and America in the second half of the eighteenth century. The wider thesis may be challenged, but so far as France is concerned, the point when Louis XVI was presented with a decisive choice between these two forces may be taken as the beginning of the Revolution. In February 1787, Calonne, Louis' Controller-General, opened his campaign to abolish privileged exemptions from taxation to save the State from bankruptcy, and in May of the following year, Loménie de Brienne tried to achieve the same object by breaking the resistance of the Parlement of Paris. Their actions provoked an aristocratic onslaught on despotism, which is the opening scene of the revolutionary drama.

This revolt of the aristocracy was not the rising of a coherent class.

[8] Grégoire, *Histoire des sectes religieuses* (1810), cit. Brunet IX, p. 656.
[9] A. Goodwin, *The French Revolution* (1953), p. 182.

Grands seigneurs and rich young magistrates deep in Orléanist intrigues or envying the political rôle of their contemporaries in England, prelates manoeuvring for the independence and safety of the clerical order, reactionary magistrates maintaining Parlement's guardianship of mythical 'fundamental laws', country squires making a last-ditch stand in defence of feudal dues or hoping to dominate local affairs in revived provincial estates of an aristocratic complexion—there was no real unity in their agitation beyond the knowledge that their privileges were in danger and a common spirit of proud independence. Most of them admitted that they would have to pay fair taxation sooner or later, but they intended to retain their honorific status, and they claimed a right of leadership, in national or in local politics, now that the royal absolutism was breaking.

Though there was genuine co-operation between nobles and commons only in Dauphiné, there was widespread public support for the aristocratic opposition during the brief period in which attention was focused on the issue of 'despotism'. Looking back twenty years later, Malouet cynically described the resulting confusions: 'The universal temper was one of independence. Clergy, Nobility, Parlement, Third Estate, each wanted an extension of privileges for its own particular group alone, and the suppression or reduction of everyone else's. The provincial nobles found the yoke of the nobles of the court intolerable; the lower clergy wanted a share of the dignities that the upper clergy monopolized; the officers, high and low, of the army argued on the same principles. . . ., and the *grands seigneurs* thought it excellent that the King should be absolute over everybody except the members of their own class, for they cast themselves for the rôle of companions of the sovereign, not his servants. From this simultaneous collision of all the different corporations, which clashed wherever they met and were in harmony nowhere, there resulted . . . a deceptive appearance of unanimity for innovations tending towards something resembling a free government, which everyone interpreted in his own private fashion.'[10]

The demand for liberty was much more sincere than Malouet ever knew, but it was certainly incoherent, so that the Crown, pushed back towards an abyss of bankruptcy by a defiant aristocracy, was able to change course, and appeal to the country at large. The promise to call the Estates General, the old assembly of the three orders which had not met for more than 170 years, reluctantly given at first, became a deliberate instrument of royal policy. 'Since the nobles and clergy abandon the King, their natural protector', said Brienne, 'he is obliged to turn to the commons and use them to crush

[10] Malouet, *Mémoires* (2 vols., 1874) I, p. 293.

the other two orders.'[11] This was the language of a revolution directed by the throne, but there was no force behind its statesmanlike and revengeful phrases. In August 1788, Brienne fell from power, and M. Egret, the latest historian of the last days of the *ancien régime*, takes this date as the true beginning of the Revolution, since from henceforward, events were no longer under the control of the government. War between aristocracy and democracy was now inevitable.

IV

'A change has come over the controversy', wrote Mallet du Pan in January 1789, 'the King, despotism and the constitution are now secondary questions: the main issue is a war between the Third Estate and the other two orders, against whom the Court has called in the towns.' The towns did not need any invitation. Once the Parlement of Paris opposed the doubling of the Third Estate in the approaching Estates General, its popularity vanished. Despotism was crumbling and the middle classes of France made no mistake about where their real enemy lay: they were determined to destroy privilege. 'Equality', said Mme de Staël, 'was the driving force of of the Revolution.'

Tocqueville was to regret that the passion for equality burned more fiercely in '89 than the nobler zeal for liberty, but educated middle-class Frenchmen did not regard these two inspirations as separable, and when they pictured the 'free government' which they would found, they saw themselves as its administrators, orators and officials.[12] Bishoprics and colonelcies would cease to be reserved for the sons of the nobility, lawyers would no longer have to pay deference to the magistrates by purchase and inheritance who lorded it in the parlements and other chief law-courts of the land, the complex, illogical code of exemptions from taxation would be ended, careers would be opened to talent, and enterprise would reap the rewards that had been reserved for birth alone. 1789 is, indeed, an impossible starting date in French history, as the whole story of the tensions within eighteenth-century society is needed to explain the vast surge of anger which swept to the assault on privilege once the barriers were down.

As civilization had advanced in Europe, wherever genius, talent or

[11] J. Egret, *La Pré-révolution française, 1787–8* (1962), p. 306.
[12] J. McManners, 'The Revolution and its Antecedents, 1774–94', in *France: Government and Society*, ed. J. M. Wallace-Hadrill and McManners (1957), p. 182.

ambition found itself excluded by inherited vested interest, resentments had multiplied. 'It is his heart that ennobles a man', wrote Mozart to his father in 1781, after quarrelling with Count Arco, Chamberlain to the Archbishop of Salzburg, 'I may not be a count, but I have more honour within myself than many a count.'[13] Significantly, to express his emotions in public form, the great musician appropriated a French inspiration, Beaumarchais' *Mariage de Figaro* (1786), with its sensational 'punch line', '*Vous vous êtes donné la peine de naître, et rien de plus*'. The crisis came in France, for of all continental European countries this was the one where an active, well-educated and cultured middle-class was rising, sharply conscious of the artificiality of the superiorities claimed by the aristocracy. The King's minister Necker, in a report of 27 December 1788 which persuaded the royal council to agree to doubling the representation of the commons in the Estates General, said that: 'Accumulated capital and holdings in government loans have associated the Third Estate with the public fortune; education and enlightenment have become a common patrimony: prejudices are declining.'[14] The mingling of birth and wealth in profitable enterprises (including well-dowried marriages), and the triumphs of the *philosophes* in the Academy and in fashionable drawing-rooms had created an egalitarian spirit in the upper reaches of Parisian society; when it suited its turn, the aristocracy itself conceded that birth was a 'prejudice', though it did not do so when pensions, embassies and bishoprics were being awarded. In France, more than elsewhere, privilege had become a manifest absurdity, and a revolt of the middle classes was becoming inevitable.

In this sense, the French Revolution was a revolution of the bourgeoisie. If we use this term, however, we must beware of allowing its Marxist implications to dominate our imaginations; we are speaking of a class that is infinitely diverse, running from Government financiers, shipowners and bankers down to very ordinary provincial *avocats*, notaries, doctors and merchants. 'It was not essentially a capitalist class: it was a coalition of the educated and the ambitious',[15] united, not against the working classes below, but

---

[13] *The Letters of Mozart and his Family* (ed. Emily Anderson, 1938) III, p. 1111.

[14] L. Villat, *La Révolution et l'Empire* (1947) I, p. 5.

[15] McManners, op. cit., pp. 181–2. Since this chapter was written, Professor A. Cobban's *The Social Interpretation of the French Revolution* (1964) has appeared. Taking up the themes of his own *Myth of the French Revolution* (1955), the author spells out in detail the arguments against the Marxist formulae used by the late Georges Lefebvre and (more especially) by Professor Soboul —that the bourgeoisie was not an homogeneous class, that it did not abolish

against the aristocracy above, a class which was fighting, not in defence of an acquired economic status, but aggressively, to bring the aristocracy down to its own level. Mirabeau, a noble rejected by his own order, summed up the aspirations of the social groups where his ambitions found a home: 'War against privileges and the privileged, that is my motto—privileges are useful against kings, but detestable if used against nations.'[16]

In this war, the spearhead of the 'bourgeois' attack was the group of deputies of the Third Estate sent by the country to the Estates General at Versailles. Its composition shows how the bourgeoisie had monopolized the national representation, and also how far we are from anything resembling a 'capitalist' class, for of the 610, only 80 are from banking or business and only 60 or so are independent landowners or rentiers; the others, fully two-thirds of the total, are 'lawyers' of various kinds. This does not mean—as the old-fashioned allegation had it—that they were a cohort of theorists. Lawyers are given, no doubt, to talk, but not, surely, except by the conventions of eighteenth-century rhetoric, to impractical abstractions. One should remember, too, that these 'lawyers' include many royal judicial and administrative officials, and many local big-wigs immersed in the affairs of municipalities, or involved in the business transactions of merchants and owners of estates, tithes or feudal dues. The first revolutionary assembly was inevitably lacking in parliamentary expertise, but it had a great deal of knowledge of the day-to-day affairs of the world; indeed, a more telling right-wing criticism would be the opposite one: that France began its career of parliamentarianism with a ready-made class of self-important politicians flocking up from the provinces. But this charge would contain only a fraction of the truth, for these men had read the *philosophes* and, what was more important, Rousseau, and with all their ambitions and self-interest, they were deeply stirred by the ideals of freedom and equality and the hope of a national regeneration.

'feudalism' of its own free-will, that its members owned much land, that its leaders did not come from business and industry, that the Revolution set back rather than hastened economic progress in France. Virtually all these qualifications are made by Lefebvre, but he did not always bear them in mind when generalizing. Since it seems excessive to follow Professor Cobban in asking French historians to abandon the word 'bourgeoisie' altogether, and since we still await a detailed analysis of what the word meant to eighteenth-century contemporaries, I have stuck to a compromise formula which—it still seems to me—reflects very much what Lefebvre and Soboul's masterly researches really imply, as distinct from their occasional doctrinaire reflections.

[16] 16 Aug. 1788, Egret, op. cit., p. 334.

V

The battle against privilege in the Estates General was joined on the question of 'verification of powers'; the nobles wished to retain their identity as an order, while the Third Estate, doubled in numbers by the royal electoral regulations, wanted to force united deliberations in which its numerical weight would prevail. On 17 June the commons declared themselves the 'National Assembly', and on 20 June, by the Oath of the Tennis Court, they swore never to disband until the constitution was established. More and more of the clergy came over to join them. Only the Crown could mediate in this quarrel. Everyone awaited a *séance royale*, a command performance in which Louis would come down—as Jefferson optimistically suggested to Lafayette—'offering a charter containing all the good in which all the parties agree'.[17] When the King did come down to the Estates General, on 23 June, it was to declare himself for the nobility; if his subjects failed to support him, he said, 'I shall do myself what is best for my people. I shall regard myself as their real representative'. The crown had thrown away its strategic advantages and had identified itself with the failing cause of reaction. Mirabeau's 'bayonet' speech and Sieyès' cold defiance have become famous, but Bailly, president of the commons, coined the most deadly riposte, a direct confutation of the royal claim to represent the people: 'I believe that the assembled nation cannot receive orders.'

Louis XVI made no attempt to enforce his injunction, and on 27 June he capitulated and commanded the first two estates to join the third. An English visitor thereupon left the capital in search of more interesting events in the provinces—'the whole business is now over, and the revolution complete'.[18] In fact, the great Parisian drama was just beginning, for the court had decided to gamble on force and regiments of German and Swiss mercenaries were closing in. On 11 July, Necker was dismissed: the scene was set for an authoritarian *coup d'état*. The Assembly was saved (almost in spite of itself, for the deputies wrung their hands at the news of disorder) by the rising of Paris—not just a rising of the working classes desperate for bread, but of the middle classes too, with mutinous troops of the French

[17] *The Letters of Lafayette and Jefferson* (ed. Chinard, 1929), pp. 126–7. For modern historians agreeing that a royal offer could have carried the day, see G. Lefebvre, *The Coming of the French Revolution* (Engl. trans., 1947), p. 74, and F. Braesch, *1789: l'année cruciale* (1946).

[18] Arthur Young, *Travels in France . . . 1787, 8 and 9* (ed. C. Maxwell, 1950), p. 159.

Guards co-operating, and the bourgeois Committee of Electors (which had chosen the Parisian deputation to the Estates General) organizing and legitimizing the arming of the city. There was no direct military significance in the fall of the Bastille, but the American, Austrian and English ambassadors all reported that it was decisive. 'Thus . . .', said the Duke of Dorset, 'the greatest revolution that we know anything of has been effected with the loss of very few lives. From this moment we may consider France as a free country, the King as a very limited Monarch, and the Nobility as reduced to a level with the rest of the Nation.'[19]

VI

Paris set up its own municipal government and National Guard, and all over France the urban middle classes followed this example—in some places they had anticipated it. No doubt their motives were mixed, for the collapse of the traditional machinery of government was hastened by an inchoate agrarian insurrection, and substantial citizens of towns, forming themselves into armed militias, may have been as conscious of the threat to property as of the aristocratic conspiracy and the German mercenaries.[20] Rather later, when the members of Assembly made a theatrical and sentimental renunciation of privileges on the famous night of 4 August, they were being driven on by the fears which this grim, autonomous revolution of the peasantry inspired. But for the moment, France was united to organize and arm to defy aristocracy and Crown. Citizen committees and bourgeois militias took over the reins from royal intendants and the old municipal oligarchies. It was 'a vast popular reaction,' writes Norman Hampson, 'whose most striking events, even the storming of the Bastille itself, were no more than isolated waves in a great storm. . . . Within the space of a few weeks, the royal government lost control over the provinces, for in matters of importance the towns henceforward took their orders only from the Assembly'.[21]

In October, Paris intervened again to force the King to recognize the sovereign authority of the Assembly. The women and National Guards who marched to Versailles did so because their families were starving and because of sinister celebrations that had marked the arrival of the Flanders regiment at court, but behind the events of

---

[19] Cit. J. M. Thompson, *The French Revolution* (1951 ed.), p. 62.
[20] J. McManners, *French Ecclesiastical Society under the Ancien Régime: a Study of Angers in the Eighteenth Century* (1960), p. 232.
[21] N. Hampson, *A Social History of the French Revolution* (1963), pp. 76, 78.

5 and 6 October there was an understanding between the revolutionaries of the capital and the 'patriots' of the Assembly to force Louis
to sanction the decrees of August and the Declaration of the Rights
of Man. The royal family was taken to Paris, and the Constituent
Assembly could now enforce its plans for the establishment of a new
order.

CHAPTER III

THE REVOLUTION: BOURGEOISIE AND PEOPLE

I

The Constituent Assembly reconstructed France on the principles of rationality, uniformity, humanity, and equality of opportunity. The defeat of the aristocracy was sealed by abolishing titles of nobility, opening careers in church and army, and by creating a single-chamber legislative assembly; the defeat of despotism was confirmed by limiting the King to a suspensive veto and by decentralizing the administration to the point of unworkability. Protestants, Jews and actors became full citizens; torture was abolished, and the jury was established (two juries in fact) in criminal cases. All men were equal before the law. If some of these reforms show an over-systematic temper—the result of inexperience and of a too-enthusiastic repudiation of the complexities of the *ancien régime* —the settlement, taken generally, was shrewdly conciliatory. The former privileged classes were not attacked in their material interests; holders of venal offices were given compensation, most feudal dues were to be bought off at full value, and it would have taken some years before the right of commoners to compete for commissions in the army or the navy could seriously have threatened the careers of sons of the nobility. 'In spite of the occasional punitive decree ...' writes Hampson, 'the Assembly in the main treated the French people as a united family.'[1]

There were choices to be made between different members of the family, of course, and the fact that the Assembly backed the interests of the owners of feudal dues is significant. Marxist historians have pointed out how the reforming inspirations of the Constituents had a 'bourgeois' bias. They refused the franchise to poorer ('passive') citizens, they abolished internal customs duties but maintained tariffs and the colonial monopoly; their basic land tax was far from being a comprehensive income tax; they made a present of ecclesiastical tithe and of the islands and rivers of crown lands to private proprietors; they made only half-hearted gestures to give small men a chance to buy church property, and they failed to organize poor relief to replace ecclesiastical charity; their *loi le Chapelier*, which

---

[1] N. Hampson, *A Social History of the French Revolution* (1963) p. 111.

Marx was to call 'a bourgeois coup d'état', forbade workmen to combine to press their grievances. There is also reason to suppose that the sense of solidarity which had been manifested against privilege above was now transforming itself into a sense of solidarity against the unpropertied masses below. Mathiez and Michon[2] have shown how a bourgeois party of order was forming, even before the flight to Varennes, and the Le Chapelier law was passed at a time when employers were petitioning the Assembly to take action against combinations of carpenters and printers to force up wages.

Evidence of this kind shows the limitations of the men of '89, but while we must recognize their 'bourgeois' prejudices, we must also remember that they would have been as horrified as Marx himself at the prospect of a victory of oligarchical capitalism. They 'did not see beyond the molecular economy of the epoch and did not think that [economic] liberty could lead to anything other than a competitive democracy of very small business enterprises.'[3] When discussing mining rights, the Assembly favoured the ordinary landowner rather than the big concessionaire, and by maintaining customary grazing rights and forbidding the exportation of grain, it looked after the poorer peasants and urban workers rather than the more successful farmers. Champions of the people like Robespierre accepted the Le Chapelier legislation for, unlike the regulations of the *ancien régime*, it forbade combinations of owners as well as of workers, and earlier decrees had swept away those nests of petty privilege, the trade guilds. Few citizens were excluded from the franchise: a constitution which defines 'active' citizens as those paying annual taxation to the value of three days of a labourer's wages is hardly an instrument of class warfare. To the best of their ability, the men of '89 had founded a free government. Jaurès, an historian whose Marxist convictions were tempered by a subtle, sympathetic mind and practical experience of politics, conceded that 'in the circumstances of the times, they spoke for all humanity'.[4]

II

By the summer of 1791, the halcyon days of the Revolution were over. Conservatives declared that they had never existed, for regeneration had been written into decrees under the shadow of violence:

[2] A. Mathiez, *Le Club des Cordeliers pendant la crise de Varennes* (1910), p. 34 especially; G. Michon, *Essai sur l'histoire du Parti Feuillant: Adrien Duport* (1924), pp. 80–91, 98.

[3] R. Mousnier and E. Labrousse, *Le XVIIIe siècle* (*Histoire générale des civilisations*, 1953), p. 389. An excellent discussion follows.

[4] J. Jaurès, *Histoire socialiste*, I (1901; ed. A. Mathiez, 1927), pp. 341–7.

'the Terror', Malouet was to say, 'dates from the fall of the Bastille.'
A few gilded courtiers left France after the July insurrection, but
numbers of army officers and deputies followed after the October
Days. The Emigration 'began as a mode, it continued as a protest,
and it gathered force as a counter-revolution.'[5] As it did so, a disproportionate fear of the plotters in Turin, Brussels and Koblenz
haunted Frenchmen, and their revolutionary zeal was embittered
by suspicions of an aristocratic conspiracy. It was easy to believe
that the King would be its accomplice; indeed, from the fall of the
Bastille Marie Antoinette had adopted the self-justificatory *cliché*
of the Emigration, '*le roi n'est pas libre*', which she interpreted to
mean that he could sign anything without moral obligation.[6]

Over the issue of the royal veto, the patriotic union of 1789 had
disintegrated. Mounier, the leader of the deputation of Dauphiné,
who finally emigrated in May 1790, said: 'We thought we needed the
club of Hercules to smash abuses, but what we really needed was the
shoulders of Atlas to bear up the monarchy.'[7] He saw that the
provinces lagged behind the radicals of Paris in their desire for
change; thus, in the constitutional debates of 29 August '89, when
Mirabeau asked for voting by name so that the spectators in the
galleries would have targets for their disapproval, Mounier called
for the publication of division lists so that the provinces would know
who were their true representatives.[8] The leaders of the Assembly
who could agree on constitutional principles were separated from
each other by feuds and ambitions; Lafayette's control of the National
Guard and Mirabeau's political genius, for example, were never
brought into partnership. Inevitably, the rapid reorganization of the
country and the sudden opening of new vistas in politics had accumulated disagreements and envy, and the Assembly, which had shrewdly
tried to smooth over aristocratic illwill, committed the startling
imprudence of pursuing an ecclesiastical policy which put half the
clergy at variance with the nation. The decision, in November 1790,
to impose an oath to the Constitution (which included the Civil
Constitution of the Clergy) was disastrous. For the first time, there
was a coherent opposition to the Revolution, based on principle
and enjoying mass support in many areas.

These disagreements weakened the revolutionary movement by

[5] D. M. Greer, *The Incidence of the Emigration* (1951), p. 29. Later figures
about the Terror are from the same author's invaluable *Incidence of the
Terror* (1935).

[6] J. A. Bouteloupe, *Le rôle politique de Marie-Antoinette* (1924), p. 153.

[7] Cit. J.-J. Chevalier, *Barnave* (1936), pp. 85–6.

[8] J. Egret, *La Révolution des notables: Mounier et les monarchiens* (1950),
pp. 138–9.

detracting from its universality, though by reaction they strengthened it. To mask divisions the ideals of unity and fraternity were proclaimed with especial fervency, and the revolutionary enthusiasts organized themselves so tightly because they were conscious of potential dangers. The naïve, idealistic unity of '89 had been lost, but in its place had arisen something harsher and more durable, a revolutionary movement directed by a large and active minority. This élite exerted its maximum force firstly, through the many new newspapers which had sprung up, especially in Paris (Marat became famous, for example, by his *L'Ami du Peuple*), and secondly, through a nation-wide network of political clubs. By June 1791, there were 400 such societies in the provinces, and the process of affiliating to the Jacobin Club in Paris was under way. When the bitter dispute over the Civil Constitution of the Clergy began, the numbers of clubs increased more rapidly still,[9] so that by the end of 1793 there were at least 3,000 of them, probably many more. Taine professed to be scandalized by the power which devolved upon these minority groups, but it was common for one in every twelve 'active' citizens in an urban area to figure on the rolls of membership, which, comparatively speaking, is an impressive proportion. In these circles, local and national leaders emerged: 'Robespierre,' says Crane Brinton, the historian of the Jacobins, 'is a classic example of a man who owed almost everything to a club.'[10] In April 1790 the Cordeliers was founded in Paris, a more democratic association than the Jacobins, as its low subscription fee showed, and various *sociétés fraternelles* arose which looked to the Cordeliers for leadership. The first of these, founded by a schoolmaster, Dansard, required its women members to take an oath not to marry an aristocrat: a significant factor in the influence of popular societies was that they took politics seriously.

The clubs, together with the new municipalities created by the law of December '89, made the towns, generally speaking, into strongholds of the new order, and the bayonets of the National Guard were a still more certain guarantee of its permanence. Lafayette, commanding the National Guard of Paris, had a force of 24,000 volunteers who, since they had to purchase their own uniforms, were unlikely to belong to the 'wrong' social class, as well as a corps of 6,000 professionals drawn from the old French Guards.

---

[9] The effect of the Civil Constitution of the Clergy is emphasized by L. de Cardenal, *La Province pendant la Révolution: histoire des clubs Jacobins, 1789–95* (1929), p. 51; see also, for the popular societies, I. Bourdin, *Les Sociétés populaires à Paris pendant la Révolution* (1937), p. 159.

[10] Crane Brinton, *The Jacobins* (1930), p. 107.

Just as the clubs were co-ordinating their activities, so, too, were the municipalities and the new militias. A meeting of Angevins and Bretons at Pontivy, on 1 February 1790, sent a deputation to the capital to urge that 'a general federation is the sole method of consolidating the Revolution', and on 14 July this wish was fulfilled by the great festival of the Federation at Paris, attended by delegates from all over the country. It was a lesson, said a patriotic Angevin priest, to those 'introverted patriots for whom the fatherland extends no further than their own backyard'—'you double and treble your own being by allying with your fellow citizens.'[11] Not all Frenchmen supported the Revolution, but those who did so were embattled to defend it.

III

On the night of 20 June 1791 the royal family fled from Paris, and with the flight—and capture—of the King, the country was compelled to face the full revolutionary possibilities of the Revolution. The people of the capital received the returning fugitives in deathly silence; republicanism had been born. The Cordeliers and the popular societies led the movement for dethronement, while the Assembly, the majority of the Jacobins (who seceded to form a new club, the Feuillants) and the bourgeoisie generally, wished to retain the crown as a guarantee against foreign invasion and against the pretensions of the lower orders, which might threaten property. In the affair of the Massacre of the Champ de Mars (17 July 1791), the National Guard fired on the people: 'the forces of order . . . shot and sabred more men in one day than the Parisian crowds had lynched in the first two years of the Revolution.'[12]

'It would have been better for liberty,' Mme Roland wrote, 'that the King had not been stopped, because civil war would then have been unavoidable . . . we can only be regenerated by bloodshed.'[13] Tension had reached the point where there were intelligent people willing to accept such an apocalyptic vision of regeneration. Fear of the émigrés, of an aristocratic conspiracy, of a treacherous court, of an onslaught by the despots of Europe, on the one hand, and the crusading belief that a people in arms would be invincible, on the

[11] J. McManners, *French Ecclesiastical Society under the Ancien Régime* (1960), p. 236. The figure of 24,000 for the National Guard, given earlier in this paragraph, refers to the period after 21 Oct. 1790 (see G. Lefebvre, *French Revolution*, (Engl. trans., 1962, p. 140).
[12] N. Hampson, op. cit., p. 107.
[13] Mme Roland, *Lettres* (1902) II, p. 313.

other, whipped public opinion into a frenzy. The Legislative Assembly, which met on 1 October 1791, consisted entirely of new men, for the Constituents had declared themselves ineligible for re-election. In its passionate inexperience, the new Assembly drifted with the tide: when war finally came, only seven deputies voted against it. For contradictory reasons the various political leaders had no interest in the preservation of peace. Brissot and his faction pushed hard for a war which would bring them into power, just as the King hoped that an early defeat would compel the nation to return humbly to its dynasty; Marie Antoinette wished to provoke the foreign intervention she had been unable to negotiate, and some of the army leaders looked forward to using their troops to impose an internal settlement. When war was declared against the 'King of Bohemia and Hungary' on 20 April 1792, Robespierre was almost alone in denouncing the folly. He anticipated, correctly, that the peoples of Europe would not welcome 'armed missionaries' and that war would lead to dictatorship; what he did not foresee was that this would be a revolutionary, and not a reactionary tyranny, and that he himself would become its most notorious agent.

On 10 August a Parisian insurrection, with National Guards from Marseille collaborating with the men of the Sections, overthrew the monarchy. The King had vetoed decrees which were believed to involve the national safety, treason was suspected in the higher command of the armies, and the enemy had issued a manifesto threatening to shoot National Guards who resisted. On 1 August a foreign observer had declared that, 'if the King be not deposed, he must soon become absolute'. With the fall of the throne the centre of gravity of the Revolution moved leftwards. 'Passive' citizens had been admitted to the National Guard when the proclamation of *la patrie en danger* had been made—now universal suffrage was introduced, measures were taken to win over the peasantry, and the new revolutionary Commune displaced the old municipality of Paris. War, and the removal of the old executive, left the way open for the invention of a new type of revolutionary government, the first steps being taken when the Assembly set up a 'Provisional Executive Council' and sent commissioners to the armies. The demand for the trial of the Swiss of the royal bodyguard who had fired on the people led to the establishment of the Revolutionary Tribunal two days after the Assembly had decreed that the wives and children of émigrés would be held as hostages. Vengeance and panic were uniting to create the atmosphere of delirium in which France fought for survival. On 1 September news arrived of the fall of Verdun, the last fortress between the capital and the invaders, and at four o'clock on the following day the prison massacres began—'*un acte de masse*', says Caron,[14] their historian, carried out by a few with the complicity of the many. The era of revolutionary government and Terror had begun.

IV

1793 was a year of desperation. The King was executed in January, war was declared on England in February; in March, exasperated by a decree calling for a levy of 300,000 men, the peasants of La Vendée rose against the Government; rebellion flared up at Marseille and Lyon, and by midsummer a federalist revolt had paralysed the administration in sixty departments. The war was accompanied by hunger and inflation. By February, the *assignats*[15] had fallen to half their original value. Food supplies ran short in the towns. The members of the Jacobin Club took an oath to abjure sugar and coffee during the emergency, though they also accepted Collot d'Herbois' amendment exempting intellectuals. A police spy with an eye for the things that vexed the public informed the Minister of the Interior on 11 June that shops were selling old stocks of chamber-pots at double the price of two years ago, and later in the month he reported a drunken man in the faubourg Saint-Antoine crying, 'Soap used to cost 12 sous and now it's 40, *vive la république*.'[16] The rounding up of volunteers for the battlefronts caused great bitterness. In April, the Department of Hérault suggested that a forced loan be levied on the rich to reward patriots who marched against the Vendéans, and a Parisian section proposed that bachelors in government offices, merchants and lawyers be conscripted first, before high-sounding appeals were made to the working classes. On 2 September, when the food shortage was at its worst, news arrived in Paris that Toulon had surrendered to a British fleet. It was against this background, and amid popular demonstrations, that the Convention voted 'Terror, the order of the day'.

The Convention, the legislative body which was facing these grim emergencies, had the advantage of a great deal of revolutionary expertise, for in it sat 96 ex-Constituents and 190 former members of the Legislative Assembly, as well as many others who had gained

[14] P. Caron, *Les Massacres de Septembre* (1935), p. 413.

[15] For the *assignats* see below, p. 60. For a sociological analysis of the tensions building up in the Vendée over the past two years before demonstrations against conscription caused 'the coalescence of a number of separate counter revolutionary movements into one great rebellion', see Charles Tilly, *The Vendeé* (1964), p. 316 and *passim*.

[16] Dutard's reports in A. Schmidt, *Tableaux de la Révolution française* (3 vols., 1867) II, p. 21.

their experience in the new local administration. With all their *cliché*-ridden oratory and faction fights, and amidst continual *déboires* and denunciations, these men hit upon the secret of the political direction of warfare by committees and dictatorship. They devised a democratic constitution, then locked it up in a cedar box until they had settled the problem of survival. In March '93 they sent 80 of their number to co-ordinate patriotic activity in the provinces, the beginning of the systematic use of *représentants en mission*; they also decreed the creation of revolutionary committees in sections and communes, with the duty of dealing with 'suspects' and handling other sinister chores of the home front; shortly afterwards they set up the first Committee of Public Safety.

Within five months this committee, in a renewed form, had become the heart of the Jacobin dictatorship. On it, Robespierre and his two allies, Couthon, crippled and stoical, and the cold, fanatical Saint-Just, represented the frightening idealism of those days. To Robespierre—the prim country lawyer who had advocated the abolition of the death penalty, the courageous politician who had protested against the declaration of war—the revolutionary government was an instrument to be used with precise ruthlessness: as one historian has said, his severities were not those of a Terrorist, like Carrier, but of a statesman, like Richelieu.[17] He was concerned, not only to win the war, but to extirpate corruption and to achieve regeneration. The theory of revolutionary government, Robespierre said, was entirely new, so that it was 'useless to look for it in the books of political writers who had not foreseen the Revolution';[18] it could be used, however, to reach an ideal which some of these writers had dreamed of, something Rousseau might have approved, that was foreshadowed in Sparta, that would be pleasing to the 'Supreme Being' whose worship was proclaimed in embarrassingly reasonable ceremonies. The other members of the Committee of Public Safety looked on their task more prosaically; some specialized in the odd jobs and oratory needed for parliamentary management, and a group of four, led by Carnot, looked after the business of supply and strategy that kept eleven armies—a million men—in the field against the enemy. These were achievements that compelled the reluctant admiration of the more patriotic of the émigrés: the Jacobins, said Chateaubriand, had come up from Hell, but brought all the talents with them.

[17] L. de Cardenal's phrase.
[18] Cit. E. Champion, *J.-J. Rousseau et la Révolution française* (1909), p. 147. Champion here is refuting, before the event, the attempt to make Rousseau the precursor of 'totalitarian democracy'.

V

There was a price to pay for victory, for the revolutionary government used Terror as its instrument—to enforce the Maximum of prices, to requisition food supplies, to break clerical influence, to punish dishonest contractors and eradicate doubtful generals, to crush civil war. Was this bloodshed necessary?

'The men of the Revolution were ruined by one mistake. They deceived themselves about the power of death; they thought it ended everything. . . . Barère's epigram, *only the dead do not return*, became more false with every day that passed.' Thus Quinet (who believed that the Revolution was the last attempt to realize true Christianity, to roll away the stone—the Church—that barred egress from the sepulchre) pilloried the Terror as the criminal abandonment of the ideals of '89. Most nineteenth-century historians, socialists included, agreed with his fastidious repudiation of the guillotine: they explained the Terror by 'the thesis of circumstances'—it was an epiphenomenon of war and a reaction against the aristocratic conspiracy. But the argument was a syllogism, not a conviction. It was left to the twentieth century to see the Terror effectively against a new background of genuinely total warfare, rationing, inflation and, as the century went on, genocide, systematic torture and concentration camps. It is also only very recently that historical research has proceeded, analytically and imaginatively, into the complexities of local circumstances and motives all over France during this period. Some time must elapse before the rich insights of Cobb's monumental study of the 'revolutionary armies'[19] can be absorbed by other historians; when this is done, the whole history of the Terror will have to be re-written with much greater subtlety than was possible before.

For the moment, some statistics about the Terror may be given, largely to guard against misconceptions. There were about 17,000 formal condemnations to death, and a total of, perhaps, 40,000 executions, formal and informal, civilian and military. Nearly three-quarters of these were in areas of civil war, and were carried out by military tribunals. The peak of killings came after the very worst danger was over, for rebels had to be defeated before they could be executed, and of all the emotions, fear provides the most in-

[19] R. C. Cobb, *Les Armées révolutionnaires* (2 vols., 1961, 1963). These 'armies' must, of course, be distinguished from the actual troops in battle; they were *sans-culotte* militias touring the countryside enforcing the revolutionary decrees, particularly concerning food supplies.

flammable fuel for vengeance. Only six or seven in each hundred victims were ecclesiastics, and only eight or nine were nobles. 'It is not a question of making some examples,' said Couthon, 'but of exterminating the implacable satellites of tyranny.' Yet the statistics of the Terror, judged by twentieth-century standards, do not bear out this fanatical statement of intention. Danton and Desmoulins were right, of course, when they courageously declared that liberty did not consist in wearing 'a red cap and a dirty shirt', but in leaving every man free under the laws, and abolishing the category of 'suspects'; one must admit, too, that comparison with our own age of mass cruelties can justify almost anything. Even so, there is a great deal of wisdom in the verdict of one of the most humane of English historians: 'The Jacobins were not theorists, but practical men dealing with an emergency. They had none of the mass-stupidities nowadays called ideological: no racialism, no anti-Semitism, no militant and exclusive nationalism. Their mild attempts to requisition the means, or to mould the minds of Frenchmen would be thought laughable by present day professors of these arts of government. Their spying was not inquisitorial, their punishments were not refined by torture, their method of liquidating their political enemies was the humanest they could devise. They retained, in their most ferocious moods, a sense of proportion and a sense of humour which saved them from the lowest depths of degradation.'[20] One might add that, if they had not been what they were, ruthlessness included, it is doubtful if they could have saved France from defeat or preserved any of the peaceful social and constitutional achievements of the Revolution.

VI

Thiers and Mignet, two of the earliest historians of the Revolution, writing during the period of the Restoration, disowned the Terror by dividing the revolutionary events at 10 August 1792. Before this date the tide had merely been hastening on the inevitable process of history, which involved the political triumph of a rising middle class; after this, 'the vile populace' (in Thiers' words), 'which has not changed since Tacitus saw it applaud the crimes of the Emperors,' took over control because it alone could win the war.[21] A quarter of a century later, when the bourgeoisie were discredited as the Bourbons had been, Michelet published an epic of revolutionary

[20] J. M. Thompson, *The French Revolution* (1944), p. 399.
[21] See J. McManners, 'The Historiography of the Revolution', *New Cambridge Modern History*, VIII (1963), pp. 618–51.

history in which the sole hero was the 'People'. 'A few men only, infinitely few,' were responsible for the bloodshed: a gang of drunken ruffians perpetrated the September massacres, and bourgeois Jacobins organized the Terror; it was the People which carried through the heroic insurrection of 10 August and repelled the enemy on the frontier lines. This myth of the sublime People which Michelet riveted on to revolutionary historiography provides illuminating insights into the heroic confusions of 1793, but it docs not correspond to social realities. Taine attacked it from one side with his frantic outpourings about the 'epileptic and scrofulous multitude': Mathiez and the Marxist historians have demolished it from the other by showing up the sharp cleavages of economic interest between the different groups in society. We have studied the upper strata of the Third Estate already when we discussed in what sense the work of the Constituent Assembly can be described as 'bourgeois' in tendency. Who, then, were the 'People', and what was their rôle in the Revolution?

Whatever popular control there may have been after the fall of the throne, this did not mean that the people took over the higher legislative and executive functions. The Convention, like the two earlier revolutionary assemblies, was 'bourgeois' in composition; it was a gathering in which 'lawyers' of various kinds predominated, and only 7 of its 749 deputies were from the working class—there were exactly the same number of *ci-devant* marquises! In theory, this new legislative body had been elected by universal suffrage, though in practice only about one million out of five million qualified voters had participated. This apathy raises interesting, though unanswerable questions as to what the majority of Frenchmen really wanted, and Aulard's 'all thinking and acting citizens participated' is an explanation that embarrasses the republican cause rather than helps it.

No doubt the political work of the world, even in wars and revolutions, is carried on by enthusiastic minorities, but in defining the 'People' of 1793, the essential fact to bear in mind is that the vast majority of Frenchmen were peasants. For most of them, the horizon of politics extended no further than their local market town. In economic interests, beyond a universal hatred of feudal dues, they were hopelessly and blindly divided; the richer minority with enough land to live on wanted to buy more acres and sell produce as dearly as may be, the poorer majority wanted land available for cheap leases, and government action to peg corn prices at low levels. In the spring of '89, peasant risings inspired by hunger and hatred of taxation and feudalism had disrupted half the country; again, in late July, the 'great fear' (of 'brigands', or of an 'aristocratic conspiracy') set rural France aflame. This autonomous, non-political peasant revolution had helped the Constituents to defeat aristocracy and despotism and had driven them to the theatrical abolition of privilege on the night of 4 August; when the Assembly got down to sober decrees, however, it merely relieved the peasants from forced labour, hunting rights and honorific dues, leaving them still burdened with the chief feudal payments. 'We thought,' said the inhabitants of one rural commune in January 1792, 'after the decree suppressing the feudal régime, that we were as free in our property as in our persons; two years experience has shown us that we are slaves.'[22]

After the fall of the throne, feudal burdens were abolished. It was the least that could be done to draw the peasants towards the Republic. Before separating, the Legislative Assembly decreed that *seigneurs* could only ask for the payment of dues if they produced the original title; in July '93, the Convention ordered the destruction of title deeds and cancelled all feudal contracts—this was taken to apply even to recent agreements that had been snobbishly titivated with scraps of feudal phraseology.

But little was done to help the mass of peasants to acquire more land. The Convention forbade associations of buyers of *biens nationaux*, though it is true that such émigré lands as were put up for sale were generally divided into small lots. The bourgeoisie and the richer peasants were the chief gainers from the auctions of church property. By removing feudal burdens and putting vast estates on the market, the Revolution widened the gap between the landowning peasants and the rural proletariat. For most peasants (and probably, if the sum is completed, for most Frenchmen) the Revolution brought hope, freedom to speak, independence, conscription, hunger and envy.

VII

When Thiers referred to the 'gloomy and ragged administration of the people' which characterized the grim epoch after the fall of the throne, he meant the urban poor, more especially the Paris crowd, the *sans-culottes*. In 1789 the poorer people of the towns invaded the revolutionary scene, driven on by desperate hunger. The harvest of 1788 had failed, and it soon became evident that the crops of '89 would be meagre. Popular opinion blamed the government, whose experiments in freeing the internal corn trade had revived the legend of the *pacte de famine*. Taine described the Parisian rioters as '*canaille*', 'vagabonds', 'scum', the 'savages of the

[22] Hampson, op. cit., p. 129.

streets', but since Professor Rudé's analysis of the composition of the crowds in the various revolutionary *journées*,[23] no-one believes any longer in this hysterical legend. Small workshop owners, journeymen, apprentices, artisans, independent craftsmen and small shopkeepers, lived together and joined together in demonstrations. The revolutionary crowds were not Taine's riff-raff, and they were no more brutal than starving, uneducated men are likely to be in an age when criminals were broken on the wheel in public executions; though they could act blindly in a mass, they were far from being mere statistical units in a mob with pathological mass emotions—in their elementary fashion they had a grasp of the realities of the political situation. Nor were the *sans-culottes* a proletariat in the Marxist sense: they did not work in big factories and they were not conscious of a sharp separation between employee and employer. Their economic ideas were those of the pre-industrial age. In hard times, their cry was, not for higher wages so much as for lower prices; they protested as consumers, and their complaints were directed towards the government which, they believed, had the paternalistic duty to fix the price of bread.

After 10 August 1792, the 48 Parisian sections (which had been set up in 1790 for electoral purposes) became centres of an autonomous *sans-culotte* movement. Each section had a salaried police official and a *juge de paix*, a *comité civil* concerned with food rationing, a *comité révolutionnaire* (with payment for attendance) dealing with suspects and corresponding directly with the Convention's Committee of General Security, and a section assembly. These assemblies met daily until the decree of September '93, which limited their meetings to two days a week, and in them voting was public, either by head or by acclamation. In some of them, business was prepared beforehand by a *société sectionnaire*, set up by militants who felt the need for a directing caucus. The National Guard, now genuinely open to all citizens and electing its own officers, was decentralized into sectional units, and in some sections there was a military committee to direct the activities of this citizen militia.

The political arrangements of the *sans-culottes* seem to have harked back to Rousseau's idyllic picture of the working of direct democracy. But whatever the ideal may have been, attendance at section assemblies was low: in one of them for which we have fairly complete figures, out of 3,200 citizens, at most 350 and sometimes no more than 60 were actually present. Not everyone was welcome,

[23] G. Rudé, *The Crowd in the French Revolution* (1959). A significant book, which opened up some entirely new sources and showed how statistical precision can be brought to the study of riots.

of course. 'Intriguers who infiltrate into the sections', Robespierre warned the Convention in May 1793, 'will be ruthlessly expelled by the patriots.' Even so, the thin attendance needs interpretation. Perhaps this is another illustration of the way in which revolutions are made by minorities, or perhaps it merely shows how ordinary people insist on living their lives to suit themselves within the mass movements which are so convenient for historians. In the margin of the operation orders for the insurrection of 2 June '93 one finds the intrusion, '*Bonsoir, ma bonne amie, vous êtes forte jolie*'; marching on the Convention was, after all, a spare-time occupation.

One word, indeed, could have been added to the agenda of all the sectional agitations during the Terror—'Bread'. The definition of *sans-culotte*, which had originally been wide enough to include almost any 'patriot', even one with 5,000 *livres* a year,[24] seemed to grow narrower as the economic crisis deepened, until it meant simply, in *Père Duchesne's* words, 'the poor b—— who lives from hand to mouth'. The fact that a Republic had replaced the King made no difference to the essential complaint of the poor, that the government was failing to peg prices at a level low enough to save them from starvation. In the faction-fight in the Convention between Montagnards and Girondins, the former enlisted the insurrectionary might of Paris by devising the first Maximum on grain prices in May 1793. The risings of 3 May and 2 June which destroyed the Girondins sprang from the initiative of the sections and were guided by the Commune and a conspiratorial committee at the Évêché; though they were not planned in the Convention, they were the natural outcome of the alliance between the Mountain and the *sans-culottes*.

It was not until July, however, that further agitation by the sections compelled the victorious Mountain to take more stringent economic measures—the imposition of the death penalty for hoarding, a forced loan on the rich (3 September), the formation of a 'revolutionary army' to requisition grain from the countryside, and a new and more effective Maximum to control prices (11 and 29 September).

These were emergency measures to placate the poor and win the war; they involved no change in the social structure; indeed, the *sans-culottes* were incapable of envisaging the machinery by which a

---

[24] A. Soboul, *Les Sans-culottes parisiens en l'An II* (1958), p. 441, refers to Varlet's 5,800 l. a year and to another *sans-culotte* owning a factory employing over 60 workers. One might add the nice reference of the Section de l'Unité, 4 May '93, to 'les sans-culottes à 10,000 livres de rente qui égarent et qui ruinent le peuple' (F. Braesch, *Papiers de Chaumette*, Soc. de l'hist. Rév. fr., 1908), p. 35.

radical social change could be brought about. In a later lecture, we will see how leaders arose to formulate their demands, and we will discuss their relevance to the rise of socialistic theory. But the *sans-culottes* were unable to protect these spokesmen from the growing power of the central government; many of their militants were now at the battlefront, or with the peripatetic 'revolutionary armies', or enjoying repose as salaried officials; others were weary of *journées* that left their families as hungry as before. The leaders themselves were mouthpieces of discontent, lacking the resourcefulness and strategic grasp required to organize a new revolution. When Robespierre and the Committee of Public Safety executed Hébert in March 1794, the *sans-culottes* looked on 'with a dramatic sense of their impotence',[25] and few of the sections moved when, four months later, Robespierre himself went down to destruction.

[25] Soboul, *Les Sans-culottes parisiens*, p. 772. Soboul's book is, of course, indispensable for all this section.

CHAPTER IV

J'AI VÉCU: FROM THERMIDOR TO BRUMAIRE

I

What would have happened if Robespierre had triumphed on the 9th of Thermidor? Long before Max Weber made reflections upon such 'might have beens' a respectable technique of their craft, historians were accustomed to make good use of this device of rhetoric and analysis; yet one finds it difficult to recollect any significant discussion of this kind about the Thermidorian crisis. Robespierre had come to speak of himself as a predestined martyr: we are tempted to take him at his word. It is impossible, for me at any rate, to imagine the emergence of a 'Robespierrist France', of a 'Maximillenium', as the dénouement of the Revolution; nor do I think that he could have hoped to exercise dictatorship except in times of peculiar hysteria and exaltation. His greatness is paradoxical. I suspect (though the weight of critical opinion would be against me here) that fundamentally he was something like Carlyle's famous caricature, an 'anxious, slight, ineffectual looking man . . . in spectacles . . . snuffing dimly the uncertain future times,'[1] one of those moral precisians who elevate the tone and prolong the deliberations of assemblies in normal peaceful days. His enormous influence sprang from the reserves of harsh moral courage which he brought to the service of the Revolution. With fear and corruption on every hand, he remained unyieldingly true to principle, and he was known to be completely disinterested. Though towards the end he may have been succumbing to a love of power, he had had the right instinct in trying to avoid it. The mere possession of power could destroy him. As a ruler, he would fail because he did not know the arts of compromise; the charismatic aura of his disinterestedness would pale when he was seen to achieve the domination which is the goal of ordinary ambitions. He was fitted to be the conscience of the Revolution, not its executive agent.

The tragedy and significance of his fall lay partly in the fact that he became the scapegoat for two unpopular institutions, the Maximum and the Terror, for which, in perspective, he bears only a fraction of the responsibility. The Maximum, once a limitation of

[1] T. Carlyle, *The French Revolution* (Everyman) I, p. 114.

wages was added to that of prices, was hated by the people. The Robespierrists went to the scaffold amid cries of 'f..... maximum'. It was a day of dupes, for ten months later the *sans-culottes* wanted the return of the war economy which they had cursed. The Terror had made men sick of cruelty. In July 1794 there were 1,285 death sentences, and there were 7,800 prisoners in the jails of Paris. One has only to try to compute the numbers of friends and relatives to see how the ending of revolutionary justice had become an almost universal, secret hope. On 26 June the victory of Fleurus left Belgium open to the French armies. The foreign menace, the essential justification of the Terror, was lifted.

Logically, Robespierre ought to have carried less responsibility for the Maximum than most of his colleagues in the government. He had much more sympathy with the people than the Thermidorians who overthrew him. Yet it was he who had destroyed the left-wing factions which most nearly represented the aspirations of the *sans-culottes*; the sections, already weakened by the departure of soldiers for the frontier and volunteers for the Vendée and by the metamorphosis of militants into salaried officials, were apathetic when the final tocsin sounded. The Terror was not Robespierre's invention. Though he used it, he wished to regulate it, and to punish bloodstained proconsuls like Fouché and Tallien who had abused its rigours in the provinces. Yet, in his pursuit of 'virtue' and in fear of plots and assassination, he had pressed for the decree of 22 Prairial (10 June 1794) which seemed to be aimed at intensifying the Terror and, by its omission of any reference to the immunity of parliamentary deputies, lost him the allegiance of frightened members of the Convention.[2]

The committees of the revolutionary government bore grim responsibilities which ought to have kept them united. In fact, however, Robespierre, Saint-Just and Couthon were estranged from Carnot, Barère and their other colleagues on the Committee of Public Safety, while there was a bitter feud between this committee and that of General Security. Fouché, his life in danger and rendered coldly desperate by the approaching death of his daughter, the only person he ever loved, went round giving general warning of a new proscription—'*Vous êtes de la fournée*'. With obtuse honesty and fanatical harshness Robespierre had drawn to himself all the hatreds which ought to have been distributed over the whole arena of the revolutionary dictatorship. And on 8 Thermidor (26 July), he

[2] H. Calvet, 'Une interprétation nouvelle de la loi de Prairial', *Annales historiques de la Révolution française* (1950), pp. 305 ff; and G. Lefebvre's reply, ibid. (1951), pp. 225 ff.

delivered the fatal speech which completed Fouché's whispering campaign and united all his enemies. The Committee of General Security, he said, had ex-nobles and émigrés as its clerks and confidants, the Committee of Public Safety was riddled with disloyalty, the 'military aristocracy' was being protected from patriotic scrutiny (this hit at Carnot), and orations of 'academic frivolity' were made on victories costing the lives of Frenchmen (this meant Barère). He proposed to intervene mercilessly, but he refused to give the names of those marked for destruction (so this could mean anybody). The Convention was alienated, and when it outlawed Robespierre, only 13 of the 48 sections were prepared to rally to his defence.

Robespierre then, was his own executioner; his very character and ideals destroyed him. 'He was never quite a leader of revolutionaries', wrote J. M. Thompson, 'but a unique embodiment of the Revolution'.[3] He was a humanitarian and a democrat; almost alone, he had stood against the gamble of war, and he had a genuine and generous social policy and sincere religious convictions from which no ridicule could shake him. In these things, he represents the noblest of the revolutionary ideals. Mathiez had the surest instinct for defending his memory, by depicting him in his self-conscious rectitude against the background of the underworld of corruption which spawned like fungus in the shadow of the guillotine. This was why Robespierre continued the Terror—against 'those who have embraced the Revolution as a profession and the Republic as their prey'.[4] Here is the justification of his personal integrity: but here too is the demonstration of the inevitability of his fall. He had no respect for that minimal co-operation with which men of differing opinions contrive to meet common dangers, or for the practical services which immoral men and speculators can make to the fighting effectiveness of a cause. Terror was to be used against all, irrespective of their revolutionary standing, of services rendered, or of potential future usefulness. He refused to recognize the right of ordinary men, in desperate circumstances, to abandon the strategy of principles for the tactics of survival, '*J'ai vécu*', said Sieyès, on his way to the final solution of saving the individuals who had made the Revolution by letting the principles take care of themselves. This sort of attitude was anathema to Robespierre. Unlike Swift, who hated mankind, but loved Tom, Dick and Harry, he embraced the paradox in its opposite and, for the statesman, more dangerous form. He loved mankind, yet could send colleagues whose loyalty to the

[3] J. M. Thompson, *Robespierre* (1934), p. 591.
[4] Cit. L. de Cardenal, 'Robespierre et le terrorisme après Thermidor', *Annales historiques de la Révolution française* (1938), p. 357.

Revolution took a different form from his own, and even his personal friends, to the guillotine.

II

It is customary to regard the Revolution as ending at Thermidor, and it is all the easier to do so since Robespierre had annexed its ideals, and by serving them with inhuman rigidity, had destroyed himself. Fouquier Tinville, the president of the Revolutionary Tribunal, followed to the scaffold, the Maximum was abolished, the Jacobin Clubs closed, the Commune of Paris disappeared, the revolutionary committees of the sections were wound up, and dandified *muscadins*, the Mods (or is it Rockers?) of reaction, ruled the streets. These *muscadins* are the symbolic figures of the Thermidorian reaction, as the *sans-culottes* were of the preceding period. One is tempted to regard them as the sons of hard-faced men who were doing well out of the war; it could be, however, that a year ago some of these 'gilded youths' had worn the red cap of liberty and sworn the oaths of Père Duchesne. Corrupt deputies like Fréron and Tallien, actors, journalists, queer fish like the *ci-devant* Marquis de Saint Huruge, once the leader of popular insurrections, and the survivors of the revolutionary bohemia set the fashion which was followed by sharpers of the Palais Royal gambling dens, office wallahs evading conscription and young men generally who had found ways of making easy money. A square-collared coat, powdered hair, and breeches so tight that their very existence was debatable were standard costume for these *muscadins*, together with a loaded stick known (from the experience of years of constitutional experiment) as 'the executive power'.

The ideals of the Revolution, now grimly associated with the Terror, were dead as creative forces, though the tangible gains they had achieved, measured in terms of possessions, power and patriotism, remained to be preserved. Thermidor had been a coalition of the survivors of purges, of frightened terrorists and of moderates regaining their courage, of men who hated bloodshed and inquisitorial government and of men whose lives were too corrupt to bear investigation—a coalition aimed simply at survival. 'On the 9th Thermidor,' said a member of the Convention, 'it was no longer a question of principles, but of killing.'[5] And behind the Thermidorians were the apprehensions of the possessing classes, who knew all too clearly by now that a war economy allied with the incongruous *clichés* of liberty tended towards a more equal division of riches.

[5] Marc Antoine Baudot, cit. P. Sainte-Claire Deville, *La Commune de l'An II* (1946), p. 189.

Yet, if reaction seemed to rule, the subterranean and incalculable insurrectionary force of Paris, which Robespierre had failed to evoke in his hour of destiny, remained unbroken. The concrete threat of starvation and the vague, hopeless dream of embodying popular sovereignty and true equality in workable institutions still remained as the motives for another rising. So it was, in April and May 1795, that the last two *journeés* of the Revolution took place, with the demand for 'bread, and the Constitution of 1793'.

Though the government introduced a new (and higher) maximum on grain prices, it refused to make rationing general. The terrible winter of Year III froze the rivers, stopping the barges and the wheels of flour mills, and made roads impassable. Farmers refused the devalued *assignats* and, paying less in dues and taxes than they had under the old régime, felt inclined to keep more of their produce for themselves. The army consumed hugely and wastefully, as armies do. Factories in the capital closed down as demand contracted and fuel became short. There was an increase in the number of suicides, and starving men dropped dead in the streets. *Muscadins* in office jobs snapped their fingers at military service. On 23 Nivôse (12 January) the Convention voted its members double salaries. The risings of 1 April (Germinal) and 20 May (Prairial) were, essentially, 'political expressions of the demand for bread'; they were not Jacobin or Robespierrist revivals, but the last surge of the autonomous, anonymous, and envious *sans-culotte* movement which in times of shortage rose against all régimes.[6]

Although in Prairial there was a manifesto, *Insurrection du Peuple pour obtenir du Pain et reconquérir ses Droits*, which called on the people to bypass the section machinery and march on the Convention in 'fraternal disorder', there were no well-known names behind the risings, no Jacobin heroes or experienced revolutionary committee-men. The old insurrectionary determination was lacking: it was the possessing classes which were willing to appear in arms, not the poor. In Prairial, the National Guards of the faubourg Saint-Antoine did move on the Convention—without their officers— but the government was ready. Regular troops stood by and invitations had been addressed to members of the National Guard throughout Paris, not by sections, but individually, to '*bons citoyens qui avaient une fortune à conserver*'. The areas of revolutionary agitation were invested by force, the poorer citizens were eased out of the National Guard and had to hand in their pikes, the more prosperous citizens took charge of the section assemblies. The main-spring of

[6] See K. D. Tönesson, *La Défaite des Sans-culottes* (1959). Essential for all this section.

revolutionary action was finally broken. Babeuf, who two years later was to lose his life in a pathetic plot for social equality, learnt the lesson and decided to put his hopes in the organization of a conspiratorial minority. Prairial showed that the days of 'fraternal disorder' and mass insurrection were over.

III

In August 1795, a new constitution was voted, the Constitution of the Year III. Boissy d'Anglas, reporting on behalf of the committee of eleven which did the drafting, defined the principle of political theory on which the new arrangements were based: 'A country governed by the proprietors is in the social order; that where the non-proprietors govern is in the state of nature.'[7] It was this same Boissy d'Anglas who, in the presidential chair of the Convention, had sat impassive while the mob produced the head of his colleague the deputy Féraud from the end of a pike and deposited it on the bureau in front of him; the state of nature for him was no dream of Locke or Jean-Jacques Rousseau. The new constitution defined the rights of citizens without suggesting the possibility of legitimate insurrection or a right to social assistance. Property was to be inviolable, except in cases of overriding public necessity, when compensation must be provided. 'Equality', the constitution lays down with complacency, 'consists in the fact that the law is the same for everybody', a formula providing an invitation for Anatole France's sardonic jest about the majestic impartiality which jails both rich and poor for stealing loaves from bakers' windows. Paris and other large cities were divided into several municipalities—there were to be no strong fortresses of resistance to the central parliamentary government.

Universal male suffrage was to operate in the primary assemblies, which appointed the local justices of the peace and municipal officers; but so far as national affairs were concerned the mass of voters merely chose an upper ring of true 'electors' from the narrow circle of men of property. There were, perhaps, no more than 30,000 individuals in France who qualified. These electors, when voting for deputies to the two legislative chambers, the Council of Ancients and the Council of 500, would presumably not go out of their way to choose Hébertist fanatics and *enragés*. They might however, in weariness of war and anarchy, choose royalists, opening the way for a return of the Bourbons. A guarantee of the sales of

[7] L. Villat, *La Révolution et l'Empire* (2 vols., 1947) I, p. 335.

Church property and of the end of financial privilege, and some sort of compromise about constitutional government might do the trick. The first to suffer would be the regicides and the other bigwigs of revolutionary politics. The Convention insured against this possibility by ruling that its own members must occupy two thirds of the seats in the new legislature, whether they were elected or not. A plebiscite ratified this Constitution. Four million out of the five million electors did not record an opinion.

A Constitution designed to keep out the left, and the emergency 'two-thirds decree' to keep out the right, with the mass of Frenchmen ominously silent—the future was unsure. The Directory, the committee of five which formed the executive under the new constitution, took office under gloomy auspices. One of the Directors describes how they were escorted to their council chamber by soldiers whose toes stuck out of their gaping boots, and how they had difficulty in getting even old straw chairs and a rickety table for furniture.[8] It was a government whose printing presses worked each night to produce the money it would spend the following morning. But it survived, and, so long as the war lasted, that was the essential task of any government in France. There was a bumper crop in 1796, and intelligent bureaucrats attempted to rationalize the administration and the finances. Above all, the armies, ill-clad and shambling as they were, by now were well organized with an effective blend of traditional and revolutionary discipline, and were led by some of the great names of military history; under Joubert, Shérer, Desaix and Moreau, men like Ney, Soult and Bernadotte were serving their apprenticeship, and the glory of Bonaparte in Italy was shared by the reckless Masséna, Murat the master of cavalry tactics, the tough egalitarian Augereau and Lannes the *beau sabreur*. But the very success of the armies created in them a spirit of independence and distrust towards the central Government. As for the Directory itself, either military defeat or a too-complete victory might end the precarious equilibrium of political forces which enabled it to rule. All the while it remained a government of regicides who feared the return of the king and a government of the bourgeoisie who feared the demands of the people.

Each year, one-third of the seats in the two Legislative Councils were vacated and the electors had their opportunity to pass judgment on the régime. In the spring of 1797, this judgment was a devastating one. The elections were a landslide to the right. Three of the Directors, Reubell, La Révellière and Barras—all regicides—called in the Army. Winnowed by desertion until it combined the characteristics

<hr/>

[8] La Révellière-Lépeaux. *Mémoires* (3 vols., 1895) I, pp. 317–19.

of a force of volunteers and professionals, rather than of conscripts,[9] the Army still saw the Revolution in the perspective of the menaced frontier lines and the crusade for liberty—abstract terms of this nature being subject to definition by popular generals. Bonaparte sent Augereau to command the garrison of Paris and do the dirty work (the coup of Fructidor). Nearly 200 deputies were excluded from the legislature. As the elections of 1798 approached, with the menace, this time, of a landslide to the left, the Councils decided to take to themselves the duty of 'verifying' the results, and on the 11 May (22 Floréal), 100 or so elected representatives, mostly Jacobins, were barred—*floréalisés* as the new euphemism had it. After this, short of heroic measures for the manufacture of consent which were unfamiliar in those rude days, the rigging of elections, through the sheer arithmetical impact of the renewal process, became impossible. Bad news from the front completed the demoralization of the Directors. On 18 June 1799 (30 Prairial, Year VII) the Councils took measures to outlaw anyone who dared to tamper with their liberty. It was the revenge of parliamentarianism; like the 9th Thermidor, it was a reassertion by the legislature of its rights over the executive. With Sieyès and two other 'florealized' deputies pushed into the Directory, the whole desperate process of steering between right and left began again—first towards the Jacobins, then against them. Swings of the pendulum were shorter and quicker now, and men wondered despairingly what sort of government would emerge from the elections of Year VIII. Would feudalism return, and would the buyers of church property lose their all? Would an inquisition be opened into all the deeds of regicide and terror? Or would the people march onto the scene again and plunder the bourgeoisie? Would the war, which had cost more than half a million dead, go on for ever? It might be best, perhaps, to run none of the risks of combination, debate and unforeseen results which spring from the electoral process, and to find an authoritative voice to give positive guarantees on these high matters. The Army, which had intervened at Fructidor and which had saved the nation from the kings of Europe, might at last save France from herself. There comes a point when even tyranny is preferable to uncertainty.

IV

The final solution was reached through the co-operation of the three most acute political intelligences of the day, three Frenchmen who, each in his own way, combined a modicum of patriotism and ad-

[9] G. Lefebvre, *La Révolution française* (1951), p. 477.

herence to the principles of the Revolution (as they defined them) with a cynical determination to ride the storm and get safely to port laden with treasure—not just decorations and applause, but hard cash and well-fenced properties. It was their business to know what France wanted so that they could get what they wanted themselves, and they knew the secrets of the Revolution with a harsh, self-interested clarity which was achieved by few of their contemporaries. I confess to being fascinated by these three masterly practitioners, so that before looking at the solution they proposed, I will turn aside to look at their careers, and at the allegiances and hatreds they had accumulated. In so doing, we can add an essential dimension to our understanding of the Revolution and to our appreciation of the interests working towards the Napoleonic denoument.

All three began as ecclesiastics. In 1789, Sieyès had been forty-one years of age, the son of a reasonably religious middle-class family which encouraged him into the Church as a sort of respectable family investment. By lending money to a vicar-general of the diocese his father had found him a patron ; a few—too few—years as chaplain to a royal princess, and some—too many—years devilling for Mgr de Lubersac, Bishop of Tréguier then of Chartres, and the Abbé Sieyès had an income of 13,500 l. from his canonries, and the *entrée* to the liberal salons of Paris. His brochure, *Qu'est-ce que le Tiers Etat* was the great manifesto against privilege in the early days of the Revolution ; behind its lapidary phrases lay his resentment against the conduct of the nobles he had met in provincial administrative circles and, it must be confessed, against aristocratic prelates like Lubersac who had used his talents but who were niggardly in promoting him. In 1789 Talleyrand, at thirty-five years of age, was Bishop of Autun, with an income of 52,000 l. from his see and two abbeys, as befitted a nobleman with a lineage as old as the Kings of France themselves. He too was a pressed man to religion, his family regarding the Church as a haven for his lameness. A young actress had been his mistress in seminary days, the Comtesse de Brionne had intrigued (unsuccessfully) to get him a Cardinal's hat at the age of thirty, the Comtesse de Flahaut . . . Talleyrand's existence had been, and remained, full of women and gaming. Meanwhile, Fouché, five years younger than Talleyrand, was a humble teacher at the Oratorian *collège* at Arras, a great reader of Masillon's devotional works and, apparently, contented with his poverty. No doubt it was from his family at Nantes and not from his own infinitesimal salary of 120 l. that he found the money to assist his friend Robespierre to attend the meeting of the Estates General.

'O années fécondes en émotions vives et douces' wrote Fouché, looking back much later.[10] 'Qui n' a pas vécu dans les années voisines de 1789 ne sait pas ce que c'est le plaisir de vivre', said Talleyrand.[11] There is also reason to believe that the Abbé Sieyès was reasonably contented.

While Fouché had the privilege of lending money to a deputy, our two other protagonists turned up in person at the Estates General. The Bishop of Autun paid his first visit to his cathedral town (his last too, except once when his carriage broke down in passing); here he persuaded his faithful clergy to elect him, then fled early on Easter Sunday lest he should be obliged to reveal his liturgical ignorance. Sieyès was turned down by the parish priests of his local constituency (they regarded this egalitarian agitator with ten times their income as one of the aristocrats), but he was accepted by the Third Estate of Paris.

Talleyrand had genuine liberal principles (though they wavered when the Bastille fell) and he had no sympathy with the emigration. To the Comte d'Artois, the first off the mark, he observed, 'Then, Monseigneur, nothing remains but for each of us to look after our own interests', which he proceeded to do. Those interests included getting rid of his ecclesiastical vocation. But first of all he used this vocation to insure himself with the new order. He proposed the sale of church property, celebrated Mass for the Federation of 1790 on the Champ de Mars (and broke the bank twice at a gaming house the same evening), he took the oath to the Civil Constitution of the Clergy and consecrated the first bishops for the Constitutional Church. And that, until the famous death-bed scene forty-seven years later, was the end of his claim to episcopal consideration. Sieyès on the other hand, though he was a friend of Talleyrand and had some peculiar Orleanist connections, acted on principle. He was the chief mover in the vote of 17 June, and pressed ruthlessly for the union of the orders and a single chamber legislature free from royal veto. While his episcopal friend proposed an 'operation' on church property, Sieyès, unbeliever and revolutionary as he was, defended his order, and protested against the loss of tithe. 'My dear Abbé', said Mirabeau, 'you're the one who let the bull loose and now you are complaining because he's using his horns.'[12] To defend tithe and, subsequently, ecclesiastical property, was courageous: as Danton said, it deprived Sieyès of the title of patriot.

Fouché came late on the political scene, in September 1792, when his home town of Nantes elected him to the Convention. Talleyrand

[10] L. Madelin, *Fouché* (1900), p. 5.
[11] G. Lacour-Gayet, *Talleyrand* (4 vols., 1928) I, p. 54.
[12] P. Bastid, *Sieyès et sa pensée* (1939), p. 81.

was out of France during the Terror; Sieyès coldly voted the death
of the King then went to ground—his reply to questions about this
period of his life is famous, '*J'ai vécu*'. Fouché too was a regicide:
like Sieyès he committed himself laconically—'*la mort*'. Apparently,
the night before he had meant to vote for clemency. But he saw the
cowardice and confusion of the moderates and, whether in fear or,
as Madelin thinks, in calculated fury, he deliberately chose the
winning side. His subsequent career, thirteen months as a *représentant
en mission* in the provinces, is a warning to those who try to explain
the Revolution by logical considerations. This ex-Oratorian dances
round bonfires of chasubles and proclaims, at the gates of cemeteries,
that 'death is an eternal sleep'. His correspondence is full of rage
against Christianity and of invocations to terrorism. They will have
the courage, he and his colleague Collot announce amid the shootings
at Lyon, 'to stride on over ruins to achieve the happiness of the
nation and the regeneration of mankind'.[13] All this may be, as
Madelin suggests, a mask, though an abominable one; and it is
true enough that Fouché abandoned the terrorists of Lyon just at
the moment that the tide turned against the Hébertist left in Paris. Yet
the sentimental egalitarianism—communism almost—of his correspondence may be sincere, secret yearnings revealed at a time when all
inhibitions were crumbling. If so, these beliefs gave an edge to the
fanaticism which was Fouché's device for insuring himself with the
Revolution. Out of self-defence he went on to knot the threads of the
heterogeneous conspiracy which brought down Robespierre at
Thermidor. By now he had lived long with danger and had become
incapable of remorse, impervious to fear and perfectly adapted for
survival.

So too, in their way, had Sieyès and Talleyrand. Since two of these
three were regicides and the other at least belonged to the Revolution
(as Bonaparte was to say) 'by his misconduct', their interest in their
own safety was inevitably bound up with the cause of the Revolution.

V

After Thermidor, Fouché was in bad odour, Sieyès could emerge
to political prominence and Talleyrand could return to France. It

---

[13] Madelin, op. cit., p. 112. With his gift for brilliant antithesis and dramatic
writing, Madelin has probably made Fouché more intelligent and sinister than
he was at this time. The Oratorians produced many enthusiasts for the revolutionary ideals (eg. see Madelin, p. 5; J. McManners, *French Ecclesiastical
Society*, pp. 212–13, 220–9; L. Jacob, *Joseph Le Bon* (2 vols., 1935), and the element of naive fanaticism may have existed and persisted for a while in Fouché.

is instructive to see how these three hardened adventurers manoeuvred towards safety. Two of them differed dramatically in their views as to how safety could be won in foreign policy. Sieyès wished to bring Europe into subjection to a revolutionary France, triumphant within her natural frontiers, laden with indemnities from the conquered, and using her dominance to close the coastline to English trade—in more ways than one, his schemes looked forward to the Napoleonic era.[14] On the other hand, Talleyrand (who became Foreign Minister of the Directory in July 1797) saw safety in a return to the atmosphere of the diplomacy of the *ancien régime*, the epoch to which his supple talents really belonged. France must seek peace within a Europe divided only by routine selfishness, and not by ideological conflict; as things are, he reported, 'our enemies regard the treaties they sign with us as nothing else but truces, like those that the Musulmans limit themselves to concluding with infidels. They . . . remain in a state of coalition against us.'[15]

In home affairs, however, the three former ecclesiastics were significantly united. They all supported the military coup of 18 Fructidor, and the Councils' re-assertion of their independence on the 30 Prairial. And both Talleyrand and Sieyès supported the appointment of Fouché as the Directory's Minister of Police in July 1799. His task, Sieyès said, was to 'crush both royalists and anarchists'. As one of the great terrorists himself, the new minister would clearly have the will to deal with the first category and the knowledge to deal with the second. The art of survival consisted in baffling the royalists, while suppressing the left lest moderate men turn to the Bourbons in despair, at the same time conciliating the Army, which barred the return of the émigrés and remained the ultimate power of intervention within. However skilfully the cards were played, the winning trick would fall to the hand that held a soldier.

Talleyrand's fête (3 Jan. 1798), in honour of Josephine, wife of General Bonaparte, was the gesture of a *grand seigneur* whose corruptly acquired wealth often went in display; it was also in the nature of an investment. The ladies wore classical costumes, the waltz, newly introduced, met with favour, and the general was genial, except to Mme de Staël. Since then, Talleyrand had helped Bonaparte with his Egyptian design and, perhaps, betrayed him a little. Sieyès and Fouché had pinned their hopes on General Joubert, who was killed at the battle of Novi. Bonaparte, however, reappeared in Paris on 16 October 1799, wearing an olive green coat and a

[14] Bastid, op. cit., pp. 158 ff.
[15] L. Madelin, *Talleyrand* (1944), p. 89.

Turkish scimitar at his waist. Sieyès was in touch with Joseph and Lucien, the general's brothers, Fouché with Josephine and Talley-rand with everyone. So the conspiracy was organized. The Minister of Police, perhaps, was not directly in it, but he showed his power by sardonically inviting the plotters all together to dinner, and his good sense by keeping all reference to them out of his reports. On the day of the coup d'état, when Bonaparte, overwrought and hysterical, brought them all to the edge of ruin, his allies, the three defrocked clerics, played their parts imperturbably.

VI

In 1789, Sieyès had seemed to embody the empiricism and dynamism of the Revolution. His writings epitomised the universal hatred of privilege. He invented the idea of a constituent power. A rationalist and a Cartesian, he believed that a new state could be constructed, like a machine. History and 'nature' are irrelevant: men do not study the history of clocks to construct one for themselves, or examine the rafts of savages when laying the keel of a warship. Yet the theorist of innovation wanted no disorder. No one desired a disciplined, intelligent revolution more than he. Representatives represent the nation, not their constituents, and ought to follow their own opinions. The people no more exercised their liberty by inter-fering in political decisions than an individual exercised his by carrying his own letters to Bordeaux, instead of putting them in the public mail. Intelligence ought to direct the state; and, as we have seen, Sieyès also became preoccupied with ideas of the power of the state abroad and national greatness. Now, things were out of joint and terrible unintelligent forces had been unleashed. Sieyès, waiting for the intervention of the sword, was concocting a constitution which would preserve something of liberty, but serve national great-ness and leave intelligence in command. Once the leading opponent of bicameralism, he was ending up with proposals for several legis-lative assemblies; instead of the constituent power he was dreaming of a 'constitutional jury', or Senate, composed of distinguished old men of the Revolution who would look after the principles of 1789 in well-paid ease. And he, the opponent of the royal veto, was prepared to join in calling in a general, well knowing the risks they ran with Bonaparte. 'Guarantees?—there are none. In great affairs, something must be left to chance.'[16]

Talleyrand had long since left things—including his own honour—

16 Bastid, p. 283.

to chance. As he said, he put himself 'at the disposition of events and, provided I remained a Frenchman, I accepted everything'. 'He will sell us all', said Carnot, when the Directors considered him in 1797 for Foreign Minister. 'Eh! Whom has he sold so far?' asked La Revellière.

'Whom? First of all, his God.'

'He doesn't believe in God.'

'Why then did he enter his service?—Then, he sold the clerical order.'

'A proof of philosophy.'

'Of ambition, rather. Finally, he sold his king.'

'But it seems to me that it's not for us to reproach him with that.'[17] There must have been many conversations of this kind in France between Thermidor and Brumaire. Though an extreme case, Talleyrand's was typical. Many people had betrayed much, and the time had come for an authoritative voice to call an end to recriminations. This is what most Frenchmen wanted, though with only half their minds. And this is what the ex-bishop of Autun sensed when meditating his next betrayal. 'I have never conspired', he once remarked, 'except when I had the majority of France for my accomplice.'[18]

If Talleyrand was the Fouché of the aristocrats (the words are Bonaparte's), Fouché was the Talleyrand of the mob.[19] A terrorist and a regicide, he was none the less a man of moderation. Even in his heyday as a master of police techniques and money-making, he retained something of his quiet Oratorian experience, as his friendships and a certain austerity of life bore witness. He had come to believe that force was kinder to the mass of men than freedom. Though he never sincerely renounced his revolutionary past, in the end, more successfully than either Sieyès or Talleyrand, he ingratiated himself with the royalists. By this incredible feat of insinuation and by a restraint that was as rare and statesmanlike as it was cynical, he was to be the ideal police chief for Bonaparte's régime of synthetic conciliation. A living example of Mirabeau's dictum that 'Jacobin ministers will no longer be Jacobins', he nevertheless could not have served the Consul and Emperor as he did without the experience and peculiar sinister standing which accrued to him from the days of his left-wing proconsulate. Unsophisticated by a preliminary apprenticeship to politics, he had come to the Revolution at the height of its crisis and had committed himself to its most extreme

[17] Lacour-Gayet, op. cit., I, p. 232.

[18] Talleyrand, *Mémoires* (ed. the Duc de Broglie, 1891) II, p. 101.

[19] I think that Bonaparte said this first, and that Benjamin Constant (see H. Nicolson, *Benjamin Constant* (1919), p. 243) borrowed the epigram.

fanaticism. Of these three ex-ecclesiastics, one remained at heart an aristocrat, at home in salons and embassies, one remained essentially a bourgeois intellectual, his mind concentrated on the constitutional machinery which could reconcile order with liberty; Fouché alone knew the secrets of a subterranean France whose ideals of equality and traditions of violence did not die.

VII

The coup d'état of Brumaire had its ambiguities. Those who contrived it were most afraid of royalism: shrewdly, they claimed to be reacting against the 'anarchists'. The seizure of power was operated without calling in the legions, in as civilian a fashion as possible: hence the near-failure. It was Lucien Bonaparte, president of the Council of 500, who saved the day by a histrionic gesture towards the guards of the legislative Councils, men who had never served under his brother and were not real soldiers. Even so, Brumaire was the definitive coup d'état of the revolutionary series precisely because it brought in the Army. 'Remember,' Bonaparte told the Ancients, 'that I march hand in hand with the God of Fortune and the God of War.'[20] The conspirators meant the coup to lead to another collegiate executive. But when the new constitution was published and the curious asked what was in it, the wits answered, 'Bonaparte'. There was, as it were, a hidden coup after Brumaire by which the general established his domination. A conspiracy to end fear, Brumaire in a sense merely created a new insecurity. 'The God of Fortune and the God of War'—without the support of these two deities, there was no future for the new order. When, six months later, Bonaparte left for the Italian front, everyone discussed who would take over if he failed. Yet, if much depended upon chance and the life of a single man, a whole concentration of ambitions and material interests was massed to accept his rule. He had been brought to power by those Vandal called 'the haunted revolutionaries'.[21] France was full of men like Talleyrand, Sieyès and Fouché. The breaking of caste barriers, war and emergency had given them administrative experience and a desire to remain in the charmed circle of those to whom public offices naturally gravitate. They hoped for a stable régime which would enlist the co-operation of moderates and disillusioned idealists of all parties. Only thus could they face the future with confidence, safe from inquisitions into their revolutionary past, and guaranteed

[20] J. M. Thompson, *Napoleon Bonaparte* (1953), p. 142.
[21] A. Vandal, *L'Avènement de Bonaparte* (1902) I, pp. 4–6.

in the possession of the property they had gained. 'We had reached the point', said Sieyès, 'when it was a question of thinking of saving, not the principles of the Revolution, but the men who had made it.'[22]

[22] Bastid, p. 239.

Chapter V

THE CHURCH AND THE REVOLUTION

I

The men of the Constituent Assembly were not a crew of freemasons and *philosophes* egged on by Jansenists and Protestants—as pious legend once had it. For the most part, they were sincere, unenthusiastic Catholics[1]—somewhat anti-clerical, but grateful to the parish priests who had joined the Third Estate; tight-fisted when it came to paying out money for benefits merely spiritual, but anxious to have an established Church all the same. Their ideals of liberty and equality—and their interests—involved the guaranteeing of religious toleration, the ending of clerical privilege in national taxation, and the breaking of the aristo-cratic monopoly of the richest ecclesiastical benefices. On these reforms virtually all Frenchmen were united. In some other respects, the Assembly was prepared to outpace public opinion, though not recklessly so. Its most radical innovation, the decrees against monas-ticism, passed after bitter debates in February 1790, was at least directed against obvious abuses, and while offending churchmen, it seems to have had a majority of lay society in its favour. In any case, here was the extreme point to which thrift and Voltairean prejudices could drive the Assembly, and this legislation, uncompromising as it was, did not cause a breach between the Church and the Revolution.

When the breach finally came about, it was not a result, directly at any rate, of the ill-will or fanaticism of the deputies—nor did it arise from clerical intransigeance. Pride, obstinacy, a tincture of anti-clericalism, the enormous pressure of circumstances and sheer miscalculation formed the ingredients in a disastrous decision, a blundering failure to rise to the heights of statesmanship on the part of the Assembly.

But first of all, let us look at an earlier decision, even more signifi-cant, which so to speak, created the materialistic core of interest at the heart of the Revolution. Ideals which attached themselves to this core could endure, régimes which anchored themselves to it could

[1] See, e.g. A. Mathiez, *Rome et le clergé français sous la Constituante* (1911), p. 7; A. Aulard, *Le Christianisme et la Révolution* (1924), p. 33; Dom Leclercq, *Les Journées d'Octobre* (1928), p. 187.

enjoy some permanence. I refer to the decision to sell church property.

II

At first sight, it may seem remarkable that an assembly which regarded property as sacred and wanted to retain an impressive established religion, should have begun its career by selling up the lands of the Gallican Church. As a preliminary to the confiscation, tithe went on the sensational night of 4 August. The story goes that the good bishop of Chartres proposed the abolition of hunting rights (which, if canon law meant anything, would be no loss to the clergy) and that the duc du Châtelet, now facing a future empty of serious employment, cried, 'Je vais lui prendre aussi quelque chose,' and added tithe to the list for cancellation. In due course, the Assembly recovered sufficiently from its altruisitic delirium to lay down heavy compensation for feudal dues, but tithe remained abolished, a gratuitous present to landowners.[2] On 10 October, four days after the King had been compelled to take up residence in Paris, a scheme for 'an operation on ecclesiastical property' was put forward by an opportunist anxious to co-operate with the inevitable —Talleyrand, bishop of Autun. Originally, he had proposed the the sale of Crown lands only, but that had been in his election speech to the clergy of his diocese, a rather different audience.

From the *cahiers*, it is clear that he was saying something that was in everyone's minds. Such an expedient for avoiding bankruptcy without putting fundholders on the rack or taxpayers to the thumb-screw was generally acceptable. According to the lawyers, church property was not that sort of property which was declared 'sacred' in the Declaration of Rights of 26 August, and which belonged to members of the Assembly; it was merely held in *usufruct*. In the past, through its monopoly of rich benefices and sinecures, the aristocracy had siphoned off the wealth of the Church; why then should the nation at large not help itself in emergency? The highest common factor in the diverse teachings of the *philosophes* had been the desire to free men from mouldy old traditions and obscurantist 'prejudices' (a favourite word of disapproval to the Enlightenment). Here then was the supreme example of the dead hand of the past tyrannizing over the present. Had not Turgot observed (Mirabeau used the famous analogy in the debates) that if everyone who had ever died was entitled to remain in his tomb there would be no land left to cultivate for the living? This argument was a favourite one

[2] M. Marion, *Histoire financière de la France depuis 1715* (3 vols., 1919–21) II, pp. 40–41.

with townspeople, who continually complained, in this age of municipal improvements, of the stranglehold which ecclesiastical property-holders maintained over schemes for new roads, quays, footpaths, orphanages, hospitals and cemeteries. The city of Angers in 1780, asking for the confiscation of two thinly populated monasteries to form a barracks, put the whole position in terms of political theory: 'The greater good is that which turns to the profit of society in general. No corporation or community can be allowed to go on living in a property which is useless to it, and which is rendered profitless to the state by the mere fact of their retaining it.'[3]

Municipal authorities were anxious to buy; there were also many private individuals who had their eye upon strategic investments. It was hardly a coincidence that the holders of venal offices of the old régime were being bought out, and thus had capital in hand, at this very moment. Certainly, there was little enthusiasm for halfmeasures like raising a vast loan on the security of ecclesiastical property (Braesch[4] has shown that this would have staved off bankruptcy just as effectively). Besides, so long as the Church held its lands, it could claim to remain an order in the State, and orders were abolished. So Church lands went on to the market, and the idea soon arose that the *assignats* (the paper currency which was the medium of the sales) would be the 'cement' of the Constitution, giving all citizens an equal interest in defending it.[5]

This was true enough. The more prosperous peasants and the bourgeousie who were the chief buyers (and who did well out of the coming inflation which reduced the burden of their instalments) became the backbone of the Revolution. At least, whatever forms the Revolution took, they stood united against a return of the old régime and the shadow of reconfiscation. A cynic might argue that, in the last resort, this is what the Revolution turned out to have been about. It was a great expropriation, a transfer of property into the hands of men with capital to invest. The Greeks have a cycle of tales, Turkish in origin, about one Nastur Djin Hodger—the equivalent of our 'shaggy dog' stories; I hope that I will not be considered frivolous if I use one of them as an illustration. Once, when Hodger was in bed, he was wakened by a thunderous knocking in the street below; forced out by his wife, he wrapped a blanket around himself and went down to investigate. Immediately he opened the door he was felled by a terrific blow. When he came to he was alone, and his

[3] J. McManners, *French Ecclesiastical Society under the Ancien Régime* (1960), p. 127.

[4] F. Braesch, *1789: l'année cruciale* (1941), pp. 169–211.

[5] McManners, op. cit., p. 243.

blanket was gone. 'What was all that about?' asked his wife when he crawled back to bed. 'I don't rightly know,' said Hodger, 'but it must have been someone who wanted my blanket.' The tumult of the Revolution had many causes, and they are difficult to analyse, but of its various and paradoxical results, one is very obvious—someone got the blanket and has held on to it ever since.

III

On 12 July 1790, the National Assembly adopted the Civil Constitution of the Clergy. Everyone agreed that the Church had to be reformed. The aristocratic monopoly of bishoprics, abbeys and well-endowed canonries was a scandal, while many parish priests were not receiving a fair income. The whole old parochial and diocesan structure was antiquated and illogical; vast sees like Rouen stood in absurd disparity to the minute dioceses of the south, while in towns a multiplicity of little parishes failed to meet the needs of growing suburban populations. In any case, since tithe was gone and church property was coming under the auctioneer's hammer, the State had to make arrangements to implement its promise to pay ecclesiastical salaries.

All this was very properly catered for, without reckless generosity. Benefices without cure of souls, and chapters, were abolished. Parish priests were to be given reasonable incomes, graded according to responsibilities, while bishops would be preserved from the temptations of affluence. Dioceses would now coincide with the boundaries of Departments, and parishes were to be combined into realistic units. The age-old abuse of non-residence, prevalent among prelates, was to be curbed by the local authorities. Aristocratic monopoly of promotion would end, for bishops would be nominated by the electors of Departments and rectors by the electors of Districts —and as for the abbeys and sinecures, they were now no more.

What then had the ordinary clergy of France to complain about? A few, perhaps, cared sufficiently about the powers of the Pope to look askance at the regulation whereby newly appointed bishops received canonical institution from the metropolitan, not from Rome. To some, the right of departmental authorities to supervise residence was humiliating and a threat to the 'parsons' freehold'. Most of them thought that the abolition of parishes before the deaths of their present incumbents was mean; older priests, whose long years of celibate existence had left them with few ties with lay society, would find a pension a poor substitute for the authority and vocation which a parish had conferred. Most objectionable of all, however, was the method of election to clerical offices. The ordinary clergy hated court influence in appointments, but they had no desire to go to the opposite extreme and become dependent on the sovereign people, that is, the local farmers, lawyers and political bigwigs. They grew particularly angry when patriots, anxious to show that learning was not a reactionary monopoly, cited examples of popular election from the early history of the Church. 'Where the name of Christian was synonymous with saint,' cried one clerical deputy, 'when the faithful, united by charity, formed one single family of brothers, when their ambitions rose no higher than their yearning for a martyr's crown—then you could have confided to the People the duty of choosing their Pastors.'[6]

Thus, there was matter for discontent in the Civil Constitution. Even so, the clergy did not dislike it sufficiently to accept the responsibility for rejecting it. There was a majority, even of bishops, in favour of finding some way of 'baptising' it. The difficulty lay, not so much in the content of the new law, as in the manner of its enforcement. The bishops insisted that the Assembly could not legislate for the Church on its own authority; 'il faut consulter l'Église'.[7] How? A national council could have done what was needed, but the Assembly would not allow the bishops to meet—that would be to present the aristocratic prelates with a counter-revolutionary platform, and would be admitting that the clergy remained an order in the State. This being so, only one resort was left. The Pope must approve the Civil Constitution. Churchmen in France believed that he would do so to avoid schism.

So far as the men of the Assembly were concerned, the Pope was welcome to act, but he would certainly receive no invitation. Collectively, they were as pig-headed as Louis XIV would have been. They regarded themselves as heirs to the Gallican tradition. Having won sovereignty for the 'nation', they felt it a point of honour to be as disobliging as monarchs of the old régime. Just at a time when the whole object ought to have been to get things done by skirting round all the issues of principle, the Assembly was engaged in demonstrating its own unlimited competence. Camus, declaring at one and the same time that it would be criminal to change religion and yet that they had the power to do so, was proclaiming the death of statesmanship. On the other hand, it seemed obvious that the Pope would have to agree. On 10 June 1790, Avignon revolted against his rule

---

[6] Ibid., pp. 261–2.
[7] For the problem see E. Lavaquery, *Le cardinal de Boisgelin, 1732–1804* (2 vols., 1920) I p. 105.

and asked for union with France. Here was a superb weapon of blackmail: the Assembly assumed that it could now lay down the law and sit back, leaving the King to persuade the Pope where his best interests lay.

In this mood of comfortable intransigeance, the Assembly went on to disaster. No public declaration came from Rome, local confusions arose over marriage dispensations and the like, tempers became frayed, a few extremists who wished to see the Church crumble made their voices heard, abetted by the supporters of Avignon, wanting a break with Rome for obvious reasons. Above all, the sale of ecclesiastical property was imminent; who would buy it if the new Church polity remained unenforced? On 27 November, the Assembly imposed an oath to the Constitution upon all office-holding clergy.

And the result? Three bishops without sees and four diocesan bishops complied. Of the latter, three had scandalous reputations and one was an eccentric. The parish clergy were divided, roughly half and half. I have tried to explain elsewhere[8] how cruel was their dilemma. Though there were some enthusiasts, it was generally not a case of for and against, so much as of bewilderment, of pathetic attempts to cling together and do the same thing, of unconvinced courage and hesitant betrayal on the part of men hoping that those in power would engineer a compromise. The intermixture of material with spiritual interests complicated the universal confusion. In Alsace, a rector and his curate appeared in church together, having agreed to refuse, but when the curate broke his word, the rector rushed to the pulpit to take the oath, crying, 'Ah, *canaille!* You think you'll get my parish. But you won't!'[9]

It is the task of statesmanship to prevent muddles of this kind from arising, to marshal disputed points in such a fashion that honest men can make honest decisions for and against them, and to separate practical issues about which reasonable men can agree from the sweeping theoretical arguments concerning ultimate authority over which consciences are bound to clash. The Assembly, basking in the glow of national sovereignty, adopted a 'take it or leave it' attitude without asking itself what it would do if there was a substantial option for the second alternative.

In due course, the Pope's condemnation of the Civil Constitution of the Clergy was made public. The schism was permanent. For the first time, the aristocratic counter-revolution had gained widespread

[8] *French Ecclesiastical Society under the Ancien Régime* (1960), chap. XIV.
[9] R. Reuss, *La Constitution civile et la crise religieuse en Alsace, 1790–5* 2 vols., 1922) I, pp. 200–1.

support among ordinary people: the emigration had been presented with a conscience.

IV

Everything now conspired to link together religion and reactionary politics. Religious scruples were known to be one of the king's chief motives for attempting to escape to the frontiers, and a decree of 29 November 1791 treated non-juring priests as 'suspects' in areas where troubles occurred. Once war was declared (April 1792), the orthodox clergy were regarded as a fifth column in league with the Emperor. One of the reasons for the fall of the throne on the 10 August was the king's refusal to sanction a decree for the deportation of 'refractory priests' who were denounced by twenty 'active' citizens; one of the results of 10 August was a tightening up of such penal legislation against the clergy. After the September massacres, a vast clerical emigration began. To their mental picture of hordes of vengeful émigrés pouring back into France behind the despots of Europe, Frenchmen now added the multitudes of priests in England, Spain and Rome, plotting the recovery of Church property and the return of the old régime.

Against this background of a war of survival, the strange phenomenon of 'de-Christianization' arose. It took the form, first of all, of abandoning and undermining the unhappy Constitutional Church. The registration of births, marriages and deaths was taken from its clergy, and divorce was legalized in September, 1792. The marriage of priests was encouraged, at any rate by threats, though not with the vision of comfortable fire-sides, for the payment of their salaries died away. Secondly, the movement took the form of attacking Christianity directly, with ridicule and persecution. The impetus came from the frenetic activity of some of the représentants en mission in the provinces, Fouché at Nevers, Laplanche at Orleans. Back in Paris, the movement was taken up in the clubs and sections. Priests were obliged to hand over their letters of ordination and abjure their vocation, and there was some sacriligeous masquerading. As usual when authority connives at disorder, buffoons and vandals seized their opportunities for exhibitionism and destruction. Thirdly, the de-Christianization took the form of inventing substitute religious observances in place of Christianity. In October 1793, the Convention adopted a new calendar, with Nature's cycle, pagan gods and botanical specimens in place of Christian martyrs; Christmas became dog day and All Saints was dedicated to the goat's-beard herb. The great national festivals were to be patriotic celebrations to the glory of the Republic, one and indivisible. Robespierre, however, went further. His strict and dignified bourgeois existence made him detest the beery demonstrators who fooled around in copes and chasubles, and—the opposite reason—he regarded atheism as 'aristocratic', the prerogative of nobles of the old régime, not of a Rousseaustic sovereign people. Besides, anti-religious buffoonery offended the peasants and gave a fighting cry to the superstitious soldiers of despotism. It was not, according to Mathiez, that Robespierre had sympathy with Christianity; he wished the de-Christianization movement to be decently controlled by the Convention, and his deism was just 'a form of his appetite for justice'. One wonders, His religious feelings had some of the ardours of his master Rousseau, and the cult of the Supreme Being (though that was not the name he himself preferred) was so foolish politically as to vouch for his enthusiasm. In effect, it was all the same; his new religion was but an episode of the de-Christianisation—as Mercier's errand boy observed, 'There's no longer a God, only Robespierre's *Être Suprême.*'

How do we account for this fantastic movement with all its overtones, atheistic or deistic, sincere or frivolous, artistic or brutal? According to Aulard, an historian who was a solid adherent of the Third Republic and an avowed anti-clerical, the idea of attacking Christianity only arose in 1793, when the priest was seen to be the obstacle to raising forces against the revolt of the Catholic Vendée and against the foreign invaders. When decrees against the clergy failed, the revolutionaries saw that they must eradicate the influence of religion altogether ; their policy was 'an expedient of national defence'. Mathiez, Aulard's pupil and an ardent socialist, broke with his master first of all on this very issue; according to him, revolutionary patriotism was itself a religion. Its ceremonies and nomenclature—drawn from masonry, the literature of sentiment, classical antiquity, and from Catholicism itself—are found early in the Revolution, running parallel to Christianity, until they finally become substitutes for it. According to Guérin, another Marxist, but much less learned than Mathiez, and wildly doctrinaire, de-Christianization was merely a vulgar diversion encouraged by the bourgeoisie to distract the working classes from their just claims to decent living standards. No doubt there is much truth in these, or at least in the first two of these explanations. From the Federation and from the first 'civic baptism' in 1790 (a patriotic baptism allied with the religious one—at Strasbourg, 13 June) we can see the Revolution manifesting itself with something of the outward trappings, as well as the inward ardour, of a religion. Without the hysteria of the war and the Terror, however, extreme fanatical outbreaks would hardly have been possible.

A psychological study both of the leaders and of the rank and file behind de-Christianization would be particularly revealing. Among the leaders, there are some interesting misfits and, more especially, the part played by clerical renegades is remarkable—of the extremist *représentants en mission*, Fouché and Le Bon are ex-Oratorians and Laplanche is an ex-Benedictine. As for the rank and file, they are fewer in number than one might imagine; their strength is drawn from the mass exaltation of war time, and the universal fear of an aristocratic conspiracy using Christianity as its instrument. It is worth noting too that some practical circumstances of wartime helped to create the atmosphere of de-Christianization. Bells were being melted into cannon, religious ornaments broken up for their precious metal, and churches used for storehouses and munition dumps. Revolutionary clubs also tended to take over churches as meeting places; men grew accustomed to making inflammatory speeches from *ci-devant* pulpits and knocking out a saint or a funeral monument to make way for busts of heroes of liberty.

All the while, however, it is important to remember—as M. Latreille points out in a masterly discussion of our problem[10]—that we are engaged essentially in investigating the play of 'obscure and marginal forces'. In the de-Christianization movement we are seeing the emergence of strange individuals and fanaticisms which would never have reached the foreground of history but for the landslide which threw open all the rifts in the social and religious order. This is one of those cases in history where the explanation of why certain things happen is broad and obvious, though the explanation of the peculiar things in themselves leads into obscure by-ways running off over the edge of the map of rationality.

V

The men of 1789 had no conception of the possibility of separating Church and State. In a sense, they were trying to bring the two into a closer alliance than before, since, with the ending of privilege, the Gallican Church lost the right to vote its own taxation, and with the sale of ecclesiastical property, the clergy became salaried servants of

---

[10] A. Latreille, *L'Eglise Catholique et la Révolution française* (2 vols., 1946). This is the best study of the Church and the Revolution. See also J. Leflon, *La crise révolutionnaire, 1789–1846* (1949). Since the publication of R. C. Cobb's monumental study, *Les Armées révolutionnaires: instrument de la Terreur dans les départements* (2 vols., 1961–3), the whole question of de-Christianization must be re-opened.

the nation. Thus the bonds binding Church and State together would be tighter, and the bias of the relationship more erastian, than under the unreformed monarchy. The Constituents, Mathiez said, were 'trying to nationalize Catholicism and put it at the service of the new order'.[11]

But by the spring of 1794, the whole traditional concept of Church-State relationships had been abolished, and something like the modern idea of the separation of the two great institutions had become official policy. This point was reached, not by theoretical re-assessments, but by necessity. When half the clergy of France refused the Civil Constitution, the idea that the assembled nation represented, in some sense, the *ecclesia*, became absurd. The orthodox Catholics led the way in urging that the *état civil* (the registration of births etc.) be laïcized. War, the fall of the throne and de-Christianization completed the divorce between the Revolution and the Constitutional Church. Therefore, on 3 Ventôse, Year III (21 February 1795), the Convention passed the decree of Boissy d'Anglas. The Republic was not to recognize nor pay for any religion but, according to article VII of the Declaration of the Rights of Man, it guaranteed the free exercise of all.

The rulers of France had entered a new world, in which there were no precedents to guide them. Nor were there theoretical principles to steer by; indeed, the Directory inherited the separation of Church and State, not as a clean new formula to solve an old problem, but as a despairing expedient. In practice, the Churches were regarded as a menace to the régime and were treated as such; the free exercise of religion in accordance with article VII of the Declaration of Rights was conspicuous by its absence. We find the Directory issuing collective deportation orders against orthodox priests and forbidding the disestablished Constitutional Church to elect its bishops by the votes of its own faithful clergy and laity. 'The liberty of religious exercise exists in Turkey,' said Grégoire, 'it does not exist in France.' Meanwhile, the old dream of the de-Christianization period, that of a substitute official religion, was kept alive. The *décadis* were to be observed instead of Sundays. Mellowed by the thought that they only had to waste one day in ten on holidays, the good citizens of France assembled in their battered local churches to hear the most recent parliamentary decrees read from the lectern, see civil marriages performed and watch school gymnastic displays. When the charming musical cult of Theophilanthropy was invented, the Directory helped it along with a subsidy from the police funds. In foreign policy, too, the Government had its bias: the armies of Italy were to

[11] A. Mathiez, *La Révolution et l' Eglise* (1910), p. 23.

swing southwards 'and make the tiara of the so-called head of the universal Church tremble'. In short, the essential pre-requisite for the amicable working of a policy of separation of Church and State, a neutral administration, a lay but not a 'laïcizing' government, was lacking.

The régime of separation posed new problems for churchmen, problems which reached their acutest form among the orthodox. They had refused the oath to the Constitution (which, of course, at that time, included the Civil Constitution of the Clergy) because they considered that the State was interfering improperly in ecclesiastical matters. However, they still had duties as citizens. How were these duties to be interpreted? Was it right to undermine a government which was anti-Christian in tendency and which had overthrown the old alliance of Church and State? Or perhaps, on the other hand, churchmen had a greater obligation than most to accept the powers that be, even if those powers had *de facto* status only. There was good apostolic precedent; and in the last resort, the teaching mission of the Church might be presumed more important to a Catholic than his preference, as an individual, for a different form of government. The various revolutionary oaths posed this question squarely.

After the fall of the throne, priests were required to take the 'Oath of Liberty'—'I swear to be faithful to the nation, to maintain with all my power liberty, equality, the security of persons and property, and to die, if necessary, for the execution of the law.' M. Emery, the tough and spiritual ex-Superior of Saint-Sulpice, regarded this oath as acceptable. The royalists challenged his ruling, and thus the orthodox were bitterly divided. A similar division arose over the oath required from priests wanting to use church buildings (September 1795)—'I recognize that the universality of French citizens is sovereign and I promise submission and obedience to the laws of the Republic.' The controversy revived again after the coup of 18 Fructidor, when a much less defensible oath was imposed, the oath of 'hatred to royalty'. The circle of émigré bishops around the Pretender in exile condemned all declarations of obedience to the Republic; the Archbishop of Paris and other prelates who had ended up in other refuges tended to be more tolerant to them; M. Emery, who had stayed in France to keep the Church alive, accepted oaths to *de facto* governments (the impropriety of 'hatred' excepted).

Thus, an understanding of the reality of the French situation was compelling some churchmen to recognize that the Church could not allow itself to be identified with royalist politics. 'The catholic religion,' said the Bishop of Boulogne in October 1797, 'can co-exist with any form of legitimate government.'[12] This was the argument of the Abbé Coste in a work, *Manuel pour Missionnaires*, whose title reveals his pastoral pre-occupations. 'The Christian religion,' he says, 'has always submitted to the different forms that revolutions have given to temporal governments, and its ministers have never had any right to take part in these revolutions. They obeyed the authorities which arose, whether they were established by God in His mercy, or permitted by Him in His wrath.'[13]

Thus, out of the Revolution, a new pattern of thought concerning the relations of Church and State had emerged. The State was to keep public order and allow the free exercise of all religious; the Church was to accept whatever form of government established itself and observed these conditions of religious neutrality. So far, however, only a minority on either side was convinced, and fewer still would be ready to fulfil their share of such a bargain. Bonaparte, with his devastating clarity of vision, saw this. Indifferent to the ideals of both Church and Revolution, but with a masterly insight into the factors of power and profit involved, he gave both sides, as nearly as possible, what each of them wanted.

VI

Bonaparte's cynical *obiter dicta* about the political uses of religion are notorious. 'Society cannot exist without inequality of fortunes, and inequality of fortunes cannot exist without religion.' 'The people have to have a religion; this religion must be in the control of the Government.' 'My policy is to govern men as the greatest number wish to be governed. That is the method, I believe, of recognizing the sovereignty of the people. . . . If I was governing a people of Jews, I'd rebuild the Temple of Solomon.' None of the twelve tribes ever came under his sceptre, but during his brief rule in Egypt he had complied with the prejudices of the followers of the Prophet. Bonaparte, indeed, appreciated well-conducted ceremonies and was not unaffected by the superficial sentimentalities of religious experience. Memories of his first Communion never faded; the faint sound of bells stealing into the silence of his retreat at Malmaison never failed to move him. He understood enough of religion to know its power over other men. His realism was unclouded by either anti-clericalism or devotion. It was obvious to him, as a technician in revolutionary expansionism, that anti-clericalism was not for export; Belgium, the

[12] C. Ledré, *L'Eglise de France sous la Révolution* (1949), p. 250, n. 16 ('la religion catholique peut subsister longtemps avec toute forme de gouvernement légitime').
[13] Latreille, op. cit., I, p. 218.

Rhineland and Italy were Catholic areas where authority needed a religious consecration. His own apprenticeship to the complexities of the Church-State problem had been served in Italy, in command of the armies. While to the Directory he was forecasting the inevitable collapse of the Roman hierarchy, he was, in the summer of 1797 (says Madelin), 'brooding on the ideas which one day would direct him to the policy of the Concordat.' 'Our religious revolution is a failure,' General Clarke wrote to him from France at this time, 'people have become Roman Catholic again. . . . Maybe we are at the point when we need the help of the Pope to bring to the Revolution the support of the priests, and consequently of the countryside, which they have succeeded in dominating once more.'[14]

From Bonaparte's trenchant observations (mostly after the event) we can see clearly the political factors which he juggled in his brain when considering the restoration of the altars in France—the Pope ('what a lever of opinion to move the rest of the world!'); foreign powers ('If I hadn't believed in God, who would have been willing to negotiate with me?'); the insurrection in the Vendée ('It was by becoming a Catholic that I finished the war in the Vendée'); the plots of the émigrés ('Fifty émigré bishops in the pay of England direct the French clergy. Their influence must be destroyed. The authority of the Pope is necessary for that'). The authority of the Pope, in fact, could silence the royalists who denied catholics the right to accept a *de facto* government, and could provide the one great assurance which the politically active classes in France required —a guarantee of the security of their purchases of Church lands.

This was how Bonaparte's mind was moving. What of the Pope's? Pius VI had been evicted from Rome by the Directory (after the murder of a French general) and died in exile. Before this, however, his entourage had drafted a 'bull' (July 1796), *Pastoralis sollicitudo*, which proclaimed the duty of submission to established governments. This document was never published, but the fact that it had been prepared is significant. The conclave of Venice (30 November 1799 —14 March 1800) elected Chiaramonti as Pius VII; he was said to have referred to the 'democratic' form as not repugnant to the gospels. The new Pope was aware that Austria and Naples were hoping to partition his dominions—Bonaparte was as good a gamble as the catholic monarchs when it was a question of looking after the temporal power. An agreement would end the schism in France, might preserve ecclesiastical property in Italy from sale, and would enhance papal authority. There were solid reasons why Bonaparte and the Pope should incline to an understanding.

[14] Ibid, p. 236.

The Concordat was finally signed on 15 May 1801. The French negotiators had been tough, though not so tough as to try to bluff Consalvi into signing a fraudulently altered copy, as the latter was to claim in his memoirs.[15] The alliance of Church and State was restored in France. Catholicism was declared, not 'dominant', as Rome desired, but simply the religion 'of the great majority of French citizens'. The Pope would delimit the boundaries of dioceses and put new titulars into the bishoprics. This meant, in effect, though the actual word was avoided, that the prelates of the old régime would be deposed—a remarkable amplification of papal power. Indeed, of the 93 survivors of the episcopate of 1789, 38 refused the invitation to resign conveyed in the brief *Tam multa*, and thus created the minor schism of the *Petite Église*. The State gained because the First Consul was to nominate the bishops, and all clergy were to take an oath to the Government; priests were expected to inform the authorities of subversive activities which came to their notice. And above all, in return for State salaries to the clergy, the Church renounced any claim to the property sold during the Revolution. This last provision was the heart of the matter.

Bonaparte had accurately weighed the interests of Frenchmen. He had, however, underestimated the psychological heritage of distrust which came to them from both the Revolution and the *ancien régime*. France insisted on remaining 'Gallican'. The Gallican cry was raised by Louis XVIII in exile, by the angry orthodox bishops and by the disappointed constitutionals, and it was re-echoed by all the submerged devotees of the old de-Christianization policies. That was why Bonaparte fraudulently added the 'Organic Articles' to the Concordat, in defiance of the Pope, their effect being to revive some, though not all of the Gallican defences against Rome that existed before 1789. Portalis, putting forward these Organic Articles, said that in the no-man's land (*zone indécise*) between spiritual and temporal, there must be a final authority, and this must be the power which 'balances all interests and defends public and general order'. 'It is an incontestable principle that the public interest— which the government maintains—ought to prevail in everything which is not of the essence of religion.'[16] And who defined what was of the essence of religion? No doubt it would be the power which balances all interests once again. The common consistent pattern of Church-State relationships in France was, that whoever wielded the secular sword—King, Assembly and King, Convention, First Consul, Emperor—in the last resort, the State must prevail.

[15] G. Constant, *L'Eglise de France sous le Consulat et l'Empire* (1928), p. 147.
[16] A. Latreille, *Napoléon et le Saint-Siège* (1935), p. 14.

VII

The Concordat came just in time. After a few more years the restoration of the traditional religious structure would have been impossible. Even in 1809, out of 32,000 priests in France, only 1000 were under 40 years of age. Now however, ecclesiastical vocations could revive, and clerical influence again exerted itself, in the parishes, and through the educational system. The schismatic Constitutional Church was ended, twelve of its bishops being pushed into the Concordatory Church with some shifty official explanations about the 'retractions' which they may or may not have made. Pius VII was to suffer much at the hands of Napoleon, but he always remained grateful to him for ending the schism and restoring the altars in France.

The story of Bonaparte's coronation and subsequent feuds with Rome does not concern us now, more especially as his conduct had little affinity with earlier erastian traditions—of the Gallican lawyers, of Josephinism and the Enlightened Despots, of the *philosophes* or of the Bourbons. His relations with the Pope were based upon impulse and the desire for immediate effects; the nuances of the *ancien régime*, whether of legalism, anti-clericalism or of devotion, were lacking. His policy—a series of ruthless incidents—did not alter the fact that the Concordat he had so intelligently devised was the only peaceful equilibrium of forces possible under the circumstances. The Bourbon Restoration tried going back to the Concordat of 1516, but within two years it became obvious that only the Napoleonic treaty was viable in France. It lasted, indeed, until the beginning of the twentieth century, and could well have lasted longer still.

Although Bonaparte re-knit the alliance of Church and State and endowed it with remarkable permanence, the whole atmosphere of the new polity differed from that of the old régime. A coronation in the presence of the Pope, not just of the French Bishops, in which the Emperor was dispensed from communion and put the crown on his own head, and in which special measures had to be taken to disassociate the head of the Church from the fraudulent Organic Articles—this was a different world from the *Sacre* at Rheims in the in the days of the monarchy. It was a world that was imperial, rather than French and Gallican, a world in which force was supreme, rather than privilege, in which the sacraments had no relevance to politics and in which ceremony was contrived, rather than traditional, The basis of the new alliance was simply a harsh coincidence of interests: the buyers of ecclesiastical property wanted security of tenure and the Church wanted status and help in its mission. During the de-Christianization movement, anti-clericalism had welled up from a thousand underground sources: once it had manifested itself so clearly, a whole pattern of long-established reverences and inhibitions was destroyed. The Revolution had created its own traditions of heroism, its own quasi-religious mythology, uniting forces of both idealism and anti-clericalism in opposition to Catholicism. 'A fine capuchinade!' said a general at the high mass of Easter 1802 which celebrated the Concordat, 'all that's lacking is the 100,000 men who gave their lives to suppress all that'. On the other side, the Church had its long roll of martyrs who had died precisely to preserve 'all that'—victims of the guillotine and the firing squad and of Carrier's drownings, of prison massacres, of cruel deportations. So from henceforward, there were to be two Frances, divided by terrible memories. The nineteenth-century alliance of Church and State did not (as did that of the old régime) represent French unity; it was rather a device of constitutional machinery and propaganda, to prevent the two bitter factions in the nation from destroying each other.

The destruction of the Church in France had begun with a crisis over the Civil Constitution of the Clergy in which the National Assembly had studiously ignored the Pope; the restoration of the Church in France was achieved by an agreement with the Pope alone. Of all ecclesiastical persons and institutions, it was the Pope who gained in power and prestige as a result of the Revolution. The plunder of his estates and the captivity of his person merely emphasized his indispensability in matters spiritual. The Imperial Council which Napoleon called in 1811 to coerce him (over the matter of bulls to vacant bishoprics) was a sycophantic assembly, but the bishops began their proceedings by admitting that they were powerless without papal agreement. The noble bearing of Pius VII in adversity, and his enforced travel outside Italy had also given him popularity. But the real reasons which added influence to his office went much deeper. With the disintegration of the normal cadres of ecclesiastical life and amid baffling conflicts of loyalties, churchmen had come to look to Rome for moral guidance. The Gallican tradition had faded. Now that the clergy were paid by the State, the old ecclesiastical Gallicanism, which had often stood by the Crown against the Pope, appeared rather like subservience. The lower clergy tended to become ultramontane, leaving Gallican attitudes to the more politic bishops. The Enlightened Despots, with their cohorts of cardinals tightly organized to rig papal conclaves and elect weaklings to the chair of Peter, were now swept away. In the interests of 'philosophy' and State power they had suppressed the Jesuits; in August 1814 Pius VII restored the Order, seeing that 'strong and experienced rowers' were needed when Peter's barque was tempest tossed. Catholic missions overseas had collapsed during the Revolution; their restoration was under the control of the Roman Propaganda, and was substantially free from the domination of secular sovereigns or of independent missionary Orders. The revolt of South America and the expulsion of Spanish bishops was to enable the Papacy to make new and more favourable agreements in an important area of the mission field. The Revolution had thrown the Catholic Churches of Europe into an equal confusion; they all now felt a common need for reconstitution and a sense of common danger. The redrawn map of Europe and the total view of the globe of missionary endeavour, memories of the Revolution and the shadow of approaching intellectual challenges all seemed to teach the same lesson. De Maistre in *Du Pape* (1817) proclaimed that the Pope was the centre of unity of all local churches: let all submit to his authoritative voice. Catholic thought was on the way towards infallibility.

CHAPTER VI

NAPOLEON

I

'I was born when my country was dying', wrote Bonaparte in June 1789.[1] 'My country', that is, Corsica; 'dying', because the French army in 1768–9 occupied the island, his father being one of the guerillas who prolonged resistance. The future Emperor of the French always remained a Corsican. France was the instrument, the accomplice of his ambitions, rather than his fatherland, and he understood the great nation so well because he studied it dispassionately; a product of its civilization and its Revolution, he had never made the last surrender to illogicality which is called patriotism.

It was as a soldier that Napoleon Bonaparte became a Frenchman. A poor Corsican noble, eligible for military education in France because of the annexation of his island, from the age of ten to sixteen his mind was formed in the academy of Brienne. Since he later pensioned his old teachers and even found a sinecure for the school porter, one imagines that these were happy years; certainly they trained a remarkable intelligence and created a vocation around which his developing personality shaped itself. He was essentially a professional soldier. 'When I was a lieutenant of artillery', he would say, in the days of his greatness, banqueting with kings; his career, in his reminiscences, was all of a piece. The veterans of his early battles had licence to say what they would to their Emperor; despite the difference in rank, it was they, and not the civilian grandees, who belonged to his world. To politics, Bonaparte brought the realism and incisiveness of the battle command. His fundamental principle was the soldier's hatred of disorder. He never forgot how, as a newly commissioned officer, he went with his battalion to suppress an insurrection of silk workers at Lyon, and how in 1789 there were riots in the town and mutiny within the garrison when he was stationed at Auxonne. A pale officer with an uncouth accent and a foreign name watched the mob invade the Tuileries on 20 June 1792 and observed that if he were King such things would not be tolerated. Apparently, he was again a spectator on 10 August, and believed that if Louis XVI had appeared on horse-

[1] *Letters and Documents of Napoleon*, ed. J. E. Howard (1961), p. 23.

back, the throne could have been saved. With these sentiments, it was fitting that he should first become a familiar of the mandarins of revolutionary politics by conducting a repressive operation, clearing the Paris streets on the occasion of the right-wing rising of *Vendémiaire* (5 October 1795).

'There is only one secret for ruling, that is to be strong, because in force there is neither error nor illusion.' The validity—and the limitations—of his soldier's outlook on politics lie in this typical *boutade*. Yet, though Bonaparte was callous—he gloated over the slaughter at Borodino and, according to Caulincourt,[2] showed no remorse for the destruction of a quarter of a million men in Russia—instances of deliberate cruelty on his part are rare. He used violence with economy, scientifically. When his dictatorial temperament and desire for quick results did not betray him, he was well aware of the limitations of armies and police, and of the importance of the intangible factors that stir public opinion. With harsh whimsicality, he assessed these factors in terms of a calculable unit of his own discipline—'treat the Pope as if he had 200,000 soldiers', 'I fear the insurrection caused by shortage of bread more than a corps of 200,000 men'.[3] Ruthlessness free from fanaticism and intelligently conscious of its own limitations served France well, and could have served her better had the driving forces of ambition been equally restrained.

An expatriate Corsican, a poor foreign noble with no real status, an officer who transferred allegiance from a monarchy whose weakness he despised to a Revolution whose disorder he detested, a man of keen intelligence and sensitivity without either religion or patriotism—Bonaparte was essentially a *déraciné*. His only roots were in the Corsican clan loyalties by which he was constantly supported or thwarted, and in the friendship of his soldiers. This is not to say, however, that Taine, whose 'scientific' method could lead to fanciful analogies, was right in portraying him as a *condottiere* of the Italian Renaissance, a mercenary of genius.[4] The conquering *élan* of the French armies was bound up with the Revolution, and Bonaparte, even when only a soldier, always looked on war with the eyes of a statesman. Hence, *déraciné* as he was, he studied the Revolution and admitted allegiance to it. In the magic days of '89 and '90, when men had believed in the dawn of liberty and equality, he had lived in officers' messes. 'Brought up in camps,' says Mignet, 'a

---

[2] See *Memoirs of General de Caulincourt* (E.T. by H. Miles, 1935), espec. pp. 528, 559 (though contrast p. 487).

[3] The quotations are in F. M. H. Markham, *Napoleon and the Awakening of Europe* (1954), pp. 102, 104.

[4] P. Geyl, *Napoleon, For and Against* (1949, ed. 1964), pp. 138–40, 422.

late arrival in the Revolution, he understood nothing but its materialistic side.'[5] This is substantially true, yet the young artillery officer
who in 1788 believed that 'there are few monarchs who do not deserve
to lose the thrones they occupy', who joined the Jacobin club of
Valence in 1791, who became a firm republican after Varennes and
who was later in some danger as a supposed protégé of Robespierre
was, in formal terms, a fully qualified revolutionary. Certainly, he
was an acute observer of the revolutionary enthusiasm. It might
serve his ambitions, and his principles of efficient, orderly government. As a general, he also came to see how the principles of 1789
could be used as the most effective of garrisons in the lands overrun
by his armies. Thus in Italy (1796–1797) he played on the republican
and national idea; in Malta, in a stay of six days he abolished titles
of nobility and most of the monasteries, and introduced religious
toleration and equality of taxation; in Egypt (May 1798–1799)
he proclaimed that men are equal to destroy the power of the
Mamelukes, and rehearsed his idea of a compromise between the
Revolution and established religion by putting the muftis into tricolour shawls and letting off fireworks for the feast of the nativity
of the Prophet.

The Revolution is often thought of as losing its ideals in a dream
of conquest, a process culminating in Bonaparte. It would be as true
to say that the Revolution disseminated its ideals, even when they
were no longer believed in at home, because they assisted expansionism and justified imperialism. At the time of the *coup d'état* of Brumaire, Bonaparte was already aware of this process: he used it for
his own ambitions, and it is this fact which gives lasting significance
to the decade and a half in which he was to rule France and dominate
Europe.

II

What sort of a man was the young general who took over control
of France shortly after his thirtieth birthday and who became
Emperor five years later? Physically, he had enormous powers of
endurance and concentration, though within a decade he was becoming unhealthily fat, not a result of easy living, but the beginning
of Fröhlich's disease, the premature failure of the pituary gland.
With all the attributes of a retentive memory and swiftness of deduction and association, his mind was a superb mechanism, geared to
action rather than reverie, and passing rapidly from one subject to
another without pause for reflection or refocusing. After the battle

[5] There is an English translation of Mignet's *History of the French Revolution*
(1824), by Everyman (1939).

of Eylau (1807), from his winter quarters in the wilds of eastern Europe, he was writing to Paris about festivities and celebrations, and reprimands to newspapers, and giving orders for the expulsion of Mme de Staël, he was devising a defence of the memory of Mirabeau and regulations for a girls' school, and giving instructions to the Empress Josephine about the best use of her leisure.[6]

The limitations of his tastes were obvious. In music, he appreciated only simple ballads, in painting the sole merit he saw was accuracy, in architecture, immensity. He—who believed that his own decisions were based upon a 'moral spark', a sort of intellectual illumination—had no reverence for inspiration in the arts; 'there are complaints that we have no literature, it is the fault of the Minister of the Interior.'[7] From the threadbare officer hanging round Paris under the Thermidorian reaction and envying the rich their pleasures to the ruler of half the Continent, his ambitions were materialistic, and interesting only because of their magnitude. The things he sought were those the majority of men esteem and desire: he differed from them only in the superb gifts of intelligence, will and energy which he brought to the quest. Nothing was impossible; the word was 'the phantom that haunts timid souls and the excuse where cowards find their refuge'.

In Tocqueville's deadly phrase, he was 'as great as a man can be without virtue'. 'He neither hates nor loves', said Mme de Staël, 'for him no one exists but himself.'[8] Yet, to his marshals and familiars, the Emperor was lavishly generous, and he was strangely loath to punish, as the careers of Talleyrand and Fouché bear witness. The famous scene in which the ex-bishop of Autun was excorciated— 'excrement in a silk stocking'—has become a bye-word to illustrate Napoleon's rudeness, when it might just as well be used to prove his clemency. Far from being a cynical amoralist, his moral outlook, like his artistic tastes, was that which we now associate with suburbia. Respectability was essential. Here is a soldier who is never recorded telling an obscene story, who forbade Mme Tallien to go to the opera dressed as a hunting nymph (or at least, he sent to warn her that 'the days of myths were over, and the age of real history had begun'), who broke with Bourrienne because of a financial scandal, who compelled Talleyrand and Berthier to marry their mistresses. An unbeliever, he defied his generals and advisors in restoring an official Church in France. Apart from his custom of laying the blame

[6] *Letters of Napoleon*, ed. J. M. Thompson (1934), pp. 172 *ff*.

[7] J. M. Thompson, *Napoleon Bonaparte* (1953), p. 202.

[8] Mme de Staël, *Considérations sur la Révolution française* (1818), in *Oeuvres complètes* (1820) XIII, p. 195.

for failures on others (on Brueys for Aboukir Bay, on Villeneuve for the English invasion fiasco, on Ney for Waterloo), he was generous: if charity really begins at home, remarkably so. While Madame Mère went round snuffing unnecessary candles and economizing on butter and warning them all that 'it won't go on for ever', Napoleon was engaged in conjuring up kingdoms for his brothers, converting barnyard roosters into eagles, as Holland Rose has it,[9] and receiving nothing but complaints for his efforts. 'From the way they talk,' he remarked, 'you'd think I'd squandered the family fortune.' Tocqueville's moral severity is harsh; indeed, it is hard to know what moral test to apply to such a meteoric career, which sprang from and was only possible because of a vast and seemingly endless state of war. Perhaps, in these circumstances, the criterion should be the avoidance of needless cruelty, and a generation which has seen the rule of Hitler may be disposed to look kindly upon Bonaparte's deficiency in the nobler Christian virtues.

More particularly will this be so for those who glimpse the introvert behind the extraverted man of action, the romantic behind the classical façade. In Cairo, when he heard of Josephine's infidelity he was already weary of glory—'A vingt-neuf ans j'ai tout épuisé.' First Consul for two months, he walked with Roederer in the dusty halls of the abandoned Tuileries.

'Général, cela est triste.'

'Oui, comme la grandeur.'

Then there is the famous melancholy reverie confided to Giradin over Rousseau's tomb at the Isle of Poplars at Ermenonville—

'It would have been better for the repose of France that this man had never been born.'

'Why so, Citizen Consul?'

'It is he who prepared the French Revolution.'

'I should have thought, Citizen Consul, that it was not for you to complain of the Revolution.'

'Well, the future will discover whether it was not better, for the repose of the World, that neither Rousseau nor I had ever been born.'[10]

The all-conquering general, the great administrator, at times became the artist, looking at his own career as if reading it in a novel. In such moments, he was conscious of the futility of the immense ambition which was so much a part of his being that he could never subject it to the realistic analysis by which he reduced the passions of others to crude fragmentary desires susceptible of manipulation and compromise.

[9] J. Holland Rose, *The Personality of Napoleon* (1912), p. 27.
[10] Citations in Geyl, op. cit., p. 387; Holland Rose, *Napoleon* (1904) I, p. 21.

III

What was the nature of Bonaparte's rule? After the coup of Brumaire, he became First Consul under the Constitution of Year VIII; by the changes of May and August 1802 be became Consul for life, was given the right to name a majority of the Senators and, through his control of the Senate, the power to suspend the constitution. In May 1804 he was proclaimed Emperor of the French. The successive steps in his elevation to supreme power were approved by plebiscites, for plebiscites had now become part of the common-law of the Revolution. There is no point in discussing the disputable details of this popular verdict, for we all know now that democratic decision-making does not consist in permission to cast a vote, but in the exercise of choice between real alternatives. Like the paper constitution of 1793, that of Year VIII was based upon universal suffrage; this suffrage, however, could only work indirectly through a hierarchy of notables, and in practice it was not allowed to work at all. The Senate, Tribunate and Legislature had interesting theoretical functions within a cunning balance; as it turned out, they really served as well-endowed clubs where the politicians of the Directorial period and other veterans of the Revolution found comfort in their retirement and an appropriate measure of popular contempt. Thus Bonaparte wielded monarchial, indeed dictatorial power.

This is a description of the extent of his authority; the question still remains, 'What was its nature?' Was he merely a war-lord, ever ready to throw his sword into the scales to outweigh the mystifications of sealing-wax and parchment that civilians devise? Or, when he assumed the ermine mantle and the golden circlet, did the Bourbon heritage fall to him also? According to Tocqueville, the main theme of French history has been the eternal centralization, so that revolutions merely succeeded in 'putting a head of liberty upon a servile body.'[11] On this view, Bonaparte may be described as doing much more than restoring the past by simply recreating its pageantry and by marrying the niece of Marie-Antoinette; his prefects will be the successors of the intendants, and his authoritarian genius would be bringing to a logical conclusion the governmental system of the old monarchy. A third possible interpretation of Napoleonic France is one which places it in the context of Enlightened Despotism. Eighteenth-century France invented the theories, which only came to fruition in other lands, in Russia,

[11] Alexis de Tocqueville, *The Old Regime and the French Revolution* (1856, Engl. trans. Doubleday, 1955), p. 209.

Prussia, Austria and Tuscany, where philosopher kings—and queens —arose. With Bonaparte, however, the heritage of philosophy at last blossoms in Paris itself. On the day he became First Consul, the password to his guard was the name of Frederick the Great, linked with that of an obscure revolutionary general. Perhaps this was meant to have significance—the Revolution has finally thrown up a soldier who is to be the last and greatest of the Enlightened Despots, one who, like Frederick II, is both a *philosophe* and a leader of armies. These are interpretations linking Napoleon with traditions of the *ancien régime*; it could be, however, that he belongs essentially to the new era, that he was the man of the Revolution, a sort of Mirabeau on horseback, the genius who canalised and redirected the great revolutionary stream when it had lost course and was drying up in deserts of corruption and anarchy. If so, it might be said that it was he who rescued the achievements of 1789 and embodied them in codes and institutions, so that they could endure. This point could be put more harshly. Tocqueville described the Frenchman of '89 as in love with liberty, but as even more in love with equality. As devotion to liberty died, they accepted a dictator who would preserve them from the return of privilege, so that they could all live equal, under a master.

These are not exclusive interpretations; some, or all of them, may be adopted simultaneously. Napoleon himself liked to think of his rule as at once French and cosmopolitan, and as embodying the whole of French history, 'from Clovis to the Committee of Public Safety'. The problem of placing the Emperor in the historical pattern, as between old régime and Revolution, is not one invented by historians—it was present to his own mind. He was aware that it was the Revolution which had made him, not just in the simple sense that it had given him his opportunity ('I should have thought, Citizen Consul, that it was not for you to complain of the Revolution'), but in the more complicated and paradoxical sense that he had been called to rule so that some of the extreme revolutionary courses might be curbed, while at the same time the dynamism of his administration came from forces that the Revolution had unleashed. On the one hand, he was accustomed to speak of the 'principles of 1789' as a constant menace, as a weapon always ready to the hands of 'the discontented, the ambitious and the theorizers of every age.' They meant individualism run riot, and he conceived it was his duty to place 'some masses of granite'[12] in French society, institutions, corporations, hierarchies, to give the nation stability. On the

[12] Madelin uses Napoleon's phrase as a chapter heading; *Histoire du Consulat et de l'Empire*, IV (1939), pp. 166 ff.

other hand, in notorious instructions to the Minister of the Interior in 1808 concerning the compilation of a history of France he insisted that there be 'no reactionary sentiments' when speaking of the Revolution. After all, it had come to reorganize a country that was bankrupt, ruled by a discredited monarchy, and politically fragmented—'rather a union of twenty kingdoms than a single state'. The historian then, would show the Revolution as necessary—and, of course, as leading inevitably to the Napoleonic dénouement.[13] Indeed, as Bonaparte saw it, the Revolution had bequeathed to him a more absolute authority than the Bourbons had ever wielded. Hence, the famous saying of 1801, when he raged against the *idéologues* who opposed his desire for repressive legislation—'I am a soldier, the son of the Revolution, risen from the people, I will not suffer myself to be insulted like a king.'

IV

'I am a soldier'. . . . The Empire was a war government throughout, which always spent at least half its yearly income on the armed forces, and which drew from conquest the revenues making more conquests possible. In 1805, a *trésor de l'armée* was formed to gather the contributions of the defeated, and in 1810, the *domaine extraordinaire* was created to hold the excess funds of the first organization —by 1811 its holdings were two milliard francs. This, at first sight, seems the sort of government over which Frederick the Great of Prussia might very suitably have presided. The tactics of the armies had changed since his day, of course, though the changes were all inventions of the old régime; the screen of snipers, the light mobile artillery, the advance in column were not devised in the revolutionary wars, but came from drill books like Guibert's *Essai général de Tactique* (1772), which had revised old concepts in the light of the lessons of the Seven Years' War. But if the monarchy had provided the tactics, the armies of the Revolution were utterly different from those of the earlier eighteenth century and derived their *élan* and will to victory from principles which would have been anathema to the Prussian king. 'It would be easy,' Guibert had written, 'to have invincible armies in a State in which the subjects were citizens',[14] and this is precisely what had occurred. True, the conscription offended against equality by allowing 'replacements', but the conscripts who reached the front after their eight days' training found themselves in the one organization in which the essential aim of

[13] R. B. Holtman, *Napoleonic Propaganda* (1950), pp. 130–1.
[14] Cit. F. M. H. Markham, *Napoleon* (1963), p. 22.

1789, the career open to talent, had been fully achieved. Promotion came from the ranks. After each battle, the colonels filled the gaps among the officers with those who had distinguished themselves in action. It was an army in which Lefebvre could rise from sergeant to marshal, and in which Couin, a general and a baron, would still trim the beards of his friends to keep his hand in at his old trade.

Essentially a soldier and superbly intelligent, Bonaparte was fully aware of the secret of the success of his armies. It was the principles of the Revolution, debased and bastardized no doubt, yet neverthe- less vital and inspiring, which made his soldiers go on to victory. And as we have seen, before he came to power he had learnt that the principles of 1789 were the most effective garrisons for the lands he conquered. They gained him support, they gilded his will to domin- ation, they provided efficient theoretical bases for reorganization and administration, and excuses for confiscations. Thus, even as a warlord, he was of necessity and by the very nature of the case much more than the last of the warrior kings or the first of the modern dictators. He was not a Frederick II grinding out a dynastic heritage, or a Hitler whose conquests would be followed by a chain of concen- tration camps. Still less was he a diplomat of the *ancien régime* playing the old game of manoeuvre, exchange and partition. He was the soldier of the Revolution, and behind his lightning forays followed French civilization and 'the principles of the modern state and modern society.'[15]

V

In this last sentence I have been quoting Professor Georges Lefebvre, who has given us a masterly interpretation of the Napoleonic era. 'The principles of the modern state and modern society'—what does this mean? The lay state, religious toleration, equality before the law, the absence of exemptions from taxation and from the ordinary obligations of citizens, careers open to talent, conscript armies, logical, instead of traditional administrative organization, pro- fessional bureaucracy, and the basic concept of the utilitarian ends of government. This is what Bonaparte gave to France—or, rather, preserved to France out of the revolutionary heritage—and offered to Europe.

The essence of his rule is summed up in the institution of the Prefects and in the Civil Code. The Revolution had swept away the old provinces, estates, dioceses, judicial and financial areas of France, and the Departments it had created in a logical pattern

[15] G. Lefebvre, *Napoléon* (*Peuples et Civilisations*, 1935), p. 1.

remained as the units of local government. Now, at the head of each was put the Prefect, an all-powerful agent of the central government. Of a hundred or so prefects, thirty had served in the revolutionary assemblies, a dozen had been soldiers and a dozen diplomats; there were a few ex-émigrés and a few former clergymen; one had been a Director and one, Jeanbon Saint-André, had been a Protestant pastor and a member of the Committee of Public Safety. In their persons, they vindicated the ideal of the career open to talents, their own being the peculiar harvest of the vast administrative experience which a decade of war and reorganization and upheaval had provided. Tocqueville was mistaken in supposing that their pre-revolutionary predecessors, the intendants, had been obsequibus agents of power, and it is now appearing that the Napoleonic prefects too, though less effectively, could represent local interests against the government they ostensibly served. Members of the Senate, Tribunate, Legislature and Council of State also seem to have offset their servility in high matters of policy by steady guerilla warfare upon the administration in matters of material concern to their own Department. One might say that Bonaparte's centralization, in so far as it was effective, was something new, but in so far as it was not, it retained something of the flavour of the *ancien régime*.

Though the Civil Code of 1804 (from 1807 called the *Code Napoléon*) owes little in detail to Bonaparte himself (except the special emphasis on parental control which he favoured), his was the driving energy which ensured that this long-matured project of the Revolution was actually completed. In pocket form, with a handy index, the Code compressed the essential guarantees of civil equality and liberty of conscience—an egalitarian document, embodying equality as it was understood by the propertied classes. In Holland, Germany and Italy, wherever the French armies marched, it exercised enormous and enduring influence.

It seems then, that the egalitarian conquests of the Revolution were preserved. But what of liberty? We have seen how the parliamentary and popular bases of the Consulate and Empire were shams. Under such a government, individual liberty and freedom of speech could hardly be observed. The notorious *lettres de cachet* of the old monarchy, by which anyone could be imprisoned or exiled by a royal signature, were revived in the form of orders signed by the Minister of Police and a judicial official. By 1814, there were 2,500 state prisoners (one might ask, however, how many state prisoners there were in Germany when Hitler fell, or in Russia when Stalin died). Article 46 of the Constitution of Year VIII declared that all prisoners, even political conspirators, must be tried within ten days.

The Senate's committee on individual liberty was the only body exercising oversight; in its ten years of existence it only once acted in a case of arbitrary imprisonment, and then it merely appealed to the Emperor. Most of the newspapers were suppressed, and the censorship was severe. It was forbidden to allude to the Bourbons, usurpers, tyrants, French defeats, the social pact, the sovereign people, the Jesuits, Napoleon's family. Tragedies like those of Corneille and Racine became comedies to the theatre-goers who followed by the text to laugh at the changes imposed. If equality was preserved, it was under something like a dictatorship.

Let us beware, however, of subscribing to the legend that Bonaparte 'assassinated' liberty in France. We have seen the state of the country on the eve of Brumaire. What was left of the ideals of 1789? What future was there for constitutional government? There is no gainsaying Vandal's decisive phrase—'Bonaparte can be blamed for not having founded liberty, he cannot be accused of having overthrown it.'[16]

At the point where the interests of liberty and equality coincide, the Emperor ostentatiously abandoned both, by recreating a splendid court and instituting a new aristocracy and a new legitimacy. Yet there was something almost inevitable about this apparent betrayal. It was with these trappings only that men could believe in permanence. To Thibaudeau, who objected to the Legion of Honour as the reintroduction of the 'baubles' of the old régime, Bonaparte replied, 'Well, it is with toys that mankind is governed.' He was providing the successful survivors of the Revolution with what they—or at least their wives—yearned for. Even under the Consulate, girls were being sent to the *pensionnat* of Mme Campan, former lady-in-waiting to Marie-Antoinette, to learn the elegant tricks of Versailles. The imperial court, with that confusion of Austrian gravity, Asiatic splendour and Caesarian grandeur which Talleyrand ridiculed, served its purpose as a substitute for the Bourbon tradition and a proclamation of the new stability of France. A scandal to faithful revolutionaries, the imperial nobility of dukes, counts and barons served as a meeting place for the *arrivistes* of two hostile and separated worlds. It became possible to have a duc de Luynes (a 'real' *ci-devant* duke) in the Senate, and at the same time pay respect to the new Duke of Danzig, Marshal Lefebvre, an ex-sergeant, whose duchess had been a washerwoman. Ney, Junot, Lannes and Augereau married women of the old nobility. One of the secrets of the success of the Napoleonic armies was the *amalgame* of new conscripts with the veterans: one of the secrets of Napoleonic government was the

[16] A. Vandal, *L'Avènement de Bonaparte* (1902) I, p. 26.

amalgame of the old aristocracy with the notables of the Revolution.

Yet the Emperor was providing a substitute for the past, not restoring it. His nobles were allowed hereditary status only if the title was supported by a sufficient guaranteed income. Feudal dues had gone, never to return. Equality before the law remained; there was no revival of privileged exemptions from taxation, or of blatant aristocratic priorities to promotion in Church, Army and State. And the court of a monarch who spent half his time commanding armies and the other half in ruling rather than reigning, could never have the peculiar magic and the illusion of permanence of Versailles. The *plaisir de vivre* of the *ancien régime*, the idyllic, aristocratic dream world of the eighteenth-century painters, was gone for ever. Greuze died in the year of Austerlitz, and Fragonard in that of Wagram.

VI

One of those who duly recorded a vote for Bonaparte in 1799 was a foreigner who had accepted honorary French citizenship, Jeremy Bentham, the philosopher of utilitarianism. The reflection arises that the Napoleonic dénouement of the Revolution was, perhaps, a utilitarian one, the nearest practicable approach to the solution of the problem of 'the greatest happiness of the greatest number'. 'My policy consists in governing men as the greatest number wish to be governed. That, I think, is the way to recognize the sovereignty of the people.'[17] In a France fragmented into bitter factions by the revolutionary events, it needed courage and intuition to decide how the greatest number did, in fact, wish to be governed. The answer had to be presented to them before they could recognize it, and it was thus that Bonaparte played a ruthlessly effective rôle as a conciliator of interests. 'If there was one art in which Napoleon excelled,' says Pasquier in his memoirs, 'it was that of balancing all interests and of combining the measure of satisfaction which had to be granted to each.'[17a]

Buyers of ecclesiastical property were guaranteed in possession of their gains. Revolutionary politicians received offices or pensions. Catholics rejoiced to see the return of an orthodox established Church, others were relieved to see that this church was kept in tutelage to the State and that religious toleration was secure. The *émigrés*—all but a few—were encouraged to return, and if their lands had not been sold, they could recover them. The assassination plot of 24 December 1800 (*La Machine Infernale*) was a royalist

[17] Thompson, *Napoleon*, p. 172.
[17a] *Mémoires du Chancelier Pasquier* (6 vols., 1894–5) I, p. 150.

conspiracy, but the First Consul insisted on taking revenge by deporting Jacobins. His duplicity reveals the essential bias of his rule: it was a conservative dictatorship directed against 'anarchy' and the social doctrines stirring among men of the extreme left. Lucien Bonaparte, in his *Parallel between Caesar, Cromwell, Monk and Bonaparte* (November, 1800) put the position without ambiguity. His brother, he said, was like Caesar, except that 'Caesar was the chief of demagogues. . . . Bonaparte on the contrary rallied the class of property owners and educated men against a raging multitude. . . . The First Consul, far from overthrowing all the conservative ideas of society, restores them to their ancient splendour.' On the other hand, however, the institution of the Empire in 1804 was prepared by the execution of the Bourbon duc d'Enghien, an act of bad faith and cruelty which had one simple justification: it bound the régime to the memory of the Revolution and reassured all those with Jacobin connexions. 'I am delighted,' said one of these, 'Bonaparte has made himself a member of the Convention'—the Convention, which had condemned the king to death.

Thus, the fears and interests of men of property and men of intelligence were captured for the service of the Consul and the Emperor. Fouché and Talleyrand—the bloodstained proconsul and the defrocked aristocratic prelate—were more than the Government's ablest servants: they were also symbols of the possibility of reuniting the fragmented nation. 'The one guards my left', Napoleon said, 'the other my right. I open a highway along which all men may go.'

Here, I think, we have an answer to our question as to the nature of Bonaparte's rule. It was pragmatic, using the traditions of the old régime and of the Revolution in so far as these traditions moved the minds of men. Essentially, it was based upon a calculation of the conflicting fears and interests of Frenchmen. These conflicts were manipulated and combined into the service of an overwhelming ambition.

VII

The kings of eighteenth-century France had been prisoners amidst the splendours of Versailles: Bonaparte was a vagabond Emperor. Of the ten years from 1805 to 1814, he spent more than seven away from his court and the seat of government. The Bourbons had waged war conscious of their own permanence as members of the trades-union of kings; Napoleon knew that a single disastrous campaign would be the end of him. He belonged to a Corsican clan and to the fraternity of soldiers, but with all his greatness, he was not an integral member of France and its society. 'Joseph,' he whispered to his brother at the coronation, 'if only our father could see us now!'—

he knew that he was a prodigy and a *parvenu*. 'When did the house of Bonaparte begin?' In the official gazette he answered this question quite simply, 'At the 18 Brumaire'. Yet the confused coup of Brumaire had made him First Consul merely on sufferance, and it was the battle of Marengo which ensured his continuance in power, a lucky triumph, won by Desaix at the cost of his life. It was not the coronation which consecrated the Empire, so much as the supreme victory of Austerlitz. 'At home and abroad, I reign only by the fear I inspire.' Representative of the Revolution, Napoleon could not disarm in face of the kings and aristocracies of Europe, and it may well be asked if his continued campaigns were not, up to a point, an insurance for his continued tenure of power at home. The armies he dared not disband were sustained by the plunder and promotions of wartime and, as the career of Henri Beyle (Stendhal, the novelist) shows, the imperial conquests provided attractive employment for civilians as well as soldiers. And to what extent were his subjects in love with glory? A study of public opinion has shown that the country, indifferent at Brumaire (it was just another *coup d'état*), was enthusiastic after Marengo, welcomed the renewal of war with England in 1803, and rose to a new peak of enthusiasm after the victories of 1805. True, from 1809 public opinion was decisively in favour of peace, but for some years, at least, France may be considered as the Emperor's accomplice. Afterwards, men became haunted more and more by insecurity, in Chateaubriand's words, by an 'existence which, because there was nowhere to stop, was put to the hazard each morning'.

'Nowhere to stop.' Was this a psychological necessity of Bonaparte's nature, or was it, in fact, a necessity of the situation? Historians who study his fantastic career naturally speculate upon alternative possibilities, and look for the 'turning point' in his fortunes. Given his soldier's drive to conquest and his revolutionary inheritance, at what stage could Bonaparte—as a realist—have called a halt? The rupture of the Peace of Amiens in 1803, followed by the formation of the Third Coalition, is taken by Pariset and Lefebvre as the beginning of an almost inevitably long period of warfare. Like the Girondins, says Lefebvre, he had thrown down the gage to the kings of Europe. Yet, though the First Consul was acting in a menacing and aggressive fashion, it is doubtful if he could have preserved peace, even if he had wished to do so; most Frenchmen did not believe that it was possible. Thiers, who had a flair for this sort of judgment, put the turning point at Austerlitz (2 December 1805), though blaming England for continually evoking new coalitions, so that Jena and the annihilation of Prussia necessarily followed. At this point, Talleyrand was suggesting a solution appropriate to the diplomacy of the *ancien régime*: a generous peace with Austria to strengthen the Habsburgs as a barrier against Russia, while France would withdraw within her natural frontiers, undertaking to make no new annexations beyond them. It would have been a gamble of course, a wager on moderation; Bonaparte preferred to gamble on force. Both then and since there has been general agreement that the invasion of Spain in October 1808 was a folly; Decrès, a contemporary, said 'the Emperor is mad, absolutely mad; he will destroy himself and all of us with him.' Talleyrand, who had cynically encouraged the Spanish adventure, and Fouché, who had opposed it, both seem to have decided at this time that they would need to make arrangements for their future without counting on Napoleon. It was the silent verdict of two acknowledged experts in the art of survival. Yet, to the very eve of the march on Moscow, it is difficult to say that the Emperor has made his decisive error. Kingdoms more riddled with treason, and surrounded by more faithless allies, have survived. As regards the Russian campaign, of course, there can be no two opinions; it was the last great gamble which brought the Empire down.

When he invaded Spain, Napoleon claimed to be the heir to Bourbon policy—'a legacy which I had to accept with the monarchy, since Louis XIV had shed so much blood to seat the same family on the two thrones'. In exile on St. Helena, his standard argument was that he had always acted in self-defence, preserving the revolutionary achievements against European reaction. Self-justifications of this kind, based upon the supposed continuity of French history, have won some acceptance among historians. According to Sorel, the monarchy aimed at the natural frontiers of Rhine, Alps and Pyrenees (he was mistaken here), the Revolution obtained them and swore never to let them go, and Bonaparte's career is explicable in terms of their defence.[18] Others have suggested that the Emperor was the heir to the policy of the eighteenth century in a different sense, in that there was an old-standing desire for revenge upon England for the loss of Canada and India; with England as the pre-determined foe, the argument can go on to show that it was England which raised up coalitions, or that it was only by continued continental conquests that France could hope to complete a system of trade embargoes to bring Albion to her knees.

The difficulty with these explanations is that they accord ill with the pattern and chronology of Napoleon's imperialism, and while

[18] A. Sorel, *L'Europe et la Révolution française* (8 vols., 1885–1904); for this and other views see Geyl, op. cit., pp. 257–326.

they make his aims more respectable, they reflect adversely upon the intelligence he brought to their realization. One feels that his aims were more grandiose, personal, and romantic. M. Bourgeois has emphasized the 'Oriental mirage' which shimmered across his imagination, the vision of an eastward march of empire in which, perhaps, the Russian Tsar could share. Another historian, Driault, follows up a contrasting theme in which the Russians are cast for the rôle of the external 'barbarians'; this is the pervasive yearning to achieve the inheritance of classical Rome, which had been present in the minds of the men of the Revolution as an heroic republican jargon, and which was embodied for all to see in the constitutional nomenclature of Tribunate, Senate, Consulate and Empire. There were, too, vague dreams of a revived Eastern Empire, and echoes of a new Holy Roman Empire are found in the imperial coronation, in the claim to a special relationship with the Pope, and in the assumption of the crown of the Kingdom of Italy. To be Caesar did not exclude being Constantine, and to be Constantine did not exclude being Charlemagne.

One wonders, however, about all this. Are we speaking of the inspiration of ambition, or merely of its archaeological dress, its scenario? Napoleon's ambitions, says Muret, are not a policy, but 'a state of mind'; their content cannot be frozen into immobility then exactly enumerated, for they change continually as new vistas open. The Emperor was a fatalist, a gambler who always played double or quits, and who did not think in terms of the achievement of a final equilibrium. There is the usual measure of half-truth in one of his cynical outbursts of bravado, '*La place de Dieu le Père? Ah, je n'en voudrais pas, c'est un cul-de-sac.*'

VIII

With all his intelligence, Bonaparte had no significant vision of the future. In this respect he was a lesser man than his dull and glassy-eyed nephew, Napoleon III, who cherished Saint-Simonian dreams of an industrial utopia. Under Napoleon I, the population increased and coal production, such as it was, tripled, but steam engines were not introduced and coal did not replace wood in the blast furnaces of Creusot until 1810. His industrial policy consisted of little more than bureaucratic regulations. The working classes owed nothing to a régime which forbade combinations and prohibited travel without a *livret* signed by an employer. Napoleonic methods of government added something to human knowledge, though not of the most useful kind. The trick of a plebiscite to confirm a political *fait accompli* was demonstrated. Fouché, in his headquarters at the Quai Voltaire, with Desmaret, an ex-priest and Jacobin as director of his secret service, exemplified the value to rulers of intelligently handled police techniques (though few of his subsequent imitators have followed his remarkable clemency). The reorganization of education under the Université showed an awareness of the possibility of manipulating the minds of youth which the Empire itself could not achieve, thanks to shortness of money and the need to conciliate the Church. Most significantly, the Emperor's masterly handling of propaganda in the *Moniteur* and official bulletins was an object lesson in the new art of mass persuasion. These devices of power have been brought to perfection under Hitlers and Stalins. But Napoleon, pursuing an ambition that is essentially personal, occupying his position by lonely individual courage and genius, rather than by the support of a party or an ideology, and being a product of the civilization of the eighteenth century, immune from nihilism and fanaticism, is only by accident their predecessor.

Though the Emperor lacked vision or ideals, his genius, working by the way of his ambitions, was responsible for scattering abroad in Europe the ideas of the French Revolution, and at home, for embodying the more materialistic of the revolutionary achievements within the legal and administrative framework of France. The Council of State, the Code, the Legion of Honour, the Bank of France, the Université, the whole prefectorial and mayorial system of local government, and the restoration of an established Church, were his work. So too, was the final guarantee of the revolutionary land sales. At his fall, he left behind him a country in which careers were open to talent while social exclusiveness and the domination of wealth remained the rule, with a highly centralized government which never knew how to master local material interests; a nation at once servile and revolutionary, thirsting for glory yet hating war, the most civilized community in the world, and unable to govern itself. This was the inheritance which the Bourbon Restoration was powerless to change. 'Louis XVIII', said de Maistre, 'has not been restored to the throne of his ancestors: he has simply ascended the throne of Bonaparte.'[19]

[19] Cit. Markham, 'Napoleonic France', in J. M. Wallace-Hadrill and McManners, *France: Government and Society* (1957), p. 188.

CHAPTER VII

DEMOCRACY, SOCIALISM AND NATIONALISM

(*The French Revolution and the Forces that shaped the Nineteenth Century*)

I

In 1821, John Stuart Mill, then a precocious genius of fifteen years of age, came upon a history of the French Revolution. 'I learnt with astonishment', he wrote later, 'that the principles of democracy, then apparently in so insignificant and hopeless a minority everywhere in Europe, had borne all before them in France thirty years earlier, and had been the creed of the nation.'[1] 'From this time,' he added, 'the subject took an immense hold of my feelings'; thus, indeed, was the future theorist of liberty and representative government born.

The actual word 'democracy' is capable of varying interpretations; Carl Becker once said that it was a conceptual Gladstone bag which would accommodate almost any collection of social facts, dictatorship included.[2] Yet even if this is so, we still have to account for its sheer evocative force, which has encouraged political designers ever since to make use of its prestige; to find this sort of explanation, we have to go back, as Mill did, to the period of the French Revolution, when 'democracy' became a word capable of inspiring both fear and enthusiasm. We have seen how, in the eighteenth century it had been developing from a neutral term of political theory, referring to an unattainable ideal, into something more potent, challenging both despotism and aristocracy. By 1791, a liberal patrician of Amsterdam could say that 'the formula, Sovereignty of the People or Democracy' meant 'the new system which admits no right of government except that arising from the free consent of those who submit to it, and which maintains that all persons who take part in government are accountable for their actions.'[3] In February 1794,

[1] *The Early Draft of John Stuart Mill's Autobiography* (ed. J. Stillinger, 1961), p. 73.
[2] Carl Becker, *Modern Democracy* (1941), pp. 4–5.
[3] R. R. Palmer, *The Age of the Democratic Revolution:* I *The Challenge* (1959), p. 2, and for Robespierre, pp. 16–17.

Robespierre widened the definition further to imply a State in which the sovereign people makes its own laws, does what it can for itself and what it cannot by its 'delegates', and in which all men enjoy 'equality and the fullness of civic rights'. 'The French,' he said, 'are the first people in the world to establish a true democracy.' Let us look at this claim of Robespierre's in more detail; here, perhaps, is the most important of all the legacies which the Revolution was to transmit to the nineteenth century.

'The principle of all sovereignty rests essentially in the nation.' This assertion of the Declaration of Rights was demonstrated most decisively by the fact that France was given a new constitution. The deputies had come up to the Estates General assuming that the country already had a traditional constitution: when they went home again they had replaced it by an entirely new one. Radical change like this fitted well with the theories of Rousseau's *Social Contract* (a book greatly in demand again), for according to Rousseau, once the sovereign people assemble, all public officials are suspended and the form of government can be utterly changed; it was congruous too with the example of America, where a convention had exercised constituent power in the name of the people. It was true, as right-wing objectors pointed out, that France was not a city state where all the inhabitants could assemble, and that, unlike the Americans, the French had not got rid of their King; even so, Sieyès prevailed with his advocacy of the *pouvoir constituant*. He succeeded because Rousseau's dreams and the American precedent were made relevant by the circumstances of the political struggle. The 'National Assembly' proclaimed on 17 June '89 was preserved in being by making the levy of taxes conditional upon its continuance, but such a safeguard could only be devised by trespassing upon the royal prerogative. From then, the way lay straight ahead to the debates on the veto and to the law of 26 February 1791 on the residence of public officers, among whom the King was included. Later on, Sieyès, the inventor of the constituent power, became anxious to tangle up constitutional innovations with 'juries' proposing changes to the electors who proposed them to the legislators—but by then the Revolution itself had become a vested interest. The original lesson of 1789 remained, however; Europe had been provided with an example of the way in which a people can start again and create a radically new order.

All this had been done in the name of the sovereignty of the people. And who were they? On Rousseau's principles, everybody. In England, where Price had pointed out that half the M.P.s were elected by a total of fewer than 6,000 voters, voices had already been raised for universal suffrage, and these demands carried on to become the platform of Chartism in the nineteenth century. The Universal suffrage was not recognized in the French Revolution until the decree of 10 August 1792, by which all men over twenty-one, except domestic servants, were to vote (indirectly) for deputies to the Convention; in the Constitution of 1793, which was never operative, the exclusion of servants was dropped and the age required for deputies was lowered from twenty-five to twenty-one. But if universal suffrage, strictly speaking, came late in the Revolution and vanished soon (the Constitution of the Year III went back to the *suffrage censitaire*), this does not mean that it was a mere expedient of crisis time. The pyramid of indirect election which had produced the deputies of the Third Estate for the Estates General had an enormously broad base— something like five million voters. Except in Paris, practically every man in France over twenty-five years of age who paid taxes and who was not an actor, a bankrupt or a domestic, had been given his opportunity to vote in the assemblies of rural parishes or urban guilds. This fact gave additional asperity to Sieyès' attack on the privileged orders; not only did the Tiers do practically all the work of the country, but it also 'represents 25,000,000 people and deliberates on the interests of the nation; the two other orders, if they meet, have only such forces as some 200,000 individuals can confer on them.'[4] In spite of what has been said about the bourgeois inclinations of the Constituent Assembly, it did not betray this argument; its tax-paying qualifications demanded of 'active citizens', 'electors' and deputies were liberally devised: of every 100 men over twenty-five years of age, 70 could vote, 50 were eligible to be chosen as electors and one to become a deputy. Even so, Robespierre, Grégoire, Marat and others objected to the limitation of the suffrage, and their protests are confirmation of the fact that the Revolution's doctrine of popular sovereignty logically involved universal suffrage as soon as practicable.

It is significant too how the principles of the Revolution involved, not only voting in depth, but also on a wide front. Judges, bishops, parish priests, municipal officers and notables, District and Department administrators were all (within certain conditions of course) to be elected. The central government had no power to nominate officials in the provinces, so that the only possible control of local actions was annulment by the Crown. The elective principle had been applied to a degree which, under normal circumstances, would have created anarchy.

[4] Sieyès, *Qu'est-ce que le Tiers Etat?*

II

According to Robespierre, the sovereign people, once its institutions were established, would 'do for itself all that it can do well, and by its delegates what it cannot'. For disciples of Rousseau, there was a difficulty here, since in the *Social Contract* it is laid down that 'a people which gives itself representatives is no longer free'—the English, for example, 'are free only at election time'.[5] Most people agreed, however, that for a large state like France, Rousseau's formulae obviously had to be modified; besides, Sieyès added, Adam Smith's principle of the division of labour applied also to politics, and was especially useful for elevating intelligence to the oversight of public affairs. Thus, he concluded—and this became the official theory of the Revolution—'the people can neither speak nor act, except by its representatives.'[6] This was the practice of the British Constitution, which Burke had expounded twelve years before without frills about popular sovereignty. The M.P., he told his Bristol constituents, was to act as his conscience and foresight dictated, and not please the electorate. Meanwhile, the voters should let their representative get on with the job. 'Applaud us when we run, console us when we fall, cheer us when we recover, but let us press on—for God's sake let us press on.'[7]

In the early days of the French Revolution this view of the representative sprinting on ahead professionally met with objections from the Right, more especially from nobles who had 'imperative mandates' from their constituents not to abandon the distinction of Orders; indeed, the very existence of *cahiers* suggested that deputies had not gone up to Versailles as free agents. Later on, during the Terror, the Sieyèsian view of the representative met with challenge from the Left. Among the *sansculottes* of Paris, publications like Bonneville's *Bouche de Fer* spread Rousseauistic ideas and, more important, the exaltation caused by participation in successive insurrections and the despair caused by economic circumstances combined to create a crude, pathetic demand for direct democracy— deputies were to be revocable, the Sections were to sit 'in permanence' and enjoy autonomy, the people were to be allowed to intervene in state affairs by insurrection and the administration of popular justice. '*Ecoutez, mandataires, un membre de votre souverain*', said an

[5] Rousseau, *Social Contract* (Everyman trans., 1961), pp. 78, 80.

[6] Sieyès, *Dire sur la question du veto* (7 Sept. 1789) in P. Bastid, *Sieyès et sa pensée* (1939), pp. 35 ff.

[7] Ernest Barker, 'Burke and his Bristol Constituency', *Essays on Government* (1945), p. 197.

orator of the faubourg Saint-Antoine to the Convention.[8] His share of the total sovereignty was only one part in twenty-five millions, of course, but whatever it was, he had come in person to exercise it.

One feels obliged to sympathise with the *sans-culottes*, who were groping for a lever of influence to move their representatives to more decisive action about the price of bread, and were unable to find one. The essential piece of machinery which gives reality to the 'sovereignty of the people' in West European and American government today was lacking then; indeed, long afterwards its importance was not realized, even by experts in the theory of democracy— Tocqueville and John Stuart Mill passed over it lightly, Bluntschli's *Theory of the State* (1875) ignored it, and Ostrogorski at the end of the century actually condemned it. Yet we now regard a coherent party system as a necessity to 'translate public opinion into public policy',[9] to 'arrange the issues upon which people are to vote', to provide predictable government and constructive criticism of its activities, to make self-consistent promises to us and be judged by their performance. By being 'free only at election time' we can evaluate our masters and the possible alternatives to them, and 'make and unmake governments'; it is not so much a question of representation as of responsibility. But there were no parties, in the modern sense of the word, in the French Revolution. There were only shifting groups, based on interest, friendship or ideals, which formed after the deputies had been elected, within the obscure recesses of the Clubs or the Legislatures. Of the Girondins (whose feud with the Mountain is the nearest thing to a party struggle that the Revolution saw) their latest historian says that the only distinction between them and their enemies 'which has any consistent validity is that of their divergent attitude towards Paris', and, indeed, 'the group became an entity only in the hour of its downfall'.[10]

From April 1792, when France plunged into war, it is unreasonable to attempt to assess the working of the country's new democratic institutions. The foolish decision of the Constituent Assembly to make its own members ineligible for the succeeding Legislature had already broken the continuity of parliamentary tradition, and once a struggle for survival had begun, there was little hope of achieving

[8] Herlaut, 'La Levée des volontaires pour la Vendée à Paris', *Annales historiques de la Révolution française* (1931), p. 391.

[9] R. M. McIver, *The Web of Government* (1947), p. 213; the following quotations are, in order, from Laski, *Grammar of Politics* (1925), p. 312, and H. Finer, *The Theory and Practice of Modern Government* (1954), pp. 219 ff.

[10] M. J. Sydenham, *The Girondins* (1961), pp. 205, 176.

that mutual forbearance which makes a party system possible. The period of the Terror was, if we wish to call it so, the beginning of 'totalitarian democracy',[11] so long as we are clear that what happened then was alien to the ideals of 1789 and to the whole spirit of Rousseau. Helvétius had once said, using by accident one of the great phrases of the coming revolution, that starving men are allowed to resort to cannibalism—'everything becomes legitimate . . . for *le salut public*'; Rousseau had replied that '*le salut public* is nothing if every individual is not enjoying security.'[12] If he had survived into the Revolution he would have said as much to Robespierre. We should remember too that Robespierre himself was fully conscious that the revolutionary dictatorship was a temporary expedient, the very antithesis of democracy, and not its totalitarian culmination.

The true contribution of the French Revolution to the totalitarianism of the future, was not the example of a war-time dictatorship —history was full of lessons of this kind—but a quasi-democratic device, that of the plebiscite. The constitutions of 1793 and of the Year III were submitted to the electorate and approved by suspiciously large majorities, and the expansionist imperialism of revolutionary war was masked by popular votes for annexation in Avignon, Savoy, Nice and Belgium, the latter being particularly fraudulent. These precedents established the plebiscite as part of the common law of the Revolution, and it became the basis of the political theory of Bonapartism. After the coup of Brumaire, the new constitution was accepted by over three million votes against 1562; in 1802 the Life Consulate was approved with only 8000 against; the Empire was floated in on a tide of over three and a half million votes as against 2579. There can be little doubt that these figures were 'cooked'; certainly, there is evidence that those who did not sign the voting registers were put down as voting 'Yes'. In the plebiscites of 1802 and 1804, moreover, there was some dishonesty in framing the terms in which the questions were put to the voters. But fundamentally, the plebiscite betrayed democracy because it presented a *fait accompli* and offered no alternative; it evoked the sovereignty of the people in unintelligent, random aggregations of voters. It was the beginning of a new kind of democracy which so far has had as long a run as that associated with parliamentary government; in it, the sovereignty of the people is reduced to the formula, 'enthusiasm is obligatory'.

[11] See J. L. Talmon, *The Origins of Totalitarian Democracy* (1952) and Lefebvre's devastating review, *Revue historique*, CCXI (1954), pp. 144–6.
[12] R. Derathé, *J.-J. Rousseau et la science politique de son temps* (1950), p. 357.

III

As Robespierre's definition made plain, democracy had two aspects: the one was the sovereignty of the people involving popular control of delegates, the other was 'equality and the fullness of civic rights' guaranteed to every citizen. Just as the American Revolution declared that men are 'created equal', and 'have certain inalienable rights', so too the French Revolution had its Declaration of the Rights of Man and Citizen. This was not a piece of abstract theorizing, but a common-sense document directed against specific evils of the *ancien régime*, like arbitrary imprisonment, limits on free speech and on freedom of worship; the Declaration was not a 'flood of theory pouring down from a mountain range of philosophy, but a canal fed by springs arising from the work-a-day soil of France.'[13] 'Civic rights' were here (except that of association), but where was equality? The privileges of the nobility were destroyed, and promotion to offices in Church and State thrown open to men of humble birth, but perhaps more than this was required. Rousseau had held that a degree of economic levelling was necessary if the General Will was to be sovereign—'No citizen should be rich enough to buy another, and none so poor as to be forced to sell himself.'[14] The demand for economic equality (in the 1830's the name 'Socialism' was to be coined to describe its most systematic manifestations) was to be one of the great driving forces of the coming century; to what extent did Frenchmen in 1789 believe in it, and to what extent did the Revolution foster the idea?

IV

'All the governments I know . . . are a conspiracy of the rich', said Hythloday in More's *Utopia*. Suspicions of this kind were current long before Marx, and were found in various guises in France on the eve of the Revolution. It is true that there is a gulf between even the most extreme thinkers of the eighteenth century and the doctrines of modern socialism, yet in some of their writings the driving force can be seen—the protest against poverty, exploitation, and the indifference of rulers. It lurks in Rousseau's transference of original sin from man's nature to society, in Mably's proposals for sumptuary and inheritance laws, and in Morelly's abstract and moralizing communism; it is evident also in startling admissions by the most

[13] J. McManners, 'The Revolution and its Antecedents', *France: Government and Society* (ed. J. M. Wallace-Hadrill and J. McManners, 1957), p. 171.
[14] Rousseau, *Social Contract* (Everyman, 1961), p. 42.

respectable of writers. An aristocrat like Montesquieu said that the State owed all its citizens an assured subsistence and healthy life; Turgot, a future Controller General, said that 'the poor have incontrovertible rights to the abundance of the rich'; Necker, another chief minister of the Crown, depicts the poor as complaining, 'What do your laws of property matter to us? . . . we possess nothing; your laws of justice?—we have nothing to safeguard; your laws of liberty? —if we don't work tomorrow we die.'[15]

These protests against economic injustice were sincere, but unsystematic, being meant to touch the hearts of administrators rather than overthrow the existing order; the communistic utopias of Mably and Morelly sounded more radical, but they looked back to a golden age in the past, a Platonic, Rousseauistic dream to exhort men to austere contentment and Spartan duty, and not to spur them to battle for equality of possessions. In 1789 then, there was no real socialist doctrine in France, yet there was a good deal of passion of the kind from which socialist theories were to be born. The Revolution was 'bourgeois' in the sense that its official documents, including the Declaration of Rights, always assumed, even at the height of the Terror, that property was sacred. Equality was defined as the destruction of social, rather than of economic privilege. But this word 'equality' had its own inherent dynamism and compulsive magic; it was impossible to use it in the hearing of the multitude and expect that they would not apply it to their own condition as contrasted with the superfluity of the rich, and it was likely that a sprinkling of educated leaders would be found who would dip into Rousseau, Mably and Morelly to give these discontents some theoretical or literary formulation.

The events of the Revolution conspired to draw attention to the dangerous issue of property; indeed, the vehemence with which official pronouncements guaranteed it owed something to the need for camouflaging the process by which the new order was financed from the proceeds of a great confiscation. To popular opinion, the sale of the lands of the Gallican Church was a demonstration that property was justified only within the boundaries of social utility—the duc d'Aiguillon made the same point about the abolition of feudal dues—'You cannot conceal the fact that these dues are property, and all property is sacred; but they are a burden on the people.'[16] Mirabeau's argument against the clergy's objections to becoming salaried servants of the State carried the definition of social utility

[15] M. Leroy, *Histoire des idées sociales en France de Montesquieu à Robespierre* (1946), p. 246.
[16] Ibid., p. 262.

further still: 'There are only three ways of earning a living; begging, stealing or accepting wages'—presumably landowners and industrialists were employees of the nation, or worse. Along with this extension of the idea that the State had eminent rights as against property owners, there was also an acceptance of its obligations towards the weaker members of society, for since the Church had been responsible for charity and, substantially, for education, by taking over ecclesiastical property the nation had automatically assumed these burdens. '*Les secours publics sont une dette sacrée*', said the Constitution of 1793.

Another debating point made when Church lands were auctioned was the desirability of making property more widespread, so that a greater number of people would have an interest in defending the new order. This common-sense calculation fitted in with a more idealistic one derived from Rousseau, for how could there be a true General Will if some men were in economic thraldom to others? In the *Cercle social*, a society founded towards the end of 1789 to educate the people, the Abbé Fauchet explained the egalitarian implications of the *Social Contract* and called for a gradual division of the land. This idea fermented in the minds of reformers who remembered from their schooldays how the Gracchi had tried to restrict the size of holdings under the Roman Republic, and of country *curés* who sympathised with the land-hunger of the peasants. Thus, throughout the Revolution, from time to time suggestions of a *loi agraire* arose; on 18 March 1793 the Convention decreed the death penalty for all who made such subversive proposals in future. By then, the King had been guillotined, France was fighting for survival, and the voice of extremists was more easily heard.

V

When the Revolution ran into war, and life in French cities became a grim story of inflation, shortages, rationing and conscription, egalitarian ideas were reinforced by the overwhelming popular demand for equality of sacrifice. More than one group of politicians expressed this sentiment, and historians have been divided as to which of them has the strongest claim to a place in the ancestry of modern socialism. Marx and Engels mention Leclerc and Roux immediately after the *Cercle Social*.[17] There was, however, a strong tradition in favour of Robespierre and his few devoted followers, a tradition which was passed on through Louis Blanc to Jean Jaurès and thence

[17] K. Marx and F. Engels *Die Heilige Familie* (1845). p. 186 (cit. R. B. Rose, see note 19 below).

to Mathiez, one of the greatest of twentieth-century historians. Beyond the Terror and the revolutionary dictatorship, Robespierre saw the hope of an egalitarian regeneration, described in his speech of 5 February '94 as 'an order of things in which distinctions will arise only from equality itself, . . . where the Fatherland assures the welfare of every individual, where commerce is the source of public wealth and not just of the monstrous opulence of a few families.'[18] But it is difficult to be more precise about his dream of a new society, more especially because the decrees of *Ventôse*, concerning the use of the property of émigrés to help the indigent, remain a subject of controversy. To Mathiez, they were 'the programme of a new revolution'; to other Marxist historians they are little more than a bourgeois device to win support in the battle against the forces of reaction. From the evidence so far we might conclude that the decrees were a sincere design to assist paupers, but that they were not directed to helping the working classes generally, that they aroused some enthusiasm in the cafés of Paris, but were never put into operation, that they fit in with Robespierre's humanitarian beliefs, but that they do not prove that he intended to pursue an advanced social policy. The *Ventôse* laws, indeed, are not the main argument of Jaurès and Mathiez in favour of Robespierre; they praise him, rather, for non-Marxist reasons, the one because he attempted to stop the mad rush into war, the other because he fought against the corruption which sprang up like noxious weeds in the fierce heat of wartime hysteria and in the dank shadow of the guillotine. Thus, in a different fashion, to both these historians, Robespierre embodies, not so much a socialist ideal, as a universal one, that of selfless rectitude.

It is significant that Marx himself had preferred Roux and Leclerc as precursors of socialism. If Robespierre embodied the ideals of the Revolution, these men stood for what Michelet was to call the '*révolution sous la révolution*'; they belonged to the anti-Jacobin left, to the demagogic lineage of Marat, who had claimed to champion the 'Fourth Estate'. Together with Varlet and a few other popular leaders, they have come to be called the '*Enragés*', a collective name which, as has recently been demonstrated, they owe to historians rather than to any common doctrines or alliances; they were individual enthusiasts who arose like prophets to proclaim the rights of the 'virtuous poor against the vicious rich'.[19] Just as a few 'red' *curés* of the country-side

---

[18] Robespierre, *Textes choisis* (ed. J. Poperen, 1958) III, p. 112.
[19] My friend Mr. R. B. Rose has a monograph on the *Enragés* in press (published by the Australian Humanities Research Council). He has been good enough to allow me to use his typescript in preparing this section of my lecture.

demanded a share-out of the land for their peasants, so Jacques Roux, a priest of the Constitutional Church in Paris, reflected the desires of his miserably poor parishioners by claiming that the produce of the land belongs to all men. In September '93, the month in which he was finally arrested by the Jacobin Government, one of the Parisian Sections carried this doctrine of the revolutionary priest to its logical conclusion: 'the only basis of property is physical need'.[20] Probably Roux himself would not have wished to go as far as this; his career as a tribune of the people was chiefly occupied in denouncing the speculators and food hoarders who were battening on the war economy— he even wished to have special clauses against them put into the Constitution of 1793. The political implications of Roux's teachings were underlined by Varlet, an egalitarian agitator with a comfortable private income, a disciple of Rousseau who saw that direct democracy would be an illusion so long as the many were subject to the tyranny of the rich. These simple theories were put into precise portable phrases by Leclerc, the journalist of the Enragés: 'the aristocracy of nobles has been succeeded by the mercantile and bourgeois aristocracy'; 'all men have an equal right to eat'.

As the Enragés declined, their place as leaders of the urban poor was taken by the Hébertists, another clique which had no real coherence or philosophy. Hébert himself was a journalist of genius who had created, as his mouthpiece, the character of Père Duchesne, a hardswearing, pipe-smoking old revolutionary, with a huge dog that barked at the mere mention of an aristocrat. In the end, this mythical personality took over entirely the mind of its creator. A well-meaning adventurer, violent only in words, Hébert faithfully reflected the aspirations, fears and hatreds of the sans-culottes, and expressed them in masterly comic narratives fortified by whimsical obscenities. Spurred on by applause, and with a deep instinctive sympathy for the disinherited, 'Père Duchesne' went well beyond the left-wing formula dividing the Third Estate into bourgeoisie and people. The peasants, he saw, were enemies—they were 'the class that had gained everything from the Revolution, the spoilt child of the new régime, while we, the unlucky inhabitants of cities, have merely been allowed to suffer for liberty's sake'.[21] One of the assumptions of Parisian insurrectionism had been that the small masters and petty shopkeepers were of the same class as the artisans and the poor, but Hébert publicised the deadly truth which rationing and shortages had revealed: 'I can see that there's a league formed of all those who sell against all

---

[20] A. Soboul, 'Les Papiers des sections parisiennes, 1790– an IV', *Annales hist. Rév. fr.* (1950), pp. 97 ff.

[21] G. Walter, *Hébert et le Père Duchesne* (1946), p. 197.

those who buy, and I find that there's as much bad faith in the little shops as in the big stores.'[22] Like the *sans-culottes* whose opinions they echoed, the Hébertists and the Enragés could not escape from the pre-capitalist assumptions of the *ancien régime*. They were preaching a war of poor against rich, yet they saw little hope of achieving any improvements save by governmental intervention to fix maximum prices. But what if the dishonest manipulations of manufacturers and merchants defeated the Maximum? Chaumette, a follower of Hébert, answered this question in October '93 by asking for the nationalization of industry. This demand has been called the first expression of the idea of nationalization in the modern sense of the word,[23] and it arose, not out of a theory about the nature of society or the trend of industrial development, but from the prosaic fact that the starving people of Paris had lost all faith in shopkeepers.

VI

The ideas of the Enragés and of the Hébertists—and of Robespierre —smouldered among the *sans-culottes* after Thermidor, and flamed briefly into life again in the conspiracy of Babeuf (1795–7). Babouvism has been called 'a product of the despair caused by the Thermidorian reaction', but if this is true of the rank and file, it hardly applies to their leader, whose mind had been formed by the full range of the left-wing inspirations of the French eighteenth century. Before 1789, Babeuf had been converted to utopian communism by reading Rousseau, Morelly and Mably, and his work as a feudist in the country-side had helped to make him an exponent of the cause of the peasants and of the *loi agraire*. During the Revolution he had reflected upon the paradox which made a motto out of equality then limited it to equality before the law. '*La révolution est à refaire*' he said, for it had merely been the forerunner of another, and greater revolution. Babeuf's speculations about this new overturn and the final reformation of society were original. Unlike the Jacobins, Enragés and Hébertists, he was a thoroughgoing collectivist, who wanted to see all property taken over by the community, industrial property included, for it would become more productive once competition was eliminated. Even education, which 'has become a species of property', was to be collectivized and made uniform. The constitutional machinery of the new order would be direct democracy, but there would be an inaugural period of temporary dictatorship, not

[22] A. Mathiez, *La Vie chere et le mouvement social sous la Terreur* (1927), p. 543.
[23] Leroy, op. cit., p. 299.

this time to win a war and evict the aristocracy, but to re-educate man and found a new social order. Utopian communism was to adopt the techniques of the Terror; a community worthy of Morelly or Rousseau, to achieve the ends of the Enragés, was to be set up by the methods of Robespierre.

Babeuf's designs were not forgotten. One of his disciples, Buonarroti, an Italian aristocrat turned communist, a great plotter who has been called 'the first professional revolutionist',[24] published an account of their *Conspiracy for Equality* in 1828 which became the handbook of social revolutionaries in the 1830's and 40's. This book combined piety to Babeuf's memory with a justification of Robespierre and the Committee of Public Safety—'it introduced into European socialism the idea of the communist state brought about by revolution and dictatorship'.[25] This decisive inspiration, shorn of the utopian dreams of Babouvism, was passed on to Blanqui, and from Blanqui the highway of theories of proletarian dictatorship leads to Marx, to Lenin and the Bolshevik Revolution.

VII

Among the forces that were to shape the nineteenth century, there was one which was as potent as democracy and socialism, but very much more mysterious: this was nationalism. Between the French Revolution and the first World War it manifested itself in various forms, idealistic, selfish or sinister, and in the twentieth century it ran on into insane demonic mutations in Nazi Germany, and into new exotic strains in the anti-colonialist movements in Africa and Asia. But limiting ourselves to the more comprehensible period of nationalism before Hitler, what definition or description can we give of this force, of this strange mass inspiration?

A modern definition would mention common descent, language, territory, race, religion, without insisting on any of them: they are objective bonds which may serve to delimit a social group within which nationality can arise.[26] A nation has been called 'the community which legitimizes the State',[27] but it is less tangible than this, for we must admit that the State in question may be one which has

[24] E. L. Eisenstein, *The First Professional Revolutionist: Filippo Michele Buonarroti* (1959).

[25] K. D. Tönnesson, 'The Babouvists', *Past and Present*, no. 22 (1962), pp. 60–76.

[26] H. Kohn, *The Idea of Nationalism* (1944), pp. 13–14.

[27] R. Emerson, *From Empire to Nation: the rise to self-assertion of Asian and African Peoples* (1960), p. 96. The qualification I have made is based on Johannet, *Le Principe des Nationalités* (1923).

disappeared, or which the community hopes to found in the future, as well as one already existing. After the experiences of the nineteenth century (and still more after those of the twentieth), a definition of nationality has to leave a large space for the sheer force of illogical emotion, feeding upon history and legend impartially, on present hatreds and on dreams of a glorious future. Renan, in a lecture, *Qu'est-ce qu'une nation?* (1887), delivered after the two greatest dramas of nineteenth-century nation-building had been played, said 'A nation is a soul, a spiritual principle. Two things . . . make up that soul. . . . One is the possession in common of a rich inheritance of memories, the other is the actual desire of living together, the will to turn to account together the inheritance bequeathed individuals.'[28] This passage is the basis of the definition of nationalism given in modern monographs: it is a 'sentiment', a 'state of mind', a 'common aspiration', and the atmosphere of the discussion generally confirms Carlton J. Hayes' thesis that it is a modern secular religion, with flags instead of relics, anthems instead of hymns and triumphal arches in place of cathedrals.[29] Having learnt how national aspirations can generate overwhelming force, often utterly disproportionate to any logical explanation which can be given of their origins, we tend now to accept as a 'nation' any group of mankind which claims to be so. As Bertrand Russell wrote in 1934, 'the sentiment, however produced, is the only essential to the existence of a nation'.[30]

To eighteenth-century statesmen, these modern discussions of nationalism would have seemed excessive, almost hysterical. Theirs was an age when diplomacy was a matter of calculation, territories being 'cut and pared like Dutch cheeses' to provide compensations and peace bribes. According to Diderot's *Encyclopédie*, which marked the highest point of eighteenth-century logic, 'nation' was 'a collective word used to denote a considerable quantity of those people who inhabit a certain extent of country defined within certain limits, and obeying the same government'.[31] 'Inhabit', 'obey': there is nothing here about 'soul' or 'spiritual principle'. It is true, of course, that nationalism was steadily developing all the while. One manifestation of the tendency was, perhaps, the way in which the cultural hegemony of France in language, the arts, literature and fashion began to crack from about 1760 onwards. Herder in Germany and Feijoo in Spain praised their native language as against French, and the Academy of

[28] Renan, *Discours et conférences* (1887, 2nd ed.), cit. Boyd C. Shafer, *Nationalism: Myth and Reality* (1955), p. 243.
[29] Carlton J. H. Hayes, *Nationalism: a Religion* (1960), pp. 394–5.
[30] Bertrand Russell, *Freedom and Organization, 1894–1914* (1934), pp. 394–5.
[31] Cit. E. Kedourie, *Nationalism* (1960), pp. 14–15.

Berlin used German as well as French for its minutes from 1786 onwards. The classical ideal in literature had been moulded in Paris, but Romanticism was arising now from a diversity of inspirations— Goethe's *Werther*, English landscape gardening, Cowper, Burns, 'Ossian', as well as Rousseau. But there were many other factors involved; the rise of historical and linguistic studies, the spread of education, the strong particularist traditions of certain churches (Orthodoxy, Gallicanism, Anglicanism, State churches in Germany), the centralizing and mercantilist policies of sovereigns, envy of the greatness achieved by French and English patriotism, and the spectacle of the founding of a new nation in America—all these influences played their part. But development seemed likely to remain slow and undramatic, spread over a long period, as it had been in France and England. And the example of America was, in spite of the glamour of the War of Independence, an unromantic one. To the European settler in the New World, said a famous commentator in the 1780s, 'his country is now that which gives him land, bread, protection and consequence. *Ubi panis ibi patria* is a motto of all emigrants'.[32] The territorial unit came first, then the nation. We have seen too many examples to the contrary to accept this dictum now, but in the eighteenth century (and indeed, later, at the Congress of Vienna) it seemed reasonable to re-adjust European boundaries by common-sense bargaining, assuming that the inhabitants would proceed to develop loyalties towards the unit to which they had been allotted and where their interests lay.

Later on, we will see some of the reasons why the idea of nationalism changed from the practical 'inhabit' and 'obey' logic of the *Encyclopédie* to Renan's brooding 'spiritual principle': the whole history of the nineteenth century is involved—railways, education, democracy, jobs in expanding bureaucracies, mass production and the search for markets, and the powerful rôle of residual hatreds, like those of the Balkan peoples for the Turks and each other, Poles against Russians, Germans against Frenchmen. For the moment, however, it is enough to point out how important the French Revolution was in forcing on the development of the idea of nationalism in Europe, both as a threat and as an example.

VIII

The French Revolution proclaimed the principle of national sover-

---

[32] Crèvecoeur, *Letters from an American Farmer* (1782), cit. D. M. Potter, 'The Historian's use of Nationalism and vice-versa', *American Historical Review* (June 1962), p. 928.

eignty, and betrayed Rousseau's ideal by making the General Will the exponent of a new imperialism. Kings had used war 'to busy giddy minds with foreign quarrels': it was now demonstrated, by Brissot, that this device had its democratic counterpart—'a people which, after a thousand years of slavery, has achieved liberty, needs war . . . to consolidate its freedom.'

This war was waged in a novel fashion. A decree of 19 November 1792 offered assistance to all peoples wishing to recover their liberty, and Cambon's decree of the following December ruled that the French occupation of foreign territory would be followed by the sequestration of noble and ecclesiastical property, the abolition of feudal dues and the imposition of the revolutionary paper money. '*Guerre aux châteaux, paix aux chaumières*'; it was ideological warfare—and self-supporting warfare too. France repelled the invader and went on to conquest because it held the home front by Terror and the battle front by mass levies; this was how war would be waged by the sovereign people in arms. The conventional, cynical bargainings of the old diplomacy were abandoned, and in their place came war on principle. The old diplomacy had destroyed its thousands, and the new destroyed its ten thousands. Kings of France had never acted on the theory of 'natural frontiers'; a few propagandists in the pay of Richelieu and one or two historians had invented the idea, and the revolutionaries adopted it to justify the annexation of Belgium, which was showing hostility to the French and to their reforms. The limits of the Republic, Danton said, 'are laid down by Nature. We will attain them . . . the Rhine, the Ocean, the Alps and the Pyrenees; there the limits of our republic ought to rest, and no human power can prevent us from reaching them. They threaten you with the displeasure of kings: but you have thrown down your challenge before them—the head of a tyrant'.[33]

In this spirit of exaltation, amid proscriptions and victories, a new and passionate nationalism was forged in France, a nationalism of the people and of the left. Its battles were glorious, even to royalists like Maistre and Chateaubriand, who praised the Committee of Public Safety and the bloodstained Jacobins who rescued the country from the invader. 'It is war', Treitschke was to say, 'that turns a people into a nation'. This was a lesson Europe learnt from France, and war, indeed, proved to be the agent in the making of all the new nations of the nineteenth century.

The influence of the French Revolution in creating nationalism in the other countries of Europe was chiefly indirect, through the admiration, envy and fear which it inspired. On St Helena, Napoleon

[33] A. Sorel, *L'Europe et la révolution française* (1927) III, p. 279.

claimed that he had followed the revolutionary teaching about nationalism more directly and intentionally, with the aim of creating a new Europe, a free federation of truly national states. This was pure invention. Bonaparte's interest in Polish, Italian, Slovene and Croat national sentiments had been superficial, just another weapon in his tactical armoury. His Empire had been a machine which turned out money and troops, a pattern of bases for his conquests. By 1813, 'France' included Piedmont, Rome, the Hanseatic towns and Holland; the kingdom of Italy was kept in economic tutelage and Italian principalities were given as rewards to Frenchmen. The Grand Duchy of Warsaw was not a resurrection of Poland, but an expedient. 'The Napoleonic Empire', writes Markham, 'was the negation of nationality'.[34] Nor was that Empire overthrown by an 'awakening of the nations', as romantic and nationalist historiography later affirmed. Spanish guerillas and monks would challenge any intruder, the Russian serfs fought against the Grand Army as blindly and as cruelly as the Russian winter; there was an outburst of patriotic feeling in Prussia, but in so far as there was a popular uprising, it was a result of French exactions for the Russian campaign; Leipzig, the 'Battle of the Nations' was, in fact, a victory of princes who had improved their organization and strategy.

Even so, Napoleon's greatness had constituted a national triumph for France, and his defeat was a matter of pride for the diverse ruling groups and their soldiers who had defied the tyrant. From the story of the Empire and its overthrow arose two myths—the myth of the liberal Emperor and the myth of the rising of the nations; the first of these illusions was to inspire Napoleon III to fight to free Italy, and the second gilded the new popular nationalism, when it arose, with a halo of idealism and heroism.

IX

The intensity of the French Revolution—as an outburst of reforming zeal and a war against privilege, as the interplay of innumerable ambitions and a struggle for survival—made it act as a sort of forcing house wherein the ideals of the future, and their perversions, were brought to early maturity. The ideals did not come solely from the reforming zeal, nor did the perversions arise solely from ambitions or the desire for self-preservation. History is always more complicated than this. It has

'. . . many cunning passages, contrived corridors
And issues, deceives with whispering ambitions,
Guides us by vanities . . .

[34] F. M. H. Markham, *Napoleon and the Awakening Europe* (1954), p. 114.

Neither fear nor courage saves us. Unnatural vices
Are fathered by our heroism. Virtues
Are forced upon us by our impudent crimes
These tears are shaken from the wrath-bearing tree.'[35]

In this lecture I have attempted to trace how democracy, socialism and nationalism came to the nineteenth century through the French Revolution. They came as inspirations that had taken to themselves something of the crude passion of the greatest revolution the world had ever seen; they had been tempered by its fires and also blackened and distorted by them too; but they were not blind, pre-determined forces, and whether they turned to good or to ill, whether the ideal or its perversion prevailed, was a matter for future generations to decide. The generation of 1789 has the lives of its own contemporaries to answer for, but it does not deserve to be saddled with the responsibility for the long-term effects of its every reckless word or desperate expedient.

[35] T. S. Eliot, 'Gerontion', *Collected Poems, 1909–35* (1936), p. 38.

CHAPTER VIII

THE OLD WORLD AND THE NEW:
METTERNICH AND SAINT-SIMON

I

On 2 August 1806, Count Klemens von Metternich, a nobleman of the Rhineland whose three square leagues of principality had been taken from him by the French Revolution,
arrived in Paris as ambassador of the Emperor of Austria. In the
same year, Claude-Henri, *ci-devant* Count de Saint-Simon, of the
great French ducal house which traced its ancestry back to Charlemagne, managed to obtain a clerk's job in the Parisian municipal
pawn shop, and one of his former servants gave him a room so that
he could go on writing his books. These two men[1] represent the most
brilliant talents of the proud, cosmopolitan aristocracy of the *ancien
régime*. In retrospect, we may also take them as sharply contrasted
representatives of two different worlds, of the old and of the new, for
while the one carried on the tradition of aristocratic eighteenth-
century diplomacy into the post-revolutionary years, the other
became a fanatical prophet of a new age of science and technology.

The French Revolution taught them both to hate anarchy.
Metternich had seen rioting in Strasbourg, and had lost his patrimony. In 1794 he published an anonymous brochure, likening the
French victories to a re-enactment of the barbarian invasions of the
Dark Ages; with a confidence in popular feeling which was not
evident in his later career, he called on governments to arm their
peoples against this new menace. In the peace negotiations of 1799,
he was present as a delegate of the Westphalian nobility, and shud-
dered at the unkempt entourage of the French plenipotentiaries.
'You'd die of fright', says this young man who had opened the ball
at the coronation of Francis II in pale green satin with silver buttons
and lace, 'if you met the best-dressed of them in a wood.' Saint-
Simon's fears were more vivid and more personal. He was arrested

[1] For Saint-Simon, see F. E. Manuel, *The New World of Henri Saint-Simon*
(1956). The basic work on Metternich is Heinrich Ritter von Srbik, *Metternich:
der Staatsmann und der Mensch* (3 vols., 1925, 1945). G. de Bertier de Sauvigny,
Metternich et son temps (1959) is an invaluable collection of material on
Metternich's ideas (there is an English translation by Peter Ryde, 1962). For
other works see P. W. Schroeder, 'Metternich Studies since 1925', *Journal of
Modern History*, XXXIII (1961), pp. 237–60.

110

in Paris during the Terror in November 1793, and was only released from the Luxembourg Prison nine months later. Luckily, he had been able to produce proofs of *civisme* from his local commune, showing he had renounced his title of 'Count' before it was necessary to do so, and had taken the unpretentious new name of 'Bonhomme'. If the Revolutionary Tribunal had been more fully informed on the previous career of its suspect, he might have been less fortunate. Was it known that, after fighting for liberty in America, he had been mixed up in the Spanish transactions of the banker Cabarrus, father of the notorious Mme Tallien?—and that he had used the Revolution as an occasion for vast speculations on the sale of Church property, in alliance with a Swiss financier, the Prussian ambassador to the Court of St James and a fashionable marquise? In jail, Saint-Simon had visions of a great destiny: he was called to be a new Charlemagne to end the revolutionary chaos. On release, however, he concentrated on dissipating his vast speculative fortune in the reckless fashion of the old aristocracy, conduct which he later justified on the ground that he had been engaged in a psychological test designed to pass him through all social classes and all possible situations. 'My actions should not be judged in accordance with the same principles as those of other people, because my active life has been a series of experiments.' By 1806, the novel experience of utter penury had been reached, and as might be expected, here the cycle closed.

In the epoch of Napoleon, both Saint-Simon and Metternich laid the foundations of their very different greatness. Shortly after his arrival in Paris, Metternich reported to his government that the next campaign against France would be a war to the death: '*Il n'existe depuis longtemps que deux partis, l'Europe et Napoléon.*' But the diplomats of the *ancien régime* did not like to think in terms of permanent enmities. After Wagram, as Minister of Foreign Affairs, Metternich was warning his Emperor not to 'fight against necessity'. Napoleon's Austrian marriage was of his devising. It was not exactly a sacrifice of a maiden to the Minotaur (for Marie-Louise was very willing), but it was a cold-blooded device all the same, to insure against the possibility that France and Russia might ally to partition Europe. When Bonaparte rushed to his ruin, Metternich 'was the first to perceive the opportunity for the containment of France and the last to agree to the destruction of Napoleon'.[2] He probably had little enthusiasm for keeping the Emperor on the throne of France,

[2] R. A. Kann, 'Metternich: a re-appraisal of his influence on international relations', *Journal of Modern History*, XXXII (1960), p. 336. See also Bertier de Sauvigny, p. 230, for what follows.

but he manoeuvred and hesitated as part of a design to frustrate Russian hegemony. In this way he maintained a dominating position in the councils of the Allies which was recognized in September 1814, when the Congress to remake the map of Europe met in Vienna.

While Metternich had thus been moving up to the summits of power, Saint-Simon, a penurious manic-depressive, living on his friends, had established the principles of his intellectual system in publications which—it is true—no one read but the police. Whatever its cultural deficiencies in other respects, the Napoleonic régime was a period of scientific creativity in France, in biology, medicine and astronomy especially. By contrast, any radical thinking on social organization was officially discouraged. Another contrast of the age was that between the religious revival, exemplified in the success of the *Génie du Christianisme*, and the simultaneous popularity of 'positivism', a doctrine eliminating mysterious origins and final causes, among the intellectuals. All these competing tendencies came to a focus in Saint-Simon's fantastic imagination. He seized on science as the key to the future; its methods were now to be applied to social phenomena, and the ultimate step would be to create a new religion for the *élite*, which would be a 'distillation into a unity of the whole body of scientific thought'.

The details of the new social order were mostly worked out later, but for the Congress of Vienna, Saint-Simon prepared a memorandum *On the Reorganization of European Society*. He urged the assembled statesmen to abandon the antiquated concept of a balance of power, and to recreate an 'organic' Europe, such as he believed had existed in the Middle Ages, endow it with an effective central government, and let this great new state, continent-wide and massive in its technological superiority, forcefully colonize the whole world.

Utopian thinking of this kind, probably fortunately, was meaningless to Metternich and the practitioners of conventional diplomacy who met together in Vienna. They had no hope of building a new civilization, and no intention of acting on any sort of abstract principles, even moral ones. When Castlereagh was challenged in Parliament about the extinction of the independence of Genoa, he was to reply, 'The Congress of Vienna was not assembled for the discussion of moral principles, but for great practical purposes, to establish effectual provisions for the general security.'[3] This is precisely what it did, and the twentieth century, for all its Saint-Simonian dynamism, can still learn lessons in peacemaking from Metternich and the cynical school of eighteenth-century diplomatists.

[3] H. Nicolson, *The Congress of Vienna* (1961), p. 187.

II

The commonest criticism of the statesmen of 1815 (though it is becoming a little old-fashioned now) is that they ignored the force of nationalism. This is true enough, but what could they have been expected to know about it? We have seen what a gulf there is between the *Encylopédie* definition of the eighteenth century and nationalism as one of the explosive factors of more recent history. There was no-one at the Congress of Vienna who could visualize the demonic potency which railways, mass education, mass marketing, mass production of armaments and mass mobilization would confer upon national sentiments, let alone the sheer determination to shake off external control which was soon to manifest itself in Greece and Belgium. Metternich and his colleagues knew, of course, the enormous co-operative energies which the French Revolution's doctrine of sovereignty in the nation had evoked; they knew something of the principle which Treitschke was to defend, that 'it is war that turns a people into a nation':[4] they had seen a people in arms, fighting for the Republic one and indivisible. But popular sovereignty, war and the whole French example were precisely what the statesmen of Vienna were planning to exorcise. The histories of France under the *ancien régime*, or of England, where strong monarchical government had, over a long period, fostered a solid respectable patriotism, or America, where the common-sense proposition, *Ubi panis ibi patria* was working itself out, were more acceptable examples at the Congress than the convulsive and ephemeral violence of the Revolution and the Empire. Napoleon's dishonest tinkering with national sentiments and his imperial reorganization of Europe, exclusively for war, were fresh in everyone's mind and helped to confirm the diplomats in their desire for a logical settlement based upon the idea of the balance of power.

This is not to say that nationalisms of various kinds were not potential forces in Europe in 1815, but simply to suggest that the statesmen of the time may be forgiven for not realizing the fact. It took time for the French revolutionary example, the confusions following Napoleon's onslaughts, the development of historical scholarship and of Romanticism in literature, the growing rage of liberals against restored legitimacy, and the impact of expanding commerce, industrialization and education to work their effect and release these underground, irrational passions. By 1830, 'nationality' was being used for the first time as a term with a special political

---

[4] Treitschke, *Politics* (E.T. 2 vols., 1916) I, p. 51. But note (p. 52) that 'the same invigorating force', comes 'into daily life by a liberal Constitution'.

significance; it was accepted by the French Academy in 1835, and a year before this was spoken of in Russia as a new word of uncertain meaning in use in western Europe.[5] It is unreasonable, then, to speak as if the Congress of Vienna could have foreseen, in 1815, the nationalism of the revolutions of 1848; Matthew Arnold's diatribe—'the treaties of Vienna, with their arbitrary distribution of the populations of Europe, their Mezentian copulation of the living with the dead, were eminently treaties of force, treaties which took no account of popular ideas'[6]—is as unjust in content as repulsive in imagery.

It is unjust in another fashion, for even if the Congress had sat down to discuss every national aspiration in Europe in sympathetic detail, what could it have done? It had met to end a war, not to fight new ones to coerce Austria (or Prussia) into accepting German unity, to evict the Russians from Poland or the Turks from the Balkans. Matthew Arnold's charges reduce themselves to one: Italy could have been unified, which is true, provided it was possible to leave Austria unrewarded for its victories and sacrifices, and provided everyone was willing to run the risk of France once more gaining control of the peninsula. The Congress could have done little for the nationalities, even had it been so minded. Its task was prescribed by the sheer weight of immediate tensions; the powers, with their clashes of interest revealed raw and naked at the end of a war for survival, had to be brought into a mutual compromise 'to establish effectual provisions for the general security'. To reach any sort of agreement and security was an overwhelming task in itself. It was no more possible to redraw the map on lines of nationality than it was to establish Saint-Simon's single super-State of technology and imperialism.

III

The first task of the Vienna assembly was to prevent renewed eruptions of the French volcano. Before the Congress met, the formula had been found: generous peace terms fortifying a Bourbon restoration—a general lowering of temperature, as it were, combined with a load of dead ash in the crater. France would be allowed to keep her boundaries of 1792 and have most of her West Indian possessions returned; she would pay no indemnity, and would even be allowed to keep the works of art her armies had looted from the cities of Europe (it is said that copies of some of the stolen pieces were on display in

[5] J. P. T. Bury, 'Nationalities and Nationalism', *New Camb. Mod. Hist.* X (1960), pp. 213–14.

[6] Matthew Arnold, *England and the Italian Question* (ed. M. E. Bevington, 1953), p. 37.

the Louvre in the hope that the wrong ones would be taken home in the baggage train of the Allies). Talleyrand gained some reputation by his skill at insinuating himself at Vienna, prising open the 'Council of Four' and making it the 'Council of Five', but in fact, he was really taking credit for a speedy achievement of the obvious. The Allies meant France to be re-instated, after due precautions, in the great community of European intrigue. 'The situation of affairs will naturally constitute England and France as arbitrators at the Congress if these powers understand one another', wrote Wellington to Castlereagh; in those days it was realized that annihilating one great power would simply leave the Continent at the mercy of one of the others.

When Napoleon met with an enthusiastic welcome in France on his return from Elba, the First Treaty of Paris was revised. The Allies now exacted an indemnity, a reduction of boundaries and a military occupation, as well as the return of the plundered masterpieces. Even so, as the Venus of the Medici went back to Florence and the horses of Saint Mark to Venice, Napoleon (in St Helena) thought Castlereagh a fool—'The peace is the sort of peace he would have made if he had been beaten.' The Prussians, indeed, wanted to seize Alsace-Lorraine and blow up the Pont de Jéna. But Castlereagh insisted that the aim was to restrain France, not to hurt or provoke her: 'I deprecate the system of scratching such a Power. We may hold her down and pare her nails so that many years shall pass away before they wound us.'[7]

Some of the other provisions of the peace settlement were devised, less directly, to hem in French ambitions. Prussia was given territory in the Rhineland, against her wish, though the obligation to defend the Rhine came to imply a 'German' destiny. Austria acquired Venetia and recovered Lombardy. Here was compensation for the loss of the Netherlands, or, putting it in the 'European' terms which Metternich affected, Austria was now to hold France in check in the south rather than in the north. Belgium, no longer under the Habsburgs, was united into a single kingdom with Holland, with clauses in the act of union guaranteeing her population religious toleration and commercial equality, 'the first minority treaties to figure in diplomatic practice'.[8] Though this union lasted only sixteen years, the idea was a reasonable one. It was hard to find safeguards for this area of political weakness and strategic importance: the solution of 1839 was to be a five-power guarantee, the notorious 'scrap of paper' of 1914.

[7] Nicolson, op. cit., pp. 257, 239–40.
[8] Ibid., p. 208.

IV

While padlocks were being devised for the front door against France, Metternich and his colleagues were not indifferent to the possibility that a bolt on the back door might be useful against Russia. One of Goldsmith's characters said (1762) that Russia, 'now at that period between refinement and barbarity which seems most adapted to military achievement . . . [was] the natural enemy of the more western parts of Europe'.[9] This opinion was widely current now. In 1791, we can first observe the germination of specific fears in the minds of Englishmen; there was the Ochakov incident, the earliest attempt by a British government to protect the Ottoman Empire against Russia; there was news of a constitution in Poland, which aroused belated resentment against the cynicism of the partitioning powers; and there was a suspicion, at least in the offices of the Board of Control for India, that the Cossacks might one day water their horses on the banks of the Ganges. In central Europe, fears of Russia went back further still, to the burning of Berlin during the wars of Frederick the Great.

The meeting of Alexander and Napoleon at Tilsit, on a raft in the Niemen, had seemed a conspiracy to partition the world. Then the events of 1812 had revealed the sheer size and invulnerability of the Tsarist Empire. Contemporaries appreciated that Napoleon was broken by one mistake, the march on Moscow. English students are too fond of anecdotes (about the French army wearing British-made greatcoats and the like) which are supposed to demonstrate the ineffectiveness of the Continental System. In fact, by 1811, Great Britain had been on the edge of ruin. This year—oddly enough, the year of the publication of *Sense and Sensibility*—marks the lowest point of economic depression in modern British history, with the South American markets flooded, the Baltic closed, the United States hostile and Napoleon's embargo effective all over northern Europe.[10] England was saved, not by the inevitability of her industrial dynamism, but by the Russian winter. Thus, the hysterical joy with which London greeted the news of the retreat from Moscow was quickly followed by anxiety about the newly revealed power of the Tsar.[11] What profit was there in victory if the Russians were left

[9] For what follows, M. S. Anderson, *Britain's Discovery of Russia, 1553–1815* (1958), pp. 93–8, 135, 183, 201.

[10] F. Crouzet, *L'Economie brittanique et le blocus continental* (2 vols., 1958) II, p. 686. For the next sentence, G. Lefebvre, *Napoléon* (1953), p. 376.

[11] J. H. Gleason, *The Genesis of Russophobia in Great Britain* (1950), pp. 50–1.

poised less than two hundred miles from Berlin, Vienna and Constantinople and not altogether out of reach of Delhi? Gentz, Metternich's literary factotum and publicist, reflected on this problem which
was causing concern in London and decided that it was folly to depose
Bonaparte: he ought to be kept for use against invasions from the
east. Russia, Gentz said, cannot be defeated, and has 'such substantially centrifugal habits, that war, which others regard as a necessary
evil, will always be to the Russians a matter of choice, emotion and
speculation'.[12]

Metternich believed in the Russian bogey and played it up too,
thus enlisting support for Austria as the bastion of central Europe.
Castlereagh suspected exaggeration, but still urged his Cabinet not to
allow 'a Calmuk prince' to become master of Europe. The French,
who had seen troops from the boundaries of Asia mounting guard on
the steps of the Opera, naturally concurred. There was thus, behind
the idle whirl of the Congress, a great deal of delicate manoeuvring.
The social incidents—the balls and the competition for the favours of
international beauties, the jewels and the Tokay a hundred years old
(and the Castlereaghs singing hymns on Sundays in the drawing
room to the sound of an harmonium)—combined to form an artificial
society, a revival of the aristocratic and cosmopolitan eighteenth
century, which kept the delegates together while the tricky business
of contriving a front against Russia and still keeping the established
front against France in repair, was organized. The French, British and
Austrian delegates wanted to keep Russia back on the fringes of
Europe. In January 1815 they went so far as to sign a secret treaty of
mutual defence. Prussia had promised to surrender most of her Polish
lands to the Tsar, and Alexander proposed to find compensation for
Prussia in Saxony, whose monarch had been a 'traitor to the common
cause': 'That, Your Imperial Majesty', said Talleyrand, the resident
expert on betrayals, 'is a question of dates'. The stand of the western
powers had some effect; even so, Prussia did get two-fifths of Saxony,
and the Tsar received Warsaw and over three million extra Polish
subjects, to whom he promised to grant a constitution within a
dependent kingdom. It has been said that the Treaty of Vienna gave
Russia too much. True, but how could things have been otherwise
without another war?

'Legitimacy' did not play much part in the Vienna discussions. The
term was prominent mainly as 'part of the tactics of the French
delegation'.[13] It was used by Talleyrand as an argument against

[12] G. Mann, *Secretary of Europe: Friedrich Gentz* (1940), pp. 276–7.
[13] M. Bourquin in preface to J. H. Pirenne, *La Sainte-Alliance* (2 vols., 1946)
I, p. x. True, Legitimacy was a respectable argument, one which helped to create

Prussian claims to Saxony, and to prevent Murat, Bonaparte's great cavalry man, from retaining the crown of Naples, as Metternich would have preferred. The delegates feared over-powerful states with ambitions of conquest: they also feared social revolution. About forms of government, they were realists. In a sense, their settlement finished up looking like a distribution of plunder; Britain's overseas power enhanced, Austria rewarded in Italy, the Tsar in Poland, Prussia in Saxony and on the Rhine, some strengthening of Bavaria and Hanover, and Norway given to Sweden as a prize for joining the coalition. But the principle which underlay the distribution was logical and, by eighteenth-century standards, civi zed. The aim was equilibrium and peace, and for these limited ends, the Congress was effective. For forty years, Europe was free from major wars.

V

Yet, if there were no great wars, the years which followed the Peace of Vienna were full of minor affrays and revolutions. One wave came in the early 1820s and another followed the French Revolution of 1830. Though skirmishes, riots and conspiracies do not fit exactly into categories, these disturbances of the 'twenties and 'thirties may be roughly classified into two kinds: those caused by 'national' aspirations and those caused by 'liberal' ones. Between 1810 and 1825, the Spanish American colonies threw off their allegiance to Madrid; in March 1821, the Greeks rose against their Turkish overlords; in 1830, the news of revolution in Paris inspired a Belgian demand for independence and also helped to cause a tragic rebellion in Poland— tragic, because it was not a rising against Russian oppression, so much as an accident.[14] These national revolutions greatly impressed European opinion. The romance of the wild warfare in South America, the appeal of memories of ancient Greece to a generation still reared on the classics, and the amazing evocation of Spartan and Athenian ideals by Balkan tribesmen whom Metternich called 'emancipated serfs and bandits', the responsible common-sense repudiation of Dutch control by the Belgians, the most progressive industrial people of continental Europe, the recollection of half a century of European treachery to Poland seen against a background of Tsarist despotism and ambition, and the brilliance of exiles like the poet Mickiewicz, the composer Chopin, the historian Lelewel—all

the atmosphere within which 'concessions appear, not as surrenders, but as sacrifices to the common cause' (H. A. Kissinger, 'The Congress of Vienna: a reappraisal', *World Politics*, VIII (1955–6), pp. 265, 279).
[14] R. F. Leslie, *Polish Politics and the Revolution of November 1830* (1956).

these things combined to create a favourable image of nationalism in the minds of many, and especially among the middle-class liberals. More than this, with the exception of the Polish rising, which faced impossible odds, these revolutions had succeeded. In the end, even the reactionary statesmen had to make the best of them: proper settlements were made, and no one was any the worse. In 1848, nationalism, generally in alliance with liberalism, was to play a dramatic part on the European stage, and its adherents were so numerous and so confident because the Spanish colonies, Greece and Belgium, each in their different fashions, had demonstrated that it was an emotion which was at once romantic and reasonable.

We will consider the 'liberal' agitations of the first half of the nineteenth century later, when we deal with the great states in turn. These diverse movements naturally looked to France as the head-quarters of the revolutionary tradition. In the early 1820s however, with the Bourbons apparently secure in Paris, various liberal move-ments arose which seem independent of direct French inspiration—military *pronunciamentos* demanding constitutional government in Spain and Portugal, an army conspiracy in Piedmont, a revolution in Naples, and the Decembrist outbreak in Russia. In all of these movements, except the Neapolitan one, the lead was taken by army officers. Tom Moore saw a cautionary tale here for Metternich.

> 'For even soldiers sometimes think—
> Nay colonels have been known to reason—
> And reasoners, whether clad in pink,
> Or red, or blue, are on the brink
> (Nine cases out of ten) of treason.'[15]

After the revolution of 1830, however, Paris once more became the centre of the forces of change, as well as the museum of the great Revolution of 1789. In November 1831, it seemed to Victor Hugo, reviewing the spectacle of oppression from Ireland to Italy to Siberia, that 'on all sides . . . the dull sound of revolt' was heard, 'deep down in the earth, pushing out under every kingdom in Europe its subter-ranean galleries from the central shaft of the mine in Paris'.[16]

Metternich shared this belief, though with very different emotions. On hearing the news of the French Revolution of 1830, he collapsed, crying, 'My life's work is ruined.'[17] He was genuinely convinced that

[15] Tom Moore, 'Fables on the Holy Alliance' in *Poetical Works* (10 vols., 1850) VII, p. 254.
[16] Victor Hugo, 'Les Feuilles d'automne',preface, *Oeuvres Complètes* (1909), *Poésie* II, p. 5.
[17] For what follows, G. de Bertier de Sauvigny, op. cit., pp. 69, 78, 88, 248; C. de Grunwald, *La Vie de Metternich* (1947), pp. 229–31.

there was a great mesh of secret societies all over Europe. Lafayette ('the most adroit technician of revolution modern times have produced'), the Carbonari and the Decembrists were all members of this 'faction désorganisatrice'. Its agents lurked in the universities; that was why he sent his ambassador to warn George IV to prohibit the foundation of London University—'or its all up with England'. Subversive groups had their eyes on Russia, hoping that the seeds of revolution might flourish in its glacial soil, unleashing a scourge of 'thirty million slaves' to conquer the world in its service. Since 'a few pirates can paralyse commerce', Metternich believed that the powers ought to intervene in any country where revolution appeared to be brewing; hence, he sponsored the 'Karlsbad decrees' of 1819 in Germany, sent Austrian troops to Naples and encouraged the Bourbons to march into Spain. One might say of him, and of the other statesmen of Vienna, that their mistake was not that of ignoring the forces of nationality during the discussions of the Congress, but that of ignoring the demands of liberalism and social reform after they had got back home. One might also reflect, however, on the possibility that Europe enjoyed freedom from major wars chiefly because the rulers were afraid of social revolution. If they had satisfied the demands of their subjects, they might have felt sufficiently secure to fight each other.

VI

The shrewdly calculated balance of the Vienna settlement and the pervasive fear of social revolution combined to create the atmosphere of a 'concert of Europe' in the diplomacy of the three decades following Waterloo. Alexander I would have claimed the credit for his 'Holy Alliance', though in the chancelleries of Europe the whole project was regarded as little more than a concession to the Tsar's mystical mania. There was an experiment in international collaboration in the system of congresses which followed the Vienna meeting, but by 1825, its ineffectiveness was evident. Congresses could do little, because English statesmen could not identify themselves with the reactionary designs of the monarchs. Before Canning withdrew altogether from such assemblies, Castlereagh had made it clear that England would not accept any obligation to act on theoretical grounds, and certainly not one to act against the 'Democratic Principles', which, admittedly, were 'but too generally spread throughout Europe'.[18]

[18] State Paper of 5 May 1820, in Camb. Hist. British Foreign Policy (1922–3) II, pp. 623–33; discussion in C. K. Webster, The Foreign Policy of Castlereagh, 1815–22 (1925), pp. 236–45.

Even so, there was a feeling of 'concert', and Metternich blandly claimed that it was the result of his 'system'. What was this famous system?[19] Though Srbik, his great biographer, accepts its existence, the general belief of Englishmen, both then and subsequently, has been that it was a myth. According to Castlereagh, Metternich was a 'political harlequin', and the bluff Duke of Wellington thought him 'a society hero and nothing more'; of the diplomatic historians, Webster regards him as 'an opportunist pure and simple', and A.J.P. Taylor describes the much-vaunted system as 'merely an elaborate masquerade for the benefit of simple-minded monarchs'. Granting, however, that Metternich's pose as puppet-master was a deception, we may still concede to him a dominating symbolic standing upon the international scene. In the nineteenth century, he represents the mellow autumn of the diplomacy of the *ancien régime*, rational, calculating, opposed to all over-weening ambitions. As an aristocrat, as a Rhinelander, German by birth and French by culture, and as the servant of a multi-national empire, he was genuinely 'European minded', pre-occupied with equilibrium, intelligent enough to see that Austria could only survive in a world where all the checks and balances were set to preserve peace.

But the concert of Europe was only to a small degree his creation. His greatest personal triumph was the Münchengratz agreement of 1833 with Russia, by which the two empires abjured adventures against Turkey or in the Balkans. Yet other powers had already made equally rational compromises; Canning had feared Russia would 'gobble Greece at one mouthful and Turkey at the next',[20] yet chose to work with Russia to restrain her; France, England and Russia co-operated to prevent the annihilation of the Greeks by Mehemet Pasha; and finally, in 1829, Russia herself had made a policy decision to respect the integrity of the Ottoman Empire. A similar restraint was shown by the five great powers when the Belgian revolution of 1830 aroused all the latent fears of French designs against the 1815 settlement. Common apprehensions of a Polish revival drew together the three partitioning powers, a devotion to liberal principles attracted England to France, a mutual fear of French aggression united everyone when emergencies arose, there was a general suspicion of Russia, and Metternich made it his business to tie together the interests of Vienna and Paris. Thus, without formal alliances, the continent was held in equilibrium by checks and counter-checks. A shrewd peace settlement, war-weariness, and fear of revolution, made statesmen cautious, and the Napoleonic adventure had left them inclined to

[19] See Kann, art. cit., *Journal of Modern History*, XXXII (1960), pp. 333ff.
[20] H. W. V. Temperley, *The Foreign Policy of Canning, 1822–7* (1925), p. 329.

sacrifice individual aggrandisement to the achievement of a balanced security. Thus, for new reasons, the old eighteenth-century technique of logical calculations of power with no permanent hatreds and no permanent enmities remained relevant in the post-revolutionary era, and of this diplomacy, Metternich was the acknowledged expert practitioner. In this sense, as a method of approach to diplomatic problems, his famous system really existed and, viewed from one aspect, the first half of the nineteenth century may still be called, without too much exaggeration, 'the Age of Metternich'.

VII

Metternich lived for another eleven years after the revolutions of 1848 had driven him from office. Henri Saint-Simon died long before him, in 1825, his name but little known in the palaces, salons and embassies frequented by the Austrian Chancellor. A descendant of Charlemagne, and a self-made millionaire, Saint-Simon finished up in penury and near-insanity. In 1823 he tried to commit suicide with a pistol, but only succeeded in blinding himself in one eye. He died two years later. Yet in this last decade of his life, his publications broke through to a large and intelligent audience, and drew to him a number of potentially influential disciples—bankers, industrialists, social theorists and economists. There was the independent genius Auguste Comte, who deserted the master in 1824 to become a rival prophet, there were publicists like Bazard, socialists like Pierre Leroux, financiers like Olinde Rodrigues and the brothers Pereire, economists like Michel Chevalier, and ingenious madmen like Enfantin—who formed an absurd 'Church' of his own, invented a waistcoat of social co-operation (you couldn't get out of it unaided) and did a good deal to inspire the cutting of the Suez Canal and the foundation of various railway companies. These men, under Saint-Simon's guidance, glimpsed the shape of the future of civilization, and some of them, by practical enterprises, hastened its coming.

In Metternich's circle, commerce and industry were regarded as existing to support the governing class engaged in the great game of European politics; among the Saint-Simonians, this great game was regarded as a fraud: the rôle of government was to build up a planned economy, bring science into mesh with industrial progress, and create a new structure of life in which every man could find opportunity for the full exercise of his capacity for both work and enjoyment. We are so accustomed now to the concept of the Industrial Revolution that it is easy for us to underestimate the originality of Saint-Simon's ideas. When he wrote, over three-quarters of the inhabitants of the continent were still engaged in subsistence farming. The astonishing interlocking progress of capitalist agriculture and industrial expansion in Britain had passed the decisive point of break-through, but this was still far from evident. No single industry had as yet achieved its complete technical transformation,[21] and the range of factory products was narrow—more than half Britain's exports were textiles. Industrial credit facilities were limited and as yet there was little attempt to link scientific investigation directly with technological innovation. The English inventions—the Watt engine, the cotton machinery and methods of rolling and puddling iron—were being appropriated on the continent, but slowly. By 1830, there were still only 29 blast furnaces using coke in France (out of more than 400); in Germany, the Ruhr coalfield was hardly touched, and Silesian industry had progressed little beyond the point to which Frederick the Great had encouraged it. Belgium, which in 1829 produced six million tons of coal (as against Great Britain's thirty and France's two) was the only industrial area which seemed likely to develop at the English pace. 'Economically', says F. B. Artz, 'the world of Metternich was much like the world of Voltaire.'[22]

Land communications and transport were still not much more effective than they had been in the more civilized areas of the Roman Empire. In 1830, the *diligence* from Paris to Bordeaux took five days; a rich man in a hurry could do the trip by stage-coach, flanked by blue-coated, yellow-trousered postillions, in forty-five hours.[23] Whenever possible, freight was sent by water. 67 per cent of French imports and over 72 per cent of exports were ocean borne. These were days when the price of bulky commodities like grain varied immensely from province to province, and when relays of post horses could ensure the success of a coup of financial speculation (except, perhaps in France, where the visual telegraph covered some main routes, not always infallibly, as the Count of Monte Cristo demonstrated). The time when the whole planet would be a single vast field of investment and trade could hardly have been foreseen.

VIII

When Saint-Simon died, the real Industrial Revolution in continental Europe was just beginning. Schumpeter describes the Kondratieff

---

[21] J. U. Nef, 'The Industrial Revolution Reconsidered', *Journal of Economic History*, III (1943), pp. 1–31. For all that follows see R. Cameron, *France and the Economic Development of Europe, 1800–1914* (1961), pp. 7–10.

[22] F. B. Artz, *Restoration and Revolution* (1934), p. 26.

[23] G. de Bertier de Sauvigny, *La Restauration* (1955), pp. 275–6.

cycle running from 1787 to the mid-nineteenth century, with its falling prices after 1817, and suggests that it was in the period of contraction in the second quarter of the century that the crucial phase comes: 'in recession, depression and revival, the achievements initiated in the prosperity phase mature and fully unfold themselves, thus bringing about a general reorganization in industry and commerce'.[24] Rostow's analysis calls the first stage on the way to a modern industrial economy 'the take-off', and places this decisive period, in Britain between 1783 and 1802, in France and Belgium from 1830, and in Germany from 1850. Elsewhere, Rostow describes the depression of 1836–42 in England as showing 'perhaps the most rapid rate of development of domestic resources throughout the whole of Britain's economic history', and Heaton has suggested that 'a similar reappraisal might be possible for Belgium, France, Germany and the U.S.A.' All in all, in the present state of expert opinion, it would seem reasonable to cease using the term 'Industrial Revolution' for the English inventions of the eighteenth century and to reserve it for the later point of decisive break-through in Western Europe generally, somewhere about the second quarter of the nineteenth century.

In 1825, the year of Saint-Simon's death, Stephenson drove the first steam train at 12 m.p.h. By 1830, there were over 1,000 miles of railway line, and by 1850 there were 14,000. By improving communications and lowering the cost of bulky goods, by facilitating exports, by creating a demand for coal and iron and engineering expertise, this new development pulled together into a single shaft of force all the diverse pressures available for accelerating the movement towards industrialization. In another fashion too, the railways were a lever of change, because their big demands for capital outlay, allied with their novel vistas of profit, were a principal factor in encouraging the extension of credit facilities for industrial expansion. The Age of Metternich was an age of international financiers[25]—the Barings of London, the Hopes of Amsterdam, the Swiss Hottinguers, the Mendelssohns and the Heines (these two latter families will remain famous for other than financial reasons), and above all, the Roths-

---

[24] J. A. Schumpeter, *Business Cycles* (2 vols., 1939) I, p. 254; for what follows, W. W. Rostow, *The Stages of Economic Growth* (1960), p. 38, and his *British Economy of the Nineteenth Century* (1948), p. 19; H. Heaton, *Economic History of Europe* (1936, rev. ed. 1948), pp. 380 ff. and *New Camb. Mod. Hist.*, X (1960), p. 47.

[25] D. S. Landes, *Bankers and Pashas* (1958), pp. 8, 30, 47. For the Rothschilds, Count Egan Caesar Corti, *The Rise of the House of Rothschild* (English trans., 1928), pp. 9, 17–19, 49, 251, 257–8; for Byron, *Don Juan* (1823), canto XII; for the change under the July Monarchy, B. Gille, *La Banque et le crédit en France de 1815 à 1848* (1959), pp. 330–69.

childs, a dynasty which began in poverty in 1770 with the marriage of
Meyer Amschel in the ghetto of Frankfurt. These great merchant
bankers had enormous political influence. According to Byron,
from international congresses to the risings of 'shirtless patriots' of
Spain, everything was ruled by 'Jew Rothschild and his fellow-
Christian Baring'. But with the exception of the Oppenheimers, who
had interests in non-ferrous metallurgy in Germany, these families
did not usually provide credit for industrial development: if they
speculated, it was on the public loans of Europe. With the coming of
the railways, however, the atmosphere began to change. The Rothschilds, Nathan in England and Meyer in Frankfurt, refused to dabble
in railway loans, but their brother James in Paris, in touch with
young engineers of the Polytechnic and the Conservatoire des Arts
et Métiers, financed the most valuable of the early French lines, the
Nord. Other bankers, more particularly Lafitte, followed this example,
and the July Monarchy saw the foundation of various *Caisses*,
lending organizations which, in a modest way, anticipated the big
industrial and agricultural credit institutions of the Second Empire.

Once railways began, with their strategic connexions with the coal
and metallurgical industries on one hand, and with the machinery of
capital extraction on the other, and their immediate impact upon the
transportation of commodities, the 'take-off' into modern industrial
society came quickly and inevitably in the advanced countries of
western Europe. The next stage, in Rostow's terminology, would be
the 'drive to maturity', the transition from a railway age to machine
tools, chemicals and electricity, leading in the end to full 'maturity',
an age of applied science and ever developing technology handling a
vast range of resources. Saint-Simon's social ideas were relevant even
more to the advent of 'maturity' than to the preliminary railway age;
his prophetic thought ranged far ahead, inspiring immediate utilitarian innovations and long-term utopian dreams. It formed some of the
technicians and managers of the first stage of the Industrial Revolution; it also provided capitalism with its most acute philosophical
justification and provided a new vision for utopian dreamers of the
various kinds of socialism.

IX

The decade between Waterloo and Saint-Simon's death was one of
reaction. 'Europe was in the control of kings, nobles and priests as it
had not been since the Age of Louis XIV.'[26] Literary Romanticism
was on the side of conservatism. In Germany, Novalis, Görres and

[26] Artz, op. cit., p. 10.

Schlegel turned their backs on the Enlightenment; in the France of Maistre and Bonald, Hugo and Lamartine were conservatives—until the late 1820s, when the Romantic movement swung towards the ideal of freedom. Reaction ruled, but under the surface, revolution smouldered; in the news from Spain or Italy, in gossip of the Paris slums or of Napoleonic veterans, in an occasional savage line in Byron, its incandescent passions glowed then died.

Saint-Simon combined the postulates of both the reactionaries and the revolutionaries. From Maistre and Bonald he inherited an admiration for the Middle Ages, a universal civilization of hierarchy and status which the new industrial society ought to imitate. This traditionalist argument he supported by the new psychological theories of the *idéologues*. Cabanis and Bichet had rejected the assumption of Locke, Helvétius and Condillac that men receive identical sense impressions from nature, and had divided mankind into types, each having different modes of sensory perception. Following these categories, Saint-Simon devised his classifications of 'scientists', 'industrials' and 'artists'. Men were necessarily and fruitfully unequal. The eighteenth-century philosophers had organized the ideal society around the claims of a common human nature. Saint-Simon's ideal was an organic society combining dissimilar individuals. 'Historically', writes F. E. Manuel, 'modern socialism has derived far more from the traditionalist denial of eighteenth-century liberalism than has been realized. Saint-Simon, who forthrightly acknowledged de Bonald's influence, was one of the most significant vehicles of transmission for this social theory'.[27] One might add, too, that Saint-Simon undermined the great Benthamite proposition which was to prove so useful to liberalism and democracy. 'What we call pleasure, what we call pain', he wrote, 'only occupy a very small space in life. To invent, to execute, to direct, to pursue, to wait, to reflect—that is how the largest part of our time is spent. Movement is far more important for us than the pleasure which is its object.'

Yet Saint-Simon did not reject the ideal of the greatest happiness of the greatest number. Originally, he had been contemptuous of the *prolétaires*, but in 1821 he assured the workers that, while their place in the ideal society would be a subordinate one, many of them would count as 'industrials'. In his later years too, he came to emphasize the aim of his utopia as being that of achieving the happiness of 'the poorest and most numerous class'. Nor was he indifferent to freedom. It is true that his three-chambered 'Parliament' looks like a potential tyranny: one house consists of engineers engaged in planning, another,

[27] F. E. Manuel, *The New World of Henri Saint-Simon* (1956), p. 320. For later quotations, pp. 127, 211.

reviewing its labours, consists of mathematicians, physicists and life-scientists, and the third, which runs taxation and administration (assuming the legislation of the scientists in the other two chambers could be administered at all) consists of 'industrials'. But, like Marx, Saint-Simon believed that the State would wither away. His dreaming was concentrated on the productive process because, in the end, the great rôle of the old State, presiding over the share-out, would not matter—there would be more than enough for everyone. Europe was on the threshold of a golden age of material plenty and spiritual release (for all men would find the full satisfaction which effective work can give them). Disputes about liberty would become irrelevant.

From 1821, these dreams were enlarged to admit psychological forces which up to then, Saint-Simon had somewhat neglected. In 1810 he had written to his nephew: 'Religion . . . has always served and will always serve as the basis for social organization. This truth is incontrovertible, but it is not more certain than the axiom: for men there is nothing absolute in the world.' From these two propositions taken together he deduced that religion must always modify itself to harmonize 'with the level of enlightenment'. Later on, he began to see that religion might be the driving force towards his utopia, and in 1821 he invented the phrase, 'a New Christianity'. This was to be something more universal and more haunting than the distillation of scientific thought which he had once imagined as a synthetic religion; it was to be the doctrine of brotherly love, shorn of its mythological origins and linking together the unequal men whose combined talents would serve the new society.

In retrospect, it is hard to decide whether Saint-Simon's utopia is a capitalist one or a communist one. In it, social relations are totally bound up in an economic structure inevitably developing towards industrialism; equality as an ideal is abandoned, but full employment in a planned economy and the abolition of inheritance provide a substitute. In the long run, it was an unrevolutionary doctrine, but in the shorter run, it had its subversive side. From observing the French Revolution, Saint-Simon deduced that history, so far, had been one long class struggle. In this struggle, the 'industrials' of the Third Estate had foolishly called on the 'bastard classes'—the lawyers, metaphysicians, rentiers and 'honourable professions'—to represent them, and these representatives had stolen the Revolution and made Napoleon a 'bourgeois king'. But this class struggle is of a different kind from that later devised by Marx: it is a fight against the drones, not against the exploiters. In 1816, Saint-Simon told the bankers and manufacturers, 'I undertake to free you from the supremacy exercised over you by the courtiers, the idle, by the nobles, by the phrase makers.' Three years later he was put on trial for a scandalous 'Parable' in his paper *L'Organisateur*. 'Let us suppose that France keeps all of the men of genius which it possesses in the sciences, in the fine arts, and in the trades, but has the misfortune to lose on the same day Monsieur, the brother of the King, Monseigneur the Duke d'Angoulême, Monseigneur the Duke de Berry, . . . all the great officers of the Crown . . . all the marshals . . . Cardinals . . . archbishops . . . prefects . . . judges . . . the ten thousand richest landowners. . . . This loss of the 30,000 individuals reputed to be the most important in the State, would only cause grief in a sentimental sense.' According to the Comte de Saint-Simon then, everyone who claimed to be anybody in the gilded world of Metternich was, quite simply, unnecessary. On the other hand, according to Prince Metternich, the danger of the Saint-Simonean theorizing was that it would arouse all those who had nothing to lose.[28]

[28] G. de Bertier de Sauvigny, *Metternich et son temps*, p. 69. The date is 1831.

CHAPTER IX

AUSTRIA AND ITALY, 1815–1849

I

The statesmen of the Congress of Vienna are commonly supposed to have ignored the forces of revolutionary nationalism. It might be truer to say that they did, in fact, recognize these forces, but that they identified them exclusively with France. Austria was therefore put in a commanding position in Italy, for the same reason that Prussia was given territory on the Rhine—to commit her to holding the cordon of steel against resurgent French ambitions. Thus Metternich and his officials could argue against liberal Englishmen who sympathized with Italian aspirations, that Lombardy 'had been forced on them by the Allies'.[1]

It was a disastrous acquisition. As national feelings grew in intensity, they tended towards the unification of Italy; on the other side of the Alps, and working among other peoples, they brought the Habsburg monarchy to the verge of disruption. For half a century after the Vienna settlement, Austria struggled to hold her Italian population against the magnetic pull from the south; hereafter, she was fighting to hold her Southern Slavs against the external attraction of Serbia. The intransigeance shown by the government of Vienna in the Southern Slav question was, in part, a result of the lessons—the wrong lessons—learnt in the earlier tensions of the Italian problem. In this sense, there was to be a direct link between the settlement of 1815 and the World War a hundred years later which brought the Habsburg empire to its end.

II

According to Metternich, Italy was but a 'geographical expression'. An Italian patriot might have replied that at least this was something, and that, geographically speaking,[2] the Austrian Empire was an unscientific, incongruous invention. The romantic Danube and its tributaries were of less importance as highways of navigation than might have been imagined; the limestone gorges of the Karst Moun-

[1] A. J. P. Taylor, *The Italian Problem in European Diplomacy, 1847–49* (1934), p. 11, n. 1.
[2] R. A. Kann, *The Habsburg Empire: a Study in Integration and Disintegration* (1957), pp. 13–14.

129

tains separated Dalmatia from the centre, as the pine-forested slopes of the Carpathians cut off Galicia from the Hungarian plains; the industrial area of Bohemia was ringed by mountains which opened northwards, and not towards the Danube valley. The Habsburg lands, indeed, had been brought together as an accumulation of heirlooms, their boundaries being determined, not by natural obstacles or economic viability, but by the lotteries of wars, marriages and diplomacy. The empire, writes A. J. P. Taylor, was 'a collection of entailed estates, not a state, and the Habsburgs were landlords, not rulers'.[3]

Yet the Habsburgs had grown so great because they had a mission, and in so far as they fulfilled it, Europe had connived at their expansion. Their historic rôle had been to defend the West against the Turks. But by 1815, this rôle was played out. The dynasty had to look for a new justification for its existence. The rising ideals of liberalism and of nationalism meant that its rule—unless there was a radical change of spirit and structure—would necessarily appear as a tyranny; an hereditary autocrat was holding together by force diverse nationalities, Germans, Magyars, Czechs, Poles, Italians, Ruthenians, Roumanians, Croats, Slovaks, Slovenes and Serbs, and each of these in turn was to be moved by the passions of independence and freedom.

The problems arising from these interlocking clashes of nationalities could hardly have been more complicated: they resembled one of those Chinese puzzles carved in ivory, in which ball lies within ball in an inextricable series. One set of problems arose from the fact that, around the frontiers of the empire there were various external forces, ready to take their turn in exercising attraction upon individual units inside. The demand for Italian unity was to be the precursor of demands of Transylvanians to unite with fellow Roumanians without, and of Southern Slavs to join Serbia and Montenegro. Though the Poles of Galicia were happier than their fellows under Russian and Prussian rule, they had not entirely forgotten the days before the eighteenth-century partitions, when Poland had been a united kingdom. The Germans of Austria had their own Austrian patriotism. Its core was loyalty to the dynasty, a feeling of superiority, and a solid satisfaction at enjoying preferential treatment for jobs in the bureaucracy; its spirit had gained an idealistic tinge between 1805 and 1810, when Stadion and the Archdukes Charles and John had prepared for a revenge on Napoleon and had sponsored patriotic pamphlets, chiefly about the heroic resistance of Spain.[4] Even so, the pull

[3] A. J. P. Taylor, *The Habsburg Monarchy, 1809–1918* (1948), p. 10.
[4] W. C. Langsam, *Austrian Nationality and German Nationalism* (1930), pp. 39–71.

of the ideal of a united Germany was felt in Austria and, of course, among scattered Germans elsewhere. Business men would have wished to be in the *Zollverein*; students frequented the northern universities as freely as northern pleasure-seekers haunted the spas of Karlsbad and Marienbad on the Bohemian border; literature and music—Goethe and Schiller, Mozart and Beethoven—were regarded as a common heritage.

A second set of national problems was essentially internal to the Habsburg empire, for the dominant Germans were being challenged by two 'major' nationalities, the Magyars of Hungary and the Czechs of Bohemia. Hungary had its medieval constitution, doubly sacrosanct since the country's famous cavalry had saved the throne of Maria Theresa from the onslaught of Frederick the Great. Political activities in the Diet and in local government were mostly the affair of the nobility, though the spirit of liberty was none the weaker for that, and flourished especially among the large class of impoverished squires. An Hungarian literary and historical movement had as its political counterpart two groups of reformers; one, of a 'whiggish' complexion, led by Széchényi, a great magnate, the other, more 'radical', inspired by Kossuth, a poor nobleman of Slovak origin.[5] Both reforming parties wished to work through the Diet, and independent action by the Diet inevitably raised the problem of relations with the government at Vienna. The Czechs of Bohemia envied the Hungarians their constitutional rights, and the Diet of Bohemia would have wished the Crown of Saint Wenceslas to achieve the sort of independence that was allowed to the Crown of Saint Stephen. Poets, historians, and grammarians were fostering a Czech renaissance; men looked back to the testament of Comenius in 1650, 'I believe that, after the tempest of God's wrath . . . shall have passed, the rule of thy country will again return to thee, O Czech nation.'[6] Bohemia, however, had strong and growing industries, which supported a middle class whose allegiance to Czech nationalism had a bourgeois motivation and flavour, unlike its Magyar counterpart, with its aristocratic and domineering recklessness.

Finally, as the third layer of the Habsburg puzzle, was the problem of the nationalities within the nationalities. The Czechs faced a strong German minority, which felt the pull of allegiances outside Bohemia, both within and without the Austrian empire. In Hungary, the Magyars had a Roumanian population in the duchy of Transylvania, as well as Croats, Slovaks, Ruthenians, Serbs and Germans elsewhere. The Croats still retained their Diet, though its powers of

[5] C. A. Macartney, *Hungary: a short History* (1962), pp. 135–41.
[6] Comenius, cit. R. J. Kerner, *Czechoslovakia* (1945), p. 31.

granting taxes had been transferred to the Hungarian assembly; for long their troops in hooded cloaks and white trousers, accompanied by their women sharpshooters, had fought for the Habsburgs in border warfare, and they would not easily relinquish the idea that they served the Emperor directly, and not as Hungarian vassals. The Croats provide an extreme example of loyalties which could tempt the government at Vienna to sinister and ephemeral triumphs in emergencies: the maxim 'divide and rule' is a degrading device when used by a monarch against his own subjects.

III

An enumeration of these tensions within the Empire gives an overwhelming impression that collapse was inevitable. One must remember, however, that up to 1848, mass support had not come in behind the aspirations of writers and the ambitions of the educated. 'The national struggle,' writes A. J. P. Taylor, with illuminating exaggeration, 'was a struggle for jobs in the bureaucracy.'[7] One of the Czech enthusiasts, in a meeting in Prague in 1848, was to say that if the ceiling fell in 'that would be the end of the national revival'. So in the generation following 1815, there was still time for shrewd policy to direct events.

What could have been done? In the comfortable retrospect of history, it is easy to propose an answer, and to forget that only supreme statesmanship could have succeeded. But assuming that genius had descended upon the Habsburgs, one might imagine that they could have turned the greatest threat to their survival into their new justification: the dynasty which had once stood as a barrier against the infidels might have become the agency of mediation, conciliation and equilibrium in a divided Danubian world.

This was the dream of the Czech historian Palacký, who in 1848 refused the invitation to send deputies from Prague to the German Constituent Assembly at Frankfurt. Only Austria, he said, could preserve the peace of central Europe and prevent the universal rule of Russia; he looked forward to an equal federation of all the nationalities in the Empire, followed by a permanent alliance and customs union with Germany. 'If the Austrian Empire had vanished long ago, in the interest of Europe, in the interests of humanity even, we'd have to make haste to create it.'[8]

Following Palacký's vision, one might imagine that an historical

---

[7] Taylor, *The Habsburg Monarchy*, pp. 29–30.
[8] Palacký, cit. R. W. Seton-Watson, *A History of the Czechs and Slovaks* (1943), p. 186.

rôle of unprecedented generosity was awaiting the Habsburgs, that of pioneering liberal constitutionalism on the banks of the Danube, and of experimenting in the free or federal association of rival national groups before they drifted out of the dynastic orbit into which the accidents of history had thrown them.

IV

What chance was there that Austrian statesmanship could rise to these heights of destiny?

'This country,' wrote the French ambassador in January 1817, 'is upheld by its own sheer weight, but the government is impotent and you seek for it in vain . . . here there is neither will nor authority and everyone does more or less as he wishes, and the underlings are the masters.'[9] The Emperor Francis (1792–1835), tall and thin, with fish-like eyes, was stupid, despotic and pedantic—though in his awkward fashion, a likeable man, who talked to his Viennese subjects in their own slang from the window of his shabby old green coach, and spent his leisure hours playing in musical quartets, stamping seals on sealing wax, or cooking toffee on a stove in his study. His successor, Ferdinand was epileptic and feeble-minded. Apart from one superb remark, made long after his abdication (from his bath chair in 1866 he saw the Prussian army enter Prague and muttered, 'Even I could have done as well as this'), he has left no impression on history. At his accession in 1835, one of his ministers, Kübeck, observed, 'we now have an absolute monarchy without a monarch. The principle of legitimacy could not have been more terribly attacked than by this foolish adaptation of it'.[10]

Under these two dim emperors, the ministers manoeuvred for power. Generally, they succeeded in neutralizing each other's effectiveness. Metternich, who in foreign affairs was engaged in decorating Austria with a European mission as the co-ordinator of conservatism against the principles of the French Revolution, was in favour of reforms at home. Without giving away any real powers of the monarchy, he wished to encourage the cultural nationalism of Czechs, Hungarians and Southern Slavs, to foster the activities of provincial estates and diets, and heighten their importance by giving them the right to send delegates to a central *Reichsrat*. At the same time he wished to keep Austria orientated towards Germany, and planned a

[9] G. de Bertier de Sauvigny, *Metternich et son temps* (1959), pp. 142–3. This work also appears in an English translation by Peter Ryde (1962).
[10] Seton-Watson, op. cit., p. 179.

reduction of tariffs as a preparation for an application to join the *Zollverein*. These were the intelligent schemes of a cosmopolitan aristocrat, anxious to gain support for the throne from the local notables, and of a cynical calculator of forces who, in the last resort, was prepared to rule by inflaming civil hatreds rather than appeasing them. 'For us revolutions will never have the sweeping danger of forest fires', he wrote in 1830, 'if the Hungarians revolt, . . . immediately we'll turn Bohemia against them—they hate each other—then the Poles, or the Germans or the Italians.'[11] It was a forecast of the policy which the Court was to employ under stress of revolution, after Metternich's fall.

But none of his more civilized projects were put into practice. The other ministers were not prepared to co-operate with Metternich. His magnificent pose and the chessboard 'system' of masterly interlinkages which he professed to detect in the tensions of foreign policy struck his colleagues as fraudulent when applied to prosaic domestic affairs. If the practical Kolowrat and the ingenious Metternich could have allied, the State would have had firm direction; but, said the former in 1839, 'he always adopts an improving tone towards me, tells me that five and three only make eight, but five times three makes fifteen, that all events are connected, and so the Anglo-Chinese opium quarrel cannot be without effect upon our finances, and so on; and he says this if I ask whether he approves the Northern Railway opening an extension to Pressburg. And then the intolerable vanity of the man, who in all his life has never been wrong, has foreseen everything and still foresees everything that happened and didn't happen. In a word, I can't get on with him.'[12]

The one consistent policy that the Emperor's ministers agreed on was the maintenance of the repressive machinery of the police state. In this respect (though Srbik, his great biographer, has tried to clear him), Metternich was no more enlightened than his colleagues.[13] Austria was the classic land of press censorship and secret police; a *cabinet noir* opened private letters, innkeepers spied on their guests and university librarians reported on the books read by professors. Francis had come to the throne during the French Revolution: the fate of his aunt Marie Antoinette haunted him. Two years after his accession, the police had unearthed a 'Jacobin' conspiracy under

---

[11] Bertier de Sauvigny, op. cit., p. 145.

[12] R. W. Seton-Watson, 'Metternich and Internal Austrian Policy', *Slavonic Review*, XVIII (1939), p. 131.

[13] H. R. von Srbik, *Metternich: der Staatsmann und der Mensch* is challenged by J. Marx, *Die österreichische Zensur im Vormärz* (1959). See the discussion in P. W. Schroeder, 'Metternich Studies since 1925', *Journal of Modern History*, XXXIII (1961), pp. 237–60.

Baron Riedel and Lieutenant Hebenstreit in Vienna and under Professor Martinovics in Hungary. Though Martinovics claimed to be in touch with the Committee of Public Safety and Hebenstreit sent the plans of a war machine he invented to revolutionary France, the roots of the plot went deep into native soil; they went down indeed to Joseph II's attempt to reform by enlightened despotism, which had evoked the support of the 'Fourth Estate'.[14] Oddly enough, Count Pergen's secret police organization, which discovered the plotters, was also a creation of Joseph's reign: when Pergen retired in 1802, the police network had been perfected, but Joseph's enlightenment had been forgotten.

The government of Austria retained henceforward the impress set upon it at the time of the Jacobin trials. The system was not meant to be brutal. Vienna was the city which had invented the waltz, where everyone was under an obligation to enjoy himself. 'Men should be merry,' wrote Baron Andrian in 1842, 'should become drunk, should tell obscene stories, or at best establish a cotton factory or read [a theatrical paper], but all interests concerning their community, their province, their state, the most important questions of the epoch, however much they affect their purse and their whole existence, they should politely leave alone, in order not to incommode the governing gentlemen.'[15] The dynasty did not appeal for intelligent general allegiance. It had its pillars of support; the great magnates, who often lived a cosmopolitan and courtly existence divorced from the crude passions of their local *milieux*, the army, whose traditions of discipline and loyalty transformed recruits of differing nationalities into 'Austrians', the bureaucratic machine, mostly staffed by Germans, and the most efficient police and censorship in the world. The Emperor ruled through official institutions. As for the rest, the good soldier Schweik was the ideal subject.

Today, when we are bitterly conscious of the destructive potentialities of nationalism and, perhaps, not as insistent as we ought to be about popular participation in government, we may be inclined to look back nostalgically upon this moribund empire and the unethical peace which lingered in its shadow. But the final condemnation of the régime consists in the fact (which has become known only in comparatively recent times) that Metternich, Kübeck and others who presided

---

[14] See E. Wangermann, *From Joseph II to the Jacobin Trials: Government Policy and Public Opinion in the Habsburg Dominions in the Period of the French Revolution* (1959).

[15] Baron Victor von Andrian-Werburg, *Oesterreich und dessen Zukunft* (first publ. anon. 1842), cit. Oscar Jàszi, *The Dissolution of the Habsburg Monarchy* (1929, repr. 1961), p. 77.

in apparent confidence over the glittering business of this vast supremacy, admitted in private that the future was hopeless.

V

The Congress of Vienna had left Austria and reaction triumphant in Italy. An Austrian viceroy, with two governors under him, ruled over Lombardy and Venetia, one of Europe's richest and most strategic areas. In Lombardy, silk production was increasing in the hill zones and breaking down the old share-cropping system; industry was developing in Milan and other towns, while on the irrigated plains an advanced agriculture supported a population denser even than that of Belgium. By contrast, Venice was in pleasing decay—

> 'In Venice Tasso's echoes are no more
> And silent rows the songless gondolier,
> Her palaces are crumbling to the shore,
> And music meets not now the ear.
> Those days are gone—but Beauty still is here . . .'[16]

This picturesque decadence—and the charms of a draper's wife—made Byron linger there, and the good-natured citizens accepted Austrian rule so long as the subsidies to operas and to the carnival continued.

By contrast, the business men of Milan and Lombardy and the nobles who were in the silk-producing industry chafed under Austrian control.[17] Only in the territories of the Habsburg monarchy did they have a free market, and there they met with overwhelming competition from the well-established manufactures of Bohemia; they saw themselves bypassed on either side by new mail routes, the French one *via* Calais and Marseille to Alexandria and its Austrian rival *via* Trieste; they complained of the state-barriers which hampered railway development, so that goods from Milan to Florence still took eight weeks in transit; by contrast, they dreamt of an Italian *Zollverein* to open up the whole peninsula as a market.

Here, in these economic disadvantages, lay the fundamental grievance against Austrian rule. The peasants were indifferent and some of the nobles and higher clergy were anxious to collaborate, but the traders and manufacturers saw that their best market lay, not within the Habsburg dominions, but in a united Italy. At the same time, they shared other reasons, of a more idealistic kind, for resenting

---

[16] Byron, *Childe Harold's Pilgrimage*, Canto IV, iii.
[17] See K. R. Greenfield, *Economics and Liberalism in the Risorgimento: a Study of Nationalism in Lombardy, 1814–48* (1934).

Austrian control. From time to time, protests were made against military conscription and police brutalities, and vain demands were put forward to obtain a say in policy for the various 'Congregations' of elected representatives which existed powerlessly alongside the alien bureaucrats. These protests could be sure of support from the ordinary people of Milan, who were willing to come on to the streets to cry '*morte ai Tedeschi*', and from liberal opinion in Europe, which was deeply moved by the publication, in 1833, of Silvio Pellico's reminiscences of thirteen years in the Spielberg prison. Yet, when all this is said, Lombardy was still the best administered area of Italy. The white tunics and yellow sentry boxes of the Austrians meant equality before the law, religious liberty to Protestants, educational opportunities and a lax press censorship, as well as heavy taxes, tariff barriers, and the application of the bastinado or belladonna at police headquarters.

South of their area of direct rule in Lombardy-Venetia, the Habsburgs exercised indirect power through the Austrian princes who ruled the duchies of Tuscany, Modena and Parma.[18] Modena, under its duke Francis IV, was a backward, reactionary little place; in Parma, under Marie-Louise, Napoleon's dissolute but enlightened widow, the changes of the French Revolution—modern legal procedures, toleration, and security of peasant land tenure—were maintained. They were very different principalities, but they were alike in being subject to tutelage from Vienna: on the death of Francis IV in 1846, and of Marie-Louise a year later, Austrian troops moved in. Tuscany, with a population of two millions (almost four times larger than either Modena or Parma) had more independence: it was bigger and not so amenable to control. More than this, 'Daddy' Leopold, who took over the ducal crown in 1824, refused to accept instructions from Vienna, the fact that he was an Austrian archduke notwithstanding. He was unwilling to expel revolutionaries from his dominions—it was convenient, he explained to Metternich, to have all Europe's conspirators kept together in one place. His reign was responsible for the death of only one of these plotters, who committed suicide because compromising letters reached him through the post with the official *visto* on them. Tuscany was a despotism, overrun by police spies, corrupt officials and unemployed monks, yet under the rule of Leopold's minister Fossombroni it was genial enough, the only place in Italy from which no one ever emigrated. Its chief exports were wines and cigars (of both, the best were consumed at home) and

[18] See G. F. H. and J. B. Berkeley, *Italy in the Making*, vol. I, *1815–46* (1932), vol. II, *1846–48* (1936), vol. III, *Jan. 1848–Nov. 1848* (1940); and for Tuscany, W. K. Hancock, *Ricasoli and the Risorgimento in Tuscany* (1926).

the numerous poor were said to be content with their manifold opportunities for watching chariot races, religious processions and fireworks.

Yet, even in Tuscany, a movement of protest was rising. There
were meetings of liberal nobles in Florence and of liberal professors
in the University of Pisa. In Leghorn, the only commercial centre, the
middle class resented their loss of trade to Genoa and Marseille, and
there were signs of working-class discontent. From 1845, Ricasoli, a
feudal baron with railway interests, a tough, thorough man who wrote
all his own text books for his daughter's education, was demanding
reforms; in Leghorn, a courageous demagogic lawyer, Guerrazzi was
encouraging the dock workers to demonstrate against foreign labour
and the employees of bakeries to refuse night work. By November
1847, popular pressure obliged Leopold to abolish his police organization, and the mob of Florence showed an untoward vindictiveness in
hunting down spies and informers.

VI

In the rest of the Italian peninsula, the Austrians did not exercise such
direct influence, but they were ready to provide troops to suppress
revolutionary movements. From 1820–27 they occupied Naples,
charging its king expenses coming to three times his annual revenue;
in 1831, the newly-elected Pope Gregory XVI called them in to suppress a rising in Bologna.

Throughout western Europe, these two governments—the Bourbons of Naples and the Papal Curia—were bywords for intolerance
and obscurantism.[19] 'The States of the Pope', wrote Macaulay in his
devastating fashion, 'are, I suppose, the worst governed in the
civilized world; the imbecility of the police, the venality of the public
servants, the desolation of the country, and the wretchedness of the
people, force themselves upon the observation of the most heedless
traveller.'[20] With old men at the top, a civil service composed of
ecclesiastics and a city population demoralized by a combination of
arbitrary rule and indiscriminate charities, the Papal States could
hardly have flourished. Their medieval government, however, had
one virtue: it exacted little in taxation, and there is some reason to
suppose that even in 1870 the inhabitants of the city of Rome would
have preferred to keep out of a united Italy.[21]

[19] For the Papal States, see Berkeley, op. cit.; for Naples, see H. M. M.
Acton, *The Last Bourbons of Naples* (1961).

[20] Lord Macaulay, letter of December 1838 in G. O. Trevelyan, *The Life and
Letters of Lord Macaulay* (1881), p. 362.

[21] E. E. Y. Hales, *Pio Nono* (1954). For 1870, see C. R. M. F. Cruttwell,
A History of Peaceful Change (1937), p. 159.

At Naples, Macaulay saw more life than at Rome: it was 'the only place in Italy that has seemed to me to have the same sort of vitality which you find in all the great English ports and cities'. Dr Arnold of Rugby, in his way, agreed when he saw there the elements of 'a fearsome drama of Pleasure, Sin and Death'. But out in the malaria-ridden countryside, the effects of heavy taxation and of grinding lords were evident in the misery of the peasantry. By its legal reforms and by the sale of Church property the French Revolution had left its impress on society, but in politics the clock had been put right back by the restored Bourbons. Ferdinand II (1830–59), a heavy-jowled young man who was up to date about railways and gas lighting, had no formula for government but despotism. With no legal means of expressing their political opinions, his subjects resorted to secret societies, so that the kingdom of Naples was full of 'Filadelfi', 'Edennisti', 'White Pilgrims', 'Faithful Hermits' and the like, as well as of branches of the mysterious Carbonari. Revolutionary tensions were strongest in Sicily, for here the hatred of Ferdinand's government was shared by all classes; they detested the rule of Naples as strongly as the Irish detested the rule of England.

This situation had a very near parallel in the States of the Pope, since the four Northern legations (Bologna, Ferrara, Ravenna and Forli) had been part of Napoleon's Northern Kingdom and hated returning to priestly rule. Revolutionary movements in Rome were directed towards reform of papal government, while in the Legations they were directed to escaping from it altogether. If Sicily was to escape from its orbit around Naples and the Legations from theirs around Rome, what new path would they trace? A final equilibrium might, perhaps, be found within a united Italy, and towards this end other gravitational forces were also working.

VII

The inhabitants of Lombardy who wished to see the last of the Austrians, those of the Northern Legations who resented papal rule, and those of Sicily who hated Neapolitan domination could all take comfort in the reflection that Napoleon had shattered the map of Italy and remade it according to his fantasy. What had been done once could be done again. This memory also gave confidence to the politicians and prophets, the business men, scholars, conspirators and idealists whose imaginations or ambitions had been caught by the idea of a united Italy. While some were devising plans for a customs league, a unified system of weights and measures or a coherent railway network, others were writing choruses for marching songs, arranging all-Italian scientific congresses, or drafting regulations for secret societies. The hand of the Carbonari was seen behind risings in Naples in 1820 and in the Papal States in 1831; Mazzini fomented conspiracies in Piedmont in 1833 and in Sicily four years later.

The vague general purpose was clear: but what was the specific first objective? The higher grades of the Carbonari kept their secret to themselves, and thus limited their movement to the cloak and dagger incidents that provide the scenario of revolutions. Mazzini 'was obsessed with two visions; one, learnt from history, was a vision of Italy's past greatness, the other, learnt from romanticism, was a vision of the infinite possibilities of a regenerated nation'.[22] Between the past and the messianic Italy, the 'Third Rome' of the distant future, was the gulf of the present. 'Tell the people you will free them from the tyranny of princes, from the insults of officials, from the oppression of the privileged and rich,' said Mazzini, 'then and then only, when the masses begin to stir, point to Lombardy and preach war against the Austrians.'[23] But this was not practical politics, for to expel the foreigner would require the co-operation of officials, the rich and the privileged and of some of the princes. Indeed, to Mazzini, 'unification was . . . secondary to the kind of Italy that would be created as a result of it'.[24] Not that he was ineffective. Today, when we have lost enthusiasm for the 'makers of nations', it is easier to see how essential the visionaries were to the final achievement. One might add that this achievement was possible only because they were deceived, and that deception coarsened the new national life, dross left behind once the fires had died.

What then were the possible practical courses of action? In a vast volume packed with curious lore, *Del primato morale e civile degli Italiani* (1843), Gioberti, a cleric of Piedmont, advocated the formation of a confederation under the Pope, beginning with a customs and currency union. Within the next three years, two other Piedmontese authors, Count Cesare Balbo and Massimo d'Azeglio published books calling on their own king to lead the movement for Italian unity. In their view, he ruled the kingdom of the marches, on which the defence of Italy against the foreigner must depend, and to which the spoils of expansion must accrue. A century ago, the Piedmontese dynasty had acquired Sardinia; by the settlement of 1815, Genoa had

---

[22] E. E. Y. Hales, *Mazzini and the Secret Societies: the Making of a Myth* (1956), p. 16.
[23] I can no longer find this particular reference, but cf. G. Salvemini, *Mazzini* (Eng. Trans. 1956).
[24] R. Albrecht-Carrié, *Italy from Napoleon to Mussolini* (1950), p. 33.

been added, bringing with it a maritime and industrial tradition and a hint of an Italian destiny.

It is true that Piedmont had none of the qualifications Mazzini would have required for leadership in a movement of liberation. It was a reactionary little state, despotically governed, where Protestants were debarred from public office, where the Jesuits controlled the universities, and the censorship forbade the press to use the words 'nation', 'Italy', 'liberal' and 'constitution'. Charles Albert, who ruled from 1831–49, fell out with Austria, but it was over matters of the salt trade, wine tariffs and railways. His correspondence with Duke Francis IV of Modena shows that he began by regarding nationalism as a threat to his throne, and only changed his mind because he feared that some other sovereign would filch his potential rôle as national leader. Though he said that, when the time came, 'my life, the life of my sons, my treasure and my army will all be spent in the cause of Italy', Massimo d'Azeglio had doubts. 'These are his words, but God alone knows his heart.'[25] In fact, when the great opportunity came, Charles Albert had no maps of Lombardy and his troops were on the French border to cordon off the forces of revolution. He was to fight for Italy reluctantly: partly from ambition, and partly from fear of allowing the movement of national regeneration to fall into the hands of the republicans.

VIII

Metternich claimed that he had insured against every disaster—except a liberal Pope. Yet the surge of national feeling in Italy in 1846–8 owed less to the advent of Pius IX and to his short-lived reputation for liberalism than to provocative Austrian actions which Metternich ought to have vetoed. With Austrian backing, Modenese troops entered the Fivizzano area of Tuscany (why hardly matters—it was a question of territorial exchanges prescribed by treaty, and the whole thing blew up when a crowd in the tiny principality of Lucca gathered to bang brass vessels outside the house of an ill-assorted newly married couple). Following the murder of a banker, Austrian forces exercised their treaty rights to enter Ferrara. Pius IX became, for the moment, a national hero because he protested against their action, and not because he granted his subjects a 'consultative assembly'. The advanced political party in Rome, the *Esaltati*, had little real hope in him.[26] Under leaders like the ex-Carbonaro, Dr Sterbini, and Prince Carlo Buonaparte, a rubicond bespectacled

[25] Berkeley, op. cit., I, p. 213.   [26] Ibid., II, pp. 72–80.

republican, atheist and bird-watcher, they encouraged the crowd to shout 'Coraggio, Santo Padre', to try to push the Pope into actions incompatible with his religious standing in Christendom.

In the autumn of 1847, there were ferments in Rome, riots against the Austrians in Milan, and in Tuscany the Duke had to disband his police spies. Edmund Lear, hiking with a sketch book in Calabria, heard crowds cheering for 'Pius IX' and for a 'Constitution'. 'There are no more keys', a drunken waiter told him when he wanted to get into his room, 'there are no more passports, no more kings, no more laws, no more judges, no more nothing! Nothing but love and liberty, friendship and the constitution.'[27] On 12 January 1848, Sicily rose. It was a particularist revolt against Neapolitan rule. In not much more than a month, constitutions of a kind were proclaimed in Piedmont and Tuscany. Ferdinand of Naples, angry at having to follow suit, decided to have a recklessly liberal one—'they have driven me to this, I will push them down'. On 17 March, news reached northern Italy of revolution in Vienna. Milan and Venice rose against the Austrians. Charles Albert of Piedmont saw no alternative but to lead the nation. Herzen, the Russian exile was there: 'I love Piedmont', he wrote, 'these folk seem younger. It is their honeymoon with free institutions, and the king wears such long moustaches and such a magnificent beard that he is willy-nilly on the side of progress.'[28] Others supported progress unwillingly too; the Pope called on the Austrians to evacuate, and Ferdinand of Naples sent a detachment of troops to join the war against them.

Meanwhile, what had happened in Vienna? Here, the revolution began as a student riot, sparked off by the news from Paris. A petition to sign, crowds on the University square, the professors assembled in the Great Hall at the Chancellor's command, ushers in academic uniform despatched to call for order and returning dishevelled and defeated, the students surging forward and battering in the doors. 'Broken was the fortress which shut up this holy of holies', wrote an undergraduate who participated in this glorious *journée*. 'The students gave orders to the professors for the first time. A topsy-turvy world was beginning. Pedants tore their hair and thought that the world was going to pieces or that the whole youth must receive a "2" in the next examination.'[29] The Archduchess Sophia, 'the only man at Court', considered these proceedings outrageous—'I could bear the loss of one of my children more easily than the ignominy of submitting to a mob of students.' She restrained the police from interfering, however,

[27] Acton, op. cit., p. 179.
[28] E. H. Carr, *The Romantic Exiles* (1933), p. 39.
[29] R. J. Rath, *The Viennese Revolution of 1848* (1957), pp. 48-9.

as she wanted to be rid of Metternich, and hoped to scare the poor epileptic emperor into abdicating in favour of her son. Metternich resigned and a constitution was promised. The student intervention in politics had widespread support from the working class, which was feeling the pinch of hard times, and from middle-class liberals. When an Academic Legion was formed, many graduates and respectable citizens hastened to join it, and stalked the streets resplendent in ostrich plumes, blue coats and grey cloaks lined with scarlet.

In Hungary, the news from Paris inspired the Diet (in session at Pressburg) to demand home rule. On 15 March, in Budapest, the 'Umbrella Revolution' took place; it was raining there, as it was, oddly enough, on the first day of the risings in Paris, Palermo and Vienna. The poet Petöfi and a group at the Café Pilvax asked for universal suffrage and radical reforms resembling those Kossuth was pressing on the Diet. To head off these radicals, and in the hope of getting Hungarian troops to fight in Italy, the Court granted Hungary a ministry of its own and a new constitution ('the Laws of April'). Nobles were no longer to monopolize political representation, but there was a property qualification for electors and candidates had to know Magyar. Nationality was becoming the new, popular substitute for aristocratic exclusiveness. In Bohemia, the liberals of Prague asked for autonomy within the Empire, for the promotion of the Czech language to equality with the German, and for a single united Diet containing the separate Estates of Bohemia, Moravia and Silesia. The government granted the last two requests but held out against autonomy.

But with Prague, Budapest, Vienna and Milan in revolt and Italy uniting against the foreigner, the Habsburg monarchy seemed on the verge of disintegration. One imperial institution alone remained standing amidst the wreckage—the army. Its obsessive, blinkered loyalty saved the dynasty by tactics of the purely military kind which, two generations later, were to destroy it.

IX

Throughout the crisis, while the Court, in flight from its own capital, lived helplessly at Innsbruck or Olmütz, the generals on the various fronts kept in touch with one another. In June, the 'Pentecost Riots' in Prague gave Windischgrätz his opportunity. He moved in to reduce the city by bombardment. It was the first time, during the revolutions of 1848, that military force had been successfully used. Marshal Radetzky, eighty-two years of age and as full of battles as of years, routed the Piedmontese army at Custozza on 13 July. On 31 October,

Windischgrätz marched into Vienna. Hungary remained in revolt, until in the end the Russian Tsar sent an army to help the Austrian Emperor to crush the defiant Magyars. Piedmont resorted to war again and went down to defeat once more at Novara, in March 1849. Thus, in a sense, the failure of the 1848 revolutions in the Austrian Empire is explained very simply: they were defeated on the battle field or at the barricades by professionals.

But why did the armies remain loyal and why did they not meet with greater resistance? The answer to both questions lies in two main considerations: firstly, that the revolutionary movements did not have mass support behind them, and secondly, that the nationalities within the Empire were at war with one another. The chief permanent result of 1848 was the abolition of the remnants of feudalism in Austria-Hungary; but the peasants—and their sons in the armed forces—showed no gratitude to the Constituent Assembly in Vienna for its law of 7 September; in Hungary, they gave little credit to the Diet for Kossuth's agrarian legislation. For the most part, the rural population took what it was given, grumbled at the unsatisfactory qualifications, and stayed at home. In Austria, some of them apparently ascribed all the praise to 'the good Emperor'.

The middle-class liberals, as everywhere, recoiled and repented at the shadow of social revolution. 'Ideas of social democracy . . . never before heard on the politically virgin soil of Vienna struck our ears', one of them wrote on 15 March, 'anarchy stood clearly before my eyes in the Michael Square.'[30] By August, the students and lower middle classes of the Austrian capital had abandoned the workers, and these, in Engels' words, 'dishonoured, disarmed, disorganized, hardly emerging from the intellectual bondage of the old régime',[31] were left helpless. Once riots began, property came in question, and all sorts of tough characters emerged into prominence, like the 'blackguards' the English captain Codrington saw at Leghorn, who paraded in arms and shot, with fixed bayonets, at sparrows. Whether it was Italian unity, Viennese constitutionalism or Bohemian autonomy that was in question, respectable citizens were anxious not to go too far.

Disorder threatened property: in the clash of nationalities, even the poor had something to lose, for the struggle for independence was also a struggle for mastery. The Germans of Bohemia sent deputies to the all-German Constituent Assembly at Frankfurt, while the Czechs refused. On the other hand, the Czechs took their part in a

---

[30] Ibid., p. 83.
[31] F. Engels, *Revolution and Counter-Revolution in Germany* in Karl Marx, *Selected Works* (ed. V. Adoratsky, 1935) II, p. 105.

Slav Congress at Prague in June; they too had hopes of greatness within a wider brotherhood. Once the Court had deserted them, the inhabitants of Vienna were horrified to see grass growing in their squares and their city becoming 'the capital of the province of lower Austria, instead of the capital of an empire of forty million people'.[32] Their joy was barely concealed when Prague fell, and four thousand volunteers enlisted to serve in the Austrian army in Italy. The Magyars of Hungary wanted independence for themselves: in other words, they would lord it over Serbs, Roumanians, Slovaks and Croats. In May 1848, an assembly at Blaj in Transylvania, inspired by Archbishop Saguna, the Orthodox metropolitan, announced that 'the Roumanian Nation declares that it will always remain faithful to the Emperor of Austria'. Serbs and Slovaks formed national councils to insist on their independence from Magyar rule. The Emperor's advisers discovered that Hungary would not provide troops for the Italian campaign; they then recognized the Croatian nobleman Jellačič as *Ban* of the kingdom of Croatia, which became 'an anti-Magyar and anti-revolutionary Vendée', whose shaggy border troops fought toughly on every front for the dynasty.

X

In Italy, the national cause was divided against itself. There were those who feared republicanism and democracy more than they feared the Austrians. The Pope and Ferdinand of Naples defected: they had only been pressed men, anyway. Ferdinand recalled his troops to suppress the liberals at home—he was 'the first to restore order in Europe'. Charles Albert held a plebiscite in Lombardy which voted for fusion with Piedmont. 'While he was collecting votes, Radetzky was collecting men.'[33] This plebiscite had other disadvantages too, for it displeased those patriots who could not bear to think of Turin as the capital and the smug, illiberal dynasty of Piedmont shaping the destinies of a new Italy.

Liberal and national enthusiasm in Italy met with approval in England and France, but there was little willingness to risk a war to help. On 13 March 1848, Palmerston told the Austrian ambassador, 'Prince Metternich thinks he is a conservative, in clinging obstinately to the *status quo* in Europe; we think ourselves conservative in preaching . . . concessions, reforms and improvements, where public opinion

---

[32] Letter of the Saxon diplomat Vitzthum von Eckstädt to his mother, in Rath, op. cit., p. 205.
[33] Bolton King, *History of Italian Unity, 1814–71* (1912) I, p. 248.

demands them.'[34] Palmerston's type of 'conservatism' meant that Italian aspirations were viewed with a benevolent eye, provided that peace was secure, the Austrian Empire kept afloat, and that the French gained no increase of influence in the Mediterranean. On 15 May, a French agent in Turin reported, 'La France est toujours populaire en Italie, mais à condition d'en être absente'. Republican statesmen were as aware of this fact as their predecessors. On ideological grounds, the prospect of driving the Austrians out of Italy was attractive: practically speaking, a war to strengthen Piedmont was flatly against French interests. In a sense, the Austrian Empire was necessary for the balance of Europe; the risks involved in encouraging its dissolution and in attempting to create a new balance were too great to be willingly accepted. That was why Palmerston and Lamartine stood aside, and why the Tsar Nicholas sent his troops to Hungary. Austria no longer had a mission, but it still appeared to be a necessity. Yet the Habsburgs had survived by force, by invoking the brutal aid of reactionary Russia, and by setting some groups of their subjects against the others: their insolence in triumph and their betrayal of their supporters was to encourage the suspicion that this apparent indispensability was an illusion.

[34] Taylor, *The Italian Problem*, p. 32.

CHAPTER X

REACTION AND REVOLUTION IN GERMANY, 1815–1850

I

N apoleon had destroyed the Holy Roman Empire. The statesmen of the Congress of Vienna and all the kings' men could not put it together again, but they produced a convincing imitation, equally fragile and as precariously balanced—the Germanic Confederation, with its Diet of ambassadors from thirty-eight states, and with the Austrian Emperor as its president. The old structure had tottered because it was a traditional monument straddling the fissures of a divided Germany: the new was doomed to be ephemeral because it was a caricature of coherence that could not give realistic embodiment to the growing sense of German unity.

While France had been overturning Europe with revolutionary ideas and with the sword, the Germans had usurped French supremacy in the arts of civilization. This was a golden age in philosophy, music and literature. Readers of Kant, Lessing, Schiller, Herder, Schelling, Schlegel and Goethe were conscious of belonging to a unique cultural complex, of their fellowship in a supreme intellectual heritage. At its highest point of expression, this heritage denied in advance all that was ultimately to give notoriety to German nationalism. In Goethe, Romantic subjectivity was allied with the clarity and transparency of Hellenism and the cosmopolitan humanism of the eighteenth century; he loved French culture and admired the genius of Napoleon, and by contrast, praised the toleration and technological progress of the United States, the new land of the future, free from tragic memories. Devoted to Germany, he was a citizen of the world. 'The German nation,' Goethe confessed in December 1808, 'is nothing, but the individual German is something, and yet they imagine the opposite is true. The Germans should be dispersed throughout the world, like the Jews, in order fully to develop all the good that is in them for the benefit of mankind.'[1]

It would be asking a great deal of a people to expect them to rise to these mysterious heights of itinerant self-abnegation. In fact, as

---

[1] Hans Kohn, *The Mind of Germany* (1961), p. 35. For Goethe's political views see B. Fairley, *A Study of Goethe* (1947), pp. 234–60.

Goethe knew and feared, at this very time a German national consciousness of a militant kind was awakening. Napoleon evoked it, not by intention, or even by tearing up the existing map of Europe, but indirectly, by reaction against his domination, and by the object-lesson of how domination could be achieved. It was 'a nationalism inspired by resistance against alien rule,' it was 'essentially a call to arms'.[2] Its prophets were crude. In Arndt, national feeling was allied to racialism and anti-semitism. These elements were also present in the doctrines of Jahn, who inspired the Free Corps movement and gymnastic associations as part of the war against Napoleon, and in 1815 founded the first of the nationalist student clubs, which excluded Jews, and swore to die for the black, red and gold flag of German unity. Looking backward at the struggle against Napoleon and, prophetically and cynically looking forward, Jahn declared that unity would be achieved by marching against France. 'Germany needs a war of her own and through her own means to feel her strength,' he wrote in 1831, 'She needs a war against Frankdom . . . Latin and Slav allies drag us into perdition . . . Germany needs her own war.'

When these brutal words were written, German national consciousness was evolving rapidly. Economic pressures were making some form of closer union inevitable. Within the space of a generation after Waterloo, the foundations of the vast industrial complex of modern times were laid. The value of industrial production tripled: from being a quarter of the English total, by 1840 it had risen to nearly three-eighths. In 1827, Alfred Krupp set up his first establishment at Essen. Twelve years later, Prussia became the first country to follow the English example in passing factory legislation—typically, because the physique of army recruits had shown sudden deterioration. The rising class of business men demanded wider markets and swifter and more uniform systems of communications and transport. In 1818, to please the industrialists of the Rhineland, Prussia ended internal customs barriers in her scattered dominions; in 1834, the *Zollverein* or Customs Union (itself a combination of smaller, earlier unions) was formed; it came to include most of Germany, and soon built up a nexus of commercial treaties with foreign powers. Railway construction began in the year of the foundation of the customs league; for seven years progress was slow, but by the middle of the century, there were 5,000 miles of track. A railway congress at Hamburg in 1847 pointed the moral: the confederation needed some central authority to unify customs, abolish tolls, and organize communications. Coal and iron, as the famous phrase has it, and not blood and iron, seemed destined to unify Germany.

[2] Kohn, op. cit., pp. 75, 92–93.

Political speculation came to focus on this problem of unity. Would Prussia lead, or Austria, or even Wurttemberg? Liberals, irked by petty tyrannies and press censorship, looked forward to a national state with free institutions; reactionaries encouraged the princes to co-operate in uniform measures for repressive purposes. The achievement of France and Russia in war, of England in politics and industry, of America in freedom and opportunity—all had needed the unified national territory as their base. Romanticism in literature added mysterious yearnings to these promptings of utility. Men looked back to the Middle Ages and beyond for an evocation of the sense of community, for traditions of the *Volk* and for ghostly memories of empire. The idea of natural law, a guiding principle of Western political theory, was displaced by Savigny's description of law as an emanation of the *Volksgeist*. Cosmopolitanism was fading; the historical outlook was rising. The cultural horizon of Germany was contracting in space, but expanding in time.

It is obviously impossible to study the manifold pressures that were moulding German nationalism without reflecting upon its potentialities for evil seen in the lurid light of two World Wars and the destruction of Europe. Yet we ought to beware of pressing the analysis too far in this early period. There is no justification for awarding sombre significance to every writer who glorified force and every entrepreneur who wanted to corner the Balkan markets, for scenting sinister meaning behind peripheral observations, for elevating ineffectual *litterateurs*, with their handful of seed and their shallow furrows, to the status of sowers of dragons' teeth in the peaceful fields of Europe. On the other hand, there is as little justification for going to the opposite extreme and indulging in speculation about the genial, unaggressive Germany which might have emerged from a different process of unification, devoted to beer, music and the technologies of peace, in that order. The harsh, inescapable facts of geography made it certain that a united Germany would be a military force—for defence, and also, potentially, for aggression. The late development of German nationalism necessarily involved the problems of adjustment which we see working today with the rise of Asian and African nations: inferiority complexes masked by truculence on the one hand, and resentment and dog-in-the-manger moralizing about the sanctity of the *status quo* on the other. German unity was inevitably a dangerous business for Europe.

By the same token, here was a nationalism which was no worse, and no better, than other nationalisms. Like others, it had its underworld of dark passions, and in Germany, these were being fostered by the operation of a sort of love-hate relationship towards France.

Napoleon's career of conquest evoked hatred of alien rule, yet French culture and the achievements of the French Revolution claimed undiminished allegiances. This pattern of attraction and repulsion continued, and is evident in its attraction (and a little, in its repulsion) in the greatest German intellect of the 'forties. Heine was a patriot, but as an artist, a Jew and a Rhinelander, he was drawn to Goethe's cosmopolitanism and love of France. He feared the day when the madness of the Nordic bards would erupt again, and the cult of the stone gods of a thousand years ago would revive.[3] In August 1848 he wrote with contempt of his countrymen who dream 'that their turn at playing the leading rôle in world history has arrived'. On the other hand, France was established as the enemy. In May 1832, at a meeting of German liberals at the ruined castle of Hambach, Dr Wirth proclaimed that, if France was aggressive, all Germans would rise against her and take back Alsace-Lorraine; it was the danger of war between France and Prussia in 1840 which inspired the poets to write the *Wacht am Rhein* and *Deutschland über alles*.

II

Thus, the national anthem was written—by Hoffman von Fallersleben, a democrat, whose opinions cost him his chair at the University of Breslau. There was an affiliation between the national idea and liberal and democratic aspirations; both were a threat to the various princes and oligarchies, and both might find simultaneous satisfaction in the acceptance of a national constitution.

Throughout Germany, there was a desire, among the educated classes, for freedom of the press and of opinion, and for some form of constitutional government. No doubt rising industrialists and business men shared this liberal enthusiasm, at least to the extent of being impatient with the snobbish hierarchy of the old régime; the entrepreneur who takes over Count Julius' estate for a factory in Karl Immermann's novel, *Die Epigonen* (1836), is driven on by a militant middle-class consciousness—'I will always strain every effort,' he says, 'to destroy the old feudal towers and castle-dungeons.'[3a] For the most part, however, liberal aspirations manifested themselves among the 'intellectuals', taking the term in a broad sense. Lawyers, unable to found bar associations and resentful

---

[3] Heinrich Heine, *Deutschland*, Kaput XXVII (*Gesammelte Werke* (1887) II, p. 113). For the reference to the 'leading rôle in world history', Kohn, op. cit., p. 113.

[3a] Ernest K. Bramsted, *Aristocracy and the Middle Classes in Germany: Social Types in German Literature, 1830–1900* (1937, new ed. 1964), p. 60.

of the bureaucratic regulation of the courts and the system of private hearings, led the way in the demand for oral proceedings, the jury system and a free press—all of which would defend the liberty of the subject and raise their own status in the community. Journalists supported them. So too did many civil servants and schoolmasters, united in their dislike of illogical systems of administration which paid starvation wages. Divided into numerous principalities, Germany had become a land of many competing universities, whose professors, as often as not, were liberals in politics. There was a large student population, for the various states needed a vast recruitment of officials, and according to the Duke of Wellington (in 1839), it was 'curious that all the mischief in Germany seems to have its rise in the universities; while in this country we look to [them] and to the state of feeling there, as one of our main sources of security'.[4] This difference was caused, he felt, by the neglect of religious education in the German Faculties, by the dependence of professors upon their lecture fees, and by the absence of the residential colleges which in England shed their civilizing balm upon reckless youth. The diversity of provincial capitals in Germany had also greatly multiplied the numbers of publishers, booksellers and writers of local celebrity; in 1831, John Strang observed that 'in a few years the names of German authors will exceed the number of living German readers'.[5] The coming revolution in Germany was certain to be well adorned with beards and big hats and the paraphernalia of the literary bohemia.

What chance was there that constitutional government might be achieved within a disunited Germany, won piecemeal, in struggles against individual princes? The answer seemed to be that, so long as the individual states subsisted, reaction was likely to remain triumphant. It is true that rulers were getting into the habit of granting constitutions based upon the formula of a two-chambered parliament, equality before the law, and the prince in charge just the same; this happened in Baden and Bavaria in 1815, in Württemburg in 1819, and in Hesse Darmstadt in 1820. Prussia, now saddled with the progressive Rhenish provinces, occasionally seemed likely to get a constitution too, as in 1821 when Provincial Diets were established, or in 1845–7 when Frederick William IV instituted his Federal *Landtag*, a sort of parliament which Metternich called 'a bad joke'.

[4] H. G. Schenk, *The Aftermath of the Napoleonic Wars* (1947), p. 89. For the rôle of conferences of scientists and scholars in fostering ideas of unity and familiarity with the procedures of discussion, see R. H. Thomas, *Liberalism, Nationalism and the German Intellectuals, 1822–47* (1951), pp. 1–6, 13, 90.
[5] L. O'Boyle, 'The Democratic Left in Germany, 1848', *Journal of Modern History*, XXIII (1961), p. 382.

From a liberal point of view, censure from such an authority was a hopeful sign; but the general flavour of government in the provincial capitals was one of inefficient tyranny. Hanover, under King Ernest Augustus, a rabid, ignorant old soldier (he had been Duke of Cumberland until the ending of the union with England in 1837) was notoriously ill-ruled, while Baden, Hesse and Bavaria, for all their charters, were states where a constitutional opposition had little chance of flourishing.

Bavaria illustrates the general position in genial caricature. King Ludwig controlled the composition of his Diet, excluding lawyers and Protestants; his army officers were promoted on the results of tests in Scripture, and university professors were paid lower salaries than the valet of the bedchamber. This latter official, however, had onerous duties, especially after 1846, when Munich saw the arrival of Lola Montez, alias Betty Watson, who signed herself '*Maîtresse du Roi*' and did her shopping with the phrase, 'My Louis will pay'. Up to now, the easy-going Bavarians had rioted only against high beer prices. A feud between Lola and the university, however, aroused all their latent passions. King Ludwig's declaration that his love affair was merely platonic convinced half his subjects that he was dishonest and the other half that he was even more foolish than they had supposed. The militia could not help the court, for their wives hid their uniforms. This was why, in February 1848, there was to be a comic-opera revolution in Bavaria, to add its quota to the tumult of real events in the other states of Germany.

It was a far cry from the cardboard scenery of Munich to the harsh, windswept city of Berlin, a city of raw contrasts, 'a compound,' says Veit Valentin, 'of all German and even, all European possibilities'.[6] A garrison town and a manufacturing centre, an administrative capital where nobles had houses but where they never found a home, a great resort for Jews and descendants of French refugees, a magnet for migrants from the Eastern provinces, who poured in at a rate which, between 1815 and 1847, doubled the city's population and more than doubled the numbers of its destitute—it was possible to imagine Berlin as the scene of an authentic revolution. Equally it was possible to imagine the city becoming the scene of an exemplary repression. Boyen's ideal of a citizen army had been useful against Napoleon: once the menace of the foreigner had been removed, the professionals took over again. A military handbook of 1826[7] assumed that the suppression of civil disorder was one of the first tasks of the

[6] Veit Valentin, *1848: Chapters of German History* (trans. E. J. Scheffauer, 1940), p. 58.
[7] G. A. Craig, *The Politics of the Prussian Army, 1640–1945* (1956), p. 81.

soldier—that was why garrisons were frequently moved, to prevent them fraternizing with the local population. In the 1830s, the famous Prussian General Staff was forming, and was engaged already in studying the use of railway transport for rapid mobilization. The army was commanded by the aristocracy: in 1842, out of 9,500 officers, over 7,000 were nobles. The world was changing underneath them, but the *Junkers* were changing with it. They had the key posts at the top of the administration: in 1842, nine out of twelve ministerial posts and twenty-nine out of thirty embassies were theirs. The peasants were freed from many of their obligations, but the *Junkers* received financial compensation and retained most of the land; they remained exempt from many taxes and exercised civil and criminal jurisdiction in the first instance. Without losing political influence, they were being set free from the traditional rural relationships which had held them back from the profitable paths of capitalist agriculture. When Provincial Diets were set up in 1821, the local aristocracies (except in the progressive industrial Rhineland) took control of their business.

Frederick William IV, the king of Prussia, was aware of his peculiar position between the aristocracy and the middle-class liberals. The dream of a liberal constitution, which had been used as an inspiration in the struggle against Napoleon, and which Hardenberg had reluctantly abandoned in 1819, lived on in his mind as a possibility— suitably amended to conform to his own autocracy. Here was a monarch with many talents and some virtues. He was intelligent, read Dutch and Sanskrit, patronized artists, had a gift for sketching and a sense of humour (his letters were often signed with one of his favourite drawings, a complacent turbot). In his contemptuous fashion, he loved the poor, and he contrived to combine megalomania with toleration and a love of peace; he was the only Hohenzollern, it has been said, who did not pose as a military chief. With all this, he was violent, unstable and neurotic, and filled with dreams of himself as some kind of new Roman Emperor. By 1845, he had decided to adopt the picturesque rôle of a liberal autocrat, hence his parliamentary experiment, the united *Landtag*, drawing together representatives of the Provincial Diets. There was no idea of granting a constitution. 'I will never permit,' said the King, 'that between our Lord in heaven and this country there be interposed a sheet of ink-stained paper to take the place of a second Providence.' However, the debates of the *Landstag* were published, so that they provided a good opportunity to by-pass the censorship. Within two years, the deputies from the Rhineland were leading in demands for a liberalization of the Government, for an ink-stained paper in the place of an unpredictable

Hohenzollern Providence. For the first time, the voice of a middle-class opposition was heard in Prussia.

III

The possibility of a constitutional régime in Prussia was significant news in other states, for it aroused hopes of leadership towards a Germany that would be both united and free. Up to 1840, the movement of constitutional opinion had little coherence: it ran from the most conservative of professorial liberals to the most extreme of republican democrats, while the very decentralization which helped to provide recruits in the diversified universities, bureaucracies and intellectual *milieux* also hampered the formation of anything resembling a nation-wide party. In the 1840s, however, two religious movements transcending state boundaries came to aid the forces of political dissatisfaction. In Prussia began the *Lichtfreunde* group, among Lutheran pastors who were tired of dogmatism, clericalism and reaction; in Catholic Germany arose the movement of *Deutsch-Katholizismus*, a protest against the superstitious veneration of relics which became a demand for a German National Church. At the same time, the enthusiasm for a united Germany was coalescing with the enthusiasm for constitutional government. In 1847, meetings were held in Lübeck, Offenburg and Heppenheim to plan for a united German Parliament or National Assembly, together with the freedoms which ought to accompany such organs. Simultaneously, the Prussian *Landtag* was defying Frederick William IV and manoeuvring for a constitution. Hopes of a free and united nation were running high in Germany at the beginning of 1848, the year of European revolution.

The explosion came when news of revolution in Paris arrived. In March, the rulers of Baden, Hesse and Württemberg capitulated to demands for a free press, a National Guard and genuine parliamentary government. Munich rose against the 'Lolamontanism' of the King, and on 20 March, Ludwig abdicated. Riots broke out in Berlin on 13 March, and there was renewed fighting later when news arrived of the fall of Metternich. On 21 March, Frederick William IV admitted defeat and promised to form a liberal ministry and to serve the cause of German unity. His intention was to appear splendidly at a congress of princes, but from all sides the intelligentsia and the middle classes asked for a provisional government of Germany with representative institutions. A meeting at Heidelberg called upon all previous and present members of diets or estates to assemble at Frankfurt; at the end of March, six hundred of them did so, and convened a united German parliament to meet there on 18 May. The Frankfurt Parliament which was thus called into being, by the 24 June had appointed a 'Vicar of the Empire' in the person of the Austrian Archduke John, and by January 1849 had devised a monarchical and parliamentary constitution for the whole nation: there was to be an Emperor and a legislative assembly elected by universal suffrage and secret ballot. Such was the main stream of revolutionary events in 1848.

More extreme possibilities loomed on the horizon, but were driven back again out of sight. The republican cause was represented by an unsuccessful rising in the south-west under Hecker and Struve, and by a raid of exiles from Paris armed with pistols and scythes, led by the poet Herwegh, magnificently sombre in black cloak and hat. In the Rhineland, Karl Marx was co-operating with the bourgeoisie, urging them on towards a German republic (and at one time, towards a revolutionary war with Russia), though his ultimate aim remained the break-through of socialism. His newspaper, the *Neue Rheinische Zeitung*, in its final number (18 May 1849) proclaimed in red letters, 'the last word, everywhere and always, the emancipation of the working class'. Marx's propaganda[8] was better known in Germany than has been supposed; in particular, a radical group around the editorial headquarters of the *Zeitungshalle* in Berlin gave publicity to the *Communist Manifesto* and provided some leaders for the March insurrection. Even so, the time was not ripe, in Germany, for either republicanism or socialism. The obvious goal of the revolution of 1848 seemed to be a united, conservative and liberal Germany, ruled by a parliamentary monarchy.

As is usual, however, in revolutions, the disorders which had shaken the grip of the reactionary princes were the result of blind discontents which nationalist and constitutional achievements could not assuage. The 'forties had been years of hunger in Germany. From 1844, the cost of foodstuffs had risen catastrophically. A wave of bread riots had swept over Prussia in the spring of 1847. By the following March, the worst was over, and prices were falling back towards the level of 1844, but the hardships of the previous years had spread discontent and bitterness among the poorer classes and had prepared them to play a rôle in the streets when the crust of order broke. Yet the demonstrators of 1848 were not the workers in the new factories and mines, for as yet they lacked the numbers, concentration and class-consciousness which could make them dangerous, nor had they been

[8] H. Meyer, 'Karl Marx und die deutsche Revolution von 1848', *Historische Zeitschrift*, CLXXII (1951), pp. 517–34; J. Droz and E. Tonnelat, *Les Révolutions allemandes de 1848* (1947), pp. 350, 527–46.

the principal victims of the shortages of the hungry 'forties. The real sufferers, and the principal demonstrators, were found in the ranks of the guildsmen and artisans, more numerous, more concentrated in the urban centres of political power. These workers belonged to a declining world; economic liberalism was abolishing their privileges and hierarchies, the new industrialism was outmoding their products and cutting their prices. Their revolutionary inspiration was conservative. They were to attack factories, iron foundries and mills, just as wagoners were to tear up railway tracks and bargees raid steamboats on the Rhine. In the fighting in Berlin on 18 March, two students and thirteen merchants were killed, together with no less than seventy-four handicraftsmen. 'The liberals,' writes Hamerow, 'gave the Revolution its leadership, but the artisans provided it with defenders and martyrs. Everywhere during the spring uprising, the hungry guildsmen fought for a restoration of the corporate system.'[9]

Frankfurt, the city of the new German national parliament, saw the meeting of a congress of artisans (which seems to have been dominated by the masters of guilds) in July, immediately followed by a conference of 'Labour', more directly representative of the lower strata of the working classes, the employees, rather than the small employers. The demands of these two assemblies were naturally incompatible in some respects, for the delegates to the second wanted shorter hours and a minimum wage; on the other hand, they were united in their opposition to 'economic freedom'. They wanted to see factory output restricted and progressive income tax applied to the fortunes of big capitalists, and state support given to the weaker members of society. What they were asking for was more likely to be granted by kings than by middle-class parliamentary deputies.

These attempts, frail as they were, to organize the artisan population, had no parallel in the rural areas of Germany, where peasant discontent manifested itself in desperate incoherence. A few enlightened rulers and, after them, the armies of the French Revolution, had pushed on the emancipation of the peasants, so that even in reactionary Hanover it had been impossible to restore the full extent of servile obligations. Yet reform in most of Germany had been carried out in strict subordination to the interests of the aristocracy. In Prussia, the so-called edicts of 'emancipation' of 1811 and 1816[10] had served to create an agricultural proletariat for the convenience of the big

[9] T. S. Hamerow, *Restoration, Revolution, Reaction: Economics and Politics in Germany, 1815-71* (1958), p. 102. Like the work of Droz mentioned above, this is an indispensable book for the subject of this chapter.

[10] W. M. Simon, *The Failure of the Prussian Reform Movement, 1807-19* (1955), pp. 98-101.

estate-owners east of the Elbe. In the smaller states of the south and west of Germany, the lord of the manor often lived on the income of his feudal dues rather than by the exploitation of his demesne; here, the grievance of the peasants was, not that traditional obligations were being wound up on disadvantageous terms, but that so many of them remained unchanged, in the form of seigneurial dues and hunting rights. It was in these areas of feudal survivals—where misery had obvious objects to demonstrate against—that the most serious disturbances took place, and in the Grand Duchy of Baden, in Württemberg and in various neighbouring principalities a series of uncoordinated rural riots broke out in March 1848. The peasants who marched on the castle of Prince Hohenlohe (in Württemberg) refused to accept the keys of the cellar—'We haven't come here to eat and drink; we only want to burn the parchments that bind us to beggary, then we are going to tell the king the reasons for our poverty.'[11]

The disturbances in the countryside brought quick results; servile obligations were abolished in Baden, easy terms were devised for their liquidation in Württemberg, and less easy terms in Bavaria, Darmstadt and Hesse-Kassel, while hunting and judicial rights of lords ended in Prussia. But the liberals and democrats of the cities failed to harness the fury of the peasants, whose servility they despised and whose terrorism they feared. When the first Prussian National Assembly (elected by universal suffrage, in two degrees) met on 22 May, no less than 68 peasant deputies appeared. They were simple folk, some completely illiterate; they kissed the hand of the official who paid their expense allowances and, indifferent to the middle-class leaders, voted with that naïve conviction which is the most extreme form of political irresponsibility. No one sought their alliance. In the Parliament of Darmstadt, a liberal orator defended the rule of law, amid the applause of his fellow deputies, by tearing up the charter a terrified nobleman had conceded to his peasants. When revolutionaries cease to strive to find excuses for the use of force, their days are numbered.

IV

The German revolution failed because it had not enlisted the fighting allegiance of the mass of the population, either in town or country-side. The 'fundamental rights' proclaimed by the Frankfurt Parliament were essentially political. For the most part, its deputies had no contact with the peasantry, and little understanding of the working-classes. Middle-class liberals naturally feared disorder. Strauss

[11] Droz, op. cit., p. 154.

(author of the famous *Leben Jesu*) renounced progressive political opinions once he found the even tenor of existence was disturbed—'it was much better under the old police-state, when we had quiet on the streets and were not always meeting excited people, new-fashioned shovel-hats and beards'.[12] Worse still was the possibility that property might be endangered. 'My liberalism has always been confined to opposition to the police-state,' confessed a professor of the University of Bonn almost a year later, 'as I belong to that class of citizens which has something of its spiritual and material patrimony to lose, I am naturally against democracy, whose folly and blindness has turned all sensible men against it. . . . Nothing remains but for us to support the government, at the risk of provisionally supporting reaction.' By February 1849, views of this kind prevailed among the intellectuals and middle classes. German historians, more especially Meinecke, have explained the all-too-easy abandonment of the ideals of 1848 by the inherent tendency of the German mind to obedience. Yet the vitality of the press, and the remarkable expansion of associations of a democratic nature all over Germany at this time suggest that, superficially at least, the middle classes were as freedom-loving as any similar class in Europe. They 'betrayed' the revolution, because they feared that they themselves would be betrayed if they adopted decisive revolutionary means. It was as if they had overheard Engels in January 1848, and made up their minds not to be hoodwinked—'Fight on bravely then, gentlemen of capital! We need your help, we even need your rule on occasions. You must draw from our path the relics of the Middle Ages and absolute monarchy. You must abolish patriarchalism, you must centralize, you must change all the more or less destitute classes into real proletarians, recruits for us. . . . Your reward shall be a brief time of rule. You shall dictate laws . . . . You shall banquet in the royal halls . . . but remember! The hangman's foot is at the threshold.'[13] They did remember and, hearing the hangman's step, handed back the royal halls hastily to their original occupants.

When we speak of the German intellectuals and middle classes, we must remember that we are referring to a whole spectrum of varied interests, which might be fused together temporarily by a common enthusiasm, but which, in the end, were likely to diverge. Some lawyers, merchants and professional men suddenly realized that, even if a united and parliamentary Germany might help industrialists, their own best customers were found in the provincial courts and garrisons.

[12] Priscilla Robertson, *Revolutions of 1848: a Social Study* (1952), p. 135.
[13] T. S. Hamerow, 'History and the German Revolution of 1848', *American Historical Review*, LX (1954), p. 29.

Officials who wanted a reformed administration also wished to retain their places. Moderate men who had fought at their first barricade reflected that the removal of a few exasperating bureaucratic regulations would be enough—the story goes that, at Berlin, after the fighting of 20 March, when the people were informed that the King granted all their demands, incredulous voices were raised, 'What? Smoking? . . . even in the *Tiergarten*?' Professors, even liberal ones, did not necessarily enjoy prolonged co-operation with riotous students. Worldly success drew a dividing line among the intellectuals. Ludwig Hausser, the historian, spoke of the left in Baden as composed of unsuccessful lawyers, lower grade teachers and examination failures; another contemporary spoke of 'those who wish to enter respectable society for the first time, and those who have been cast out [of it.]' Professional and literary men who had achieved good incomes had more to lose than these in a general overturn.

Religion, too, was a divisive force. Orthodox Lutherans were alarmed at the *Lichtfreunde* groups, as orthodox Catholics were at *Deutsch-Katholizismus*, and both were aware that liberals and democrats contained many rationalists and adherents of the neo-Hegelian philosophy in their ranks. Ludwig von Gerlach, in alliance with the aristocracy, led a Pietistic crusade against the revolution in Prussia, at the same time naïvely exhorting the *Junkers* to recognize that their property ought to be at the service of the poor and of the State. On 23 October, the German Catholic bishops, convoked by the reactionary Archbishop of Cologne, met in congress at Würzburg. They condemned the course the revolution had taken, and asked for the freedom of the Church, in full communication with Rome, to run its own affairs, a crafty manoeuvre, which revolutionaries were obliged to support on principle and which reactionaries supported as allies.

According to Engels,[14] another reason for the failure of the revolutionary movement was that it had no great urban heart, like Paris or London, so that, inevitably, the isolated combats degenerated into futility. Even so, Berlin might have turned Prussia, and Prussia was the key to the future of Germany. Unluckily for the success of the revolution, however, the liberal forces were weak and the reactionary forces were at their strongest at this point of decision. When the Prussian aristocracy found that only thirteen noble proprietors had been elected to Frankfurt, and twelve to the first Prussian National Assembly at Berlin (as one of these was an avowed republican he did not count), they began to organize. In August, a *Junkerparlament* of four hundred nobles met at Berlin; its leaders were in touch with the

[14] F. Engels, *Revolution and Counter-Revolution in Germany in 1848* (ed. Eleanor Marx Aveling, 1896), p. 5.

Pietists, the Army and the camarilla of advisers around the king. By September, preparations for a *coup* were under way—'if they don't do it this time,' wrote young von Moltke, a junior officer on the General Staff, to his brother, 'then I am ready to emigrate with you to Adelaide'. Windischgrätz bombarded Vienna on 28 October: General Wrangel marched on Berlin on 10 November. There was no resistance. The militia handed in its weapons, and the Assembly's decree calling on the country to refuse to pay taxes met with no response. The king invented his own constitution, the 'Dictated Constitution' of 5 December. Men looked back on the March days as an inexplicable accident.

Once the cause of liberty was dead in Prussia, what chance had it in Germany? What relevance could the constitutional crown which the Frankfurt Parliament was devising have to the autocrat who had re-established his power in Berlin by military force?

V

It is customary to say that the Frankfurt Parliament contained too many lawyers, intellectuals and officials. Too many—for what? Presumably, to frame realistic policies, but in that case, what policy could have succeeded? Afraid of republican and socialistic agitations and peasant disorders, the deputies dared not destroy the old dynastic machinery, and thus they were doomed to attempt to stick together an old Germany instead of fusing and moulding the white-hot alloys of a new. Veit Valentin's description of the Parliament as 'too much of a university and too little of a political stock-exchange' is exact, not because the deputies were impractical dreamers, but because they were, in the nature of the case, a debating society, rather than the gathered representatives of dynamic forces. They did not come to Frankfurt with the sense of overwhelming mass opinion behind them. Voting methods had varied from state to state; in some, workers and farm labourers had been denied the franchise, in most, voting had been indirect; only in Baden, Saxony and the Rhineland had there been an electoral battle along party lines. In most areas, less than half the eligible voters had recorded an opinion. By European standards of the mid-century, this was a respectable show of public opinion, but it was hardly an unleashing of revolutionary forces. What the deputies lacked, essentially, was not expertise, but authority. While they grandly decided to build a battle fleet and plotted the far-flung frontiers of a new nation, they were dependent upon the armed forces of the old dynasties; while they devised a constitution, they were unable to call out the shock troops of riot to storm the Bastilles and

Tuileries of Germany; while they discussed who was worthy to wear the constitutional crown they had invented, it was becoming less and less likely that any possible nominee would accept it.

Before this crown could be offered, the Frankfurt Parliament faced a brutal choice between two desperate alternatives—an Austrian Germany, or a Prussian one? On this issue, by tradition, and economic and political aspirations, the deputies were hopelessly divided; more than this, the whole force of religious hatreds was inevitably involved in the disagreement, for an Austrian Germany would be predominantly Catholic, and a Prussian Germany would be predominantly Protestant. Either way, the choice involved problems of the utmost difficulty. Could the king of Prussia be expected to conform, honestly, to a genuine parliamentary régime? Dare he risk accepting the crown if the offer was not accompanied by the manifest common consent of both Catholic and Protestant deputies? Would the Polish populations won by Prussia as her share of the loot in the eighteenth-century partitions remain within the new boundaries? Could Austria be detached from the Habsburg monarchy to join, or could some or all of the nationalities in the Habsburg orbit become connected with a united Germany? What would happen to the Germans of the dispersion outside the present frontiers? What would happen to the rulers of the smaller states? How would foreign nations react? There were multifarious problems.

These problems bedevilled the whole proceedings of the Frankfurt Parliament. The discussion of boundaries was dangerous. The support given by the assembly to a Prussian invasion of Schleswig-Holstein, expansive talk about German influence in the Baltic, the Danube basin and in Poland, the enumeration of the exiled Germans in Alsace-Lorraine, Courland, Limbourg and some of the Swiss cantons caused alarm in Europe,[15] and further divided the Parliament by driving many deputies of the left to protest against this 'lust for conquest'. So intractable was the religious issue that, when the imperial dignity was finally offered to the Prussian king, the only South Germans who voted 'Yes' were Protestants, while most of the Prussian Roman Catholics abstained. A majority of the Parliament would have preferred a constitution with the suffrage limited to an élite of well-to-do and educated voters; the partisans of Austria, however, threw their weight into the scale for universal suffrage simply to make the constitution unpalatable for the king of Prussia.

They succeeded. On 27 April 1849, Frederick William IV refused

[15] Roy Pascal, 'The Frankfurt Parliament, 1848, and the *Drang nach Osten*', *Journal of Modern History*, XVIII (1946), pp. 108–22; Hans Rothfels, '1848—One Hundred Years After', ibid., XX (1948), pp. 291–319.

the proferred crown. It was, he said, a 'sausage sandwich', a cryptic saying, but clearly contemptuous. His refusal revealed the full implications of General Wrangel's easy march on Berlin in the previous November. That had been the beginning of the end of the German revolution of 1848. At first, the revolution had been moved by the ideals of unity and freedom, for men had not yet learnt to disassociate them; but the hope of their conjoint realization had depended upon an illusion, the dream of a liberal parliamentary régime in Prussia.

VI

Some German liberals were inclined to blame the rest of Europe, more especially England and France, for the failure of their revolution. It is true that no one gave them any help. On the other hand, there is no gainsaying Russell's reply (22 November 1850)—'It is not for forty millions of people to complain that they could not obtain good government because England has looked coldly upon them.'[16] England had an interest in promoting a unitary and liberal Germany, but felt no obligation to take risks to support any particular German definition of either unity or freedom. On 10 April 1848, Prussian troops marched into the duchies of Schleswig and Holstein. These duchies were under Danish suzerainty, though Holstein was German in population and a member of the Confederation, and Schleswig had some Germans in the south; the question at issue was, whether the rights of Denmark would remain intact once the male line of its royal succession ended. The Frankfurt Parliament, and opinion generally in Germany supported Prussia. The rights and wrongs of this diplomatic tangle are inextricable (everyone knows the famous joke about the three men who had understood it—one dead, one mad and one had forgotten); enough to say that England, by accumulated obligations and through commercial and naval interests in the Baltic, was necessarily on the side of Denmark. Had the Germans 'set to work heart and mind to throw off the old Metternich *incubus*,' said Russell, 'they would surely have succeeded. But they set their wits to work and their courage to fight for a bit of conquest—to deprive the King of Denmark of Schleswig, which neither justice nor England could tolerate.'

In the cafés of republican France there was plenty of enthusiasm for freeing the oppressed nationalities of Europe: in the bureaux of the Foreign Office there was a harsh appreciation of realities. 'German unity,' wrote Bastide (31 July 1848), 'would make of this people

[16] W. E. Mosse, *The European Powers and the German Question, 1848–71* (1958), p. 44, n. 1.

of more than thirty-five millions a power very much more redoubtable to its neighbours than Germany is today, and therefore I do not think we have any reason to desire this unity, still less to promote it.'[17] A powerful new nation in the centre of Europe was a potential ally—and a potential enemy. One day, it might ask for Alsace; in pursuit of its own freedom it might sabotage the aspirations of other peoples, more especially the long-suffering Poles. Even if France had retained the warlike ardour of her first Revolution (as apprehensive conservatives supposed), her armies would hardly have marched to serve so doubtful a cause.

Russia had all the motives of England and France, together with others of her own, for distrusting the German revolution. Like England, she had a traditional interest in the Schleswig-Holstein problem and its implications for the balance of power in the Baltic; like France, she ruled over a German-speaking population in her Baltic provinces. A liberal Germany was anathema to the Tsar on ideological grounds; a unified and liberal nation might provide England with a dangerous ally, and might even set free the Polish subjects of Prussia, thus raising a menace to the security of the whole western frontiers of Russia. Yet Nicholas I did not yield to the temptation to intervene in Germany. His advisers, themselves Germans (his Chancellor, Nesselrode, was a German Jew born in Portugal, who never learnt to speak Russian, and his ambassador at Berlin was a Baltic baron), foresaw that there might well be no need to do so. What the Tsar did do, however, was to intervene, in 1849, to save Austria, by crushing the Hungarian rebels. His motives were various, but the essential one was to maintain Austria intact to keep Germany divided.

The Russians marched because the Tsar was taking precautions for the future; when they entered Hungary, the German revolution was over. Its failure had nothing to do with the advent of hordes of disciplined serfs from the boundaries of Asia. The German liberals (and some historians subsequently) who complained that Europe failed to help the Germans in 1848 were being unreasonable, as if other nations were not entitled to their own foreign policies. What might well have unified Germany in 1848 would have been a war for survival against an invasion by the Russian autocrat. Then—one may speculate—Germany might have seen a fusion of all states and classes in a national effort, the destruction of the dynasties, the co-ordinating force of dictatorship, and terror used for national, and social ends. Marx himself might have essayed the rôle of Robespierre.

[17] A. J. P. Taylor, *The Struggle for Mastery in Europe, 1848–1918* (1954), p. 16.

CHAPTER XI

AUTOCRACY AND SERFDOM: RUSSIA TO 1850

I

The history of Russian Tsardom reveals a strange alternation between terrifying realists and fantastic eccentrics, and a case could be made for the unbalanced rulers showing deeper insight into their country's needs that the sane. Catherine II, who died in 1796, was a realist. She had played with constitutionalism, but in fact had established her autocratic power by conciliating the nobility at the expense of the serfs. Her reign brought to its harsh and logical conclusion the alliance between the crown and the gentry which had been developing throughout the eighteenth century. Once the iron hand of Peter the Great had been removed, the first half of his formula—that the nobles serve the State and the peasants serve the nobles—was abandoned. Under Anne, it was the gentry who saved the autocracy by defeating the designs of the great aristocrats for oligarchical government: the monarchy rewarded them by a series of concessions, culminating in Peter III's abolition of the obligation of State service altogether. Catherine II accepted and improved upon this lesson taught by her mad husband, and in her reign the compact between the autocracy and the provincial nobles was sealed—at the expense of the rural masses of Russia. The terrors of Pugachev's rebellion came to bind together the monarch and the serf-owners; the news of the French Revolution confirmed their mutual fears, and Catherine's reign ended in black reaction.

From her death to the accession of Nicholas I, another harsh realist, in 1825, Russia was ruled by two men of fantasy, Paul I (1796–1801) and Alexander I (1801–25).

Paul is commonly spoken of as mentally deranged, though the instances cited as proof arouse sympathy—some of us might envy a despot who threw jam tarts at people he disliked and forbade new-fashioned dances; others might concede that the despatch of a force of Cossacks to conquer India (while England had other pre-occupations) was far from foolish; his proposal that all European rulers and their foreign ministers should settle disputes by single combat in an arena was as good a device for ending war as many of the more complicated ones subsequently invented.

164

More significantly, with the instinctive sympathy of the mentally deficient towards the socially disinherited, the Tsar Paul took reckless action on behalf of the peasant. Radischchev in *A Journey from Saint Petersburg to Moscow* (1790), had described in grim terms the lot of the people. 'Have you no time to work in the week then?' he had asked a peasant whom he found ploughing on a Sunday. 'In the week, sir, there are six days, and we go six times a week to work on the master's fields; in the evenings, if the weather is good, we haul to the master's house the hay that is left in the woods. . . .'

'But how do you manage to get food enough, if you have only the holidays free?'

'Not only the holidays: the nights are ours too. If a fellow isn't lazy, he won't starve to death.'[1]

Perhaps the new Tsar was aware of this passage. Certainly, he released Radischchev from prison, gave him official employment, and published a decree forbidding the lords to work their serfs on Sundays, and limiting the *barschina* (forced labour) to three days a week. The reform caused unrest in the countryside, but it was so obviously necessary that it endured. As for the poor mad Tsar, within four years he had been assassinated, and ridicule accumulated round his memory.

II

Alexander I, it seems, had been implicated in the conspiracy that destroyed his father. 'This ineffaceable stain', says Czartoryski, one of his closest friends, '. . . settled like a vulture on his conscience, paralysed his best abilities . . . and plunged him into a mysticism sometimes degenerating into superstition.'[2] From his grandmother Catherine II, and from his father, Alexander inherited the blind self-willed determination of the autocrat; at the same time, from Catherine and the tutors she had employed, he had picked up the jargon of liberalism, and from Paul he had inherited an act of mad generosity which he felt he must emulate. Here was a despot who spoke continually of constitutions and told Napoleon that hereditary right was an abuse, but who also had a pathological fear of losing the merest rag of his power; a warlord who vacillated between the duty of freeing the world from tyranny and the preoccupation of annexing as much as he could for himself. This was Byron's

'. . . Coxcomb Tsar,
The autocrat of waltzes and of war . . .

---

[1] A. N. Radischchev, *A Journey from St Petersburg to Moscow* (trans. L. Wiener, ed. R. P. Thales, 1958), p. 47.

[2] Czartoryski's *Memoirs*, cit. M. Kukiel, *Czartoryski and European Unity, 1770–1861* (1955), p. 24.

> With no objection to true Liberty
> Except that it would make the nations free.'[3]

Alexander was, indeed, a man divided against himself and, essentially an exhibitionist, he was unable to settle his conflicts secretly, within his own mind. With all his goodwill and perversity, he needed, more than most rulers, the guidance of a minister who would impose consistency upon his policies; but as Speransky, the ablest of his advisers confessed, he was 'too weak to rule and too strong to be ruled'.

The reign began with reforms directed by a cabal of enlightened aristocrats around the Tsar; the chief were Prince Adam Czartoryski, a Polish nationalist who had been brought up as an hostage at the Russian court, a close friend of Alexander and a much too close friend of his Empress, and Count Paul Stroganov, the richest noble in Russia, who had seen the early days of the French Revolution and had joined the Jacobin Club in Paris. To some extent, the reforms were merely the ephemeral changes which Russian autocrats usually had to make to gear the creaking administrative machine to their personal will. What was genuinely new and constructive was the attempt to develop education as the basis of further progress. The chief emphasis was on the extension of facilities at the top—the creation of new universities, of advanced centres of theological study, and of a *lycée* for scions of the royal family and the sons of great aristocrats. It was an attempt to form the administrators, experts and higher ecclesiastics who might be expected to co-operate with the liberal régime which the Tsar, half-sincerely, meant one day to institute.

As things were, coherent initiative in Russia could come only from the autocracy, and the execution of such designs must depend simply on the blind obedience of the army and such incompetent compliance as could be extracted from the bureaucracy. That was why the Tsar was all-powerful, and that was why his power was so ineffective. The attempt, in November 1806, to call out a militia for national defence proved to be a dangerous farce—it required qualities of independence and social virtues which were not to be found in Russia. In a memorandum four years earlier, Speransky, a brilliant young civil servant, had declared that there were 'only two estates in Russia: the slaves of the Sovereign and the slaves of the landlord. The former are called free in relation to the latter; but in fact there are no free men in Russia, except beggars and philosophers.'[4] The government, he argued, must create a class of educated 'mediators', who would

[3] Byron, *The Age of Bronze* (*Works*, ed. E. H. Coleridge, 1905) V, pp. 563–4.
[4] M. Raeff, *Michael Speransky: Statesman of Imperial Russia, 1772–1839* (1957), pp. 121–2.

inform the throne of the people's needs and steer its policies towards the abolition of serfdom.

Six years later, Alexander called on Speransky to undertake the direction of the next stage of the reforming movement, and it looked as if the wayward Tsar had at last found the minister who could give consistency to his projects.

III

To a later generation, Speransky's name was to become synonymous with moderate liberalism and constitutionalism. Yet essentially, he was a pliable bureaucrat, out of touch with both aristocracy and people, and content to serve a despotic government, provided it was enlightened. He did not wish to limit the power of the Tsar, but to make logical and predictable the relations of subjects to the State and to each other. Precise legislation consolidated into an unambiguous code, impartial justice working through the jury system, the career open to talents and machinery for providing the autocrat with good advice, were the sum of his intentions.

Speransky's tenure of power lasted for four years. In this brief period, he contrived to make a few significant changes. An enlarged State Council became the Sovereign's advisory body for legislation, and the new institution of ministries under a single head was given a pattern of organization which remained unchanged until the beginning of the twentieth century. No direct attack was made on serfdom, but another of its glaring abuses was corrected: the sale of serfs as substitutes for army recruits, which had gone on in spite of previous legislation, was now virtually brought to an end.

But this was all. The logically articulated society Speransky hoped to create remained as far off as ever. To a degree, his plans had been unreasonable: the chaos of Russian law was not to be sorted out in a few years by experts fishing around for fragments that would fit into the Napoleonic Code. Another reason for his failure was the desperate state of the finances, weighed down by the debts of Catherine II and by Alexander's vast expenditure on warlike preparations. By the time Napoleon was defeated, the paper currency which Catherine had instituted had fallen to one-fifth of its original value. Speransky would have used the crisis as an excuse for further measures of reform —for selling State domains to the peasants and replacing the salt and alcohol monopolies by a land tax, fairly based on the wealth of the countryside. But these proposals brought down on him the wrath of the nobility, who had no desire for fair taxation, and who were finding inflation a profitable experience.

Here, in the uncompromising hostility of the nobility, lay the final reason for Speransky's fall. His schemes represented a reformed, bureaucratic version of autocracy in which the interests of the gentry would be sacrificed. Eventually, the serfs would be freed, and the privilege of service in the higher ranks of army and administration, the great support of younger sons, would be awarded to talent alone. The proposal of 1809, to institute examinations as a test for higher promotion, was greeted by the nobility with incredulous rage. Magistrates and administrators, said Karamzin, would have to recite Homer and Theocritus, and know the properties of oxygen. Nothing could be more unreasonable than this, and the court was full of rumours that so desperate an egalitarian minister must surely be a masonic conspirator. The Tsar was warned of his danger by his sister, the Grand Duchess Catherine, by Joseph de Maistre, the Sardinian ambassador (whose name was to be famous in the annals of conservatism), and by agents of the French *émigrés*. When Napoleon began mustering armies for a march on Russia, Alexander decided that his safest course was to fall back upon the well-tried old social compact with the privileged classes, and Speransky was sent into honourable exile.

IV

A palace intrigue against a reforming minister was an ordinary occurrence in Imperial Russia; in this case, however, the activities of the Grand Duchess Catherine have proved singularly illuminating, for she called on Karamzin, the great historian, to produce a memoir for the instruction of the Tsar. Karamzin, a noble of middling fortune, had travelled in Western Europe and had seen for himself the beginnings of revolution in France. Though he believed in cultural liberty, he considered that 'civil order is sacred', and that time alone can bring changes for the better. As a patriot, he had come to regret the frantic passion for westernization associated with the memory of Peter the Great, and he feared equally the western notions of liberal constitutionalism and of bureaucratic egalitarian efficiency. Speransky's attempt to codify the law was a transplantation to the Russian scene of alien French ideas, at once pedantic and revolutionary. Why should we 'bow our grey heads to a book pasted together in Paris by six or seven ex-lawyers and ex-Jacobins?' In his *Memoir on Ancient and Modern Russia*, Karamzin defended what he regarded as the traditional Russian form of autocracy which, he claimed, bore some resemblance to the aristocratic polity of Montesquieu. The monarch legislated, but in due form and mindful of precedent; the higher posts of army and administration were reserved for the gentry, whose loyalty sustained the throne. 'The gentry and the clergy, the Senate and the Synods as repositories of laws; over all—the Sovereign, the only legislator, the autocratic source of authority: this is the foundation of the Russian monarchy.'[5]

The gentry supported the Crown, and they in their turn were supported by the serfs: it followed that the Crown itself was at stake if any attempt was made to set the peasants free. In any case, the bureaucracy could not hope to rule the countryside: only a traditional, universal mesh of social custom—as serfdom was—could entrap the blind forces stirring in the mysterious underworld of rural Russia. Emancipation would mean nothing to the serfs without the land, and Karamzin tacitly assumed that there was no question of giving it to them. The peasants would have to buy their freedom: those on the estates of generous landlords would not wish to do so, and those on the estates of grasping ones would be too poor anyway. And, once freedom had been obtained, the former serfs would sink back into misery through drink and litigation, the miseries of freedom. It would be far better, Karamzin argued, for the autocracy to exert its full powers, and encourage the gentry to use theirs. Let the serfs be kept virtuous by restoring the old threat of recruitment into the army: let the nobles be constrained to be just by the ruthless intervention of the Tsar's provincial governors.

This *Memoir* is an intelligent summary of the ethical and political principles of the forces of reaction in Russia. Its modern editor emphasizes that its 'ideology' of 'gentry conservatism . . . supplied the monarchy with a new set of aims to take the place of that liberal, pro-western programme which it had hitherto espoused. Basically, this programme was the same as that with which the monarchy was to go to its grave a hundred years later.'[6] One ought to add that the westernizing programme which had haunted the Tsars ever since Peter the Great had, up to the French Revolution, been associated more particularly with the leadership of enlightened despotism. Now, however, the liberalism of the West meant constitutionalism and, increasingly, middle-class rule and freedom of opinion. No Russian autocrat had ever believed in these.

V

After Speransky's departure, Alexander's reign sank into reactionary twilight, lit by fitful gleams of the old reforming enthusiasm. While

[5] R. Pipes, *Karamzin's Memoir on Ancient and Modern Russia* (1959), p. 204.
[6] Ibid., p. 21.

the censorship stifled political discussion in the press and the universities, a federal constitution for Russia was devised—and duly pigeonholed. Poland actually was given a constitution, which the Tsar did not observe:

> 'How nobly gave he back the Poles their Diet
> Then told pugnacious Poland to be quiet.'

Another abuse of serfdom was abolished in 1822, when the sale of peasants without land was forbidden. Yet the government itself ignored this principle in Esthonia, Courland and Livonia: here, the serfs, at the request of the nobles, were emancipated without land, a fate which Karamzin had described as worse than bondage. Meanwhile, the odious device of 'military colonies' was creating a new kind of slavery, sponsored by the State. For this sinister invention, the Tsar himself was to blame. General Arakcheev, who supervised the system and has often been held responsible for its brutalities, did in fact recommend its abolition as uneconomical; his own proposal was to devote the profits of the vodka monopoly to buying up private estates and freeing their serfs, an emancipation process which would expand automatically, borne on the self-supporting cycle of alcohol and liberty.

Yet, while reaction triumphed, men remembered that the Tsar himself had once believed in freedom. On hearing of a conspiracy, Alexander instinctively turned to self-inculpation: 'I shared and encouraged these illusions.' This was in 1821 when, at the age of forty-four, he was out of touch with the younger generation of army officers and intellectuals. Griboyedov's play, 'Tis Folly to be Wise (written in 1823, though not performed until 1831), portrayed the conflict between the servile, corrupt older set and the brash young people, with their carping criticism, justified, but useless. It is significant that the central figure, Chatsky, the 'superfluous man', the intelligent critic who has no real point of contact with Russian society, is depicted as newly returned to Moscow after a long stay abroad. As hopes of freedom declined in Russia, those who were young looked to western horizons, to England with its immemorial constitution and Byron, to France with its Charter and Saint-Simon. Many young Guards officers had seen western Europe in the campaigns of 1812–14; they had lived in Paris, had read Rousseau to understand the ideals of the Revolution, had called on Mme de Staël, Benjamin Constant, Sieyès and Saint-Simon, had been dazzled by the rich complexity of occidental civilization and its instinctive swing towards the magnetic pole of freedom.

Now they were dissatisfied: with themselves, as petty serf-owners and as officers ruling over brutalized conscripts, with their country in its bleak ignorance and crudity, with their reactionary Tsar and his cheap parade of nobler feelings. Among these army officers, two linked conspiratorial societies formed, the moderate Northern Society in St Petersburg, and the Southern Society under Colonel Pestel, a republican extremist. Both groups wished to abolish serfdom, but while the northern conspirators wanted constitutional monarchy, a free press and religious toleration, the southern ones proposed to assassinate the royal family and set up a republican dictatorship, intolerant in religion and ruthlessly centralized in administration.

The plotters' influence was confined to a limited section of the army, and it is probable that little would have been heard of them but for the sudden death of Alexander I, followed by some weeks of confusion about the succession to the throne. Possibly Alexander really did die on 1 December 1825 or, possibly, as 'Fedor Kousmitch' he vanished into Siberia to brood over his mad, dead father and the wasted years of empire. Whatever the truth, his brothers Constantine and Nicholas were unprepared, and vacillated, offering each other the throne (Constantine was the elder, but had renounced his claims earlier). During this disastrous confusion, the 'Decembrist' revolt flared out—and was as quickly suppressed. The Decembrists might have influenced the succession to the throne: they could not possibly have changed Russian society. Their desire to free the serfs was incomprehensible to their contemporaries. 'I can understand the French bourgeois bringing about the Revolution to get rights,' said the military governor of Moscow, 'but how am I to comprehend the Russian nobleman making a revolution to lose them?'[7] The peasants, a police spy reported, heard the news of the suppression of their would-be emancipators and said, 'They have begun to hang the masters.'

Yet the December conspiracy had an influence out of all proportion to its scale and chances of success. Its romance, ideals and tragedy stirred the men of letters—Pushkin, Griboyedov, the poet Ryleyev. Young Gogol passed out of school in 1828 with top marks, but was put in a lower grade of the public service than his results had earned, because of his association with masters who admired the Decembrists. At the age of fourteen, Alexander Herzen swore to devote his life to the Decembrist cause. The plotters of 1825 had no real successors, yet Lenin was to hail them as ancestors. A sort of inhibition had been broken. From now onwards, the police expect to encounter subversive machinations. Faced with an attack whose inspiration was idealistic, which was neither a palace revolution nor a serf revolt, the

[7] J. H. Billington, *Mikhailovsky and Russian Populism* (1958), p. v.

autocracy faltered. Always on Nicholas I's desk was the richly bound book containing the list of the 570 involved in the Decembrist movement and the other volume containing the summary of the reforms they had desired. In 1828, he recalled one of the condemned from Siberia to write a memorandum explaining what his motives had been. The new Tsar never forgot the scene on the frozen Senate Square in St Petersburg, in the shadow of Falconnet's gigantic bronze statue of Peter the Great—the crowds of demonstrating soldiers and the cannon fire: 'Emperor, at the price of my subjects' blood.' Nor did he ever forget that even the privileged servants of the Crown had conspired against it. There was no one left to trust. The autocracy became more ruthless: ruthless from fear and from an evil conscience.

VI

'A sovereign has no right to pardon the enemies of the State,' Nicholas I had written in an essay of schoolboy days. He never did. Even Russian opinion was appalled by this Tsar who interrogated the Decembrists himself, who understood their ideals, and who nevertheless exacted ruthless punishment. The officer who was brought back from Siberia to prepare a memorandum on the rising, was kept in jail for another four years, then sent to serve as a private in the army. The Tsar's enemies admitted that he was just: what friends he had could not deny that he was merciless.

The third son of Paul, Nicholas had not been expected to succeed to the throne. He had therefore heard a lot of gossip which would have otherwise been concealed from him, and which was now stored up in his memory as a confirmation of his suspicious and gloomy view of human nature. Since his great destiny had come upon him unawares, he believed that it had been the result of a more particular intervention of Providence than that which had conferred divine right upon the Romanov dynasty generally. Too little confidence in man and too much confidence in God formed a fearful combination. In his most brutal actions, Nicholas could conscientiously invoke the Deity. After going in person to the scene of a mutiny and ordering 2,600 rebels to be forced to run the gauntlet (so that 129 of them died), he said, 'God rewarded me for my journey to Novgorod.' Clearly, God had not rewarded anyone else.

There was thus something peculiarly sinister about this Russian Tsar, convinced of divine favour, charming and devoted in family life, an enthusiast for ballet, and the handsomest man in Europe, yet with a soul that pity could not touch. To enlightened opinion of the day he was 'Nicholas the Flogger', with 'eyes as cold as winter'. Yet there was no sadism in him; only harsh devotion to what he thought was duty and, perhaps, something of his father's madness. Married to an Hohenzollern princess and bound in ties of friendship with her family, Nicholas took the Prussian tradition of State service and military discipline as his ideal. 'I consider the whole of human life as service to the State': he required this standard from his subjects and lived up to it himself. Without desiring war, he loved the parade, precision and ruthlessness of armies. He always wore military uniform, and drilled his Household Guard himself with a thunderous voice. Every sector of life where his personal intervention was felt was afflicted by his Midas touch of useless order and was reduced to regimented farce. Smoking was forbidden in the streets of the capital; a royal portrait was sent back to the artist because of a single missing button; only soldiers were allowed moustaches, and these had to be black, dyed if necessary.

And yet, amidst his glittering surroundings and the servility which his imperious nature demanded, Nicholas remained immune from the temptations of personal vain-glory. In the Winter Palace (which he rebuilt, after a fire, on a vast scale) he lived in a single room, decorated with a few portraits and the ikon Peter the Great had at Poltava. Like Peter, he moved easily and courageously among the ordinary people, whom he was prepared to assist with his own hands —or send to jail—on the slightest provocation. Life for him consisted of duty, and greatness was a burden. Queen Victoria described him, in her peculiar fashion, with remarkable insight (this was after his visit to England in 1844). 'The Tsar Nicholas is stern and severe— with fixed principles of duty which nothing on earth will make him change; very *clever* I do not think him, and his mind is an uncivilized one . . . but he is *sincere* even in his most despotic acts, from a sense that that is the *only* way to govern. . . . He is *not* happy, and that melancholy which is visible in the countenance made me sad at times.'[8]

VII

Nicholas I was not an out and out reactionary. In certain respects he was keenly aware of the need for reform. His reign began with the dismissal of Arakheev and the mad monk Photius who had encouraged the illiberal policies of Alexander's later years; in their place, he recalled Speransky, and set the reforming General Kiselev to work devising measures to improve the lot of the serfs. Had he ruled two

[8] Queen Victoria, *Correspondence* (ed. A. C. Benson and Visc. Esher, 1908) II, p. 14.

generations earlier, Nicholas would have qualified as a respectable member of the clan of 'Enlightened Despots'.

With all this, however, Nicholas was essentially a man of order, ruthless order, and a fanatical believer in his own autocracy; it is this aspect of his reign which is remembered and which influenced the future. Uvarov, his Minister of Education, summarized the official theory of social organization when he declared—'Political religion, just as Christian religion, has its inviolable dogmas; in our case they are: autocracy and serfdom.' Why serfdom?—he went on to say that the peasants had to be kept in bondage to satisfy the gentry, lest they 'start looking for compensations, and there is nowhere to look except in the domain of the autocracy.'[9] Gogol, who joined the conservative camp in 1847, put the case for authoritarian rule more subtly—'The law is wooden . . . we need supreme grace to mitigate the law, and it can come to men only in the form of absolute power.'[10]

But it is doubtful if Nicholas thought of his duties in terms of the mystique of a political religion or of supreme grace; with his complete distrust of human nature, he felt called by God in a grim utilitarian way as a wielder of force upon recalcitrant and selfish slaves. He had no urge to awaken the interest of his subjects or to seek their advice: projects of reform were considered by secret committees with fraudulent names, so that public opinion, baffled, could have no chance to join in the discussion. A committee on the serf question, for example, was apparently dealing with 'the equalization of local government dues and charges in the western provinces'. For the whole vast bureaucracy, the Tsar had open contempt, from the Senate downwards. Surprise has sometimes been expressed that he attended the first performance of *The Government Inspector* in April 1836, and laughed at the portrayal of the corruption and shifty, greasy confusion of provincial officialdom; but the Tsar, no less than Gogol knew all this, hated it all, and was glad to see it pilloried. Wherever he could, he broke through the cadres of bureaucratic routine by emergency interventions. His Majesty's Private Imperial Chancery was expanded as a direct agent of the Sovereign's will, and army officers were seconded to act as special emissaries, or to direct the Post Office, preside over the Holy Synod or (possibly more incongruous still) to run the navy.

One new branch of the Private Chancery which Nicholas created was the notorious 'Third Section'. Russia had long been a land of spies, informers and brutal interrogations, but so far there had been

---

[9] N. V. Riasanovsky, *Nicholas I and Official Nationality in Russia, 1825–1855* (1959), p. 140.

[10] N. V. Gogol, *Letters to Friends* (1847).

no political police in the strict sense of the term. Alexander had been impressed by the efficiency of the Austrian system at the time of the Congress of Vienna, and had introduced its methods into the army; it was left for Nicholas to set up the independent organization. The result was rather comic and very Russian. General Benckendorff, the head of the new Third Section, was a brainless, humane courtier who used his position to extract dignified formal bribes from commercial firms. As for a 'secret police', he regarded such a thing as 'unthinkable; honourable people would be afraid of it, and scoundrels adapt themselves to it easily'. 'I liked you as a man of talent: now I respect you as a man of honour,'[11] said this amateur police chief to a vaudeville actor who refused his request to insert lines in praise of the monarchy into his script. The terrible brutalities of the Russian repressive system went on, but the new organization formed to ferret out conspiracies kept its hands fairly clean; it was, said Mérimée, 'the Inquisition in a pink peignoir'.

In one form or another, however, under Nicholas the inquisition prevailed. Jews and Old Believers (schismatics from Orthodoxy) were persecuted. The government controlled the universities, reviewing lecture courses and limiting enrolments (with the especial object of excluding non-noble students). The censorship had its agents in every department, and in 1848, the Buturlin Committee was created, to censor the censors. Subversive passages were unearthed in the prayers of the Orthodox Church, atheistic expressions like 'the forces of nature' were expunged from physics books, and poets who confessed that their mistresses held sovereign sway in their hearts were reminded that 'no law-abiding citizen ought to put anything above God and the Emperor'.[12]

VIII

Why was it that this age of unintelligent repression was a golden age of Russian literature? The resplendent totalitarian Tsar patronized music, for melody has no political bias, but the written word could be dangerous, and he discouraged its practitioners. Even Pushkin, at a time when he was being officially favoured, found himself urged to rewrite *Boris Godunov* as a novel 'in the manner of Walter Scott'.

Herzen suggested that the educated men of his generation turned to the inner realm of the spirit to escape the world around them—'We devoted ourselves to science, philosophy, love, the art of war, mysticism, to forget the overwhelming emptiness of existence.' It could be,

[11] S. Monas, *The Third Section: Police and Society under Nicholas I* (1961), p. 96.
[12] M. L. Slonim, *The Epic of Russian Literature* (1950), p. 126.

however, that great literature and political repression ran their parallel courses by mere coincidence, the autonomous working of cultural evolution bringing together the mannered style of the eighteenth century, derived from foreign influences, the new influence of Byron, and the folklore and traditions of a more distant, Russian past, in readiness for the advent of Pushkin's genius. Whatever the reason, this was a brilliant age, and it also prepared the way for the even greater age to follow. An educated public assimilated George Sand, Balzac and Stendhal and looked for their Russian counterparts; Lermontov in character drawing, Gogol in satirical burlesque and Goncharov in comic realism perfected the techniques of the novelist; before Nicholas died, Turgenev, Dostoievsky and Tolstoy had each published a first work.

By a sort of tacit consent, historians allow that a great age in cultural development sheds lustre upon the political régime of the time. But in this case, the conclusion is reversed, and when everything else about the government of Nicholas I is forgotten, it will be remembered for the part its folly and cruelty played in the lives of authors. Chadayev was certified insane and locked up. Pushkin was followed everywhere by police spies and there were more police than friends at his funeral. 'Pushkin died in the middle of a great career,' said the Minister of Education with regard to these obsequies, 'What *was* this career of his?' And, above all, there was the infamous scene of 22 December 1849, on the ice-bound Semenovsky Place, when the white-shrouded, blindfolded prisoners waited on the scaffold, not knowing that their sentence had been commuted. It was thus that Dostoievsky escaped an even more ruthless form of official obituary.

IX

'Autocracy and serfdom' were Uvarov's inviolable dogmas. The compact between the monarchy and the serf-owners which Catherine II had ratified, which the mad Tsar Paul had threatened to break, and for which Karamzin had provided historical and theoretical justification, was the foundation of the social order. Nicholas I believed that this was so, but he also knew that desperate reforms were necessary. Before considering his attitude, however, let us ask what sort of social order this was which the alliance of autocracy and nobility was preserving.

The strange world which the institution of serfdom made possible is an infinite distance away from us today, but we can still revisit it in the brilliant writings of 'conscience-stricken' noblemen, who described it with a blend of bitterness and sympathy, with the nostalgia of exiles and the wrath of reformers. Prince Kropotkin[13] remembered growing up in a fashionable Moscow suburb in the 'forties—the great sledges gliding over the snow, the sumptuous carriages, the brilliantly lighted windows, a footman behind every chair at dinner and an orchestra—of household serfs—playing. His father, owner of 1,200 'souls' (i.e., male serfs) regarded himself as a just man because he never sold his people to strangers. He kept his fifty domestics in order, however, by the threat of conscription into the army; for minor offences, like breaking plates, a flogging would be inflicted, either at the police station, or at fire-brigade headquarters. On these occasions there would be a great silence upon the house, and the children would go round with haunted faces. Once, when the butler was flogged, young Kropotkin tried to console him: 'Leave me alone,' said the victim, 'you too when you are grown up, will you not be just the same?' At worst, there was cruelty: at best, there was an insufferably patriarchal atmosphere. Herzen[14] describes how, on the eve of Ash Wednesday, all the servants had to appear before his father:

> 'Who is that decent old man standing in that corner?'
> 'Danilo the coachman.'
> 'Dear dear, how changed he is! I really believe it is drinking too much that ages them so fast. . . . Well Danilo, God in his mercy has permitted me to meet you yet another year. I pardon all your offences . . . your waste of my oats and your neglect of my horses; and you must pardon me. . . . And now that Lent is beginning, I advise you to take rather less spirits: at our years it is bad for the health, and the Church forbids it.'

Most serfs, however, lived far from the range of these compulsions and civilities, tilling the soil in fearful poverty under the control of the village community, and paying the lord his dues in money, kind or labour. For these (and numerically speaking, they virtually constituted Russia) Turgenev's *Sportsman's Notebook* is a permanent memorial. These famous essays, written mostly in Paris from 1848–50, and published in St Petersburg in 1852, had an impact upon enlightened opinion comparable with *Uncle Tom's Cabin* in America. Yet, though one motive for writing them was to atone for the cruelties of the author's mother towards her peasants, the sketches were not crude propaganda. Harassed by grasping bailiffs and degraded by the contempt of the landowners, the peasants are revealed, not primarily

[13] P. A. Kropotkin, *Memoirs of a Revolutionist* (2 vols., 1899) I, pp. 32–5, 58–59.
[14] A. Herzen, *Memoirs* (trans. J. D. Duff, 1923), pp. 110–11.

as victims of shocking oppression, but as simple, good-natured human beings, deserving of treatment as men. And this does not mean being patronized by reforming enthusiasts. Ovayanskov the freeholder remembers the 'good old days' when the lord took some of his father's land and flogged him for protesting, but he is still not happy with the younger gentry, who repudiate these old ways, but 'treat the peasant like a doll: they turn him this way and that, they break him and throw him away. And the agent, who is a serf, or the bailiff, who is of German origin, gets the peasant into his clutches once more.'[15]

There were other serfs, neither house servants nor peasants, and their lot was worst of all. These were serfs employed in industrial undertakings. Of them, it is enough to say that misery bred an ignorance and lack of initiative which ensured that factory owners would not increase their numbers, for experience had shown that free, paid labour was more profitable than unfree. By the 'forties, the iron and woollen cloth industries, which retained servile labour, were declining, in spite of high tariff protection, while cotton factories were developing, without special privileges, and using wage labour only.

In theory, given the connivance of his master, a serf could become rich, and a peculiar and rare phenomenon in some areas of Russia was the rise of serf industrialists, who built factories and bought 'souls' to work in them, all in the name of their lord. It was a profitable business for the lord, who drew heavy fines from the profits and retained the permanent ownership of the factories, as well as exacting huge indemnities when the time came for a serf to ask to buy his freedom. A crafty noble might refuse to ransom one of the family, so as to qualify for another slice of the industrialist's profit at a later date.

The fantastic injustice of these arrangements is a revelation of the total subjection which serfdom implied. One is reminded of Kropotkin's story of his father blandly accepting the Cross of St Anne for himself because his batman saved a child from a burning house— 'Was he not my man? It is all the same.' There was no reciprocity in serfdom: the serf existed for his master's convenience. If the peasant question had simply been one of cruel lords abusing their authority, Karamazin's remedy—ruthless protective intervention by the Tsar's governors—might have brought peace. But Turgenev, Kropotkin and Herzen emphasize, by implication, that serfdom, whether well administered or not, treats men as less than human. The Third Section hit upon this truth when engaged in analysing the information about the rising tide of riot and discontent over rural Russia: in 1834, Benckendorff gave the Tsar a report which ought to have rendered all further

[15] Turgenev, *A Sportsman's Notebook* (trans. C. and N. Hepburn, 1950), p. 72.

reports unnecessary. 'Every year the idea of freedom spreads'; this insubordination, he said, is not a result of ill-treatment, but 'purely from the idea of obtaining the right to freedom'.

X

'Serfdom is a powder cellar under the State', Nicholas I wrote in the margin of a police report: he knew that he must act before the explosion came from below. This was in 1839, and during the next decade, peasant disturbances intensified. Rumours swept the countryside that the Tsar was at last to free his people from the yoke of the nobility. This yoke was appearing heavier, for in some areas, a sort of 'feudal reaction' was in progress. From the second half of the eighteenth century, serf-owners whose estates were near to extensive markets, like Moscow, had been increasing their demands for forced labour, rather than money dues. After 1840, there was a great increase in the export of grain, and the advent of railways seemed to open up vast possibilities for estate owners who were willing to adopt the techniques of capitalist agriculture. Thus, the greater or more strategically placed landlords intensified labour demands because of hopes of expansion; at the same time, the lesser serf-owners clung to their rights simply to survive. By 1843, more than half the demesnes of Russia were mortgaged to State credit institutions; some small landowners were having to sell out, and those who remained could not afford to be generous to their peasants. Count Tolstoy, a conscience-striken nobleman, offered his serfs their freedom on the hire purchase system for a sum that would simply cover his mortgage. They found it too expensive. 'Went to the peasants,' his diary recorded on 4 June 1856, 'They don't want their freedom.'[16] They did, but they had reached the dangerous stage when they were not willing to pay for it.

Between an indebted nobility and an angry peasantry, what could be done? The question at issue in the end was—to whom does the land belong? Nicholas I accepted uncompromisingly the hypothesis of the nobles, that the land was theirs. Within this limitation, and granted his indifference to the idea of freedom, the Tsar did what he could to civilize the institution of serfdom. Under General Kiselev, the State peasants were given schools, medical services and enlarged

[16] Quoted by Stephen Graham, *Alexander II* (1935), p. 35. For the economic background of serfdom see P. I. Lyashchenko, *History of the National Economy of Russia* (1939, Engl. trans. 1949), and M. Confino, 'Problèmes agraires: le système des redevances mixtes dans les domaines privés en Russie', *Annales Économies, Sociétés, Civilisations* (Nov.-Dec. 1961), pp. 1066 ff. For the 'serf industrialists', R. Portal, 'Aux origines d'une bourgeoisie industrielle en Russie', *Rev. d'hist. mod. et contemp.* VIII (1961), pp. 35 ff.

plots of land, making them models for the rest of the nation. By a succession of decrees, it was forbidden to sell serfs apart from the land, or apart from their families, and at public auctions they were given the right to bid themselves for their land and freedom. But none of this would do. A government report of 1835 says—'The unfortunate idea, almost universally held among peasants on private estates, that they belong to the landlords but that the land belongs to them, is one of the fundamental obstacles standing in the way of ... introducing improvements in their conditions.'[17]

As the nobility declined, leaving the monarchy alone with its bureaucracy, army and police, the 'unfortunate idea' of the peasants came to mean much more. They believed that the soil of Russia was theirs, and to render homage to this conviction was the revolutionary weapon which could be used to overthrow the autocracy.

[17] F. Venturi, *Roots of Revolution* (trans. Francis Haskell, 1960), p. 61.

CHAPTER XII

RESTORATION, REVOLUTION AND SOCIAL THEORY IN FRANCE, 1815–1848

I

The life-span of the Bourbon Restoration was about the same as that of Napoleonic France. On 12 April 1814, the comte d'Artois rode into Paris to claim the throne on behalf of his brother Louis, and the *Moniteur* reported his superb epigram, '*rien n'y est changé, si ce n'est qu'il s'y trouve un français de plus*'—a pure fabrication by one of Talleyrand's hired journalists. Sixteen years later, the same Artois, now King Charles X, fled for the coast with a vast entourage packed into twelve state carriages: there were fifteen cooks and no provisions. According to ancient usage, the king ought not to dine at a round table, so when the party stopped at Laigle a table had to be sawn up to make it rectangular.[1] From the beginning to the end there was something artificial and contrived about the Restoration. France had never really wanted the Bourbons to return and the Bourbons had not wanted to return on the terms they accepted. Charles X had sworn that he would 'rather saw wood than rule like a King of England'; his determination did not cost him so much, though in the end, at Laigle, his courtiers had to saw a table .

Why had the Bourbons been brought back? The royalists had little support. According to Joseph de Maistre, in 1812 the old dynasty was as unknown as the Ptolemies. Realizing this, the Allies intended to leave the responsibility for the final decision to the French themselves. But what was the alternative? Napoleon was out of the question, even if the Allies would have accepted him. 'He must be brought down,' Talleyrand had told the marquise de Coigny in November 1812, 'no matter how. . . . He has destroyed equality, that's good; but we must hang on to liberty, we must have laws; with him that is impossible.'[2] Conceivably, a Regency might have been devised, but the Emperor's intransigeance and Talleyrand's crafty handling of the revolutionary patriarchs in the Senate and of the invading Tsar ensured that this dubious solution was never tried. So the first

---

[1] Catherine Charlotte, Lady Jackson, *The Court of the Tuileries* (1883) II, p. 350; F. C. Sieburg, *Chateaubriand* (Engl. trans. 1961), p. 307.
[2] Lacour-Gayet, *Talleyrand*, II (1930), pp. 314–15.

Restoration was sponsored by Talleyrand, serving his ambitions by taking the credit for facilitating the uninspiring obvious.

It is important to remember, however, that the Bourbons were brought back twice, with little glory after Leipzig and with none at all after Waterloo. The second Restoration, after the Hundred Days, was Fouché's work, a 'job' contrived by Napoleon's regicide Police Minister, who was rewarded by being continued in the same office by the King. When, on 6 July 1815 Talleyrand presented Fouché at court, 'vice supported by crime', the bankruptcy of the Revolution and of Legitimacy were simultaneously evident: both Carnot and Chateaubriand were in despair.[3] This time, the Bourbons really had come back in the baggage train of the Allies. When the King returned the first time there had been 'neither victors nor vanquished'. Now there was a proscription list drawn up by Fouché ('he has forgotten none of his friends,' said Talleyrand); a White Terror raged in the South; Marshal Ney was shot. The Allies imposed harsher peace terms, which constituted a public avowal of the fact that the French people's affections were with the house of Bonaparte.

The contrast between the greatest soldier of modern times and Louis XVIII could hardly have been sharper. Chateaubriand saw the Imperial Guard present arms to the new King when he entered Paris, an old, red-faced, lame and bloated figure, 'an invalid of time, not war', passing in review the soldiers who had marched into every capital in Europe. 'I do not think that human faces can ever have expressed such terrible emotions . . . they showed their teeth through their moustaches like tigers.'[4] Louis XVIII did what he could to play his rôle portenteously, taking refuge from ridicule behind a carefully-rehearsed, scatalogical wit and an exaggerated insistence upon ceremony (the story goes that once, when he fell down, he refused to be helped up except by the captain of the guard). But it was impossible now to reawake among Frenchmen the cult of majesty, for they had become accustomed to the more intoxicating worship of glory, soon to be revived in memory by the Legend of St Helena and the songs of Béranger.

One gift, however, the new monarch had, and it insured the dynasty for his life-time, that sense of realities which is often vouchsafed as compensation for physical weakness. So far as their material interests and immediate fears were concerned, he gave the respectable classes of France what they most wanted to retain from the conquests of the Revolution. The Charter of 1814 granted parliamentary control of taxation, individual and religious liberty, the security of tenure of

[3] L. Madelin, *Fouché*, pp. 485 ff.
[4] Chateaubriand, *Mémoires d'outre tombe* in Sieburg, op. cit., p. 188.

judges, the admissibility of all citizens to office (though the old and new nobility kept their titles); finally, and most important, the alienation of the *biens nationaux* was guaranteed 'irrevocable'. The royal concessions stopped short of true parliamentary government and a long way short of democracy: the ministers could not be overthrown by the Chambers, while only the 90,000 richest citizens could vote and only the 10,000 very richest were eligible as deputies. This surprised nobody. The sting of the Charter was in the foolish claim to inherit the old authority of the kings of the *ancien régime*, and the declaration that the constitutional provisions were 'voluntarily granted, conceded and prescribed to our subjects . . . in 1814, the *nineteenth* year of our reign'. Louis XVIII was too weary and cynical to do more than state this theory: when Charles X acted upon it, the dynasty was doomed.

II

With his gross dignity and senile passions, Louis XVIII is an unattractive figure. Yet, within his limitations, he served France well. He gave her internal peace under a thrifty administration, something that had not been seen for a quarter of a century. The notorious balcony story is probably untrue—how he stood there blowing kisses to the crowd and muttering 'scoundrels, Jacobins, monsters' under his breath—but it gives a fair impression of his policy: he knew how to separate his private opinions from his public conduct. His reign began with moderate ministries presided over by the duc de Richelieu and Decazes; the 'Ultras', the extreme royalists, were excluded from power. After 1820, however, the Right could no longer be kept at bay, and since the murder of the duc de Berry, Louis was more inclined to yield to them. Under Villèle as chief minister, the true 'royalist' Restoration seemed to have been achieved. For the first time, the army and public opinion showed enthusiasm for the White Flag, the result of a cheap military triumph engineered by Chateaubriand at the Foreign Office. Divisions under old imperial marshals, provisioned by a contractor of the Directory, marched into Madrid and settled the affairs of Spain, a country where Napoleon himself had failed. The elections of the spring of 1824 were a sweeping success for the royalists. The polls confirmed Stendhal's verdict, 'You cannot say that the Bourbons have been restored in France before the recent Spanish war.'[5]

But in its hour of triumph, the Right split. The years when they had been kept out of office, in spite of their parliamentary majority, still rankled with some royalists. '*Vive le Roi quand même*' they had

[5] Cit. G. de Bertier de Sauvigny, *La Restauration* (1955), p. 260.

learnt to say. Among these *frondeurs* were some like Chateaubriand, who had conceived a genuine desire for parliamentary government. Villèle monopolized power and was afraid of ability in others, a disastrous trait in a leader whose following was beginning to disintegrate. On Whit Sunday, 1824, Chateaubriand was called out of the Tuileries Chapel by a servant bearing his letter of dismissal. He immediately ordered four cabs and removed his possessions from the Ministry of Foreign Affairs. 'They have turned me out,' he said, 'as though I had stolen the King's clock off the mantlepiece.'[6]

Thus, when Louis XVIII died three months later, the most brilliant theorist and propagandist of the royalist side was in opposition, leading a schism which deprived Charles X of all the youth and enthusiasm of the right-wing cause. It is true that Chateaubriand could have brought the monarchy down more quickly by adventurism at the Foreign Office: to that extent, Villèle's mistake is understandable.

III

It is worth while pausing to analyse Chateaubriand's discontents, for they throw light on the essential weaknesses of the Restoration régime. He wanted the monarchy to do two things: to accept liberalism in politics, and to be liberal to its own supporters. 'Adopt the constitutional form of government openly . . .' he said, 'but entrust official posts only to royalists.' The second proviso arose from bitter personal experience. Chateaubriand had brilliant talents, he and his family had suffered during the Revolution, and he had taken the risk of writing a pamphlet on behalf of the Bourbons which was on the streets the day the Allies entered Paris. Yet all he was given was a minor embassy, and that was only because the duchesse de Duras pleaded his cause with Talleyrand. At Ghent, during the Hundred Days, he was given a higher post, then lost it at the second Restoration. This sort of thing was happening on every rung of the ladder. Returning functionaries of the crumbled Empire and returning émigrés competed with the stay-at-homes for office. Young men who had achieved rapid promotion in the revolutionary turmoils now blocked the way for the next young generation. Henri Beyle (the novelist Stendhal) had been Director-General of Reserve Supplies on the retreat from Moscow, living through an epic, he complained, in the company of people whose presence would have robbed the Colosseum of its grandeur;[7] in the character of Julien Sorel he depicted the ambitions of the generation which followed his own, still

---

[6] Sieburg, pp. 277–8.
[7] F. C. Green, *Stendhal* (1939), p. 103.

inspired, as he had been, by the Napoleonic mirage, but in a land where the horizons had contracted and society was closing its ranks against adventurers from below. An economical government had very few Civil Service posts to bestow—these were the days when a Foreign Ministry was run on a staff of eighty-eight and a Ministry of Education on rather fewer. The monarchy had not enough patronage to provide an outlet for even modest ambitions, and in France, said Mme de Staël, 'the First Article of the Declaration of the Rights of Man ... is the necessity for every Frenchman to occupy a public post'.[8]

It would be unjust to Chateaubriand, however, to suggest that the main reason for his feud with authority was self-interest or vanity. With passion and intelligence he really believed in the necessity 'to adopt the constitutional form of government openly', and his plea goes to the root of the failure of the Restoration. The monarchy needed a free press and parliamentary institutions to survive. Grudging compliance with the Charter was not enough: the King must make himself an integral part of a constitutional order. One might go further still and say that a *pays légal* of 90,000 electors was too narrow a foundation to support a dynasty. In his more imaginative moments, Villèle himself realized this, and speculated on the possibility of using the lower classes to annihilate the bourgeoisie in elections.[9] 'The list of the electors of Paris has just been published,' a royalist wrote in his diary in January 1824. 'They are all butchers, masons, lodging-house keepers, bakers, grocers. ... What a shame! If I had a licence as a stocking merchant I'd be an elector. I'm not, because I'm just an inspector of schools.'[10]

It is true, however, that a wider franchise would have had to be very much wider, for it is doubtful if the Crown had many supporters in the income bracket represented by school inspectors. The way to change would have been to put everything to the hazard and call on the peasant masses to support the throne. They were to do this again for a Bonaparte, but would they have done as much for a Bourbon?

IV

When Charles X came to the throne, the grim realities of the revolutionary and Napoleonic era were misting over in memory. Bonaparte dominated the horizon of the century, as Vesuvius the horizon of Naples: behind him lay the confused epoch of the prophets of liberty,

[8] G. de Bertier de Sauvigny, op. cit., p. 100.
[9] R. Rémond, *La Droite en France de 1815 à nos jours* (1954), pp. 36–7.
[10] G. de Bertier de Sauvigny, p. 399.

whose story was now being compiled to form the canon of an Old Testament of freedom. Thiers and Mignet had just published histories of the Revolution, in which they regretted the fatal chain of circumstances which had thrown France into the power of terrorists, and looked forward to the completion of the respectable revolution of the bourgeoisie, just as 1688 had completed the work of the Great Rebellion in England. By 1827, Frenchmen who had been twenty years of age and over in 1789 constituted only a ninth of the nation (the expectation of life was less in those days) and a quarter of those who had known the Empire were dead. The new generation knew the revolutionary chaos only at secondhand, and was willing to risk its recurrence to preserve the conquests of freedom.

Within three years, Charles X and Villèle had provided *prima facie* evidence of their intention to overturn these conquests and go back to the *ancien régime*. Not that they really thought they could do so. Charles, handsome, white-haired and dignified, had lived down a stormy youth and become a decent, obtuse old man who wanted his theoretical 'rights' without expecting to be able to make anything of them. He had himself crowned at Rheims with the ceremonies of the old monarchy. The omission of the oath against heresy and the presence of Napoleonic marshals bearing the insignia did nothing to reconcile public opinion to this anachronism. A law against sacrilege, prescribing the death penalty for theft of the sacred Host was another sensational gesture which pleased the few in proportion as it angered many. 'The religious hatred brought about by the Restoration,' said Tocqueville, was 'the chief cause of the downfall of the Bourbons.'[11] The law was never applied of course: its only victim was the dynasty. The inheritance legislation of 1826, designed to discourage the equal division among heirs which the Code Napoléon made normal practice, and the draconian press law of that year both had to be withdrawn because of the hostility of the Chamber of Peers. In the following April, when the King reviewed the National Guard of Paris (a conservative institution with a revolutionary pedigree), there were cheers for the Charter and shouts of 'Down with the Ministers, down with the Jesuits'. Villèle proceeded to dissolve the whole organization, to the chagrin of many stout citizens who had bought new uniforms specially. '*Habit à vendre, fusil à garder*,' said the wits.

These ill-judged proceedings were repudiated by many royalists. Chateaubriand and the liberally-minded opposed the sacrilege, succession and press laws, and complained of Villèle's delay in helping the Greeks against the Turks; some of the older generation retained the Voltairean spirit of the eighteenth century, and applauded a

11 *Memoir, Letters etc. of Alexis de Tocqueville* (1861) II, p. 12.

violent *Mémoire* of the tough, reactionary comte de Montlosier against the Jesuits and all their accomplices. In October 1827, Castellane noted in his journal, 'M. de Villèle has as many supporters . . . as the plague would have if it awarded government pensions.'[12]

Villèle fell; then, after a conciliatory interval, came the Ministry of Polignac, son of Marie Antoinette's old favourite, a name redolent of the *ancien régime*. Wages were falling and the price of bread was rising. The usual anthropomorphic explanations of economic crisis were current—'the King and the Jesuits force up the price of grain.'[13] Instead of providing food for the people, Charles and Polignac were supposed to be plotting the rebuilding of the Bastille and the abolition of the metric system. What they did do was to dissolve Parliament, lose the elections, then issue four ordinances (25 July 1830) ordering new elections on a narrower franchise, and establishing a strict press censorship. They knew they were playing for the highest stakes— 'life or death', said the King—yet they had made no military preparations. A protest of journalists and students, a Parisian uprising, the troops wavered and the era of the Bourbons was over.

V

'The trouble with this country is that there are too many people like you who imagine that there has been a revolution in France,' said Casimir Périer,[14] replying to a complaint that political life had been virtually unchanged by the substitution of the Orleanist for the Bourbon monarchy. The July Revolution had been undramatic. Nearly 2,000 Parisians had been killed, but disorder had been brief and unsensational. John Stuart Mill, writing from Paris in August, described the workers, amidst their dead, taking 'equal care of the soldiers who had opposed them and of the citizens who had aided them. Surrounded by every temptation that perfect licence could offer, not one excess was committed. Vast treasures passed through their hands untouched . . . these men were actually starving, and yet they would take no recompense.'[15] He might have added that no-one had any intention of giving them one. Disturbances in the provinces, caused by hard times, had not been directly linked with events in the capital. 'We despatched our revolution to the departments by coach,'

[12] G. de Bertier de Sauvigny, p. 333.

[13] D. H. Pinkney, 'A new look at the French Revolution of 1830', *Review of Politics*, XXIII (1961), p. 496.

[14] Gordon Wright, *France in Modern Times* (1960), p. 144.

[15] J. S. Mill, 'Letters on the French Revolution of 1830', *Victorian Studies*, I (2) (1957), p. 145.

said a contemporary, 'they had only to acknowledge the receipt.'[16] Such a tame revolution could hardly herald sensational changes. Lamartine, on his way out of the royalist camp now, and looking on events with the professional eye of a poet, regretted that the coup had lacked that 'breadth, exaltation and dignity appropriate to measures of desperation'.[17]

What then were the results? Under the new king, Louis Philippe of the house of Orleans, government proceeded in much the same old fashion. Ministers were still not responsible to the Chamber. By a law of March 1831, the electorate was expanded to a mere 166,000 (increasing wealth brought the total of voters to 241,000 within the next dozen years). The hereditary peerage became a nominated one. The National Guard was restored, its membership limited to direct tax payers who could afford the uniform. The new Charter of 1830 guaranteed freedom of the press, but a system of heavy fines and unfair court procedure became equivalent to a severe censorship, so that the editors of adventurous newspapers maintained bookings on special quarters in the Saint-Pélagie prison. Apart from Guizot's education law of 1833, no concern was shown for the common people. For most Frenchmen, 1830 was merely a change of dynasty.

We should beware, however, of that 'merely', for the change of dynasty was a startling one. The new King had fought at Valmy under the flag of the Convention, had ostentatiously accepted the new France, and sent his sons to study at ordinary *lycées*. The crown was awarded to him amid scenes of coarse familiarity—students tramping up and down his stairs and urchins charging passers-by for shouting him out on the balcony (extra to make him sing the Marseillaise), and his 'coronation' was a civil ceremony in the Chamber of Deputies —with, it is true, a salvo of 300 guns. Thereafter he went round armed with an umbrella. 'He is too complacent to the rage of equality,' said an English observer, 'and stoops more than he needs to; in fact he overdoes it.'[18] Clever, experienced and determined to play an effective rôle in politics, Louis Philippe none the less remained essentially a king by grace of revolution, who had inherited none of the mystique of the old monarchy. His high office was held on a contractual basis. France had not made a choice between two dynasties; it had got rid of one dynasty and then had accepted the house of Orleans as a substitute, not for the Bourbons, but for a Republic. Lafayette, who presided over the change, rejected the republican solution because he did not want it said that he had personal ambitions, because he was

[16] J. Lucas-Dubreton, *The Restoration and July Monarchy* (1929), p. 170.
[17] P. Quentin-Baucourt, *Lamartine: homme politique* (1903) I, p. 8.
[18] Greville in T. E. B. Howarth, *Citizen King* (1961), p. 173.

afraid for property, and because he thought it 'an experiment which was too hazardous for the success of republican ideas themselves'.[19] A convenient caretaker was available.

Louis Philippe was not the only high official who 'arrived' in 1830; the July Revolution, indeed, marks a decisive change in French governing circles. A purge of administrative officials was carried through, only seven prefects being left in office. Of the new ones, 53 came from the old prefectorial bureaucracy, 32 of them of Empire vintage and the others from the early 'liberal' era of the Restoration; 15 had been deputies, and these too were Imperialists or Restoration liberals; the entirely new men were mostly distinguished by large fortunes. 'If you compare the lists of the Restoration and those of 1830,' writes Pouthas, 'the true character of the latter is illuminated: it is the substitution of one class for another. Guizot expelled the nobility from the control of the administrative machine and handed it over to the bourgeoisie. This fact, among others, helps us to understand how contemporaries regarded the Revolution of July as completing the Revolution of 1789.'[20]

On Shrove Tuesday 1831 began a riot which formed an epilogue to the events of 1830. A mob wrecked the church where a legitimist congregation had assembled to hear a mass for the murdered duc de Berry, celebrated by the priest who had attended Marie Antoinette on the scaffold, and a tumult began which lasted three days and included the sack of the Palace of the Archbishop of Paris. The police did not interfere. Those who watched the Carmagnole danced in ecclesiastical vestments or fished books of the archiepiscopal library from the Seine reflected that the old interdependence of throne and altar had ended. It was to revive again under the Second Empire, but uneasily, for traditional loyalties inclined many Catholics to feel that the alliance could not continually be re-invented for the benefit of new thrones, but belonged only to Legitimism.

VI

In 1830, the July Revolution was not the only Parisian event of importance. There was a dispute between Cuvier and Geoffroy Saint-Hilaire about the diversity of species (which Goethe thought much more significant than the fall of the Bourbons); Lamartine was elected to the Academy, publications by Balzac, de Musset and Saint-Beuve were on sale in the bookshops; La Mennais founded

[19] Charles de Rémusat, *Mémoires de ma vie* (ed. C.-H. Pouthas, 1959), p. 346.
[20] C.-H. Pouthas, 'La Réorganization du ministère de l'intérieur . . . par Guizot', *Revue d'histoire moderne et contemporaine*, IX (1962), p. 258.

L'Avenir; the Romantic movement reached its dramatic victory in the 'battle of *Hernani*', Victor Hugo's lurid drama which broke all the classical rules; some of the stalwarts who built the barricades in the blazing heat of July were typographers who had abandoned chapter thirty-eight of *Le Rouge et le Noir* to perform their revolutionary chores. France in the nineteenth century declined—comparatively speaking—as a European power, but in art and literature French domination became more obvious than it had been in the days of Louis Quartorze or in the age of Voltaire. In these lectures devoted, not to chronicling the grandeurs of the nineteenth century, but merely to providing a framework within which they can be studied, we can do no more than note the fact.

One aspect of the efflorescence of French culture, however, must concern even those whose responsibilities are limited to the erection of scaffolding. In the first half of the century, Paris became a laboratory of social and political theory. One of the inspirations was the need for explaining the great Revolution: 'I have witnessed an end and a beginning of a whole world,' said Chateaubriand. Then came the obligation to explain the new revolutions which tried to complete the first but never did, until men became tired of mistaking cloud banks for the shore, and began to despair. An inspiration of another kind may be found in the conditions of internal peace which the Restoration, for all its follies, achieved. 'The National Convention had stifled the *ancien régime* in blood,' wrote Guizot, 'the Empire had condemned both the old France and revolutionary France to silence. These two worlds found themselves face to face once again under the Restoration, but in conditions which did not allow either of them to oppress the other. For the first time since 1792, the French Revolution and the old society of France met, and fought each other in argument, over a period of fifteen years, in full and unbroken liberty.'[21]

In the early stages of this debate, the cause of conservatism had the most brilliant exponents. When Napoleon fell, de Maistre and de Bonald were both sixty years of age. Both were provincials, out of sympathy with revolutionary Paris (Maistre, indeed, was a Savoyard); both had been nobles of the robe until the Revolution blasted their careers; both began to write in exile. Their defence of hereditary absolute monarchy went on obvious lines: that man is radically evil, that society, religion and the family create the individual, who has no rights, only duties; that in the last resort, 'the executioner is the corner stone of society'. These were well-known arguments, but Maistre and Bonald said a great deal more than this, and what they said was

[21] D. Bagge, *Les Idées politiques en France sous la Restauration* (1952), pp. 20–21.

remembered. With them began the process by which the Right accepted the patriotic glories of the Revolution, whose blood-stained dictatorship had saved France from the invader.[22] More important, from these writers and from Chateaubriand comes the idea of a dialectic between liberty and equality: how men make revolutions grasping at both, only to find that by its very nature, equality brings slavery. Under the old monarchy there were checks upon despotism, effective ones, because they were part of the social fabric, while during the Revolution there were proclamations of freedom which were mere words, referring to individual men whose standing was unguaranteed by any traditional social order. 'The Rights of Man . . . are signs of desolation and death,' said Bonald, 'like cannon shots at long intervals from a sinking ship.' 'No nation can give itself liberty,' concludes Maistre, 'that has always been the gift of kings.' Certainly, liberty would not be the achievement of political theorists, and these two publicists provided reactionary thought with one of its most sinister weapons when they took up and made intellectually respectable the 'plot' theory of the Revolution put out originally by the abbé Barruel. Amid the splendours of eighteenth-century thought lurked the seeds of cruel anarchy, like plague in precious cargoes from the Levant. Ever since, right-wing thinkers have clung to the argument that revolutionary thought, and more especially that of poor, peace-loving Rousseau, is somehow indissolubly linked with Terror, rather than Terror being the result of desperate circumstances.

One sombre, recurring theme of conservative publicists was that of social disintegration. The Revolution had destroyed the organic unity of France and left a collection of individuals, liable to fall a prey to either despotism or anarchy. It was against these dangers that Bonald prescribed a return to social hierarchy, and Chateaubriand a revived aristocracy and a genuinely parliamentary monarchy. Balzac, a legitimist, was describing in his huge series of novels the grim acquisitive society which had arisen from the sale of the *biens nationaux*, with every family fighting for itself—or as he sometimes thought, every single individual—'*il n'y a pas de famille aujourd'hui, il n'y a que les individus*'.[23] In his early royalist and ultramontane days, La Mennais saw no hope of unifying Frenchmen except through Catholicism—'France is an assembly of thirty million inhabitants amongst whom the law recognizes no other distinction than that of riches'.[24]

[22] Joseph de Maistre, *Considérations sur la France* (1797; ed. R. Johannet and F. Vermale, 1936), p. 21.
[23] H. de Balzac, *Béatrix*, in Bagge, op. cit.
[24] Bagge, p. 275.

On these brilliant paradoxical margins of right-wing thought, we can detect the possibilities of very different conclusions from identical premises. An anarchist, perhaps, lurks in the soul of every aristocrat: Chateaubriand, beneath his conservatism, believed that all government was essentially an evil; Bonald's idea of an organic society was passed on, through Saint Simon, to socialism; La Mennais was to revolt, leftwards and democratically, against a society whose only hierarchy was riches; Balzac's *Comédie humaine* was a quarry of information to support a total condemnation of bourgeois society and was, indeed, Karl Marx's favourite recreational reading.

VII

The idea that the great Revolution had destroyed liberty was accepted by liberals as well as reactionaries, though as Talleyrand said on another occasion, it was 'all a question of dates'. Almost everyone repudiated the Terror, but only hardened reactionaries disowned the Fall of the Bastille, so that there was a general admission that somewhere between, things had gone wrong, and the strength of a man's liberal convictions could be tested by the date he chose—early or late—for this betrayal. Liberalism is, of course, a vague term, and covers a wide spectrum of ideas. After the event we may detect two main tendencies, which may be called 'individualistic' and 'bourgeois'. The first title may be applied to thinkers who did not care intensely about the form of government, provided individual freedom was safe under it. 'I will always avoid overturning an existing institution which is compatible with liberty,' said Benjamin Constant, and he even conceded that 'old governments are more favourable to liberty than new ones'.[25] Like Mme de Staël and, later, her son in law, duc Victor de Broglie and his circle, he would have preferred a government of the English kind, not so much because it gave men a say in politics, but because it freed them from political interference in their private lives. The menace to individual freedom in France was, they thought, the centralized administrative machine with its omnicompetent prefects, and this had arisen, said Royer Collard (annexing a favourite right-wing argument) because the Revolution had disintegrated society leaving only isolated individuals. 'From the dust of an atomized social order centralization was born.'[26] The remedy, said Barante, was to revive local loyalties or even, as Broglie argued, to

[25] H. Nicolson, *Benjamin Constant* (1949), pp. 260–1.
[26] Bagge, p. 120.

restore the old provinces and reorganize everything, including the army, on a territorial basis.

The other tendency in liberalism, which we have called 'bourgeois', was exemplified by Thiers and Guizot, historians and politicians,who interpreted the Revolution as the decisive battle between the bourgeoisie and the aristocracy; according to Guizot, it was the end of a war which had begun with the Franks oppressing the Gauls, thirteen centuries ago. A free press and representative institutions were necessary, not just to ensure individual freedom, but to prevent the return of the *ancien régime* and to guarantee that the State was controlled by the middle classes; to be fair to this view, it meant, in theory, control by intelligence and capacity, not wealth. 'Representative Government,' said Guizot in his *Du gouvernement de la France* (1820) 'is not like Legitimism, impartial and neutral in its nature. It belongs to whoever has desired it and achieved it. It is an instrument of triumph, a fortress of security. If this instrument falls into the hands of enemies —one thing alone is urgent, that is to reconquer it.'[27] That is what the middle classes did, in 1830.

As we have seen, this reconquest of the fortress did not involve concessions to the lower classes. The time was ripe, however, for the rise of a thinker who had absorbed the brilliant theorizing of liberals and reactionaries in France, but who could make this theorizing relevant to the future by his own acceptance of democracy. This conjunction of opportunity with the chance that produces genius accounts for Alexis de Tocqueville's astonishingly perceptive volumes on *Democracy in America* (1835). Sainte Beuve's famous gibe, 'He began to think before he had learnt anything' was justified in that Tocqueville, who had long meditated on the liberty-equality dialectic, knew what he meant to discover before he embarked for America; an inspired social psychologist, he had arrived by analytical intuition at a coherent philosophy of history. For him, behind all history lay a 'providential fact', a 'divine decree', an 'unknown force', which men can hope to regulate, but which they cannot defeat, which 'has annihilated feudalism and will not spare the capitalist'.[28] This force is the drive of men towards equality.

An aristocrat to his finger tips, scornful of the bourgeois temperament and fearful of the dangers of mass tyranny and plebiscitary dictatorship inherent in a situation which gave power to the lower orders, Tocqueville none the less accepted democracy as inevitable. The aristocracy represented elevated passions, but its day was over. Perhaps it was God's wish to shed 'a mediocre happiness' upon a

---

[27] C.-H. Pouthas, *Guizot pendant la Restauration* (1923), pp. 257–8.
[28] Alexis de Tocqueville, *Democracy in America* (1835).

greater number of participants. This Norman nobleman therefore made himself the 'prophet of the mass age'[29] and bent his mind to devising safeguards—mostly spiritual ones—which would preserve some elements of liberty in the Gadarene rush down to equality which democracy implied. We must consider Tocqueville's thought later when its full influence was being felt; it dazzled his contemporaries, but as the events of 1848–9 were to show, he had uttered his prophecies too late to save them from disaster.

VIII

Tocqueville and Marx, the two most intelligent sociological observers of the day, hit upon the same analogy to describe the July Monarchy. It was a 'joint stock company,' an 'industrial combine' run for the profit of the shareholders.[30] These shareholders were few: only the 241,000 richest citizens had the right to vote. 'The middle classes,' wrote Tocqueville (he meant the upper bourgeoisie), 'continually exposed to the solicitations of the government, have gradually assumed towards the rest of the nation the position of a little aristocracy, with all the corruption of the ancient aristocracy, and without its higher feelings.'[31]

This régime had neither glamour nor generosity. Guizot[32] as chief minister was well-intentioned, but Frenchmen forgot the value of a peaceful foreign policy when it proved so inglorious, more especially when it came to being led by the nose by Metternich. 'French nowhere, counter-revolutionary everywhere,' Lamartine complained. A crop of scandals gave the impression that public life was untowardly corrupt: frauds over the salt monopoly and naval stores, a duke killed his wife, a peer stabbed his mistress and an aide-de-camp of the King was caught cheating at cards. The government was indifferent to the lot of the working classes. Its one piece of labour legislation, on the hours of work of children, was never enforced. Unemployment was irrelevant to the well-heeled legislators: 'we are here to make laws, not to provide work'. Thus the ministers of Louis Philippe had no resources of public good will to draw on to rescue them from the blame for the severe economic depression, which began in 1846 with crop failures and intensified in 1847 as heavy investment in railways

[29] J. P. Mayer, *Alexis de Tocqueville: Prophet of the Mass Age* (1939).
[30] K. Marx, *The Class Struggles in France* in *Selected Works* (1951) I, pp. 128–9; A. de Tocqueville, *Souvenirs* (1942), pp. 26–7.
[31] *Memoir, Letters etc. of Alexis de Tocqueville*, II, p. 83.
[32] There is a superb biography of Guizot which does much to rehabilitate his memory, Douglas Johnson, *Guizot, Aspects of French History, 1787–1874* (1963).

(not yet yielding profits) deprived the money market of elasticity.

While discontent accumulated, a new leaven of revolutionary idealism fermented among the reading public. Until the late 1820s, Romanticism had been right-wing in political inclination. Perhaps this was because the great Revolution had had no original literature, leaving inspiration to the Emigration; whatever the reason, literary fashion had come to follow Rousseau, not in his enthusiasm for equality or liberty, so much as in his rôle of the prophet of solitude and introspection. But by 1830, the Catholic, medieval and authoritarian aspects of Romanticism had given place to a new and picturesque vision of emancipation. Now, the mysteries of incense and candlelight beneath the vaults of Notre-Dame stirred the emotions less than the hopeless passion of the poor twisted devil who swung the mighty bells. The key word became the 'people', whose virtues and idealism Michelet was to hymn in his essay *Le Peuple* (1846) and in his history of the Revolution.

To this generation, the Terror was half a century away, so that its red shadow no longer cast twilight fears of damnation over every radical enthusiasm. In a study of the *Girondins* which 'raised history to the level of a novel', Lamartine proclaimed a national reconciliation over the graves of all those of all parties who had died for posterity. As revolutionary ideals came back into fashion, Frenchmen heard them invoked by the exiles of Poland, Russia, Italy and Germany, to whom Paris was the city of refuge. When news arrived of disturbances elsewhere in Europe—of Poles rising again in Cracow, of the victory of the Protestant cantons of Switzerland over the Catholic *Sonderbund*, of the Sicilian rising of January 1848—there was intense interest in the cafés of Paris. For six months a campaign of 'banquets' had been waged against Louis Philippe—'a revolution of contempt against the Bourgeois King', said Lamartine. It was unlikely that France would forget its own traditions and allow itself to be outstripped by other countries in the race for freedom.

The efficacy of these banquets as a revolutionary instrument is something of a myth, but at least they served to reveal the sheer isolation of the governing clique. Legitimists and Bonapartists retained their old allegiances. Liberal monarchists were either in factious opposition like Thiers, or anxious to enlarge the social basis of political life. There were growing numbers of republicans, some anxious for change merely as a 'grammatical satisfaction'; others, like Ledru-Rollin and a group around the newspaper *La Réforme*, wanting a very much wider suffrage. Thus, given the unpopularity and isolation of the monarchy, the Revolution of February 1848 was an easy affair, as revolutions go. The National Guard, mostly consisting of members of the lower bourgeoisie, quietly abandoned Louis Philippe, who set off for England as Charles X had done, only without an entourage and calling himself 'Mr Smith'.

When the King had gone, it seemed harder to explain why his rule had lasted than why it had been overthrown. Yet it was not long before the answer was obvious. In 1830—as in 1789—the people had fought in the streets and had received no reward. The *raison d'être* of the July Monarchy had been, quite simply, the defence of property (for that was the only place where the people's reward could come from). With the advent of the Second Republic and the dissolution of the bonds of order, fear came upon everyone who had anything to lose. 'You can only compare this fear,' said Tocqueville, who shared it to the full himself, 'to that which the inhabitants of the civilized cities of the Roman world felt when they suddenly found themselves in the power of the Goths and Vandals.'[33] The next four months in France were to pose decisively the great new dominating question of European history: they were too, in a vicious, unforgettable fashion, to give one possible answer. On 22 March, Blanqui described the position with lapidary precision: 'The Republic will be a lie if it is only going to mean the substitution of one form of government for another. It is not enough to change words: you have to change things. The Republic must mean the emancipation of the workers.'[34]

[33] Tocqueville, *Souvenirs*, p. 80.
[34] Cit. J. Dautry, *1848 et la IIe République* (1957), p. 92.

Chapter XIII

THE JUNE DAYS OF '48 AND THE GREAT EXHIBITION OF '51

(*Socialism and Industrialism*)

I

Two tremendous events—contemporaries found the one terrifying and the other stupendous—stand like symbolic landmarks in the middle of the nineteenth century: the June Days of 1848 and the Great Exhibition of 1851. The street fighting in Paris revealed the full and ultimate implications of the history of French revolutions: here was an object-lesson to prove the case for revolutionary socialism and the doctrine of class warfare. The Great Exhibition in London three years later revealed the astonishing potentiality of the new industrialism, 'wonders far surpassing the Egyptian pyramids, Roman aqueducts and Gothic cathedrals', as Marx had said, in venomous praise of the bourgeoisie, in the *Communist Manifesto* three years before. In fact, both these great symbols were deceptive: they do not reveal to us precisely what they seemed to be revealing to contemporaries. The June Days were not, strictly speaking, the proletarian uprising which some imagined them to be, and the Great Exhibition was summing up the romantic achievements of a first stage of industrialization whose wonders were soon to become obsolete.

Even so, one can see how reflections upon the new industrialism and upon the revolutionary tradition could come to a burning focus. Marxism has been called 'a German theory about French revolutions'.[1] One might go further and say that Marx brought the German tendency towards broad philosophical interpretations of history to bear on the two great social units of western Europe, France and England; from the recent history of England he deduced a pattern of industrial civilization, and from the recent history of France a pattern of revolution, which he combined into a forecast of the great goal to which history inevitably moves.

---

[1] Though with the qualification 'It would perhaps be extravagant to say that the Marxian account of the class war is a German theory about French revolutions' (J. Plamenatz, *German Marxism and Russian Communism* (1954), p. 117).

II

'How swiftly Providence advances thus
    Our flag of progress placing in the van!
This double decade of the world's short span
    Is richer than two centuries of old.
Richer in helps, advantages and pleasures,
    In all things richer—even down to gold . . .
All wonders of the world gladden the sight
    In that world's wonder-house the Crystal Palace,
And everywhere is Might enslaved to Right.'[2]

In retrospect, it is easy to smile at Martin Tupper's enthusiasm. The locomotives, textile machines, Applegarth's vertical printing press which turned out 10,000 sheets of the *Illustrated London News* in an hour, Nasmyth's steam hammer that could crack a nut or swing a blow of 500 tons, the diving suits, hydraulic presses, seed drills and the like are antediluvian memories now, as curious as the 'cricket catapulta for propelling the ball in the absence of a first-rate bowler'. And though much of the machinery and Paxton's prefabricated palace of cast iron and glass were beautiful in their sheer dramatic utility, the exhibits meant to reveal the artistic achievements of the age were atrocious—'wonderfully ugly', said William Morris. *The Times* had just condemned the Pre-Raphaelite paintings, especially Millais' 'Carpenter's Shop'; one would have wished that these thunders had been reserved for the manifold crimes of the Exhibition, the ancient Egyptian ornamentation in cast-iron, the Elizabethan sideboard in gutta percha, the stuffed cats' tea-party, and the vulgar refinement of the statuary. One of the few voices raised in protest was that of a writer in Chambers' *Papers for the People*, who acutely diagnosed the disastrous artistic effects of a sudden plethora of new materials and quick mechanical methods of moulding them upon a generation intoxicated with technical progress. 'The present is the age of shams. . . . Works of art are *tacked on* to works of utility. . . . Instead of an article *itself* ornamental, it must be, if 'decorative', *something else*. . . . Everywhere, if not frightful, our forms are tame, overloaded, or broken up. . . .'[3]

Yet these were the ebullient errors of a wonderfully vital generation, which was creating a new world for both good and evil. Its explorers were adventuring into unknown lands: in the year of the

[2] From Martin Tupper's (1810–89) verses on the Great Exhibition.
[3] Cit. J. W. Dodds, *The Age of Paradox: A Biography of England, 1841–51* (1953), p. 467.

Exhibition, Livingstone reached the Zambesi. In its schools, the games that were to form the civilizing core of modern mass culture were being developed; an all-England cricket team played in 1846; three years before this Oxford had beaten Cambridge in the boat race, with one oar missing; football was gaining in popularity, though the 'carriers' and the 'dribblers' did not part company for another dozen years. In the course of the last decade, the reading public had added *Wuthering Heights* and *Jane Eyre* to its shelves, and *David Copperfield*, *Vanity Fair*, Macaulay's *History*, Ruskin's *Seven Lamps of Architecture*, Layard's *Nineveh*, as well as *Lavengro* and *In Memoriam* —writings that lost none of their appeal from being read amid tartan and trellised wallpapers and wax flowers behind glass, and under the melancholy scrutiny of Landseer's 'Monarch of the Glen'.

To contemporaries on the mainland, Britain's achievements in literature, law and constitutional government were overshadowed by the grim ambiguous triumphs of her unplanned industrialization. Behind the rows of identical houses in the factory towns and the obelisks of chimneys whose smoke blackened the cathedrals (the description is Michelet's[4]) lay astonishing power and wealth. Since the beginning of the century the population had almost doubled, the fastest rate of growth in Europe, except for Russia, and in the year of the Exhibition, the urban population at last exceeded that of the countryside. In 1851, Britain produced 57 million tons of coal, as compared with Germany's 6 million and France's $4\frac{1}{2}$, and $2\frac{1}{4}$ million tons of iron, five times as much as the U.S.A., six times as much as France and ten times as much as Germany. Half the world's tonnage of ocean-going shipping was British, and half the world's total of railway mileage, and this, concentrated in a small island, formed the basic outline of the modern network. To Kinglake's Pasha, who was presumably too far away to appreciate the evil aspects of industrial expansion, all this was prodigious. 'The ships of the English swarm like flies; their printed calicoes cover the whole earth. . . . All India is but an item in the ledger-books of the merchant whose lumber rooms are filled with ancient thrones! Whirr! Whirr! all by wheels! Whiz! Whiz! all by steam!'[5]

III

Why had British industrialization raced ahead of the rest of Europe and, more particularly, ahead of France? At the time of the Great Exhibition, France had a larger population than any European nation

[4] Michelet, *Journal* (for 1834; ed. P. Viallaneix), I (1959), pp. 151–2.
[5] A. W. Kinglake, *Eothen* (1844), (introd. by P. H. Newby, 1948), p. 30.

except Russia; in absolute terms she was still the world's wealthiest nation, enjoying unsurpassed agricultural resources and coming second to Great Britain in industrial production. There were then over 6,800 steam engines in the country—more than in the whole of the rest of continental Europe. Yet France was industrially far behind Britain, and by the end of the century was falling well behind Germany and the U.S.A. in population, industrial production and real *per capita* income. The French 'take off' came later than Britain's, and there was no meteoric burst of expansion subsequently, like that which was to make Germany Europe's greatest industrial power. Why was this so?

The factors assisting the 'take off' in Britain—geographical position and resources, stable government and religious toleration, a preliminary revolution in agricultural methods along with the enclosure of scattered strips and commons, a long maritime tradition with its growing pattern of overseas trading interests, an increasing population and an accumulation of capital and technical expertise—have often been discussed, though it is impossible to be certain about their relative importance. One way of proceeding would be to ask in which of these respects France was deficient. It is clear at once that she had no shortage of high-level technicians or of capital. The best scientific and technological education in the world was available in Paris, an inheritance of the *ancien régime* which the Revolution had fostered. Foreign students came to study at the École Polytechnique, and French engineers trained in its classes were found all over eastern Europe, Russia, Egypt and the Levant. With them went the metric system, which was being gradually adopted by the rest of the world, for example by the Austrian railways in 1855 and by the German ones six years later. Throughout the century, Frenchmen made vast placements of capital abroad, more especially during years of comparative prosperity, 1835–8, 1852–6 and, later, 1878–81. By 1867 the point was to be reached when foreign investments were yielding enough income to provide for all new investment abroad and also to finance part of the commodity import surplus as well. Yet, active though they were abroad, French engineers and French capital did not lead in the development of the home railways.

One explanation of this backwardness lies along political lines. French energies had been diverted by Revolution and conquest, and Napoleon had interrupted the development of scientific education by centering all its activities on war. The restored Bourbons played for safety: their position was not secure enough to risk an expansionist gamble in economic policy. For all its hoarded capital, France lacked credit institutions to direct investment towards industry and legislation which would facilitate the formation of joint stock companies. Yet the governments of the first half of the century limited their intervention to the unimaginative expedient of trying to encourage industry by tariff protection. The effect was to discourage initiative and invite reprisals. All this is true, but one may ask what effect expansionist policies characteristic of the Second Empire could have had if they had been tried under the Restoration? It may well be that the essential basis for later development lay precisely in that undramatic growth of national income by 2 to 3 per cent a year in the first half of the century.

Population growth in France, like economic expansion, was steady, but relatively modest. From 1800 to 1850, there was an increase of 29 per cent (from 28.2 millions to 35.8 millions), a much slower rate of growth than Britain's. Whether this difference can be ascribed to the loss of life in the wars, the prudent tradition of the bourgeoisie, the peasants' determination to own their own land, the spirit of agnosticism or any of the other reasons that have been advanced, one hesitates to say. The results, however, are easier to assess than the causes. From 1750 to 1850, the ratio of rural to urban population remained constant at about 3 :1 ; there was an increasing density of population in the countryside, and this was possible only because a delicate balance between agriculture and handicraft industry was preserved. One clue to the relative backwardness of France, then, may be found in the agrarian structure. The revolutionary land sales and inheritance laws encouraged the subdivision of the land : in the hundred years following 1789 the number of agricultural proprietors doubled. Small farms were under-capitalized and uneconomical, so agricultural productivity was lower than it might have been—so, too, was the rural demand for industrial products. Equal division among heirs has usually been supposed to retard population growth; this is doubtful, but it certainly did encourage the peasants to stay on the land. In England, in most of Germany, and in the west of Bohemia, where the single-heir system prevailed, younger sons would naturally move to the cities, and industrialists could assume that labour would migrate towards the factories they founded. In France, the geographical distribution of industry was for long determined by the immobility of labour.

When all this is said, however, the essential reason for the comparative backwardness of French industrialization remains—inadequate and ill-sited resources. France was rich in wood and water power, the driving forces of the old technology, but not in coal, the essential source of energy for the new. More than this, her iron ores were not conveniently accessible to the established centres of population and industry. In 1853 Cobden wrote, 'Whilst the indigenous coal and iron in England have attracted to her shores the raw materials of her industry . . . , France, on the contrary, relying on her ingenuity only to sustain a competition with England, is compelled to purchase a portion of her [coal and iron] from her rival.'[6] When, later on, Germany goes ahead of all Europe, we must look again at the same criterion for the explanation—the immediate availability and convenient location of coal supplies.

IV

By the time of the Great Exhibition, Britain was exporting her Industrial Revolution. Railways were being built in other lands by British engineers, heroic entrepreneurs like Thomas Brassey, who was in Norway in 1851, having built the Paris-Rouen line ten years earlier, and later was to fulfil railway contracts in Canada, Italy and Queensland as well as supervising drainage schemes for Rio de Janiero. The lines surveyed by men like him were often financed by British capital: nearly half the money behind the 2,000 miles of railway in France at the mid-century had been raised in London. By this time, there were rather more than 6,600 miles of track in Britain and about the same amount in the rest of Europe, ranging from a toy line in Naples with a chapel at every station to the developing, scientifically planned Belgian network. The railway revolution was fully launched. Within twenty years the length of track in Europe was to be quintupled. The iron rails and the embankments became a feature of the countryside, and the girders of the stations were the standardized sight greeting travellers arriving in almost any city. In 1849, Ruskin had been divided between a sensation of awe at the fiery vitality which throbbed through the land in iron arteries, and one of regret at finding mankind 'thrown back in continually closer crowds upon the city gates'.[7] Literature continued to reflect this dichotomy. Victor Hugo hymned the 'brazen hydra of smoke and lightning' speeding through the night; Flaubert, typically, demythologized progress by discovering the tedium of speed. 'After five minutes I bay with boredom. They

---

[6] Cobden, *Political Writings* (1867) I, pp. 467, 469, cit. R. Cameron, 'Economic Growth in France, 1815–1914', *Journal of Modern History*, XXX (1958), p. 12.

For all this section see Cameron's book *France and the Economic Development of Europe* (1961), H. J. Habakkuk, 'Family Structure and Economic Change in Nineteenth-Century Europe', *Journ. Econ. Hist.* XV (1955), pp. 1–12, and A. L. Dunham, *The Industrial Revolution in France* (1955).

[7] Cit. Asa Briggs, *Victorian Cities* (1963), p. 57.

think it's a lost dog shut in the carriage; it isn't though, it's M. Flaubert groaning.'[8]

Wherever the railways penetrated, they joined rural producers to urban consumers, breaking monopolies and opening new markets for agricultural products. In 1848, the price of wheat in France varied from area to area by as much as 26 francs per hectolitre: after 1870 the variation was never greater than 3½ francs. The railways also carried loads of the new-fashioned fertilizers to agricultural areas. First there was bone manure (a British enterprise exploited the resources of the old Napoleonic battlefields); then from 1840 there was guano from the Pacific coast of South America and potassium salts from the Harz Mountains and Alsace. The effective operation of the railways in central Europe coincided with the freeing of the peasants from serfdom in the 1848 revolutions. These two factors together helped the rise of the big estates, using the techniques of the English Agricultural Revolution, hiring wage labour and selling in distant markets. Similar developments were seen in Italy, Denmark and Germany east of the Elbe. The market for foodstuffs was expanding; the population of Europe had risen from 187 millions in 1800 to 266 millions in 1850 and the rise was accelerating; in 1800 there had been only twenty-two cities with a population over 100,000, while at the half-century there were forty-seven. As steam navigation was still confined to passenger traffic, heavy freight charges prevented American grain from competing in the European market, though the European farmer could borrow the latest American agricultural machinery, like McCormack's reaper, which was on display at the Great Exhibition. Russian grain exports trebled in the thirty years following 1840, and the greater landowners of the Danubian basin enjoyed a brief period of intense prosperity. After 1850, there was also a sudden expansion of the cultivation of sugar beet, so that the European industry ousted the cane sugar of other continents from the profits of rising consumption. For a brief space, European agriculture enjoyed the exclusive benefits of the revolution in transport, until in the 'seventies railways and steamships poured in the overwhelming production of the American prairies.

Just as bulky agricultural products could easily be moved by rail, so too could coal, ores, raw materials and heavy machinery, whose transportation so far had been uneconomical except by canals and waterways. Thus, like agriculture, industry received a stimulus. The railways brought with them a demand for skilled engineers and for

---

[8] V. Hugo, *Le Satyre, La Légende des siècles* (1859), (ed. P. Berret, 1922) II, p. 613; Flaubert, *Correspondance* (for 1867), III (1903), p. 325; see A. Dupay, *L'Information historique* (Jan.-Feb. 1961), pp. 9–16.

metallurgical products, creating a reservoir of expertise and materials which overflowed into other industrial enterprises. In an elementary fashion we can gauge the resultant pace of change in Europe by looking at the figures for the rise of productivity in coal and iron in the twenty years following the Great Exhibition. British production doubled (reaching 112 million tons a year for coal and six million tons for iron), French production nearly tripled (13 millions tons and 1.2 million tons, respectively), while the German output increased nearly six times (34 million tons and 1.3 million tons). France was making up some leeway now, but Germany, from a less favourable start, was heading for supremacy.

V

Though in 1845 the Pasha said that everything in Britain whizzed by steam, he was mistaken. Mechanization and expansion were so far limited to a small number of basic industries, principally textiles, coal and iron. The world was changing rapidly, but it is important not to exaggerate the scope of the transformation. In 1851, only 45,000 men and boys in Britain were employed as engineers; steel was 'a semi-precious metal',[9] and remained so until the advent of the Bessemer convertor (1856). Twelve times as much British shipping was moved by sail as by steam: not until 1883 were the two tonnages equal. Indeed, the period up to the late 'eighties was the golden age of sail, of American tea clippers like the *Flying Cloud* which, in the year of the Exhibition, did the Horn passage from Canton to London in eighty-nine days.

The near future was to see the victory of the steamship and the completion of the railway networks—this much contemporaries could foresee. What was concealed from them, however, was the vision of the boundless possibilities—possibilities of change in the conditions of change itself—which would open up once scientific research became a planned activity and was put into mesh with technology, medicine and agriculture. At the official ceremonies at the Crystal Palace Prince Albert had talked of science discovering the laws and of industry applying them, but the exhibits all around him were conspicuous, not as the end-products of the investigations of scientists, but as the culmination of empirical technology. The vision of the age, writes A. R. Hall, was 'limited to coal, iron and steam until the intervention of the scientific inventor between 1855 and 1870 brought in fresh materials and methods', and he adds that the effects

[9] H. Heaton, 'Economic Change and Growth', *New Camb. Mod. Hist.* X (1960), p. 30.

of this intervention were at first slight.[10] In the Crystal Palace, the dynamo and arc lamp were shown merely as curiosities. As yet little industrial use had been made of electrolysis and catalysis, though the principles of the one had been known for forty years, and of the other for fifteen. Practical men were hardly aware of the profits that the processes of laboratory synthesis might bring to them, and they remained comparatively unenlightened until 1856, when Perkin accidentally synthesized the first aniline dye. Science afforded little help, as yet, to farmers faced with plagues which destroyed their cattle or blights which rotted crops. Doctors had no knowledge of the causes of diseases or the means of their transmission. Chloroform had recently been used as an anaesthetic, but carbolic acid, discovered in 1834, had still not been used as an antiseptic. In 1846, a plant disease ruined three-quarters of the Irish potato crop and, directly and indirectly, famine took nearly a million lives. In 1830, cholera, sweeping westwards from China, reached Moscow; within two years it had killed 18,000 people in Paris and had crossed the ocean to Quebec and New Orleans; in the autumn of 1848 the Counter Revolution was assisted by another onslaught of the same scourge which terrorized and exhausted the inhabitants of the principal cities of Europe. Before these visitations, mankind was still helpless.

It was possible then, before Pasteur in the 'sixties did the decisive work which began the attack on the diseases of men, animals and plants, before the factories were turning out a flood of consumer goods and before the new means of transport had had their full effect on the provisioning of cities, to wonder at the speed of modern conveyances and the complexity of the new devices, and yet still to doubt if the bulk of mankind would ever be able to share in the comforts of the new civilization. At the time of the 1848 revolutions, the economist Sismondi anticipated that capitalism would suffer from a permanent disequilibrium between supply and demand, and that this, inevitably, would lead to the triumph of some form of socialism.[11]

VI

The condition of the urban working classes of western Europe seemed to prove Sismondi's analysis. There has been much controversy about their standards of living (more especially of the poor in the English towns) in the first half of the nineteenth century, turning on the question of whether or not the 'Industrial Revolution' or 'Capitalism'

[10] A. R. Hall, 'The Scientific Movement and its Influence on Thought and Material Development', *New Camb. Mod. Hist.* X, pp. 52, 73.
[11] Cit. R. Schnerb, *Le XIXe siècle* (*Hist. gén. des civilis.* VI, 1957), p. 45.

made the workers better off or worse off than they would have been·
But the task of defining which features of the economy are 'capital-
istic' and of unravelling conditions in trades directly influenced by
the new industrialism from those less directly affected, is not an easy
one; it is difficult to know how to compare the picturesque old dirt
with the new and abominable filth of the factory towns, or to distin-
guish the misery caused by the stranglehold of the British fundholders
on the national revenue (a result of the wars) from that imposed by
unrestricted industrial enterprise. What we can say, however, is that
the price fall of the years 1816 to 1846 had been generally associated,
in the whole of western Europe, with unemployment and misery.
The poor eat less well than their eighteenth-century ancestors, a grim
fact which would have been more obvious but for the sheer belly-
filling qualities of potatoes. Clothes, shoes and other necessities for
ordinary people were not greatly cheapened by machine production
before 1850. The rapidly growing population was drawn into many
English towns, and in the case of France, into Paris, but hygienic
reforms before the mid-century were rare. Governments made little
attempt to change factory conditions. The English legislation of 1833
had some effect in limiting child labour, but the Prussian regulations
of 1829 and the French law of 1841 were useless.

The real improvement of working-class life began somewhere about
the mid-century. In England, the decisive intervention of government started then, while the rise of Co-operatives, Friendly Societies
and even of Trades' Unions were hopeful signs that the working
classes might be able to fight for themselves. At about 1850 we can
place the beginning of a new Kondratieff cycle, within which there is
a period of rising prices up to 1873. This period of rise, with its
stimulating effect upon business, was one of prosperity, though
marred by a major crisis in 1857. The causes of this prosperity-
inflation were, no doubt, various: the release of immobilized capital
as the profits of the technological innovations in which it had been
invested began to come in, in this case especially from the railways;
the increase of fiduciary circulation by central banks; and the discovery of gold in California in 1848 and in Victoria in 1851. More gold
came on to the markets in the next twenty years than America had
produced since Cortés and Pizarro. Within this period the tonnage of
the world's merchant fleets almost doubled, the railways went everywhere, world trade swung from limited turnovers with high profits
to huge turnovers with low margins. The riches of lavish industrial
production and of imported wheat and meat, and the triumphs of the
new bacteriological medicine of prevention and cure were evident for
the working classes of western Europe only from 1870 or so. At the

time of the Great Exhibition, the wonders of the new mechanical era had conferred only limited benefits upon the mass of mankind.

VII

'When people on Turkey carpets, with their three meat meals a day are wondering, forsooth, why working men turn Chartists and Communists—Do they want to know why? Then let them read *Mary Barton*.'[12] This advice of a writer in *Fraser's* in April 1849 is relevant to us today. We ought to look at Mrs Gaskell's revelation of conditions in Manchester—and at Kingsley's *Yeast* (1848), at Hood's *Song of the Shirt* (1843), at Mayhew's *London* (1851), perhaps even at Chadwick's *Sanitary Condition of the Labouring Population* (1842), so that we may not forget the dark satanic foundations on which the civilization of the nineteenth century was reared. These horrors were not exclusively phenomena of the new industrialization; certainly, they were not confined to the poor of English manufacturing towns. Howard's *Enquiry into the Morbid Effects of Deficiency of Food* (1839) spoke of 'protracted starvation'[13]: similarly, in France, Fourier wrote of '*faim lente*', which Proudhon defined with deadly precision: 'Hunger, at every minute, all the year round, life-long; hunger which does not kill quickly, but which is built up of accumulated privations and accumulated regrets, which continually undermines the body, decays the mind, demoralizes the conscience, bastardizes the race, engenders every illness and every vice . . . causes revulsion from work and thrift, baseness of soul and coarseness of conscience.'[14] It was against this terrifying background that the idea of socialism was developed, chiefly in France (though to some extent in England), during the thirty-five years following Waterloo.

The history of these years accounts for Marx's ingrained and erroneous conviction that there was a 'law of increasing misery', and for his tendency to discover a proletarian spirit among workers who did not fit into his own definition of a proletariat. 'If the workers of the world in 1848 had answered Marx's call to unite, only a small minority would have been factory proletarians.'[15] This is true: even so, many urban workers, quite apart from the factory areas, were becoming rootless and depersonalized, and bound together in a vicious new

[12] Cit. K. Tillotson, *Novels of the Eighteen-Forties* (1956), p. 207.

[13] E. J. Hobsbawn, 'En Angleterre: révolution industrielle et vie matérielle des classes populaires', *Annales Econ. Soc. Civilis.* (1946), p. 1056.

[14] Proudhon, *La Guerre et la Paix* (1861), cit. L. Chevalier, *Classes laborieuses et classes dangereuses à Paris pendant la première moitié du XIXe siècle* (1958), p. 140.

[15] H. Heaton, op. cit., *New Camb. Mod. Hist.* X, p. 43.

community of slum existence. In Paris, the great hive of small traders of the *ancien régime* type, the marriage registers prove that the old amalgam of shopkeepers, small masters, workmen and domestic servants still constituted the 'people', as it had constituted the *sans culottes* of 1793. Marx was mistaken in calling them a proletariat, yet their condition of living was such that they had many of the character-istics of his proletarian formula. Hard times and the flooding in of population from the countryside created a terrifying multitude. From 1815 to 1850 Paris increased, by sheer immigration, from 700,000 to 1,000,000 inhabitants. In 1846, one person in every thirteen in the French capital was in receipt of official poor relief and one in every four lived on the margin of survival. One child in three was illegitimate. The crowd does not figure much in Balzac's novels, but when his eye roves the narrow streets he seems to see only pallid, prematurely aged, 'exhumed' faces, born for crime. In England, Chadwick described the urban masses as 'an encamped horde': Lecouturier in 1848 said, 'There is no Parisian society, there are no Parisians. Paris is but an encampment of nomads'.[16]

It was in face of poverty like this that an interpretation of all history in terms of the class struggle was formulated. From our comfortable armchairs we can see, now, how Marx was mistaken: the classes need much more subtle definition than he gave them, and his insistence upon economic motivation is too single-minded. As Chesterton said, 'a Catholic association is more coherent than a union of window cleaners'. Yet in 1848, intelligent men had no doubt that they were on the verge of a war to the death between the haves and the have-nots. These were Disraeli's 'two nations . . . as ignorant of each others' . . . feelings as if they were . . . inhabitants of different planets . . . THE RICH AND THE POOR'.[17] In France, the analogy commonly used was that of barbarians lurking on the frontiers of the Roman Empire. Girardin used it in describing the rising of the starving silkweavers of Lyon in 1831, which, he said, 'has revealed a terrible secret, that there is a war in society between the class with possessions and the class which possesses nothing'.[18] The sociologist Buret in 1840 spoke of the workers, isolated in society with neither rights nor duties, 'like the barbarians to which they have been compared, . . . brooding upon an invasion'.[19] When in June 1848 the great invasion came in Paris,

---

[16] Lecouturier, *Paris incompatible avec la République* (1848), cit. Chevalier, op. cit., p. 459.
[17] Disraeli, *Sybil or the Two Nations* (1845), Bk. II, chap. v (The World's Classics, 1950), p. 67.
[18] Schnerb, op. cit., p. 70.
[19] Chevalier, op. cit., p. 453.

Tocqueville described the sinister mass solidarity of the disinherited multitude. 'The whole of the working class was engaged, either in fact or in spirit, in the struggle. . . . Women took part in it as much as men. . . . They hoped for a victory to make life easier for their husbands to help rear their children. They took pleasure in this war as they might have taken pleasure in a lottery. . . . It was not a political struggle . . . but a class war, a kind of slave insurrection.'[20]

VIII

Modern research on the June Days is revealing that, literally speaking, the working classes of Paris were not united in a mass insurrection of helots, as contemporaries like Tocqueville imagined. A substantial minority of the workers was on the side of order. This is not surprising: 'unanimous' uprisings of the poor can seldom survive the test of statistical analysis. By contrast, we now know something of the widespread rioting which took place outside the capital—the destruction of railway lines and power looms, attacks on Jewish money-lenders in Alsace and risings against the forest laws in the Pyrenees. The fact was that the lower half of French society was in despair. This was a year of severe economic deprivation. At the beginning of summer the grain of last year's crop was exhausted and the new harvest was still in the fields. But starving men are not necessarily unanimous about the remedy for their ills. Dussardier the idealist (in Flaubert's *Sentimental Education*) fought in the end on the side of the authorities: 'Perhaps he ought to have gone over to the other side of the barricades, with the workers, for they'd been promised a whole heap of things and the promises had been broken.'[21]

In Paris, the surge of mass feeling which frightened Tocqueville owed much to what he called 'chimerical ideas on the relations between labour and capital, extravagant theories as to the degree in which the government might interfere between the working man and the employers'.[22] Under the July Monarchy, France had been a sort of intellectual laboratory where the ideas of socialism were being invented, distilled and blended. Against the grim background of poverty, the new theories were more revolutionary than Saint-Simon's: they challenged riches as well as idleness, and concentrated on the share-out instead of leaving the problem of distributive justice to the easy solution of an inevitably rising productivity. Yet few

[20] Alexis de Tocqueville, *Souvenirs* (1942), pp. 140, 136, 135. There is an English translation, ed. J. P. Mayer (1949).
[21] Flaubert, *L'Education sentimentale* (1869), Pt. III, chap. i.
[22] *Memoir, Letters and Remains of A. de Tocqueville* (2 vols., 1861) II, p. 87.

writers preached class warfare, though a bitter phrase like 'Property is theft'—quite contrary to its author's argument—stuck in people's memories.

And what was the effect of these various socialist doctrines upon the popular mind? There were, perhaps, three main inspirations that were communicated and, without being logically consistent, were simultaneously welcomed. From Cabet, Fourier and Prudhon came a vision of a utopian colonization of the wilderness of industrialization: the simple healthy life in a *phalanstère* with Fourier or with Cabet in Icaria or, more realistically, in Prudhon's world of small landowners and humble tradesmen, enjoying interest-free loans on the way to independence and exercising democratic privileges in the parochial politics of a small commune. From the tradition of Babeuf and from writers like Blanqui and Considérant came a harsher idea, one that led necessarily, perhaps, to class warfare—the idea that the great French Revolution had never been finished, that the 'Fourth Estate' must have its turn, and that another night of the 4 August was needed, this time to end the privileges of the bourgeoisie. This theme of the unfinished revolution did not need publicists to imprint it on the popular consciousness. The tide of migration which flowed into Paris came chiefly from the departments of the north and east, where the traditions of 1793 were strongest: the city was not allowed to abandon its revolutionary memories. A third inspiration, and the most practical one of all, was that of Louis Blanc's *L'Organisation du Travail* (1839), which depicted a democratic state planning for the public welfare, setting up government workshops to drive the private industrialists out of business, and calling on talent to sacrifice itself for the masses: 'From each according to his capacity; to each according to his needs.' In 1848, the practical action that the working class called for in its misery was that recommended by Louis Blanc. '*Organisation du travail*', '*droit au travail*', were the slogans of the submerged Fourth Estate.

What response did the Provisional Government of the Republic make to all these yearnings? It established voting by universal suffrage, recognized the *droit au travail*, set up National Workshops under Emil Thomas and the Minister of the Interior, and a *Commission pour les travailleurs* under Louis Blanc. But so far as the workers were concerned, all this was camouflage. The National Workshops were a device for giving a dole to the unemployed, not a lever to break down the profits of private enterprise, and Louis Blanc resigned from the Commission when he realized that it was powerless to do more than pass resolutions. The elections to a Constituent Assembly on 23 and 24 April showed that the rural voters were not prepared to support the left and the dream of *la république sociale*. Blanqui, the most determined heir of the revolutionary tradition, had foreseen this disaster. 'For the space of sixty years, the Counter Revolution has had a monopoly of free speech in France. . . . In consequence, we ask for the indefinite adjournment of the elections and the despatch into the departments of citizens charged with the mission of spreading democratic enlightenment.'[23] There could hardly be a better summary of the arguments for a dictatorship of the proletariat. Georges Sand had already threatened, if the elections went wrong, to call on the people to 'adjourn the decision of a false national sovereignty'. On 12 May, Louis Blanc's proposal for a 'Ministry of Progress' was turned down. There was an abortive *journée* on 15 May; then, when the Executive Commission tried to wind up the Workshops, the barricades went up again in Paris on 23 June, and civil war began.

It was not the men of the National Workshops, however, who formed the bulk of the insurgents, nor were there any obvious leaders. Those who fought seem to have been a representative cross-section of the starving workers of Paris. There can be little doubt that many who did not fight and some who fought against them were really on their side. The total allegiances involved were far more extensive than an analysis of actual numbers engaged at the barricades would suggest, and the far-reaching discussion of social ideas that had gone on in France for a generation meant that the total hopes involved went far beyond the incoherent demands which were all the insurgents could formulate. Thus the tragedy of the June Days had an enormous symbolic significance. In industrial England, the Chartist movement expired quietly, while in pre-industrial France a desperate rising occurred which Marx was glad to take as a prototype and forerunner of his proletarian revolution.

IX

The repression was ferocious. By 25 June the possessing classes, peasants included, were pouring into the capital to shoot down the men who were threatening property. 'Had the revolt shown a less radical character', Tocqueville mused, 'it is probable that the greater part of the bourgeois would have stayed at home. France would not have come to our aid.'[24] Many of the cruelties were committed by the

[23] Cit. J. Dautry, *1848 et la IIe République* (1957), pp. 121–2. For 1848 in France generally see P. Amann, 'The Changing Outlines of 1848', *American Hist. Rev.* LXVIII (1963), pp. 938 ff.
[24] Tocqueville, *Souvenirs*, p. 141.

Gardes mobiles, young militiamen drawn from the poorer classes. Balzac saw them swarm over a barricade, 'like lice on the head of a beggar', while the generals debated upon its impregnability.[25] Marx reserved his greatest hatred for these traitors of the *Lumpenproletariat* who, like the *lazzaroni* of Naples, gratified their lust for violence in the pay of reaction.[26] About 1,500 insurgents were executed without trial, and the numbers killed in the fighting were never counted. 'The excesses were practically exclusively the work of the defenders of order', Renan wrote from Paris to his sister. 'Something hard, ferocious and inhuman is coming into our conduct; . . . The men of order, those that are called "respectable folk", ask for shootings, nothing but shootings. And they think that they are victors for always.'[27]

Herzen, the Russian exile, watched the events in Paris and regarded liberalism as doomed and the advent of socialism as inevitable. The liberals had ignored the question of 'daily bread' and had 'rewarded the people for a thousand years of suffering by declaring them sovereign'; but now it was proved 'that a representative system is a cunning device to transmute social needs and readiness for energetic action into words'. On the evening of 26 June, he heard the volleys of the firing-squads—'moments like these make one . . . seek revenge all one's life. Woe to those who forget such moments!'[28]

X

On 15 October 1851, Prince Albert declared the Great Exhibition closed. Massed choirs sang the Hallelujah Chorus in thunderous valedictory. Seven weeks later, Louis Napoleon seized power in France. The Republic that had crushed the workers fell into the hands of a plebiscitary dictator using the doctrine of popular sovereignty against the liberals. Of the overwhelming majority which voted for him, many did so because they feared the red spectre and trembled for property, and others because the democratic Republic had done nothing to relieve their miseries. Two years later, the long era of peace among the great powers ended; England and France fought Russia—the new world of industrialism and democracy against the old world of serfdom and autocracy. The processes of industrialization

[25] Balzac, 'Lettres inédites sur la révolution de 1848', ed. R. Pierrot, *L'Année Balzacienne* (1960), p. 49.

[26] K. Marx, *The Class Struggles in France, 1848–50* in *Selected Works* (1951) I, p. 142.

[27] Renan to his sister, 1 July 1848, in *Oeuvres Complètes* (ed. Henriette Psichari), IX (1960), p. 1084.

[28] Herzen, *From the Other Shore* (Engl. trans. 1956), pp. 64, 93, 82, 47.

pioneered by England were to sweep over Europe, releasing tremendous productive forces and vast riches. But how would men share these riches, and how would they rule themselves in an era of massive technology, jingoistic nationalism and urban multitudes? The June Days, the failure of the 1848 revolutions, and the Crimean War made it hard to give an optimistic answer.

CHAPTER XIV

NAPOLEON III

I

On the threshold of the century stood Bonaparte, his gigantic shadow falling across the future generations. The words are Victor Hugo's, eight years after the Emperor had died at St Helena. Had Napoleon lived out his exile on Elba amidst Ruritanian splendour, he might have been more easily relegated into ordinary history: on a rock in mid-Atlantic he could create the Promethean myth of a peaceful and democratic soldier who would have liberated and federated Europe.[1] The most conspicuous dupe of this legend (if 'dupe' is the word, for the deception made him great) was its inventor's nephew, Louis Napoleon, son of Louis Bonaparte, King of Holland and his queen Hortense de Beauharnais. When he was only twenty-four years of age we find him publishing books claiming that France can be regenerated by a return to the tradition of his uncle, 'the People's Emperor', who had ruled in the interests of all classes, who had intended to make Poland and Italy into national States, and to crown his work by giving France herself a liberal constitution. These fictions became a creed, an incitement to a mission. Three years later, in 1836, in a private letter, Louis Napoleon writes of his efforts to make himself worthy of the cause, to 'raise myself to a height at which I may still be lit by an expiring ray from the sunset of St Helena'.

In appearance and conversation, the man who wrote in terms of this romantic obsession was unconvincing as a candidate for the Napoleonic heritage. He was, said Greville (who saw him in exile in England) 'a short thickish vulgar-looking man, without the slightest resemblance to his Imperial uncle, or any intelligence in his countenance'.[2] In later life, in his days of greatness, more than one observer was to suspect that, behind the mysterious mask, the man himself was dull. Here, said Bismarck maliciously, was 'a sphinx without a riddle . . . a great unfathomed incapacity'.[3] Yet if the talents were commonplace and the exterior undistinguished, they were transfigured by the faith in the Napoleonic legend which was Louis Napoleon's substi-

[1] Cf. F. A. Simpson, *The Rise of Louis Napoleon* (1909, ed. 1950), pp. 7–12.
[2] Cit. J. M. Thompson, *Louis Napoleon and the Second Empire* (1954), p. 51.
[3] Cit. L. Namier, *Vanished Supremacies* (1958), p. 56.

tute for religion. In this faith, and with no apparent hope of success, he risked his life, though it must be conceded that he revelled in conspiratorial intrigues and had a shrewd idea that it is the initial success of a *coup d'état* which produces most of its accomplices. In 1836 he made an attempt to stir up mutiny in the garrison at Strasbourg; in 1840 he sailed from Gravesend in a chartered steamer (with a tame eagle, bought from a boy at the docks, on the mast) to exhort anyone around Boulogne who would listen to join in a march on Paris. Condemned to perpetual imprisonment, from the fortress of Ham he writes five years later—'I believe that there are certain men who are born to serve as a means for the progress of the human race. . . . I await with resignation, but with confidence, the moment when I will either live my providential life or die my predestined death, persuaded that in either way I shall be useful, first of all to France, then to humanity.'[4] He was living instinctively, like a sleepwalker; he had achieved the certainty that is given only to complete self-dedication.

Yet the humility of Louis Napoleon before his uncle's memory should not deceive us. Superbly intelligent, the great Napoleon had been blind to the pattern of the future, while his nephew, with the 'extinct look in his eyes', succeeded in detecting the leading issues of the nineteenth and, indeed, of the twentieth century. There was a generation between them, of course, and the waging of war distracted the one just as exile and imprisonment gave the other leisure for reflection. More than this, Louis Napoleon had the insight which goes, not with analytical reason, but with sympathy. Napoleon I saw into the ideals of men, and used them; his nephew understood them instinctively because he shared them. A true son of the Romantic era, he had wanted to fight for Greece in 1829 (in the Russian army— *Madame Mère*, still alive, was thunderstruck), for Italy in 1831, then for Poland. The oppressed nationalities, which his uncle had stirred up by accident, were his concern, and he dreamt of a revision of the map of Europe to give them their liberty. He foresaw, too, the inevitable advance of the French Revolution's principle of the 'sovereignty of the people', and he consciously annexed the democratic future to the Napoleonic heritage. Advancing on the dumbfounded soldiery at Strasbourg, and on trial after the Boulogne fiasco, he proclaimed himself the representative of popular sovereignty. Only by incarnating their wishes in one man can the masses reconcile their desire for order and their desire for liberty. Or, looking at the problem from the other

[4] A. Dansette, *Louis-Napoléon à la conquête du pouvoir* (1961), p. 203 (letter to Mme Cornu, 18 Sept. 1845: this correspondence is published by M. Emérit, 2 vols., 1937).

side, only by basing itself upon the will of the masses can a monarchy hope to exercise the strong government that the age demands. In a letter of 1837, Louis Napoleon makes this point vividly. 'My conviction is that Europe will not be at peace until France has a strong government. Now in France, the only basis upon which a throne can be consolidated is democracy. If a new dynasty is not settled upon the broadest foundations, the man in power will never be more than the head of a party. There will be victors and vanquished, and not a people of brothers.'[5]

This fraternal language from the heir to the Bonapartist tradition was not dishonest. Louis Napoleon sympathized with ordinary people; he had wandered around the Anglo-Saxon world and in prison (at the 'University of Ham', as he liked to call it) he had studied practical matters like electrical power, sugar beet, canals, pauperism and land settlement. These sentiments and insights combined to form his vision of the future, which went far beyond the formula of a democratic dictatorship. His dream was a Saint-Simonian one of a technological utopia, of a France undergoing an industrial revolution of the English kind, but one inspired by the State and controlled, to protect the working classes. A history of modern Europe could be written around these five key words— 'nationalism', 'democracy', 'dictatorship', 'industrialization' and 'socialism'; Louis Napoleon sensed the importance of all of these, and dreamt of uniting them all in the service of France, humanity, and his own ambitions.

II

The Frenchmen who elected Louis Napoleon President in November 1848 knew little about his progressive visions, though his propaganda had referred to canals and railways and measures to help the sick and aged. As his enormous majority shows ($5\frac{1}{2}$ million out of $7\frac{1}{2}$ million votes), he drew support from all classes and all opinions. Property and religion would be safe under a 'man of order'; all the same, he had been absent from France during the June Days, and none of the blood of repression stained his hands. Conservative politicians thought they could use him; those who sympathized with the proscripts of the left awaited his clemency; the peasants, puzzled by this era of great passions and little men, voted for the magic of his name, for the legend of the Napoleonic past. His candidature, said Victor Hugo, dated from Austerlitz.

Thus, power was obtained: there were no Bonapartist precedents

[5] Dansette, op. cit.

or relinquishing it. In the late spring of 1852, France, once again, had to elect a President—necessarily a new man, for by the Constitution, the outgoing President was not re-eligible. That was why, on 2 December 1851, Louis Napoleon seized power by a *coup d'état*. Tocqueville denounced these 'military saturnalia'. In theory, one is obliged to sympathize with him, yet the fact is that Tocqueville, Broglie, Montalembert and the other aristocratic and intellectual friends of liberty were left high and dry in their *salons* and the Academy, as the popular tide set overwhelmingly towards the Empire. The conservative Assembly had changed the electoral law to exclude three million voters (May 1850); it was Louis Napoleon who made the master-stroke (all the more masterly because he was sincere) of asking for the restoration of universal suffrage. There was force in his denunciation of the Assembly (in a speech at Dijon, 1 June 1851)— 'I have noticed that I can always count on the backing of the Assembly when there is any question of combating disorder by means of repression. But whenever I have tried to do good, to ameliorate the conditions of the people, I have found apathy and inertia'.[6] The rule against re-eligibility was a barrier to the will of the country. A strong majority of the Assembly (though not enough for a constitutional amendment) admitted as much by voting for its cancellation. Thus, when the machinery of the *coup* went into action, there was little resistance. Walter Bagehot saw barricades erected in Paris by urchins, directed by 'a few old stagers . . . men whose faces I do not like to think of, yellow, sour, angry, fanatical'. But it was all over soon. Then it was a question of accepting the *fait accompli*. An English visitor saw the customers in a barber's shop—'republican' until Louis Napoleon rode past, then saying he looked 'every inch a king'.[7] And in any case, what was now the alternative? 'To vote against Louis Napoleon,' admitted Montalembert, 'is to approve the socialist revolution.' So Frenchmen gave easy acquiescence to the 'military saturnalia'. The actual figures of the plebiscite were 7,439,215 for; 646,735 against.

By the standards of modern purges, or compared with the brutal repression of the Commune twenty years later, the coup of December 1851 was a mild affair—27,000 provisionally arrested and of these 239 deported to Cayenne and 9,000 to Algeria. The principal beneficiary of these limited severities averted his eyes from what was going on. Dictators who disinterest themselves in the fate of their opponents are not unaware of the fact that some of their understrappers are not

[6] F. A. Simpson, *Louis Napoleon and the Recovery of France* (1923, ed. 1960), p. 119.
[7] Ibid., pp. 149, 138.

likely to be squeamish. There is evidence, however, that Louis Napoleon felt a genuine revulsion against the actions done in his name, and that the memory of 2 December haunted him.

While others attended to sordid details of transportation and police registers, the President was engaged in organizing the new government, with a speed and self-confidence which show that his theories of politics had been matured long beforehand. On 14 January 1852, he proclaimed the new constitution; on 9 October, in a speech at Bordeaux, he made it clear that the Empire was coming and defined it as peace and economic progress; on 7 November the Senate agreed and on 21 November a plebiscite recorded over 7,800,000 votes in favour of the Second Empire, whose constitution was promulgated on Christmas Day. The arrangements were such as the new Emperor had dreamed of—the masses incarnate in one man, democracy allied to the Napoleonic heritage. There was a Legislative Assembly elected by universal suffrage, and a Senate of marshals and cardinals and those the head of State delighted to honour. But the secret of the working of the constitution lay in the fact that the ministers depended entirely on the Emperor. The Assembly, with no ministers sitting in its precincts, no power to initiate legislation, and no publicity for its debates, was a sort of adjunct to the executive, a peripheral institution.

This constitution represented the theories Louis Napoleon had meditated in exile and prison. In one respect only did he depart significantly from them. By the decree of 17 February 1852, severe restraints were put upon the press—a system of caution monies, warnings, suspensions and trials without juries. Yet the Emperor had believed in freedom of expression, more especially because, to him, dictatorship had the duty of navigating according to the currents of the vast democratic sea upon which it floated. Expediency prevailed: it was easier to rely on the reports of the prefects and the *procureurs* of the Courts of Appeal for a knowledge of public opinion than to allow the discontented a forum for their mutual encouragement. Popular as he was, the Emperor was respecting the freedom of the masses only in so far as he served their wishes as isolated individuals. He would not allow them to formulate their demands in coherent organizations, for coherent organizations can produce alternative governments. Plebiscitary dictators prefer to see voters confined to a choice between their own rule and the nameless confusions of the Hobbesian state of nature.

III

The government was a dictatorship. But where lay the realities of power?—with one man, or with a group of men, with a party or with a class? By way of answer, one may notice: firstly, that with Napoleon III a new group of individuals ousted the old politicians at the top of the hierarchy; secondly, that the Emperor's entourage had no coherence, no common policy or ideology. 'How could you expect the Empire to work smoothly?' Louis Napoleon once observed. 'The Empress is a Legitimist, Morny is an Orleanist, my cousin Napoleon is a Republican, I am a Socialist, only Persigny is a Bonapartist, and he is crazy.'[8] Certainly, the Empress Eugénie, a supporter of the Papacy and a fanatical believer in the divine right of the dynasty, was nicely balanced by cousin Prince Napoleon, an anti-clerical left-wing *frondeur*. Closer to Napoleon III, politically, than either of them was his half-brother, the duc de Morny, an illegitimate son of Hortense by the comte de Flahaut, who was himself a natural son of Talleyrand. An army officer of distinction, a speculator who made a fortune out of sugar beet before his twenty-seventh birthday on capital provided by his mistress, the wife of the Belgian ambassador, a writer of light verse and comedies, a patron of art and sea-bathing, Morny had the brilliant talents, frivolity and cynicism of his ancestry. It was he who planned and executed the *coup d'état*. Paradoxically, it was Morny, too, bohemian and aristocrat that he was, who tried to push the Emperor further along the path of social reform and liberalism. But to Napoleon, this half-brother, with his vices and perpetual need for money, was something of a liability. '*Je traine deux boulets*,' he said (referring to the iron weights on the fetters of criminals), '*Morny et Persigny*.' This other *boulet*, Persigny, was the most intelligent of the adventurers who had suffered for the Bonapartist cause in exile; he now served the régime recklessly and imaginatively as an ambassador and Minister of the Interior, until his originality proved too much for his master and he was removed into a dukedom. There were some others who counted as of the inner circle—some friends of exile and one more close relative, Walewski, the natural son of the great Napoleon and a Polish countess, a soldier, journalist, diplomat and *bon viveur*, whose influence was added to Morny's in favour of a liberalization of the régime.

By contrast with this inner circle (where, except for the Empress, liberalism in politics—and in morals—prevailed), there was an outer group of expert executives, who served the Empire without illusions, and preferred its authoritarian bias to its liberal potentialities. The bourgeois lawyers, Baroche and Rouher, were ministers of this kind, fearful of freedom at home and of adventures abroad, Gallican in their attitude to Rome, able and cynical instruments of their master's will, and great amassers of money and offices. Both had been 'republicans'

[8] Thompson, op. cit., p. 249.

in 1848; that is, they had sought a career in politics. Then the June rising had scared them—Rouher had voted for Cavaignac as President —'*avant tout, il fallait voter pour le gagnant*'—but had hastily scrambled out of the ditch on the winning side in time to receive high office. From his speeches and correspondence we can reconstruct his unheroic, bourgeois version of Bonapartism. He agreed with the Emperor's social ideas in so far as he favoured free trade, technical education and legislation for better working conditions; he disagreed with the official foreign policy, for he opposed all war, since Western Europe must abandon its quarrels to be able to face the two great powers of the future, Russia and America; he believed in authoritarian government because he distrusted universal suffrage, always at the mercy of the 'ready-made passions served up to it by the press'. 'Parliamentary government,' said Rouher, in March 1866, 'is a worn-out coat . . . its day-to-day task is to survive, stay there, avoid defeat, and not to lead towards progress. . . . Parliamentary government is not suited to work with the immense sovereignty of ten million voters.'[9] It was unfortunate that Napoleon III intervened in Italy and Mexico against the advice of Rouher, but that in the decision to delay the liberalization of the régime he found support in Rouher's tough administrative genius. The Emperor had not weighed sufficiently the merits of systems in which ministers are expected to have consciences.

There was no question, of course, of cabinet solidarity. The Emperor usually consulted ministers individually, and the others read about the result in the *Moniteur*. In foreign affairs and home affairs alike, the momentous decisions were Napoleon's; the changes of Foreign Ministers in May 1855 and in January 1860, the Commercial Treaty with England, the confiscation of the property of the Orleans family, the financial measures of 1861, the reforms of 1867–8—all these were his personal work. The economic policy of the régime, its essential claim to originality and greatness, was the reflection of the Emperor's Saint-Simonian dreams of an industrial utopia. Haussmann, the Prefect of the Seine who transformed Paris, Michel Chevalier, engineer and free-trade economist, the brothers Pereire, Portuguese Jews prominent in railway speculation and credit operations, Fould, rich from both land and banking, who planned the new economic policy—these men, more than any others, may be described as consistently influencing the Emperor's policy. But the original vision was his own. They had the experience and practical ability to translate his dreams into realities. Without intellectual distinction, administrative ability or moral elevation, a great *coureur des femmes*, a kindly, well-intentioned vulgarian, Louis Napoleon had glimpsed a

[9] R. Schnerb, *Rouher et le Second Empire* (1949), p. 56.

political goal and, somehow, he knew how to rule. He believed in himself, in his mission, in his duty to take decisions, and he still was not proud. In his way, he had greatness.

IV

'We all thought France wedded to class division and constitutionalism: he saw that the equality for which the French are passionate is Asiatic equality—one ruler and everyone prostrate below him ... that they do not wish for a leader, but for a master, under whom every man may have a chance of becoming minister.'[10] These words of Montalembert sum up the liberal aristocratic explanation of the advent of Napoleon III and his destruction of liberty. Democracy is inevitable, it means equality, and equality brings with it the menace of tyranny—at best, the tyranny of the majority, at worst, of a dictator. In *L'Ancien Régime et la Révolution* (1856), that masterpiece of analytical history, Tocqueville used this formula to dissect the recent past of France. Under the eighteenth-century Bourbons, a decadent but proud aristocracy, an independent Gallician Church, the privileged *pays d'états*, the magistrates who had bought their offices—the very abuses of society—had served to maintain a fragmentary liberty. Then the Revolution had atomized society, so that the machine of power could grind unhindered over the pulverized dust of disassociated individuals. As Mirabeau told Louis XVI, the Revolution had completed the work of Richelieu, '*cette surface égale facilite l'exercise du pouvoir.*'

Like Tocqueville, Louis Napoleon had foreseen that democracy was inevitable; but while the former talked of the Gadarene rush down to equality as inevitably leading to dictatorship, the Emperor congratulated himself on the necessity whereby the vast sovereignty of the masses could only become real when incarnated in one man. In practice, both of these broad generalizations fail to describe the régime, which lived by influence, manipulation and manoeuvre, very occasionally resorting to arbitrary measures, and not infrequently creating the illusion of leadership by finding out what everyone wanted to do then ordering them to do it. When the administration was ruthless, it generally rendered itself ridiculous, as when, during the Crimean War, the actor Grassot was arrested for complaining of the service in a café, '*C'est ici comme à Sebastopol, on ne peut rien prendre.*' The excessive measures of military precaution taken after Orsini's attempt on the Emperor's life (1858) had to be abandoned in a few months. Force was alien to the genius of the Second Empire.

[10] Thompson, pp. 92–3.

In its peculiar way, the régime depended upon public opinion, even if it had to manufacture it. It was a civilized government, though an unedifying one—'an admirable government for present and coarse purposes,' said Bagehot, 'but a detestable government for future and refined purposes.'[11]

The Emperor believed in universal suffrage: he also knew that the majority of men like to have their thinking done for them. In the Parliament of 1857, out of over 260 deputies, there were only a dozen opponents; government candidates polled 5,471,000 votes as against 665,000 to the right and left opposition. This was the Emperor's standard for voting figures—rather over 7 millions in a plebiscite for himself, and rather over 5 millions for his parliamentary majority. Majestic statistics like these are virtually impossible in the workings of democracy. How was it done without resort to the more odious forms of manufactured consent? The great secret was that there was no obvious alternative form of government within the horizon of vision. So far as Parliament was concerned, the government frankly encouraged the tendency of Frenchmen (especially in rural areas) to regard national politics as a distant battlefield from which representatives return laden with booty in the form of state money for local needs, like roads and bridges. In the countryside, the web of influence was tightened by rumours of the prefect's frown and by the closer authority of the mayor, and by the correct attitudes necessarily demonstrated by government employees, the schoolmaster, constable, road man, tax collector, tobacconist and bill-sticker.[12] There was no doubt about whom to vote for: Persigny had established the theory of the 'official candidature', and the *Moniteur* published the names of those recommended to the electors. There was, too, some 'gerrymandering' of constituency boundaries, generally to ensure that a town was under-represented, or to engulf the republican voters of a working-class suburb in rural cohorts from the neighbouring countryside. We should beware, however, of supposing that the government was 'imposing' its men on the constituencies. The prefect (under the Minister of the Interior) nominated candidates, and while the object was, no doubt, to pick supporters of the régime, it was more important still to name someone who was certain to get in. Thus, especially in legitimist areas, prefects were often allowed great latitude, and local notabilities of varying allegiances became official candidates, provided that they were willing to co-operate. What Bonapartists received as a reward, others might receive as an

[11] From Bagehot's essay on *Caesarism* (1865), in Thompson, p. 254.
[12] For all this paragraph see Th. Zeldin, *The Political System of Napoleon III* (1958), pp. 85 ff.

incentive. The Second Empire was a broad easy highway where no questions were asked of the multitude of travellers who found it convenient.

On their journey, these travellers were to be kept reasonably happy. Though the policies of Napoleon III were tortuous, they were calculated to conciliate influential opinion and to ensure the applause of the masses when it was most needed. The expansionist economic policy provided plums for the provinces and opportunities for the enterprising. It also enabled the Emperor to appear in two potentially contradictory rôles: as the defender of the bourgeoisie against disorder, and as the patron of the workers. The former rôle was, of course, the crucial one. Zola's grim 'Rougon–Macquart' series of novels gives a scarifying picture of the sort of blind support the Empire received—Legitimists, Orleanists and bourgeoisie in the little town of Plassans all going Bonapartist because of the danger to property, while the talk in Felicité Rougon's salon runs on 'massacring the Reds'; the sordid speculators around 'Son Excellence Eugène Rougon', who has crept into the sunlight of power; the Parisian shopkeepers who are happy because 'trade is doing well', because they 'can sleep without being woken by gunfire'; the peasants, land-hungry and promiscuous, who ask 'What blasted good has it been to us, their liberty and equality?'[13] Nor does Zola fail to note the electioneering support given by the clergy; indeed, in its early years, the Empire made especial efforts to win over the Church. The salaries of the clergy, especially of the bishops, were increased, the expansion of religious education proceeded unhindered, the laws which could have restricted the growth of religious orders were not enforced. The Legitimists saw their popular following in the countryside vanishing as a new throne and altar alliance developed. When the Emperor had less need of clerical support, he could manoeuvre more freely. In 1856 the taking over of communal schools by religious congregations was forbidden, and the Italian campaign of 1859, with all its implications for the papal temporal power, was universally unpopular among churchmen. Yet Napoleon knew what he was doing. For the most part, Frenchmen were indifferent to the fate of the papal dominions and had an instinctive distrust of clericalism in their rulers.

The Second Empire has been described as 'essentially Parisian',[14] and the régime lost nothing by co-operating in the frivolities of the

---

[13] *La Fortune des Rougon: La Conquête de Plassans: Son Excellence Eugène Rougon* (see R. B. Grant's 'An Historical and Critical Study' of this novel, 1960); *Le Ventre de Paris* (Engl. trans. 1955); *La Terre* (Engl. trans. 1954).
[14] P. Guedalla, *The Second Empire* (1922, ed. 1964), p. 201.

day, which preserved the capital from boredom. This was the generation of Offenbach, the can-can and the great courtesans, pink cham-
pagne at the Moulin Rouge, all-night dancing at Mabille's and tumults
in the theatres led by young men of the Jockey Club. 'Who does not
keep a carriage these days?', wrote the Goncourts, 'What a society!
Everybody is determined to bankrupt himself. Never have *appearances*
been so despotic, so imperious and so demoralizing.'[15] Literature and
the arts gave rise to more than their usual meed of controversy, even
for Paris, as if joining in the bohemian conspiracy to add spice to
existence—Flaubert prosecuted for *Mme Bovary* and the Goncourts
and Baudelaire before the courts for 'immoral' publications, Renan
losing his chair over the *Vie de Jésus*, Manet's *Déjeuner sur l'herbe*,
and riots (for from the start the French suspected Wagner) over the
first production of *Tannhaüser*. The imperial household, steering
between the stuffy exclusiveness of Legitimism and the parsimony and
bonhomie of Orleanism, splendid and not undecorous, was the only
court in French history which really managed to integrate itself with
the social life of the capital.

It was, indeed, a cardinal principle of Napoleon III's dictatorship
that the government should have wide contacts and be accessible to
representations, and the Emperor had his machinery all over France
to ensure that he knew what the provinces, as well as Paris, were
thinking. The erratic fluctuations in his foreign policy are, to some
extent, explained by his flair for sensing the direction in which public
opinion was moving. France was apathetic at the outbreak of the
Crimean War and hostile to the English alliance, but became bellicose
once hostilities began. The Italian adventure was unpopular at first:
'They only think of the effect the war can have on bonds and railroad
stocks,' said Mérimée, 'It goes without saying that no one thinks of
glory or humanity. The Emperor appears to be rather wrought up
over the general cowardice.'[16] Then the Austrians marched, and
France broke into flame. Yet when Napoleon made an armistice at
Villafranca, he was acting like a telepath, for the reports coming in from
the prefects back in France were already indicating a general yearning
for peace. Then to crown all there was a great outburst of enthusiasm
at the acquisition of Savoy and Nice. Napoleon had understood what
the French wanted better than they themselves. Intractable problems
lay ahead, but for the moment, the Emperor, by his oscillations, had

[15] *The Goncourt Journals, 1851–70* (Engl. trans. ed. Lewis Galantière, 1937),
p. 42. For other details see Roger L. Williams, *Gaslight and Shadow: the World
of Napoleon III* (1957).
[16] Cit. L. M. Case, *French Opinion on War and Diplomacy during the Second
Empire* (1954), p. 65.

satisfied the mutually contradictory ambitions of France, the desire for peace and the lust for glory.

V

'To those who might regret that larger concessions had not been made to liberty, I would answer: Liberty has never helped to found a lasting political edifice; it crowns the edifice when time has consolidated it.'[17] This is what Napoleon III said in 1853. Presumably, he meant, in his own time, to liberalize the régime. Persigny, Haussmann and Morny urged him to do so. The adventurers were for it: the administrators, Rouher, Baroche and Fould, were against. By 1860, the Emperor was in the mood for change. After a practically unanimous plebiscite for the annexation of Savoy and Nice, no one could say that concessions implied weakness. He had come to realize that he could not control the vast administrative machine himself, and that publicity and discussion in areas beyond his own grasp were to his advantage. More reasoned explanations of policy were required, both in parliament and in the country at large. In the chancelleries of Europe the heir of the Bonapartist tradition was regarded as a conspiratorial firebrand; it would be as well to demonstrate that he could not spend money secretly on military preparations. According to Thiers, the contrast between foreign policy and its constitutional base at home was becoming a public embarrassment—'it was impossible to continue the contrast of France giving liberty to all the world and refusing it for herself'.[18] There was a young Prince Imperial now, and long views must be taken to ensure the future of the dynasty.

For these reasons, in November and December 1860, Napoleon made constitutional concessions. The Legislature and Senate could vote an address in reply to the Emperor at the opening of the session; reports of debates could be published; three ministers were named to take part in the deliberations of the lower house; a formal law was required before the government could obtain supplementary credits, and a decree of the *conseil d'état* was needed to authorize the transfer of funds from one heading of the budget to another. What did these changes add up to? The budgetary provisions were not strictly observed, for money was still spent by special decree and asked for later. The other changes did little more than oblige the government to explain itself more often, more fully and more publicly. They did not create a 'liberal Empire'. In retrospect, it became obvious that the great opportunity had been missed. Later, Napoleon admitted, to

[17] Th. Zeldin, op. cit., p. 102.
[18] Ibid., p. 106.

Emile Ollivier, '*J'aurais dû donner la liberté au lendemain du Congrès de Paris.*'

VI

In this same year 1860, when the Emperor let slip the moment of destiny in politics, he finally brought his economic design to its definitive formulation. In his reading and dreaming and in conversations with Saint-Simonian economists and business men, he had been groping towards coherence. The famous Bordeaux speech of 9 October 1852 had defined the Empire as meaning roads, canals, communications with the New World, the assimilation of Algeria, and the comforting of those who 'in the richest country in the world, remain poor'. In power, he had taken isolated measures towards these ends. Finally, in January 1860, in a letter to Fould, the integrated policy was defined. Industry would be freed from restrictions and, conversely, compelled to face the brusque stimulus of competition; commercial treaties would be negotiated, communications improved, consumption increased, and capital made available; the government would lead and would deliberately incur debt to finance the expansion.

It was a plan based upon the realities of the French situation. France had the most logical system of law and administration in Europe; a nation of thrifty peasants and bourgeois, she had an abundance of capital; her financiers were expert, at least in the exchanges and public loans of Europe. Yet in 1850, there was little more than 2,000 miles of railway in the country, coal production stood at $4\frac{1}{2}$ million tons and iron at 1 million, and the industrial labour force still consisted chiefly of artisans or independent workshop owners—there were only 1,300,000 factory workers. With all its logic, the legal framework was conservative, suited to maintain an individualistic and static economic order. On the one hand, apart from limitations on the hours of work of children, there was no legislation to protect the working class; on the other, the formation of new enterprises was made difficult—labyrinthine procedures were needed for an authorization by the *conseil d'état*, while simple ones led to the unsatisfactory *société en commandite*, in which the shareholders had no control. Deposit banking was limited and the banks fought shy of industrial investments; there were no appropriate institutions to siphon off the great reservoir of savings to promote expansion.

Napoleon's policy was designed to break through the circle of routine in which his country's economic life moved. It was not a question of putting France into the hands of business men—as under the July Monarchy—but of subjecting the business men to State leadership, and of changing their mentality, which had become used to protectionism, and to an interior market dominated by the idea of local consumption. They were to be encouraged to take risks for the big prizes, yet the interests of the whole community would be safeguarded. What was intended was a State-directed industrial revolution.

How was the design of the letter of January 1860 translated into practical measures? The most striking achievement was the revolution in communications. By persuading small companies to amalgamate and by offering long-term concessions and State guarantees of a minimum return on investments, the basic railway network of modern France—some 12,000 miles of line—was completed. Canals were taken over by the State; the electric telegraph extended its wires all over France, and its cables out to Dover and Algeria; the first of the big navigation companies was formed. The flow of trade was increased and the pressure of competition intensified by commercial treaties with foreign powers, beginning with the major treaty of 1860 with England. Institutions to draw capital into industrial expansion arose, like the Crédit Foncier and the ill-fated Crédit Mobilier. Taxation was heavy and wars were paid for by loans, so that government money was available to prime expansion. Towns were encouraged into debt for the sake of improvements and found a magnificent official example in the person of Haussmann, who gave Paris its boulevards, parks and pure water supply, and completed its gas lighting, by resort to fantastic financial expedients.[19] Over the whole expansionist gamble, the government presided intelligently: the crisis of 1857 was weathered by raising the rate of interest, and that of 1863 was handled by an intensification of public works. Industry was helped by international exhibitions, and by legislation of various kinds, especially that of May 1863 and July 1867, which introduced the principle of the English type of joint stock company.

What effect had these measures upon the French economy? It would be safer to begin by answering a more straightforward question—what was the extent of economic progress under the Second Empire? The population increased by $1\frac{1}{2}$ millions, the numbers of factory workers more than doubled, exports and imports more than quadrupled, coal and iron production tripled, the value of shares quoted on the Bourse (excluding government bonds) increased nearly five times. In business and professional circles, there was an air of prosperity. The peasant, with a growing market, internal and external, for his produce, was satisfied.

[19] See J. M. and Brian Chapman, *The Life and Times of Baron Haussmann* (1957) and D. H. Pinkney, *Napoleon III and the Rebuilding of Paris* (1958).

It is more difficult to assess the lot of the industrial workers. The common factor in the condition of the hopelessly apathetic proletariat of *L'Assommoir* and the militant revolutionary miners of *Germinal* is misery, starvation, drink, immorality and isolation from the whole world of culture and civilization; and a great deal of the repulsive detail of Zola's terrifying novels (written, one should remember, under the Third Republic) can be substantiated by grim contemporary evidence from the 'sixties. The question is, however, were conditions, bad as they were, improving? Recent research[20] has emphasized how greatly the lot of the workers varied in different areas and at different times—in big cities like Lyon as compared with compact, urban units like Orléans, in big industrial organizations like Le Creusot as compared with the domestic weavers of the countryside; in the harsh years from 1852–8, in contrast with the time of rising real wages from 1858 to about 1864. Many of the workers were more 'respectable' and had more spiritual resources within themselves than Zola's crude 'naturalistic' analysis allowed. Statistics suggest that rural families coming to work in factory areas were often bettering their lot, so far as nutrition and health were concerned, even though their new surroundings were sordid. It is no longer possible, however, to accept Levasseur's picture of an industrial working class obtaining a solid share in the rising prosperity of the Second Empire, for from 1865, prices outpaced wages again, and the Empire declined, as it had arisen, in a period of hardship. Napoleon III had a genuine interest in the working classes, but in fact did not take decisive action on their behalf. He was unwilling to put obstacles in the way of capitalist expansion, and he was jealous of pressure groups which might challenge his power. Thus, while workers' co-operatives were encouraged, and *conseils de prud'hommes* were set up to settle labour disputes, and strikes were allowed, the government forbade the establishment of trades unions. The Emperor feared all organizations which might infringe his own monopoly of leadership in politics.

We have described the official policy and the economic transformation that took place under the Second Empire. Was the second the result of the first? Obviously, to some extent; yet to give a more precise answer is difficult. What metaphors do we use? Was it an unleashing of forces, or their diversion, or their combination; was it a mechanical process or a catalytic one? Were the interventions of the government effective in key areas of the economy, or were they more useful as general propaganda creating a new spirit of enterprise? Was policy creating something new, or co-operating with the

[20] G. Duveau, *La vie ouvrière en France sous le Second Empire* (1946), espec. pp. 113–23, 279 ff, 372, 541–50.

inevitable, or simply intelligently claiming credit for what was certain to happen anyhow? It is safest, perhaps, to evade these questions and to describe the policy alongside the progress, making no inferences beyond the obvious one—that here is the first government of modern times to grasp coherently the administrative implications of economic and technological progress.

VII

The Second Empire was like a vaudeville entertainment; there was something to please everybody—except the republicans, who formed an irreconcilable core of opposition. For a decade, they were power-less. Their historians defended 1848 or denigrated the memory of the first Napoleon, while Victor Hugo, from exile, poured coruscating vituperation upon the third. Vacherot in *La Democratie* (1858) and Jules Simon in *La Liberté* (1859) elaborated the theory of parliament-tary government, the lay state and freedom of association. But until the elections of 1863, no serious political challenge was made. Then, the republicans obtained 17 seats—few enough, but significantly, they were all in constituencies of Paris or other big cities. Six years later, 30 republican candidates were returned, nine from Paris. The tide was rising and leaders of the future were emerging. Gambetta made his name in 1868 defending a newspaper editor on a political charge. In the salon of Juliette Adams, amidst the company in evening dress, he appeared in his flannel shirt to urge open warfare on the Empire—'Visitors to the sewers should wear scavengers' boots.'[21]

Meanwhile, discontent was showing itself in conservative *milieux*. Clerical opposition finally held up the official policy of secular educa-tion. In the 1869 elections, 131 deputies were returned (mostly government candidates) who had taken an engagement to support the temporal power of the Papacy. More important still was the rise of a 'Third Party', which by the end of the Empire had 80 deputies in its ranks. This was a Bonapartist group, Catholic, conservative and loyal to the Empire, but anxious to see the press freed and a measure of parliamentary control.

Against this knitting together of political interests in criticism of the régime, the Emperor could appeal to the weight of mass consent upon which his throne was founded. But the gossip of cafés and dinner parties—less dangerous, but also less responsible than a free press would have been—naturally tended to judge the heir of the Bonapartist tradition by facile tests of foreign policy. And here, the glorious days were over. After its Crimean and Italian triumphs, the government might be allowed an unlucky foray in Mexico, but the

[21] G. P. Gooch, *The Second Empire* (1960), pp. 275-6.

rise of Prussia on the northern horizon, the defeat of Austria, and French isolation caused dismay. Napoleon gave a bellicose speech to test public opinion and discovered that France was not willing to fight for territorial compensations. Then, when it was too late, the secret reports showed that all but four departments were for war. 'Everybody says,' observed a minister, summarising the situation, 'that greatness is a relative thing, and that a country can be reduced while remaining the same, when new forces increase around it.'[22] The Empress foresaw 'the beginning of the end of the dynasty'. Yet when an attempt was made to strengthen the army the prefects reported a general unwillingness. True, the rearmament loan of 1868 was thirty-four times oversubscribed. The Emperor was always successful in his appeals to the 'universal suffrage of capital', and even his Mexican loan of 1864 had received offers a dozen times in excess of what was asked. Investment was one thing: conscription, taxation and a falling stock market were another. France wanted peace—'*l'Empire, c'est la paix*.' When trading on the Bourse reflected the danger of war with Prussia, Rothschild's jest, '*l'Empire, c'est la baisse*' was taken gloomily at the Tuileries. At first, France had wanted both peace and glory, and Napoleon in his prime had kept the balance. Now, it was peace and security that were desired, and an ageing ruler failed to convince the country that a price must be paid to make the two compatible.

Constitutional concessions ought to have been made in the days of glory. Now they came under the shadow of decline. In January 1867, the *Moniteur* announced a liberalization of the régime. 'Interpellations' would be allowed in parliament, and laws would be proposed to free the press. But the Emperor was being haunted by the reactionaries, particularly Rouher and the Empress, prophesying doom; he was ill, suffering agonies from the stone; he was unwilling to make his concessions appear like 'asking pardon for Mexico and Germany'. In the Legislature, the new-found privilege of interpellation was recklessly used, even against the Emperor's right to concede interpellation at all. So press reform was delayed, then grudgingly given. When the restrictions were lifted, the outburst was the more sensational: Henri Rochefort's *La Lanterne* on 31 May 1868 opened its career with 'France contains thirty-seven million subjects, without counting the subjects for discontent.' In the elections of 1869, the government vote was down by more than a million, and the Bonapartist 'Third Party' led the way in asking for responsibility of ministers. On 8 September this was granted, together with other constitutional reforms. The Emperor was known to be acting unwillingly.

[22] Case, op. cit., p. 217.

Yet the point of decisive change had been reached, and on the eve of its downfall the Empire achieved a form in which it might have endured. In December, Emile Ollivier, who had been in touch with the Emperor's circle since 1861, was invited to form a ministry. A republican and the son of a republican fanatic, Ollivier had regarded Napoleon as 'not the representation of the Revolution, but its exploitation'. Yet, by 1860, he was writing in his journal, 'Liberty, even with him, will give me more joy than a palace revolution operated by the generals or a popular revolution which might well end up only in another despotism. We need time to educate universal suffrage.'[23] Behind his unprepossessing exterior ('the face of the defrocked priest, his squint, the dirty nails, the shabby appearance,' said an enemy),[24] Ollivier was an intelligent lawyer, a superb orator and a genuine liberal. When he took office, he insisted upon true cabinet government. The constitution of April 1870 made France into a parliamentary régime and in May, a plebiscite gave approval with over 7,350,000 armffiative votes. Napoleon was happy. '*J'ai mon chiffre*'—he had roughly the same number of votes as he had collected after the *coup d'état*. A parliament with new powers met on 18 May: the Empire then had three months to go.

It could have endured. War, and not the logic of internal developments ended it. The final crisis had its ironies. In an anachronistic return to personal government, Grammont sent off the fatal telegram after consulting the Emperor, not the Cabinet (though Ollivier added an irrelevant pacific phrase). The Chamber, with its new power and responsibility, was swept by a wave of unreasoning warlike passion. The Empire had been feared in the world as a military régime and Frenchmen were confident in its arms: in fact, out of deference to public opinion, Napoleon had economized on the army and defeat was certain.

[23] Th. Zeldin, *Emile Ollivier* (1963), p. 60.
[24] Gooch, op. cit., p. 190.

CHAPTER XV

GERMAN AND ITALIAN UNITY,
1849–1866

I

In civil wars, total victory is a dangerous achievement. The Habsburg monarchy did not have to compromise with the revolutions of 1848; it survived through its military triumphs, a régime hardened, but not tempered, by adversity, more unyielding and more brittle than before.

Poor Ferdinand had to abdicate in December 1848, not so much because he was feeble-minded, but because he was bound by promises made to the insurgent Hungarians.[1] The young Francis Joseph, son of the termagant Archduchess Sophia, became emperor in his stead. Real power was in the hands of Prince Schwarzenberg, a bitter opponent of the principles of 1848, on personal as well as political grounds, for his sister, married to Windischgrätz, had been killed in the Pentecost riots in Prague. An ex-cavalry officer and diplomat, sardonic and frivolous, Schwarzenberg was an intelligent aristocrat who was as contemptuous of the stupidity of his own class as he was of the lower orders' inferior status. He had none of Metternich's eighteenth-century poise, European sense or tolerance: politics to him, at home and abroad, meant domination.

At home, his principles were absolutism and centralization. A liberal-seeming constitution was devised in 1849, but withdrawn in 1851. Meanwhile, under the cover of its parade of free institutions, the Empire had been given a single administrative system, and local liberties were suppressed. Hungary was divided into 'provinces of the Austrian Crown'. The Croats, who had fought so bravely for the monarchy, also lost their Diet—'they received as a reward what the others received as a punishment'.[2] The German language was established as official usage in the army, in the rapidly expanding bureaucracy and in institutions of higher learning, a crowd of German and German-speaking Czech officials descended upon the Hungarian

[1] James Joll, 'Prussia and the German Problem, 1830–66', *New Camb. Mod. Hist.* X (1960), p. 498.

[2] As a Croat leader observed to an Hungarian friend, cit. C. A. Macartney, 'The Austrian Empire, 1848–67', *New Camb. Mod. Hist.* X, p. 537.

territories to vex the Magyars and their subordinate nationalities alike.

In Germany and Italy, Schwarzenberg restored Austria to the position she had held before 1848, even though this meant the permanent hostility of Piedmont, and the even more bitter enmity of Prussia, brought to heel and humiliated by threats of war. Faced on either side by the tremendous forces driving towards German and Italian unity, a wise statesman would have manoeuvred for disengagement, at least on one front. In such circumstances, Metternich would also have tried to get a settlement which had the goodwill, or if possible, the guarantee, of Europe. Yet, by its unwillingness to yield ground in Italy and by its brutalities in Hungary, the Austrian government seemed to be going out of its way to offend liberal sentiment in England and France. In a provocative circular, Schwarzenberg proclaimed his indifference to foreign opinion, and pointed out that Lord Palmerston did not have to undergo gratuitous advice from Vienna on the treatment of Ireland.[3] This thrust of aristocratic insolence was part of the technique of the diplomatic duellist, rather than the statesman; Schwarzenberg was putting up an aggressive front and, in a sense, it could be said that at his death in April 1852, Austria had been restored to the status of a great power—but the price was high. The country was committed to maintaining a huge army against Prussia and to hold down Italy, and had only one friend in Europe, the Tsar of Russia.

Thus, the Crimean War (1854–56) was a disaster for the Habsburg monarchy. Francis Joseph kept out of the slaughter, and tried to play the civilized rôle of a mediator between France and England on the one hand and Russia on the other. But to Nicholas I, who had suppressed the Hungarian rising and supported Austria against Prussia in Germany, this was black ingratitude. Alexander II inherited his bitterness. Austria now had no ally: she faced the renewed challenge of German and Italian nationalism alone.

II

What had been happening meanwhile in Germany and Italy? In Germany, Prussia had lost the opportunity of leading the liberal and national cause. After suppressing left-wing movements in Rhenish Prussia, Baden, Bavaria and Hesse, Frederick William IV decided to make a bid for the leadership of a reactionary Germany, and called on the princes to form a federal state. Schwarzenberg replied by con-

[3] A. J. P. Taylor, *The Italian Problem in European Diplomacy, 1847–49* (1934), p. 190.

voking a counter-assembly under Austrian tutelage. In September 1850, the Elector of Hesse was driven out by his subjects; though he was a member of the newly formed Prussian Union, he appealed to the Council of the Diet, where Austria predominated. In November, war between Prussia and Austria seemed certain. It was avoided only by the 'capitulation of Olmütz', whereby Frederick William ignominiously withdrew his troops from the Hessian dominions. The Russian policy of supporting Austria had certainly succeeded in its main objective, preventing the unity of Germany; but the stage was now set for a unification by force, by a war of revenge of Prussia against Austria.

Reaction was triumphant. The old Confederation was resurrected and on 23 August 1851 it annulled the 'Fundamental Rights of the German People' of the Parliament of Frankfurt. The red, black and gold flag was abandoned, and the new national navy was sold by auction. Finding that even the 'Dictated Constitution' of 5 December was irksome, the King of Prussia amended it to ensure that a parliament could not tamper with his freedom to levy taxes and issue ordinances. Reactionary revisions of the constitution took place in Saxony, Hanover and Mecklenberg. After its tough, paternalistic fashion, the Prussian government also led the way in showing rulers how to win over their working classes and peasants, acting on General Radowitz's principle that the masses are 'natural allies' of princes.[4] Artisans and handicraftsmen were pleased to see the guild system strengthened, religious holidays enforced and child labour in factories forbidden. Easy terms were devised to enable the peasants to buy off their remaining servile obligations; on the other hand, they were allowed no share in rural government, which was kept in the hands of the nobles. The peasants were given what they wanted, and so too were the estate owners, only the former did not know their own real interests.

A brisk breeze of economic recovery came to fill the sails of reaction. During the decade following 1848, industrial production in the area of the *Zollverein* doubled, and the production of coal and iron tripled. By 1850, real wages had reached their highest average for twenty years, though they were shortly to fall back again to harsher levels. The German output of coal passed the French in 1860: it was clear that even a reactionary Germany was destined for industrial greatness.

To an earlier generation, speculations about unity had been interlaced with vague dreams of freedom: now they were entangled with

[4] T. S. Hamerow, *Restoration, Revolution, Reaction: Economics and Politics in Germany, 1815–1871* (1958), p. 73.

the idea of power. In 1853, the word *Realpolitik* was used for the first time.[5] Political realism dictated a single goal and adequate force to drive through to it. If the issue of freedom was postponed, the forces of reaction themselves might lead the conspiracy for unity. The problem remained, however—Austria or Prussia? Catholics clung to their hope that Austria would remain in the Confederation until closer ties evolved to bind her twelve million Catholics into the full life of Germany. A new school of thinkers arose favouring a federal structure for central Europe. Klopp, the Hanoverian historian, was one of these, out of fear of 'Prussianization'; Constantin Frantz and others saw in federalism an instrument of unlimited expansionist possibilities. But the main tide of opinion was setting towards Prussia. The rise of Napoleon III made Germans think of the defence of the Rhine; Austria was entangled in Italy and was to be defeated there, a confirmation both of her weakness and of the danger of her pre-occupation with extra-German interests. The great industrial boom swept upwards, while the *Zollverein* continued to exclude Austria. The sight of constitutional arrangements in Vienna gave liberals little to hope for; in the end, things began to look better in Berlin. Here, in the elections of 1861, a new Progressive Party, asking for parliamentary control over military expenditure, gained over 100 seats. From January of this year, William I was King (he had been Regent for two years before); a simple, honest conservative, he believed that 'where constitutions exist they ought to be observed'. While the historians Droysen, Sybel and Treitschke glorified the realism of Hohenzollern policies in the past, men of differing aspirations hoped that under the shadow of Prussian might their private hopes might come to flower in Germany.

The ideal of liberty was to be sacrificed to the ideal of nationality, for an indefinite period. For most of Europe, 1848 had been a sort of combined dress rehearsal for a number of individual dramas which were to be played to their dénouement in due course. France was to be a republic again, Italy was to be unified, the nationalities of the Austrian Empire would gain independence, the Balkans would be freed, Germany would become a single nation state. But for one drama the caste had lost its nerve and transferred to other parts elsewhere. The victory of German liberalism was no longer on the programme.

III

In Italy, revolutionary agitation collapsed after Novara. Charles Albert abdicated the throne of Piedmont after his defeat, and his suc-

[5] Joll, op. cit., p. 504.

cessor, Victor Emanuel II, proved his conservative intentions by bombarding radical Genoa into submission. Radetzky allowed him favourable terms for ending the war with Austria: after all, the Piedmontese monarchy was to be preferred to republicanism rampant all over Italy. The Roman Republic collapsed on the first day of July 1849; inflation and insoluable social problems had sapped it from within[6] and foreign troops cleared out the rearguards of patriots who had rallied to its defence. In April 1850, Pius IX returned, escorted by French bayonets. The Roman jails filled with prisoners and the Austrians shot agitators in the Northern Legations. Typhus, cholera and Radetzky's guns brought Venice to surrender at the end of August 1849. Lombardy and Venetia were put under the control of the Austrian army, and Austrian garrisons marched into Parma and Modena again. The Grand Duke of Parma, Charles III, instituted brutal reprisals on rebels and forced university professors to remove their beards as a gesture of renunciation of dangerous opinions—until in March 1854, his assassination ended this threat to academic freedom. Leopold was hoisted back onto the ducal throne of Tuscany, but he had to pay heavy expenses to an Austrian occupation force, and these, together with bad seasons and cholera, completed the financial ruin of his dukedom. His old popularity vanished, and his straw hat and gaiters and benevolent mien became subjects for ridicule in the cafés of Florence. Ferdinand ruled as he pleased in Naples. His piety was undimmed and his family life blameless; his children ran all over the palace eating lollipops and their washing hung out to dry in the marble halls. But amidst all this evidence of domestic virtues, Ferdinand was presiding over the most notorious police state in Europe, 'the negation of God erected into a system of government'. Mr Gladstone erred, no doubt, in not being analytical and comparative in his study of the Neapolitan prisons, yet his pamphlet of 1851 gave the world substantially true facts: something between 15,000 and 30,000 political prisoners housed in appalling conditions and brought to trial—when they were tried—before judges who were 'not monsters, but slaves'.[7]

With defeat, realism came to the national cause. The revolutionary statesmen of 1848 had been, very often, men whose fame rested chiefly on their writings, while among the rank-and-file there had been a great deal of unco-ordinated, undirected enthusiasm. As

[6] D. Demarco, *Una rivoluzione sociale, la repubblica romana del 1849* (1944), pp. 9, 324–38.

[7] W. E. Gladstone, *Two Letters to the Earl of Aberdeen on the State Prosecutions of the Neapolitan Government* (1851), in *Gleanings of Past Years* IV (1879), pp. 7, 31,

Cavour observed, there had been 'too many songs about freeing Italy'. The future was to lie with men of practical action in politics and war. Cavour himself became Minister of Trade and Agriculture in Piedmont in 1850, and Prime Minister two years later. Long ago, he had noted in his diary a French phrase as a motto for his career, '*Pour être un homme d'état utile, il faut avant tout avoir le tact des choses possibles.*' While Cavour, with the aid of his unfailing realism, was making his way in politics, a war leader had arisen to whom nothing was impossible. After fighting as a corsair and a soldier of fortune in South America, Garibaldi had laid the foundation of his legendary reputation as the gucrilla general of the *Risorgimento* in the last-ditch stand of the Roman Republic. These two were to be the leaders, and the aims of the next Italian revolution were clear to everyone.

The dream of unity around a liberal Pope was gone for ever. 'For many centuries,' wrote Massimo d'Azeglio (especially angered by papal objections to the abolition of ecclesiastical courts and the introduction of civil marriage in Piedmont) 'the Pope has governed three millions of subjects. Over them he exercises in all its fullness a double authority, the temporal and the spiritual. What has been the result? Four armies were required to put him on his throne, and two foreign powers are necessary, and always will be necessary, to keep him there.' Italian patriots now turned universally towards Piedmont. It had fought Austria, it was the only state with a constitution, and it was the refuge for thousands of political exiles from the rest of the peninsula. 'Piedmont today is all of Italy,' said Ricasoli.[8] Significantly, he added, 'I would rather be a Jesuit than an Italian liberal . . . with the national idea there can be no compromise. Face to face with this the other liberties must yield place.' Thus, in Italy, the defeat of the revolution of 1848 had something of the effect that was evident in Germany. Ideals had coarsened. If freedom and unity could not be pursued together, men would choose unity and hope that time and chance would take care of liberty.

IV

Count Camillo Benso di Cavour was one of those tough business men, at once calculators and speculators, who take over from theorists and idealists and, with crude effectiveness, produce results. Before he became the Piedmontese Minister for Trade and Agriculture, he had established a solid reputation for himself as an expert in big-scale

[8] W. K. Hancock, *Ricasoli and the Risorgimento in Tuscany* (1926), pp. 163, 170, 175.

agricultural management and as a director of the Bank of Turin and of the Turin-Genoa railway. Not that he had proved himself a dull dog: he had been expelled from the rank of a royal page in the Military Academy for 'Jacobin' opinions, had gambled on the Paris Bourse and lost money equally effectively in bohemian adventures in London and the French capital, where his love affair with Melanie Waldour was publicised by the lady herself in a boring romantic novel, *Alphonse et Juliette*. These youthful follies turned out to have been a good investment. A knowledge of France, of its Stock Exchange and of the *demi-monde* where half the business of politics was transacted were useful qualifications for the politician who desired to create a united Italy.

Cavour's patriotism was none the less robust for having its roots deeply struck into his personal interests. As a business man and a railway promoter, he was fully aware of the economic advantages of a united Italy, and as an ambitious politician he wanted a big sphere in which to operate. 'In my dreams I already see myself minister of the kingdom of Italy,' he wrote in the eighteen thirties, '. . . Ah! if I was an Englishman, I would be already of some importance.'[9] His knowledge of his own country was of the statistical, portable kind that is handy for solving economic problems: he was not inclined to study its literature, and had virtually no first-hand experience of its provincial life except in his native Piedmont. The unification to which he looked forward was to be a practical achievement; he did not wish to preserve local traditions or idiosyncrasies, nor did he wish to promote a regeneration. His political theories were borrowed from the conservative aspects of Tocqueville's *Democracy in America*: democracy was inevitable, but the great art of statesmanship was to limit it; government by discussion and social reform were ideals, to be applied judiciously by conservatives. Though he had applauded the war against Austria in 1848, the last thing he desired was a repetition of that year of revolutions, with republican enthusiasm bubbling up within the national movement. 'The time for conspiracies is past,' he said, 'the emancipation of nations can no longer be effected by plots or surprises; it has become the necessary consequence of the progress of Christian civilization.'[10]

By 'Christian civilization', Cavour meant industrialization and railways. Even so, his words must be cautiously interpreted. 'Plots and surprises' were his speciality: though of a different kind from those favoured by Mazzinians and the Carbonari. Austria would be evicted by a masterly stroke of foreign policy followed by a conven-

[9] A. J. Whyte, *The Early Life and Letters of Cavour, 1810–48* (1925), pp. 74, 96.
[10] Whyte, op. cit., p. 304.

tional war. The key to success was France. 'We shall be either aided or sacrificed according as it will suit Louis Napoleon to oppose or be friends to Austria,' Cavour wrote to a correspondent in September 1852. 'As you have said to me many times, it is upon France, above all, that our destiny depends. *Bon gré, mal gré*, we must be her partner in the great game that sooner or later must be played in Europe.'[11]

V

The opportunity for playing the great game came in July 1858, when Cavour and Napoleon III met in secret at Plombières. Here, the French Emperor promised that he would make war on Austria, if opportunity arose, with the object of obtaining Lombardy-Venetia for Piedmont, and setting up a kingdom of central Italy composed of Tuscan and other territories. This was far short of what Italian patriots desired: on the other hand, it was a remarkable achievement to have brought the brooding Emperor to the point of offering to shed French blood for the Italian cause.

Why, indeed, did he do so? Basically, the answer is that an adventure of this kind fitted into his Napoleonic dreams, his myth of a generous Bonapartist imperialism devoted to the cause of freeing the nationalities of Europe, his desire to emulate the conquests of the First Empire, and to overturn the hated settlement of 1814–15. But the explanation needs to be more specific. Why was this the time when dreams seemed to have come into the realm of action? For one thing, the Plombières' agreement included a substantial bribe— Savoy and Nice and a marriage alliance with the oldest dynasty in Europe. For another, Napoleon, like many others, had been impressed by Cavour's economic policies in Piedmont over the past six years; this little state was becoming the industrial leader of Italy. In other ways, too, the government of Turin had gained a reputation for respectability. Extremists were kept out of office and the death sentence had once more been pronounced against Mazzini—*in absentia*, of course. The Orsini bomb plot of January 1858 against Napoleon had endangered relations with France, but Cavour and his monarch gave a demonstration of submissiveness and proud independence, a combination of nicely calculated reactions which impressed the sombre and sentimental Emperor. Perhaps there was, too, some feeling of gratitude for Piedmont's contribution of troops to the Crimean alliance. If so, this was luck, for it is no longer possible to believe that Cavour had joined the war against Russia out of long-term Machiavellian purposes; the truth is that the king insisted on

[11] Cit. Whyte, *The Political Life and Letters of Cavour, 1848–61* (1930), p. 95.

war, partly to distract the minds of patriots from Lombardy, and that the minister 'was reluctantly indulging a royal whim to avoid being dismissed'.[12]

These were the considerations which moved the Emperor at Plombières. One ought to add that, while Napoleon went on to make his preparations, more especially by buying Russian neutrality, in typical fashion he had still not made up his mind. There were reservations to his promises, and he was already backing out when, with incredible folly, the Austrians called on Piedmont to disarm and, four days later, marched. Rescued from ruin by their armies in 1848-9, the Habsburgs in emergency too easily resorted to the gamble of war.

Napoleon III defeated the Austrians at Solferino (23 June 1859), then made peace as quickly as he could. The carnage of the battlefield sickened him, and his slow-moving reflective, brain was incapable of the quick decisions required by war. Russia had promised neutrality (for a revision of the Black Sea clauses of the 1856 Treaty), but the Tsar's advice was to end the fighting: if Austria cracked, the Poles might rise again, including those under Russian domination. There had been revolts in Tuscany, the papal states, Modena and Parma, arousing the usual fears of republicanism and social disruption. 'I made peace,' Louis Napoleon told the Austrians, a little disingenuously, 'because I didn't like opening the way for revolution. I was going to be regarded as the leader of all the scum of Europe.'[13] The French Catholics and the Empress opposed the war, and even in Piedmont there were investors in Austrian funds, estate owners fearful of plundering armies and local patriots reluctant to see Turin reduced to a 'frontier town' who regretted Cavour's adventure. So the French Emperor made peace. Austria was to keep Venetia; the Dukes of Tuscany, Modena and Parma and the Pope would rule again over their rebellious subjects.

The difficulty about these arrangements was that the Italians would not accept them. Ricasoli called an assembly in Tuscany (with a restricted franchise to stop the peasants voting for the return of the old régime) and persuaded it to propose union with Piedmont. Parma, Modena and papal Romagna allied to form a new revolutionary state, Emilia. It was unthinkable that France should use force against the Italian nationalists, or allow Austria to do so. So Napoleon

---

[12] D. Mack Smith, 'Italy', *N.C.M.H.* X, p. 569.

[13] F. Valsecchi, 'La paix de Zurich, 1859', *Rev. d'hist. mod. et contemp.* VII (1960), p. 117. For the English attitude, wanting the Austrians to defeat the French, then (as second priority) the Italians to be free and 'grateful to us for doing nothing towards it', see the quotation from Monckton Miles in D. Beales, *England and Italy, 1859-60* (1961), p. 68. Miss R. Cooper drew my attention to this reference.

once more made a deal with Cavour. Plebiscites, of suspicious unanimity, voted the union of Emilia and Tuscany with Piedmont. France was given Savoy and Nice. This cynical diplomatic bargain was also sealed by a plebiscitary decision. It is interesting to speculate on what would have happened if the voting had gone the wrong way. Though the commercial middle class was in favour of France and the clergy and schoolmasters stood to gain almost double salaries by the transfer,[14] it was a theoretical possibility. But the Piedmontese officials departed and the voters knew what was expected of them. As the *Courier des Alpes* had prophesied a year earlier—'A people never gives itself before it has been taken over; on the other hand, once it is annexed, it never refuses to sign the treaty. Consent is simply a matter of knowing how to go about getting it.'[15]

VI

Nice voted for union with France on 15 April 1860. By then, revolution had blazed up in Sicily. The new King of Naples, Francis II, a simple young man with none of his father's toughness, pottered around giving ineffectual orders in face of the rising storm. Three weeks later, Garibaldi and rather more than a thousand red shirt volunteers sailed southwards to aid the rebels. Nice, which Cavour had presented to France, was Garibaldi's home town: he had been made 'a stranger in Italy', and he was now determined to break through the web of subtlety and sordid bargaining which he regarded as a disgrace to the national cause. Theoretically, he remained a republican; the names of his three donkeys on his island retreat of Caprera reminded him of his hatreds, not only of 'Pius IX' and 'Francis Joseph', but also of 'Louis Napoleon'. But there was no 'Victor Emmanuel' there; in practice, he accepted the Piedmontese monarchy, and reserved all his detestation for Cavour. Paradoxically, it was the hatred between these two men, the guerilla of genius and the crafty politician, which created the new Italy. In August, the victorious Garibaldi crossed the Straits and marched on Naples. On 15 September, Cavour sent the Piedmontese army into the Papal States and southwards to anticipate him. 'His aim is . . . not to acquire more provinces,' wrote a foreign observer, 'but to stop Garibaldi.' France, and the powers generally, reluctantly condoned these actions, for the alternative might have been Garibaldi in Naples or even at the gates of Rome, with Victor Emmanuel discredited as the leader of the

[14] C. R. M. F. Cruttwell, *A History of Peaceful Change in the Modern World* (1937), pp. 160–1.
[15] P. Guichonnet, 'La droite savoyarde et piémontaise devant les événements de 1859', *Rev. d'hist. mod. et contemp.* VII (1960), p. 85.

national cause and, maybe, a wave of republicanism sweeping southern Italy.

Then came the question of consent. Cavour proved again that it was 'simply a matter of knowing how to go about getting it'. The Garibaldians would have preferred to see elected assemblies meeting in Sicily and Naples, for in this way conditions could have been imposed upon a vote of union with the north. Lawyers who feared that justice would be centralized in Turin and the clergy who feared Piedmontese anti-clericalism would have welcomed this solution. But Garibaldi was no politician, and he and his followers, in their confusion, missed their opportunity. On 2 October, in the Parliament at Turin, Cavour vetoed all solutions other than a plebiscite.

On 21 October, Sicily and Naples voted to form a united Italy, by 432,052 against 667 in Sicily, and 1,302,064 against 10,312 in Naples. Many peasants kept away from the polls, suspecting that they would be registering for conscription, others voted because they thought they were supporting their hero Garibaldi, not knowing of his feud with Cavour, while others gave their assent because it was a public ballot with National Guards on duty and it seemed only wise to comply. Illiterate folk were baffled by the enthusiasm expected of them—'Long live Italy'—'Italy, what's that?' According to Lord John Russell, the proceedings showed that universal suffrage operating through a plebiscite was a menace—'a few sweating Madonnas and canting friars might pervert that mode of voting into a machinery for restoring Francesco II of pious memory.'[16] The only choice was that between the plebiscitary formula and chaos. 'There is no clear, positive annexationist opinion,' said a French observer, 'but annexation is the only possible solution.' There was no means of expressing a desire for the preservation of local liberties, no opportunity for reflection or delay.

The result was a tragedy. Cavour's vague promises of decentralization were not kept and the laws, the heavy taxes, conscription and free trade policy of Piedmont were extended to the south, ruining its precarious economy and evoking civil war. A legacy of permanent bitterness was bequeathed to the new Italy.

VII

When, on 3 October 1860, Prussia had protested against the Piedmontese invasion of Roman territory, Cavour had replied, 'I am setting an example which Prussia, in due course, will probably be very

[16] Lord John Russell to Sir Henry Elliott (British minister in Naples), cit. D. Mack Smith, *Cavour and Garibaldi: 1860* (1954), p. 387.

glad to imitate.'[17] Eight months later, he died, having lived long enough to see the creation of the kingdom of Italy, a nation of twenty-one millions, an achievement which was regarded with envy in Prussia and, indeed, throughout Germany.

At the time of Cavour's death, Bismarck, the future architect of German unity, was Prussian minister in St Petersburg; in March 1862 he moved to the Paris embassy, and in the following September he became Minister President, director of the policies of the Prussian state. His appointment owed nothing to the surge of national feeling; indeed, many who had come to look on Prussia as the Piedmont of the north were disillusioned at the news. William I sent for Bismarck as a last resort: the Liberals and the Progressives in the parliament were out of hand, defying the Crown on a matter of pre-eminent importance to an Hohenzollern heart, the army laws. It was not easy to find a minister willing to govern in defiance of the constitution and with sufficient ability to do so.

In 1847, Bismarck had come into politics as a sarcastic, provocative spokesman of the Junkers. During the revolution of 1848 he had been such a rabid supporter of the prejudices of his class that the king had not dared to give him office. 'Red reactionary,' ran the marginal note on his papers, 'still smells of blood, to be used later.' This rôle of a reactionary was one that Bismarck played consciously—'I am a Junker and wish to profit from it.' He had been born at the manor of Schonhausen and inherited it in 1845, 'an old haunted castle with pointed arches and walls four feet thick,' a few rags of tapestry, rats, and a bayonet hole in a door made by the French after Jena. The gigantic young man with the heavy walking stick, white bulldog and huge pipe who had fooled around the universities of Göttingen and Berlin, fighting twenty-five duels and rioting in the front seats of the opera, had matured into a Pomeranian estate manager in leather breeches, stroking his moustache and selling two thalers cheaper on the Stettin wool market to anyone who called him 'Baron'.[18] In 1847. he had married—for love—in the process adopting the pietistic religion of his wife's family—unless we are to believe that this was the first and longest-sustained of his great diplomatic deceptions. To this religion he gave a harsh utilitarian twist (or affected to do so), speaking of God as the sanction of the soldier's obedience, 'somebody who sees when the Lieutenant is not looking'. Then, as revolution approached, he moved into politics as the defender of the jurisdiction

[17] L. M. Case, 'Thouvenal et la rupture des relations diplomatiques Franco-Sardes en 1860', *Rev. d'hist. mod. et contemp.* VII (1960), p. 175.
[18] This is from Bismarck's own comic account of how he proposed to carry on F. Darmstaedter, *Bismarck and the Creation of the Second Reich* (1948), p. 23.

of landowners and of the superiority of all those who enjoyed 'that revolting privilege of having the particle *von* prefixed to their name.'

Yet behind this Junker façade, which was, in some ways, a mask ironically assumed, a self-conscious caricature of his own opinions, there was another Bismarck, sophisticated, acutely intelligent, a master of prose style, nurtured on Goethe, Shakespeare, Scott and Byron, highly sensitive and finely drawn. These qualities came, perhaps, from the academics and professors of his mother's side of the family, though in the son, all these gifts were adjusted to the service of an implacable realism. Like Cavour, Bismarck had '*le tact des choses possibles*'; more than that, he had the divinatory faculty to guess at the various possibilities of the future, and the insight into situations which enabled him to see the interests of others before they were fully conscious of them themselves. His conservatism was not a blind Junker prejudice, but a belief intelligently assessed and flexibly held. As a realist, he could not believe in the 'will of the people' invoked by liberals in 1848. 'Generally they mean a random mob of individuals whom they have succeeded in winning for their views.' This realism, combined with his romantic pessimism and cult of personality, and with his peculiar Christianity, made him sceptical of all attempts to transform the political scene. One doubts if this great practitioner of the arts of government can be said to have had a continuous goal, but if he had one, it 'was and remained the preservation and the elevation of the Prussian military monarchy'.[19] But his quick and observant mind continually attuned goals to possibilities. The events of 1848–9 had at least convinced him that in the long run there could be no return to the old régime. From Louis Napoleon's example, he learnt how majority rule and liberal ideas could be harnessed to serve authoritarian government; from observation of Prussian affairs he realized how easy it was to use the conservative countryside against the radicals of towns, and how a resounding foreign policy could persuade the people 'to put up with a good deal at home'. Thus, called to office in 1862 to sabotage parliamentarianism in Prussia, Bismarck was even then meditating launching out on the uncharted sea of universal suffrage; he would be glad, he said, to see a German confederate parliament based on a wide franchise, for 'Prussia needs a counterweight against the dynastic policy of the governments, and can only find this in national representation.'[20]

This scheme for a national parliament (which the Crown Prince was to call 'a criminal game with the most sacred matters') was, for

---

[19] Hajo Holborn, 'Bismarck's *Realpolitik*', *Journal History of Ideas*, XXI (1960), p. 91.
[20] Darmstaedter, op. cit., p. 226.

Bismarck, a device of Prussian foreign policy, to push Austria out of Germany. He had not always wanted to do this. At the time of the capitulation of Olmütz, he had been one of the few Prussians who had dared to praise Austria and look forward to an alliance of Hohenzollerns and Habsburgs. It was because he was a supporter of Austria that he was sent as Prussian minister to the Federal Diet, in May 1851. Then the change came. Was it a logical decision, or a passionate one? Austrian airs of superiority at the Diet were vexatious, and a new arrival anxious to make his name would be self-assertive; hence the flourishing of a cigar case at the Federal military commission meetings to break the Austrian monopoly of smoking. There were neurotic undercurrents beneath Bismarck's realism: the spring which triggered off the clockwork process of his reasoning might have been his personal reaction to opponents, for his anger was never blind, his rage was always cerebral: however this may have been, the logic of his decision, from his own point of view, was impeccable. He could see how his own ambitions and his country's interests could tie together in a great design of foreign policy, in which the popular passions of the day could be harnessed to give the Prussian Crown power and glory externally and, internally, control over its own people. Strictly speaking, at this time at least, he was not a German nationalist,[21] but an ambitious and intelligent servant of the Prussian state and monarchy preparing for desperate courses. 'If there is to be revolution,' he was to say in 1866, 'we would rather make it than suffer it.'

These ideas matured in Bismarck's mind. He thought of a Russian alliance against the Habsburgs, then of a French one, though accepting the help of Louis Napoleon would be an 'escape through a sewer'. When Austria and France were at war in 1859, he wrote to the Prince Regent advising him to 'allow Austria's war against France to eat . . . deeply into her substance. Then let us march southwards with our whole army, with the boundary posts in the soldiers' knapsacks.'[22] Was this what he meant by his notorious first speech as Minister President—'The great questions of the day will not be decided by speeches and the resolutions of majorities—that was the great mistake of 1848 to 1849—but by iron and blood'?

VIII

In his memoirs, Bismarck claims that he engineered a breach with Austria: on the other hand, he once told the Austrian historian

[21] O. Pflanze, 'Bismarck and German Nationalism', *American Hist. Rev.* LX (1954–5), pp. 548–66. See Pflanze's book, *Bismarck and the Development of Germany: the period of unification, 1815–71* (1963).
[22] E. Eyck, *Bismarck and the German Empire* (1950), p. 43.

Friedjung that a firm alliance with Vienna had always been his hope.[23] The two statements are not entirely incompatible. Bismarck was not one of those men of bronze who stride robot-like over obstacles towards a fixed goal: it was his method, in diplomacy, to move into a central strategic position which opened up various alternative possibilities for future advances. He was not contriving war, except in the sense that he was viewing it dispassionately as a reasonable course of action, and was edging his opponent into a position of inferiority from which the gamble of war would be the only escape.

In August 1863 he managed, with great difficulty (this was the famous interview of the broken door-knob) to dissuade his monarch from going to a meeting of the German princes to discuss the reform of constitutional arrangements under the presidency of Francis Joseph. In this way, Bismarck preserved Prussia's independence of action and let Austria identify herself with the tarnished gilding of the old Germany of the princes; for Prussia, he was ready to claim the emotive dream of a Germany of the people. The next step was to co-operate with Austria—on carefully chosen ground. The death of the King of Denmark caused a revival of the notorious Schleswig-Holstein question, and Austrian and Prussian armies marched together into the disputed duchies. An edifying impression of Prussia's willingness to serve the national cause was given to the smaller states of Germany; Austria had shown her willingness too, but the sheer facts of geography meant that she had got herself into a joint venture in which none of the profits could be hers.

Meanwhile, Bismarck pulled all the strings of diplomacy to keep Austria isolated. The Polish rising of 1863 gave an opportunity for the courtship of Russia, and Prussia signed a convention to join in action against the rebels. Though in later life Bismarck claimed that this ruthless gesture of friendship was a masterpiece, it appears that there was an elephantine importunity about his offer to St Petersburg which offended the Tsar.[24] It was effective, however, in comparison with the Austrian reaction, one of half-hearted disapproval of Russia, a repetition and reminder of the neutrality of Crimean War days, which deprived Francis Joseph of all hope of assistance from the east in a crisis. England was angry over the Schleswig-Holstein business and had no sympathy to spare for either of the aggressors; if Vienna fell out with Berlin, English statesmen would be delighted to say 'We told you so'. An Austria which still held on to Venetia in defiance of the Italians and which had just filched Holstein from Denmark had little hope of support from London or, for that matter, from Paris.

[23] K. S. Pinson, *Modern Germany: its history and civilization* (1954), pp. 135–6.
[24] A. J. P. Taylor, *The Struggle for Mastery in Europe* (1954), p. 134.

In October 1865, Bismarck met Napoleon III at Biarritz. Unlike Cavour at Plombières, he was not inveigling the French Emperor into his affairs: he was politely ushering him out. Each party vaguely suggested that it would leave the other free to act against Austria. Napoleon had two aims, summed up by the British Ambassador as '1° to turn the Austrians out of Venetia 2° to get a bit of the Rhine'[25]. The Prussian Minister President carefully avoided committing himself to the second half of this formula, and the first half was enough to give him French neutrality and the military alliance of Italy.

By 8 April 1866, when Prussia and Italy concluded their alliance, Austria was completely isolated. Military problems conspired to make her diplomatic position hopeless. Prussia could mobilize in three weeks, half the time required by the Habsburg armies, while the threat from Italy drew Austria into warlike preparations which made her look like an aggressor in the north, and brought upon her the odium of breaking the peace. On 1 June, Austria invoked the Federal Diet to deal with disputes with Prussia over the duchies of Schleswig and Holstein, and a fortnight later obtained a vote for a federal mobilization. Within a week, the Prussian armies were pouring over the frontiers.

IX

By the Peace of Prague (August 1866) the old Germanic Confederation was dissolved, Austria was excluded from German affairs, and Prussia annexed Hanover, Nassau, Frankfurt and the Electorate of Hesse. In the following year all the Germanic states north of the river Main were organized into a North German Confederation, dominated by Prussia. 'There is nothing more to do in our lifetime,' Bismarck wrote to his wife. He proceeded, however, to make alliances with the South German states so that their armies would come under Prussian control in time of war. Through Napoleon III's offices, Venetia was transferred from Austria to Italy. But French troops maintained the Pope in Rome; thus it happened that Bismarck's next great enterprise, the war against France of 1870, which was to create the German Empire, gave Italy its last piece of booty and its capital.

There was a time when this interlocking story of German and Italian unity aroused the enthusiasm of English historians, who praised Bismarck and Cavour as 'makers of nations'.[26] Subsequent

---

[25] W. E. Mosse, *The European Powers and the German Question, 1848–71* (1958), p. 204.

[26] For a startling example, see Sir Charles Grant Robertson, *Bismarck* (1918), pp. 493–4: 'Canonization . . . by a people is a more exacting inquest than

events—one might take the Rome-Berlin Axis of Mussolini and Hitler, which Salvatorelli calls 'the final apostacy of the *Risorgimento*',[27] as an extreme example—reinforce one's suspicions that the creation of great nation states may not be such a self-justifying activity as the 'makers of nations' enthusiasm implied. How these things are done may matter as much as the fact that they are done: means may affect the quality of the end. 'It was a different Italy that I had dreamed of all my life,' said Garibaldi in 1880, reflecting on the shabby treatment of the South and the domination of the rich, 'not this miserable, poverty-stricken, humiliated Italy that we now see, governed by the dregs of the nation.'[28] In the next lecture we must consider the Germany which Bismarck created. Though it was far from being miserable, poor or humiliated, from the start there were who those thought something was lacking, that something had been destroyed amid the heroic din of the unification. It is true that this was the opinion of a very small minority. Most Germans would have agreed with the historian Baumgarten, who at the end of 1866 renounced the old liberalism of words and said that Bismarck was now vindicated by his deeds—'complete liberty rests upon complete power'. Only a few would have echoed Johann Jacoby's bitter reply, 'Unity (*Einheit*) without Liberty (*Freiheit*) is a unity of slaves.'[29]

canonization by a church. . . . In the sanctuaries of a nation's Valhalla there will be niches without number for the heroes and the saints . . . but the corner reserved for the Makers of the Nation will be a scanty and awful plot. . . . Of the Makers, the nation is the supreme judge . . .'

[27] L. Salvatorelli, *Pensiero e azione del Risorgimento* (1959), p. 194.
[28] D. Mack Smith, *Garibaldi* (1957), p. 195.
[29] Pinson, op. cit., p. 152

CHAPTER XVI

BISMARCK'S GERMANY, 1867–1890

I

After meeting Napoleon III in 1863, the great German historian Theodore Mommsen confessed, 'I left with a feeling of envy that fate never throws up such a *grand criminel* amongst us. What could such a man do with a healthy nation like ours?'[1] As it happened, fate had already fulfilled his wish. Within three years Austria was defeated and within seven, Germany's *grand criminel* had overturned the French one, and in so doing had created the German Empire. In an earlier lecture we studied Bismarck's responsibility for the first of these wars, let us now look at his responsibility for the second, the Franco-Prussian War of 1870, a struggle which cost 600,000 lives and prepared the way for even more desperate wars in the future. Was he really the criminal adventurer that Mommsen had dreamed of?

After the victory of 1866, Bismarck's outlook became German rather than Prussian. On various occasions he is recorded as saying, 'My highest ambition is to make the Germans into a nation.' 'He had spoken contemptuously of German nationalism even after Sadova,' writes A. J. P. Taylor; 'by the beginning of 1867 he was talking as though he had taken the patent out for it.'[2] The practical problem of incorporating Hanover into Prussia had a lot to do with his conversion. 'The decisive factors which the governmental press will have to stress in its efforts to conquer particularism,' he wrote to the Governor of Hanover, 'lie in the German and not in the Prussian nationality.'[3] It was also a conversion which harmonized with the whole direction of his ambitions as a statesman; for him, success in foreign policy was at once the test of a state's greatness and the secret for keeping political control over the multitude at home. In the Luxemburg crisis of 1867, Bismarck would have been glad to hand over the territory to Napoleon III, but what would have been a wise concession for a Prussian minister was an impossibility, in view of the public outcry, for a leader of Germany. Power

[1] H. Kohn, *The Mind of Germany* (1962), p. 186. I have ventured to change the wording to a freer form of English.
[2] A. J. P. Taylor, *Bismarck* (1955), p. 93.
[3] O. Pflanze, 'Bismarck and German Nationalism', *American Hist. Rev.* LXX (1954–5), p. 55.

politics could be conducted more effectively by playing on nationalist emotions than by defying them. 'The Luxemburg affair,' writes Eyck, 'was the turning point in Bismarck's development from a Prussian to a German statesman.'[4] This is not to say that he ever became a romantic nationalist, still less a racialist or a Pan-Germanist. He simply transferred to Germany the idea of the State, monarchical, aristocratic and military, which he had served in Prussia, and to which he proposed to harness the forces of democracy and nationalism.

As a German—and indeed, as a Prussian—statesman, Bismarck was aware that the south German states might slip away from him. They were his military allies, no more. The Catholic majorities in Bavaria and Baden and the strong minorities in Württemberg and Hesse-Darmstadt were unhappy with the idea of a final unification into a Prussian-dominated *Kleindeutschland*, of becoming absorbed into an organization which Bismarck referred to as 'old Prussia with somewhat broader shoulders, a somewhat stronger back, and a light German overcoat.'[5] Catholicism was becoming a potential force with the masses through the clubs and co-operatives of its social movement and its many newspapers. Narrow particularists who were against unity altogether, *Grossdeutsch* enthusiasts who were unwilling to leave out Austria, and all the others who, for widely differing reasons, feared a Prussianized Germany, were finding a basis for popular support in the Catholic suspicion of the policies of Berlin. In Baden, a *Katholische Volkspartei* arose; in Bavaria, a *Patriotenpartei* of 'Ultramontanes', opponents of the 'Prussian bloodsuckers', won the *Landtag* elections towards the end of 1869. When the four southern states elected deputies, by universal suffrage, to a *Zollparlament* (in connection with the *Zollverein*, or Customs Union), their representatives turned out to be mostly clericals and particularists. From Bismarck's point of view, things were becoming progressively worse in South Germany; in his memoirs, he says that he saw a national war was needed to draw the north and the south together, and that he engineered one.[6] His own story then, makes him responsible for the Franco-Prussian War as a masterly and merciless design; according to his confidant Lothar Bucher, the Hohenzollern candidature for the Spanish throne was 'a trap which Bismarck laid for Napoleon'.

But was it? Like most of us, Bismarck preferred to be praised for

[4] E. Eyck, *Bismarck and the German Empire* (1950), p. 156.

[5] C. G. Windell, *The Catholics and German Unity, 1866–71* (1954), p. 69.

[6] *Reflections and Reminiscences of Otto Prince von Bismarck* (ed. A. J. Butler, 1898) II, pp. 56–7.

his intelligence rather than his integrity, and his memory operated the meshes of selectivity accordingly. Nor was he ever inclined to share the credit for achievements. A contemporary speaks of him as regarding 'the glory of creating the German Empire as an enormous cheese which is his sole property, anyone who cuts off a slice is a thief'.[7] Having this proprietary interest, Bismarck tended to portray himself as more fanatically dedicated to the national cause than he had been. His own story of far-sighted ruthlessness may be exaggerated.

At one time, it looks as though his object was to do a deal with France, rather than defeat her. A war would have dangerous long-term consequences: 'once started,' he said, 'it will never cease.' In 1869 he was advising Napoleon III to take Belgium, while the North German Confederation would take the southern states as compensation; since England was more concerned over the Low Countries than over south Germany, he blandly confessed this *politique de brigandage* to the astonished British ambassador. Probably, he embarked on the Hohenzollern candidature with motives something like those he put to the King on 9th March 1870—a prince on the Spanish throne would be a distinction to the dynasty; Spain had some value as a market, and in war against France would be worth two army corps; hence, once the initial risk was run, France would be more securely tied down to a peaceful policy.[8] These views were reinforced when, on 15th March, Moltke and the soldiers advised acceptance. That Bismarck expected to get through without a war is suggested by the fact that on 4th June, in his conversations with the Tsar of Russia at Ems, the possibility was not mentioned; also his retirement to his estate at Varzin gives the impression, not of a conspirator waiting for his mine to explode, but of a politician taking a risk and leaving the King to carry the blame if anything went wrong.

Things went wrong in an unexpected way on 12th July, when Prince Leopold's father withdrew his son's acceptance of the Spanish throne. France had won a diplomatic victory. Rather than accept this humiliation, Bismarck wanted war. Hence the provocative, though reasonably accurate statement of the facts in the Ems telegram as he edited it.[9] As it happened, the French leaders, lusting for prestige, made impossible demands, 'reopening the gates of

---

[7] Reference mislaid.

[8] G. Bonnin, *Bismarck and the Hohenzollern Candidature* (trans. I. M. Massey, 1957), pp. 68–73.

[9] See A. J. P. Taylor's excellent discussion of the Ems telegram in *The Struggle for Mastery in Europe, 1848–1918* (1954), pp. 205–6. Bismarck's

the Temple of Janus'.[10] It suited Bismarck to give them the war they wanted. The southern states joined in the national war effort, and after victory, Bismarck's manoeuvres culminated in the ceremony in the *Salle des Glaces* at Versailles on 18th January 1871, when the German Empire was constituted. No doubt he had long foreseen this way to unification, but until the last moment, he had probably considered it as a strictly marginal possibility.

II

Where would the realities of political power be within the new united Germany? At the end of 1866, after the defeat of Austria, Bismarck had planned a constitution for the North German Confederation which would 'kill parliamentarianism through parliament'; there would be a *Reichstag* elected by universal suffrage, but there would also be an upper house with an absolute veto over the lower, a Chancellor responsible only to the Crown, and a permanent military budget. His supporters had insisted, however, that this was hardly a constitution to exercise magnetic attraction upon the states of south Germany, so Bismarck had changed his scheme; in particular, the military budget was to expire in December 1871 and become subject to parliamentary control in future. Even so, contemporaries still made sardonic remarks about this constitution. It was said to consist of three articles—'Pay up'; 'Be a soldier'; 'Shut up.' This is the point, it has been argued, at which Bismarck's baleful domination sabotaged the possibility of the rise of a liberal Germany. On the other side, it ought to be said that here was the widest franchise in Europe and the only effective secret ballot, and that true parliamentary government would have become inevitable if a party possessing a stable majority had demanded it. 'If no majority ever emerged,' writes Taylor, 'the blame must lie as much with the politicians as with Bismarck.'[11]

The federal constitution of 1871 for the German Empire was modelled on the principles behind that of the North German Confederation. The twenty-five states kept their old internal form of government and retained power over education, justice and police,

famous story of dining with the generals on 13 July, of their gloom, of his editing the telegram and Moltke saying, 'It sounded like a parley, it is like a fanfare now', is exploded. They had dined together the night before and knew already what they wanted to do about French 'arrogance' (W. L. Langer, 'Bismarck as a Dramatist', *Studies in Diplomatic History in Honour of G. P. Gooch*) (ed. A. O. Sakrissian, 1961), pp. 199–213.

[10] R. H. Lord, *The Origins of the War of 1870* (1924), p. 80.

[11] Taylor, *Bismarck*, p. 98.

drawing their revenue from direct taxation (leaving the indirect taxes to the central imperial authorities). The executive power of the federation was in the Emperor, acting through his Chancellor, who was directly responsible to the Crown, not to parliament. Legislative power was exercised by a *Reichstag*, elected by universal suffrage, and a *Bundesrat* of delegates of State governments. The army swore allegiance, not to the constitution, but to the Emperor; this symbol of direct dependence upon the crown assisted it to remain, from henceforward, a state within the state, selecting its own officers and conducting a good deal of its important business in secret sessions of the Military Cabinet and the General Staff.[12] Yet the machinery for parliamentary control existed in article 60 of the constitution, and though Bismarck persuaded the *Reichstag* not to make the army dependent upon an annual vote, the law of 1874 fixed the strength of the armed forces for seven years only.

Constitution makers seldom display the altruistic aloofness of the shadowy legislator in Rousseau's *Social Contract*, 'knowing all human passions but moved by none of them'. By appropriate choices of machinery, they try to make themselves indispensable. Bismarck's arrangements were of this kind, 'tailored to fit the personal relationship' between himself and his Emperor.[13] Yet there was nothing in the constitution to prevent the parliamentarians taking over control. The Chancellor did not have to resign if he was in a minority, it is true, but had to scrape together a majority every time he wanted a piece of positive legislation. In the long run, he was financially dependent on parliament and in 1877, the *Reichstag* added the 'Franckenstein clause' to a law reforming the customs duties, to ensure that any increased revenues were kept out of the coffers of the Empire. The army law ran for seven years and the law of 1878 against the Social Democrats, which Bismarck regarded as almost equally important, was limited by parliament to three years. Thus, for the Chancellor, politics became a juggling act—of routine tricks to get ordinary business done and of special acrobatic exertions to renew the army or the anti-socialist laws. In his way then, Bismarck had to become a master of parliamentary tactics; unfortunately for Germany, his ultimate constitutional dependence upon the legislative assembly never led to parliamentary government.

[12] G. A. Craig, *The Politics of the Prussian Army, 1640–1945* (1955), pp. 219–32.
[13] K. S. Pinson, *Modern Germany* (1954), p. 143.

III

Why was this so? One reason, as we have seen, was that no united party capable of holding a stable majority in the *Reichstag* arose. Reading from the ideological right to left, the assembly of 1871 contained six main groups: the Conservatives, essentially the Protestant Prussian landowners from east of the Elbe; the Free Conservatives, a broader based party of smaller Prussian estate owners, some bigger ones from other states, and a few industrialists; the Liberal *Reichspartei* (which was to vanish within three years); the National Liberals; the Progressives, led by bourgeois intellectuals, and the Catholic Centre. In addition there were the dissident nationalities, Poles, Danes and the deputies of Alsace-Lorraine, and the Hanoverians who still deplored the annexation of 1866; finally, there were the Socialists, as yet only two of them and divided at that, for one was a Marxist and the other was a follower of Lassalle.

Of these parties, Bismarck's chief supporters were the National Liberals: his most dangerous opponents, the deputies of the Catholic Centre. The National Liberals believed in *Freiheit* in that they would have been glad to see a growing measure of parliamentary control, but they had decided that *Einheit* was more important for the time being. Their hour of decision had come soon after the victory over Austria, when Bismarck had asked for and had obtained a Bill of indemnity for his infringements of the Prussian Constitution. This legacy of compliance the National Liberals brought with them into the new *Reich*, and to them gravitated the rising class of leaders of industry, exponents of the doctrine of *Realpolitik* in economic affairs, who would accept any sort of government, provided it paid occasional dividends in the form of tariff protection (an issue which caused a split in the National-Liberal Party) or anti-socialist laws. The Centre Party had about 60 deputies, only half as many as the National Liberals, but its potentialities for expansion were great. Though its strength in 1871 came from the Rhineland, it could hope to draw on the reservoir of Catholic votes in south Germany, and to have for its allies the Poles, Hanoverians and every other group dissatisfied with 'Prussianization'. Tradition gave it a grip on the peasantry in some areas, and the developing ideals of Social Catholicism gave it a foothold among the urban workers. The Centre Party really was 'central': it occupied a position from which it could reach out to draw together conservative, bourgeois and radical interests. It had too, within it, an ideological core that guaranteed permanence.

Its deputies, together with the two Socialists, differed from all the others in the *Reichstag* in that they stood, not merely for interests, but for causes, for the 'black international' and the 'red' one, and these causes were capable of evoking mass support. As a threat to his own monopoly of power, as a 'state within a state', and as a rival which used his own tactics of employing radical means for conservative ends, Bismarck detested the Centre Party. As so often happened with him, the designs of foreign policy and his personal prejudices (he hated Windthorst, the Catholic political leader) coincided with the logic of politics; in 1871, he began the *Kulturkampf*, a war, not only against the Centre, but against Catholicism in general.

Up to 1877, Bismarck ruled with the aid of the National Liberals and the Free Conservatives. Then he changed course. The National Liberals were for free trade and laissez-faire and were hostile to Catholic claims; the Chancellor had decided upon tariffs and social insurance, and by now he saw that the *Kulturkampf* had been a miscalculation. 'Honest but awkward Prussian gendarmes, with spurs and trailing sabres' pursuing 'dexterous, light-footed priests through back doors and bedrooms',[14] were becoming a ridiculous spectacle. Devout Protestants were dismayed at a furore which was beginning to look like an attack on all religion. 'Baptism will go next,' muttered the old Emperor. A feud with the Vatican was no longer useful as an instrument of foreign policy, now that there was no danger of a clericalist régime in France, and the fact was to become very obvious later on when Germany became allied (October 1879) to Catholic Austria. Pope Pius IX died in February 1878, and his successor Leo XIII was willing to hasten on the process of compromise. There was reason enough then for Bismarck to call off the *Kulturkampf* and even to begin courting the Centre Party. But why did he go beyond this, however, and split the National Liberals, the only group consisting essentially of his supporters? The logic of this apparently short-sighted ruthlessness was purely personal. The Emperor was not expected to live much longer and the Crown Prince was a patron of the Liberals: if he had a strong party in the *Reichstag* he might get delusions of grandeur and think that he could change his Chancellor.

After the 1884 elections, the ruffled birds of Bismarck's over-crafty tactics came home to roost. His slaves, the right wing National Liberals were only 50 strong, and though the Pope himself urged them to support the new army law of 1886, the Centre deputies refused. True, Bismarck ran new elections on the cry, 'The Father-

[14] Bismarck, *Reflections*, II, p. 141.

land in danger', and carried them for his 'Cartel' of Conservatives, Free Conservatives and National Liberals, but the Cartel disintegrated in 1890 and its constituent parties lost heavily in the elections. At the time of his fall, the Chancellor had played out most of his winning cards so far as parliamentary management was concerned, and his only hope of controlling the *Reichstag* would have been the very doubtful one of winning the Centre Party.

The general effect of Bismarck's political strategy was to keep German parliamentary life incoherent. Germany had been united suddenly and harshly: its political parties represented raw conflicts— capital versus labour, industry versus agriculture, Catholic versus Protestant, Prussian centralization versus federation. The cohesive effects of friendly traditions, of the hard necessities of compromise and the responsibilities of power had not had time to operate, and thus the clash between the parties was one which did not provide the electorate with broad national issues or with that real choice between alternative governments which is the essence of democracy. This could not have come about at once, of course, but in spite of its impressive machinery of parliamentarianism, Germany was hardly on the way at all. To a certain degree, the responsibility was Bismarck's. To him, internal politics were largely a matter of keeping in power, though he believed that he did so as a means to loftier ends—maintaining an intelligent continuous foreign policy immune from the fluctuation of opinion, or even, he once said, educating Germany for democracy. To stay in office he played off the Emperor and the *Reichstag* against each other, bribed the press through his 'reptile fund' and cynically manipulated the political parties. He neither led them nor followed them, he used them, and he had a natural bias against allowing any of them to become too great, that is, great enough to claim to direct policy. He was so pre-eminent himself, that others tended to accept the inevitability of his rule, with the parties merely fulfilling the duty of limiting it occasionally, and this is precisely the attitude which Bismarck himself fostered.

Crown Princess Victoria put a very small part of the truth about him very naïvely in 1875 when she wrote, 'he is medieval altogether and the true theories of liberty and of government are Hebrew to him, though he adopts and admits a democratic idea or measure now and then when he thinks it will serve his purpose.'[15] The trouble with Bismarck really was that he was so intelligent and up to date that he could turn almost any device of liberal machinery to the service of his revolutionary brand of conservatism. Nor had he that loyalty to colleagues which creates an atmosphere of parliamentar-

[15] Eyck, op. cit., p. 199.

ianism. Holstein maliciously described his attitude to people—
'not friends, just tools, like knives and forks which are changed
after each course'.[16] In 1881, another German contemporary, with
remarkable insight, explained why Bismarck had 'no gift for domestic
politics. He does not understand the power that intellectual movements have for good and for evil. He always operates by schemes
based on a purely mechanical balance of forces, and supposes that
other people are solely motivated by calculations of loss and gain.'
It was the technique of foreign policy applied to home affairs, it
was getting things done, indifferent to the effect upon the instruments
used, and overlooking the fact that the instruments were not foreign
states, but homogeneous units within the German body politic.
Bismarck was not building for the future; he was using the tendencies
of the future for temporary purposes—more especially to keep himself in office. No doubt this is true of many statesmen, but Bismarck
is open to extraordinary criticism because he is so much superior to
them all. He did not cause war in 1870, but he alone could have
prevented it: this is the standard by which he must be judged.
He did not destroy liberalism in Germany, but he was so great and
intelligent that he alone could have created the conditions in which
it might have revived.

IV

'Bismarck's Germany', like 'Napoleonic France', is one of those
convenient text-book phrases whose meaning must not be pressed
too far. These men set their imprint on a generation, created the
style and tone of politics, acted the drama which everyone talked
about, and sent some of their compatriots to death in war. But
France made Napoleon and Germany made Bismarck, rather than
vice-versa. Bonaparte was the heir to the Revolution (though as
Talleyrand said, he had no intention of being its continuator);
Bismarck was the manipulator of German nationalism rather than
the creator of German greatness. In the Rhineland-Westphalia area,
in Upper Silesia, South-West Saxony, the Saar Basin and in the
factory belt around Berlin—areas which Bismarck never visited and
never understood—the enterprise of many individuals and the
misery of countless more was creating an inferno of mines and
factories which was making Germany rich, and a military force
capable of defying the rest of the world. 'The German Empire,'
said Keynes, 'was built more truly on coal and iron than on blood
and iron.' The inferences to be drawn from statistics of bloodshed
are debatable, but the figures of coal and iron speak for themselves.

[16] *The Holstein Papers* (ed. W. Rich and M. H. Fisher, 1957) II, p. 228.

The production figures of 34 million tons of coal and 1·3 million tons of pig iron in 1870 had risen to 89 millions tons and 4·1 million tons respectively twenty years later. After 1890, this industrial boom was to accelerate, to race onwards and upwards at a greater pace, giving Germany, on the eve of the World War, the greatest metallurgical, chemical and electrical industry in Europe, and a textile industry second only to that of England.

The rapidity of this development has been variously explained. Political causes go so far; the unification of the country, the huge war indemnity paid by the French, the annexation of Alsace-Lorraine with its efficient textile industry and its iron ore deposits (becoming valuable after the invention of the Thomas-Gilchrist process), no doubt gave some encouragement to industrial expansion. So too did governmental policies. After the defeat of Austria, Bismarck abandoned the theory of a monarchy protecting artisans and guildsmen against the factory system; guild regulations were jettisoned in 1868, and the free movement of labour was allowed.[17] It is true that as Chancellor of the *Reich* after 1871 Bismarck looked on economic questions from a narrowly political point of view: yet, as his aim was to overcome particularism, he inevitably served the cause of industrialization by his attempts to co-ordinate and integrate the national life—though his designs to unify the railway network were, for the most part, frustrated. His conversion to Protectionism was probably a matter of destroying the National Liberals, strengthening the power of the central government and defending his own revenues as a landed proprietor; even so, the erection of tariff barriers in 1879 came at a strategic moment. It gave the industrialists a breathing space in face of the competition of English steel made by the Bessemer process and the agriculturalists time to lower production costs against the challenge of American and Russian grain.

It would seem, however, that the great German expansion was chiefly the result of factors of a more obvious and strictly economic nature. The groundwork of industrialization had been laid in the first half of the nineteenth century. The expansion figures for 1870 to 1890 may seem impressive, but comparatively speaking they represent a slowing up after the slump of 1873, with the advent of a new boom delayed until after 1890. From this point of view, Bismarck may be described as ruling 'during years of depression and stagnation',[18] and the great expansion of his epoch and the much more

[17] T. S. Hamerow, *Restoration, Revolution, Reaction: Economics and Politics in Germany, 1815–71* (1958), pp. 250–1.

[18] Werner Conze, 'The German Empire', *New Camb. Mod. Hist.* XI (1962), p. 286.

rapid development of the Wilhelmian period may be taken as natural sequels to the breakthrough prepared before. We may notice, however, that all the while the rise in population continued—from 41 millions in 1871 to 67 millions in 1913, continually providing an expanding market. This was particularly the case for agricultural products, and in Germany, agriculture and industry raced on together in harness. The anonymous indispensable labour of draining and manuring the poor soil and been done in the two decades before the 1848 revolutions, and the steady rise in the price of agricultural products had encouraged the enterprise of the big proprietors— the Junkers were reputed to be the best agriculturalists in Europe. After 1870, grain prices fell because of the competition of the American prairies and the Russian steppes, but the big estate owners had the economic strength to ride the tide by going in for mechanization and chemical fertilizers—a demand for new products which industry was glad to satisfy.

To be late in the field of industrial expansion had its compensations. Thorstein Veblen in a famous book, *Imperial Germany and the Industrial Revolution* (1915) pointed out that German industrialists did not have to adapt traditional structures to new machines: they began by obtaining the most modern plant and putting it down in the most suitable locations. The dynamic possibilities of new beginnings were also seen in other ways, more obviously after 1890. German chemical firms employed trained scientists on a scale unknown elsewhere; the banks went into mesh with the big industrial companies, providing 'production credit' rather than the more traditional 'circulation credit'; large-scale 'vertical' or 'horizontal' grouping of industrial organizations began; German consuls and other agents abroad made careful surveys of the needs of customers or of the possibilities of 'dumping' before the attempts to break into new markets were launched. A late start gave more opportunities for planned production and logical marketing techniques in Germany's industrial revolution.

When all this is said, however, one ought to reflect that we are merely assuming that the German expansion needs special explanations. This may not be valid. Amid the dynamism of economic change in the nineteenth century, it is hard to decide what we ought to call 'natural'. Comparing Germany with France in total figures, for example, provides a startling contrast, which may be misleading. Breaking the figures down, we find that in the Pas de Calais, where coal was easily and economically extracted, French development was going ahead at the 'German' rate, while in Aachen, where coal seams were hard to work, German development was at the 'French'

rate.[19] It may well be that the rapid German expansion was condi-
tioned essentially by the fact that many of the German coal fields,
at that stage of their development, could be worked more quickly
and efficiently than those of other countries. If this is so, the glittering
undemocratic ceremony in the *Salle des Glaces* at Versailles in January 1871 is at once a landmark in its own right and also by coincidence; it was then approximately, that the era of the industrial
'take off' in Germany ended and the drive of the autonomous
forces of capitalist production began to produce their spectacular
results on the apparatus of national power.[20]

V

Germany became rich, but not all Germans. The industrial and
commercial bourgeoisie and the professions gained, so too did the
skilled workers. The condition of the unskilled, the true 'proletariat', improved but little, and they were more than half the
industrial population. The expansion of factories drew multitudes
to the cities, with the usual results of overcrowding and vile conditions. The concentration of workers into factories and the growing
inequality of wealth had their inevitable political result: in 1874
there were nine Social Democrats in the *Reichstag*, and in 1877,
there were a dozen, representing half a million votes.

Bismarck's reaction—typically—was ambivalent. As a Junker
and a conservative he acted quickly, 'to destroy the eggs' before they
hatched their brood. The good fortune of two attempts on the Emperor's
life (this, apparently, was how Bismarck viewed them) provided him
with arguments for severity—somewhat devious ones, for the attempts
had no connexion with Socialism; he coerced the *Reichstag* into passing a law forbidding socialist meetings and newspapers. Yet, as a man
of sensitivity and intelligence, Bismarck adopted something of a socialist policy himself. This was not simply a device to steal the clothes
of the Social Democrats before they could get out of the water;
it was a seriously considered policy, derived from his correspondence
with Lassalle in the early 'sixties, and from conversations with
intellectuals of the *Kathedersozialismus* movement. 'The working

[19] E. A. Wrigley, *Industrial Growth and Population Change* (1961), pp. 38–45.
[20] The 'take-off' date is 1850–73 in W. W. Rostow, *The Stages of Economic
Growth* (1960), p. 38. J. H. Clapham, *The Economic Development of France and
Germany, 1815–1914* (4th ed., 1955), p. 278, takes the years 1852–61 as laying
the basis of German industrialism.

classes are instinctively inclined towards dictatorship, if they can be fully convinced that this dictatorship is exercised in their interests,' Lassalle had written to him in June 1863 '. . . the Crown is the natural bearer of social dictatorship, in contrast to the egotism of bourgeois society.'[21] Bismarck kept this possibility in mind. From 1850 to 1868 the Prussian monarchy had acted as the patron of artisans and guildsmen: the day might come when the German Emperor might take his stand as the Dictator of the Proletariat. In a letter of 1883, Bismarck confessed that he hoped that his social policy might lead to the grouping of the workers on corporative lines, and that this might become the basis of popular representation in the future, either parallel to the *Reichstag* or in place of it. Universal suffrage, the German Chancellor was finding, was a two-edged weapon to handle; it is interesting to see that he had reflected upon one possible method of controlling it, the device of 'corporations' which (for widely differing motives) Catholic social thinkers and Fascists after them were to imagine could be used to bridge the class war in society.

Yet, in his oblique, brusque and logical fashion, Bismarck was a humanitarian. After 1871, his vast designs of foreign policy were not moved by the desire for aggrandizement but for security. This longing he accepted as the rightful instinct of every human being: indeed, he was not entirely able to understand how idealists could ever bring themselves to defy their own interests. Schemes for the limitations of working hours and the like he regarded as utopian: they would simply leave industry at the mercy of foreign competitors. But what he did want—and he was a generation ahead of his age in this—was a comprehensive system of social security for the whole population —insurance against sickness and accident and provision for old age. His social insurance laws, passed between 1883 and 1889 were not as generous as he would have wished to make them; even so, it was twenty years before significant measures of this kind were adopted in other countries. This was Bismarck's most original and intelligent contribution to progress, yet in his memoirs he is silent on the subject. Giving people what they needed was an important task of the statesman, but it was essentially a preliminary, to buy their co-operation while the great game of international power politics was played. Foreign policy was primary to Bismarck. With all his openness to modern social ideas and all his skill at utilizing revolutionary tendencies and working through parliamentary procedures, he remained at heart a statesman of the aristocratic eighteenth-century type, his mind fixed on the diplomatic map of Europe, a calculator

[21] Lassalle to Bismarck, 8 June 1863, cit. Pinson, p. 202.

of forces and a manipulator of balances, like Choiseul, Kaunitz or Metternich.[22]

VI

For twenty years, from the Franco-Prussian War to his fall in 1890, Bismarck dominated the diplomatic scene in Europe. How did he achieve this mastery?

When he wished, he could make the whole business look very complicated, a proof of his own indispensability; but in basic terms there was no mystery about it. United Germany was the greatest military force of the Continent. Without being a militarist, he put a high valuation on armed force; it was a simple necessity—'the pike in the European fish pond prevent us from becoming carp'. Overweening power is dangerous to its possessors, for it raises up coalitions against it. Under the Iron Chancellor, however, Germany's armed might achieved its maximum diplomatic leverage because it was manifestly bridled by moderation, it was an instrument of manoeuvre in the hands of a statesman whose object was to avoid raising up enmities against his own country. The Germans (partly because they were too quickly united into a nation) had the trick of making power look crude and blatant: Bismarck at least gave it an appearance of solid predictability. He had an aversion to war, not least because, once hostilities started, the Prussian generals would undoubtedly usurp the powers of the civilian Chancellor; in the Franco-Prussian War he had been reduced to picking up progress reports from the correspondent of the London *Times*. In any case, he had got what he wanted; to be sure of keeping his gains he had to maintain peace in Europe. This gave him a potential rôle of leadership which he accepted, and which others, relieved to see power directed by moderation, accorded to him. When all this is said, however, one must also add that Bismarck's mastery was partly due to the highly intelligent nature of the leadership which he gave. Granting that his hand was a strong one, it was superbly played. Perhaps it was played too effectively, for the spectacle of his imagination and finesse convinced everyone that his 'system' could not outlast him. It might have been better for Germany if he had bequeathed some more conventional diplomatic traditions to his inferior successors.

In the day to day tactics of diplomacy, Bismarck was an opportunist. In preserving peace, as in preparing war, he was accustomed to move on to the dominating heights of any situation, ready to strike

---

[22] See F. Schnabel, in *German History: Some New German Views* (ed. H. Kohn, 1954), pp. 74-5.

out from thence along roads leading to various alternative possibilities.[23] Even so, we may learn a great deal by trying to guess at the broad strategic rules of the game as they were observed by this most intelligent of all diplomatic practitioners. At the risk of reckless oversimplification, I think that we may suggest that Bismarck followed four rules; firstly, that the basis of foreign policy is the power structure, not ideological issues; secondly, that the aim must always be strictly limited, concerned only with the essential interests of the State; thirdly, that one of the best ways to serve one's own nation is by providing outlets for the ambitions of others; and finally, that while it is legitimate to inspire fear or wage war, it is important to avoid raising up permanent hatreds.

One of the clearest expositions of the first 'rule' was given by Bismarck early in his career, when an alliance with Napoleon III was in question. Admitting that it would be 'an escape through a sewer', he considered the possibility on its merits all the same. 'France counts for me merely as a piece, but an unavoidable one, in the game of political chess,' he said, 'not even the king has the right to subordinate the interests of the country to his own feeling of love or hate towards the foreigner.'[24] After 1871, an equally distasteful government in France posed the same problem. While his Emperor tried to encourage the monarchists and was in touch with Marshal MacMahon, the Chancellor did his best to ensure that France remained a republic, and was in touch with Gambetta. From an ideological point of view, monarchy was desirable in France, but as Bismarck saw things, a republic would not be *bündnisfähig* (capable of contracting alliances), more especially with Tsarist Russia. It was more important to keep France isolated than to inveigle her into the trade union of kings. Religious preferences and policies were as easily abandoned as political ones when the great interests of international power were being manipulated; the *Kulturkampf* began when Bismarck feared that Austria and France and the Poles and the Centre Party were all likely to league up against him, and it ended once he had decided upon an alliance with Catholic Austria. Going rather beyond these particular examples, one might suggest that Bismarck contrived to have two views of the world, which he kept isolated from each other in separate compartments. In one, there was the chessboard pattern of power, and in the other, the picturesque map of his own opinions. The latter was full of superstitious Catholics, cigar-smoking Popes, Balkan sheepstealers,

[23] Cf. the remarks on the 'strategy of alternatives' in O. Pflanze, 'Bismarck's *Realpolitik*', *Rev. of Politics* XX (1958), p. 512.

[24] Eyck, op. cit., p. 38.

stinking Wallachians, cowardly Italians, Russian *Schweinehunde* and the like, but none of this was relevant to his foreign policies. These policies were calculated solely on the logic of power and were unaffected by his prejudices.

The realism of the calculation was assured by the strict limitation of the aims. There was no place for romantic dreams, for that lure of distant horizons and the temptations of *Weltpolitik* which were to haunt the imagination of William II when the Great Chancellor was gone. Germany's interests, according to Bismarck, lay essentially in Europe, and they consisted, not in gaining anything new, but in always being able to prevent an overwhelming military coalition forming against her. The scramble for Africa, rivalries in the Far East and even, in the Balkans, were fields for diplomatic intrigue which would provide bribes and prizes for other people. It may seem strange to say this, seeing that under Bismarck Germany gained a colonial empire of a million square miles, but an examination of motives shows that this is the exception that proves the rule. 'For Germany to possess colonies would be like a poverty-stricken Polish nobleman acquiring a silken sable coat when he needed shirts,' said Bismarck in 1871.[25] Later on, he changed his mind—or, one ought to say, his views were much the same, but there were reasons for saying something different. He saw that there was a growing public opinion in Germany interested in the doings of explorers, mission- aries and traders (like the Godeffroy firm in Samoa); he also realized that colonial claims could be used as a bargaining counter in Europe. In 1884, he launched the great diplomatic furore which established German claims on South-West Africa, the Cameroons and Togo, East Africa and North-West New Guinea. Why? He did not want any of these unpleasant steamy territories. They would become hostages in enemy hands in event of a war with France and would in any case furnish a standing argument to fools like Admiral Albrecht von Stosch who wanted a battle fleet, not only to 'document our position as a world power', but even to challenge England.[26] It was not the territories themselves that Bismarck wanted, but a dispute with Great Britain about them, and an appropriate outburst of German public opinion. He was engaged in an attempt to end the feud with France, and this could only be done by persuading the French to accept German co-operation in the colonial sphere; he wanted to convince them 'that he had grievances of his own and

[25] M. E. Townsend, *Origins of Modern German Colonialism, 1871–1885* (1921), p. 18.

[26] F. B. M. Hollyday, *Bismarck's Rival: General and Admiral Albrecht von Stosch* (1960), pp. 162, 273.

therefore actually needed French help'.[27] A quarrel between Berlin and London was also of some use to Bismarck in knotting together German and Russian interests. But above all, it was valuable, in a very selfish way, for domestic purposes. William I was 87 years of age. The Crown Prince had a political party (the *Deutsch freisinnige Partei*) ready to serve him and a predilection for a new foreign policy, based upon an English alliance. But with public opinion inflamed against Britain, the hope of a new foreign policy vanished, and with a public demand for colonies, the *Deutsch freisinnige Partei*, which opposed them was sure to decline in influence. In short, it would be very hard to dispense with Bismarck.

Apart from these peculiar circumstances, Bismarck did not ask for territorial gains; generally, he was to be found smoothly offering them to other people. During his artificial crisis of 1884, he was telling France that he would help in Egypt or in any other part of the world except on the Rhine. Three years earlier, the French had seized Tunisia with his blessing. A year before that, he had suggested that Austria could take Salonika and Russia Constantinople. 'I flatter myself on having been the first, in Europe, to break with the old tradition with which the Western powers have innoculated all the Cabinets, namely, that Constantinople in the hands of Russia would be a European danger.'[28] True, France gained the hostility of Italy by taking Tunisia and was running grave risks with England over Egypt, while if the Russians moved into Constantinople they would have another Crimean War on their hands. Bismarck was willing to help everybody towards their ambitions (provided they lay away from the German frontiers) knowing that each one was bound to become embroiled with some of the others. By being the honest broker, and asking nothing for himself, he hoped to stand outside the web of jealousy and rivalry.

This brings us to Bismarck's fourth rule—the avoidance of permanent hatreds. He allied with Austria after defeating her, and did his best to cajole defeated France. In a sense, one might say that the whole of his diplomacy was devoted to averting the natural outcome of the victories of 1866 and 1870, that is, an alliance of revenge between the defeated against the victor. In 1888, in a memorandum for William II (shortly before he ascended the throne) he said that a war against Russia would be folly, as Germany would subsequently be caught between a defeated France and a defeated Russia; the only war Germany could fight would be a preventive one, against

---

[27] A. J. P. Taylor, *Germany's First Bid for Colonies, 1884–5* (1938), p. 23. For the domestic reasons, see Eyck, op. cit.

[28] W. L. Langer, *European Alliances and Alignments, 1871–90* (1950), p. 206.

France, which was irretrievably hostile anyway.[29] At this point, perhaps, we can see where Bismarck's one great blunder had lain, the one occasion when he had infringed the rule forbidding permanent hatreds. The annexation of Alsace Lorraine had made ordinary relations with France forever impossible. 'I have no illusions, it is absurd,' he told the first French diplomat in Berlin after the war. Yet though Bismarck had opposed the taking of Metz, he had supported the demand of the soldiers for Alsace. Perhaps he was glad to bind the Germans together in a common complicity; perhaps he expected that a defeated France would seek revenge anyway. Certainly, he had overestimated the impact of the financial indemnity, which he had assumed would be crippling. But however his calculations had run, the result was that one major piece on the European chess board remained fixed in hostility, and the task of German foreign policy was one which would inevitably grow more difficult, that of working the other pieces so as to keep France in isolation.

VII

Bismarck's observation about 'the importance of being one of three on the European chessboard so long as the world is governed by the unstable equilibrium of five great powers' is too obvious to be worthy of him as an expression of theory about foreign policy. Nor was it. It was just another argument inflicted on the Russian ambassador in the course of the long-sustained juggling act by which both Austria and Russia were retained by Germany as allies. The whole point of this remarkable swindle is seen when we consider the combination of three that really did haunt Bismarck—the possibility of a revival of the 'Kaunitz coalition' of the eighteenth century: Austria, Russia and France, the major land powers leagued together to annihilate Prussia. The next worst thing that could happen would be a military alliance between France and one of the other two, the more dangerous being Russia, whose vast barbarous distances afforded it a sinister invulnerability. As Austria and Russia were bitter rivals in the Balkans, it would be difficult to satisfy both of them simultaneously. Therefore, the obvious course for German foreign policy seemed to be an alliance with Russia, leaving defeated France and defeated Austria to league together and seek revenge if they dared.

Bismarck did not accept this obvious course. He was well aware of the key importance of Russia; 'the secret of politics,' he said in

[29] Langer, op. cit., p. 485.

1863, 'make a good treaty with Russia.' But he was reluctant to abandon all freedom of manoeuvre and to allow Europe to fall decisively into two armed camps. He therefore adopted a policy of masterly brinkmanship, allying with Austria, his old enemy and his least necessary friend, then using his dominating strength within the partnership to force Austria to accept an understanding with Russia. Putting things so simply falsifies what really happened, of course— everything was more complex and more tentative. At the time of the Austrian alliance, there is some ground for thinking that Bismarck's judgment was clouded by illness; it was not until afterwards that he seized the implications towards which he had groped, and pulled his ingenious system into coherence.

In some ways, the better position for Germany to hold would have been that established by the Convention of Schoenbrunn in June 1873, a tripartite agreement with Austria and Russia to keep the peace, but behind it a German-Russian military convention that was a real fighting alliance. Yet in 1879, Bismarck allied with Austria-Hungary, to the despair of his Emperor, who declared, 'those who drove me to this will bear the responsibility for it in the world to come'. Why did Bismarck do this?—tying up the trim steel-plated Prussian battleship to the worm-eaten Austrian galleon. We have said that his manoeuvre turned out to be an exploit of masterly brinkmanship, but there were some fairly commonplace reasons, approaching necessity, involved as well. For one thing, Russia was already showing distrust; the Tsar held Germany responsible for the affronts he had suffered at the Congress of Berlin—'a coalition of Europe against Russia,' he had said, 'led by Prince Bismarck.' This estrangement was peculiarly dangerous, since a military group in Austria around the Archduke Albrecht was proposing a desperate leap in the dark, an alliance with Russia. If this happened, the 'Kaunitz Coalition' would be near at hand; the German government had to come to a firm understanding with one of the two autocracies immediately. Quite a different possibility was that Austria might drift into the old 'Crimean coalition' of France and England against Russia; this would mean that France would come gloriously out of her isolation in a big international venture which might turn against Germany in the end. Bismarck claimed that he acted to head off Austria-Hungary out of this danger-ous company—'I wanted to dig a ditch between her and the Western powers.'[30] A paradoxical and complicating factor in the situation was that Bismarck had suspicions that both the great eastern empires

[30] A. J. P. Taylor, 'International Relations, 1870–1898', *New Camb. Mod. Hist.* XI (1962), p. 551.

were not far from disintegration. A Russian collapse need not concern him beyond the difficulties attendant upon the loss of an ally, while the break up of the Habsburg Monarchy would involve him in desperate problems—the reconstruction of central and southeast Europe, and possibly even, the changing of the structure of the German Empire itself. Informed opinion in Germany was anxious to avoid these hazards; on the other hand, opinion generally was hostile to Russia. The Catholics complained of the persecution of the Poles, the left and the liberals hated Tsardom because of the repressions of 1848–49, fanatical nationalists feared the Slavs, the Junkers resented the competition of the steppeland cornfields. Given the feeling of Germany, it was easier to do a quick deal with Austria; having done this, it was also easier to coerce Austria to come to an understanding with Russia than the reverse process would have been.

And this—bringing Austria to an understanding with Russia—is what Bismark forthwith proceeded to do. It was in 1880 that he was impressing on the Russian ambassador 'the importance of being one of three', and talking expansively about letting Russia have Constantinople. In June 1881, he got what he wanted, the Alliance of the Three Emperors, substantially at the expense of his ally Austria, which was now unable to intervene if France attacked Germany or if England attacked Russia. In the following year, the Triple Alliance of Germany, Italy and Austria was made to complete French isolation, and in 1887 an alliance of Great Britain with Italy came as a final touch to tie up the Mediterranean. Four months later, in June 1887, came the Treaty of Reinsurance with Russia, which Langer calls 'the keystone of the Bismarckian structure',[31] and which, its author claimed, gave Germany security. It is true indeed, that the treaty did complete a web of alliances which put a premium on the keeping of the peace; in particular, it was calculated to prevent France from knowing beforehand that Russia would support her in an attack on Germany. Being unknown to Austria, the agreement also constituted a sort of recognition that Russia was Germany's essential military ally. Even so, remove Bismarck from the scene, and the Reinsurance Treaty (though Russia, as it happens, was very willing to renew it) became worthless. After all, Russia could ally, defensively, with France any time she wished, just as Germany was allied with Austria. Germany had two allies, but whenever tension grew high between Russia and Austria, she would be obliged to choose between them. There was no real security in reinsurance itself: the treaty was simply a glittering illuminated address on the

[31] Langer, p. 425.

part of the great Bismarck assuring the Tsar that he would bottle up his ally Austria to keep the peace of Europe.

In the Bulgarian crisis of the autumn of 1887 we can see how reinsurance had to be operated in practice. Bismarck published the Austro-German treaty of 1879 to scare Austrian opinion by showing it was strictly defensive and Russian opinion by its mere existence; he refused the General Staff's proposals for a preventive war on Russia, but told Austria to arm, and cut off all German loans to St Petersburg. In short, it was proved that the Bismarckian system depended upon its founder's ability to coerce his allies and to stop the Balkans from boiling over. Something else was also proved, since the Russians detected that, in the last resort, Germany would fight for Austria and not for them; and as money from Berlin was cut off, they turned to Paris for their loans. Two years before Bismarck's fall from office, his system was shaking, and the shadow of a Franco-Russian alliance was creeping onto the horizon, bringing to an end two decades of German diplomatic supremacy.

Chapter XVII

WINDS OF CHANGE IN RUSSIA, 1850–94

I

'The Emperor Nicholas is Master of Europe', said Prince Albert in 1851. This was the year of the Great Exhibition in London, which revealed a whole world of technology and industry to which Nicholas was a stranger. Only in simple and brutal terms was the Tsar predominant on the continent or, indeed, at home; one by one he had trampled on liberal or national movements which might have threatened his authority. First, the Decembrists had been crushed, then the ill-fated Polish Revolution of 1830. Meanwhile, by police measures, censorship and a modicum of authoritarian reform, Nicholas was keeping Russia itself in order. In 1848, the year of revolutions, the empire of the Tsars was unmoved. It was, said Tyutchev, the reactionary poet, like a cliff towering above an angry sea of war and riot. From this base, apparently secure, Nicholas sent an army to help the Austrian Emperor to triumph over his rebellious Hungarian subjects, comfortably playing the rôle of the altruistic friend of brother-monarchs and at the same time guarding Russia from the menace of a united Germany.

It was thus, in the mid-century, that an external observer could regard the Tsar as master of the continent. But within four years Nicholas was plunged into the disasters of the Crimean War. He died in 1855, amidst defeat, inflation, administrative chaos and bitter criticism. At his death, he was no longer the master of Europe, and it could be asked if the very mastery of Russia was not now at stake, so long as autocracy and serfdom remained unreformed. His son and successor Alexander II ascended the throne at a time when the old system was breaking and when the demand for reform, among the educated minority of Russian society, had reached a revolutionary intensity.

II

How had this reform movement developed? It was inspired principally by the contrast between the achievements of Western Europe and Russia's backwardness. Reformers reacted to the stimulus of this contrast in differing ways; some declared that Russia must simply imitate and follow the Western nations, while others wished to challenge and out-vie the West by rediscovering the traditions and spiritual resources which they believed lay hidden in the vast morass of their country's barbarism. By the reign of Nicholas I these divergent reactions had hardened into separate intellectual fashions claiming the allegiance of two warring parties, the Westernizers and the Slavophils. Both opinions had been reinforced by the Russian forays in pursuit of Napoleon: one side remembered the cultural superiority of the world of Mme de Staël and Saint-Simon and despaired, while the other reflected complacently upon the triumphal advance of serfs and Cossacks into the heart of Western civilization. For long, the educated section of the gentry had lived, not disagreeably, in two worlds. 'Like spreading oaks, these families grew in the easy soil of serfdom, their roots invisibly intertwined with the life of the people and drawing life from its waters, while their topmost branches reached up into the atmosphere of European culture.'[1] The time was bound to come when something of a choice had to be made.

Yet the differences between Westernizers and Slavophils were not great; at least, there was much more common ground than either would allow at the time. Both belonged to the same small class of intellectuals, isolated amidst a chaos of ignorance; both were influenced by German Romanticism and Idealism which they applied in different ways; both saw history in Hegel's terms of the progressive revelation of the Absolute, leading to a universal culture, though one side saw this culture coming from the Atlantic seaboard and the other from the eastern marchlands. If the Slavophils were opposing the cosmopolitan outlook of their rivals, perhaps, in this age when national feeling and historical consciousness were intensifying in the most civilized countries of Europe, they were merely showing themselves the most up to date of Westernizers. If the Westernizers were less 'natural' than their opponents, less rooted in the soil of their homeland, it was the Slavophils who displayed most of the affectation. Chadayev (a Westernizer who was sent to a lunatic asylum for opposing the Crimean War) said that Constantine Aksakov wore a costume so national that the peasants in the streets took him for a Persian, and that foreign visitors to Russia had the Slavophils pointed out to them like animals at the zoo.

In a sense, it is true to say that the Westernizers were radical, while the Slavophils were conservative. If so, however, the terms need careful definition. Both condemned serfdom unreservedly, the

---

[1] M. Gershenzon, cit. M. B. Petrovich, *The Emergence of Russian Pan-Slavism, 1856–70* (1958), p. 42.

Slavophils more particularly insisting that the peasants must be given most of the land when their bondage was ended. The Slavophils like the Aksakovs, the Kireyevsky brothers and Samarin had no love for autocracy, which they gloomily contrasted with the old traditions of freedom, the Cossack assemblies and the *Zemsky Sobor*, a sort of Estates General. To them, the Tsars were out of touch, not only with the past, but also with the future of their country: as Samarin said, the ideal of Nicholas I was 'not the Russia of tomorrow but the Austria of yesterday'. On the other hand, it was possible to find Westernizers who had come to see no alternative to autocratic government. 'A liberated Russian people', Belinsky wrote in 1837, 'would not take its place in any parliament . . . They would rush off instead to carouse in the vodka shops . . . and to hang all noblemen who shave.'[2] Slavophil doctrines might be used to enhance the mystique of authority around the Tsar; on the other hand, Westernizers were more likely to turn to the autocracy in despair as the only force, in a wilderness of inertia, that could initiate reform.

What then were the differences of opinion and outlook which separated Westernizers and Slavophils? In a notorious letter published in 1836, Chadayev declared that the Russians were vagabonds and nomads, united only by their religion, a religion which, unlike Christianity in the West, had come to them without an attendant culture. Thus, they had nothing to add to the common stock of civilization. As against these extreme views and their less extreme variants, the Slavophils believed that the Russian past provided two great traditions around which the whole world could be remoulded. One was Orthodoxy, with its conviction of the mystical union of all believers, living and dead, and its doctrine of brotherhood, superior far to western individualism and democracy. This is what they said: their opponents, looking at Orthodoxy from a different angle, saw only (in Herzen's words) 'fresh oil for annointing the Tsar, new chains laid upon thought, new subordination of conscience to the slavish Byzantine Church'. The other great Russian tradition was the co-operative principle exemplified in the *mir*, the peasant community, which tilled the land in common and periodically redistributed it in accordance with the need of families. Both Westernizers and Slavophils wished to free the serfs, but they differed in their attitude to the rural community. According to the Slavophils, once the tyranny of the lords was removed, the *mir* would achieve its real perfection as a progressive communal institution. Ogarev, a Westernizer, tried the experiment and reported that once his serfs had been freed they refused to improve their agriculture; the only equality the

[2] R. Hare, *Pioneers of Russian Social Thought* (1951), p. 43.

mir produced, he concluded, was 'equality of slavery'. Turgenev, another friend of the peasants, also denounced the Slavophils' worship of the 'sheepskin cloak', and their failure to realize that freedom could only be achieved by following the way of Europe. 'The peasantry', he said, 'are conservative to the core and carry within themselves the makings of a bourgeoisie, with their stuffy, dirty huts and their reluctance to share any civic responsibility.'

III

Rivals though they were, Westernizers and Slavophils were both contributing to the growing reform movement in Russia. 'Like Janus', said Herzen, 'we looked in different directions, while one heart beat within us.'[3] The conflict between the two schools formed a pattern of thesis and antithesis out of which a revolutionary synthesis was born, compounded of the Westernizers' hatred for a backward social order and the Slavophils' hope in its hidden potentialities for good. Both opinions seemed to be converging upon a sort of socialistic ideal; on the one hand were the dreams of Western writers like Owen, Fourier, Saint-Simon, Proudhon and Louis Blanc, and on the other was the vision of an indigenous utopia, the communal life of the *mir* freed from the shackles of serfdom.

The new revolutionary generation was to be inspired by Herzen's periodical *Kolokol, The Bell* (from 1857 onwards) and by Cherny-shevsky's novel, *What is to be Done?* (1863), and these two writers derived their 'socialism' from a combination of Westernizing and Slavophil influences. Though Chernyshevsky claimed to be indebted to the concept of the *mir*, he was essentially a Westernizer, who ridiculed the Slavophil analogy of the barbarians who brought 'vitality' into a decadent Roman Empire. With him, the influence of French and English writers was sharpened to the edge of rebellion by his observation of events, not so much in Russia, as in Europe, in 1848, when ideals were defeated. 'You think the matter depends on the word republic', he wrote in his diary, 'but there is no power in that word. What matters is to relieve the lower class from slavery, not to law, but to the inevitability of things . . . Freedom . . . freedom for what? . . . It is no question of whether there should be a Tsar or not, but a question of whether one class should suck the blood of another.'[4] The effect of 1848 on Herzen (who saw the Parisian *débâcle* with his own eyes) was similar—but with one great difference. The memory of that defeat, recollected in the shadow of personal

---

[3] J. H. Billington, *Mikhailovsky and Russian Populism* (1958), pp. 9 10.
[4] R. Hare, op. cit., pp. 180–1.

unhappiness and in the bitterness of exile, brought him to hate the West, a civilization of gross vaudeville and unscrupulous money-changers, whose democratic ideal would inevitably crush individualism, and whose socialism would finish up as insufferably bourgeois. Thus Herzen, whose intellectual roots were all in the West, virtually became a sort of Slavophil socialist, believing that the seeds of the European doctrines of socialism could grow in Russia in the soil of traditional institutions, notably the rural commune.

In Herzen and Chernyshevky, the doctrines of Westernizers and Slavophils were synthesized to inspire a new revolutionary generation. In terms of practical action, what did this mean? With regard to the autocracy, the prophets were divided. The Crimean War had provided a terrible revelation of the inefficiency of despotism: even so, Herzen greeted the accession of Alexander II with appeals to the Tsar to lead a peaceful revolution, and to the nobility, to co-operate with the autocracy in the abolition of serfdom. As a disciple of Fourier and Saint-Simon (and not of Marx and Engels), it was perfectly logical for him to appeal to the throne and, disillusioned with the West, he was inclined towards a 'Russian' solution. But Chernyshevsky denounced this reliance on the Tsar, whom he regarded as 'merely the pinnacle of an aristocratic hierarchy to which he belongs body and soul'; he angrily regretted that the people were so foolish as to 'regard their aggressor as their protector'. On one thing, however, Herzen and Chernyshevsky, Slavophils and Westernizers, and the reforming intellectuals generally all agreed—serfdom must be ended. Here was the point at which, as Herzen told the new Tsar, the autocracy could fulfil all their hopes and itself take the lead of the forces of reform.

IV

Alexander II was dictatorial and haughty, a true Tsar in that he did not know the meaning of freedom. But he had none of his father's unselfish and dedicated inhumanity. Unlike Nicholas, he was given to pleasure—smoking, cards and mistresses. He had the trick of enjoying life, and was not impervious to the idea that his subjects might like to do so as well. There was a sentimental vein in his nature: it is said that, in a burial ground for serfs he recited Gray's *Elegy*:

> 'Perchance in this neglected spot is laid
> Some heart once pregnant with celestial fire'

and wept. Gifted with human sympathy to inspire intervention and the autocratic will to override obstacles, he seemed to have the temperamental qualities necessary for the great task to which Herzen called him, the abolition of serfdom.

It was unfortunate however, that the Tsar had his sentimentality well under control, and that he followed its dictates only when they accorded with political expediency. He was to free the peasants—but in an ungenerous fashion, at their own expense, as it were. Essentially, Alexander's motives for ending serfdom were calculated and logical. This was something that had to come, it was inevitable: as he said, 'it had better come from above than below'. He had seen revolution in Vienna and Berlin in 1848, and could recognize the stirrings of danger in the chaotic Russia which he had inherited in the midst of a disastrous war. Reforming criticism, now reaching revolutionary intensity, had fixed on the abolition of serfdom as its first and most obvious demand, and under Nicholas I, both paternalism and ruthlessness had failed to silence the continuous rumbling of discontent in the countryside. On any view of Russia's future greatness, liberal or autocratic, serfdom stood condemned: the labour force it provided was virtually useless for industrial development of the English type, or for the settlement of the vast new lands of Siberia on the American pattern. Indeed, what had already been achieved by free settlers in the east may have provided the argument which clinched the case for emancipation with the hesitant government. 'It was probably the growing prosperity of Siberia', said the Scotsman Alexander Michie, in 1864, 'and the marked superiority of the condition of the population there, that induced the government to emancipate the serfs of Russia proper.'[5] All the arguments of national interest and of expediency favoured freedom; the only reason for delay was that the nobility might be angry. But by now, the serf-owners were reconciled to the inevitable—it was merely a question of haggling about the price.

From 1858, when the Tsar took the first steps towards freeing the peasants on crown lands, to 1861, the year of the general emancipation, this haggling went on, very successfully from the point of view of the proprietors. By the Edict of 1861, the household serfs were liberated: their owners received no compensation, nor did they. The masses of rural peasants were also set free, and in their case, a land settlement of some kind had to be made. Those who were prepared to renounce all other claims could take a tiny portion of land as a free gift; as these plots were too small to sustain existence, the option was useful only to those who wished to sell out and go to the towns. Families which wanted enough land to live on had to buy

[5] *The Siberian Overland Route from Pekin to Petersburg* (1864), cit. D. W. Treadgold, *The Great Siberian Migration* (1957), p. 88.

it from the estate-owner, and until an agreement was made about this redemption payment, dues in money and labour had to be rendered as before. Most of the purchase money would be advanced by the government, and the peasants would have to repay it with interest over the next forty-nine years. Allotments would belong, not to the individual or the family, but to the village community. The *mir* thus remained in existence, with increased powers, more especially police and judicial powers which had formerly belonged to the lords; within it, the peasants were bound together in a collective responsibility to the State, for repayment of their instalments on the land and their ordinary taxes.

What did the peasantry think of this edict of liberation? They firmly believed two things; firstly, that even if their bodies belonged to the lord, the land was theirs, and secondly, that when the nobles had been freed from State-service by Peter III in the eighteenth century, the Tsar had intended to concede reciprocal freedom to the serfs. The Edict of emancipation therefore came to them as a terrible disillusionment—in so far as they were being given freedom, the gift was tardy: in so far as they had to pay for their land, the obligation was unjust. This was the basic, major injustice, made all the more obvious by the minor injustices perpetrated in detail. The assumption of noble proprietorship hit the peasants in other ways, excluding them from gathering fuel in the woods or exercising traditional grazing rights on wasteland. Payments to the lords, in theory for the land, were in practice calculated, not on what the peasant was getting, but on what the lord was losing. In the black soil areas, the landlord got the value of the land plus 36 roubles for each 'serf soul', while in areas of poorer soil he got the value of the land and an additional 62 roubles for each soul. 'The peasant', G. T. Robinson observed, 'was really renting, not only his land, but his own person from his former master.'[6] On matters of this kind, the illiterate inhabitants of rural Russia were not deceived. In 1881 there were still one and a half million peasants who had not complied with the Edict and who were ordered by the government to accept a settlement.

The emancipation was loaded to favour the nobles—and the peasants knew it. Yet, if the object was to preserve the gentry, even this selfish aim was unrealized. Before 1861, seven-tenths of the serfs were already mortgaged to State-credit institutions; afterwards, the nobles continued to sink into debt as rapidly as before. Most of them had neither the skill nor the resources to turn to large-scale capitalist farming, especially in an era of agrarian crisis. Once the unmortgaged part of the redemption money was gone, they had to sell the land

[6] G. T. Robinson, *Rural Russia Under the Old Regime* (1932), p 83.

itself. The influence of the nobles waned in the countryside, and the peasants could accumulate their hatred against a new objective, the central government.

The Tsar and his advisers had missed the opportunity to change the course of Russian history. They ended serfdom, but failed to create the conditions within which either freedom or prosperity could come to rural Russia. The *mir* tyrannized over the peasants more than the lords of the last generation; defaulters to the annual redemption payment were flogged, conscripts were sent to the army, travel was impossible without a passport signed by a village elder. Slavophil visions of the *mir* looked very different when the rural commune came to be used essentially as an enforcement agency of the central government, an 'engine of an over-priced redemption'. Agriculture remained obsolete and unproductive; the holdings were too small and there was no provision for the consolidation of scattered strips save the impossible one of action by a substantial majority. As the rural population of European Russia kept on increasing, the poorer peasants were driven to desperate short-term renting of land at high prices; from 1880, the competition of the American prairies brought down the price of grain, taking the profit out of agriculture for the lucky minority which had a surplus to sell. Thus, agriculture was unimproved and the peasants were disillusioned, ready to give their allegiance to a revolutionary movement which would promise them the land.

V

Alexander II's claim to both liberal sentiments and greatness rests, not on his emancipation of the serfs, but on his relaxation of the police state built up by Nicholas I, and on his creation of a new and voluntary system of local government. He did not intend to relinquish his autocratic authority: he wished to bring the more intelligent classes into co-operation with it. Even so, this change of course was of the utmost significance. The atmosphere of life in the capital changed. Citizens found they could smoke in public, and writers could send their books to press without fear of the censorship. Nekrasov hailed this dawn of freedom with an ode

> 'My favourite idea
> That the Petersburg climate is terrible
> I can now insert
> In every article without fear.

Having undergone the blows of fate,
At length in old age I have achieved happiness
I have smoked cigars in the street
And written without censorship.'[7]

But one did not need to have succumbed to the vices of smoking or authorship to appreciate the new era. The educational system, the army and the law courts all bore witness to the transformation of the spirit of government. The universities regained their autonomy, and students of non-noble birth were once more admitted to higher education. New schools were founded under secular control, entirely independent of the Holy Synod. In place of the old system of long-term military service, universal conscription (by lot) was instituted, with generous reductions of service for the educated classes; the cruel military punishments of knouting and 'passing under the sticks' were abolished. Legal procedure was reformed, judges were given security of tenure, hearings were made public and the jury system was introduced. The old vision embodied in Karamzin's *Memoir*, of an absolute monarchy supported by a serf-owning aristocracy, had been finally abandoned: the ideal now pursued was to establish the existing autocracy at the summit of a modern state, with equality before the law and secular education as its basis. There was a danger here, however, for education and equality may foster ideas of liberty. Of the obligation of universal military service, Trotsky was to observe that it 'introduced into the army all the contradictions proper to a nation which still has its bourgeois revolution to accomplish'.[8] The modernization of Russia inevitably increased the revolutionary forces working against the autocracy.

In 1864, Alexander promulgated the most significant of his liberal measures, the creation of a new system of local government. This was only three years after the emancipation of the serfs, and the two reforms were connected. Once serfdom ended, new provincial institutions were needed to integrate the atomized multitude of village communities into a convenient pattern for administration. The method chosen was to set up elected assemblies representing, not the people of their areas, but the property-holders, and to give these assemblies power to act locally in matters of education, health, communications and public welfare generally—so long as there was no trespass on the autocratic powers of the Tsar. These assemblies (*zemstvo*) were of two kinds. In the districts, townsmen and peasants

[7] Cit. S. R. Tompkins, *The Russian Intelligentsia* (1957), p. 26.
[8] Leon Trotsky, *History of the Russian Revolution* (trans. Max Eastman, 1932) I, p. 37.

elected some deputies, but the preponderant voting power belonged to the estate owners, and that strictly in proportion to the amount of land they held. Representatives from the district assemblies went up to the provincial *zemstvo*; these met for short sessions, but had standing committees to maintain continuity of policy in the intervals.

No sooner were these institutions set up than they were successful. So far, all reforms in Russia had derived their force from the central government, which took a global view, indifferent to local needs and idiosyncrasies. The decree of 1790 prescribing the election of a 'marshal of the nobility' among the wild Yakut tribesmen of Eastern Siberia is an extreme example, but it serves to illustrate the tendency which had prevailed for more than a century. Thus the change of administrative organization which allowed reforms to spring from local inspiration was a radically new departure and it evoked unexpected enthusiasm and interest. Up to now, the great curse of Russian provincial life had been the sheer inertia of so many of those who ought to have been leaders—the disease of 'Oblomovism'. In Ivan Goncharov's famous novel (1858), Oblomov has reached a perfect equilibrium of happy inactivity; letters are put away unopened if there is a suspicion they may contain awkward news, and the house-serfs go round in awe-struck silence, as if there was a death in the house, on the rare occasions when their master writes a reply. 'For unforeseen contingencies, though they might turn out well in the end, were disturbing,' they said in Oblomovka; 'they involved constant worry and trouble, running about, restlessness, buying and selling or writing—in a word, doing something in a hurry, and that was no joking matter.'[9] So they did nothing, and lived on for years, yawning, talking, drowsing, laughing. Now, however, the opportunity came, and the more active and politically conscious gentry came forward to lead their provinces. The *zemstvo* quickly put on foot remarkable improvements in education and public welfare. Their zeal surprised the Tsar, and not entirely pleasantly. Very soon, the government was jealously cutting back the authority of its newly-founded assemblies—within four years, limits were put on their powers of levying local taxation, and on their publications.

From his autocratic point of view, the Tsar's mistrust was justified. Around the *zemstvo* gathered the first generation of Russian liberals. 42 per cent of the district assembly seats and nearly three-quarters of the provincial assembly places went to the gentry, and the gentry had their grievances. Their economic decline, their hatred of the bureaucracy, their distrust of a government which had taken away their serfs and was now busily engaged in favouring industry at the

[9] I. Goncharov, *Oblomov* (Penguin, 1954), p. 134.

expense of agriculture—all these were matters for resentment, making them a discontented element in the state. With the ending of serfdom, they became less isolated from the other classes of society; as they were driven to sell their land, they became more anxious to conciliate the middle classes and richer peasants who were buying it. 'It was no mere coincidence', writes the historian of Russian liberalism, 'that after the Great Reforms the gentry was for many years the major force of Russian liberalism.'[10] Some of them, inspired by utopian and revolutionary literature, and working in close touch with the '*zemstvo* intellectuals' (the doctors, teachers and engineers sent by the assemblies to enlighten the countryside) came to see, in Alexander II's new form of local government, the beginning of freedom for the whole of Russia.

Though their first request was for the creation of a central office at St Petersburg to co-ordinate *zemstvo* policy, they really wanted much more than this. They wanted to give a 'parliamentary roof' to the *zemstvo* structure. Assemblies for districts and provinces existed: it remained to create a national assembly.

VI

In 1866, a student, Karakozov, tried to assassinate the Tsar. Alexander was disillusioned now: the liberation of the serfs had excited more criticism than applause, the *zemstvo* were ungratefully undermining his authority, during the last five years there had been outbreaks of arson and student riots in Petersburg and insurrection in Poland. He was no longer prepared to experiment with liberalism. The press censorship was re-established, the government once more took over control of the universities, and special judicial procedures were devised to try crimes against the State. A mist had crept across the new sunrise: Russia was back in the twilight days of Nicholas I. But there was a difference. Alexander still shrank from the lonely exercise of power, still yearned for a veneer of consultation and consent to disguise his autocracy. A camouflage constitution was needed, 'to harness the formal aspects of a representative order to an essentially unchanged absolutism',[11] and the search for it went on throughout the rest of the reign. On 1 March 1881, a few hours before he was murdered, Alexander II approved such a plan, drawn up by Loris-Melikov, the tough Governor of Kharkov, who had been called in to reorganize the machinery of State security. The object of this pro-

[10] G. Fischer, *Russian Liberalism* (1958), p. 6.
[11] Hans Heilbonner, 'Alexander III and the Reform Plan of Loris-Melikov' *J. Modern Hist.* XXXIII, 4 (1961), p. 385.

posal was to bring the *zemstvo* into mesh with the autocracy, but in a purely advisory capacity; they would have no new powers. 'It would be unthinkable', Loris-Melikov said, 'for Russia to have any form of popular representation based upon western models.' These words may almost serve as a justification of Alexander's assassins. Though they were committing an act of cruelty and folly, it was also a logical symbol of the battle they were waging. The emancipation of the serfs and the creation of the *zemstvo* had merely served to focus and clarify the objective of revolutionary opinion in Russia. It was no longer a question of this reform or that, of good Tsars or bad ones. War was declared against the principle of autocracy itself.

Karamzin's myth of an omnipotent sovereign upheld by his loyal nobles in a land of obedient serfs had vanished, and for a moment it had seemed possible that the myth of the 'Tsar Liberator' would replace it. Slavophils, out of reverence for the past, and Westernizers, out of hope for the future, might have been willing to serve an autocracy genuinely devoted to liberal reform. Even Bakunin, anarchist and professional revolutionist, was haunted by the vision of 'a strong dictatorial power . . . which would concern itself exclusively with the elevation and enlightenment of the masses, a power which is free in tendency and spirit but without parliamentary forms . . . a power which is surrounded, advised and supported by the free co-operation of like-minded men, but which is not limited by anybody or anything.'[12] Herzen too, was under the spell: as we have seen, he appealed to Alexander II when he first came to the throne.

But by the end of the reign, the myth of the 'Tsar Liberator' was destroyed. The first to proclaim that the emancipation of the serfs was a fraud was Herzen himself. 'A new serfdom', he wrote in *Kolokol*, 15 June 1861. 'The Tsar has cheated the people.'[13] In the following year Bakunin published *The People's Cause, Romanov, Pugachev or Pestel*; he was through with his 'dictatorial power' now, and wanted to see the calling of the *Zemsky Sobor*, the old, almost forgotten assembly of the nation. Tocqueville's famous dictum, that the most dangerous moment for a bad government comes at the point when it tries to reform, was proved right again. Half measures aroused the demand for full measures, and a glimpse of the shadow whetted the imagination which yearned for the reality. By dabbling in freedom, the autocracy had demonstrated its own obsolescence without being able to adapt itself to the new age.

---

[12] Cit. H. Kohn, *Panslavism* (1953), p. 77. Bakunin was in jail, and was addressing the Tsar. Yet his courage is sufficiently proved for most historians to accept his sincerity.

[13] F. Venturi, *Roots of Revolution* (1960), p. 109.

Ironically enough, the bomb explosion of 1 March 1881 offered the Romanov dynasty its last chance of coming to terms with the ideals of the future. It was still not too late for some romantic, quixotic gesture. The three greatest minds of the day in Russia, Mikhailovsky the philosopher, Tolstoy the novelist and Vladimir Solovev the theologian appealed to the new Tsar to forgive his father's murderers. Alexander III, a man of sobriety and honour, but a ruthless absolutist, refused. He did not know the meaning of mercy. Yet he meant well by the mass of his subjects who did not ask for liberty. His reign, with Bunge at the finances, saw some improvements on behalf of the ordinary people; the hated poll tax was abolished, a State Bank was set up to help the peasants, and the first decrees limiting the hours of work of women and children in factories were published. But for the more intelligent part of Russian society, this was an era of black reaction. A rigid censorship silenced opposition, secondary education was limited to the upper classes and university fees were quadrupled, church schools were multiplied and the lay schools set up by the *zemstvo* were discouraged; Catholics, Lutherans and other dissenters from Orthodoxy were persecuted, and the non-Russian nationalities in the empire were subjected to 'russification'. There was further government interference in the law courts, and the principle of the security of tenure of judges was abolished. Even within their local sphere of action, the *zemstvo* became subject to surveillance. So too were the peasants, for in 1889, a 'Land Captain' was established in every canton to preside over the village assemblies and cantonal courts. 'No single act of government in the reign of Alexander III stirred the Russian peasant to more bitter resentment', writes Charques; 'it brought back the breath and being of serf law.'[14]

VII

As Karamzin had been the political theorist of monarchical conservatism under the first Alexander, Pobyedonostsev, Professor of Civil Law in the University of Moscow, became the theoretical justifier of reaction under Alexander III nearly eighty years later. Pale, austere and solemn behind his horn-rimmed spectacles, and endowed with an incongruous gift for vituperation (he called the ministers of the last reign 'flabby eunuchs and conjurers'), Pobyedonostsev was one of those clear-sighted pessimists who are ruthless in the cause of reaction without any real enthusiasm. If the times had been propitious, he would have preferred radical changes—the peasants to be made

[14] R. Charques, *The Twilight of Imperial Russia* (1958), p. 32.

independent of the *mir* and given the land in freehold, and the whole administrative system to be reorganized and freed from arbitrary interference. In private letters, he reveals doubts about the future of the autocracy itself. He was critical of Alexander I's foreign ideas, of Nicholas, whose administrators had been lackeys and whose court had been isolated from the people, of Alexander II and his irresponsibilities. Autocrats only deserved to rule if they observed high standards of Christian duty and knew how to choose intelligent servants. Pobyedonostsev did not delude himself about the possibility of his ideal being realized. His defence of the *status quo* in Russia was founded on negative arguments: it was better than the proposed alternatives.

While wishing to see the adoption of western efficiency and ideas of property, Pobyedonostsev had inherited from the Slavophils a hatred of western liberalism, which he criticized with insight and acuteness. A 'free press' simply means that any 'vagabond babbler' can make himself heard, and that all debate will be conducted at the level of hysteria; parliaments are 'fetishes', assemblies of individuals each following his own secret path of self-interest, mere façades of talk behind which bureaucracies rule; universal education 'pulls young people out of their natural environment' and leaves them rootless; democracy is inherently chauvinistic and will bring the world to war.

Yet this ruthless critic of liberalism was not a fanatical nationalist and Slavophil like his friend Dostoevsky. He knew the West from genteel trips to London and Salzburg, not from sojourns in its slums: his detestation was theoretical. To him, Russia had no battles to fight outside its own boundaries, no duty to the scattered Slavs, no mission to promote Orthodoxy. He confessed that his own country-men were hopelessly backward—beyond the imperial palaces lay 'an icy desert and an abode of evil men'. An ignorant population could not hope to work the jury system and to live freely under the rule of law. The British themselves only apparently held law in great es-teem, Pobyedonostsev once observed—'apart from a handful of lawyers, nobody knows what the law is. What they really mean is respect for authority, the authority which for centuries has enforced and still enforces, with a great latitude of sound interpretation, laws and customs which are often antiquated. In our own country, it is nonsense to speak of respect for the law, as our organs of legal administration do not function properly.'[15] In short, each country had its traditional institutions, suited to it by use and appropriate

[15] P. O. Schilovsky, 'Remniscences of K. K. Pobyedonostsev', *Slavonic Review*, XXX (1952), p. 364.

for the level of education of its inhabitants; these institutions could not be transplanted into alien soil. Pobyedonostsev did not say that Russia was superior to the West: he merely said she was entirely different.

What sort of government did he think was fitting for Russia? The ideal was 'calm, humane, indulgent and arbitrary administration'.[16] The Tsar would keep his people at peace with the outside world, for states ought to meet 'only at the top', through their kings. He would choose intelligent servants from the middle class; for Pobyedonostsev, the day of the nobility was gone for ever. There would be no representative institutions, only efficient and honest administration. The inspiration of the régime, and the mystical bond which united the people to the State would be Orthodoxy; the whole nation would be transformed into a living community by the educational pressure of a vast network of parish schools controlled by the Church. Through the unifying force of religion, the nationalities in Russia would all be absorbed; the Poles, giving up Catholicism, would cease their agitations, and the Jews (not without some ruthless encouragement) would be converted or would 'wander away'.

In many respects, these ideas of Pobyedonostsev resemble those of his ally Dostoevsky. The two men had come to their opinions independently; then their minds had interacted closely for a decade, and finally the great novelist died just before his friend was promoted to be the 'grey eminence' of the reactionary Alexander III.[17] Yet there is a significant contrast between their viewpoints, a contrast between intelligence and genius, between theory and dark, overwhelming experience. Dostoevsky had himself been seared by the passion of revolutionary ideals and had suffered for them in Siberia before he became a conservative; Pobyedonostsev knew them only from books of law and history and official dossiers. Thus, his well-argued system was bloodless; his ideal bureaucrats did not exist; the doctrines of the Church had not the enormous influence on men's minds which he postulated; his theories ignored the rôle of army and police, on which, in the last resort, the régime was founded; he had no appreciation of the importance of either glamour or discussion in the governance of men. Yet, even today, Pobyedonostsev's conservatism retains some of its old compelling, sinister logic, an irrefutable half-truth founded

---

[16] R. F. Byrnes, 'Pobyedonostsev on the Instruments of Russian Government', in E. J. Simmons, *Continuity and Change in Russian and Soviet Thought* (1955), p. 119.

[17] R. F. Byrnes, 'Dostoevskii and Pobyedonostsev', in J. S. Curtiss, *Essays in Russian and Soviet History* (1963), pp. 85–104.

on a sombre view of human nature. According to him, men are incapable of goodness or rationality; most of them ought to be confined to a knowledge of the sacred books and an official view of history, and be compelled to live decent, happy lives. It was the creed of the Grand Inquisitor of *The Brothers Karamazov*, who gave men bread, blind worship and the unity of the ant-heap in place of the Saviour's dangerous gift of freedom. 'They will remember the horrors of slavery and confusion to which Thy freedom brought them. Freedom, free thought and science will lead them into such straits . . . that some of them . . . will destroy themselves . . . while the rest . . . will crawl fawning to our feet and whine, "Yes, you were right, you alone possess His mystery, and we come back to you; save us from ourselves!" '[18]

The arguments in favour of autocracy had gone through their full circle, from the Tsar as head of the social hierarchy to the Tsar Liberator rescuing the disinherited. Pobyedonostsev now went back to the oldest of arguments in favour of authoritarian rule—the unworthiness of men, and their original sin.

VIII

During the reign of Alexander II, for the first time the revolutionary movement in Russia gained a degree of coherence. About 1870, the word 'Populism' (and 'Populist'—*narodnik*) came into use as a description, not of an organization, but of a common spirit that united a congeries of revolutionary groups. Their members were called 'Populists' because they had faith in the people, in human progress, individuality and freedom. From the Slavophils they had inherited a belief in the peasant communism of the *mir*; they were predisposed towards an early seizure of governmental power, since they feared that the autocracy would sponsor capitalist development and attempt to buy off the intellectuals by the opportunity of joining a Saint-Simonian *élite*. From the Westernizers they drew their belief in the infinite possibilities of progress, and their desire for representative institutions. In Proudhon they found the intellectual

[18] F. D. Dostoevsky, *The Brothers Karamazov* (trans. Constance Garnett, 1912, 1945), pp. 263–6. This is not to say that the Grand Inquisitor represents Dostoevsky's or Pobyedonostsev's views, or the views of either as interpreted by the other. The novelist was referring to 'our modern *negationist*' and to the coercive implications of socialism. For his opinions and Pobyedonostsev's grave concern at this 'powerful' piece of writing, see D. Magarshack, *Dostoevsky* (1962), pp. 476–9, and Jessie Coulson, *Dostoevsky: a Self-Portrait* (1962), p. 224.

middle term to unite their conflicting aspirations, a vision of a western type of progress embodied in a State composed of a free federation of a multitude of peasant communes. After the failure of the 1861 Emancipation, both Herzen and Chernyshevsky (united now on the futility of relying on the Tsar) appealed to the younger generation to go directly to the people, and to devote themselves to solacing its sufferings. Their writings had enormous influence, especially among university students. Chernyshevsky's *What is to be Done?* (1863) and Lavrov's *Historical Letters* (1868–9) taught the duty of intellectuals towards the people, in recognition of the debt which civilization owes to the anonymous masses; after the defeat of the Paris Commune, Mikhailovsky turned his disciples away from admiration of a decadent France—the land of 'Darwinism and the operettas of Offenbach'—and urged them to go with open hearts to the unspoilt Russian peasants. In 1874, some 2,000 idealists, students, 'repentant noblemen' and the like, actually did go to the people in a sort of kenotic crusade, a 'collective act of Rousseauism'. The result was a tragi-comic disaster. Nobody wanted the intellectuals to come and share their miseries. The people ridiculed their saviours, got them drunk, or handed them over to the police. Turgenev, who had lost his faith in the peasants since their emancipation, finding them addicted to hair grease, patent leather shoes and vodka, wrote *Virgin Soil* (1877) to demonstrate the failure of the *narodnik* ideal: founding a model factory in the Urals is constructive, going to the people with brotherly affection is plain folly.

With the collapse of this crusade an element of romantic, Slavophilic idealism vanished from the revolutionary movement. Though the great gesture of 1874, like the Decembrist failure fifty years before, left behind it a haunting memory of self-sacrifice, its main effect was to serve as a warning: success would only come to those who followed harsher and more logical courses. Indeed, the movement back to the people came too late; when it occurred, it was an anachronism, for the 'sixties had seen the 'iconoclastic revolution', the victory of 'realism' and of 'nihilism' among the intellectuals. Bazarov in Turgenev's *Fathers and Sons* (1861) exemplifies the new tendencies, the rejection of tradition allied with a brutal self-assertiveness. Of the novel *What is to be Done?*—the great inspiration of Populist altruism—the theologian Solovev acutely observed that the fraternal duty of sharing the lot of the disinherited was hardly deducible from the atheistic and nihilistic presuppositions of the characters: 'man is descended from monkeys, let us therefore give our souls for the salvation of our friends'. 'Bazarovism' drew a more logical deduction from the initial premises. The new nihilism found its philosophy in Pisarev, who taught that the only reality was the material world, and that aesthetic and emotional interpretation of it ought to be discarded. Nihilists did not believe in the 'people' or the *mir*; they believed only in those who thought 'scientifically'. They united despair with the will to action, for the task of the present generation was to criticize and destroy, and some of them were inclined to regard their own rôle as leadership, not towards an ideal, but in a Darwinian struggle for existence.

What did this new philosophy of revolution mean in terms of practical action? To some of the revolutionaries, their underlying pessimism seemed to call for almost pointless violence, a protest without thought of the future. 'Bloody and hopeless revolution', like the serf rising of Pugachev in the eighteenth century, was the formula of a manifesto of Moscow students in 1862. 'The revolutionary is a lost man', said the *Revolutionary Catechism* drawn up by Nechaev and Bakunin in exile: he has no interests, possessions or name, no morality, enthusiasm or sentiment. Yet this romantic, defeatist nihilism was generally allied with a grim sense of realities. Nechaev returned to Russia to build up a nucleus of conspirators, whom he was apparently prepared to rule by the weapon of murder. Zaichnevsky, the author of the Moscow students' manifesto, was planning for a rising which would capture and maintain the centralized machinery of the State, and exercise dictatorial control of elections until a new order was firmly established. This system of his —an interim revolutionary dictatorship—he called 'Russian Jacobinism'. The Jacobin idea and Nechaev's concept of ruthless discipline among conspirators were taken over by Tkachev, the son of a poor noble, who studied at the university of St Petersburg and finally fled from Russia in the year before the Populists 'went to the people'. Tkachev rejected Populist idealism; he also rejected Bakunin's anarchism and the scientific socialism of Marx and Engels. In essentials, his master was Blanqui. What he cared about was the seizure of power in a strictly political sense. Zaichnevsky and Nechaev helped him to put Blanqui's insurrectionist theories into a Russian context; he thought in terms of disciplined conspiracy, a violent overturn, then a revolutionary dictatorship carrying through a gradual educative programme. Lenin's seizure of power in 1917 did not conform to Marxist orthodoxy, but it followed closely the technique advised by Tkachev. One wonders whether, in the end, Marxist theories provided the Russian revolutionaries with good reasons for what they were going to do anyway.

The failure of the Populist crusade in 1874 helped to turn the revolutionary intellectuals towards realistic and violent theories, and towards the industrial working class as allies. In 1876, the government took cruel measures against intellectuals who had joined in a workers' demonstration on the Kazan Cathedral Square in St Petersburg. In the next dozen years, the numbers of factory workers in Russia doubled, reaching a total of $2\frac{1}{2}$ millions, and at the same time, individual factories were becoming bigger, concentrating their employees together. Town and country were becoming more separate, so that now only 18 per cent of factory workers went back to their villages in summer. Rudimentary unions of workers were forming, assisted no doubt by the rise of real wages which took place from 1883-96, though this improvement may also have done something to blunt the edge of grievance. None the less, conditions were terrifying. Whole families had no home but the factory, sleeping on looms, or building themselves beds on heaps of boxes in the yard, going up high to escape the fleas. Others slept in industrial barracks, two families in a room, with no furniture but beds, a cheap clock, an ikon and a woodcut of the Tsar.[19] Russia had not reached anything like the stage of capitalism Marx had postulated for a revolution, but at least it had produced an industrial proletariat living in unparalleled misery.

The Kazan Square demonstration of 1876, which symbolized the new enthusiasm of the revolutionary intellectuals to link themselves with the industrial workers, was significant in another sense. It provoked the government to severities, and these in their turn provoked the declaration of open warfare upon the throne. Terrorism became a revolutionary institution. Karakozov, who fired at Alexander II in 1866, had belonged to a conspiratorial ring called 'Hell', a small, isolated group which most revolutionaries would have disowned. But when Vera Zasulich assassinated General Trepov on 24 January 1878, there was widespread approval of her action, and a wave of terrorist outrages followed. Two years before, something like a central organization of Populist groups had arisen, called 'Land and Liberty' (*Zemlya i Volya*); now, a powerful terrorist group arose within it, 'The People's Will' (*Narodnaya Volya*). After various attempts, this organization succeeded in blowing up Alexander II on 1 March 1881. In the police repression that followed, *Narodnaya Volya* was crushed, but its tradition of unreasoning violence continued. A young student, son of a school inspector, who won the gold medal of the University of St Petersburg for a treatise on the anatomy of worms worked on a bomb to destroy Alexander III, was caught, and at 3.30 in the morning of 8 May 1887 was taken out of his cell and hanged. His brother, Vladimir Ulyanov, decided to find

[19] Pokrovsky, *Brief History of Russia* (2 vols., 1933) I, p. 211.

out more about the strange fanaticism which had made 'Sasha' throw his life away, and started by reading Chernyshevsky's *What is to be Done?* This was the beginning of Vladimir Ulyanov's conversion to revolution; to serve this dangerous cause he took the pseudonym of Lenin.

CHAPTER XVIII

THE NEAR-EASTERN QUESTION AND THE BALKANS

I

T
he essence of the Near-Eastern Question was the long slow decline of the Ottoman Empire. If Turkish decadence had merely involved difficulties about keeping order, the European powers might have seen to them, in the spirit of the English naval officer who wrote home, after putting through some negotiations with Mehemet Ali in 1840, 'I do not know whether I have done right or not in settling the Eastern Question'.[1] Unfortunately, however, preventing chaos in the Ottoman dominions was only a small part of the task of statesmen. As the grip of the Sultans faltered, rich spoils became available for the taking. Who would annex Constantinople and the Straits, and to whom would the domination or leadership of the Christian subjects of the Turks in the Balkans fall? The 'Sick Man' was dying amidst covetous neighbours, incurably suspicious of each others' designs.

But there was more to the problem than this. The balance of force among those neighbours was steadily changing. If the decline of the Ottoman Empire was the essence of the Near-Eastern Question, its intractability and complexity derived from the rise of the Russian. And the increase of Russian power was not viewed dispassionately by western Europe, for this was the rise of something incalculable, autocratic and Asiatic, a menace to civilization. These fears, which Tocqueville was to express soberly, were voiced by the marquis de Custine, a visitor to Russia in the late 'thirties, in terms of brilliant hysteria. 'In the heart of the Russian people an immense, boundless ambition is fermenting, the sort of ambition which could only be conceived in the soul of the oppressed, and could feed only on the unhappiness of an entire nation. Bent on conquest, greedy because of the privations it has endured, this nation lives in a state of degrading subjection by which it does penance in advance for its hope of exercising tyranny over others. . . . Russia sees in Europe a prey which will fall to her sooner or later as a result of our dissensions.'[2] Fears about Russia and its vast potential force accumulated, and

[1] H. M. V. Temperley, *England and the Near East: the Crimea* (1936), p. 133.
[2] Le Marquis de Custine, *La Russie en 1839* (2nd ed. 1843) IV, pp. 354–5.

these fears formed a barrier to logical thought about the fate of south-east Europe. As the shadow of the Tsars lengthened over the Golden Horn, it became impossible to consider the decline of Turkish domination in cool isolation. Through Russian ambitions the Straits and the Balkans were linked with the balance of forces in central Europe and the Mediterranean and with European rivalries in Asia.

This wider background explains much that would otherwise be mysterious about the Crimean War. It was a war reluctantly fought. The fighting was grim enough, but neither side wished to annihilate the other. Great Britain gave Russian ships ample time to sail home after hostilities began. Russia continued to pay interest on English bonds, borrowing the money in London, and the French government invited Russia to participate in the Paris Exhibition. So far as its ostensible causes are concerned, the war could almost be described as 'unnecessary'. It is true that the Tsar had gone to unwarranted extremes in his demands on the Turks (over the Sultan's favour to French religious orders in the Holy Places), but he never intended to deny that the principles of the 'Concert of Europe' ought to apply to the Near East, as Great Britain and France insisted they should.[3] Napoleon III wanted glory and an English alliance, though these prospects alone would not have moved him to fight. The British government was confused and divided, and ill-prepared to resist the gigantic ground-swell of unreasoning passion against Russia which swept the barriers of common sense away. Yet, beneath it all, as wars go, this was a logical conflict. When Great Britain and France opened hostilities in 1854 they were conscious of the total problem presented by Russia, dominant in central Europe since 1849. They were not only preventing the Ottoman Empire from becoming a client state of Nicholas I; they were also striking a blow to bring to an end five years of Russian hegemony. 'The Crimean War', writes A. J. P. Taylor, 'was fought for the sake of Europe rather than for the Eastern Question; it was fought against Russia, not in favour of Turkey.'[4]

To define the Near-Eastern Question more precisely then, we may say that it arose from the determination, from time to time, of one or more of the great powers to prevent Russia gaining a new accession of strength from the spoils of the decaying Turkish Empire. And who

[3] F. H. Hinsley, *Power and the Pursuit of Peace* (1963), pp. 227 ff.
[4] A. J. P. Taylor, *The Struggle for Mastery in Europe, 1848–1918* (1954), p. 61. For a history of the discussion on the causes of the war, see Brisson D. Gooch, 'A Century of Historiography on the Origins of the Crimean War', *American Hist. Rev.* LXII (1) (1956), p. 47.

would lead? This depended upon which of the two prizes was immediately at stake. If the Straits were in danger, Great Britain and France would be most concerned; if the mastery of the Balkans was involved, Austria must take their place.

II

Having defeated Russia in the Crimean War, Great Britain and France came to the peace conference of Paris in 1856 with two complementary objectives. One was to ensure that Russia did not regain the power she had wielded in international affairs from 1848 to 1854; the other was to bolster up the Turks to prolong the life of their empire. But how were these aims to be achieved? The neutralization of the Black Sea was a remarkable attempt to impose partial disarmament on a great empire, yet it was impossible to entertain illusions about its long-term efficacy. In March 1856, Palmerston wrote, 'The Treaty will leave Russia a most formidable Power able in a few years when she shall by wiser internal Policy have developed her immense National Resources to place in danger the great Interests of Europe. But the future must look after itself'.[5] Another clause of the peace treaty laid down that no foreign state would be allowed to intervene between the Sultan of Turkey and his subjects; on the other hand, the Sultan was required to put into effect western reforms, in particular, he was to grant equal treatment to Christians and Moslems. Was there any chance of his happening, or was this another case where the future had to look after itself?

Twenty years ago, when Mahmud II was still on the throne, an answer might have been hazarded in the affirmative. Under this strong ruler, 'the Peter the Great of the Ottoman Empire', the turbulent Janizaries had overturned their soup kettles (a sign of rebellion) once too often and had been disbanded. Feudal fiefs had been abolished. Officials had been put into frock coats and set to preside over the first Ottoman census and the introduction of a postal system. Though these reforms had been imposed from above, they were not without support from below. Since their armies had been turned back from the gates of Vienna at the end of the seventeenth century, the Turks had envied the growing technical and military superiority of the west. The French Revolution, in so far as it implied a logical and secularist reorganization of society, had drawn attention: it was 'the first great movement of ideas in Christendom that had any real effect in the world of Islam'.[6] The innovating passions

[5] Taylor, op. cit., p. 88 n.
[6] B. Lewis, *The Emergence of Modern Turkey* (1961), p. 40.

which were ultimately to transform the structure of Turkish life were already beginning to stir. A strong ruler might have used the terms of the Treaty of Paris as an excuse for continuing the policies of Mahmud II.

By now, however, the Sultan was the violent and profligate Abdul Azziz. In 1876, he was deposed; Murad V lasted a few months before he too was removed. Then Abdul Hamid ascended the throne, to begin a reign noteworthy chiefly for its crazy programmes of railway construction and palace building and its creation of a useless fleet which lay permanently at anchor under the command of a retired British rear-admiral. The *Tanzimat*—the reforms sponsored by the European powers—had little immediate effect, though the establishment of an Imperial *lycée* at Galatasaray in 1868 helped to create an educated class of westernized officials in a later generation.

In any event, the attempt to push the Ottoman Government into reform was risky. One of the reasons for its survival through so many vicissitudes had been its inefficiency, which gave so many warring interests the illusion that they could work out their own ends within the structure of the régime. Corruption had played the rôle of delegation of power in encouraging private initiative, and a miserable stability prevailed in the provinces, where successive generations of officials had pragmatically established the limits at which extortion defeats its own object. To persuade the Sultans to rule efficiently would have been the ultimate disaster for their subjects. A British naval officer discussing the westernizing reforms of Mahmud II, observed, 'In scanning over the riches of civilization, spread out before him for acceptance, he contemptuously rejects those calculated to benefit his people, and chooses the modern scientific governing machine, result of ages of experiments, with its patent screws for extracting blood and treasure, conscription and taxation. . . .'[7]

The western powers who wished to reform the Turkish government to enable it to survive, and to liberalize it to make it civilized, were trying to square the circle. The incompatibility of these aims became dramatically obvious when nationalism and the desire for independence stirred up the Christian peoples of south-east Europe who were subject to Ottoman overlordship. Prudence might continue to prescribe support for a Sultan who held the Straits against Russia: principle suggested that he could not much longer be allowed to remain as the scourge of the Balkans.

---

[7] Adolphus Slade, *Record of Travels in Turkey, Greece etc.* (1831), in B. Lewis, op. cit., p. 73.

III

The word 'Balkan', which has come to be associated with political fragmentation and fanatical rivalries was, in origin, a Turkish word meaning 'mountain'. The political characteristics followed from the geographical ones. Invasions of the Balkans swept in easily from the north, following the valleys of the Danube and its tributaries. Thus the Slavs had come down and displaced and absorbed the original Illyrians (except the Albanians) and the original Thracians (except the Roumanians), though stopping short of the jagged southernmost part of the peninsula, where a race of herdsmen, fishermen and pirates had never quite forgotten its descent from the Greeks of classical antiquity. Yet, while invaders entered easily, the rugged mountain terrain kept each group of settlers apart from the others. This combination of 'inner fragmentation and outer accessibility' meant that conquests had not brought about unity, but had piled up diversities, which would be sharply revealed when national feelings began to awake in the Balkan area.[8]

As we have seen earlier, it is difficult to give a full explanation of this rise of national sentiment; at the moment, all we need is a statement of the fact and some significant illustration of its working. In the Balkans, all sorts of local loyalties and feuds were tying together, within the context of common traditional memories, into wider patriotisms and more permanent hatreds, with detestation of the Turks and a feeling that the Ottoman Empire was cracking acting as a general inspiration. The slow development of literacy and of more effective administration brought wider loyalties, cultural and political, and also created teaching and administrative posts to interlock men's ambitions with their enthusiasms. The increasing use, within national limits, of a common language, reasonably standardized among the different dialects, was probably the most significant factor, indicative of change, if not causing it. Its importance can be seen when Albania is contrasted with the other Balkan states. In Albania, the rise of independent national feeling was delayed, virtually until the twentieth century. Islam had been substantially victorious here, and the Christian minority was divided, these religious divisions being reflected in linguistic backwardness. The Moslem majority spoke Turkish, the Orthodox in the south spoke Greek; only among the northern Catholics was Albanian spoken, and this

[8] For the whole of this section see especially, R. L. Wolff, *The Balkans in our Time* (1956), esp. pp. 55 ff. See also L. S. Stavrianos, *The Balkans, 1815–1914* (1963).

did not become a written language until the British and Foreign Bible Society came in to spell it into Latin characters in the 1860s. This was late indeed; the Serbian and Roumanian linguistic revivals took place towards the end of the eighteenth century, and the Bulgarian early in the nineteenth.

As elsewhere, nationalism in the Balkans was nourished by a revival of an interest in history, and this seems to have shown itself in simple popular ways as well as in scholarly production known to the intellectuals. History reminded its devotees of accumulated traditions of particularism and hatred. Roumanians looked back to Trajan and imperial Rome, and preserved their 'Latin' tradition by borrowing their culture from France. The Greeks claimed to be heirs of both Athens and Byzantium. They remembered the Emperor Basil II, 'the Bulgarian killer'; they remembered too how the Phanariot Greeks of the lighthouse quarter of Constantinople, had infiltrated the administration of the Ottoman Empire and had ruled the Balkans for their Turkish masters. Bulgarian memories were identical, but opposite. They idolized the inveterate foe of Basil II, their own Samuel, who had grasped at empire and had fallen down dead at the sight of his 15,000 blinded warriors; they detested the Phanariot Greeks as collaborators with their oppressors. The Serbs, for their part, looked back to Stephen Dushan, who in the fourteenth century, had ruled over territories corresponding to those held three hundred years before by the Bulgarians in their hour of greatness. These were divisive memories. Only to fight the Turks could the newly awakened Balkan peoples be united: if the Ottoman power collapsed, they would fight each other.

IV

The revolt of the Greeks in 1820, resulting in their achievement of full independence twelve years later, set the pattern for the aspirations of the Balkan peoples. National consciousness was most highly developed among the Serbs; it had been kept alive by the example of the tiny principality of Montenegro, which had never given in to the Turks, and it was revived towards the end of the eighteenth century by a linguistic and literary movement of which Rayich's history of the Serbian people was the most significant production. In 1804 and 1815, the Serbs had risen in revolt, and the Turks finally granted them autonomy under their own prince in 1830. Michel Obrenovitch, the son of the hero of the revolt of 1815, who ruled from 1860–68, was successful in reducing the Turkish control to the occupation of a few fortresses, and he started reforms which made Serbia talked of in western Europe as 'the Piedmont of the Balkans'.

These achievements impressed the wild mountaineers of Bosnia-Herzegovina, who spoke the Serbian tongue, though unlike the Serbs, many of them adhered to Catholicism or Islam rather than to Orthodoxy. An English traveller in this romantic wilderness was impressed by the shapely legs of the women and the independent spirit of the men—so much so that he paid the country the highest compliment he knew by saying that it was fit for parliamentary institutions.[9] One may doubt if the conventions of debate at Westminster would have been accepted, but the spirit of freedom was there; in 1831, 1845, 1850 and 1875, the mountain peoples rose against the Turks and demanded union with Serbia and Montenegro. Here was the powder magazine of the Balkans. It was commonly said among diplomats (who tended to be cynical about enthusiasms for liberty) that 'anyone who wished to raise the Eastern Question had only to spend 300,000 francs in Herzegovina'.

Like the Serbs and the inhabitants of Bosnia-Herzegovina, the Bulgarians were Slavs, though they felt no particular attraction towards the Serbian complex. Indeed, among this dour, illiterate peasantry, national consciousness was slow in arising. It was only in the 1830s that the national idea came into the schools, and a class of revolutionary intellectuals was created, not at home, but in the Russian universities, among students sponsored by Russian Pan-Slav organizations. Here was a land where national self-awareness was derived in the first place from hatreds, of the Turks, and also of the Greeks, who for long had monopolized posts in Church and administration in Bulgarian territory. In 1870, the Turks craftily allowed the creation of a new Exarchate within the Orthodox Church, to take over ecclesiastical control in areas where two-thirds of the population was Bulgarian—a manoeuvre which increased the enmities among Greeks, Serbs and Bulgarians and which added the Macedonian problem to the Balkan imbroglio.

The Roumanian national movement was a blend of impulses. Like the Serbian, it began in a cultural and linguistic revival at the end of the eighteenth century; like the Bulgarian, hatred of the Phanariot Greeks was a factor, as were the activities of a foreign-trained intelligentsia, though in this case Paris, not Odessa, had been the place of their studies. Roumanians too were drawn together by suspicion of the surrounding Slavs—of the Serbs, the Bulgarians and of Russia. There was one great difficulty in the way of the formation of a national state and this, as sometimes happens, was the great incentive to action: Roumanians lived under Ottoman overlordship

[9] Arthur Evans, *Through Bosnia and Herzegovina on foot* ... [in] *1875* (1877), p. CI.

in two separate provinces, Moldavia and Wallachia, and the agreement of the Turks and of the powers was needed before they could be united. By 1856, Turkish sovereignty had become merely nominal; in 1858, the provinces came together in a sort of federation; then, by the device of both electing the same prince, Alexander Cuza, a real union was achieved. Alexander ruled in a corrupt but enlightened fashion, modelling himself on Napoleon III, until 1866, when a palace revolution put Charles of Hohenzollern on the throne. The Turks then conceded full independence conditional upon the payment of tribute monies.

Here then is the Balkan scene: Greece, Roumania and Albania, and the Slav groups, Bulgaria and Serbia, with Montenegro and Bosnia-Herzegovina moving into the Serbian orbit. This mountainous peninsula was a wild and picturesque world, a strange complex of feuds and assassinations, of kings with their bags permanently packed against the next revolution,[10] of tribesmen and sheep stealers, of great poets writing in strange tongues, of Bulgarian peasants in their ox-carts and Roumanian officers in corsets and dyed moustaches. Unfortunately, however, the rise of national feeling in the Balkans involved the destiny of two great empires, and this scene of Ruritanian farce brought on the tragedy which ended Europe's predominance in the world.

V

The two great empires, were, of course, Russia and Austria-Hungary. The Habsburgs were shepherds presiding over a fold in which many different flocks were penned—and shorn; their task became difficult if invitations and bleatings resounded on every hand from the free moorlands outside. There were one and a half million Roumanians in the Transylvanian area of Hungary, resentful of Magyar domination and looking hopefully towards Bucharest. More dangerous still were the Slavs within the empire. There were the 'Prechani' Serbs who had come into depopulated Hungary at the end of the seventeenth century when the Turks were driven out, Orthodox in religion, obeying their own Patriarch at Karlowitz; there were the Croats, speaking a dialect of the Serbian language, though using a different

---

[10] In 1884, Milan of Serbia wrote to Alexander of Bulgaria, 'We must support one another mutually for the peoples of this peninsula are apt to change their rulers like their shirts. If ever you have to pack your bags, you can always pass through Belgrade and I will give you part of my luggage, and *vice-versa*. We will say the same to Carol of Roumania' (Egon Caesar Conti Corte, *Alexander von Battenberg*, Engl. trans. 1954, p. 144).

alphabet; there were nearly two million Slovaks, who from the mid-century were changing to an independent Slovak literary language, under the influence of the Protestant scholar L'udovit Stur.[11] Among these minority peoples the nostalgia of exile gave a romantic force to nationalist dreams: indeed, it is significant that both the Serbian and Roumanian literary and linguistic revivals of the eighteenth century had begun inside the Hungarian boundaries, among the Prechani Serbs and the Transylvanians respectively.

In 1861, it still seemed as if the Habsburgs were going to take the enormous risk of transforming their dominions into a unitary state, but after being defeated by Prussia, the government at Vienna adopted a form of internal organization which was easier to maintain—in the short run—by the so-called 'Compromise' of 1867. Francis Joseph would be Emperor in Austria and King in Hungary, and each state would have its own parliament and administration, though with joint departments for foreign affairs, war and finance. 'It may truly be described', writes Gordon A. Craig, 'as a "deal" between the German minority in the western half of the empire and the Magyar minority in the eastern at the expense of all of the other peoples.'[12] Since Habsburg policy was sacrificing the interests of the Serbs, it was inevitable, as national feelings rose, that many Croats and Serbs and some Slovenes should regard themselves as 'South Slavs' or 'Yugo Slavs' (the terms were in use in the 1840s) and should seek their destiny with Serbia outside the Dual Monarchy.

Short of imaginative experiments with federalism or 'trialism' (instead of dualism)—experiments which one suspects could never have been worked by the old Habsburg machine—there was no way out of the dilemma. To avoid disintegration, Austria-Hungary must fight to prevent the Southern Slavs from uniting. This was why Metternich's old dictum, that the Ottoman Empire was necessary to Austria's security, remained a rule of policy at Vienna. In January 1875, on the eve of the great Balkan crisis, Andrássy said, 'Turkey possesses a utility almost providential for Austria-Hungary. For Turkey maintains the *status quo* of the small Balkan States and impedes their aspirations. If it were not for Turkey, all these aspirations would fall down on our heads . . . if Bosnia-Herzegovina should go to Serbia or Montenegro, or if a new State should be formed there which we cannot prevent, then *we* should be ruined and should ourselves assume the role of the "Sick Man".'[13]

[11] J. Lettrich, *History of Modern Slovakia* (1955), p. 27.
[12] G. A. Craig, *Europe since 1815* (1961), p. 232.
[13] G. H. Rupp, *A Wavering Friendship: Russia and Austria, 1876–78* (1941), p. 39 (in Taylor, op. cit., p. 231).

VI

It was natural that the Southern Slavs should gradually come to look to Russia as their protector, and it was natural that Russia should use this fact as a demonstration of prestige and a lever of influence. What was less obviously inherent in the situation was the rise of a Pan-Slav ideology,[14] based on the untenable assumption that the Slavs of Western Europe would profit by being incorporated into the empire of the Tsars. Ukranians and Poles made haste to point out how little they had gained by being the first: a Polish newspaper welcomed delegates passing through to the Moscow Slav Congress of 1867 with the words, 'Travel this red sea, this sea of Polish blood... observe our Hell: it leads to your Paradise.' Voices from the revolutionary left made the same point. Bakunin told the Slav Congress in Prague in 1848, 'You ask for life and there (in Russia) is only the silence of death.' 'We have never heard,' said Herzen, 'that the Christians in Turkey were more oppressed than our peasants.' For their part, the autocrats Alexander I (after the Congress of Vienna) and Nicholas I rejected Pan-Slavism too; they stood for legitimacy and the rights of sovereigns over their subjects, and if the Sultan of Turkey and the Emperor of Austria were not legitimate sovereigns, who was?

The doctrine of Pan-Slavism arose originally outside Russia. Two Lutheran Slovaks were its prophets; Jan Kollár the poet, who at Jena University had seen and envied the German national uprising against Napoleon, and the scholar Pavel Josef Safařík, whose imagination had been captured by Herder's vision of a coming age of leadership by unspoilt Slav peoples. The actual word 'Pan-Slavism' was first used in 1826 by a Slovak philologist, Jan Merkel, in a Latin volume published at Budapest. There is an artificial ring about this enthusiasm among the Slavs of the dispersion. 'All the other peoples have said their last word; now Slavs, it is our turn to speak,' was one of Kollár's famous phrases. But what did he mean? One doubts if Slovak poets and scholars really wished to exchange Hungarian for Russian domination. The Balkan Slavs would be glad to have Russian aid to achieve freedom, and that was all. As Bismarck was to say, 'the people you set free have no gratitude, only pretensions'.

It is not difficult, however, to explain why Pan-Slavism was taken seriously in Russia. Slavophil messianism could easily be corrupted into a crude doctrine of world domination—though to do them justice, most Slavophils refused to debase their ideals. Pogodin,

---

[14] See H. Kohn, *Pan-Slavism: its History and Ideology* (1953).

professor of history in Moscow University, one of the few Pan-Slav writers tolerated by Nicholas I, produced a text book for the heir to the throne—'Emperor Nicholas,' he said, 'quietly sitting in Tsarskoye Selo, is nearer the realization of Charles V and Napoleon's dream of a universal empire than the two ever were at the zenith of their power.'[15] Then came the Crimean War against the western powers which the Pan-Slavs envied and despised. Nicholas had saved the Habsburg dynasty in 1849, yet he was left to fight alone. Fifteen years later, his wife, the Tsarina, said on her death-bed that she forgave 'everyone except the Emperor of Austria'.[16] With the portrait of Francis Joseph turned to the wall, relations between Russia and the Balkan Slavs could become closer. From 1858, the Moscow Slavic Benevolent Committee paid for foreign students to attend Russian universities; at the Moscow Slav Congress of 1867, there were sixty-three delegates from the Austro-Hungarian Empire. A shrill press campaign and books by writers like General Fadieev and Danilevskii whipped up enthusiasm for the exiled Slavs—and for imperialist expansion. Danilevskii's *Russia and Europe* (1871) even included Greece, Roumania, Hungary and Constantinople within the legitimate bounds of Slavdom.

Such was the state of Russian public opinion (a minority phenomenon, it is true, but a potent force upon a government that had to think continually of its prestige), when in July 1875, Herzegovina rose against the Turks. The Bulgarians followed suit in May 1876, and the Turks let loose their irregular troops in an orgy of massacre. Serbia and Montenegro declared war. The Balkans were aflame and the Slavs called on the Russian Tsar to march to their aid.

VII

In November 1876, driven forward by Pan-Slav pressure, Alexander II declared war on Turkey. Fighting was bitter. Karl Marx prophesied from London that the Russian army would go down and the dynasty with it—'this time the revolution will begin in the East'. But after the fall of the fortress of Plevna in December 1877, the Turkish resistance was broken. The Russian forces came within sight of Constantinople. Now was the great crisis of the Near-Eastern Question. The Turks were no longer able to defend the Straits or to hold the Balkans. How would the other powers react to this total Russia victory?

---

[15] M. B. Petrovich, *The Emergence of Russian Pan-Slavism, 1856–1870* (1956), p. 27.

[16] C de Grunwald, *La vie de Nicolas III* (1946), p. 289.

In Great Britain, public opinion erupted in indignation against Turkish barbarities. Gladstone expressed the feeling: he did not create it. Spurgeon, Manning, Dale and the bishops, Bryce, Freeman, Lecky and J. R. Green, William Morris, Burne Jones, Ruskin, Trollope—the outcry was universal. Yet there remained a deep, underlying suspicion of Russia. The opening of the Suez Canal in 1869, the completing of the Bombay, Aden, Suez cable a year later, and the proclamation of the Queen as Empress of India had turned men's minds eastwards. Travellers' accounts, like Burnaby's *Ride to Khiva* (1876), told of the Russian drive into Central Asia and of Cossack officers waiting for 'the day' on the banks of the Oxus. Cynically indifferent to the fate of the Balkan Christians, Disraeli decided that the Straits were vital to the security of India, a logic which owed part of its force to the use of large-scale maps, though there was a real connexion, which he underlined by sending Indian troops to Malta. The British battle fleet moved to the Dardanelles. Its presence helped to deter the Russian army from marching into Constantinople, though the fact that the general in command had eleven different sets of orders—from the Foreign Minister forward in Roumania, from the Foreign Office back in St Petersburg, and from the Tsar in his field chancery—may have contributed to slowing his reactions.[17]

The British navy was of some slight use off Prinkipo, but as a French statesman once said, it was not equipped with wheels, and it was incapable of preventing a Russian settlement of the Balkans. The fact was, however, that Russia had been able to get a free hand to smash the Turks only by buying Austrian neutrality, and Austria's price had been, inevitably, security against the Southern Slavs. So guarantees had been given that no large Slav state would be created (this was ambiguous, but as promises also given to England suggested, it meant a single, large, independent Bulgaria would not be set up), and that Austria-Hungary would be allowed to annex Bosnia-Herzegovina. This Austro-Russian understanding was the key to the whole situation. Failure to guess at its existence early in the game deprives Disraeli of all claim to be a master of foreign policy,[18] since he brought England to 'the dizzy brink of war' without hope of an effective ally. The Russians only had to make peace with the Turks in conformity with their promises to Vienna, and Disraeli was helpless.

What happened, however, was that Ignatyev, a reckless Pan-Slav

[17] B. H. Sumner, *Russia and the Balkans, 1870–80* (1937), pp. 305–6.
[18] R. W. Seton-Watson, *Disraeli, Gladstone and the Eastern Question* (1935), pp. 329 ff.

expansionist, was put in charge of the negotiation of the Treaty of San Stefano, and he imposed terms on Turkey which ignored all these obligations. A single large Bulgarian state, extra territory for Serbia and Montenegro, Russia to collect Bessarabia from her luckless ally Roumania—and no reference at all to Bosnia-Herzegovina for Austria. This was an act of childish cupidity. It proved Disraeli right, after the event, with English public opinion, and it brought England and Austria together to demand a European congress. So the whole Near-Eastern Question was back in the melting pot.

The Congress of Berlin (1878) was a picturesque affair.[19] Old Gorchakov, an octogenarian aristocrat, made his last appearance on the international scene for Russia, bowling around in his wheel chair, throwing his paper knife down petulantly, and spreading out his confidential maps so that everyone could see them. Disraeli used his deafness and ignorance of French to be suitably intransigent and left the manoeuvering to Salisbury—who had made a secret compromise with Russia beforehand. Andrássy, wearing a different and more brilliant uniform every day, represented Austria, with a team of able diplomats under him. The defeated Turks muddled along with one representative who drank himself to death in the course of the negotiations, and another (a German converted to Islam) who was hardly *persona grata* with the managers of the conference. Bismarck presided blandly, though worried in case he lost Russia, eating shrimps with one hand and cherries with the other and complaining of indigestion.

By the Treaty of Berlin, everyone got something—except the Turks, of course. Russia was given Bessarabia and Batum, Austria-Hungary was to be allowed to occupy Bosnia-Herzegovina, Britain got Cyprus (Disraeli's *pot de vin*, said Bismarck sardonically), Bulgaria was divided into three, and one part, Macedonia, was put back under Turkish misrule.

Disraeli claimed he had won 'peace with honour', but there is some point in the reply that it was 'the peace that passeth all understanding and the honour that is common among thieves'. What had happened was that by their folly, the Russians had thrown away the fruits of their victories. Austria had been strengthened in the Balkans; Roumania was enraged by the loss of Bessarabia; Greece and Serbia were jealous of Bulgaria and complained against its giant patron. Within seven years, Russia had fallen out with the Bulgarians as well, and the failure of her Balkan schemes was complete.

[19] See W. N. Medlicott, *The Congress of Berlin and After, 1878–80* (1938).

VIII

The disintegration of the Ottoman Empire continued. In the thirty-six years between the Congress of Berlin and the first World War, the Bulgarians united into a single state and declared their independence, Austria annexed Bosnia-Herzegovina, Crete declared its union with Greece, Italy occupied Tripolitania, and in 1912, the Balkan states leagued together and virtually expelled the Turks from the peninsula. Abdul Hamid lived hidden behind the high walls of his palace Yildiz on the heights overlooking the Bosphorus; his sole object was survival. An international commission took over the huge state debt: by 1911 this *Administration of the Ottoman Public Debt* employed more clerks than the Ministry of Finance itself.[20]

Yet here were signs that the decline of the Turks was coming to an end. Earlier reforms had produced a generation of educated officials, schools on western lines developed and in 1900 a university was founded. The first through train from Paris steamed into the Sirkeji station in Constantinople in 1888. For the convenience of its arbitrary and irresponsible rule, the Sultan's government ran out telegraph lines to the most fantastic corners—'it is no longer necessary', said Sir Charles Elliot in 1900 'to leave a province to the discretion of a Governor, and trust that he will come home to be beheaded when that operation seems desirable.'[21] A new literary movement based on French models, the introduction of western style journalism by Englishmen, the impact of western Turcological research upon Turkish scholars, the rediscovery of texts in the Koran supporting government by discussion—all these strangely blended tendencies combined to create a new atmosphere—revolutionary and nationalist. From 1864, a 'Young Turk'[22] movement produced a journal in London, *Hurriet* (Liberty). Twenty years later, the movement was extending its influence in the army, and in 1908 a military coup, ostensibly for constitutionalism, put power in the hands of an oligarchy of young Turk leaders. This military conspiracy aimed to save the empire from disintegration: in that sense it was retrograde, for an 'Ottoman nation' was no longer possible now that the Christian nations of the Balkans were inflamed. What was happening, however, was that a new 'Turkish' nationality, independent of Islamic sentiments, was making its appearance; the foundations were being laid

[20] See D. C. Blaisdell, *European Financial Control in the Ottoman Empire: a Study of the Administration of the Ottoman Public Debt* (1929).
[21] Lewis, op. cit., p. 183.
[22] See E. E. Ramsaur, Jnr., *The Young Turks* (1957).

for the idea of a territorial nation state which was the form in which Turkey (as distinct from the Ottoman Empire) was to be regenerated after the First World War.

In Europe generally, nationalism implied expansion, in the sense that scattered fragments yearned to be united into a larger whole. Nationalism in Turkey implied concentration. The Turks had to get rid of their sense of imperial mission and of Islamic leadership before they could consolidate as a national state. There were two prizes at stake in the Near-Eastern Question: the Straits and the Balkans. In the end the question was settled by the Turks becoming strong enough to hold the Straits because they had been obliged to relinquish the Balkans, and because the nationalism, which had been characteristic of the Balkan peoples in the nineteenth century, finally became an inspiration to the defeated Turks themselves.

IX

After swindling Russia at the Congress of Berlin, the least the powers could do was to leave the affairs of the two Bulgarias (East Roumelia and Bulgaria proper) to be settled at St Petersburg. As a result, Russia learnt by hard experience the two laws of Balkan politics: firstly, that these little nations loved their independence above everything—'no gratitude, only pretensions'—and secondly, that favours done to one of them made the others jealous.

The Tsar gave Bulgaria a constitutional régime, a strange present from an autocrat, but he could not afford to risk comparisons with Serbia and Roumania. Besides, after five centuries of direct Ottoman rule, there was no landed aristocracy or native bureaucracy to support a despotic national prince. Alexander II also put his wife's brother, Alexander of Battenberg, on the Bulgarian throne, it being understood in Europe that he was to obey orders. 'If he wants to be something more than Russian *Statthalter*', wrote Bismarck, 'he has misjudged his position.' Everything went wrong. The new ruler blamed Russia for the misfortune of a liberal constitution, then involved his Russian advisers, more especially Generals Sobolev and Kaulbars, in his intrigues to subvert it. The Russians kept all posts of captain and above in the army for themselves, they nagged to have their occupation costs paid, and they tried to impose on Bulgaria a pattern of railway development which suited Russia's strategic interests but was of little economic value. Feelings ran high and finally the union of the two Bulgarias took place in 1885 in defiance of the wishes of the Russian government. All this so soon after the Treaty of San Stefano, when Ignatyev had defied the world to defend Bulgarian unity!

The unification of Bulgaria was the signal for an armed onslaught by the Serbs, ostensibly disputing for a say in Macedonia, but in fact, expressing their pent-up rage over what they regarded as their betrayal by Russia, which had been 'a mother to Bulgaria and a step-mother to Serbia'.[23] Austrian troops had occupied Bosnia, and Kallay had built up an even-handed administration there—just, but devoting its efforts to outwitting the Serbs by fostering a spirit of 'Bosnian' nationality. Prince Milan of Serbia, in despair, threw in his lot with Austria. From a commercial point of view, this was very sensible, for 75 per cent of Serbian exports went to the lands of the Dual Monarchy. It was Austria which intervened to rescue Milan from his disastrous attack on Bulgaria, and which performed services for him like persuading the Patriarch of Karlowitz to consecrate his personal candidate for Metropolitan of the Serbian Church, a prelate whose vices are catalogued by a modern historian as 'wine, women and song, and in addition, cards'.[24]

Thus Serbia moved into the Austrian orbit. So too did Roumania, which was to be expected since Russia had so dishonestly filched Bessarabia. Roumania was now on the eve of a great and corrupting economic expension—railways, canals, oil—and beneath the glitter of imported technology the peasants continued to be ground under by absentee landlords and Jewish moneylenders. In 1907 they rose—the last great serf revolt of European history, one might call it—and were shot down in thousands. In Bulgaria and Serbia the peasants owned the land: in Roumania, they were a depressed majority. Roumania's nationalism therefore had less popular driving force behind it, and King Carol was able to overlook the grievances of the Transylvanians in Hungary, and to spite the Russians by secretly allying with Austria-Hungary and Germany.

By the end of the nineteenth century, Russia had salvaged some of the wreckage of her shattered Balkan policies. Rather painfully and uneasily, she became reconciled to Serbia and Bulgaria. By now, however, under the impact of disillusionments in Europe, her states-men were turning to the Far East, where Japan was the enemy. But in the East, further disasters were waiting, and once again, Russia was to swing back to the Balkans, finding there her only avenue of glory. This would inevitably mean a clash with Austria-Hungary, an

[23] Count Chedomille Myatovich, *The Memoirs of a Balkan Diplomatist* (1907), p. 36.

[24] C. Jelavich, *Tsarist Russia and Balkan Nationalism: Russian influence in the internal affairs of Bulgaria and Serbia, 1879–86* (1958), p. 181.

empire facing disintegration under the pull of the powerful magnetic forces of national feeling radiating from Serbia. The Southern Slav movement, said Bismarck, was an internal problem for Austria-Hungary, but for Russia a question of foreign policy. This would suggest that it was tension between Russian aggrandizement and Austrian survival. But the Romanovs, like the Habsburgs, ruled at the dangerous apex of a pyramid in unstable equilibrium, and social discontents threatened the emperor in St Petersburg just as nationalist ones threatened the emperor in Vienna. Neither could afford to lose prestige.

In the end, their clash destroyed the old Europe, and left the way open for new and more potent ideologies and imperialisms. The last of the old-fashioned Pan-Slav congresses, held in Sofia in 1910, was a failure: the next meeting of the Slavs was at Belgrade in 1946, under the auspices of world Communism, and in praise of Comrade Stalin.

CHAPTER XIX

CHURCH, STATE AND SOCIETY

I

The nineteenth century saw the decay of the venerable assumption that Church and State are necessarily and properly in alliance. By 1815, there were two startling breaches in the tradition; during the Revolution, from 1795 to 1801, the French Republic had abandoned all ecclesiastical connexions and obligations, and in America, the First Amendment to the Constitution (1791) had laid down that 'Congress shall make no law respecting an establishment of religion, or prohibiting the free exercise thereof'. The Napoleonic Concordat, which the Bourbons found they could not alter, might be said to have disproved the wisdom of the policy of the French revolutionaries, but as observers in Europe, guided by Tocqueville, came to look at trans-Atlantic democracy as foreshadowing the pattern of the future, the American example grew significant.

Once the Church-State alliance was dispensed with anywhere, the whole concept was thrown on the defensive. Except in England and Russia, the turmoils of the Revolution had broken many of the old usages associated with it. States, even monarchical ones, now justified themselves by Rousseauistic and Benthamite principles, by the ideas of the General Will or of Utility, both providing excellent grounds for claims to omnicompetence; and churches, progressively purged from the nepotism and excessive riches of the eighteenth century, became correspondingly more strict in their dealings with civil society; with the spread of literacy and the rise of the Press (and of ecclesiastical journalists as violent as secular ones), the affairs of both states and churches became subject to the mass pressures of their adherents. Everything conspired to make disputes on matters of principle more likely, and less susceptible to settlement by those aristocratic compromises which theologians and the vulgar regard as hole-and-corner bargains.

While the maintenance of the alliance between secular and spiritual was becoming more difficult, the assumptions that underlay its theoretical justification were crumbling. Hooker's ideal, that the same men, looked at from different points of view, constitute both Church and Commonwealth, was clearly unrealistic. What did seem reasonable, however, was the principle laid down—in the Age of Reason a century ago—by Bishop Warburton, in his *Alliance of Church and State* (1736): that is, the established religion should remain established only so long as the greater number of citizens followed it. The same idea, perhaps, was implicit in Napoleon's Concordat, where it is stated that Catholicism is the 'religion of the great majority of French citizens'. But the nineteenth century brought with it a crisis of belief, and the question could well be asked, how many Englishmen really believed the doctrines of the Anglican Church, and how many Frenchmen were sincere Catholics?

II

There was a crisis of belief, but the nineteenth century was not an irreligious or sceptical age: it was an age of tremendous religious vitality. Up to now, the centre of missionary activity had been Rome, and the heroes of the mission field had been members of religious congregations; in the nineteenth century, the outburst of Protestant missionary endeavour swept the whole globe. This, in the phrase of the historian of the expansion of Christianity, was 'the great century'.[1] It is a fallacy to consider religion in terms of military tactics, and to assume that fighting enthusiasm on distant frontiers depends on the security of the home base: probably the very opposite is true.

The intellectual attack on the foundations of Christian belief was serious, but it did not run through the moods of materialism, nihilism and indifference characteristic of the generations that followed the first World War. Many nineteenth-century thinkers abandoned Christianity because they wanted a more ethically satisfying belief; they were in revolt against 'the apparent immorality and inhumanity of the Christian scheme of salvation (divine favouritism, the substitutionary atonement, everlasting torment in hell, etc.) and also its barefaced next-worldliness which seemed to deny both the possibility and the duty of improving the conditions of life in this world'.[2] This was true of Francis Newman, J. A. Froude and George Eliot in England, and of Musset, Vigny, Lamartine and Leconte de Lisle in

[1] K. S. Latourette, *A History of the Expansion of Christianity: IV The Great Century, 1800–1914* (1947). Cf. 'At the dawn of the nineteenth century Protestantism was a regional faith. By the mid-century it was world-wide and was displaying more vigour than any other branch of Christianity' (Latourette, *Christianity in a Revolutionary Age: the Nineteenth Century in Europe*, I (1958), p. ix).
[2] A. R. Vidler, *The Church in an Age of Revolution* (Pelican, 1961), p. 113; D. G. Charlton, *Secular Religions in France, 1815–70* (1963), pp. 19–22.

France. In so far as Christian churches have got rid of crude perversions of doctrine, they owe a debt to these ethical rebels who saw the implications of the gospels more clearly than some of the theologians.

Behind the ethical problem, and affecting a wider circle of doubters was, of course, the more strictly intellectual one, which came to turn around the two poles of historical criticism and 'science'. The 'warfare between science and religion', essentially a nineteenth-century concept, is one which has been waged generally by the second-rate intellects on either side. With the outbursts of some churchmen against Darwinism in the 1860s, the idea that such a war existed gained popular currency—at the very moment that more enlightened Christians were welcoming Darwin's aid to end the old Genesis myth of special creation ('a theory of occasional intervention implies as its correlative a theory of ordinary absence'[3]), and other thinkers of a religious kind were finding their escape from the alien universe which science so far seemed to have imposed upon them. 'Here, in the very heart of "science" itself, was obviously the new faith . . . so greatly yearned after. There is a purpose in the world

> "Some call it Evolution,
> Others call it God." '[4]

The impact of historical criticism on the Biblical documents was more serious than skirmishes with scientists, for even at the midcentury, after Ranke and the German universities had established the ideal—more than half illusory, as we now realize—of 'scientific' history, the majority of educated Christians remained simple fundamentalists. Ewald's history of the Israelites, which treated the patriarchs as legendary figures (1843), and Strauss' *Leben Jesu* (1835), which made the New Testament story a myth, the product of communal imagination, showed the way in which the currents of explanation were setting. In 1845, Renan abandoned his faith: 'A single error proves the Church is not infallible; a single weak link proves a book is not revelation.'[5] But his *Vie de Jésus* (1863), which caused such a scandal by its rejection of the supernatural, also

[3] Aubrey Moore (in Vidler, op. cit.).
[4] J. H. Randall Jnr., 'The Changing Impact of Darwin on Philosophy', *Journ. Hist. Ideas* XXII (1961), repr. in S. A. Burrell, *The Rôle of Religion in Modern European History* (1964), p. 124. Cf. 'The religious managed to find in Darwin a variety of consolations and virtues not dreamed of even in natural theology' (Gertrude Himmelfarb, *Darwin and the Darwinian Revolution* (1959), p. 325).
[5] E. Renan, *Souvenirs d'enfance et de jeunesse* (*Oeuvres*, ed. H. Psichari 1947–61) II, p. 866.

romantically recaptured the rich humanity of the teacher who was 'resurrected by love'. This insight was fortified by the Liberal Protestant picture of the true humanity of Jesus built up by German historical scholarship; then it was shattered by the rediscovery of the apocalyptic element in the gospels;[6] then all these themes and others were taken up by theologians who had inherited the great German tradition of religious philosophy deriving from Schleiermacher (1763–1834) and Ritschl (1822–89), and who fully accepted the methods of historical criticism. The result was the founding of a new apologetics. By the coming of the first World War, Christian thinkers, at least within the more progressive of the Protestant churches, had annexed historical criticism and were using it as an aid to biblical interpretation. The defence of Christian belief would never again be a simple matter, but the faith would have an intellectual depth which had been concealed by the old assumptions of fundamentalism. Intelligent Christianity today is, indeed, in many respects very like the religion which the nineteenth-century rebels were seeking, though it is true that many of them gave up hope of finding it in the future, and looked back nostalgically at the last gleam of the bright sea of faith which had ebbed away from the 'vast edges drear and naked shingles' of their world. 'We live', said Renan sadly, 'by the shadow of a shade, by the perfume of an empty vase'.

III

The crisis of belief of the nineteenth century, in so far as one can generalize about so complex an affair, was not like our modern 'drift from religion': it was, rather, a passionate dissatisfaction and disappointment with dogma and institutional churches in the interests of the religious ideal itself. Even so, it necessarily weakened the churches in their conflicts with secular authorities. What weakened them still more, however, was the absence from their congregations of the mass of the industrial workers, and this had little to do with questions of belief or intellectual difficulties. The vast increase of population and its movement into the industrial towns cut off whole generations from the traditional parochial cadres of religious existence. Unthinking absence from the observances of religion became a feature of the new popular mores, just as unthinking presence had been a feature of the old. Here was a phenomenon, terrifyingly new, which gave especial point and acerbity to disputes between Church

---

[6] See A. Schweitzer, *The Quest of the Historical Jesus* (Eng. trans. 1910). Generally, see Stephen Neill, *The Interpretation of the New Testament, 1861–1961* (1964).

and State about education. The advent of technology and democracy made mass elementary education an absolute necessity, and the question arose, could the State allow the churches to work through the schools to recapture the industrial population which now lived and died outside the traditions of Christianity? But an even more urgent question was that of the condition, physical and moral, of the working classes in the industrial slums, for this involved not only the tactical question of regaining their allegiance, but also the application of the most fundamental of Christian duties, that of charity.

In England, both within the established Church and outside it, the social gospel was preached, by a minority, it is true, but in a fashion that made it possible for the politically organized labour of the future to be impregnated with Christian influences. On the continent, however, the hope of an effective Christian social movement rising contemporaneously and in step with the development of industry perished in the shootings of the June Days of 1848.

Up till then, France had been the laboratory for the production of Christian social ideas, as well as of socialist ones, but these ideas were diverse, lacking an anchorage to strong, united bodies of Christian opinion. There was La Mennais' *De l'esclavage moderne* (1839), 'one of the great documents in the history of the class struggle';[7] there was the Abbé Gerbet's denunciation of 'the new feudalism, the feudalism of riches' (1830); there was the philosophy of the great Liberal Catholic, Ozanam, founder of the charitable Society of Saint Vincent de Paul; and the radical, democratic socialism of Buchez, journalist and historian of the French Revolution. But none of these writers could command a party in the Church. La Mennais had been disavowed by the Pope in 1832, Gerbet finished up a conservative bishop denouncing socialism as 'barbarism', most Liberal Catholics did not follow Ozanam in social matters, and Buchez, an ex-carbonaro who announced his religious faith without attending masses, was regarded as a dangerous firebrand. Only half a dozen bishops (including Mgr Affre of Paris, who was killed in the June Days) and one theologian, the Abbé Maret, showed any interest in social designs which went beyond ordinary almsgiving. The only effective foothold which the social movement obtained within the laity was among the aristocratic Legitimists, who wished to see a paternalistic state taking measures that would show

[7] G. D. H. Cole, *A History of Socialist Thought* (1953) I, pp. 199–200. For Gerbet, see J.-B. Duroselle, *Les Débuts du Catholicisme social en France, 1822–70* (1951), p. 59. For the well-meaning but vague pronouncements of bishops see P. Droulers, 'L'Episcopat devant la question ouvrière sous la Monarchie de Juillet', *Revue historique*, CCXXIX (1963), pp. 335–62.

up the bankruptcy of the revolutionary tradition; this did not mean, of course, that their motives were solely political—the comte de Villeneuve-Bargemont, one of the first politicians to demand state intervention on behalf of the working classes, had been a prefect in an industrial area, and retained terrible memories of the misery he had seen.

The events of 1848 intensified the divisions of the social catholics, isolating Ozanam, Maret and Buchez, who accepted the Republic and asked for social measures, from the main 'party of order'. The June Days reinforced the conservative majority and completely destroyed the influence of the left-wing minority. When the social movement revived in French Catholicism, it would be devoted to 'counter revolution' and 'paternalism'—a movement to exhort owners to treat their employees fairly, not to encourage workers to seek their rights under the banner of Christianity. Yet France, with its plethora of tiny workshops and an unusually large proportion of women in the industrial labour force, was a country in many ways ideally suited for 'moral', as distinct from 'revolutionary' socialism. Catholicism might have provided this, instead of allowing its inspirations to be appropriated by others: 'I have collected the oddest of quotations from the so-called men of progress', wrote Flaubert to Michelet in 1869, 'beginning with Saint-Simon and ending with Proudhon. They *all* start from the religious revelation.'[8]

IV

We have seen how La Mennais was one of the first of the visionaries of the nineteenth century who drew attention to the socialism implicit in the gospels. Though his discovery came home to him most vividly after he had left the Church, its bitterness was there beforehand; he spoke of the workers as the serfs of the new industrialism, and of the priest as 'the friend, the living Providence of the unfortunate'. It was then, in the 1820s that this prophetic thinker was striving to give Catholicism the leadership of the forces of the future. He had become a liberal in reaction against the régime of Napoleon, whose Université was moulding the new generation, 'as if he would rob the human race even of hope', and he had become an ultramontane because he saw the Pope standing alone against the Corsican tyrant. The old principle, that religion was essential to society, was defended by La Mennais in 1817, in an *Essay on Indifference* which gave him the reputation of 'the chaplain of the Romantic move-

[8] Flaubert to Michelet, 2 Feb. 1869 (*Correspondance*, III (1903), p. 387).

ment';[9] but to him, religion was socially necessary, not because it hallowed the majesty of secular coercion and gilded the legal code, but because it provided the only possible basis for the ethical conduct of individuals. Thus, La Mennais drew a new conclusion from old premises: Church and State, he held, ought to be separate, and within the social order there ought to be entire freedom of association, of worship, of education and of publication. If the Church was allowed to fulfil its mission to educate children and inspire society, the forces of freedom would be harnessed to beneficent and peaceful ends. 'Men tremble before Liberalism', he said, 'make it Catholic and society will be reborn.'

La Mennais' concept of the separation of Church and State (in formal principle, though hardly in ideal results) was first achieved in Belgium, where Catholics and Liberals united in the national revolution to achieve independence, and in 1831 put their alliance into the only constitutional terms that both sides could accept. Though the Belgian polity was condemned at Rome, one of its immediate effects was to hasten the breakdown of the old eighteenth-century 'Gallican' tradition by which secular rulers had supervised communications between their national clergy and the Pope. The '*Placet*', missing from the Belgian constitution, was abolished in Prussia and Bavaria in 1841, in the Netherlands in 1847, in Austria in 1850 and in Württemberg seven years later, though Spain retained its '*pase regio*' until 1883, and Tsarist Russia did not relax its regulations so long as the Romanov dynasty endured.[10]

According to the Liberal Catholics, this freedom of the Church to receive messages and directions from its head was a proof of the spiritual value of the principle of the separation of Church and State. Montalembert, the French Liberal Catholic leader, speaking in 1863 (appropriately, at Malines, in Belgium), said that the Church gladly accepted the principles of 1789, and would flourish in the atmosphere of 'modern liberty, democratic liberty'.

The Pope repudiated him. Among the propositions condemned by the Syllabus of 1864 (accompanying the encyclical *Quanta Cura*) was one denying the necessity of having Catholicism as the established state religion, and another objecting to the refusal of religious toleration to immigrants who entered Catholic countries. This disastrous document which, among other things, seemed to proclaim a fundamentalist view of the Bible and the right of the Church to be intolerant, has been variously explained by Roman Catholic writers

[9] A. R. Vidler, *Prophecy and Papacy: a Study of Lamennais, the Church and the Revolution* (1954), p. 72.
[10] R. A. Graham, S. J., *Vatican Diplomacy* (1959), pp. 277–99.

at the time of its publication and subsequently:[11] it represents the 'thesis' but not the practical 'hypothesis'; it consists of fragments of earlier pronouncements that can only be understood in context, and by expert theologians; it is a document that has no real authority, being the work, not of the Pope, but as Newman said, of 'an anonymous author'. Since the Syllabus of Errors is manifestly not *ex cathedra*, there is no reason why it should be a subject of controversy today. It was a foolish outburst that can no longer be taken seriously, though it had the effect, in its time, of rejoicing the hearts of anticlericals and of destroying all hopes of a triumph for Liberal Catholicism. Of the causes La Mennais worked to promote within The Roman Church—socialism, liberalism and ultramontanism, —only the latter was to prevail, and the effects on the spiritual and intellectual history of Europe have been incalculable.

V

To understand how Pius IX could have issued a document like the Syllabus, one must remember that this was a collection of his earlier fulminations, and that most of them referred to the activities of the men who had created a united Italy, filching the temporal possessions of the Papacy in the process. The formula on which Cavour professed to be acting in religious matters (and which Rome naturally rejected) was that of 'A free Church in a free State', and this had been derived from the book of a French Protestant, Vinet, *Essai sur le manifestation des convictions religieuses et sur la séparation de l'Eglise et de l'État* (1842). 'A free Church in a free State' was to be one of the great phrases of the century: but what did it mean? Giolitti later said that it implied that Church and State were like parallel straight lines, always in relationship but never meeting. Though this is the sort of thing acute politicians say to keep the peace, the metaphor hardly bears examination. In the last resort, the State's duty as the arbiter between different groups in society forces it into religious affairs. It was because the law upheld private patronage that the Free Church of Scotland broke away in 1843, causing a schism in Scottish Presbyterianism; the State exercised its rights over property when Gladstone disestablished the Church of Ireland; in 1845, the English Parliament, by the Dissenters' Chapels Act, awarded possession to Unitarians of bequests originally given for the promotion of Trinitarian doctrine. Clearly, the powers of the State to arbitrate or define must be extensive. Even so, there were still stronger arguments, in continental Europe, against taking the words 'a free Church'

[11] See espec. E. E. Y. Hales, *Pio Nono* (1954), pp. 256 ff.

too literally. 'Experience shows that the Church is more than an opinion, it is an authority', Charles de Rémusat told Cavour in November 1860. 'To abolish Concordats . . . is not to give liberty to an opinion, it is to unleash in society an irresponsible authority (*une autorité sans contrôle*)'.[12] Cavour himself seems to have half agreed with Rémusat, for in the following March, his proposals to the Pope (who was being invited to hand over Rome) included a grant of property to maintain the clergy and a governmental veto on the nomination of bishops. The State was to be generous, but the Church was not to be free.

In 1870, the definition of papal infallibility and the Italian seizure of Rome brought Church-State relationships in Italy to their crisis. Politicians and theorists now had to produce a working definition of Cavour's formula.[13] To a few, it meant a genuine separation of spiritual and secular; to many, like Minghetti, it meant that Catholicism would be the official religion, protected against hostile propaganda, but that politics and the legal code would be strictly secular; to others, the 'jurisdictionalists', the Church had to be kept in tutelage—the State should appoint bishops, supervise communications with the Pope, inspect education and police the meetings of councils. The arguments for this one-sided, erastian definition of 'freedom' were that the liberty of the Church was merely composed of 'the individual liberties of believers in the field of religious doctrine' or, conversely, that the Church was a social institution, not a private one. But these were merely syllogisms of political theory, and the real reasons were practical ones—the danger of clerical 'despotism' and the desire to ensure that the younger clergy were brought up in touch with modern ideas.

The Italian 'Law of Guarantees' of May 1871 was, in fact, much more liberal than the jurisdictionalists desired, for the State was to have no control over the regulations, councils or episcopal appointments of the Church. This law, however, was not recognized by the Pope. Italian Catholics were forbidden to take part in their country's politics, though from 1904 Pius X did little to enforce the rule. Luzzatti might talk in romantic terms of 'the modern State' addressing itself 'to all those Gods who die only to be born again' and guaranteeing to their worshippers 'the freedom to indulge in their dreams',[14] but in fact, the Italian experience of the free Church in

[12] Charles de Rémusat, 'Entretiens avec Cavour', p.p. C.-H. Pouthas, *Rev. d'hist. mod. et contemp*. VII (1960), p. 187.
[13] For what follows, A. C. Jemolo, *Church and State in Italy, 1850–1950*. (Engl. trans., 1960).
[14] Jemolo, op. cit., p. 150.

the free State was a chapter of disillusionments. In the communes, battles over burials, schools and taxation took the gloss off popular memories of the Risorgimento, and the abstention of Catholics from democratic politics helped to create the state of mind which eventually made possible the Concordat between the Church and Fascism.

VI

The balance of power in Church-State relationships was changed in the nineteenth century by the vast expansion of elementary education under secular control. Before 1870 Holland and the new countries across the seas, the United States and Australia, set an example of state-controlled, religiously neutral schools, and in the following decade the educational systems of Switzerland and Germany were secularized; in Belgium, the State took over the supervision of communal schools in 1879 (an action which a Catholic government reversed later); in England and France, where the established churches controlled many educational institutions, State schools were created—to compete with those of the Church, or simply to take care of the growing population which religious schools could not accommodate.

What sort of religious teaching—if any—should be given within a secular educational system? The problem was hotly debated. From Denmark (where elementary education had long been under State control) came the principle, 'Children must become persons before they become Christians'.[15] But how was this logical formula to be translated into psychological terms? In the French parliamentary debates of 1880 over Jules Ferry's Education Laws, Bishop Freppel said that to teach a child for six hours a day for seven years without telling him there was a God was tantamount to saying that God did not exist, and that to separate the instruction of the home from that of the school was as destructive to the mind as the judgment of Solomon would have been to the body.[16] The weakness of Mgr Freppel's argument, however, was that agreement on the content of religious teaching for all children could no longer be obtained. Jules Ferry himself was a 'religious' propagandist, but of a religion of Humanity, 'an endless procession striding on towards the light'; he objected strongly to the belief in original sin and insisted that morality was entirely separate from those 'high metaphysical

[15] The phrase of Holberg (died 1754) cit. V. Murray, 'Education', *N.C.M.H.* XI, p. 187.
[16] See R. P. Lecanuet, *Les Premières années du pontificat de Léon XIII, 1878–94* (1910, new ed. 1931), p. 122.

questions . . . about which theologians and philosophers have disputed for six thousand years'.[17] Significantly, Ferry's two chief advisers, Buisson and Pécaut, were Protestants: the divisions of Christians, as well as the spread of agnosticism, were weakening the case for religious education. This was evident also in England, where the Dissenters hotly opposed the Forster Education Bill of 1870, which increased the money given to voluntary schools (chiefly Anglican).

The obvious resource for churchmen who were dissatisfied with secular education was to maintain schools of their own; this is what Catholics did in Belgium and both Catholics and Protestants did in Holland. If the State was willing to provide subsidies, as in England, so much the better. In France, however, as so often happened, problems common to Europe became heated and fused into their most extreme and incandescent form; thus it was, under the Third Republic, that the question became, not 'should the State subsidize denominational education?', but 'ought the State to permit such education at all?'. The Falloux Law of 1850 had reduced governmental supervision of religious schools to questions of hygiene only, and had allowed members of religious orders to teach without any qualifying examinations. Twenty years later, the French religious orders were teaching one and a half millions of the four million children receiving primary education, and 70,000 out of 186,000 secondary pupils were in religious establishments. According to Ferry and the republicans, this vast educational structure under ecclesiastical control was undermining the national life; in 1870, its inefficiency had left the armies at the mercy of troops trained by Protestant Prussian schoolmasters, and its continued existence served to perpetuate divisions which withered the roots of patriotism. Putting this latter argument in political, rather than national terms, one could say that the attack on clerical education was part of the tactics of survival of the Third Republic, for in France it was easy to see how the education given to the new generation might decisively change the nature of the political régime of the future.

VII

'In a moment, by my vote I'll take my place in the ranks of this republican majority which backs the spirit of the French Revolution, expressed in the Declaration of the Rights of Man, against the counter revolution of the Roman Church, whose formula is in the

[17] M. Reclus, *Jules Ferry* (1947), pp. 117, 202.

Syllabus (Very good! and applause from the Left, murmurs on the Right)'.

This was Clemenceau, speaking in the Senate in October 1902, on the usual theme of the republican anticlericals: that the Roman Catholic Church was the handmaid of political reaction. There was better evidence for the accusation than the irascible ambiguities of the Syllabus, for at the time of Louis Napoleon's *coup d'état* the Pope and most of the French clergy had made no secret of their satisfaction with the man of order. 'These few months of dictatorship', writes Maurain, 'fixed for long the position of Catholics in French political life.'[18] After a preliminary hesitation, Montalembert warned his co-religionists against seeking the precarious advantages which an ephemeral despotism could confer upon its acolytes. 'When I am weakest', he depicted the Church as saying, 'I ask you for liberty because it is your principle; when I am strongest I take it away from you, because that is my principle.' This was the lesson which the republicans learned under the Second Empire. It was no accident that the word 'anticlerical' was first used in 1852, and that Gambetta's famous phrase *Le cléricalisme, violà l'ennemi'*, is an echo of a sardonic remark by Peyrat under the Empire—'You have to judge men, not by the principles they profess in opposition, but by those they practice when they are in power: *c'est là l'ennemi.'*[19]

After the fall of Napoleon III, churchmen did their best to ensure a royalist restoration, and it was not their fault that the comte de Chambord made his coronation impossible by insisting on the white flag of the Bourbons. 'Henry IV said Paris was worth a mass,' the Pope complained, 'Henry V finds France not worth a serviette'. Though the republicans won the elections of 1876, they were kept out of power, since Marshal MacMahon manoeuvred until the beginning of 1879 with ministries that bore small relationship to the parliamentary majority. The Catholic press applauded his policy, and there were rumours of ecclesiastical pressure for a military coup. The republicans therefore regarded the Church as an accomplice of the régime of 'moral order' as it had been of the Second Empire, as a reactionary institution that must be broken if the Republic was to be secure.

After Italy seized Rome in September 1870, and Pius IX excommunicated all concerned, the French Church rallied unanimously to the defence of the papal temporal power. This outcry deprived the

---

[18] J. Maurain, *La politique ecclésiastique du second Empire de 1852 à 1869* 1930) pp. 81–2, 944–5.

[19] Maurian, op. cit., pp. 637–9; cf. R. P. Lecanuet, *L'Englise de France sous la Troisième République*, I (1906), p. 22 n.

nation, still smarting from its defeat by Germany, of all hope of restoring its prestige by pursuing an active foreign policy. 'France must bear the responsibility for this reaction', said an Italian states-man after the Italo-German rapprochement of 1873, 'and her isola-tion will be her condemnation. Clericalism generates solitude.'[20] A renewed outcry in the Catholic press of France against Italian anticlerical legislation in 1877, led to further discussions between Italy and Germany; it was then that About launched his gibe against 'maniacs drunk with holy water', and Gambetta said that clericalism was the enemy. Both at home and abroad the Church seemed to be a menace to the security of the Republic. Clearly, there were good reasons—reasons of self-defence—for the anticlerical policies of the Third Republic. These policies also had their ideological justification; various inspirations, atheistical, deistical, Protestant or Positivist, creeds of science, progress or even of pessimism, were proclaimed in defiance of Catholicism, and prophets like Quinet, Michelet, Renan and Taine were invoked. Never had religious apologetics been so helpless. Quinet's appeal to the clergy to reply, as patriots, to the German biblical critics went unanswered. Lenormant's book, de-fending the teaching but denying the historicity of Genesis, was put on the Index (1887), and the encyclical *Providentissimus* declared that divine inspiration of the Scriptures 'excludes all error'.[21] Meanwhile, there was an outburst of popular devotion of the more sensational kind (the cult of the Sacred Heart and mass pilgrimages by railway), and the majority of the clergy swung towards Rome in defiance of the episcopate. Republican intellectuals wrote of Catholi-cism as a colourful popular superstition with foreign headquarters and a reactionary line in politics, and in place of its outworn creeds they proclaimed their doctrines of humanistic optimism or despair. 'Two things are certain', said Renan, ironically, from a position between the conflicting forces, 'Catholicism cannot perish: Catholi-cism cannot remain what it is. It is true also that we cannot imagine in what way it could change.'

These are logical explanations for the anticlericalism of the Third Republic. Its virulence, however, suggests that supplementary explanations are needed at a sub-logical, possibly at a sub-conscious level. Many of the peasants and lesser bourgeoisie (though generally not their wives) were brought up within the tradition of the feud be-

[20] Luzzatti to Minghetti, 3 Sept. 1873, in S. W. Halperin, *Italy and the Vatican at War* (1939), p. 326.

[21] A. Houtin, *La Question biblique chez les catholiques de France au XIXe siècle* (1902), pp. 106–10, 130. For the encyclical *Providentissimus*, Lecanuet, IV (1930), pp. 356–60.

tween the Revolution and the Church, and inherited the philistine Voltaireanism which would have shocked Voltaire and which Flaubert satirized in the person of M. Homais in *Madame Bovary*. Tensions between different geographical areas and social classes were involved; industrial workers and the poorer middle class hated the churchgoing rich; metropolitan dwellers distrusted the inhabitants of the mountains of Franche Comté, the Massif Central and the Pyrenees; the educated ridiculed the devotion of the peasants of the Vendée and Brittany as fear of hell and of the priest.

The politicians were generally above these prejudices—and had more sophisticated ones of their own. 'To govern France you need violent words and moderate actions', Gambetta said; on another occasion he remarked, 'There is no social question.' Taken together, these statements are illuminating. The basis of the Gambettist tradition on which the Third Republic was run was anticlericalism, for this was the cheapest way to find the 'violent words' required, this was the only revolutionary drum that could be beaten without endangering property; it was the only device which the republicans could use to evoke memories of 1789 and attract votes on the left without having to put their hands into their pockets to pay for social reforms. In the end, that was why clericalism had to be the enemy.

VIII

The republicans did not intend to break the Concordat; the separation of Church and State, Gambetta said, would mean 'the end of the world'. But they did mean to reduce the power of Catholicism in the political life of the next generation by undermining its educational system and disbanding the religious orders upon which its schools depended. When the Senate turned down Article VII of Ferry's Education Law of 1880 (directed particularly against the Jesuits), the government, under pressure from the Deputies, expelled this order, together with some other non-authorized congregations, by making use of existing legislation. Further anticlerical measures followed: teachers in religious schools were subjected to State examinations, hospitals were laïcized, prayers on official occasions were abolished, and divorce was legalized.

Catholics grew exasperated, though in fact the moderate republicans were becoming half-hearted about the guerilla warfare they were waging, as politicians, not as enthusiasts—as prisoners, indeed, of left-wing parliamentary groups whose alliance they distrusted. 'The radicals gave the orders', said Albert de Mun in savage reproach, 'the opportunists carried them out. Religious war has been the cement of your union, . . . it is on you like the poisoned shirt of Nessus, you cannot escape from it.' When Clemenceau made definite proposals for the separation of Church and State in the election campaign of 1885, the more cautious republicans panicked. In these elections, the conservative vote came to over three and a half millions, less than one million short of the republican total. Religion, it appeared, could still evoke mass support, far beyond the social circles of magistrates, naval officers, upper civil servants and the immortals of the Academy where it was known to be highly influential. Friendship with Rome, which not long ago would have been a liability in foreign policy, would now be an asset, for Pope Leo XIII was achieving some eminence in European affairs, and was being courted assiduously by the German Emperor. The only available ally for France was Russia, and for the Tsar to feel at home with a republic, it would have to appear respectable. In colonial affairs, French influence often depended upon missionaries and on the protectorate over missions in China and the Near East which was in the gift of the Papacy. 'Anticlericalism', Gambetta had said, 'is not for export.' With the rise of Boulangism, there were more urgent reasons still for conciliating Catholics, whose chief newspaper, the *Univers*, vociferously declared its unconcern at the crumbling of the Republic. By the end of 1888, Jules Ferry himself was proclaiming the end of anticlericalism. 'It is too late,' said Albert de Mun, 'there are men from whom we could accept advances, from you never.'

Albert de Mun was mistaken. There was a party in the French Church which welcomed overtures. A group of realistic bishops wanted to come to terms with the Republic. The two most arresting figures in this party of compromise were Guilbert of Bordeaux, 'the red archbishop', a man of humble peasant origins who believed that the Church could work with any form of government, more especially with democracy, and Lavigerie, archbishop of Algiers, who had been an imperialist and a legitimist, but was now ready to accept the Republic, partly because he feared socialist revolution, partly because he wanted the maximum assistance for his missionary work among the Arabs. In 1880, Lavigerie had made a crafty deal with the moderate republicans, which would have saved many congregations from expulsion, but a royalist paper had betrayed his manoeuvre. Czacki, the smooth and worldly papal nuncio at Paris, wrote to Lavigerie in March 1881 shrewdly analysing this treason—'there is a coterie which wishes to play all the cards in the Church's hand after they have lost all the other possible tricks'.[22] The royalists *wanted*

[22] Czacki to Lavigerie, in J. Tournier, *Le Cardinal Lavigerie et son action politique* (1913), p. 117.

Catholicism to be persecuted, to enhance the odious reputation of the Republic.

Leo XIII, who had ascended the papal throne in 1878, was a politic prelate who had studied Church-State relationships as nuncio in the liberal atmosphere of Belgium. The events of 1880 seem to have convinced him that he must manoeuvre to end the alliance between churchmen and legitimists in France. Lavigerie was given a cardinal's hat; the encyclical *Immortale Dei* (1885) declared that there was no one exclusive form of just government. In 1890, Lavigerie travelled between Rome and Paris, and warned the moderate republican leaders to expect 'the explicit adhesion of the . . . episcopate to the republican form'. Then, in November, he proposed the famous toast of Algiers, declaring that when the will of a people is clearly affirmed, one must adhere, without reservations, to the form of government established; 'in so saying', he added, 'I am certain of not being disowned by any authorized voice'.[23]

Thus the *Ralliement* was launched. Its immediate effect was to divide and disorganize the Catholics of France. The republicans did not disarm. 'They say they have rallied, I say they have resigned themselves,' said a politician in 1893, 'they have learned something but they will be the first to recognize that they have forgotten nothing. . . . I'm all for them submitting to the Republic: what I ask them is, will they defend it?' The 'new spirit' which for a year or two crept into politics vanished in the chaos and bitterness of the Dreyfus Case. In a few more years, the alliance between Church and State would be ended for ever. But Leo XIII had made the great gesture which severed the cause of religion from the cause of conservatism; he had established the principle, which he reaffirmed in an encyclical of February 1892, of the political neutrality of the Church. In short-term results, the *Ralliement* was but an incident in the Church-State battle; yet its long-term importance is great. The Roman Church would not, in fact, pursue the policies of the Syllabus: in practice, if not entirely in theory, it would recognize the lay State, and accept the political verdict of the voting majority in a democratic government.

IX

Flaubert had spoken of the connexion between socialism and the religious revelation. To Leo XIII, who laid down the formulae which reconciled Catholicism with democracy, also belongs the honour of producing the great encyclical which lifted the Church beyond the obvious obligations of almsgiving on to the plane of broad social

[23] C. S. Phillips, *The Church in France, 1848–1907* (1936), p. 229.

action.[24] His inspiration came from Germany, where Bishop Ketteler campaigned for the formation of Christian trade unions and for State intervention to improve working-class conditions, and from France, where Albert de Mun, an aristocratic army officer, and Léon Harmel, a pious industrialist, founded the *Oeuvre des Cercles*. The Paris Commune of 1871 had as significant an effect upon the development of Christian social ideas as it had on socialist ones, for it was a revelation both of the grim tensions of class hatred and of the hostility of the workers to Christianity. Albert de Mun found his 'social vocation' in the ranks of the Versailles army, when he saw how the communards died.

In the encyclical *Rerum Novarum* (1891), Leo XIII proclaimed that the State had a positive duty to intervene in economic life to improve the conditions of the people, more especially of 'the unhappy multitude, which has no security through resources of its own'. In retrospect, it is all too easy to see how this pronouncement, and the whole social Catholic movement which inspired it, were remote from the needs and passions of the industrial workers. The theory behind the *Oeuvre des Cercles*, that of the corporative unity of workers and owners (embarrassingly called 'la classe dirigeante'), was an alternative to class warfare, but hardly a realistic one; *Rerum Novarum*, which limited State action to the remedy of evils or the removal of dangers, seemed to preclude the emotive, utopian hope of a complete remodelling of society—indeed, Leo XIII believed that 'the diversity of classes and conditions' was to be accepted 'with religious resignation and as a necessary fact'. But the Pope was obliged to speak in the colourless terms in which official pronouncements, more especially infallible ones, must be couched, and within those terms, without any concession to the ideas of violence or class warfare, he succeeded in imposing on the Church the abandonment of the old bourgeois Christianity of economic and social laissez-faire relieved by private charity.

What he did not say was said by those within the Social Catholic movement who did not have to restrain themselves to cautious officialese—by men like Ketteler, de Mun and Léon Bloy. This Christian protest against inequality (uniting with similar protests from Protestant social movements, especially in England) surged on, a moral fermentation which, together with the threat or inspiration of socialism proper, has exerted a continuous and successful pressure for social reform in western Europe. Here is the conclusion of Bloy's *La Femme Pauvre* (1897), when Clothilde, listening to a sermon to a

---

[24] For this section see especially H. Rollet, *L'Action sociale des catholiques en France, 1871–1901* (1948).

respectable congregation, hears with the ear of the imagination what the preacher really would have wished to say.[25]

'It is true that you have no idols in your houses; . . . You don't blaspheme—the name of the Lord is, as a matter of fact, so far from your thoughts that it would not occur to you to take it in vain. On Sundays you pay God the overwhelming honour of your presence. It is the respectable thing to do and sets a good example to the servants. You do not murder with sword or poison—that would be disagreeable and might scare away your customers! You don't indulge in vice in too open and scandalous a fashion, you don't tell mountainous lies that are sure to be detected, you don't hold up people on the highways where you might easily get hurt, nor rob banks, which are so well guarded. . . . [But the poor meanwhile] cry, *What time is it, Father? for we watch without knowing the hour or the day . . . When will this suffering be finished? What is the time by the clock of thine unending Passion? What time is it?*

It is time to pay the rent or to get out and die in the gutter with the dogs, replies the landlord.'

[25] Léon Bloy, *La Femme Pauvre* (1897), pp. 370–3.

CHAPTER XX

SOCIALISM

I

Napoleon III and thirty-nine generals surrendered at Sedan on 1 September 1870: Paris fought on until the end of the following January. In these four months of siege, a time of starvation, fear and elation, the people of the French capital recaptured the fighting republican spirit of 1793, the great days of *la patrie en danger*. When the inevitable capitulation came, the Parisians were enraged—and proud. Every able-bodied man had served in the National Guard, and citizens who had no war stories of shooting at Prussians had others, about menus featuring dogs and rats, or luxury joints from the Zoo, and near misses in the bombardment.

Rural France passed judgment on Parisian heroism in the elections of 8 February 1871. Four hundred monarchists and nearly two hundred conservative republicans were elected; of radical republicans, men of the left who had inspired the desperate, futile continuance of resistance to the invader, only forty were returned. 'The vote was largely a plebiscite for peace.'[1] To Parisians, the Bordeaux Assembly was a flock of reactionary and rural *capitulards*, elected by accident at a time of panic and disintegration. The men of Bordeaux reciprocated by deciding to transfer their Assembly, not to the capital, but to Versailles. They also ended the wartime moratorium on rents and promissory notes, as if, a few weeks after manning the forts against the Prussian army, the small tradesmen and shopkeepers of Paris could be expected to pay their debts as usual. This conduct of the Assembly was doubly foolish, for in the capital there were 200,000 men who still retained the muskets they had used against the Germans—'What other revolution had such arms?'[2] On 17-18 March 1871, the Versailles government sent a force of troops on a stealthy nocturnal expedition to seize some of the artillery belonging to the National Guard. The attempt failed, amidst scenes of riot and exasperation. The Versailles executive thereupon ordered all constituted authorities to withdraw and leave the Parisians alone in their insubordination. Paris had, quite literally, stuck to its guns, but it did not revolt until the government of France left it with no alternative but to set up an illegal

---

[1] A. Cobban, *A History of Modern France* (1961) II, p. 205.
[2] F. Jellinek, *The Paris Commune of 1871* (1937), p. 195.

authority to rule itself. In origin, the terrible seventy-two days of the Commune of 1871 were not a revolution, but a 'show down', called for by the established order.

The responsibility for the attempt to seize the guns and for the abandonment of the capital falls on Thiers, the chief of the Executive. Seventy years of age, dapper, brisk and parsimonious, a prolific historian and a practised politician, a patriot yet a realist, he was well fitted to wind up the business side of the defeat and to persuade peasant and bourgeois France to get back to business as usual. But, except in a sinister fashion, he was the last man to handle Paris in a revolutionary mood. His foible was omniscience (once on a Channel steamer he told the captain how the steering worked—'When is he going to climb the mast?' someone muttered[3]), and having written many volumes on wars and revolutions, he was satisfied that he knew all the answers. Elected by no less than twenty-six departments, Thiers had the additional confidence that the country had called on him; he had a personal mandate, almost, for dictatorship. And this was the man who feared and hated all socialist ideas, that 'swarm of insects from the decomposition of all governments'. When the Empire had cracked and the resistance to the invader had been led by left-wing extremists, in Lyon and Marseille and in Paris stirrings of social revolution had been heard amid the din of patriotic proclamations. 'Il faut en finir'—this seems to have been the instinctive reaction of the conservatives of the Assembly and of the possessing classes generally, in face of social danger. Thiers, with his facile knowledge of history and of military tactics, decided to do what Mirabeau had tried to get Louis XVI to do, what he himself had tried to get Louis Philippe to do, and what Windischgrätz had done with Vienna: evacuate the capital and return at the head of an army.

This fatal decision put France at war with Paris, and made Versailles the headquarters of an emigration, 'the Koblentz of the bourgeoisie'. Fear of socialism prompted otherwise responsible statesmen to incur the risks of civil war and this war, when it came, hardened and concentrated a socialist ideology in a way that would have been impossible before. 'Socialism was the result, and not the cause of the revolution of the 18th of March,' wrote Lepelletier, a soldier of the Commune, 'it profited from a communal régime which it had not created.'[4]

[3] F. H. Brabant, *The Beginnings of the Third Republic* (1940), pp. 23–4.
[4] Lepelletier, *Histoire du Commune* (4 vols., 1911–13) III, p. 30, cit. E. S. Mason, *The Paris Commune* (1930), p. 243.

II

What was this 'swarm' of socialist ideas which Thiers feared and which came to the surface in Paris during the civil war between the Versailles government and the Commune? Once the fighting was joined, as in the June Days of '48, the possessing classes convinced themselves that they had to do with a great slave or barbarian insurrection. On 28 March, Edmund de Goncourt noted in his journal, 'What is happening is, quite simply, the conquest of France by the working-class population, and the enslavement under its despotism of the noble, bourgeois and peasant'.[5] From the opposite point of view, Marx and Engels understood the Commune in much the same terms: it was the first example in history of the dictatorship of the proletariat.[6]

In retrospect, these converging descriptions from right and left seem surprising. Apart from fighting the Versaillais, what revolutionary actions did the Commune perpetrate? Marx was mistaken in thinking that it restricted official salaries to those of skilled workmen; its social innovations went no further than forbidding night work in bakeries and ending the system of fines in factories. Many ordinary people supported the Commune for political, rather than social reasons. The posters of the revolutionary government emphasized the charge that the Versailles Assembly was going to impose a king on France: 'the royalist conspirators have attacked!'[7] The electoral basis of the communard régime was reasonably broad, for 230,000 votes were registered, which bears comparison with the 322,000 for the Government of National Defence in the previous November. The common motives uniting these voters were republicanism, patriotism, pride in Parisian heroism and contempt for the 'cow peddlers' and gentry of Versailles. The Commune which they elected was composed of 'revolutionaries', but the extent to which these were 'socialists' is a matter for argument. Only twenty-five of the ninety were workers, so strictly speaking, it was not a proletarian assembly. Only thirteen were members of the International, and most of these were disciples of Proudhon—only one was a Marxist. Of the rest, fifteen have been described as 'Blanquists' and thirty or more as 'Jacobins'. Men of the International, Marxists and—more significantly from the point

---

[5] *Journal des Goncourt*, IV (1911), p. 239.
[6] Marx, *Civil War in France* (1871) and Engels' introduction to it (1891), in Marx and Engels, *Selected Works* (Moscow, 1951) I, pp. 440, 463, 473.
[7] A. Adamov, *La Commune de Paris: anthologie* (1959), pp. 27, 30, 31.

of view of the history of the Commune—Proudhonists, Blanquists
and Jacobins; let us pause a while to define these groups. In so doing,
we can trace the pattern of socialist thought up to 1870. It is possible
too, that we may glimpse what the future of socialism might have
been if Thiers and the Versailles Government had not provided
devastating evidence in support of the cruel myth of class warfare
and of the necessity for a revolutionary dictatorship of the proletariat.

III

In 1871, a 'Jacobin' was a republican of the tradition of 1793. In
the last ten years, books had been published glorifying Danton,
Robespierre, Marat and the Hébertists; though they all belonged to
the high Revolution, these men had destroyed one another, so that
the Jacobin faith could run through a wide spectrum of contrasting
allegiances. But on one thing all Jacobins agreed—they rejected the
bourgeois interpretation of the French Revolution which Thiers,
as a young historian, had put forward nearly half a century ago.
Beslay, a member of the Commune, wrote to Thiers on 26 April to
reproach him with his blindness. 'A whole world has passed before
you—the world of the Revolution! And you who have studied it,
researched on it, written of it, you still have not understood it!
The word 'Revolution' means a regeneration in the conditions of
government, in social institutions, in the organization of labour and
of exchange. . . .'[8] To Jacobins, the Revolution had not gone wrong
after 1789: it had been left unfinished in 1794. The regeneration that
was still to come was pictured variously, and there were varying
proposals for action to accomplish it. There were also varying
degrees of courage and seriousness, for in the words of a contemporary, describing the communard movement at Marseille, some were
revolutionaries of 'the picturesque school, the dilettanti of insurrection'.[9]

At the very core of Jacobinism, however, like a steel rod giving
rigidity to the revolutionary tradition, was the fanatical determination of a single individual. August Blanqui[10] was the eternal conspirator; of his seventy-six years he spent thirty-three in jail and ten
in exile. From 1830, he lived only for the coming revolution, which

[8] Ch. Rihs, *La Commune de Paris: sa structure et ses doctrines* (1955), p. 207.
[9] Bertin, cit. A. Olivesi, *La Commune de 1871 à Marseille* (1950), p. 55.
[10] For what follows see M. Dommanget, *Les Idées politiques et sociales d'Auguste Blanqui* (1957).

he continually tried to hasten on. '*Il faut durer, systématiquement*', he said, in the prisons of the Empire. In 1870, he was free again, preaching revolutionary resistance to the Germans, and though he was arrested before he could join the Commune, his followers formed the dourest group of the Parisian fighters. This grim, heroic figure has hardly had justice done to him. On the one hand, he was the terror of respectable society; Tocqueville saw him in May 1848 and was revolted by his dirty pallor and air of emaciation and decay— 'he seemed to have lived in a sewer'. On the other hand, socialists who saw how few devoted followers he could muster, overlooked their debt to his ideas. 'Blanqui, basically', said Engels in 1847, 'is a political revolutionary who is a socialist only by sentiment.' But this political insurrectionist prepared men's minds for Marx's doctrines and, probably, taught Marx something too.

Idealists like Tocqueville, who praised freedom above equality, or like Mazzini, who held up their hands in horror at materialism, faced Blanqui's deadly riposte—'where there is hunger there is no liberty'. To the utopian socialists, 'arguing on the river bank whether the field on the other side was maize or wheat', he simply said, 'Let us cross and see'. Revolutions, he believed, needed no utopian goal, since insurrection itself would generate new ideals. But, you say, somebody has to carry on the routine work of the world, so how can we ever have equality? 'When communism is discussed,' Blanqui replies, 'it's magnificent to see how your opponent's fears instinctively direct him towards a fatal domestic utensil. *Who will empty the chamber-pot?*—that's always the first cry. *Who will empty my chamber-pot?* he really means, but he is too crafty to use the possessive pronoun, and so he generously devotes his solicitude to the difficulties that will haunt posterity.'

With his empiricism, and his indifference to plans for the ideal society of the future, it is easy to see how Blanqui came to be regarded as a purely destructive *putschist*. Yet he was one of the few socialists who had really clear ideas on the actual technique of revolution itself. His vision was limited to one thing: the achievement of material equality by the most direct method, the seizure of the State by a conspiratorial minority, and the establishment of a popular dictatorship which would not relax its grip until society had been changed and man re-educated. The type of *coup* Babeuf and Buonarroti had dreamed of was defined in precise terms, as a wholly logical insurrection, by Blanqui, and from him came to Marx the idea of the dictatorship of the proletariat and, quite possibly, the very phrase itself. Even so, Marx and Engels disliked the Blanquist idea of minority action. Lenin, who in the end put the dictatorship of the proletariat into practice in a way that changed history, went back to Blanqui's view of it.[10a]

IV

The official doctrine of the Paris Commune was not the Jacobin-Blanquist-Marxist theory of a revolutionary dictatorship. According to the 'Declaration of the French People' of 19 April, France would become a voluntary and spontaneous federation of communes, each in charge of its own budget, police and National Guard, a federal scheme which reflected the Parisian yearning for municipal autonomy. Throughout the century, the capital had been closely supervised by the central government; during the Second Republic it had been under a nominated commission, and during the Second Empire under the Prefect of the Seine and the Prefect of Police. To most Parisians, federalism meant self-government, with romantic over-tones of the revolutionary Commune of 1793 and of the medieval city states. To members of the International, however, the word implied more, being a specific choice against the doctrines of Marx and in favour of those of Proudhon and Bakunin. From its founda-tion, in 1864, the First International Working Men's Association had been divided between Marxists and Proudhonists. Proudhon, one of the few prophets of socialism who came from a working-class milieu, was an individualistic anarchist, proclaiming a socialism which included a belief in marriage, the family, small properties and independent businesses, and communal self-government. This shrewd, self-taught thinker in knitted jacket and clogs regarded Marx's communism as tyranny, while Marx, who never had time to spare for ignorance, however sincere, devastated his rival's homespun amateur philosophy.

After Proudhon's death in 1865, the leadership of the federalist majority of the International fell to Bakunin, an exiled Russian nobleman, a gigantic, reckless man who wandered Europe deep in half-imaginary conspiracies and looking for opportunities to harangue the crowds in other peoples' revolutions. His anarchism was social, rather than individualistic, for after the overthrow of all established authorities, he proposed to re-organize the world on the basis of collective property and co-operative association—a utopia which was something like an idealized version of the peasant community in Russia, or of the localized co-operative production he had admired among the watchmakers of Switzerland. Certainly, his theories excluded all dictatorships, including that of the pro-

[10a] For Lenin's debt to Blanqui's ideas via Tkachev, a 'Russian Blanquist', see above Chap. XVII (Sect. VIII).

letariat, and he ridiculed Marx as 'a State worshipper, triply so, as a Jew, a German and an Hegelian', an elaborate insult which throws revealing light upon the personal factors operating behind this ideological feud.

At the Basle Conference of the International in 1869, Marx was absent, and Bakunin reigned triumphant. Socialism had begun in Italy with the foundation of the newspaper *Il Proletario* four years before, and in Spain with the journal *Federación* in 1867. In both these countries the new movement was essentially anarchistic and federal; this was true also of Switzerland, Bakunin's personal headquarters. In Germany, the Communist Manifesto, which had some influence when it first appeared, was soon forgotten, and until it was reprinted in 1872, most revolutionaries had not even heard of it. In England, trade unions, active in pursuit of ideals or practical benefits, but unresponsive to systematic theories, were taking over control of the working-class cause. Marx was less well-known in Belgium than Jacob Katz, the tobacconist and playwright, who carried on a tradition of reformist socialism founded by the eccentric Baron de Colins, who had advocated, with equal fervour, the causes of public ownership, atheism and reincarnation. At the time of the Paris Commune's declaration in favour of federalism on 19 April 1871, it looked as though Marxism would be only a minor tendency within the broad developing movement of socialist thought in Europe.

V

For many, the anarcho-syndicalist type of socialism was discredited by the failure of the Paris Commune. If the Commune was, as Engels said, the dictatorship of the proletariat, it had acted in a Proudhonist fashion, not a Marxist one, for it had neither destroyed old machinery of government nor set up an effective machinery of its own. Above all, it had failed to seize the Bank of France or to march on Versailles, two decisive omissions which Lenin seized upon in an article, *The Paris Commune and the Problem of a Democratic Dictatorship* (1905). By reflections of this kind, Lenin clarified his mind in preparation for the revolution which was to follow Russia's defeat in war, just as revolution had come in France after Sedan. Thus Marx's 'dictatorship of the proletariat', seen through the bloody haze of the street fighting of 1871, was drawn back to its origin and retempered in the heat of the Blanquist ideal of minority action and decisive ruthlessness.

The justification for ruthlessness and the validity of Marx's fundamental doctrine of class warfare seemed to be established by the ferocity of Thiers' repression. There were 20,000 to 30,000 executions. In one week, the government of Thiers killed, imprisoned or exiled more people than the Terror of 1793–4. These terrible events confirmed intellectuals like Taine and Flaubert in Darwinian pessimism; they converted Albert de Mun, an officer with the Versailles army, to the task of refounding Christian Socialism in France; and they left an ineffaceable belief in the reality and necessity of class warfare in the memories of the working-class of Europe. Every Whit Sunday, thousands still march to the Père Lachaise Cemetery where 147 communards were shot on 28 May 1871, and the red banner of the Commune hangs beside Lenin in his tomb in the Kremlin. If one were listing the names of the men who did most to make revolutionary socialism a force in European history, a case could be made out for awarding a high place, perhaps immediately after Marx, Engels and Lenin, to Adolphe Thiers, the most astute of conventional politicians, an historian who in a lifetime of study had failed to learn the quality of mercy.

VI

Perhaps the history of the Commune would not have seemed to prove Marx's doctrines so conclusively if Marx had not written that history so brilliantly himself. Taken together, his studies of the June Days of 1848, of Louis Napoléon's *coup d'état*, and of the Commune have been described as 'one of the great cardinal productions of the modern art-science of history'.[11] They are certainly masterpieces of interpretation and invective. Contemporary history, so far as it is possible, can best be written by fanatics—or at least by men with powerful motives for operating some trenchant system of selectivity, by men with a formula, provided it is big enough. Marx had invented such a formula which, in its pristine freshness, must have seemed a veritable incantation bringing lucid explanation out of the most chaotic happenings. This is what Engels said over Marx's coffin in 1883: 'As Darwin discovered the law of evolution in organic nature, so Marx discovered the law of evolution in human history: the simple fact, previously hidden under ideological growths, that human beings must first of all eat, drink, shelter and clothe themselves before they can turn their attention to politics, science, art and religion',[12] a summary which, it is true, makes Marxism a great deal easier to understand and believe in than it ever was.

As a logical system, as a description of reality, and as prophecy,

[11] Edmund Wilson, *To the Finland Station* (1940, new ed. 1960), p. 199.
[12] F. Mehring, *Karl Marx* (1918, Eng. trans., 1936), p. 531.

Marx's thought abounded in errors and inconsistencies. His basic concept of class is shaky, he over-emphasized the domination of economic motives, his dialectic is a mystification, his stages of history do not square with his own theories, his economic technicalities are sometimes just complicated mistakes. But when all this is conceded, his doctrines have a majestic unity and a driving force that invite comparisons with great religious movements. Marx, a quarrelsome and ferociously learned German doctor of philosophy, married to a courageous wife whose family belonged to the top class of Prussian officialdom, and Engels, the son of a wealthy textile manufacturer, a dabbler in poetry and music and an expert in riding and drinking, with his Irish mill-girl mistress, were a strange and brilliant combination. One can well imagine them following devious paths of investigation into social worlds far removed from their own, writing ingenious history, and devising labyrinthine philosophies, as indeed they did. But their greatness and the secret of their power is found only when erudition, ingenuity and complexities are stripped away and we are left with what they wrote in sheer pity and indignation. The miseries which Engels saw in the factories and which Marx himself endured in Soho as an exile after the '48 revolutions were, by this stage of European history, avoidable miseries, even if the Marxist sociology to demonstrate the fact was disputable. Ways and means have since been found, in the fortunate third of the world, to eradicate many of these miseries by peaceful means, though one does not need to be a cynic to reflect that these means might have been harder to discover and apply but for the forces disciplined by the harsh theories of class conflict and the terror that the prophets of revolution inspired.

'Philosophers have previously offered various interpretations of the world. Our business is to change it.' Marx's description of capitalism, in appearance a fully-rounded philosophical, historical and economic analysis, was, in fact, an emotional one, wholly directed towards its transformation. It was 'preaching, in the garb of analysis'.[13] The age revered science and craved for certainty, and in this apparently scientific system was concealed a substitute religion. The march of history was portrayed as deterministically assured, so that men could look forward in certainty to the ultimate victory of socialism; yet, the bourgeoisie were hated for performing their necessary, predestined rôle, and the proletariat were called to united action to bring on the inevitable, perhaps to shorten the birth-pangs of the new era. Just as religious men believed in Providence and at the same time accepted the heavy burden of personal responsi-

[13] J. Schumpeter, *Capitalism, Socialism and Democracy* (1947 ed.), p. 6.

bility for the outcome, so too did Marxism contrive to unite the opposites, to bring together the negative and positive poles of determinism and of individual enthusiasm. From this contact, given the opportunity, electrifying results could flow.

VII

With its passion and its strange materialistic and scientific messianism, Marxism, after the Commune and before the first World War, became the most significant ideology in continental European socialism. This statement needs qualification, however; for one thing, it does not mean that socialist movements were all impregnated with Marxism, but that, when ideological arguments were needed, Marxist ones were generally adopted. For another, no sooner did massive socialist parties arise than Marxism itself became modified by 'revisionism', and revisionism had many more adherents than the original doctrine. The corpus of Marx-Engels writings achieved the status within socialism that the Bible had within European civilization: some accepted the book in the spirit of fundamentalism, some in the spirit of the higher criticism, some with heretical reservations; others respected without believing, others neither respected nor believed, but often quoted significant passages all the same. Yet, when all qualifications are made, it is clear that the discussions which from henceforth were conducted within the chief socialist parties were discussions which revolved around Marx's original inspirations.

At one time, it had seemed that anarchism and federalism would prevail over Marxism; now, however, they declined into picturesque and peripheral doctrines. Bakunin died at Zürich in 1876. '*Michel de Bakounine, rentier*', was the entry in the police registers,[14] for after all, he had latterly enjoyed a small private income. Some of the force of anarchism went off into utopian dreams that had little influence, though their magic is not exhausted and future centuries may revive them. It is a sad commentary on our age that Prince Kropotkin's decentralized and semi-rural world, based on 'mutual aid' and electricity, is still as far from us as the most novel creations of science fiction. Another tiny minority of anarchists followed the path of 'propaganda by deeds', and their bombs and assassinations caused some grim sensations in the 'nineties. Practically speaking, however, the force of the anarchist tradition lingered essentially in the syndicalist movement, a doctrine of despair, an abandonment

[14] E. H. Carr, *Michael Bakunin* (1937), p. 488.

of hope in coherent political action in favour of strikes and sabotage. Though it attracted some sophisticated interest (more particularly from Georges Sorel, who turned it into a gospel of creative violence that looks forward to Fascism), in reality it did little more than carry on into the industrial age the blind traditions of Luddism and the *Jacquerie*. Even so, anarcho-syndicalism helped in the formation of the French trade unions and was the dominant influence in Spain and Italy among peasants and workers too ignorant and down-trodden to be able to organize to fight scientifically. Bakunin had fled to the West from a land of serfs, and it was on the Mediterranean peasant fringe of industrial Europe that his doctrines of anarchical socialism retained their relevance and force.

In France anarcho-syndicalism had its stronghold in the C.G.T. (*Confédération Générale du Travail*), a confederation of small trades unions which, in its Amiens Charter of 1906 repudiated all political alliances and proclaimed the duty of 'direct action'. The reply of the Socialist Party, at its Toulouse Congress in 1908, was to retain the right of revolution, but to point out that 'these vast collective movements which can only arise from the deep and general emotion of the proletariat' must not be confused 'with the skirmishes in which workers throw themselves haphazardly against the massed forces of the bourgeois state'.[15] In the following two years the inevitable outcome of such 'skirmishes' was demonstrated, when Clemenceau broke the great postal strike and Briand got the railways running again. The contrast between these failures and the success of the Carmaux strike of 1892 (coming only eight years after the French workers had received the right to combine) was an object lesson. At Carmaux, the miners forced the owners to withdraw an unjust dismissal, and there were those who drew the moral that the strike could achieve specific objectives against industrialists, but could not defy the State.

A socialist political party in France was the creation of Jules Guesde, a convert from anarchism to Marxism in 1880. The next twenty years were a history of fragmentation, so that in 1899 there were six socialist parties, not counting the Anarchists. Though by 1905, all the socialist groups were united under Jean Jaurès, there were still only 35,000 card-carrying party members. France was no longer the metropolis of European socialism. By now, Germany was the country with the greatest industrial proletariat; its Social Democratic Party had 384,000 members and in the parliamentary elections of 1903 it had polled over 3 million votes. Engels, who liked French wines, had called Germany 'a land of beer and schnapps

---

[15] P. Louis, *Histoire du Socialisme en France* (5th ed. 1950), pp. 303–4.

and rye bread, of rivers and revolutions that both run into the sands'.[16] But he and Marx, whatever their doubts about the revolutionary potentiality of their own country, had cast their thought into typically German patterns, and when German industrialism raced ahead, Marxism found unique acceptance in the homeland of its originators.

VIII

The great German Social Democratic Party was founded in 1875, by the union of the Marxists, led by Liebknecht, with the Lassallians. Lassalle had died eleven years before, a German-Jewish adventurer who equalled Marx in courage, but fell short of him in self-dedication. In his thought, ideas of earlier German writers, like Fichte and the 'professorial socialists', were distilled into a more radical essence, an ideal of Prussian State Socialism which would buy over universal suffrage by plucking the bourgeoisie to satisfy the workers. Schemes like these had their influence upon Bismarck's decision to introduce social insurance. The Gotha Programme (1875) of the new united Social Democratic Party said nothing about revolution, and much about universal suffrage, civil liberties and improvement of working-class conditions, and Marx was particularly angry because it accepted Lassalle's scheme of State co-operatives in place of the 'revolutionary dictatorship of the proletariat'. In the Erfurt Programme of 1891 the Lassallian ideas were jettisoned and it was formally laid down that the working-class must obtain political power, though without any clear directions as to whether this would be by violent or by parliamentary means. By now the Social Democrats had 20 per cent of the total vote and 35 seats in the *Reichstag*: it seemed a pity to throw away this peaceful progress for the hazards of revolution.

So far, in contrast to the pattern of events in England, the trade unions had played little part in founding the working-class political movement in Germany. In 1893 the party had eight times as many voters as the unions had members. But this was at the end of a period of economic depression, and during the prosperous years 1895–1904, the balance changed, so that by 1912 there were 2,530,000 trade unionists as against 4,250,000 party voters. Like the industries on which they were based, the unions were huge concerns, with their insurance schemes, strike funds and secretariats, and they soon came to have overwhelming power in party affairs. After handling the severe strikes and lock-outs of 1904–5 they refused to allow the party theorists to impose a doctrine of the general strike, saying that this was not a matter for socialist 'literati' or for conferences working

[16] Wilson, op. cit., p. 175.

up steam in spas and summer resorts. From 1905 the party, like the unions, developed a bureaucracy, and congresses fell into the control of the executive. This situation led, in 1910, to Michel's famous sociological analysis of the life-cycle of democratic party systems—how working-class officials and parliamentarians succumb to the attractions of managerial power and bourgeois status, until a new Left is invented to replace them, and becomes corrupted in its turn.[17] Even so, if Social Democracy was becoming institutionalized, it was enormously powerful. In 1912 it had four and a quarter million voters (a third of the electorate) and 110 members in the *Reichstag*. Nowhere else had socialism come so near to the peaceful conquest of the State.

Not without exasperation, the other socialist parties of Europe had to concede to the Germans their right to leadership. A Second International had been founded in 1889 at meetings held in Paris for the centenary of the Fall of the Bastille; typically, there had been two rival French congresses, accusing each other of posting touts on the railway stations to kidnap unsuspecting foreign delegates. Unlike the First International, which had been destroyed by the feud of Marx and Bakunin, the Second proved an effective organization for bringing together the leaders of European and American socialism. In their debates, the German view of Marxist orthodoxy and tactics generally prevailed, and it is easy to see why. Jaurès, who in 1904 was complaining of the inflexibility of the theoretical formulae which the Germans imposed on others, in 1910 was proclaiming that 'four million German socialists will rise like one man and execute the Kaiser if he wants to start a war'.[18] These four million Social Democratic voters and their mythical zeal were the most glorious of the socialist illusions in the decade of bright hopes before the War.

IX

While German Social Democracy accumulated its peaceful electoral triumphs, what was happening to the Marxist doctrine of revolution? In a preface to a German edition of the *Communist Manifesto* in 1890, Engels spoke of 'the European and American proletariat . . . reviewing its fighting forces, mobilized for the first time, mobilized as *one* army . . . for *one* immediate aim. . . . If only Marx were still by my side to see this with his own eyes'. It comes as an anti-climax to know that this one aim was 'the standard eight-hour working day, to be established by legal enactment'. Marx and Engels were, indeed,

[17] See C. E. Schorske, *German Socia. Democracy, 1905–17* (1955), pp. 116–18.
[18] J. Joll, *The Second International 1889–1914* (1956), pp. 103, 157.

much too civilized to want violence for any but necessary ends. It was within the logic of their system when Engels declared, in 1895, that the socialist cause was triumphing through universal suffrage, and that its leaders were not such fools as to break legality. Besides, he pointed out, in an age of railways, percussion shells and factory-produced cartridges, revolutionary enthusiasts could no longer hope to hold their barricades long enough to shake the morale of the soldiers.[19]

If revolution was to be achieved through the ballot-box, how were Marxists to conduct themselves in the interim period before an absolute parliamentary majority was theirs? Obviously, where universal suffrage did not exist, they would have to fight to obtain it, and in Belgium, Sweden and Austria, the socialists from time to time organized general strikes for a wider suffrage. In Sweden, the results were significant, for four years after the electoral reform of 1907 the Social Democrats obtained 64 seats out of 230. But fighting for constitutional changes, or to win elections, needed alliances with bourgeois political parties. How could these be reconciled with Marxist orthodoxy? Many socialists decided that compromises of this kind were not only inevitable, but desirable; they would obtain their objectives, not necessarily by capturing power, even peacefully, but by extracting piecemeal reforms gradually from a bourgeois order. Karl Kautsky, the pontiff of Marxist orthodoxy in Germany, repudiated alliances with the bourgeoisie yet, as his opponents were quick to point out, all his theoretical rectitude led to immobilism—he was no more going to start a revolution than they were, but was waiting for the development of capitalism to ripen the time.

The best thinkers of European socialism—Emile Vandervelde in Belgium, Jean Jaurès[20] in France and Eduard Bernstein in Germany—were gradualists and revisionists. They claimed, not without reason, that had Marx still been alive he would have supported them against Kautsky's rigidity and literalism. The contrast between Jaurès and Bernstein, two of the noblest figures in the history of socialism, is fascinating. The one was from the lesser bourgeoisie of the Midi, the other from a poor family of Berlin Jews; by birth, both belonged to the disinherited classes, but while Bernstein began as an apprentice in a bank and educated himself as he worked his way up to the editorship of the Social Democratic newspaper, Jaurès was a brilliant young intellectual, who graduated from the

---

[19] Marx and Engels, *Selected Works* I, p. 31; Engels' introduction to Marx, *The Class Struggles in France* (Marx, *Selected Works* (Martin Lawrence, London) II, p. 183).

[20] See H. Goldberg, *The Life of Jean Jaurès* (1962).

École Normale second only to Bergson. Yet it was the self-taught German who became the theorist and publicist of revisionism, and it was the French acɔdemician who lived out revisionism in practice, recklessly, as 'a whole man' (in Romain Rolland's phrase) 'harmonious and free'. The writer of a 'socialist history' of the French Revolution which, in fact, was remarkably impartial, a touchy aristocrat of politics who fought a couple of pistol duels (one on a Christmas morning), a genial family man who defied most of his party by allowing his wife to send their daughter to her first communion, a superb orator and parliamentarian, Jaurès was a socialist because he wanted to give every man the same fullness of life and richness of experience that he himself enjoyed. Socialism, he said, 'seeks to develop all the faculties of man, his power to think, to love and to will'; it consisted, not only of Marxism, but of the entire 'revolutionary and idealistic tradition of France', and he believed that it was compatible both with small property and with democracy. Equality was more than an end in itself: it was also a step on the way to true freedom, for the people must be freed from the domination of the feudal lords of the new industrialism, like the Baron René Reille and his son-in-law the Marquis de Solages, iron masters who tyrannized over Jaurès' constituents in the Midi. Jaurès accepted Marx's doctrine of class warfare, but he held that it did not prevent co-operation between men of goodwill. Millerand was justified in taking office (in 1899) in Waldeck Rousseau's government if he believed that he could serve the interests of ordinary people by doing so; socialists were obliged to fight for Dreyfus, for he was 'no longer an officer or a bourgeois; in his misery he has been stripped of all class character, he is nothing less than mankind itself in the deepest pit of despair'. So Jaurès' belief in class warfare was limited, he accepted it only in so far as it was necessary in achieving justice for suffering humanity.

The sympathetic and individualistic socialism which Jaurès practised was codified and given a theoretical justification by Bernstein. Reformist ideas were strong in German socialism. The trades unions wanted better conditions for their members, not strikes and starvation for the defence of theories, while in south Germany, away from the industrial slums, the Social Democrats found it easy to consider themselves as just another left-wing party, and as early as 1894, they were voting for the state budget in the Bavarian *Landtag*. But Bernstein's chief inspiration came from England, from the history of the quaint utopian groups of Levellers and Diggers in the seventeenth century, from the quiet successes of the Fabian Socialists, from the tolerance of a régime whose police

protected revolutionary agitators and whose queen subscribed £10 to
a fund for the widow of a communist. Bernstein set himself to study
philosophy, and found that he disbelieved in the dialectic; when he
turned to economics, he found that value must be based on demand,
not labour; he studied the evolution of capitalism and saw that the
condition of the working class was improving, and that the rise of
managers and technocrats on one hand and of small shareholders
on the other was transforming industrial organization in ways Marx
had not foreseen. 'What is crucial in Socialism,' he wrote, 'is its
philosophy of history: . . . Marxism is an insight, not a receipt.'[21]
Instead, therefore, of a dictatorship of the proletariat which would
either wreck the industrial machine or bureaucratize idealism, he
looked forward to the victory of 'the common interest' within the
cadres of capitalism, while the workers stood by, ready to use the
general strike simply as a safeguard against any attempt to deprive
them of their voting rights.

X

In practice, Bernstein was no less revolutionary than most other
German socialists. They were waiting for a majority in the *Reichstag*.
So Kautsky argued in 1910 when Rosa Luxemburg demanded a
general strike for universal suffrage in the State of Prussia. What was
true of Germany was true of the whole of Western Europe. 'In
effect,' wrote Cole, 'west European socialism, whatever it called
itself, was a reformist, not a revolutionary movement.'[22] Theoretical
allegiance to the dictatorship of the proletariat, when the electoral
process made this possible, had become a conventional, catechitical
formula, and the real test of revolutionary idealism lay elsewhere—
in the deadly question—'What will you do if the nation goes to war?'
Judged by this test, Bernstein, with Rosa Luxemburg and Liebknecht, was one of the courageous and very small minority. In spite
of all the brave talk of the Second International, in 1914 socialism
did nothing to save Europe from disaster. Christianity, the other
great international organization with peace inscribed in its charter,
was equally helpless. In face of war, the ideals of Western Europe
died, and in the East, out of the chaos of defeat, something resembling
the long-talked of dictatorship of the proletariat was born.

[21] P. Gay, *The Dilemma of Democratic Socialism: Eduard Bernstein's
Challenge to Marx* (1952), p. 76.
[22] G. D. H. Cole, *A History of Socialist Thought*, III, pt. II (1960), pp. 975–6.

CHAPTER XXI

RUSSIA TO 1905: THE APPROACH OF REVOLUTION

I

'Nicholas II inherited from his ancestors not only a giant empire, but a revolution.' Trotsky's deterministic judgement was echoed, from a very different point of view, by another acute observer. 'Autocracy,' said Sir Bernard Pares, 'really ended in Russia in November 1894 when the last autocrat died. The question was, what was to succeed it?'[1]

The new Tsar who ascended the throne of Alexander III was a smooth young Guards officer who spoke English, French and German, had travelled splendidly in the Far East, and had many private virtues. But he lacked a conviction which had gripped and inspired even the most tyrannical and foolish of his predecessors—a sense of involvement in the destiny of his people. On the evening of his Coronation, after a terrible accident in which hundreds of his celebrating subjects had lost their lives, he thoughtlessly attended a ball at the French embassy. On some of the great days of crisis for the régime, his diary is full of tea-drinking, crow shooting, promenades and boating. Nicholas was kind to children and individual peasants, but had no interest in men in the mass—and being an autocrat, that was all he had to deal with. His Tsarina, Alexandra Fedorovna, was a Princess of Hesse brought up by her grandmother, Queen Victoria. The domestic virtues of Kensington Palace and the gossip of petty German courts were of little help to her in the great arena of St Petersburg; in an alien environment she desperately embraced the harsh old traditions of autocracy, as if thus she could make herself a true Russian. Her influence reinforced her husband's natural inclinations. Without ill-will, without deep thought, without conviction, the reign of reaction in Russia was prolonged by the new Tsar. To the *zemstvo* representatives who waited on him to greet his accession, he declared that schemes for the participation of their assemblies in government were 'senseless dreams'. A day or two after this the conservative historian Kliuchevsky was heard to remark that 'the Romanov dynasty will end with Nicholas II'.

[1] L. Trotsky, *History of the Russian Revolution* (trans. M. Eastman, 1932) I, p. 52; B. Pares, *The Fall of the Russian Monarchy* (1939), p. 29.

II

A survey of Russia at this time, on the threshold of the most significant period of its history, might well begin by adopting Trotsky's formula for the inheritance of the last of the Tsars. Here was 'a giant empire' and 'a revolution', and we may consider each in turn. First of all, the 'giant empire'.

By 1890, the Russian population, which had been 57 millions at mid-century, had grown to 95 millions; by the beginning of the twentieth century it was well over the hundred million mark—nearly double that of Germany and much more than double that of Great Britain or France. Europe looked with awe, excessive awe indeed, upon this demographic giant on its eastern borders. In 1890, Russia had a standing army of a million men and spent as much as France or Germany on her armed forces. She was one of the three great military powers, though the most problematic of them all, secure, perhaps, in her vast spaces, yet so far behind in organization, transport and industrial potential that it was impossible to assess her offensive force in modern war.

Territorially, Russia had been expanding ever since Peter the Great had forced through to the Baltic. Under Catherine II, huge areas of Poland, the Crimea and other lands around the Black Sea had been acquired; in 1801, Georgia had been taken, Finland in 1809, Central Poland in 1815, the rest of Transcaucasia and the Northern Caucasus in the first half of the nineteenth century. By 1850, the military frontier was creeping forward past the mud-walled fortresses and over the endless steppes of Central Asia. In 1864, Gorchakov issued a note to the powers excusing the use of force against wild tribesmen, citing the analogy of the French in Algeria and the British in India, but promising not to overthrow organized states. Yet within the next dozen years Russian columns had stormed Tashkent and brought the Emir of Bukhara and the Khans of Khiva into subjection. In 1880, Transcaspia was annexed. By then, within the short space of half a century, Russia had taken control of a region the size of western Europe, at a cost of only 4,000 casualties.

The railway followed the Cossacks. The first train went down the iron road to Samarkand in May 1888; the line reached Tashkent in 1906. Von Kaufman, Governor General of Turkestan from 1867 to 1882, had presided over this expansion, which he would have wished to see go on through the snows of the Khyber Pass to the teeming plains of India. Under his governorship and subsequently, once the railway had arrived, Tashkent developed out of all recognition. In 1914, there were six cinemas, three theatres and a skating rink. A visitor sitting in a coffee house watching the Armenian hawkers, barbers and shoeblacks come and go in their cheap western suits with their long hair hanging down beneath their black felt hats was astonished at the pace of change; idly opening the *Courier of Turkestan* his eye fell upon the leading article—on 'The State of Affairs in Ulster'.[2]

Central Asia provided Russia with a sphere for the exercise of something like the west European nations' colonial imperialism; Siberia provided her with the equivalent of North America, a vast new land to which an immense tide of migration flowed. There was, of course, this difference, that the European migration was building up another nation, while the Russian was simply strengthening the empire of the Tsars. The motive for the Siberian migration was obvious: land hunger. The peasants who moved came chiefly from the over-populated centre and middle-Volga areas; figures for 1895–6 show that a third of them were landless, and another third had not enough land to support their families. A survey of sixteen years later shows what they were gaining, for a farm in Siberia was shown to be, on the average, eight times larger than a holding in the home-land. Before the Emancipation, there had been a movement of peasants eastwards, some of them state peasants furnished with official permission, others serfs from private estates in illegal flight. The decree of 1861 freed the rural population from technical bond-age, but made movement difficult, since a man could not leave the *mir* until he had discharged all communal obligations. Seven years later, when the Minister of the Interior granted permission for entire communes to transplant themselves, the rush from the central provinces was so overwhelming that the edict was withdrawn. From 1890, however, the great continuous surge of migration began. The government encouraged colonists by granting some exemption from taxation and, above all, the Trans-Siberian railway was completed and from 1898 was offering cheap migrant fares. The population of Siberia, which had been three millions at the Emanci-pation, was over thirteen millions by the end of the century, and in the first nine years of the twentieth century, another four million new settlers came in.

Travellers from France, England and America were astonished at the progress they saw in the wilderness: museums and newspapers at Omsk and Tomsk, American harvesters pulled by horses in the

[2] R. A. Pierce, *Russian Central Asia, 1867–1917* (1960), pp. 103–4.

cold north and by camels on the fringes of the Gobi desert.[3] More
significant still was the high standard of living of the peasants, who
dined on eggs, salt cabbage and mutton broth with an abandon
unknown in the crowded homeland. In the tradition of the frontier,
the well-fed men of Siberia were of an independent spirit. George
Lynch, writing in 1903 about the Russian 'Path of Empire', observed that the migration was 'a safety valve to the revolutionary
unrest in Russia proper'. But seven years later, Stolypin, a minister
of the Tsar who was a great supporter of the migration policy,
visited the east and expressed his fears—'the democracy of Siberia
will crush us'.

III

The growth of a free and prosperous peasantry in the empty lands
of the east was, however, but the least of the problems which two
centuries of expansion had created for the autocracy. Expansion had
brought with it an accumulated diversity which continually challenged
the idea of uniform bureaucratic centralization which was the
tradition of the Tsars. The first proper census, taken in 1897, revealed
that 55·7 per cent of the people of the Empire were, strictly speaking,
non-Russian; 17·8 per cent were Ukrainians, 6·3 per cent Poles,
10·8 per cent of Turkic stock, 4 per cent Jews, and there were also
Finns, Lithuanians and Latvians, Germans, Georgians, Armenians,
Mongolians and so on. Mostly, these nationalities were divided from
the officials of St Petersburg and Moscow by a sharp consciousness
of independent religious traditions. Until 1874, the Ukrainians had
their Uniate Church (that is, a church apparently Orthodox in its
externals, but in communion with Rome). The Poles—or at least the
nobility and upper classes—were predominantly Catholic, as were
the Lithuanians; the Latvians and Esthonians were Lutheran; the
Georgians were Orthodox, but under their own Exarch; the Armenians followed a variety of monophysite Christianity; the four million
scattered Jews were still bound together by a sense of religious
uniqueness; while the fourteen million Turks (more than in the
Ottoman Empire itself) were all Moslems.

Thus, around its borders and honeycombing its inner structure
the Tsarist Empire had this pattern of diverse nationalities and
religions, ranging from the highest to the lowest levels of civilization,
from Polish nobles and Warsaw industrialists to peasants of the
Ukraine, from Jews of the ghetto to Jews of the university, from
Tartars of the Volga with their widespread network of commercial

[3] R. L. Wright and Bassett Digby, *Through Siberia: an Empire in the Making*
(1913), cit. D. W. Treadgold, *The Great Siberian Migration* (1957), p. 220.

connections to the nomadic Kirghiz of the steppes. It was impossible to devise any one policy relevant to all of these, unless indeed, it was the most useless policy of all, the unimaginative requirement of uniformity.

It was towards this solution of 'Russification', futile and potentially cruel, that the autocracy had been tending throughout the nineteenth century. The policy became defined in exasperation and contempt against two of the nationalities in particular, the Poles and the Jews—the inhabitants of the newly acquired territories in the west with their proud traditions of culture and independence, and the unhappy internal minority which had been oppressed since time immemorial. Jews, except those who were very rich, could not buy land, or settle outside the towns, or enter government service. Alexander II relaxed these restrictions, but under Alexander III they were re-imposed, and brutal *pogroms* in certain areas set the seal of popular approval upon official intolerance. So it is not surprising to find Jews prominent in the revolutionary movement: in 1897 they founded their own underground organization, the *Bund*, allied to the Social Democratic Party.

Towards the Poles, Russian governments had a bad conscience. Since Catherine II had presided over the first partition in 1772, official policy had run through various phases. Alexander I, romantically influenced by his friend Czartoryski, a patriotic Polish aristocrat, dreamt of a Poland recreated from her ashes. In practice, however, the Tsar did not stand to his generous constitution of 1815: he legislated by decree and refused to submit his budgets to the Diet. After the Polish revolution of 1830, Nicholas I treated the country with his own peculiar brand of iron-handed equity. He deported families of the gentry from the eastern provinces to Siberia or the Caucasus and abolished the Diet; at the same time he granted the Poles their own independent administration and the personal liberties of religious toleration and freedom from arbitrary arrest. Alexander II began with liberal designs, but after the rising of 1863 he attempted to cut the roots of this recurrent demand for liberty by extirpating the Polish language—in future, all education was to be conducted in Russian.

This was a measure taken in exasperation, for as Alexander well knew, the Russian autocracy had done more for most of the Poles than it had for its own subjects. The rising of 1863 (caused by a sudden levy of recruits for the army) had not been joined by the peasants. They remembered how earlier revolutionary movements had shown no interest in their grievances. 'We do not like the Russians,' a peasant is reported as saying in 1830 '. . . but will it be better for us peasants if we drive them out? . . . As we have been up to now, so we shall be afterwards. Our misery will not change. Even now in time of war the manor drives out to field services the wives and children of households from which the farmers have gone to join the army. . . . Indeed, it will be better for the lords when they defeat the Russians. So let them fight them.'[4] Since then, the autocracy had manoeuvred to separate the rural masses from the national cause. This was particularly easy in some of the eastern provinces, where only the landlords were of Polish stock. When the peasants were emancipated in 1861, those of Russian Poland received more land than their contemporaries.

For the moment—though not, perhaps, for long—Russian rule in Poland was secure. The peasants were conscious of their gains, and the new commercial class recognized that the developing textile industry of Lodz and the machine industry of Warsaw had their best outlet eastwards into Russia. True, there was a growing revolutionary movement in Poland aimed at national independence (though in the Socialist Party, founded in 1892, there were some internationalists who believed independence was an illusion and put all their hopes in socializing the partitioning powers). There was still time, however, for the autocracy to plan for the future and to design a *modus vivendi* between Russian strategic interests and Polish national feeling. The policy of Russification, intensified under Alexander III, threw away the opportunity and, indeed, by disturbing the ordinary tenor of existence, did much to awake a national feeling in rural *milieux* which might have remained somnolent for another generation.

Under Alexander III and under Nicholas II (up to 1905) Russification reached its most ruthless intensity. In Poland and in the Ukraine it was merely a question of maintaining the policies of Alexander II's later years. Now however, in all the borderlands of north and south—in Lithuania, Latvia and Esthonia, in the Grand Duchy of Finland and in Armenia and Georgia, the Russian language was imposed in all schools. Russians took over the higher administration of Finland, military conscription was introduced, and finally, in 1903, the old constitution of the country was entirely suspended.

At the same time, revolutionary and nationalist movements were rising in opposition. Ukranians cherished the memory of their poet Taras Shevchenko,[5] the glorifier of Cossack traditions, who had

---

[4] R. F. Leslie, *The Polish Revolution of 1830* (1956), p. 228. See also, Leslie, *Reform and Insurrection in Russian Poland, 1856–65* (1963).

[5] J. S. Reshetar Jnr., *The Ukranian Revolution* (1952), pp. 6–7. On the nation-

been exiled in 1847 to the Kirghiz steppes; in 1891, a meeting at his tomb formed a secret brotherhood to fight despotism and demand autonomy. The Poles had Dmowski's National Democrats and the Socialist Party, whose nationalist wing produced (from 1894) a newspaper, edited by Pilsudski. Jews had their *Bund*, Finns and Armenians had terrorist organizations. The impoverished Georgian nobility, already distrustful of autocracy and contemptuous of the bourgeoisie, welcomed the advent of Marxist doctrines in the 'eighties. Even among the Turkic peoples, a national consciousness was awakening, fostered by their own newspapers.

To all this diverse agitation, the old government of Russia had nothing to offer. Nor indeed, strictly speaking, had the theories of Marx and Engels, who believed in centralization, efficiency, and the absorption of fragmented racial groups by the greater nationalities. But the socialists of the Habsburg monarchy were engaged, in face of their own problems, in devising a solution which the Russian revolutionaries could adopt as their own. In 1899, the Brünn Congress of the Austrian Social Democrats voted for the transformation of the Habsburg dominions into a 'democratic federation of nationalities'. The idea of federalism and cultural autonomy could also be applied to the empire of the Romanovs.

IV

Russia was one of the great military and imperialist powers, ruling over subject nationalities and expanding her control rapidly over vast areas: yet in social and economic structure, she was herself an underdeveloped country.

Since the Emancipation, the peasants were buying more land. Freedom was assisting a tiny and lucky minority towards affluence. One can imagine their jubilation. 'If only my father and my grandfather could rise from their graves to see the whole affair,' says Chekov's Lopakhin,[6] 'how their Yermolái, their flogged and ignorant Yermolái, who used to run about barefooted in the winter, how this same Yermolái has bought a property that hasn't its equal for beauty anywhere in the whole world; I have bought the property where my father and grandfather were slaves, where they weren't even allowed into the kitchen.' Yet the mass of the peasantry was becoming poorer, for the increase of the rural population was forcing down the size

alities generally, R. Pipes, *The Formation of the Soviet Union: Communism and Nationalism, 1917–23* (1954).

[6] Chekov, *The Cherry Orchard* (produced in 1904), trans. G. Calderon in *Two Plays by Chekov* (1912), p. 139.

of holdings, while the communal tenure of the *mir* made agricultural progress impossible. The Kovalevsky commission of 1899 was to ascribe the poverty of the black soil regions to the constricting grip of the rural commune; later, the government of Nicholas II accepted this finding and abandoned the *mir* to take 'a wager on the strong', on the more prosperous minority of peasant households.

The poverty of the countryside meant that industry had a restricted internal market while, except for the fastnesses of Central Asia, there was no external avenue where Russian manufactures could compete with British. In the United States of America, where the working classes could afford to buy the products of the factories, industrial and commercial development went forward in a surge of homogeneous expansion. In Russia, however, where the mass of the population had no purchasing power, industrialization had something 'unnatural' about its growth. It staggered forward, impelled by speculation and government encouragement or restrained by the collective manoeuvres of the owners whenever prices were in danger of collapsing.[7]

The foundations of a modern metallurgical and, to some extent, textile industry, had been laid by Peter the Great, for the purposes of war. There had been significant progress afterwards in the eighteenth and early nineteenth centuries. From 1800–1850, the foreign trade of Russia had more than doubled, and there was an increase of manufacturing productivity, mostly through the work of peasant craftsmen organized in co-operative *artels*, though the cotton textile industry became fully mechanized after 1842, when Great Britain repealed her prohibition on the export of machinery. Even so, Russia was falling far behind western Europe. In the metallurgical works of the Urals the new English inventions were unknown, and the smelting was still done by charcoal; in 1870, the Russian production of pig iron was one third that of France or Germany and one fifteenth that of Great Britain. At the death of Nicholas I, the conditions to create the momentum for an industrial revolution seemed lacking. Serfdom prevented mobility of labour, rural poverty reduced effective demand for manufactures, there was little capital for investment in industry, and communications were suited only to a world of annual fairs and petty market days. In the whole vast empire, there were only 650 miles of railway, very little more than in the tiny kingdom of Piedmont.

As in so many other respects, the reign of Alexander II marked the beginning of modernity, and the changes were made which unleashed

[7] See Fr. X. Coquin, 'Aperçus sur l'économie Tsariste avant 1914', *Rev. d'hist. mod. et contemp.* VII (1960), pp. 54–71.

a chaotic industrial revolution in Russia. The serfs were emancipated, the formation of private banks and the import of foreign capital was encouraged, a return was made to the policy of high tariffs and, backed by western investment, a great railway boom began. Under Alexander III and Nicholas II these developments raced forward jerkily, interlocking but unco-ordinated. In 1881, there were 14,000 miles of railway; ten years later (by which time the Russian metallurgical industry was supplying a large part of the equipment) the Trans-Siberian line was started; by the beginning of the first World War there were over 50,000 miles of track. Foreign capital poured in; the national debt shot up and about half of it consisted of loans raised abroad, while one third of the issued stock of the banks and a good deal of the holdings in the new joint stock companies paid their dividends abroad. 'Railways, tariffs, foreign investment and state encouragement of western capitalism—combined with the results of the emancipation of the serfs,' writes Sumner, 'to effect a revolution in Russian economy.'[8]

The dimensions of this revolution may be assessed by looking at industrial Russia fifty years after the emancipation of the serfs, on the eve of the first World War. A sugar beet industry had arisen from nothing; so too had a vast oil industry at Baku, which in 1900 had been producing half the world's supplies, though by now it was far outstripped by America. The textile factories had expanded to occupy nearly a million workers, and exported great quantities of cheap cotton goods to the Asiatic borders. A new metallurgical industry based on the iron ore of Krivoi Rog and the coal of the Donetz basin (founded in 1869 by a Welshman, John Hughes) had ousted the Ural forges from the place of first importance and produced nearly 70 per cent of Russia's coal, iron and steel. In fifty years, the total iron production had risen ten times, and the value of manufactured products twelve times.

What did these figures mean in comparative terms? Russian production of iron in 1913 was one third that of Great Britain, one quarter that of Germany and one ninth that of the United States; in coal production she was much further behind. In terms of consumption per head or of productivity per worker, the contrast was even more striking. The Russian expansion was also subject to periods of 'Malthusian' restriction imposed by industrialists who were unsure of their markets and had excessive power over the government. Thus, from 1900, coal and oil extraction lagged, and in the winter of 1912–13 the whole country was short of fuel. On the other hand, with all its inefficiency and crudity, the Russian industrial

[8] B. H. Sumner, *Survey of Russian History* (1944), p. 327.

expansion was now beginning to overhaul that of the more advanced nations, though there was still an enormous distance to go. From 1885 to 1913, British industrial production increased at an annual rate of 2·1 per cent, German at 4·5 per cent, Russian at 5·72 per cent, rather faster even than the American. The Tsarist empire remained predominantly a land of peasants, but it was the most rapidly growing industrial country in the world.

In this period of 'take off', Russia needed above all a government capable of planning and of evoking popular support. The régime of Nicholas II could do neither. In attempting to control monopolies, it only succeeded in legalizing them. The rising public debt deprived the government of its independence in economic affairs, so that it lived from hand to mouth, chiefly concerned with putting up a façade to impress foreign creditors. It was the sort of government that fell into the hands of cartels in its concentration on armament production, and which was continually surrendering its policies to the demands of the industrial feudalists who seemed to be replacing the landed ones, which was unable to foresee or remedy shortages of food and fuel, and which exported grain when its own people were starving. Meanwhile, the industrial revolution in Russia was creating a proletariat in some of the great cities. An army was gathering whose miseries might one day serve the cause of political revolution and end the rule of the Tsars.

V

We have seen something of the desperate problems which Nicholas II inherited along with his 'giant empire': they provided the groundwork of the 'revolution' which Trotsky regarded as the other half of the Romanov inheritance. Through all these confusions ran the developing patterns of revolutionary ideas, moulding and directing the heterogeneous discontents. Recklessly oversimplifying, we may classify these ideas into three main trends, two indigenous to Russia —Populism and zemstvo liberalism—and one a foreign importation —Marxism.

The Populist tradition was now shorn of the utopian and Slavophil elements which had graced its doctrines in the writings of Herzen and Chernyshevsky, Lavrov and Mikhailovsky. The idealists had gone to the people and had been rebuffed. In the great famine of 1891, the intellectuals again tried to help the peasants, but were disappointed to find that rural Russia was indifferent to their theories. In any case, the generation which followed the years of realism and nihilism was determined to pursue its ideals by a tough, realistic policy. Victor Chernov provided it. He stood for out and out revolution, going directly towards its goal. In controversy with Marxists he pointed out that, if Bernstein was a revisionist of the right, he himself was a revisionist of the left, who hated the bourgeoisie and was not prepared to stand aside to allow them to fulfil an historic rôle. In Russia, capitalism was a parasitical hothouse novelty introduced by the autocracy: the bourgeoisie it had produced was an appendage of the throne and would vanish with it. So the immediate goal was the seizure of power. After that the policy of revolution would be simple: to give the vast majority of Russians exactly what they wanted—the land. Chernov believed that Russia contained within itself immense spiritual forces (Marxists alleged that he was virtually returning to Slavophil Messianism) and that these forces would be released once the land belonged to the people. By 1897, the various Populist groups were coming together under the influence of Chernov's programme; by the end of 1901 the Social Revolutionary Party was formed, the party which in 1917 was to have a majority in the All-Russian Constituent Assembly and elect Chernov to its presidential chair—for a single day.

The S-R's constituted the sort of party which the logic of the Russian situation demanded. On the one hand, they were revolutionary extremists (they had an autonomous 'Battle Organization' which kept the tradition of terrorism alive): on the other, they had chosen the policy, radical yet conservative, which the peasants desired. Thus, though they claimed to be the most revolutionary of parties, in a sense they were the least. Their historian, Radkey, speculates that, if the Bolsheviks had not destroyed them, the S-R's might have developed by shedding socialism but retaining their peasant following, until they became a party representing the small democratic cultivators, like the French Radical Socialists south of the Loire.[9] If one cares to be wise after the event, it is easy to see the weakness of this neo-Populist party with its ambiguous revolutionary standing, and, it must be confessed, its tendency to internal factions and divisions. None of its leaders knew what procedures to follow between the overthrow of the old régime and the distribution of the land to the people.

Yet if the S-R's were lacking in revolutionary tactics, this was precisely because they were democrats. In 1904, they were represented at a conference of Russian opposition groups in Paris and agreed that democratic government, universal suffrage and national self-determination would be the formula for a new order in Russia. Here, they were at one with the zemstvo Liberals, though some of the latter,

[9] O. H. Radkey, *The Agrarian Foes of Bolshevism* (1958), p. 44.

like Shipov, chairman of the *zemstvo* board of the province of Moscow from 1893 to 1906, wished to go no further than representative machinery for local government and for giving good advice to an omnipotent Tsar. The *zemstvo* demands for participation in government, which Nicholas called 'senseless dreams', could indeed, be interpreted in various ways. Their significance lay in the fact that they came from a series of organizations around which the best intelligences of Russia were gathered. By 1899, the *zemstvos* employed over 65,000 doctors, teachers, engineers, statisticians and veterinary and agricultural experts. The declining gentry, whose sons, in any case, were now going into the professions in increasing numbers, were thus drawn into close touch with the intellectuals and with professional associations like the Pirogov Society of doctors or the Moscow Society of Jurisprudence (closed by the government in 1899). Another institutional link in the chain of liberal development was provided by the universities, whose students, like those of the universities of Latin America or the Arab world today, provided the discontented professions with 'a sort of mass base and striking force'.[10]

Zemstvo liberalism became a broad, inclusive movement. On the one side, through leaders like Petrunkevich, contacts had been built up with desperate extremists. 'When the squire Ivan Petrunkevich descended into the alley hide-aways of Kiev to talk as an equal with some outcast terrorists in 1879,' writes Treadgold, 'it was the beginning of a new epoch in the annals of the Russian opposition.'[11] By contrast, there were conventional respecters of the throne like Shipov, and the worthy philanthropists on the Committees on Illiteracy which Lenin liked to ridicule. Populists and liberals were allies, sometimes the same people. Into this alliance came the 'Legal Marxists'; in 1899, their leading thinker, Struve, condemned the 'Jacobin-Blanquist' idea of a seizure of power and preached gradual social evolution. Along with these moderates were the 'Economists', principally Prokopovich and his wife Kuskova, 'the Sidney and Beatrice Webb of Russian socialism', who wanted a trade-union movement dedicated to the achievement of piecemeal gains and under the leadership of real workers, not reckless intellectuals. In 1901, the wide spectrum of liberal co-operation was made visible in a series of regional conferences of *zemstvos* and the professions, and in the foundation of the magazine *Osvobozhdenie*, edited by Struve, Petrunkevich and the historian, Miliukov. Two years later, a

[10] G. Fischer, *Russian Liberalism* (1958), pp. 53, 56.
[11] D. W. Treadgold, *Lenin and his Rivals: the Struggle for Russia's Future, 1898–1906* (1955), p. 8.

'Union of Liberation' was formed, consisting of all groups willing to accept democracy and self-determination for the nationalities. In the following year, at the Paris conference of opposition groups, the S-R's were also represented.

Only one main revolutionary group was conspicuous by its absence from this federative movement, the Marxists. They remained aloof, one party among many, and no one could guess at the great destiny which was to fall to them in the lottery of revolution.

VI

The first Marxist groups sprang up in Russia in the 'eighties. As a result of their preparatory work, the 'League of Combat for the Liberation of the Working Class' was formed in St Petersburg in 1895. Lenin, whose brother had been executed eight years before and Martov, the son of a rich Jewish family of Odessa and a former university student, were members. Within a year, both had been caught by the police and sent to Siberia. They were still there in 1898 when a congress of Marxist groups was held in Minsk to establish the Social Democratic Workers Party. This was intended to be a loose federation, but proved to be even less centralized than intended, for the Tsarist police net trapped the whole of its directing committee almost immediately. It appeared that it was only possible to organize the movement and discuss its theoretical bases in the comparative safety of exile; this was the experience of Lenin and Martov who returned from Siberia in 1900 and, finding European Russia too dangerous, moved to Munich. Here they were able to co-operate with an earlier group of refugees, former Populists who had been converted to Marxism since their flight from Russia. One was Vera Zasulich, who had shot General Trepov; another was Akselrod, the son of a poor Jewish tavern keeper of the Ukraine, deeply conscious of the latent idealism of the popular masses from which he himself had arisen. Then there was the greatest theorist of them all, Plekhanov, a noble trained at the Military Academy and at the St Petersburg Metallurgical Institute, who had fled to the west after addressing the crowd at the Kazan Square demonstration of December 1876. Lenin, Martov, Plekhanov and Akselrod, a team of brilliant and diversified talents, joined together to edit a journal, *Iskra*, which was smuggled into Russia and distributed by the Marxist underground. Its title meant 'Spark' and reflects the editors' despair at their puny forces allied with their hopes for an ultimate conflagration from small beginnings.

The cutting edge of Marxist theory was whetted in acrimonious controversy with the Populists. In 1884, Plekhanov summarized the points at issue in a pamphlet entitled *Our Differences*; the Populists still believed socialism could come in Russia through the rural commune, while the Marxists held that the commune was an anachronism, and that an advance to socialism must await the triumph of capitalism and the full development of an industrial working class. As Struve was to say, only those blinded by 'national vanity' could argue that Russia might take a 'short cut' to Utopia. This confrontation between Populists and Marxists was one variant of an intellectual schism that seemed to be inspiring all political theorizing in Russia: it was Slavophils versus Westernizers all over again and, oddly enough, it was also a reflection, in conspiratorial circles, of a contemporaneous paper war going on in the corridors of the Tsarist bureaucracy, with the Ministry of the Interior supporting the rural commune and the Ministry of Finance denouncing it in favour of capitalist development.

Another irony of the situation was that Karl Marx himself, who died in the year before *Our Differences*, had ended as a thoroughgoing Populist, and not a supporter of Plekhanov. In 1864, Marx had regarded Russia as 'the gendarme of European reaction' and had ridiculed the Slavophils. Since then, he had fallen under the spell of the Populists, and was especially gratified when Danielson, one of the *narodnik* intellectuals, translated *Das Kapital*. By 1877, he was speculating that Russia might go directly from feudalism to socialism, with the rural commune as the agency of the transformation, though he made the qualification that western Europe must go socialist simultaneously.[12] Thus the Populists were trounced by Plekhanov for their terrorism, their reliance on the *mir*, their failure to see that industrialization must precede socialism—for precisely the things which Marx and Engels found so romantically attractive. In strict theory, there was no doubt that Plekhanov was right: Marx himself was not a Marxist.

Though Lenin called the Populists 'stinking carrion', he learnt a great deal from their malodorous doctrines. They taught him the importance of the peasants. Their idea of using the discontents of rural Russia to leap directly into socialism struck him as revolutionary 'adventurism' and 'pyrotechnics', but he realized that the connivance of the peasant masses would be indispensable for the overthrow of the autocracy. From the Populists he also learnt how important in history can be the purposeful intervention of individuals; their idealism, recklessness and terrorism suggested the hope that

[12] I. Deutscher, 'Marx and Russia', in *Russia in Transition* (1957), p. 162.

historical evolution could be speeded up. There was, indeed, a remarkable affinity between Populists and Marxists. This was not surprising: one group consisted of intellectuals hoping to call out the peasants and the other of intellectuals claiming the leadership of the proletariat.

Lenin's idea of a short cut towards the revolutionary seizure of of power arose in controversy, not only with the Populists, but also with other rivals. Struve and the Legal Marxists, with their gradualism, acted as an irritant, a warning against the possibility that Marxist orthodoxy might degenerate into a smug, non-revolutionary determinism. The Economists, who wanted a spontaneous workers' movement manoeuvring for bread and butter victories and independent of the intellectuals, goaded Lenin towards his ruthless theory of revolutionary leadership. In *What is to be Done?* (1902) he declared that 'the working class, exclusively by its own effort, is able to develop only trade-union consciousness . . . the theory of socialism, however, grew out of the philosophic, historical, and economic theories elaborated by educated representatives of the propertied classes, by intellectuals . . . and would have been brought to them [the workers] from without.'[13] The intellectuals must lead: if so, however, they must 'dedicate their whole lives to the revolution, not just a free evening,' they must surrender their individual wills to form an iron party, obeying commands with military precision.

Lenin put forward his doctrine to the Second Congress of the Russian Social Democratic Party in 1903 (in exile, of course), and the dispute about the nature of the party which followed was one of the chief reasons for the split between Bolsheviks and Mensheviks. At the time, Trotsky said that Lenin was betraying Marxism, by setting himself up as a sort of farcical version of Robespierre and by inventing the heresy of 'Substitutionism', putting the party in place of the proletariat. Yet all the while Lenin was on his way towards one of the great decisions which change history. He was developing a system of revolutionary tactics for which texts from *Das Kapital* merely provided a theoretical justification. Adherence to the strict tenets of Marxist orthodoxy would have made the seizure of power in 1917 impossible.

[13] V. I. Lenin, *What is to be Done?* in *Collected Works* (ed. V. Jerome, 1961) V, p. 375. For the development of Lenin's thought see R. Pipes, *Social Democracy and the St Petersburg Labor Movement, 1885–1897* (1963); and D. W. Treadgold, *Lenin and his Rivals* (1955).

VII

According to Plehve, who was Minister of the Interior from 1902–4, Russia needed 'a little victorious war to stop the revolutionary tide'.[14] As things happened, an unnecessary, big and disastrous war with Japan led directly to the 1905 Revolution. The inefficiency of the autocracy stood revealed for the world to marvel at. Count Kokovtsov's memoirs[15] paint a ludicrous picture of a once-great empire on the eve of the fall of Port Arthur—the manoeuvres of profiteers had driven to war a court which had not made serious preparations to fight and which still blindly ridiculed the Japanese as 'monkeys'; a Commander-in-Chief directing hostilities without stirring from the carriages of the Chinese Eastern railway and claiming large forage monies for horses he never rode; an admiral shaving off his beard and going in transparent disguise to Paris to purchase some non-existent Chilean battleships. Such was the incompetence of the government that its very machinery of police repression served as an encouragement to revolutionary demonstrations. Zubatov, the head of Moscow security, had encouraged the formation of tame unions of workers under police surveillance, and it was one of these official trade unions, founded by a priest, Father Gapon, which was infiltrated by Social Democrats and which organized the great demonstration of 9/22 January 1905, 'Bloody Sunday'.

It was then that the soldiers fired on the petitioners marching to the Winter Palace and the Revolution began. Yet for five months before this, all the discontents of the country had been coming to a focus. An S-R terrorist murdered Plehve in the summer of 1904. In November, a congress of *zemstvo* delegates asked for a representative assembly. At the end of that month and in December industrial strikes broke out in Baku and St Petersburg.

The massacre of Bloody Sunday fused these discontents in a white-hot rage. Even Conservative newspapers defied the censorship and demanded an enquiry. A new wave of strikes swept the country, and work ceased on the railways, in the factories, universities, secondary and primary schools.[16] Teachers, lawyers and doctors formed associations, which in May 1905 combined into a 'Union of Unions', to co-operate with the working class movement and demand universal suffrage and parliamentary institutions. Peasant risings, chiefly

---

[14] H. Seton-Watson, *The Decline of Imperial Russia, 1855–1914* (1952), p. 213.
[15] N. V. Kokovtsov, *Out of my Past* (ed. H. H. Fisher, 1935).
[16] R. Girault, 'La Révolution russe de 1905 d'après quelques témoignages français', *Revue historique*, CCXXX (1963), p. 107.

under S-R leadership, flared up, and in the same month of May a meeting in Moscow set up an All-Russian Peasant Union. This illegal organization demanded the land for the people and openly encouraged resistance to the government. Everywhere, the nationalities were in agitation. In Poland, it was the two branches of the Socialist Party uniting to demand constituent assemblies for both Russia and their own country; in the Ukraine it was the non-Socialist groups, the nationalist People's Party and the Radical Democrats, who called for a separate legislative assembly at Kiev; in Lithuania, Socialists and non-Socialists, meeting in separate congresses, passed resolutions for national autonomy; there were strikes and peasant risings and demands for the use of the national tongue in Latvia; there was a boycott of the government in Georgia, led by the Mensheviks; in Finland, the autocracy, faced with terrorist activities and a general strike, was obliged to suspend its policy of Russification; a first all-Russian Moslem congress was held, illegally, at Nizhnii Novgorod on a steamer on the river Oka.

This universal revolutionary fermentation was, in the end, quelled with comparative ease—or so it seemed to the Tsar. His October Manifesto, promising a Duma (or Parliament) was gratefully accepted by the moderates; having so easily regained the initiative, Nicholas proceeded to make arrangements to prevent the Duma from interfering with his 'supreme autocratic power'. Yet Russia had seen the face of revolution—a modern revolution, not a serf rising or a guards' conspiracy—and the lesson that the Tsar had refused to learn was there for his enemies to study. Men had seen how defeat in war can leave the armed forces open to propaganda, and how the apparently inert peasant masses could be organized to fight for the land; they had seen the coercive power of a general strike, provided that its factory committees were organized into a central council for political action, like the 'Soviets' of workers' deputies which had arisen in St Petersburg and Moscow. The cause of revolution had gained new heroic memories, more inspiring to practical action than the long annals of suffering in jails and exile or of sporadic terrorism. There had been street fighting in Moscow, peasant risings in the countryside, mutinies in regiments and on the battleship *Potemkin*. Trotsky defying his judges was a symbol of the alliance of the intellectuals and the proletariat.

Defeat imposed a lesson in insurrectionary strategy. As the 'black hundreds', gangs of thugs hired by reactionaries, attacked Jews, strikers, peasant demonstrators and left-wing intellectuals, the theorists of revolution were driven to reflect again upon the problem of the take-over of power. Perhaps in Russia a bourgeois revolution would always slip back under the talons of the autocracy. Maybe the conspiratorial minority ought to seize the State machinery and hold it fast, from the death of the last Tsar to the advent of utopia. By other paths of argument, Lenin was already on the verge of this conclusion. For the majority of Russians, who had neither revolutionary purposes nor theories, 1905 marks the end of an ancient illusion. The myth of the paternal autocrat, separated from his people by nobles, bureaucrats or industrialists, was shattered. Though he was a police agent, Father Gapon summed up the universal disillusionment after Bloody Sunday—'Nicholas Romanov, formerly Tsar and now destroyer of souls'.

CHAPTER XXII

IMPERIALISM, DIPLOMACY AND WAR

I

'Here is a diplomat of the future', said Bismarck when, as ambassador to St Petersburg, he introduced his attaché to Prince Nesselrode, a survivor of the Congress of Vienna. 'In the future,' said the Prince, 'there will be no diplomacy and no diplomats.'[1] Though this prophecy—the *boutade* of a retired statesman growing old ungracefully—need not be taken very seriously, it retains some point as an observation that the diplomatic milieu and the presuppositions of international relations were changing. Let us look at the diplomatic scene in 1890, when Bismarck fell and when Holstein, the attaché of St Petersburg days, succeeded unworthily to the control of German foreign policy.

The practitioners of foreign affairs remained, as they always had been, a 'small intellectual élite who shared the same sort of background and who desired the same sort of world';[2] except in the service of the Third Republic, most of the great embassies were filled by men of high birth or great wealth—'degenerate members of the high aristocracy or sons of big industrialists who were incapable of carrying on their fathers' work',[3] said Admiral Tirpitz, in a bitter moment, of the envoys of Wilhelmian Germany. Yet diplomacy, like everything else in this century of progress, was becoming more highly organized and professionalized. Bismarck, himself a master of languages and of despatch writing, reformed the Prussian diplomatic corps, though he made his ambassadors too dependent upon his own leadership for them to be able to exercise a restraining influence on the government after his departure. Oddly enough, it was republican France, with its growing proportion of unfashionable envoys and its unstable ministries that was developing the most efficient organization.[4] The Quai d'Orsay reclassified its files into

[1] Gordon A. Craig, *From Bismarck to Adenauer* (1958), p. 33.
[2] H. Nicolson, 'Diplomacy then and now', *Foreign Affairs*, XL (1) (1961), p. 39.
[3] Craig, op. cit., p. 103.
[4] See J. E. Howard, *Parliament and Foreign Policy in France . . . during the Third Republic* (1948); C. W. Porter, *The Career of Théophile Delcassé* (1936); and K. Eubank, *Paul Cambon, Master Diplomatist* (1960). In 1900, of the eight major embassies, three (Berlin, Vienna and St Petersburg) were held by aristocrats.

a thoroughly logical system in 1896, press contacts were fostered, and an efficient secret deciphering service was established. The bourgeoisie proved as skilful at the great game of international politics as the aristocracy. Europe's ablest foreign minister between Bismarck and the World War was Delcassé, a journalist who financed his way in politics by marrying a wealthy widow; and in spite of his refusal to wear knee breeches to please Edward VII, the ablest ambassador may well have been Paul Cambon, who rose through the prefectures and the Tunis Residency to the embassies of Madrid, Constantinople and, from 1898 onwards, London.

The old assumption that autocracies are likely to be more efficient in their foreign policies than parliamentary governments, began to appear doubtful by the early twentieth century as, from time to time, some example of German vainglory, Russian incompetence or Austrian ruthlessness drew attention to the consistency of British designs or to the steady *Realpolitik* of the French. In particular, the chaotic operation of parliamentarianism under the Third Republic had much less effect upon the coherence and continuity of foreign policy than might have been expected. In theory, the Committees of Foreign Affairs in the Senate and Deputies could demand explanations, as any deputy could by interpellation, and as ministries changed 'like opera scenery', relations with other countries might have been at the mercy of every new combination. In practice, however, foreign ministers were removed less frequently than cabinets— Delcassé was in continual tenure for 84 months (from 1898 to 1905), Pichon for 52 months, Decazes for 48, Ribot for 34. For patriotic reasons, or because they had other fish to fry, deputies generally left foreign affairs alone: from 1906 to 1912 there were only seven interpellations, and the biggest decisions were kept secret from Parliament—the military convention with Russia, the text of the 1902 treaty with Italy, the letters interpreting the 1904 treaty with England. Beneath all their domestic scandals and confusions, Frenchmen were realists about national security, and the possibility rather than the actuality of parliamentary control preserved their governments from the reckless words and hesitant aggressiveness which were to serve Germany so ill.

II

When Nesselrode prophesied that diplomacy (as well as its practitioners) was dying out, he probably meant that the 'Concert of Europe' of Metternich's day had collapsed and that no alternative idea of a European order had replaced it. Though this theme has been adopted by historians writing under the shadow of the great wars of the twentieth century, it is important to notice that concert diplomacy outlived the Age of Metternich, and to look for the circumstances which eventually brought it to an end. After 1848, 'Europe' could still act to settle Near-Eastern crises: the Crimean War and the Russo-Turkish War of 1877 were both followed by general congresses, the latter, the Congress of Berlin, being hailed by *The Times* as 'the first instance of a real Parliament of the Great Powers'.[5] Significantly, however, the French defeat of 1870 led, not to a congress, but to dictated peace terms, which the neutral powers did not moderate and did not guarantee. 'Who is Europe?' Bismarck once asked.[6] The answer might have been that it consisted of all the powers in matters which did not affect their vital interests. But once Germany was united and at bitter enmity with France, fear tended to drive both parties into firm, embattled alliances which would share the other hatreds of the continent between them—a process which Bismarck contrived to delay for two decades. Once two armed camps formed, few European matters were left which were not 'vital', for maintaining the good-will of an ally might be concerned. That was why no European concert revived to save 200,000 Armenians from massacre in the 'nineties,[7] and that was why, in the end, a pistol shot in the Balkans could throw the whole continent into war.

Yet all the while, in tragic contrast, educated opinion was becoming more internationally-minded, and diplomatic practice was becoming more dextrous and more civilized.[8] The Red Cross was founded in 1863, conferences to advocate peace and international organizations of various kinds, like the Inter-parliamentary Union (1892) were multiplying. The settlement of disputes by arbitration (Great Britain and the U.S.A., 1842 and 1871; Germany and Spain, 1885), the exchange or purchase of territories (Germany and Great Britain in 1890; the U.S.A. and Mexico and Russia in 1853 and 1867), or even its free gift (Great Britain and Greece in 1864), conventions for freedom of navigation (the Baltic, 1857; the Congo, 1885; Suez, 1888) and the establishment of neutral zones (Switzerland, 1815; Belgium, 1839; Corfu, 1864; Luxemburg, 1867; the border between Norway and Sweden, 1905) gave evidence of the improvement of diplomatic techniques and hope that many minor occasions

[5] F. H. Hinsley, *Power and the Pursuit of Peace* (1963), p. 137.
[6] G. Barraclough, *European Unity in Thought and Action* (1963), p. 13.
[7] A. O. Sarkissian, 'Concert Diplomacy and the Armenians, 1890-7', in *Studies in Diplomatic History in Honour of G. P. Gooch* (1961), pp. 60, 75.
[8] See C. R. M. F. Cruttwell, *A History of Peaceful Change in the Modern World* (1937).

of friction could be eliminated. On the other hand, there were signs that international law could easily be violated. In 1870, Russia denounced the Black Sea clauses of the Treaty of 1856, and in 1886 fortified Batum in defiance of the Treaty of Berlin; Austria-Hungary broke her engagements when she annexed Bosnia in 1908, and for long Germany matured a war plan that involved violating the neutrality of Belgium and Luxemburg. There was a will to peace in Europe, but none of the great states was willing to sacrifice to this end any degree of national security.

It was this determination to achieve security, rather than the will to aggression, which was characteristic of the movements of public opinion which pressed continually upon the deliberations of the diplomats. After the first World War began, the catastrophe was blamed on the 'new nationalism' of the 'militaristic type' which had 'permeated the masses of the population'.[9] To be sure, nationalism in the Balkans provided the occasion for war, but it is doubtful to what extent the power tensions of the great states were inspired by the leaven of aggressive nationalism working in the masses. The masses did not want war, nor indeed, did the statesmen, though a few of them, more especially in Vienna and Berlin, were willing to risk it. Perhaps the most significant thing about the nationalism of the masses towards the end of the nineteenth and the beginning of the twentieth century is, not that it was jingoistic when appropriately stimulated, but that it was uninformed and sensationalist. Mass circulation daily newspapers began in the 'nineties, and foreign policy was news. The issues were often simplified, even by *The Times*, whose famous correspondent Bourchier, wandering the Balkans with ear trumpet and bug-proof sleeping-bag, was denied an assistant on the ground that 'as a rule, the British public only care for one thing at once, and two things in the Balkans would be more than they could stand'.[10] In France, England and Germany, popular journalism created its effects by juggling with brightly coloured counters, easy and unflattering stereotypes of foreign nations. It is true that the racial doctrines of Gobineau (1853–5) and Houston Stewart Chamberlain (1899) were not current—they were left for Hitler long afterwards—but Frenchmen spoke of Germans as barbarians and Germans spoke of Russians as worse, without 'scientific' jargon to justify their fears, unless it was crude versions of Darwinism that Darwin would have spurned.[11] 'The intervention

[9] J. Holland Rose, *Nationalism as a Factor in Modern History* (1916), p. 151. Cf. Arnold Toynbee, *Nationality and the War* (1915), p. v.

[10] *History of 'The Times'* (4 vols., 1935–52), III (1884–1912), p. 715.

[11] J. Barzun, *Race: a Study in Modern Superstition* (1938), p. 234; for

of the Press in international disputes tends daily to become more and more hostile to peace and civilization', wrote an English journalist in 1898. 'If there is one thing more than another which I found that everyone was agreed in my tour around Europe, it was that much of our modern journalism is the most potent weapon yet invented by the devil for banishing peace and goodwill from the earth.'[12] Yet the press knew its public too well to incite to real warfare when the conscripts would have to march: it incited to hatred when it thought that war was far away, and in so doing compelled the diplomats to play their rôles before a vast audience that would be quick to anger if prestige seemed to be lost and quick to panic if security seemed to be threatened. This dual attitude of the newspapers, jingoistic yet pacifist, is also evident in their reporting of that projection of nationalism upon the world screen which is called 'imperialism'—inciting to defiance in distant arenas and at the same time demanding peace and safety on all home borders. As we shall see, the two were by no means incompatible; the world was a less crowded place then, and clashes of interest in Europe could sometimes be 'adjusted peacefully' at the expense of weaker states elsewhere.[13]

III

The last quarter of the nineteenth century is commonly called the age of 'imperialism', for it is then that the great powers of Europe were competing with each other to grab territories in the backward, defenceless areas of the world, more especially in Africa, the Pacific and S.E. Asia. From 1871 to 1900, Great Britain annexed over four million square miles, an area one third the size of Europe, with over sixty million inhabitants, France took more than three million square miles, Germany and Belgium one million each, and Italy, to her chagrin, substantially less. This mania for expansion needed interpretation, and in 1902, J. A. Hobson provided a brilliant, one-sided explanation which has enjoyed a long run and still remains a ghost which no amount of statistical incantation can exorcise. The working classes, the argument went, were getting too small a share of the profits of the Industrial Revolution, and because they were underspending, the machines were producing more than domestic markets could absorb, and the owners were accumulating savings which

'Darwinism' see W. L. Langer, *The Diplomacy of Imperialism* (1 vol., 1951 ed.), pp. 85–6.
[12] Langer, op. cit., p. 85.
[13] *Nationalism* (Royal Institute of International Affairs, 1939), p. 187; E. H. Carr, *Nationalism and After* (1945), pp. 10–17.

could no longer be profitably invested in their own country. 'Imperialism', Hobson concluded, 'is the endeavour of the great controllers of industry to broaden the channel for the flow of their surplus wealth by seeking foreign markets and foreign investments to take off the goods and capital they cannot sell or use at home.'[14] As might be expected, this idea was adopted by Marxist writers, and Lenin in 1916 defined imperialism as 'the highest stage of capitalism'.[15] In this stage, he argued, an 'aristocracy of labour' in the advanced countries went into alliance with the bourgeoisie to exploit the backward peoples of the world. Hobson had said that the foreign policies of the European powers were 'primarily a struggle for profitable markets and investments'; the Marxists, writing later and more recklessly, held that it was this clash of imperialisms which had caused the first World War.

What truth is there in the theory that imperialism was 'the highest stage of capitalism' and the essential cause of war? Obviously, there were profits to be won out of annexations, by the manufacturers, for example, of munitions and mosquito nets, and of products made from rubber or ivory. A 'financial conquistador' like King Leopold II of Belgium, who sponsored Stanley's explorations, made a sinister fortune out of exploiting his private apanage in the Congo. It is also true that empire provided interesting administrative and military employment: radical politicians who had become a menace at Paris could be sent off to misgovern Indo-China, and heroic soldiers could win promotion fighting against North African tribes; public-school men could exercise what John Buchan called 'the gift of responsibility, the power of being in a little way a king' within 'the closed circle of British power, where everyone knew everyone else, where everyone knew where everything was—"the pass on your right as you go over into Ladakh".'[16]

But jobs and profits can be found in every expansionist movement, from evangelistic campaigns to international socialism. If Hobson (who later retracted his extreme views) and Lenin are right, there would have been a big-scale flow of capital into the areas which the imperialist powers were annexing. This is precisely what did not happen. French capital went, not to the colonies, but to Russia, encouraged over the edge of that abyss by the government of the

[14] J. A. Hobson, *Imperialism* (1902, 6th ed. 1961), p. 85.
[15] Lenin, *Imperialism, the Highest Stage of Capitalism, Selected Works* (London ed. 2 vols., 1947) I, pp. 630–725.
[16] A. P. Thornton, *The Imperial Idea and its Enemies: a Study in British Power* (1959), p. 92. See the quotations in R. Winks, *British Imperialism: gold, God, glory* (1963).

Republic, for reasons of national security. In the decades before 1914, over half British overseas assets were invested outside the Empire, and another quarter of the total was placed in Canada, Australia and New Zealand. Unluckily for Africa, the European powers were not partitioning the Continent because they had surpluses to invest or markets to develop—they could do much better elsewhere.

Though our information is limited (since it comes mainly from the diplomatic archives, rather than from the secret files of capitalist enterprises), it does not support the supposition that the clash of rival imperialist ambitions can be blamed on financial and industrial interests. No doubt Schumpeter went too far in saying that 'capitalism is by nature anti-imperialistic' and hostile to war,[17] but his generalization is at least as applicable to some segments of capitalism as the Marxist hypothesis may be to others. When the workings of big business are revealed, its chiefs can sometimes be seen detaching themselves—all too easily, one might say—from national hatreds. In 1909, at the height of the Bosnian crisis, when French statesmen ought to have been concentrating on maintaining the Russian alliance, there were Franco-German talks over Moroccan mining interests, inspired by Schneider-Creusot and Krupps and their allied banks in the two countries.[18] International capitalism knew the arts of combination as well as of competition. If its leaders had dominated the destinies of Europe, as some have supposed, they would have prevented the first World War, when sellers were engaged in destroying their best customers and buyers in destroying their best sources of supply. Indeed, the big rifts of imperialist rivalry outside Europe had been patched up before 1914—even Berlin–Bagdad and Morocco; it would seem that imperialism, by encouraging the powers to seek compensations in distant lands, had delayed a major war rather than caused one.

IV

The connection between capitalism and imperialism was not, for the most part, direct. The faceless manipulators of finance and factories were concerned with present profits, and these were generally highest and appeared most secure in economies where transport and sources of power were already developed. It was politicians and visionaries reflecting upon the expansionist dynamic of industrial society and on

[17] J. Schumpeter, *Imperialism and the Social Classes* (1951), pp. 96–8.
[18] E. W. Edwards, 'The Franco-German Agreement on Morocco, 1909', *Eng. Hist. Rev.* LXXVII (1963), pp. 493 ff.

its possible need for raw materials and markets in the future, who were the prophets of imperial expansion. Jules Ferry, the greatest French exponent of colonies as fields for investment and exploitation (a policy which he adopted only when he became head of a government in 1881 and saw from the dossiers the possibilities that lay open) said, 'It is a question of fifty or a hundred years' time . . . of the future heritage of our children.'[19] The rise of protective tariffs in most European countries gave new point to fears about future supplies of primary products like vegetable oils, rubber, coffee and cocoa, and about markets for manufactures; 'the protectionist system', said Ferry in 1890, 'unless accompanied by a serious colonial policy, is like a steam engine without a safety valve.'[20] Beneath the surface of the most forbidding territories the basic ingredients for future industrialization—coal, iron and other metals—might lie concealed, and unskilled labour under European technical direction might become an effective means of working them. It was the possibility of capitalist exploitation, as envisaged by nationalist dreamers, rather than the ambitions of actual capitalists that inspired imperialism.

These dreams necessarily involved a military element, for those who will the end must will the means, and the means included the defence of what had been won—coaling stations for warships, depots for troops, supply areas, frontiers pushed forward to strategic natural lines, buffer states suitably manipulated, linkages between one territory and another. Lord Salisbury said that he feared the military would advise him to garrison the moon—a jest which events are rapidly overtaking. And military arrangements to defend visions of economic expansion brought with them military visions of defence transmuted into overwhelming power. The example of the British in Egypt and in India (tarnished, it is true, by the terrible memories of the Mutiny) suggested that an imperialist state that learned the art of raising native armies might one day astonish Europe. France, perhaps, could throw North African legions onto the Rhine, and an English publicist in 1899, writing under the significant title, *From Peking to Petersburg*, said that in China, 'we could raise in twenty years an army that would hold the world at bay'.[21]

Economic and strategic arguments for grabbing new territories were many, and whether the reasoning was sound or not, once the grab had started, no nation which wished to be insured against the

[19] M. Baumont, *L'Essor industriel et l'impérialisme colonial, 1874–1904* (2nd ed., 1949), p. 60.

[20] H. Goldberg, *French colonialism: progress or poverty?* (1959), p. 3.

[21] E. V. G. Kiernan, *British Diplomacy in China, 1880 to 1885* (1939), p. 214.

future could afford to stay out of it: 'taking as much as possible, without knowing what to do with it', said a sardonic Frenchman, 'taking what others want because they want it and to prevent them getting it.'[22] In a speech to the Colonial Institute in 1893, Lord Rosebery admitted that the Empire was large enough as it stood, but added, 'we are engaged, at the present moment, in the language of mining, "in pegging out claims for the future". We have to look forward beyond the chatter of platforms and the passions of party to the future of the race of which we are . . . trustees, and we should . . . grossly fail . . . did we . . . decline to take our share in a partition of the world which we have not forced on, but which has been forced upon us.'[23]

Speeches like this represent attempts to capture, for the benefit of the nation, a vast surge of activity which sprang from other allegiances or from the interests of individuals. This was the age of Europe's self-conscious superiority to other peoples and to its own past, an outlook which gained crude force from popular versions of Darwinism (though not from Darwin's writings themselves). Western society and culture was expansive in its very nature. Its industrialism was making it the centre of a world-wide web of exchange, and making agricultural regions its tributaries; its technological advances were spiritually neutral achievements that could be adopted (as the Japanese were demonstrating) by alien civilizations; its explorers, scientists and journalists were everywhere, agents of its insatiable curiosity. Aided by the printing press, better methods of transportation, improvements in medicine, and the increasing prosperity of their adherents, the Christian churches had entered upon the greatest period of missionary activity in their history, or in the history of any other religion or movement. About 40,000 Roman Catholic and 20,000 Protestant missionaries were at work in Asia and Africa; the great missionary societies, especially in America and England, were raising sums of money that would have appeared incredible earlier in the century, and as men looked at the statistical results (figures like one and a half million Catholics and a quarter of a million Protestant communicants in China) they believed that the conversion of the whole world had become, for the first time, a real possibility.

The missionary effort, whose deeper effects remain after the European proconsuls have withdrawn, had an enormous, though superficial influence upon contemporary public opinion at home, and gave to imperialist aspirations an ethical tinge which was neither

[22] M. Baumont, op. cit., p. 59.
[23] W. L. Langer, op. cit., p. 78.

cynical nor insincere. This moralizing of expansionism is equally
evident among the opponents of Christianity, more particularly
in their favourite argument that the mass conversions of the mission
field were merely adhesions to material goods and to a superior
culture: 'how could I refuse to believe so good a man, who gave me
soup with meat in it?'[24] Christians and anti-Christians alike made a
common assumption, that of the superiority of European civilization.
Hence, with its ethical overtones and its undertones of future profit,
with its sense of power and its invocation of distant, exotic worlds,
the imperial idea was eminently suited to stir the minds of the masses,
newly enfranchised and easily influenced by the expanding popular
press. Late nineteenth-century imperialism, it might be said, was not
the 'highest stage of capitalism', but the 'highest stage of nationalism'. Nationalism plus democracy equals imperialism, *vox populi,
vox diaboli*, a French historian concludes.[25]

V

A listing of pressures and motives, however, must always fall short
of an explanation of an historical phenomenon; this can be found
finally in the chronology of events as they happened, a pattern which,
in the case of imperialism, is formed by the interweaving jealousies
and fears of the great powers. Great Britain was acting to support an
already existing empire. The security of India involved the routes to
the East, so that the collapse of the Khedival régime in Egypt led to
a British occupation (1882); this in turn gave a new urgency to African
problems, whether of trade and missions in Nyasaland, or of white
settlers in South Africa. 'From start to finish,' it has been said (no
doubt with some exaggeration) 'the partition of tropical Africa was
driven by the persistent crisis in Egypt.'[26] In the Far East, outside
the strategic lines of imperial communications, Britain was hostile
to proposals of partition or 'spheres of influence', being anxious to
keep the whole Chinese market open to trade, though not willing to
take any startling action to ensure this. 'We have never had and we
have not any policy towards China', wrote Curzon to St John

---

[24] See Clemenceau's anticlerical short story *Mokoubamba's Fetish*. For
statistics of the missionary effort, K. S. Latourette, *A History of the Expansion
of Christianity* (7 vols., 1944–5) VI, p. 356.

[25] Baumont, op. cit., p. 5. 'Imperialism owed its popular appeal, not to the
sinister influence of the capitalists, but to its inherent attractions for the masses'
(D. K. Fieldhouse, 'Imperialism: an Historiographical Revision', *Econ. Hist.
Rev.* Ser. 2, XIV (1961), p. 209).

[26] R. Robinson, J. Gallagher and A. Dennis, *Africa and the Victorians*
(1961), p. 465.

Broderick in 1899. 'No one knows that better than you or I who have successively had to conjure up make-believe.'[27]

The imperialisms of the other powers revolved around the British Empire, which aroused their envy and whose manoeuvres for security were not easily distinguishable from manoeuvres to grow mightier: by the resulting rivalries, British imperialism itself was sharpened. One of these rivalries was geographically inevitable, arising from marginal contacts with Russia, as the Tsarist Empire, without order or design, expanded towards India, and as its shadow (from 1892 to 1902) fell heavily over China. But British fears of Russia, though pathologically easy to arouse, were lacking in urgency: as Bismarck had said, 'Russia is more an elemental force than a government, more a mastodon than a diplomatic entity, and she must be treated like bad weather, until things are different.'[28] Whatever the reasons may have been, neither party in this confrontation was anxious to go to extremes. The Anglo-Japanese alliance of 1902 was a device to end Japanese flirtations with St Petersburg, rather than an attempt to score off an enemy. 'It is after all, only a wooden leg', said a British journalist.[29] And it is remarkable how easily the British and Russian empires made some sort of agreement in the end, after the one had been humiliated in war by the Boers and the other by the Japanese. Perhaps the whale and the bear had been ostentatious of their mutual hatred because they knew that neither could venture into the other's territory to do decisive damage.

The other principal imperial rivalries—between Great Britain and France and between Great Britain and Germany—were less necessary and more accidental than the Anglo-Russian feud. The imperialist spirit in France arose in political, literary and geographical circles, not in industrial or commercial ones, and it fed upon a morbid craving for prestige which was born from the defeat of 1870. To bring the dream into the realm of reality, leadership and opportunity were needed. Ferry, who gained the protectorate over Tunisia (1881) and over Annam and Tonkin in Indo-China (1885) provided the first, and Bismarck the second, on the ground that he was anxious to give his defeated enemy 'satisfaction in all possible directions except that of the Rhine'. That the advance of the tricolour in North Africa would cause anger in Rome (there were more Italian settlers in Tunisia than French), and that advances almost anywhere would cause apprehension in London, made German generosity suspect. When France and England are at each other's throats, said the

[27] Earl of Ronaldshay, *Life of Lord Curzon* (3 vols., 1928) I, p. 282.
[28] Craig, op. cit., p. 11.
[29] Chung-Fu Chang, *The Anglo-Japanese Alliance* (1931), p. 85.

French ambassador at Berlin, Bismarck will 'rub his hands and swear that he never wanted anything but concord'. The peasants and the lesser bourgeosie, who constituted the vast majority of Frenchmen, were unmoved by glowing mirages on far horizons; significantly, in this century of emigration, the French were stay-at-home patriots. Leroy-Beaulieu could evoke a romantic *frisson* with his declaration, in 1874, that 'either France becomes a great African power or, in a century or two, she will be a secondary power in Europe',[30] but deserts and jungles and their inhabitants were no substitute for the blue line of the Vosges and the fellow-countrymen of the two lost provinces. 'I have lost two children and you offer me twenty domestic servants', cried Déroulède. Thus it was, in the words of a contemporary, that 'the country saw its aversion for colonies and its overseas empire grow at the same time by a parallel progression'.

As a possible policy—though not, perhaps, as a nationalist dream —the imperialist idea in France died on 21 March, 1899, when a convention with England ratified the failure of Marchand's expedition to Fashoda. France got nothing: no territory, no conference to discuss the Egyptian question. How it had been possible for republican politicians to decide on such a mission (this was in November, 1894), to persist in spite of Grey's specific warning that it would be 'an unfriendly act', and to send a second expedition when the first had broken down, knowing all the while that the navy could not fight, passes comprehension. But a lesson was learned in time. Just as England and Russia were to settle their differences after each had faced the bitterness of imperial disaster, so too did France and Italy, for Italy had lost an army in an Abyssinian ambush three years before Fashoda; this understanding with Italy was soon followed by one with England.

In the colonial sphere, where nations were not fighting for existence and where there were alternative avenues of action, a compromise could always be devised. In 1900, France agreed to turn a benevolent eye on Italian ambitions in Tripolitania, in return for support over Morocco; in 1904, France left Egypt to England and abandoned her rights in the Newfoundland fisheries, England in return leaving Morocco and other African possibilities to France; in 1907, Great Britain and Russia balanced out their conflicting demands in Tibet, Afghanistan and Persia. These were all real interests that were being bartered, but not vital ones. German imperialism was more difficult to assuage, as its basis was not interest, but pride. As we have seen,

[30] S. H. Roberts, *The History of French Colonial Policy, 1870–1925* (1929; reprinted one vol., 1963), p. 18.

for shabby reasons of internal policy and to suit his European designs, Bismarck had coolly moved into the colonial fracas in 1884, unleashing passions which he did not share. After his fall, these passions crept into policy-making; they came to constitute a shadowy, lurid imperialism, not in the sense that they were directed towards building up a realistic structure of overseas territories, but because they constituted a will-to-power, a far-ranging vision of *Weltpolitik*, whose limits could not be foreseen and whose demands might become insatiable.

VI

Unluckily for the reputation of Germany, her struggle for national unity was belated, so that historians have been able to speak of her nationalism as a sinister deviant from a comparatively respectable tradition. It was the confined nationalism of the power State, lacking the messianic universalism which cast a halo over French revolutionary expansionism;[31] it was a peculiar accretion around the 'hard crystal' of militaristic Prussianism;[32] it was a derivative from Romanticism, which regards the nation as a 'natural, primitive organism', unlike the nationalism of France, Italy and Poland, based upon 'spiritual community' formed by the 'voluntary association of free men';[33] it was a passionate sentiment which, by the accidents of history, especially in 1848, became divorced from the love of liberty.[34] There is truth in all of these views, though one must concede that, up to the very outbreak of war in 1914, no one in the German General Staff or in the Wilhelmstrasse had seriously planned a conquest of Europe such as Napoleon had nearly achieved with the aid of the 'spiritual community' of free Frenchmen.

Germany continued to be unlucky when nationalism moved into its imperialistic phase, for her imperial ambitions reached their apogee at a time when other nations were becoming disillusioned and cautious; she was unfortunate too in having a plentiful supply of humourless philosophers and generals who prosaically systematized floating visions of sombre Wagnerian greatness until they took on the air of official prospectuses. 'World Power or Destruction', said General Bernhardi in 1911, in a book that ran into six editions

[31] P. Geyl, 'The Historical Background of the Idea of European Unity', *Encounters in History* (1963), pp. 378–84.
[32] A. Cobban, *National Self-Determination* (1944), p. 8.
[33] Ch. Pouthas, 'The Revolutions of 1848', *N.C.M.H.* X (1960), p. 391.
[34] H. Kohn, *The Age of Nationalism* (1962), pp. 4–5, 11–12. Note especially the quotation from John Stuart Mill, *Westminster Review*, April 1849.

immediately. Every healthy organism must expand, argued Professor Dr Ernst Hasse of the Pan-German League in his *Deutsche Politik* (1905), so that Germany would draw to itself all the German-speaking peoples of Europe, and the Swiss and the Dutch, she would establish her supremacy over Poles, Czechs and Magyars, and would extend her influence in S. America, Africa, Morocco and the Near East.[35] It is difficult to assess the influence of this propaganda. Before the War, the Pan-German League never had more than 22,000 members and its highest total of deputies in the *Reichstag*, taking all parties together, was 34 (out of 397); on the other hand, numerous professors, and Kardoff the great industrialist were on its Central Council, and the Emperor himself led the way in proclaiming the necessity for thinking in terms of 'a world horizon'.

When the actual content of German ambitions is examined in more detail, they turn out to be strangely lacking in precision, a fact which enabled the Germans to preserve a self-righteous complacency about aims which were regarded by everyone else with the deepest suspicion. The idea of a *Mitteleuropa* existed, either as a union of all Germans or as an economic entity, so that other nations could well believe that Bismarck's *Kleindeutsch* settlement was meant to be but a temporary stage on the path to new greatness: as Max Weber said, 1871 was 'a beginning, not an end'.[36] Yet *Weltpolitik* and *Mitteleuropapolitik* were contradictory, and the Kaiser knew it. When war came in 1914, the Central Powers had no official war aims, though the way in which the public mind was setting may be gauged from Friedrich Naumann's *Mitteleuropa* (October 1915), the greatest publishing success since Bismarck's memoirs.[37] Naumann's idea of a federation of Central Europe around a German 'nucleus' was defensive, to form an impregnable barrier against Russia; it was only after the war began, during the eastern campaigns, that Germany became bewitched by the spectacle of the vast resources that could be plundered from a disintegrating Russia, and *Osteuropa*, Hitler's dream of *Lebensraum* in the east, took root in the minds of industrialists, and generals like Ludendorff. Dreaming of world power, the men who ruled Germany were compelled to think in terms of acquisitions in Europe that would form a basis for an empire that equalled Great Britain, Russia or the United States in its command

[35] M. S. Wertheimer, *The Pan-German League, 1870–1914* (1924), p. 46. A. Kruck, *Geschichte des Alldeutschen Verbandes, 1890–1939* (1954), considers that Wertheimer underestimated the League's influence.

[36] G. Barraclough, 'German Unification: an Essay in Revision', *Historical Studies*, IV (1963), p. 65.

[37] H. C. Meyer, *Mitteleuropa in German Thought and Action, 1815–1945* (1955), p. 206.

of potential resources. Yet, until war came, no one knew, they did not know themselves, what they were going to try to get. Instead of defining their objectives they 'gambled on general changes in the entire status quo',[38] arousing universal apprehension.

In areas of the world where German ambitions clashed with British, a similar disproportion between the vastness of the vague, potential menace and the limitation of the concrete objectives which any reasonable statesman could pursue, is apparent. Germany was acquiring solid interests in the Near East; from 1880 to 1910, her share in the Turkish debt rose from 5 per cent to 20 per cent, and from being fifteenth in the list of traders to the Ottoman Empire, she became second; further east, there were possibilities of investment in railways and in irrigation works, for as Dr Sprenger pointed out in 1886, Babylon had been 'the richest land in ancient times'.[39] But high-sounding strategic talk about 'Berlin-Bagdad', the Kaiser's ludicrous Jerusalem speech of 1898, declaring himself the friend of 300,000,000 Moslems, and finally, the arrival of German military experts in Constantinople combined to give legitimate interests a reckless flavour of aggression. A German understanding with France and Russia in 1895 (to deprive Japan of the fruits of her victory over China) was a policy contrived to entangle potential European foes in Far-Eastern puzzles, a policy whose benefits were thrown away two years later by the seizure of Kaio-Chow as a naval base, which aroused English suspicions and committed Germany herself in an area where she ought to have been satisfied to entangle others.

By strict logic, a Germany which acted undramatically in pursuit of her interests would have been a natural ally for Great Britain. The evidence of English trade journals makes it clear that trade rivalry between the two empires did not constitute a threat to peace. Germany, the U.S.A. and Japan were Britain's most dangerous commercial competitors: they were also her most promising markets, and Germany, from 1911, was the best market of all. But the 'natural' course of diplomatic relations between two enormously powerful states whose vital interests clashed nowhere was diverted by the supreme, exhibitionist folly of William II's *Weltpolitik*, the building of a vast and unnecessary navy. Under Admiral Tirpitz, State Secretary of the Imperial Naval Office from 1897, a long-term

[38] L. Dehio, *Germany and World Politics in the Twentieth Century* (Eng. trans. 1959), p. 15. There is a recent and harsh analysis of German ambitions in F. Fischer, *Germany's Bid for World Power* (1961, Eng. trans. 1965).
[39] W. O. Henderson, 'German Economic Penetration of the Middle East, 1870–1914', *Econ. Hist. Rev.* Ser. 1, XVIII (1948), p. 56.

ship-building programme began. When Britain launched the *Dreadnought* in 1906, all previous battleships were rendered obsolete, and the naval race became desperate. For Germany, a fleet was a luxury: for Britain, it was a question of survival. No one at Berlin expected to be able to pin down the British battle-fleet and conquer an overseas empire; the object, according to Tirpitz's 'risk theory', was diplomatic blackmail, and in the mind of the Emperor the whole project was a superb gesture of power. As any intelligent politician could have guessed, the blackmail misfired and had the effect of bringing Great Britain to discussions with France and Russia, while money was wasted that could have been spent on the armies. If the Germans had invested in land forces only, says A. J. P. Taylor, 'they might have won British neutrality and would certainly have won the continental war'.[40]

If imperialism is defined as the 'disposition on the part of a state to unlimited forcible expansion',[41] one might say that the movement reached its ultimate point of absurdity in the *Flottenpolitik* of Wilhelmian Germany—a proclamation of a will to domination when there was, in fact, no one to dominate. It was the nemesis Kipling had feared for his own country, the drunkenness of power, 'such boastings as the Gentiles use'. Whether the Lord of Hosts was also forgotten does not concern us; what had been forgotten was clear—the balance of forces in Europe upon which Germany's safety ultimately depended.

VII

Bismarck would never have embarked upon a long-drawn feud with England, and if he had felt obliged to quarrel, it would have been part of a manoeuvre to use Asiatic and colonial issues to persuade France to forget Sedan or Russia to remember the Crimea. But such dividends could accrue only to a Germany which was manifestly peaceful in its intentions, and under William II foreign policy was braggart, covetous and unpredictable. The Emperor, someone said, was 'like a cat in a cupboard', liable to leap in any direction when a door was opened. With his withered arm and his inferiority-superiority complex, his neurotic sensitivity barely protected by his bristling military panoply, with his brilliant, incisive instability and his lack of common sense, William II had no idea how to win friends and

---

[40] A. J. P. Taylor, *The Struggle for Mastery in Europe* (1954), p. 461.

[41] Schumpeter's definition (*Imperialism and the Social Classes*, p. 7), but omitting the prefatory word 'objectless' in view of Murray Green's criticism of the logic of Schumpeter's argument (*Social Research*, XIX (1952), pp. 453–6).

wrong ideas about how to influence people. He genuinely believed that his suggestion that England concede victory to the Boers in the spirit she had conceded victory to Australia in the Test Match[42] would be welcomed; he convinced himself that by filling the North Sea with his battleships he could make the English respect him, then love him. To do justice to the Kaiser, however, his spectacular irresponsibility was less harmful to his country than the carefully pondered blunders of his advisers. Holstein, with patriotic assiduity, presided over the collapse of Bismarck's system without realizing what was at stake; Bülow, behind his theatrical façade of carefully rehearsed speeches allowed diplomatic *gaffes* to accumulate, the most dangerous being his approval of the letter of the Chief of the General Staff guaranteeing support to Austria in January 1909; Kiderlen-Wächter sent the stupid ultimatum to Russia about Bosnia and the *Panther* to Agadir with the schoolboy bravado which had inspired him, in early days, to lead an anti-German mob in Copenhagen to attack the *wrong* embassy. But to do justice to all of them, the Kaiser and his advisers, one must add that, with Bismarck's departure, genius would have been needed to reconstruct the bases of foreign policy, for he alone could have kept both Austria and Russia together in orbit around Berlin, and probably even he could not have continued to do so much longer. Once France and Russia drew together, German foreign policy lost its freedom of manoeuvre, and these changed circumstances showed in high relief the incompetence of its directors and the folly of their rhetoric and brusque excursions.

The Franco-Russian alliance was desired by France and reluctantly accepted by Russia. 'The tree is planted', said Ribot after the negotiations of August 1891, but it was not until December 1893 that the government at St Petersburg finally ratified the military convention of 1892, after a delay of ten months. 'Strasburg and Metz to Germany means, in the next war, that the French must necessarily be on our side', said a Russian diplomat, implying that his country could afford to wait. This was not true in the financial sense, however, for Paris had become the only source for loans. The savings of democrats, one might add, could be borrowed with an easier conscience after the *Ralliement*, when the Third Republic began to look respectable—until November '92, when the Panama scandal broke. It also seemed doubtful if Russia could afford to wait for an ally against England, for links between Great Britain and the Triple Alliance were forming, revealed in July 1890, when Heligoland was given to Germany in exchange for Zanzibar, and in June of the

42 P. Magnus, *King Edward VII* (1964), p. 264.

following year when the Mediterranean agreement with Italy was referred to in the Italian Parliament. Thus the Tsar became doubly anxious to be certain that Germany would hold back Austria from adventures, but after Bismarck's fall, the German government had refused to renew the secret treaty of 1887, and by the summer of 1893 was devising a new army law to cope with the danger of 'war on two fronts'. 'It was the German policy', wrote Langer, 'that drove Russia into the arms of France';[43] his point is, not that William II and Holstein were mistaken in believing that they could no longer continue the juggling act which the Reinsurance Treaty involved, but that the game was lost when they got rid of the Iron Chancellor. As a challenge to the solid Austro-German front, a Franco-Russian understanding was in the nature of things; the inefficiency of German diplomacy is revealed, not so much in the failure to prevent or delay this understanding, as in the unsubtle policies over a longer period by which the French and Russian governments were encouraged to consolidate their alliance once it had been concluded.

It is true that the French did not give up hopes of recovering Alsace-Lorraine, and that they regarded Germany as their pre-destined enemy—all the more so because their old ideas of a land of romantic dreamers and mild scholars had been destroyed in 1870, when, said Flaubert, we saw 'the invasion of Doctors of Letters breaking mirrors with pistol shots and stealing clocks'.[44] Even so, the idea of *revanche* played a subordinate part in French policy and stirred public opinion only to a limited extent. There were signs that the inhabitants of the two stolen provinces were losing their enthusiasm to return, for the Catholics of Alsace detested the anti-clerical ministries in Paris, the new metallurgical industry of Lorraine was tied up with German enterprises, and exporters of wine and textiles were doing well in the German market. In 1898, there were twelve 'autonomist' deputies (as against 'protesting' ones) returned to the *Reichstag*, whereas in 1890 there had been only four. There were signs too that Frenchmen generally were unwilling to resort to the gamble of war to redeem their lost compatriots; they were aware of the dangers of pitting a population of 40 millions against one of 67 millions in a more highly industrialized country, and they feared militarism, which might undermine the Republic. *Faites un Roi, sinon faites la paix* (1913) was the title of a pamphlet by Sembat, the socialist millionaire. The climate of opinion was at once passionate and realistic, and the press fairly reflected the views of the mass of

---

[43] Langer, op. cit., p. 183.
[44] Cit. C. Digeon, *La crise allemande de la pensée française, 1870–1914* (1959), p. 168.

ordinary people: that *revanche* was to be desired, but that no amount of glory could compensate for the horrors of war.[45]

Public opinion, therefore, was not pressing to make the Russian alliance into a conspiracy for revenge. Essentially, it was a guarantee of security, a precaution against the possibility that Germany (as had seemed likely in 1875 and in 1886–7) would embark upon a preventive war. Over the Armenian massacres of 1895 and the Greco-Turkish war of 1897, France made it clear to Russia that diplomatic support was all that could be expected, and that was all Russia gave to France over Fashoda. Up to 1899, theirs was a passive alliance, regarded by both sides as a last resort against the ultimate danger; then, in that year, Delcassé persuaded the Tsarist Government to add to the aims of the agreement the maintenance of 'the equilibrium between European governments', and in the following two years there were military staff talks and new loans were arranged to develop Russian strategic railways. If Bismarck had still been in control, he would have spent the past seven years in reassuring Russia and in ensuring that her alliance with France was directed mainly against England: his successors had spent their time devising a naval policy calculated to drive England into the arms of France and towards a grudging understanding with Russia.

VIII

The crisis of German fortunes came in 1904–5, when the Tsar was fighting his disastrous war with Japan. The situation held two logical possibilities: either winning Russian good-will by neighbourly sympathy, or striking down France while her ally was helpless. William II had the good sense to pursue the first and most civilized policy, but Holstein forced his Emperor into the Moroccan crisis of 1905 without being able to bring about the preventive war which alone could have 'justified' a sensational foray into sabre-rattling. The Conference of Algeciras, which wound up this episode, revealed Germany's unpopularity, for only Austria-Hungary supported her. Just as fear of isolation made France dependent on the Tsarist Empire, sapped by revolutionary agitations, so fear made Germany dependent on the Habsburg Monarchy, which was liable to disintegration under the centrifugal tensions of its nationalities. As Austria became more necessary to Germany, so the control of the alliance began to slide from Berlin to Vienna. Thus those who should have

[45] See E. M. Carroll, *French Public Opinion and Foreign Affairs 1870–1914* (1931). For the German adventure of Tangiers as swinging French opinion towards war see Digeon, op. cit., pp. 492 ff.

led because they were strongest and because they had most to lose, became the followers and, in the end, went down to destruction with the weak and reckless.

The national problems of the Habsburg Monarchy, which the alliance system made into the problems of all Europe, were grave, but only one was urgent. The Poles (10 per cent of the population) had little hope, for their subjection was a bond of union between three empires; the Roumanians (6·4 per cent) had no great external protector; the Italians (2 per cent) were too few; the Czechs were numerous (12·6 per cent) but willing to be patient if allowed concessions, like those of Count Taaffe (1879–93), whose aim was 'to keep all the nationalities in a balanced state of mild dissatisfaction'.[46] The urgent threat was posed by the Southern Slav problem. 'As long as the Catholic pro-imperial Croats, with their "military frontier" traditions against the Turks, had the upper hand an intra-empire solution . . . was not entirely beyond the limits of possibility', writes Kann;[47] but the monarchy had sacrified the Croats to the Magyars in 1849, and again in 1868. In 1905, it was proclaimed in public meetings that 'Croats and Serbs are one people' (the Slovenes were less active), and two years later, when Magyar was made the sole language in use on the Hungarian railways, even in Croatia, the Southern Slavs openly talked of their great hope of escaping to join Serbia.

Then, in 1908, came the fatal blunder by which the government at Vienna flung down its challenge to the Slavs—the annexation of Bosnia-Herzegovina. So much for Serbia becoming a 'Piedmont': it was the Dual Monarchy which would absorb any Southern Slavs that were not spoken for. The annexation was a unilateral action which, in Grey's words, 'struck at the roots of all good international order',[48] and it was a step taken in circumstances which constituted a peculiar affront to Russia, the protector of the Slavs of the dispersion. In 1897 and 1903, Austria-Hungary and Russia had made very sensible mutual arrangements to avoid clashes over Balkan affairs; suddenly, this new-found concord vanished in the course of a dramatic public duel between the two foreign ministers which lost nothing of its tragi-comic intensity from the contrast between their two personalities—Izvolsky, intriguing and vain, who 'strutted on

---

[46] But the Czechs were worried by the alliance with Germany once the Franco-Russian alliance was concluded (Elizabeth Wiskemann, *Czechs and Germans* (1938), pp. 46–7).

[47] R. A. Kann, *The Habsburg Empire* (1957), pp. 52–3.

[48] J. P. T. Bury, 'International Relations, 1900–12', *N.C.M.H.* XII (1960), p. 322.

little lacquered feet', surprisingly and scandalously outwitted by Aehrenthal, 'an unwieldly man, with heavy hapless jaws, a stubble head of hair and sad turbot eyes'.[49] Russia, evicted from the Far East by Japan, had swung back into European affairs only to be rendered ridiculous; the Tsar would not dare to lose prestige again where Slav affairs were concerned, and Izvolsky spent the rest of his career trying to engineer revenge. Matters were made worse by the action of Germany, which forced Russia to accept the Austrian coup by the despatch of a gratuitous ultimatum. Yet Aehrenthal had given Bülow only a month's notice of his intentions and deserved to be disowned by Berlin, as he would have been in days before German foreign policy had lost its grasp of principles, and the tail had started wagging the dog. To crown his folly, Bülow approved a letter of the Chief of the German General Staff to his opposite number in Vienna, giving an assurance that the army would prevent Russian intervention. The great German war machine would underwrite the gambling risks of Vienna. It was a deadly precedent.

IX

At the time of the diplomatic crisis of 1909, the phrase a 'war machine', to us a gruesome cliché, served as an exact description of something terrifying and new, the transformation of man's oldest occupation by the application of the methods and materials of the Industrial Revolution. In 1830, the world's battle fleets were little changed from those of Nelson's day[50]—wooden sailing ships firing broadsides almost within hailing distance—and armies still relied on the smooth-bore flint-lock musket, firing two rounds a minute and accurate up to fifty yards. Fifty years later, navies had iron-clad steam-driven ships with heavy guns firing explosive shells, and by 1906, battleships were becoming floating artillery platforms with huge 12-inch guns mounted in turrets—as a counter to them, submarines were being built and mines and torpedoes were being used. Meanwhile, armies had been equipped with repeating, magazine-fed rifles, artillery had improved to the point where it could break up infantry concentrations at 7000 yards, and the machine-gun had been invented.

[49] H. Nicolson, *Sir Arthur Nicolson, first Lord Carnock* (1930), pp. 216, 265.
[50] M. Lewis, 'Armed forces and the art of war: Navies', *N.C.M.H.* X (1960), p. 274. For what follows about armies see T. S. Ropp, *War in the Modern World* (1959), Cyril Falls, *A Hundred Years of War* (1953) and B. H. Liddell Hart, 'Armed forces and the art of war: Armies', *N.C.M.H.* X, pp. 302–30.

It was not, however, the improved devices for killing which transformed the art of war, so much as the improved methods of transportation. The French Revolution had invented the myth of the people in arms, but it was the railways which made real mass warfare possible, and it was the Germans who carried the idea to its logical extreme with their universal military service, short-term training and rapid mobilization. The Prussian victory of 1866 was the fruit of Moltke's twenty years' reflection upon methods of deploying conscript armies by use of the railway network, and the defeat of France four years later was another triumph for a system which moved up three armies in eighteen days against an enemy whose concentration plans had broken down. With well-drilled precision, German manpower could be switched from peace to war. 'I *was* going in the middle of September . . . to Ammergau to see the Miracle Play,' wrote an English visitor in 1870, 'but the chief person is taken off to serve in the artillery, with Judas Iscariot as his superior officer.'[51] Of necessity, the other continental countries followed the German lead, and among the great powers only Great Britain and the U.S.A. retained voluntary enlistment. Thus, while standing armies were huge and were getting still bigger, they were only part of the vast forces that would be available to the generals within a few weeks of the first shot being fired. Once anyone issued a mobilization order, therefore, everyone must do so, and a state whose arrangements were swift and effective was not likely to allow a slow and inefficient rival to erode its advantage. So mobilization meant war.

What effect had these new conditions upon strategy and tactics? Napoleon's principle, that a commander's objective is the destruction of the enemy in the field, was carried on, with refinements, by theorists like the Swiss Jomeni (1829) and the German Clausewitz (1832). But Clausewitz's doctrine of rapid concentration and surprise seemed to be limited by technical considerations to the actual machinery of mobilization, for in this period between the steam locomotive and the effective use of the petrol engine, armies which could be rapidly amassed at the railheads were dependent entirely upon horse transport for further deployment, and were less mobile than Napoleon's had been. The generals seem to have paid little attention to the possibilities of long-range reconnaissance or raids to disrupt mobilization; they thought in terms of mass attack, so that the striking of the first blow became all-important. It was assumed, officially at any rate, that the next war would be

[51] T. W. Reid, *The Life, Letters and Friendships of Richard Monckton Milnes, first Lord Houghton* (2 vols., 1890) II, p. 232.

short;[52] the elder Moltke's warning, given in 1870, that hostilities might last for seven years, was ignored, and Bloch's six volumes, published at Paris from 1898–1900, predicting stalemate and the horrors of trench warfare, were regarded as sensational fiction. Thus everyone had plans for the total mobilization of men, and no-one had plans for the total mobilization of economic resources, and military thinking was geared to the achievement of decisive advantages in the first weeks of fighting. This meant that in a crisis, the time available to the diplomats would, very probably, be cut short. Once a certain point was reached, the military would clamour to take over and run things according to their timetable.

Of all the military timetables, the German was the most drastic. The German Army at this period has been called a 'State within the State'. Parliament, except by blindly-imposed financial restraints which would have been generally regarded as unpatriotic, had no control, and the middle-class officers who swelled the battalions were won over to the aristocratic traditions of the caste they had joined: an officer was 'his imperial master's *man* in the old German sense of the word'.[53] It is against this background of an army regarding itself as beyond the control of society that the German war plan, drawn up by the General Staff in complete independence of the politicians, can be understood. Between 1891 and 1905, Count Alfred von Schlieffen,[54] the Chief of the General Staff, perfected the design of an all-out onslaught on France through Belgium and Luxemburg; he appears to have made light of the political dangers of violating Belgian neutrality and of the political wisdom of earlier war plans which gave priority to an attack on Russia without any attempt to hold new territories. By the Schlieffen plan, any Balkan fracas which brought Russia and Austria to mobilization point would compel the German generals to advocate a march on Brussels and Paris; the planners of the General Staff had left no viable alternative, no escape hatch for the negotiators, and the politicans were allowed no say in the Army's designs to preserve the Fatherland. In the last resort, it was not Germany's swashbuckling imperialism which menaced the world, but its pitiless determination to have a hundred per cent security.

As it was, over the Bosnian affair of 1908–9, Russia did not

[52] The younger Moltke, German Chief of Staff in 1914, knew otherwise (Corelli Barnett, *The Swordbearers* (1963), pp. 33–4). Yet the German plan was unchanged.

[53] G. A. Craig, *The Politics of the Prussian Army, 1640–1945* (1956), p. 236.

[54] For the Schlieffen Plan, G. Ritter, 'The Military and Problems in Germany', *Journal of Central European Affairs*, XVII (1957), pp. 259–71, and 'Le Plan Schlieffen', *Rev. d'hist. mod. et contemp.* VII (1960), pp. 215 ff.

mobilize; if and when she was driven to do so, the structure of alliances and the pattern of military planning were there to ensure that the lights would go out all over Europe and ten million men would die.

CHAPTER XXIII

MEN AND MACHINES

I

In these last two lectures we revert to the formula with which we began: 'Men, Machines and Freedom.' Could the growth in population and the rise of a machine civilization be combined with an extension in the area of liberty? The problem was part of a wider dilemma which is still with us and may yet destroy us. Long before most people had realized the dynamic possibilities of the Industrial Revolution, Southey had posed the question upon which the future of humanity would depend—

'*Montesinos*: You would make me apprehend, then, that we have advanced in our chemical and mechanical discoveries faster than is consistent with the real welfare of society.

More: You cannot advance in them too fast, provided that the moral culture of the species keep pace with the increase of its material powers. Has it been so?'[1]

II

Though increasing power in the hands of undiminished selfishness is a proper subject for moral reflections, the sudden accession of mastery over natural environment was a gain which western European society could neither renounce nor, except in a limited sense, control: it was something inevitable that could be used for good or for evil. The interlocking and mutually supporting expansion of railways, metallurgy and machine production, the new civilization founded upon steam power and iron, continued according to its own inbuilt logic. Between 1870 and 1910, European coal and iron production tripled, the percentage of iron made into steel rose from about 15 per cent to over 90 per cent, and the output of manufactures generally quadrupled. The means of transportation kept pace with the expansion of production, the railway network almost trebling, and the tonnage of shipping using the ports doubling; this was the era of the Trans-Siberian Railway, the St Gothard and Simplon tunnels (1882, 1906) and the Kiel and Panama canals (1895, 1914).

[1] Robert Southey, *Sir Thomas More: or, Colloquies on the Progress and Prospects of Society* (1829), cit. Raymond Williams, *Culture and Society 1780–1950* (1958), p. 25.

In 1870, the new industrialism had still been a British phenomenon which other nations were enviously imitating. Great Britain then produced more coal and iron, and her cotton industry had more power looms and spindles, than the whole of the rest of the world, and she was the principal maker of the machinery which others bought in the hope of growing rich by following her example. Forty years later, though British coal and iron production had doubled (coal rather more, iron rather less), it was outstripped by that of the United States, and while Germany had not caught up in coal extraction, she was well ahead in iron and, more especially, in steel output; by then, Great Britain had only a third of the power looms that worked in the world's cotton factories, and both the U.S.A. and Germany had surpassed her output of machinery—significantly, while the British sold nearly half their machines abroad, the Germans and Americans were installing most of theirs at home. France was being left far behind; even so, her coal and iron output tripled between 1870 and 1910, and still remained ahead of Russia's. On the eve of the first World War, though America was already the world's leading economic power and there was evidence that Russia would one day become her chief rival, the heartland of the Industrial Revolution was still situated in western Europe, where the greatest collection of riches history had ever recorded awaited the moment when human folly would decree its dissipation.

In 1913, half the trade of the world consisted of the imports and exports of the United Kingdom, France, Belgium, Germany, Holland, Switzerland and Denmark;[2] these countries were closely and profitably interlocked with each other in trade, and around this central core of industry and wealth the network of commerce went out to the primary producers of the world—the U.S.A., India, Malaya, Australia, Russia and China; from the central core capital was exported for investment on the periphery to the extent of £350,000,000 a year. The axis of the internal commerce of western Europe ran between London and Berlin, for Great Britain exported more to Germany than to any other country except India, and bought more from Germany than from anyone else but the U.S.A.,[3] while Germany was the best customer of Belgium, Holland, Switzerland and Norway, as well as of Italy, Russia and Austria-Hungary. After France adopted the Méline tariff in 1881, most countries of

---

[2] Asa Briggs, 'Economic Interdependence and Planned Economies', *N.C.M.H.* XII (1960), p. 502.

[3] First pointed out by J. M. Keynes, *The Economic Consequences of the Peace* (1919), p. 15, cit. D. Thomson, 'The Transformation of Social Life', *N.C.M.H.* XII (1960), p. 44.

Europe, with the exception of Great Britain, Belgium and Holland, abandoned free trade; yet in spite of tariffs the years from 1894 to 1914 saw international trade flowing smoothly—in Professor Asa Brigg's words, this was 'the golden age of economic specialization and exchange'.[4]

The nodal point of the external commerce of western Europe was London, for Great Britain drew two-thirds of its imports from outside Europe, offsetting an adverse balance of trade with the U.S.A. and the Argentine against a favourable balance with India, Turkey and Japan.[5] London was the home of sterling, in which most international financial transactions were conducted, and the centre of insurance and capital advances. From 1896 or so, the sunlight of prosperity shone upon the great industrial and capitalist complex of the Atlantic seaboard, for the depression years were ending and a steady price rise began. The rise had obvious causes—the exploitation of the gold mines of the Transvaal, the extension of banking facilities and the rise of population—and less obvious ones, connected with the way in which inventions tied in with each other to form 'clusters of innovations' that ultimately brought in their profits. Whatever the causes, this limited tendency towards inflation oiled the wheels of business enterprise, and in the dozen years before the War the world trade in manufactured goods doubled, and in primary products increased by two-thirds. The age of steam and iron, disfigured as it was by ugliness and injustice, could provide a single generation with more material goods than all mankind had acquired in all its previous history.

III

This was an astonishing spectacle of progress; yet in retrospect, the significant thing is that within the Industrial Revolution which coal, iron and railways had fostered, developments were taking place which were laying the foundations of what has recently been called the 'new' or the 'second' Industrial Revolution.[6] The motive power for the machines of the new era would be provided by electricity and oil. Siemens invented an industrially viable dynamo in 1867 and Edison the incandescent light bulb rather later; in 1890 the first electric underground railway began to operate in London, and by 1900 electric vacuum cleaners and sewing machines were in use.

[4] Briggs, op. cit., p. 502.
[5] C. Wilson, 'Economic Conditions', *N.C.M.H.* XI (1962), p. 55.
[6] D. Thomson, op. cit., p. 42; G. Barraclough, *Introduction to Contemporary History* (1964), pp. 36 ff.

Germany took the lead in exploiting the potentialities of electricity, as England had exploited those of coal, and was soon exporting hydro-electric machinery, especially to Switzerland and Italy. A beginning was made of tapping the world's underground reservoirs of oil in the eighteen sixties, and from this new fuel began a revolution in transport when the petrol engine and the diesel engine were invented in the 'eighties and 'nineties. By the end of the century there were about 100,000 automobiles and motor cycles in England and something like a fifth of this number in France—there were many more, of course, in America. Three years later a petrol driven aeroplane kept aloft for 59 seconds, and six years later still Blériot flew over the Straits of Dover.

Along with oil and electricity, machine tools and chemicals were to be the bases for the apparently limitless possibilities of the second Industrial Revolution—machines to make more machines, and an endlessly increasing number of new products that became necessities in almost every aspect of life: pharmaceutical materials, dyes, explosives, fertilizers and so on. Invention was now moving forward on a broad front—telephone (1876), wireless, gramophone, bicycles, pneumatic tyres (1889), artificial silk, celluloid, motion pictures, aluminium (produced by the electrolysis of bauxite) and the first plastic (1908); soon, it was no longer going to be a question of trying to give men more of what they already desired, but also of offering them comforts and amusements that they had not so far dreamed of. For the first time, science was being deliberately harnessed to the promotion of industrial progress. The whole history of electricity was an illustration of technological advance derived originally from disinterested experiment, and in Germany especially the chemical industry took the lead in employing research experts rather than leaving advance to disinterested experiment again. It is true, of course, that co-operation between science and industry was still 'haphazard and on a small scale'[7] when viewed from the vantage point of the mid-twentieth century, which has seen the world resources allotted to scientific research doubled between 1930 and 1938, and doubled again from 1938 to 1950. Yet what was happening about 1900 was a pointer to the whole trend of the twentieth century.

When we speak of the beginning of a deliberate alliance between science and technology, to keep the picture in perspective we must remember that scientific research had by now far outrun all possibilities of immediate technological applications. Modern European history is less the story of highly successful materialistic barbarians,

[7] C. F. Carter, 'Economic incentives for and consequences of Technical Invention', in A. C. Crombie (ed.) *Scientific Change* (1963), p. 681.

than of a uniquely brilliant flowering of the intellect in all sorts of ways, but especially in science, whose accidentally useful discoveries, coming to an era industrially prepared to use them, are permanently changing the whole condition of human life. Along with the second Industrial Revolution, the nineteenth century saw what has been called a 'second', and even, a 'third' Scientific Revolution,[8] which may be considered, in crude 'heroic' terms, as linked respectively with the names of Darwin and Clerk Maxwell. After Darwin[9] had established that natural selection has been the chief agent in evolution, Weismann showed the independence of the germ cells from their environment ('a hen is just an egg's way of producing another egg', Samuel Butler commented); De Vries rediscovered Mendel's principles of particulate inheritance; Morgan, in 1910, by experiments with generations of fruit flies, established the nature of mutations— all steps on the way to the modern theory of natural selection operating on the random variations caused by mutation. Clerk Maxwell may be taken as the scientist who laid the foundations of the view of the universe which was to replace Newton's world of indestructible atoms. In the 'nineties, the work of Mme Curie on radio-activity, and of Lorentz and J. J. Thompson on electrons, completed the idea of a new world of sub-atomic particles, and Einstein was soon to add to this the mathematical description of a four-dimensional space-time continuum. But the significance of these new insights for ordinary life was not immediate, and some of their enormous practical possibilities still lie ahead of us, bright sunshine or black shadows on the horizon of our future.

Another development of the late-nineteenth and early-twentieth centuries which foreshadows the pattern of the second Industrial Revolution is the leaguing together of industrial organizations to rationalize their activities and plan their production. Germany led the way with her 'cartels', beginning with the Rhine-Westphalian coal alliance of 1893, organized by Kardoff. This was an 'horizontal' combine: others, like the Krupp complex of mines and metallurgical works running through to arms factories and naval construction yards were 'vertical', attempts to control specific products from the extraction of the raw materials to the buyer's final cheque. Before 1914, the German industrialists were deep in schemes for big-scale planning, and Walther Rathenau was learning, in his father's *Allgemeine Elektrizitäts Gesellschaft*, the biggest industrial company in Europe, the techniques by which he was to transform the German

[8] H. F. Kearney, *Origins of the Scientific Revolution* (1964), pp. 151, 155.
[9] For this summary I have used my friend Professor C. L. Birch's articles in the *Australian Journal of Science*, XXI (2) and XXII (1) (1958–9).

economy into a sort of State-socialism to face the stresses and privations of the first World War.

A world market whose news circulated among buyers and sellers by virtually instantaneous means, big-scale planning at the top of industry, an expanding, probing arc of scientific investigation and a vast reserve of skills and precision tooling to refine and redirect the machines; and, at the bottom of the pyramid, the monotonous, vastly prolific routines of mass production—by 1913, the year in which Ford began his conveyor-belt system, the shape of the future in the era of the second Industrial Revolution could already be foreseen.

IV

'Men, machines and freedom': like the machines, the men were multiplying rapidly. In the second half of the nineteenth century, the population of Europe rose from 266 millions to 401 millions, in spite of a great drain of emigration overseas. The industries of Great Britain and Germany were drawing upon an expanding labour force, as the British population rose, by 1900, to forty millions and the German to fifty-six; France, which in Napoleon's day had been the most populous nation after Russia, by then had fallen slightly behind Great Britain. This population explosion ran parallel to the Industrial Revolution, though the complicated relationship between the two movements was far from being one of cause and effect, for Russia, still on the threshold of industrialization, was growing rapidly. There was, however, a sharp distinction between eastern and western Europe. A decline in fertility which had begun in France (Queen Victoria took only two of her children to Paris on her visit of 1857, to avoid Gallic jests about the 'ménage Anglais'), became general among France's neighbours by the eighteen-seventies, so that on the eve of the first World War, Russia's birth rate was three times higher than that of the West. In industrial Europe, the population continued to rise, not because more people were being born, but because the death rate was falling. In the second half of the nineteenth century, the average expectation of life in France, England and Germany rose by ten years, reaching a point about twenty years higher than the Russian average. The interpretation of statistics of this kind is notoriously difficult, but if any sort of Benthamite 'felicific calculus' is possible, here is the starting point for a discussion of the real progress, in human terms, achieved by the first Industrial Revolution.

The population explosion and the advent of industrialism made this the age of a *Volkerwanderung*—or rather, of an *Auswanderung*—

such as had not been seen since the barbarians overwhelmed the frontier lines of the dying Roman Empire. Through the cadres and patterns within which history is normally comprehended, the moving tides of humanity flowed crosswise, in defiance of structure, and for once, ordinary men could make a decisive choice and change entirely their own fate and the lives of their children. By comparison with our own times, obstacles to migration were few. Most countries did not close their doors to foreigners; after 1870, there was an influx of Germans, continental Jews and Poles into England, especially into London;[10] France, whose indigenous population was growing comparatively slowly, naturalized nearly a million foreigners between 1872 and 1911, and the census of that year showed over a million aliens, mostly Italians and Belgians.[11] Nor did European countries normally prohibit their own people from leaving. The precautions taken by the French government in 1860, the imposition of licensing on emigration agencies in Germany, and the King of Sweden's proclamation warning his subjects against the American Emigrant Company in 1865[12] were limited measures, directed only to discouraging the flight of skilled labour.

It was possible to move to a new country, and railways and steamships made travel quicker, safer and cheaper. Within Europe, the prospect of higher wages and of an escape from the constraints of rural society drew country folk into the new industrial areas, and outside Europe, the opening up of virgin continents set families on the move on longer journeys, especially to America or, for the Russian peasants, Siberia. The pulls of industrial development and of new lands were complementary, not only in the obvious sense that the U.S.A. itself raced into an industrial boom which carried on after the frontier had ended, but also because overseas migration was often the final stage of an uprooting which had begun with a much shorter local move. 'An industrial boom in distant cities', writes the historian of German emigration, referring especially to the one and a half millions who crossed the Atlantic from Germany between 1871 and 1885, 'pressed the countryman to break up housekeeping and leave his community; and once he made the break, he often found his way to America.'[13]

Between 1815 and 1914 over 40 million people left Europe, mostly for North America; the tide of emigration flowed higher after 1880

[10] Carlton J. H. Hayes, *A Generation of Materialism, 1871–1900* (1941), p. 104.
[11] A. M. Carr-Saunders, *World Population* (1936), pp. 145–55.
[12] C. Erikson, *American Industry and the European Immigrant, 1860–85* (1957), pp. 18, 24, 26–7.
[13] M. Walker, *Germany and the Emigration, 1816–1885* (1964), pp. 190–1.

and from 1900 to 1914 the yearly average of sailings to the U.S.A. alone was over a million. Before 1890, most of the emigrants came from northern and western Europe. At certain periods sheer want drove them out of their homes; famine in Germany and Ireland in the 'hungry forties', the Norwegian crop failure of 1847, the spread of large-scale capitalist agriculture on the estates of German aristocrats in the 'fifties, and the grim three years of disastrous crops in Sweden from 1864–7. But the folk who were driven out thus were not, for the most part, people who were normally either starving or improvident, and Emma Lazarus' verses on the base of the Statue of Liberty about the 'poor', the 'huddled masses', the 'wretched refuge of your teeming shore' are hardly suitable as a description of the 'old migration' before 1890. Certainly, it was not the hopeless drifters of city slums who departed. 'Proletization, that final failure, precluded even escape.'[14] And quite apart from famine years, there were periods when huge numbers of enterprising country folk emigrated; from 1871 to 1885, for example, only 13 to 18 per cent of the emigrants from Germany were leaving industrial areas. There is evidence too that the migrants from the English towns, at least in certain periods, included many skilled artisans and 'reading families' who were being 'pulled' to America, not 'pushed'—drawn by letters from friends and propaganda literature, hoping to better themselves in a land where there were more apples rotting in the orchards of Ohio than 'would sink the British fleet'.[15] Nor did the peak periods of emigration always coincide with economic crisis in Europe. Sometimes they coincided with peaks of prosperity, when full bellies made men feel reckless and high wages left a surplus to save for the fares of the family; at other times, there was general prosperity, but the United States looked the most prosperous of all, and relatives who had gone there beforehand felt rich enough to remit to Europe the passage money of those they wished to join them.

Towards the end of the nineteenth century began the 'new migration'; in 1896 the numbers leaving south and south-east Europe were greater than those of the 'old migration' from the north and west, and between 1900 and 1914, 70 per cent of the emigrants came from

[14] Ibid., p. 51.
[15] M. L. Hansen, *The Atlantic Migration* (1945), pp. 152–7. Two-fifths of the British migrants in the 'fifties and 'sixties were skilled artisans (R. Hofstadter, W. Miller and W. Aaron, *The American Republic* (1959) II, p. 171). Of more than 1¼ million British working people who disembarked in America, 1873–1918, over 40 per cent said they had been skilled in trades, and only 25 per cent said they had been unskilled labourers (R. J. Berthoff, *British Immigrants in Industrial America, 1790–1950* (1953), pp. 21–3).

the Slav and Mediterranean countries. Italians leaving their over-taxed homeland, where population had outrun industrial expansion, worshippers of the Uniate Church fleeing from persecution in Russian Poland,[16] Jews escaping from Russian pogroms, Poles of Prussian Poland weary of the struggle against Germanization, Croats abandoning their blackened vineyards after the blight of 1887, Balkan peoples fleeing from the scourge of cholera—here at last were the 'huddled masses yearning to breathe free'. They were arriving in an America which would absorb them and mould them into its own character, a nation which had been founded within the cultural traditions of western Europe and had recruited its citizens for three crucial, formative generations from the same source. By the end of the nineteenth century, a million Europeans were landing on the shores of the U.S.A. every year, and the earlier waves of the vast immigration were multiplying in their new country; in 1900, the total population stood at 76 millions; thirteen years later it was 96½ millions, so that here, in potentiality, was the most powerful nation in the world. This vast, anonymous migration had thrown up no heroes and its records are barren of dramatic incident, but its effects will be remembered long after the achievements of even the greatest nineteenth-century statesmen are forgotten.

V

Some statistics from Germany, in the heyday of its industrial expansion, will illustrate how the first Industrial Revolution drew the rising population into the towns—Europe's internal migration, on a vaster scale even than the movement overseas. In 1890, there were only seven German cities with populations over 200,000, and greater Berlin had about two million inhabitants; by 1910 there were twenty-three towns over 200,000 and Berlin was well over four millions. Perhaps the most overwhelming statistical example, however, is that of the growth of industrial towns in the Ruhr,[17] where between 1871 and 1910, Essen rose from 52,000 to 295,000, Düsseldorf from 69,000 to 359,000, and Dortmund, Duisburg, Hamborn and Wupper-tal in similar proportions—all running into one another in a grim confusion for which the geographer Geddes, in 1915, coined the name 'conurbation'.

What had happened in England tended to happen wherever the new industrialism extended. The monuments of the age of iron and steam

[16] J. Zubrycki, 'Emigration from Poland in the 19th and 20th Centuries', *Population Studies*, VI (3) (1953).
[17] Griffith Taylor, *Urban Geography* (1949), p. 380.

were barbarous enough in their own right—blackened factories, slag heaps, smokestacks, railway lines and stinking canals; great unplanned concentrations of population piling into tenement rows and rent barracks completed a sordid picture, and life in these 'Coketowns', by any humane or aesthetic standard, was appalling. 'Every man for himself', Lewis Mumford has written, 'and the Devil, if he did not take the hindmost, at least reserved for himself the privilege of building the cities.'[18]

Things were not quite so bad, however, as Mumford believes, at least after 1870. By then, governments were enforcing minimum standards of hygiene and building, and police and educational organization was catching up with the crowded masses. Not all factory development took place in seething 'Megalopolis' or in the conurbations which Geddes likened to fungus on the jam, a spore-like life battening on inadequate resources of space, light and air.[19] A town like Toulouse, to which the railways brought tobacco, boot and clothing factories, grew from 52,000 in 1821 to 150,000 in 1906 without losing its agreeable character as a regional, ecclesiastical and university centre.[20] Nor were the big cities the mere 'man-heaps' and 'machine warrens' that figure in Mumford's pages. 'They had large numbers of voluntary organizations, covering a far wider range of specialized interests than was possible in the village or the small town. They were more free of aristocratic "influence"'; they had clubs, institutes, newspapers, music halls, choirs and municipal pride.[21] Before 1914, cars, wireless and refrigerators had not come into general use, the new cinema was a purely urban entertainment, and the railways were more efficient at bringing a range of foodstuffs into big centres than at exchanging them between smaller ones. It was not an ideal age to be living in the country.

The argument has often been put forward that mortality was highest in the towns and that the fertile countryside replenished the unhealthy urban work force; in the late nineteenth century, at least, the truth was more complicated.[22] Expectation of life was lowest in the biggest cities, but no lower than in remote agricultural areas like East Prussia and Finisterre; in coalfields and industrial zones (as distinct from very large cities) the death rates were higher than the national averages earlier on, but by the end of the century were

[18] L. Mumford, *The City in History* (1961), p. 449.
[19] P. Geddes, *Cities in Evolution* (1915), p. 52.
[20] R. E. Dickinson, *The West European City* (1951), pp. 111–16.
[21] Asa Briggs, *Victorian Cities* (1963), pp. 22–3.
[22] For what follows, E. A. Wrigley, *Industrial Growth and Population Change* (1961).

well below them, and it was in agricultural areas nearest to the industrial centres that life expectation was highest. Fertility was lowest in very big cities, but was high in coalfields and industrial places, and it varied widely in the countryside. One might conclude that rural areas were not necessarily healthier than industrial ones, and that if statistics condemn 'Megalopolis', they return a reasonably favourable verdict on 'Coketown'.

By 1900, however, it was clear that western Europe would not tolerate the building of further Coketowns, and that the growth of Megalopolis would be regulated by attempts at scientific planning. For long, the dream of the planned city rising gloriously on its virgin site had pleased men's imaginations, but while L'Enfant could draw up blue prints for Washington and Colonel Light for Adelaide, where could new beginnings be made in the long-settled, thickly populated lands of Europe? In 1898 Ebenezer Howard published *Tomorrow*, his design for a 'garden city' of 30,000 inhabitants; it would need the electricity of the second Industrial Revolution, however, to decentralize industry sufficiently to make his romantic schemes practicable. The urgent problem was to plan for cities that were already immense and still growing, and in the 'sixties, there were three capitals in Europe where a beginning of enlightened planning could be seen—Paris, Brussels and Vienna. In Paris, Haussmann was demolishing slums to put through his new boulevards; in Brussels, the river Senne was being driven underground, and the old mills, tanneries and breweries that had propped up its fetid banks were being replaced by dignified commercial buildings, and a system of zoning and of taxing building materials was pushing population into outer suburbs;[23] in Vienna, the medieval walls were being pulled down and four-fifths of the land recovered was being devoted to parks and public buildings, new bridges over the Danube were being planned, and tax exemptions were allowed on buildings which reached a high architectural standard.

These examples attracted attention. Systematic town-planning legislation began in Sweden in 1874; in Holland an act of 1901 made planning obligatory on all municipalities of over 10,000 souls, and an innocuous, lukewarm planning act was passed by the British Parliament eight years later.[24] But a real beginning of the scientific organization of urban living came in Germany where, wrote F. C. Howe, the American author of *European Cities at Work* (1913), the towns were being built 'as Bismarck perfected the army before Sadowa and Sedan; as the empire is building its warships and

[23] Dickinson, op. cit., pp. 156 ff.
[24] Montague Harris, *Comparative Local Government* (1948), pp. 92–4.

merchantmen'.[25] In Essen, he admired the Krupp housing estates, in Dresden and Frankfurt the railway stations, in Cologne the deliberate eccentricity of the pattern of suburban streets, while Düsseldorf, since Dr Marx became burgomaster in 1898, had been made into 'the garden City of Germany'. On a more extensive scale than their English counterparts, the cities of Germany had adopted schemes of 'municipal socialism', shedding benefits and making profits out of publicly owned gas and water works, tramways, labour exchanges, pawnshops, theatres and symphony orchestras. Municipal authorities in America had not sufficient independent powers, and in England they had not sufficient control of the big landlords who owned the ground rents, to be able to press on with reforms so swiftly, nor did their elected councils have the force and pushfulness of the despotic German burgomasters. Some dividends, then, accrued to Germany from her lack of progress towards true democracy. Tocqueville's dictum, that 'town meetings are to liberty what primary schools are to science'[26] was an uncomfortable ideal for the mass industrial society.

The inventions of the first Industrial Revolution had been more suited to increase production than to contrive a cadre for civilized living, but planning was now beginning in the wastes of urban industrialism at a time when the circle of invention was widening. Automobiles and electric trams and trains, and electric power for machinery would henceforward make it possible to build residential suburbs apart from the factories, and to combine town and country modes of living. The banal and monstrous era of architecture, which had lasted for most of the nineteenth century, with its neo-Gothic churches, neo-Classical counting houses, and medieval turrets and Doge's palaces packed with solicitors and shipping clerks, came to an end; so too did some fearful experiments in preciosity by a school of reformers at Munich. The functional beauties of the iron frames of the Crystal Palace and the steel girders of the Forth Bridge and the Eiffel Tower became an architectural ideal. By 1900, steel and reinforced concrete (and the invention, in America, of the elevator) had made possible the first experiments in the massive and daring simplicities of 'modern' architecture. Skylines and ground-plans were changing, and men could now glimpse the shape of the cities of the future, of the second Industrial Revolution.

[25] F. C. Howe, *European Cities at Work* (1913), p. 4.
[26] A. de Tocqueville, *Democracy in America* (Eng. trans. ed. Phillips Bradley, 1953) I, p. 61.

VI

What share of western Europe's increasing riches went to the ordinary man? This is a safer question than more sweeping variants that mention 'happiness', a rare commodity with its own laws that defy both logic and statistics. In broad terms, the answer is obvious: the dividends of industrialization were coming in for everybody, but their incidence was uneven and fluctuating, and the Socialists were right when they said that the shareout was unequal.

Real wages in Great Britain rose by 50 per cent between 1850 and 1900. In Germany, during the comparable period of growth from 1871 to 1913, they rose by 64 per cent—during this time, the consumption of sugar per head increased nearly fourfold and the deposits in savings banks multiplied twelvefold.[27] Even so, the German workers still had not caught up with the English standard of living;[28] indeed, it was partly at their expense that their country was accumulating the force to overhaul and pass Great Britain in the industrial race. Though the actual benefits of increasing specialization and improvements in social organization far exceeded those that are reflected only in increased purchasing power, it is also true that, by whatever criterion the total wealth of western Europe is reckoned, the wage-earner's share was disproportionately low. According to Money's *Riches and Poverty* (1905–6) thirty-eight million people in Great Britain had only half of the national income, while one and a quarter millions enjoyed a third of it.[29] Parallel figures for Germany were more startling still. The increased purchasing power which had fallen to the working class was also very unevenly distributed among its members. Industrial employees were, generally speaking, better off than those in agriculture,[30] and the 'aristocracy' of industrial workers, the skilled men who were indispensable to the machines, also did much better than the rank and file majority of wage-earners. Though progress was continuous, sometimes it became exasperatingly slow. The depression years of the 'seventies and 'eighties, which by definition had been bad for business, had seen an improvement in working-class conditions, for prices fell without a corresponding fall in wages.[31] In the 'nineties, for most workers things continued to improve, the rise of wages in

[27] E. S. Pinson, *Modern Germany* (1954), p. 249.
[28] F. A. Ogg, *Social Progress in Contemporary Europe* (1912), pp. 314–15.
[29] J. H. Clapham, *An Economic History of Modern Britain* IV (1951), p. 497.
[30] C. P. Kindleberger, *Economic Growth in France and Britain, 1851–1950* (1964), pp. 229–34.
[31] H. Heaton, *Economic History of Europe* (rev. ed. 1948), pp. 666–7.

Germany being particularly steep. Thereafter, prices rose and incomes tended to become stagnant, so that real wages moved up slowly or, sometimes, declined.[32] For all the benefits it was conferring, the economic process worked mercilessly; there were bitter battles between capital and labour, and there were, occasionally, waves of mass unemployment.

Yet the basic statistics of sheer existence are in favour of this harshly competitive society as against the small-scale, less impersonal social organizations of previous centuries: men were eating better and living longer. With the invention and perfection of evaporation, refrigeration and canning,[33] the new means of transport, which had flooded western Europe with the grain of the American prairies, now became capable of bringing in a whole varied range of products from other lands, like beef from the Argentine and fruits from the tropics. About the same time, in the 'seventies, margarine was introduced, and vegetable and whale oils from overseas were used in vast quantities to provide the poor man's substitute for butter. In 1889, when French farmers at the first International Agricultural Congress complained that 'a sack of corn can be moved from America to Europe more cheaply than from Dijon to Paris',[34] it had seemed that European agriculture must necessarily decline. What happened, however was that a successful balance was achieved between the potentialities of west European farming and those of more distant lands. From 1896, the price of grain, which had fallen to half the average level of the years 1851–75, started to rise again, and continental European agriculture began to reap the benefits of the rationalization which the depression years had imposed on it— mechanization, greatly increased use of fertilizers, drawn especially from industrial waste, and the switching of resources to market gardening and the production of milk, meat and sugar beet. In Denmark and the Low Countries rural co-operatives co-ordinated the efforts of primary producers, while in Germany the revival was dominated by the big capitalist farmers, who between 1890 and 1914 almost doubled the productivity of their acreage. The people of the industrial cities, drawing a great variety of foodstuffs both from the rural hinterland and from a wide range of different climatic zones overseas, were—in the midst of their grey and unlovely surroundings— better fed than the mass of men had ever been before.

[32] Ibid., p. 669; Clapham, op. cit., p. 73.
[33] Each the result of a series of inventions and experiments throughout the century (R. J. Forbes and E. J. Dijksterhuis, *A History of Science and Technology* (2 vols., 1963) II, pp. 500–5).
[34] M. Baumont, *L'Essor industriel et l'impérialisme colonial* (1949), p. 422.

They were better clothed and equipped too; perhaps only those who have never been without them would sacrifice a plentiful supply of cheap cotton shirts, woollen stockings and metal and china utensils for fresh air and rural landscapes. Fear of contagion and Christian, humanitarian and aesthetic sentiments had stirred up the governing classes to hygienic reforms, so that the vast nomad encampments of the cities were now caught within a web of official edicts about scavenging, sewage, and water supplies. Here probably, was the most important contribution to the reduction of the death rate, and these essential reforms had been made before medicine became a science.[35] In 1870, the means by which typhus and cholera are transmitted were still unknown, and the theory that bad smells cause disease was widely believed; with the exception of mercury for syphilis and quinine for malaria, few effective remedies were in use. The way had been prepared for future advance, however, for both dentistry and nursing had become professions in their own right, medical investigators had become skilled in statistical analysis of mortality (that sure lever to force governments to reform), Lister had begun using antiseptics in surgery, and Pasteur was doing work on putrefaction which was later to lead to the germ theory of disease. In the twenty years after 1890, scientific medicine began; aspirin and the first anti-biotic, Salvarsan, were marketed, forerunners of a stream of new drugs from the chemists' laboratories, vitamins and hormones were discovered, the rôle of mosquitoes in carrying malaria became known, and the usefulness of X-rays for medical diagnosis was tested.

As a result of an accumulation of improvements in food, clothes and hygiene (and, ironically, on the eve of a war which was to kill the best young manhood of the continent), the expectation of life in western Europe was fifteen years higher than it had been in 1850. By now, the machinery of public order was more effective, elementary education was universal and compulsory, and governments had followed the example of England in factory legislation and of Germany in social insurance. The factory, grim as it remained, was by now conceding to the workers a degree of leisure—a predictable pattern of free hours—which had been unknown in the days of peasant agriculture and cottage industry. The railways made seaside weekends possible and, in Catholic Europe, pilgrimages to Rome and Lourdes. England, which had exported its industrial revolution, also began to export the antidote for some of its evils, team games,

[35] R. H. Shryock, 'Medicine and Society in the 19th Century', *Cahiers d'histoire mondiale*, V (1959), pp. 116–46; D. McKie, 'Science and Technology', *N.C.M.H.* XII (1960), pp. 109–10.

more especially association football, to be played, or to be watched as gladiatorial shows.[36] Between 1863 and 1886 national associations were founded in Great Britain for soccer, rugby, cycling, boxing, hockey and tennis. Germany remained faithful to its gymnastics (the *Deutsche Turnerschaft* increased its membership from 170,000 to one and a quarter millions between 1880 and 1914), but also set up associations for cycling in 1884, soccer in 1900 and tennis two years later. When a team of working men, Blackburn Olympic, defeated the Old Etonians in 1883, the days of professional soccer had arrived; by the beginning of the twentieth century, the Cup Final drew over 100,000 spectators. By then, the game was played all over central Europe, though no-one as yet could foresee the days when the fire would sink on dune and headland and an Hungarian team would defeat England. In the 'nineties, the French Baron de Coubertin persuaded the nations to set up the Olympic Games again, with association football as one of the founding sports. For some reason continental Europe never took to cricket, and the English were left to find opponents for themselves within the spacious confines of their empire. Historians have been too austere in assessing the rôle of the new games in the lives of those who played or watched them, or read about them in newspapers and gambled on their outcome. They probably made a significant contribution to civilizing the wastes of industrial barbarism, by creating local and provincial patriotisms and establishing—along with trade unionism—a popular morality of partisan loyalty.

The new security, leisure and predictability of existence was offset, in some ways, by a break-up of the tight traditions of small communities which in earlier centuries had preserved the individual from loneliness and assisted him in adversity. Emigration overseas and migration to the towns, the increasing specialization required of the industrial labour force, the shift system in mines and factories, social services and compulsory schooling, cheaper travel to entertainments and holiday resorts, the possibility of civil divorce and the cheapening of the legal proceedings necessary to obtain it, and the fall in the birth rate all combined—for good as well as for ill— to loosen the bonds of family life. Two hundred years ago, most people had lived and died in the place where they were born, having no independent life outside their family and local community; the average duration of a marriage had been twenty years and a man

---

[36] For what follows, P. C. McIntosh, *Sport in Society* (1963), pp. 61–5, 85, 88, 92; Terence Delauney, *A Century of Soccer* (1963), pp. 30, 38; H. S. Altham, *A History of Cricket*, I (1962), pp. 29 ff. (England toured Australia in 1861, and lost the Ashes in 1882).

would expect to see half his large family of children die before they reached the age of fifteen, so that death was at the centre of life as the graveyard was in the centre of the village.[37] With the advent of the routine of the factory had come a new freedom from the routines of family and community and, to a degree, from the routine, universal imminence of death. There was more time to live, both to apply acquired skills to increasing production and, so far as an unattractive environment allowed, to seek personal fulfilment. In a sense, then, the machines were bringing freedom.

But the greatness of modern European history consists in the fact that the definition of freedom in terms of longevity, leisure or well-being or as mastery over natural environment, has never been exclusively accepted; since the seventeenth century in England and since Rousseau in France, freedom has meant the right to share in political rule and, in a paradoxical fashion susceptible of varying interpretations, to give only voluntary obedience. In what sense then was it possible and to what extent were attempts made to make this ideal a reality for everyone? We have seen how the masses received material benefits, impressive in their way, but less than they might have been: what share would they have in freedom?

[37] The phrase comes from J. Fourastie, 'De la vie traditionelle à la vie 'tertiaire", *Population* (July-Sept. 1959), pp. 415–32.

CHAPTER XXIV

FREEDOM

I

Almost every liberal writer of the first half of the nineteenth century had wanted to limit the suffrage, using tests of economic status to exclude those presumed to lack 'intelligence' or 'independence'. Yet as Hobbes had said long ago, 'there are very few so foolish, that they had not rather governe themselves, than be governed by others,'[1] and in any case, compulsory education was coming in. At the Frankfurt Assembly, the historian Waitz had argued that factory hands would vote as their employers dictated; it was soon evident, however, that the industrial workers, emancipated from the hierarchial and paternalistic traditions of the countryside and at feud with the capitalists, were 'free' men as their ancestors had never been and, given a chance, they could vote as freely as they could starve. Tocqueville had summed up the whole tendency of modern history as one long drive towards equality. The French Revolution had defined this drive as a political ideal, and in April 1848, when eight million Frenchmen went to the polls the ideal was realized. 'By what procedure do citizens all participate by entitlement in government and legislation? By universal suffrage. Universal suffrage is, then, democracy itself.'[2]

This is what Lamartine had said—a naïve politician in an age of enthusiasm. Since then, by this definition, Napoleon III and Bismarck had qualified as great democrats. They ensured the triumph of universal suffrage because it was a revolutionary ideal that could be harnessed for conservative ends. It was, too, an essential tendency of the age, being the link that brought into harmony the ineluctable forces of industrialism and nationalism—industrialism, which was atomizing mankind into free, rootless individuals in an undifferentiated swarm, and nationalism, which strove to fuse this mass into a patriotic, spiritual, organic community. Whatever the form of government, no State can be great, or even secure, if its citizens do not feel that they belong to it and it to them. In the new society, only universal suffrage could create this conviction; it was the

[1] Hobbes, *Leviathan* (1651), Part I, chap. 15.
[2] Lamartine, *Le Passé, le présent, l'avenir de la République*, II, p. 4; cit. P. Robert, *Dictionnaire* (1957) II, p. 1168.

indispensable, unifying myth behind the State in an era when the social changes wrought by the Industrial Revolution and the population explosion were working themselves out in parallel with the ideals the French Revolution had fostered.

The actual dates at which various national communities gave the vote to virtually all adult males have their significance, though they do not tell the whole story. After France came Greece (1864), the North German Confederation (1867), then the German Empire (1871), Switzerland (1874), Great Britain (1884), Spain (1890), Belgium (1893), Norway (1898), Sweden and Austria (1907), Italy (1912) and Holland (1917). The decisive year however, at which enlightened public opinion came to recognize the inevitability of the expanding franchise was 1867, when the electorate of Great Britain was doubled to two millions. In practice, this extension of the franchise did not bring about a startling change in political life, for there were still over a hundred corrupt constituencies, and normally only about half the parliamentary seats were contested.[3] What was significant was the widening of the franchise down to skilled trades-men within a genuine parliamentary system of government, as distinct from Bonapartist or Bismarckian variants. From this time, the demand for universal suffrage became general in western Europe and, in the next decade, extensions of the franchise came in Italy and Holland.

It was in the 'sixties too that John Stuart Mill raised problems of principle that had so far been avoided: the questions of votes for women and of preserving the political rights of minorities by the use of Proportional Representation.[4] Many conservatives regarded votes for women as just another reckless innovation, and many men of the Left (though Shaw, Zola and Bebel are interesting exceptions) feared that the feminine mind would shrink from the class struggle or succumb to clerical domination; it was on the pioneering frontiers of western civilization that women first received political rights, in Wyoming, Colorado, New Zealand and Australia. The first European states to follow these examples were Finland (a Grand Duchy of the Tsar) and Norway, in 1902 and 1907. Proportional representation, which had so far been used in various Swiss cantons, was introduced into Belgium in 1899 in a form devised to encourage the rise of a third party, for the Catholics were unwilling to see the Liberals disappear, leaving them to face the Socialists alone. By this time, still

---

[3] H. J. Hanham, *Elections and Party Management: Politics in the time of Disraeli and Gladstone* (1959), pp. 263, 191.

[4] J. S. Mill, *The Subjection of Woman* (1869), pp. 99–100; *Considerations on Representative Government* (1861, ed. 1905), pp. 125–54.

more effective means of giving a voice to minorities were being
employed in Switzerland, through the referendum and the initiative;
but only a happy country which had no dreams of national greatness
could afford to risk giving its people the opportunity to impose
policies of detail on the rulers, irrespective of total coherence.

II

These experiments to make mass voting a more precise instrument of
representation were peripheral. This was not surprising, for almost
everywhere, the wider suffrage was being introduced, not as the basis
for a new constitution, but as a novelty to be tacked onto constitutions that existed already. The masses were marching onto a battlefield in which the strategic heights of power were already occupied
by others. For one thing, peculiar tricks could be played when
extensions of the suffrage were granted. Right up to the first World
War, the dictated Constitution of January 1850 was in force in
Prussia, by which the male population went to the polls in three
classes, according to wealth, a vote in Class 1 having forty times
the weight of a vote in Class III. This system was imitated in
Roumania and, from 1873 to 1907, in Austria; it is interesting to
note that it was not applied in Hungary, where a narrow franchise
left the Magyars in command and universal suffrage was the cry,
not of democrats, but of subject nationalities.

More significant than the rigging of electoral machinery were the
constitutional provisions which in some countries were devised to
preserve vested interests at the top. The votes of the masses could
not be a lever to move the State unless they operated around the
fulcrum of genuine parliamentary government. In the German
Empire, the Chancellor depended on the Emperor alone. It was all
the same to him, said William II (in a telegram which, typically, he
sent in clear over the public network) whether red, black or yellow
monkeys gambolled in the *Reichstag*. 'If only I could see the *Reichstag* strung up like that!' he exclaimed, in a less genial mood, at the
sight of skulls on poles outside the house of a negro king on display
at a colonial exhibition.[5] His indifference and hostility is a sad
commentary on German politics, for if a resolute majority in
Reichstag and *Bundesrat* had ever emerged, the Emperor could not
have continued for long choosing his chancellors from a narrow
circle of aristocrats unconnected with the political parties. Even
after universal suffrage was introduced into Austria, the Emperor

[5] Prince von Bülow, *Memoirs* (Eng. trans., 1931) II, p. 5; *Holstein Papers*
cit. M. Balfour, *The Kaiser and his Times* (1964), p. 159.

Francis Joseph could still rule by decree. The parliamentary régime set up in Russia after the 1905 Revolution was a fraud; ministers were not responsible to the Duma, there was no control over military or court expenditure, and the government issued decrees between sessions—besides, even this ineffectual constitution was violated by the Tsar when he pleased. In some of the smaller states of Europe parliamentary institutions were also slow to develop— there was little progress in Denmark until the lower Chamber defeated King Christian IX in 1901, and in Portugal until the assassination of the absolutist Carlos I in 1908. Even in Sweden, it was not until 1902 that the chief minister was allowed by the Crown to choose his own colleagues.[6] According to Leopold von Ranke, the great German historian, the 'fundamental problem of the day' in the eighteen-fifties had been 'the conflict of monarchic with popular sovereignty, with which all other conflicts are connected'.[7] Given the qualification that the monarchies themselves were façades for concealing the interests of changing complexes of conservative forces, Ranke's dictum remained true for more than half of Europe, even so late as the early years of the twentieth century.

III

At the beginning of the new century, true democratic parliamentary government, or something approaching it, existed in the U.S.A., Great Britain, France, the Low Countries and Scandinavia, while the *Reichstag* had enough power to have demanded it in Germany. The map of constitutional progress coincides almost exactly with that of industrial expansion. Outside the boundaries of western industrial civilization, parliaments were either subject to autocracies, as in the Austro-Hungarian and Russian empires, or were forums for professional politicians manoeuvring independently of the real life of their countries; in Spain, Portugal, Greece and Roumania the spoils of office were shared in rotation, while in Italy, the art of mere ruling, indifferent to principles, but mindful of persons and conciliating local interests, was brought to perfection.

In the countries of western Europe where democratic government was progressing effectively, the sort of problems Tocqueville had foreseen were arising, though the age was too vital to find them as intractable as he had imagined. 'At every moment', he had said, 'the people are falling under the control of public administration, . . . So the very men who on occasion overturn monarchies. . . . obey

[6] D. V. Verney, *Parliamentary Reform in Sweden, 1866–1921* (1957), p. 122.
[7] R. C. Binkley, *Realism and Nationalism, 1852–71* (1935), p. 140.

increasingly . . . the least order of a clerk.'[8] Since those words were written, States had taken over education, set up social insurance schemes, enforced factory legislation, instituted systems of posts and telegraphs and, in some cases, had nationalized their railways. In Great Britain, Germany, Italy, Austria and Norway, an income tax was levied; bourgeois France refused to submit its profits to such precise calculations, but soon, in 1901, adopted progressive death duties. 'Public administration' had extended its grip further even than Tocqueville had foreseen. 'As a tolerably integrated, comprehensive and efficient organization of power', writes a modern historian, 'the State existed hardly anywhere before 1890.'[9] The Industrial Revolution and the population explosion had forced sovereign power to intervene in the most ordinary details of daily life, and Liberals in the succession of Tocqueville protested that freedom was in danger. 'How shall we meet the pressure which the centralized social order exerts upon us', wrote Friedrich Naumann, the theorist of German Liberalism, shortly before the first World War; 'that is the problem of human rights within the framework of modern industrialism.'[10]

Centralization and bureaucracy, however, are not evil in their very nature; indeed, in the context of the new industrialism they were necessary to make some sort of popular control of public policy possible and to create safeguards for an environment within which individuals could exercise their freedom. From the mid-century to 1890, the numbers of civil servants in the chief countries of western Europe doubled, and the increase was still more rapid afterwards. By 1911, one worker out of every thirty in Germany was a direct employee of the State. The higher posts in this vastly expanding bureaucracy of the German Empire were still a preserve of privilege: the most useful qualifications for candidates, along with a university degree and some experience of the law courts, were noble birth, a private income, membership of a student corps and rank as a reserve officer. From 1888 to 1914, nine of the twelve *Oberpräsidente* of provinces and a third of all the *Landräte* were nobles.

Elsewhere in western Europe, however, posts in the state bureaucracy were being thrown open to merit. Great Britain led the way by instituting competitive examinations, though it is a significant comment on the social and educational system that 74 per cent of

[8] J. Lively, *The Social and Political Theory of Alexis de Tocqueville* (1962), p. 91.

[9] F. H. Hinsley, *Power and the Pursuit of Peace* (1963), p. 281.

[10] Theodore Schieder, *The State and Society in our Times* (Eng. trans., 1962), p. 63.

successful candidates between 1905–14 were from the public schools and only a minority from State educational institutions. In France,[11] the situation was peculiar, for the bureaucracy of the Third Republic remained the highly centralized machine which France had inherited from the first Napoleon. Except for mayors and employees of municipal councils, all officials were chosen by the central government or its representatives, and thus a sort of parliamentary nepotism arose—'deputantism' it has been called—whereby the members of Parliament tried to manipulate the allocation of appointments and promotions. Yet the system was never as corrupt as it appeared to be, for ministers and deputies evolved a crafty protocol of official replies which took the credit for underhand intervention on behalf of the successful candidates appointed by merit and evaded all blame for the failures. The civil servants themselves also did a good deal to prevent favouritism by taking advantage of the law of 1901 and forming professional associations; what looked like revolutionary syndicalism was really a device to ensure promotion by seniority. From about 1900 onwards, the sons of industrial workers and peasants were entering the bureaucracy, partly because of their improved educational opportunites and the waning of nepotism, but also, it must be confessed, because the salaries of *fonctionnaires* were not keeping pace with those of other professions, and the better-class bourgeoisie was looking elsewhere for careers. But whatever the reasons, throughout western Europe the general tendency was clear: the civil service of the twentieth century was taking over the rôle that the Church had played in the Middle Ages, providing a ladder of 'meritocracy' linking the lower and higher levels of society.

The function of these vast new bureaucracies was variously interpreted by political theorists. In Germany, the jurists regarded the State as sovereign, with public administration existing to serve its interests. An utterly contrasted point of view was that of the syndicalist thinkers who exercised a great influence on the working-class movements in Spain, Italy, France and Belgium; according to them, state employees, leagued together in a collective labour contract, ought to form a self-governing corporation. In either case, the interests of the public at large were likely to be sacrificed. The theory which came nearest to serving the interests of representative parliamentary democracy was that of the jurists of the French Third Republic, who regarded the nation as sovereign and as delegating its powers to elected politicians, who would control the public officials. 'Thus', said Duguit, 'the notion of public power is replaced

[11] For what follows, W. K. Sharp, *The French Civil Service* (1931), pp. 5, 9, 75, 85–6.

by the notion of public service; the state ceases to be a power which commands and becomes a group which works. and those in authority can legitimately use it only in order to ensure general co-operation.'[12]

Within the limits of a theory of this kind, or of the traditions of parliamentary control of Westminster, the extension and increasing efficiency of Civil Services smoothed the way for democracy. If promotion by merit produces 'brahmin' administrators, it also runs threads of alliance through the classes, for even the most austere 'man from the ministry' has friends and relatives somewhere. Systematic procedures, however irritating, are necessary for freedom: as someone has said, 'red tape properly used is the best guarantee of the liberty of the citizen'. Many things were moved out of politics into the realm of administration, and many of the decisions of politics were simplified by the guidance of technical expertise. 'The value of political heads of departments', said Harcourt, 'is to tell the officials what the public will not stand',[13] and this could be done as effectively by a man risen from the people as by an aristocrat brought up in the arts of ruling. With the rise of a politically neutral administrative 'meritocracy', the highly complex industrial State could be more easily run by politicians than the comparatively small and inefficient States of a century before. '*On gouverne avec un parti*', Gambetta had said, '*on administre avec les capacités*.' Elected politicians could rule, but the question that remained was—how and in what sense could the mass of newly-enfranchised voters exercise control over its rulers?

IV

'Popular government without popular education is the prologue to a farce or a tragedy.'[14] Popular education was also essential for industrial and technological progress, possibly also for success in war—after the defeat of 1870, it was commonly said that the Prussian schoolmaster had defeated France. Whatever the reasons, whether it was nations developing their reservoir of human talent, or politicians educating their 'masters' or employers educating their 'slaves', between 1868 and 1884, practically all European governments set up free primary schools, and by 1900, the vast majority of the adult population of western Europe was literate.

The number of newspapers rose in almost exact proportion to the increased number of readers. For long, Liberals had insisted on the

[12] Brian Chapman, *The Profession of Government: the Public Service in Europe* (1959), pp. 25–38.
[13] Cit. H. J. Laski, *A Grammar of Politics* (1925), p. 245.
[14] Words of President Madison of the U.S.A.

freedom of the press: in the 'eighties, the Industrial Revolution made this freedom effective through the invention of linotype and the use of wood pulp for newsprint, so that cheap newspapers became accessible to everyone. Dailies with circulations going on for a million, like the *Daily Mail*, the *Petit Journal* and the *Lokal-Anzeiger*, arose in the 'ninties, and there was also a great increase in the number of specialized publications catering for particular interests, churches, hobbies, trades and so on. By 1914 there were 41 daily papers in London, 40 in Paris, 22 in Berlin, 19 in Brussels and 20 at St Petersburg.[15]

The new journalism was generally vulgar and sometimes mendacious. This was the heroic age of advertisement, when travellers reported recommendations for margarine on the walls of fiords within the Arctic Circle, and Prince Henry of Bourbon praised Bantam bicycles—'*Jamais je n'ai eu de bicyclette plus agréable.*'[16] Towards the end of the nineteenth century newspapers were deriving something like half their revenue from advertisements and, as Walter Lippmann said, how could the public, reading its subsidized news, expect the fountains of truth to bubble—free of charge?[17] Advertisements and circulation went hand in hand, so editors had to pander to the masses, with their yearning for simplicity, sensationalism, sentimentality and 'the vicarious thrill of gorgeous vices'. The atmosphere of politics, national and international, became embittered by irresponsible revelations, by 'scoops' like the Berlin newspapers' photographs of visiting German generals paralysed with mirth at the Swiss manoeuvres.[18] Articles about public affairs were often ill-informed (though less so in France, where journalism became a testing ground for ambitious young men seeking careers in politics—it lead to everything, provided you got out of it);[19] sometimes they were dishonest, for it was well-known that Russian and Italian bribes reached the pockets of French editors, and that steel and shipbuilding interests bought propaganda space in German newspapers to help the Navy League.

Yet, with all its shortcomings, the new mass-circulation press was indispensable to democracy. Parties of the Left could at last break through to their audience—in the columns of *L'Humanité*, *Vorwärts*, *The Daily Herald* and *L'Avanti*—broadcasting the day-to-day

[15] Sell, *The World's Press* (1914 ed.), pp. 147–8, 406 409, 414.
[16] E. S. Turner, *The Shocking History of Advertising* (1952), pp. 113, 111; see also the lecture by H. A. Innes, *The Press: a neglected factor in the Economic History of the Twentieth Century* (1948).
[17] W. Lippmann, *Public Opinion* (1921, ed. 1957), pp. 321–2.
[18] Princess Marie Radziwill, *This was Germany* (1937), p. 221.
[19] C. J. Hayes, *France: a Nation of Patriots* (1930), p. 154.

guidance and exhortation suitable to political action in a parliamentary régime, just as the fireworks of occasional manifestos and pamphlets are fitted for inspiring revolutions. Most people preferred to read the 'capitalist' press, but the competition of different newspapers and the common sense of the ordinary man ensured that, on home affairs at least, few were taken in. The press put a spotlight on big issues and initiated processes of discussion which, if elementary in nature, were at least calculated to bring about the simple decisions which are all the electoral process can cater for. 'It is the newspaper press', Lord Bryce said, 'that has made democracy possible in large countries.'[20]

V

Though the press kept the electors informed and haunted politicians with the shadow of popular censure, the actual machinery through which the voting masses were to influence government was provided by the political party. The press propagated ideas crudely, and supplementary means were needed to correct its distortions. Wireless had not yet become a popular medium of entertainment and communication, and television was not thought of. 'Perhaps in retrospect', writes an historian of parties, 'it will be evident that the mass party saw its heyday during the period when the extension of the franchise had created a mass electorate, but there was as yet no effective means of reaching the voters in their own homes.'[21] More important still, Party had an indispensable rôle to play in shaping opinions. 'Raw opinion is elusive, . . . formed opinion alone can be expressed';[22] multiple differences have to be narrowed into clear, possible policies, or no-one is really represented. In a two-party system it is also possible to vote for the small group of men put forward by the party as its governing 'team' and to punish them, if they are unsatisfactory, by deprivation at the next election.

This was the pattern towards which democratic parliamentary government was moving, and it is odd that the political theorists—Gierke, Jellinek, Dicey, Esmein and Duguit—did not see it. One reason for their blindness was the prejudice against the idea of party, especially in Germany. Here, the view put forward by Bluntschli (1869) and Treitschke (1871) prevailed, that the State was an ethical unity standing above the dialectic of political strife; if the party system was to provide the government, Treitschke argued, there

---

[20] James Viscount Bryce, *Modern Democracies* (1921), p. 104.
[21] R. J. McKenzie, *British Political Parties* (1955), p. 591.
[22] M. Duverger, *Political Parties* (Eng. trans., 1954, pref. by D. W. Brogan, ed. 1964), p. 380.

would be no reality in debate, for it could never influence members of parliament to change their opinions, and no reconciliation of opposites, because they would simply alternate in power.[23] Even where Party was more favourably regarded, its rôle was often misunderstood; its highest duty, many held, was to represent ideals in their abstract purity, rather than to provide the machinery for government with something like consent or for criticism of government with something like responsibility. This misconception lies behind Michel's grim enunciation of the 'iron law of oligarchy' by which the achievement of power necessarily corrupts all idealists and behind Ostrogorski's famous volume on *Democracy and the Organization of Political Parties* (1902). Horrified by what he saw happening in England and America, Ostrogorski denounced all the apparatus of the mass party—the rule of 'caucus', the 'omnibus programmes' to which the individual must sacrifice his integrity, the 'apostolic succession' of leaders and the 'standing army' of organizers—and he called for the foundation of new 'temporary, single-issue organizations', each marching forward under the banner of a single ideal.[24] He was apparently unaware that under his system all governments would be concocted in the lobbies of legislatures, and that the people at large would vote for precisely what they thought they wanted without knowing if it was possible, and at the cost of having no say in who would actually govern them, no coherent national policy and no-one to take responsibility for failures.

In Great Britain, the political system reacted undramatically to the advent of universal suffrage, for the traditional parties were accustomed to claiming to represent the general interest and psychologically prepared to organize the new voters and 'take them in socially', while the flourishing trade unions and co-operatives could easily move into an alliance to found a socialist political machine. In the multi-party systems of France and Germany, the elaboration of party organization began on the Left—another reason, perhaps, why the political theorists were distrustful. The French elections of 1871, when the Second Empire's arrangements for managing the electorate had lapsed, were a warning, for the voters had turned to the notables and landlords. From then onwards republican groups organized electoral committees to make their candidates known to a mass electorate that might relapse, if left unguided, into the morass of conservatism.[25] But above all, it was the socialists who had to

[23] Schieder, op. cit., pp 185–96.
[24] Ostrogorski, *Democracy and the Organization of Political Parties* (Eng. trans., 1902) II, pp. 647–8, 659, 667.
[25] See Brogan's introduction to Duverger, op. cit., p. vii.

organize, for newspapers would not be on their side unless they founded their own, and contributions would not flow into their coffers unless they arranged for collections among vast numbers of small subscribers. The German Social Democrats set the example, building up an organization of a million members, with a vast budget and 150 local and regional secretaries. Once one party organized, the others had to follow suit in self-defence, unless indeed they had allied bodies to do their political work unofficially, as the People's Union of Catholic Germany did for the Centre Party and the Agrarian League for the Conservatives. In 1906, the National Liberals employed a staff of three, but seven years later they paid two general and fifty provincial secretaries.

VI

According to the British ideal of parliamentary government, political parties must be great comprehensive organizations 'divided by broad issues of policy rather than by sectional interests'.[26] In continental Europe, however, the advent of a broader suffrage led to the rise of parties founded upon narrower and more intense allegiances—to religion, class or nationality or, even, to locality. In Holland, from 1848 to 1868, a Catholic-Liberal coalition confronted a Conservative–Calvinist alliance; thereafter, a religious front of Catholics and Calvinists formed on the educational issue, against Liberals and Radicals, an alliance that remained unbroken until the 'Christian Historical Party' went over to the Conservatives. Scandinavia in particular saw the rise of agrarian parties. After the four Estates of Sweden were replaced by a two-chambered Parliament of the modern kind in 1866, for twenty years there was only one effective political group, the Farmers' Party, which had no policy beyond keeping down the taxes. Austria, by contrast, was the classical instance of a country in which political divisions were multiplied by the cross-fragmentation of nationalities: in 1914, Andrássy complained that there were no less than twenty-five parties, though he might have reflected that it was these very divisions which made it possible for his Emperor to remain a virtual autocrat. 'Free institutions', John Stuart Mill had said, 'are next to impossible in a country made up of different nationalities.'[27] Indeed, a political system whose parties are based upon such sectional and overwhelming allegiances must always be in danger; in the service of

[26] *Joint Committee on Indian Constitutional Reform* (1934), cit. F. C. S. Wade and G. S. Phillips, *Manual of Constitutional Law* (5th ed. 1955), p. 121.
[27] J. S. Mill, *Considerations on Representative Government*, p. 287.

religion, class or nationality, a party can easily forget the broad
common interest, or refuse to make the compromises necessary to
produce a stable government, while the principle of toleration will
be imperilled if political victories or defeats are too closely identified
with the fortunes of particular churches or racial or economic
groups.

Pope Leo XIII had shown awareness of the dangers of identifying
religion with a political cause when he proclaimed the Ralliement.
But he had not carried his principle far enough, for he had tried to
persuade the French Catholics to found a new political party,
accepting the Republic but serving the interests of Catholicism none
the less. Fortunately for the Church, the design failed. Keller, its
chosen leader, refused to abandon his royalist convictions and Lamy,
the Pope's next choice, was too naïve and good a man for politics
('We must act—strike a great blow. I'm going to write an article in
the *Revue des Deux Mondes*.') There was also a good deal of discussion in Italy about the feasibility of forming a Catholic political
party, more especially when the papal ban on voting virtually lapsed
in 1904. Don Luigi Sturzo, a Sicilian priest with great political talents,
was quick to seize upon the essential precautions that must be taken:
a Christian party, he said, must be Christian only in its ideals; the
hierarchy must have no power in its affairs, nor must it serve clerical
interests.[28] Another sort of warning was provided by the example
of the Centre Party in Germany, a great mass party which weakly
collaborated with the imperial government from 1894 to 1906, years
in which the country ought to have been moving towards parliamentary government. This was neither the first nor the last time that
the Centre preferred the interests of Catholicism to the principles
of democracy. The lesson seemed to be that political parties ought to
be essentially political, appealing to all men, united by 'broad
issues of policy rather than by sectional interests'—even by religion.

VII

There was a dilemma here, however, that parliamentary democracy
must always face and that can no more be resolved than children
can both have their cake and eat it: the more precisely an individual
voter's opinions are represented, the less effective is that representation likely to be. In the English-speaking countries, a two-party
system prevailed, 'the natural concomitant of a political tradition
in which government, as such, is the first consideration'.[29] The

[28] R. Webster, *Christian Democracy in Italy, 1860–1960* (1961), p. 18.
[29] L. S. Amery, *Thoughts on the Constitution* (1948), p. 17.

disadvantage was that the voter's enthusiasms might not be engaged
in the meaningful and momentous choice which was forced upon him;
also, to some extent the great parties were opportunistic and un-
principled—'All has been lost', said Bryce of the electoral struggle
in the U.S.A., 'except office and the hope of getting it.'[30] In continental Europe, a multi-party system generally prevailed, bringing
with it the opposite disadvantages. Long ago, in 1842, Tocqueville
had forecast what would happen: 'Momentary needs, intellectual
fantasies, the smallest particular interests can create at any time small
and ephemeral factions, whose caprices and sterile freedom of action
end by sickening men of their own independence, and liberty is
threatened with extinction, not because a party tyrannically abuses
governmental power, but because no party is in a position to
govern.'[31]

Something like this might have been said half a century later by
an Englishman commenting on the politics of the Third French
Republic, for Tocqueville had a prophetic vision, and the trick of
putting the Anglo-Saxons' point of view with more logic than they
themselves could muster. But what if some continental countries,
especially France, did not accept the English theory of government
being 'the first consideration', and others, especially Germany, had
doubts about parliamentary control of the executive? Perhaps the
multi-party system gave them what they really wanted.

It has been argued[32] that the multiplicity of parties in continental
Europe was the creation of the electoral device of 'second ballot',
and it is true enough that there is 'an almost complete correlation . . .
between the simple–majority single-ballot system and the two-
party system.'[33] Denmark, with majority ballot and four main
parties, and Belgium before 1894, with second ballot and only two
parties are only apparent exceptions, for the battle over religious
education kept Belgian politics circling round a single theme,
and the majority ballot in Denmark operated to keep down the
actual numbers of candidates to two in many constituencies. Yet, as
M. Duverger has observed, 'Ballot procedure . . . has no real driving
power'; it merely served to maintain established patterns of party
strife, majority ballot helping to eliminate third parties if they arose
in two-party systems, and second ballot assisting a multiplicity of
parties to retain their independence rather than drifting from

[30] Bryce, *American Commonwealth* (1888), cit. V. O. Key Jnr., *Politics, Parties and Pressure Groups* (1962), p. 255.
[31] Lively, op. cit., pp. 138–9.
[32] R. K. Ensor, 'Political Institutions in Europe', *N.C.M.H.* XII (1960), p. 75.
[33] Duverger, op. cit., p. 217.

coalitions into unification. The multi-party system, in fact, corresponded to what people wanted, just as, in different countries, the two-party system did.

In Germany, all legislation had to be got through by a coalition. Under Chancellors Hohenlohe and Bülow, the Conservatives, National Liberals and Centre allied in a 'Cartel' to support the government, and from 1907–9 the 'Bloc' of Conservatives, Liberals and Progressives fulfilled this office; thereafter, the imperial government had to make do with shifting, *ad hoc* majorities. But did not this situation correspond with what the German middle classes subconsciously desired? They would not ally with the Social Democrats and they did not know how to fight them; they wanted glory, expansion and peace, all simultaneously; they wanted the *Reichstag* to have power to coerce the executive, but never to use it; they wanted to be free without accepting responsibility.[34] Instead of moving towards universality in their appeal, the German parties were becoming, if anything, more highly sectional; from 1906–10 the Catholic Centre was racked by doctrinal disputes on the question of co-operation with Protestants in social legislation; the Social Democrats were doctrinaire Marxists considering themselves as strictly representative of the working classes: the National Liberals, once the party of university professors and the bourgeoisie, were being bought up by the big industrialists.[35] Apart from the S-D.s who, in theory at least, did not accept the system at all, the parties seemed to consider their rôle as being to advise, exhort and warn the government and, maybe, on rare occasions to check it, but never to take over power themselves. To Germans, as to Englishmen, the issue of government was primary, but they did not believe that the effective, superior, world-defying executive they wanted could ever emerge from parliamentary assemblies.

Equally, it is probable that the party system of the Third Republic (the longest-lived régime France has had since 1789) corresponded to what most people wanted, at least with part of their minds and strongly enough to make any alternative impossible. The two-party system demands a basic agreement to differ; English parties, said Amable de Franqueville enviously, in 1887, are two disciplined

---

[34] Cf. L. Krieger, *The German Idea of Freedom* (1957), pp. 463–4, 'Freedom would be realized by a people's state, unified by the Emperor, equalizing economic benefits at home and asserting the national interest powerfully abroad.' Cf. J. Alden Nichols' description of Caprivi's ideal of 'a nationalistic, middle-of-the-road policy' based on a 'Single-party system of frock-coated totalitariansim' (*Germany after Bismark: the Caprivi Era, 1890–4* (1958), p. 371.

[35] J. L. Snell, 'Imperial Germany's Tragic Era, 1888–1918', *Journ. Central European Affairs*, XVIII (1959), pp. 58–9.

armies always fighting yet never annihilating each other, like the Romans and Carthaginians in the theatre.[36] In France, however, the forces of the Right would have wished for nothing better than to annihilate the Republic, and in times of scandal, like the Panama affair, or of crisis, like the Boulangist movement, they had hopes of succeeding. There was, too, a feud between Catholicism and the spirit of the French Revolution, which the Ralliement had not appeased, and which the Dreyfus Case forced into the forefront of politics once again, a feud which reached its climax in the breaking of the Concordat and the final separation of Church and State in 1905. In a sense, therefore, on the occasions when the Republic was in danger or at various stages of the mean and cynical attack on the Church (and taking these two together meant practically always), the republican political groups were at one; this included even the Socialists, for they wished to exhaust the republican programme of anti-clericalism so that they could have a free run for their own demands on the social question. Politics then, said Robert de Jouvenal, were 'a matter of taste', and government was a game of 'replastering', of shifting in and out republican groups of varying opinions while keeping intact the anti-clerical, anti-royalist façade. All this manoeuvring could go on for long periods within the precincts of the assemblies, undisturbed by movements of opinion in the electorate, for the presidential power of dissolution had been discredited by Marshal MacMahon's attempt to use it in favour of the royalists in 1877.

That successive governments were thus kept impotent in everything except republican defence and sabotaging the Church did not cause undue concern, for the Third Republic 'was based on the predominance of a great vested interest and the discredit or exhaustion of the rival social forces'.[37] The bourgeoisie and the landowning peasants did not want active government: they wanted a system which would give them security from the incursions of the monarchist Right and against the demands of the industrial workers. On a higher plane, they also wanted individual freedom; this was the dominant theme of 'Alain's' writings in defence of the régime and the explanation (rather than the search for sheer political advantage) of the astonishing persistence of the Dreyfusards. The Dreyfus Affair, indeed, which revealed so much that was rotten in French society, blew up in time to provide the Republic with a *mystique* which had been lacking so far in its history; in all the con-

---

[36] M. Baumont, *L'Essor industriel et l'impérialisme colonial* (1949), p. 488.
[37] P. M. Williams, 'From Dreyfus to Vichy', in *France: Government & Society* (1957), p. 228.

fusions and corruption of its politics, France remained the land of
the Revolution so far as the rights of the individual were concerned.
But on more general issues, where broad decisions of governmental
policy would have been needed, propertied Frenchmen were wedded
to immobilism, since their pride and their interests pulled in directly
opposite directions. They wanted to glory in the determination to
avenge Sedan and yet not have to fight a war; they wanted to belong
to parties with left-wing names and be heirs of the Revolution yet,
with hearts on the left and wallets on the right, they did not wish
to pay taxes for social improvements. They hoped to achieve a
government that would not embark on aggression abroad or social
changes at home, yet they insisted on voting for 'glory' and 'revolution'. The only way to achieve this was to allow politics to become
an agreed and open conspiracy between deceiving politicians and
deceived electors, with do-little cabinets composed of coalitions
in which no-one was responsible. Here was one way of solving the
problem of representation and achieving 'the form of government
which divides us least'.

VIII

The immobilism and cynicism of parliamentarianism in France, its
distance from the levers of power in Germany, and its corruption in
Italy made some of the most brilliant minds of the early twentieth
century distrustful of the prospects for democracy. On one hand,
the Marxists challenged universal suffrage as a poor substitute for
social justice, on the other, Liberals in the succession of Tocqueville
feared that the advent of democracy would bring on a movement
towards social equality which would destroy liberty. Hence the
title of a gloomy work by Lecky, *Democracy and Liberty* (1899),
which forecast an era of governmental extravagance, corruption,
and interference with private property and individual freedom.

But behind these two perennial critiques of democracy, more subtle
challenges were developing, ambiguous, strangely combining alternative possibilities for good and evil. Nietzsche, whose 'blonde
beast' was leonine, not Nordic, and whose 'will to power' was nothing more perverse than a striving towards self-transcendence by
suffering and self-sacrifice, was the very antithesis of a progenitor
of Fascism; nonetheless, he exercised a disturbing influence upon the
bourgeois, rational, egalitarian traditions of thought to which
parliamentary democracy appealed for its justification. An existen-
tialist in philosophy, an aristocrat in politics, a pessimist who foresaw the 'brotherhoods of robbery' that would arise in the wilderness
of barbarism to which our materialism will condemn us, Nietzsche

forced men to examine the moral foundations of their society and to despair at what they saw. Without having read his writings, or those of his philosophical predecessors, Schopenhauer and Kierkegaard, Freud came by his own experimental means to discover in man what was already implicit in Nietzsche's theories—the irrational 'drives', the sexual masochism, the weight of guilt and the machinery of repression and sublimation. With Freud's discovery of the unconscious, the established conclusions of political thought, in so far as they were anchored on the premise of man's rationality, became problematical and uncertain.

Nietzsche had said that the age was 'decadent': by this he meant that 'life no longer resides in the whole', that thinkers had become mere experimenters dealing self-consciously with a narrow segment of reality, lacking the cosmic vision characteristic of Shakespeare, Goethe, Beethoven and Hegel.[38] Walter Pater meant something like this when he defined 'the tendency of modern thought' as being 'to regard all things . . . as inconstant modes or fashions';[39] so too did Paul Valéry,[40] who in 1897 complained that 'the heroic age' of philosophers, musicians and 'speculative scholars' was over, and an age of science, 'fertile only in patents of invention', was beginning— this in a France adorned by the writings of Claudel, Gide, Proust, Péguy, Anatole France and the symbolist poets, the paintings of the Impressionists, Rodin's sculpture and Debussy's music! There was then, a 'failure of nerve', a sophisticated, introspective withdrawal of faith in the prophetic, universal qualities of art and literature, and this tendency was met and reinforced by a converging, opposite kind of pessimism, the retreat from reality and the doctrine of 'art for art's sake'.

No doubt fastidious introversion is necessary, in some degree, in all ages of cultural achievement. Paul Bourget in his *Essais de Psychologie contemporaine* (1883) was being unreasonable when he complained of the new *mal du siècle*, the disease of the will implicit in the sensualism of Baudelaire, in Renan's ironical detachment and in Flaubert's nihilism. It is true also that this tendency was only one of many currents in the deep and brilliant surge of ideas that rolled through the late nineteenth and early twentieth centuries. Gerhard Hauptman, Shaw and Anatole France were as deadly earnest about social evils as Romain Rolland was about the problem of nationalism, or Claudel about religion or Gide about morals. Even so, there is

[38] W. A. Kaufmann, *Nietzsche* (1950), pp. 52–3, 64–5.
[39] Cit. G. Bruun, *Nineteenth-Century European Civilization* (1959), p. 191.
[40] C. Digeon, *La Crise allemande de la pensée française, 1870–1914* (1959), p. 485.

something significant about Rimbaud's flight from democracy and industrialism into the more congenial society of gunrunners in the Persian Gulf; in Proust insulating himself from life in his cork-lined bedroom to write his masterly and utterly pessimistic analysis of 'the Heartbreak House of capitalist culture'; in the suicide of Villiers de l'Isle d'Adam's hero on the verge of love and happiness—'We have exhausted the future. . . . Live? our servants will do that for us.'[41] It was Croce, the great Italian philosopher and historian, whose own life was later to be devoted to the courageous defiance of anti-liberal forces, who summed up the temper of the pre-War age as one that had to make thought its substitute for hope.

'We no longer believe . . ., like the Greeks, in happiness of life on earth; we no longer believe, like the Christians, in happiness in an other-worldly life; we no longer believe, like the optimistic philoso-phers of the last century, in a happy future for the human race. . . . What we have alone retained is the consciousness of ourselves, and the need to make that consciousness ever clearer and more evident, a need for whose satisfaction we turn to science and to art.'[42]

There is no redemption, only the struggle for self-awareness. It was but a short step to Spengler's proud, grim formula for the declining West, to 'go downhill, *seeing*'.[43]

Against the background of a subtle pessimism, with its abandon-ment of religious hope and its suspicion of man's rationality, its search for self-awareness and its withdrawal from the life of the multitude and from industrial society, new political theories arose, theories of rule by an *élite*, which would triumph over the ignorance of the voting masses and the selfish mediocrity of bourgeois politi-cians. In Italy, these ideas were put forward by Mosca and, later, by Pareto; in France, they were associated with Sorel, who followed a strange course, from preaching violent action by a proletarian *élite* to a flirtation with monarchism and, finally, after the War, with Fascism. A more consistent and powerful thinker was the German historian, economist and sociologist Max Weber, whose pessimism was heightened by his struggle to reconcile his belief in reason and the values of the Enlightenment with his acceptance of the irration-ality of human conduct and the provisional, highly personal nature of historical judgments. The mass industrial society needed a vast

[41] Edmund Wilson, *Axel's Castle: a Study in the Imaginative Literature of 1870–1930* (1936), pp. 164, 262.
[42] H. Stuart Hughes, *Consciousness and Society: the Reorientation of European Social Thought, 1890–1930* (1959), pp. 428–9.
[43] O. Spengler, *The Decline of the West* (1918), Eng. trans. by C. F. Atkinson, 2 vols. (1926).

apparatus of bureaucracy and, by contrast, charismatic leadership; Weber held that democracy would never escape from the fetters of these two necessities, and that its normal pattern of government would be rule by officials under an *élite* of professional politicians alternating with the occasional emergence of a charismatic dictator. In either case, true freedom would be submerged. Like Croce, Weber anticipated Spengler, this time by the vision of an iron Ceasarian age that would complete the cycle of European history: 'not summer's bloom lies ahead of us, but rather a polar night of icy darkness and hardness'.[44]

Behind Weber's pessimism lay a subconscious sense of the hopelessness of the political situation in Wilhelmian Germany, for even the most cosmopolitan of European thinkers in this era could not escape from the limitations of their national situation and allegiance. Freud himself, a German-speaking Jew born in a Czech province and brought up in Vienna, a man apparently 'above nation, beyond class, outside time', turned out to be an Austrian patriot when war was declared.[45] Patterns of thought tended to take on a national colouring, and France in particular produced its idiosyncratic type of anti-democratic theory.

In the 'nineties, the Third Republic, anti-clerical and highly centralized, began to look drab and inglorious. Religion was coming into fashion again with the intellectuals. On Christmas Day, 1884, in Nôtre-Dame, Claudel had been converted by the lightning-flash of an intuition of 'the Innocence, the eternal infancy of God';[46] ten years later, Brunetière went to Rome and came back saying that 'a morality is nothing if it is not religious'; Huysmans left black magic for the shadow of the cathedral; later, Péguy became a Catholic— and remained a republican. For some time, there had been a growing revulsion against the centralized administration: Le Play, Vidal de la Blanche the geographer, and Mistral had talked of provincial revivals and regional federations; Durkheim praised the corporations and guilds of the *ancien régime*, which had given men integration in a social order and preserved them from despair; Duguit advocated 'pluralism'—'the great error of the French Revolution, inspired by Rousseau, was to wish to destroy and forbid all secondary groupings'.[47]

[44] Stuart Hughes, op. cit., p. 332.
[45] E. Jones, *The Life and Work of Freud* (3 vols., 1953–7) II, pp. 191–2. (The quotation about Freud's cosmopolitanism is from Schoenwold, cit. Stuart Hughes, p. 126.)
[46] L. Chaigne, *Paul Claudel* (1961), pp. 49–50.
[47] M. H. Elbow, *French Corporative Theory, 1789–1948* (1953), p. 116.

Against this background of disillusionment, royalism revived in France. In 1899, Charles Maurras founded the *Action Française*, to preach the cause of civilization and national greatness—a civilization that was impossible without inequality, and a greatness that had perished through intestine divisions and could only be restored by hereditary, authoritarian monarchy. These were old arguments, but Chateaubriand would not have recognized Maurras' brand of royalism. It was a political system deduced from critical appraisal of historical precedents, not a traditional loyalty inspiring romantic devotion. French Royalism had been rural, Catholic, pacific, aristocratic: the new Right was urban, agnostic, militaristic, journalistic.[48] Though Maurras was glad to make use of the revulsion against anti-clericalism and centralization, he himself moved in a world of thought which was illuminated by a harsher and brighter light than the twilight glow of religious sentiment or nostalgic corporatism or regionalism. He was a declared foe of every kind of individualism which, he said, in religion had caused the Reformation, in politics the French Revolution, and in literature Romanticism—all three being evil. Seeking freedom we impoverish our spirits: 'we must come out of liberty as out of a prison'. His sentimentality was reserved for nationalism alone: Barrès' cult of the dead and the earth that had borne them. The intellectual traditions which he claimed to inherit were those of Classicism and of Positivism; the Classicism of Greece and Rome and of the French seventeenth century, ages of civilization and discipline, and the Positivism of Comte and Taine that claimed to study facts scientifically and considered that the Revolution was the point at which Frenchmen had abandoned the paths of reason. With his austere and fastidious culture, it is hard to equate Maurras with the repulsive practitioners of totalitarianism of the inter-war years, yet in his nationalistic fanaticism and his unequivocal adherence to authoritarian rule, he is nearer to twentieth-century Fascism than to the traditions of French Royalism.

Thus, even as universal suffrage and parliamentary democracy were triumphing in western Europe, disillusionment was being manifested among the intellectuals, and anti-democratic movements of thought were arising. There were too, especially in Germany, racialist doctrines and some vicious anti-Semitic propaganda,[49] as well as more widely diffused theories of a Darwinian struggle for survival. Even intellectuals who held freedom as the greatest good

[48] R. Rémond, *La Droite en France de 1815 à nos jours* (1954), p. 152.
[49] For anti-Semitism, G. L. Mosse, *The Culture of Western Europe in the 19th and 20th Centuries* (1963), pp. 80 ff.

were inclined to abase its claims before the insistencies of national power: 'Is Weber not right?' wrote Naumann in 1895. 'Of what use is the best social policy if the Cossacks are coming?'[50] All these could come together to form a sinister amalgam, and it has been easy enough to look into Europe before 1914 and detect there the hidden roots of the Nazi and Fascist movements. Yet there is a world of difference between authoritarian government and the nationalistic State as envisaged by thinkers before the first World War and as practised by Hitler and Mussolini after it. It is sometimes said that western Europe did not know the reality of democracy, as distinct from nominally democratic institutions, until the levelling experience of years of trench warfare; it might be added that western Europe did not know the immense potentialities of mass industrial society for tyranny and rapine, or seriously consider using them for such, until a bitter and useless war had revealed them, and that ordinary men would not have abandoned their simple faith in progress and rationality to serve demonic ends and nihilistic leaders if war had not impoverished society and blunted consciences, and if the trenches had not left their legacy of despair. 'Our intellect is a feeble and dependent thing', wrote Freud in December 1914, 'a plaything and a tool of our impulses and emotions. ... And now just look at what is happening in this wartime.'[51] It was the eclipse of the great creative conviction—or was it just an illusion?—which had made west European history original and fecund in a fashion never seen before and, maybe, never to be seen again: the belief that man is rational and that by the exercise of reason he can master both his environment and his passions, and achieve true freedom.

[50] J. P. Mayer, *Max Weber and German Politics* (1944), p. 35.
[51] Letter of 28 Dec. 1914, cit. Stuart Hughes, p. 143.